Essentials of
Strategic Management
The Quest for Competitive Advantage

John E. Gamble
Texas A&M University–Corpus Christi

Margaret A. Peteraf
Dartmouth College

Arthur A. Thompson, Jr.
The University of Alabama

Mc
Graw
Hill
Education

ESSENTIALS OF STRATEGIC MANAGEMENT: THE QUEST FOR COMPETITIVE ADVANTAGE, FIFTH EDITION

Published by McGraw-Hill Education, 2 Penn Plaza, New York, NY 10121. Copyright © 2017 by McGraw-Hill Education. All rights reserved. Printed in the United States of America. Previous editions © 2015, 2013, and 2011. No part of this publication may be reproduced or distributed in any form or by any means, or stored in a database or retrieval system, without the prior written consent of McGraw-Hill Education, including, but not limited to, in any network or other electronic storage or transmission, or broadcast for distance learning.

Some ancillaries, including electronic and print components, may not be available to customers outside the United States.

This book is printed on acid-free paper.

2 3 4 5 6 7 8 9 LWI 21 20 19 18 17 16

ISBN 978-1-259-54698-3

MHID 1-259-54698-5

Senior Vice President, Products & Markets: *Kurt L. Strand*
Vice President, Content Pesign & Delivery: *Kimberly Meriwether David*
Director: *Michael Ablassmeir*
Lead, Product Development: *Kelly Delso*
Freelance Product Developer: *Michelle Houston*
Marketing Manager: *Casey Keske*
Digital Product Analyst: *Sankha Bas*u
Director, Content Production: *Terri Schies*l
Program Manager: *Mary Conzachi*
Content Project Manager: *Mary Powers (*Core*), Keri Johnson (*Assessment*)*
Buyer: *Laura Fuller*
Design: *Matt Diamond*
Cover Image: *John Lund/Getty Images*
Content Licensing Specialists: *Michelle Whitaker (*Image*), DeAnna Dausener (*Text*)*
Compositor: *SPi Global*
Printer: *LSC Communications*

All credits appearing on page or at the end of the book are considered to be an extension of the copyright page.

Library of Congress Cataloging-in-Publication Data

Names: Gamble, John (John E.) author. | Thompson, Arthur A., 1940- author. | Peteraf, Margaret Ann, author.
Title: Essentials of strategic management : the quest for competitive advantage / John Gamble, Texas A&M University Corpus Christi, Arthur Thompson, Jr., The University of Alabama TUSCALOOSA, Margaret Peteraf, DARTMOUTH COLLEGE.
Description: Fifth Edition. | Dubuque : McGraw-Hill Education, 2016. | Revised edition of the authors' Essentials of strategic management, 2015.
Identifiers: LCCN 2015045630 | ISBN 9781259546983 (alk. paper)
Subjects: LCSH: Strategic planning. | Business planning. | Competition. | Strategic planning—Case studies.
Classification: LCC HD30.28 .G353 2016 | DDC 658.4/012—dc23 LC record available at http://lccn.loc.gov/2015045630

www.mhhe.com

John E. Gamble is a Professor of Management and Dean of the College of Business at Texas A&M University–Corpus Christi. His teaching and research for nearly 20 years has focused on strategic management at the undergraduate and graduate levels. He has conducted courses in strategic management in Germany since 2001, which have been sponsored by the University of Applied Sciences in Worms.

Dr. Gamble's research has been published in various scholarly journals and he is the author or co-author of more than 75 case studies published in an assortment of strategic management and strategic marketing texts. He has done consulting on industry and market analysis for clients in a diverse mix of industries.

Professor Gamble received his Ph.D., Master of Arts, and Bachelor of Science degrees from The University of Alabama and was a faculty member in the Mitchell College of Business at the University of South Alabama before his appointment to the faculty at Texas A&M University–Corpus Christi.

Margaret A. Peteraf is the Leon E. Williams Professor of Management at the Tuck School of Business at Dartmouth College. She is an internationally recognized scholar of strategic management, with a long list of publications in top management journals. She has earned myriad honors and prizes for her contributions, including the 1999 Strategic Management Society Best Paper Award recognizing the deep influence of her work on the field of strategic management. Professor Peteraf is on the Board of Directors of the Strategic Management Society and has been elected as a Fellow of the Society. She served previously as a member of the Academy of Management's Board of Governors and as Chair of the Business Policy and Strategy Division of the Academy. She has also served in various editorial roles and is presently on nine editorial boards, including the *Strategic Management Journal,* the *Academy of Management Review,* and *Organization Science.* She has taught in Executive Education programs around the world and has won teaching awards at the MBA and Executive level.

Professor Peteraf earned her Ph.D., M.A., and M.Phil. at Yale University and held previous faculty appointments at Northwestern University's Kellogg Graduate School of Management and at the University of Minnesota's Carlson School of Management.

Arthur A. Thompson, Jr., earned his B.S. and Ph.D. degrees in economics from The University of Tennessee, spent three years on the economics faculty at Virginia Tech, and served on the faculty of The University of Alabama's College of Commerce and Business Administration for 25 years. In 1974 and again in 1982, Dr. Thompson spent semester-long sabbaticals as a visiting scholar at the Harvard Business School.

His areas of specialization are business strategy, competition and market analysis, and the economics of business enterprises. In addition to publishing over 30 articles in some 25 different professional and trade publications, he has authored or co-authored five textbooks and six computer-based simulation exercises that are used in colleges and universities worldwide.

Dr. Thompson spends much of his off-campus time giving presentations, putting on management development programs, working with companies, and helping operate a business simulation enterprise in which he is a major partner.

Dr. Thompson and his wife of 54 years have two daughters, two grandchildren, and a Yorkshire terrier.

Brief Contents

The standout features of this fifth edition of *Essentials of Strategic Management* are its concisely written and robust coverage of strategic management concepts and its compelling collection of cases. The text presents a conceptually strong treatment of strategic management principles and analytic approaches that features straight-to-the-point discussions, timely examples, and a writing style that captures the interest of students. While this edition retains the 10-chapter structure of the prior edition, every chapter has been reexamined, refined, and refreshed. New content has been added to keep the material in line with the latest developments in the theory and practice of strategic management. Also, scores of new examples have been added, along with fresh Concepts & Connections illustrations, to make the content come alive and to provide students with a ringside view of strategy in action. The fundamental character of the fifth edition of *Essentials of Strategic Management* is very much in step with the best academic thinking and contemporary management practice. The chapter content continues to be solidly mainstream and balanced, mirroring *both* the penetrating insight of academic thought and the pragmatism of real-world strategic management.

Complementing the text presentation is a truly appealing lineup of 12 diverse, timely, and thoughtfully crafted cases. All of the cases are tightly linked to the content of the 10 chapters, thus pushing students to apply the concepts and analytical tools they have read about. Eleven of the 12 cases were written by the coauthors to illustrate specific tools of analysis or distinct strategic management theories. The Robin Hood case was not written by the coauthors but was included because of its exceptional pedagogical value and linkage to strategic management concepts presented in the text. We are confident you will be impressed with how well each of the 12 cases in the collection will work in the classroom and the amount of student interest they will spark.

For some years now, growing numbers of strategy instructors at business schools worldwide have been transitioning from a purely text-cases course structure to a more robust and energizing text-cases-simulation course structure. Incorporating a competition-based strategy simulation has the strong appeal of providing class members with *an immediate and engaging opportunity to apply the concepts and analytical tools covered in the chapters in a head-to-head competition with companies run by other class members.* Two widely used and pedagogically effective online strategy simulations, *The Business Strategy Game* and *GLO-BUS,* are optional companions for this text. Both simulations, like the cases, are closely linked to the content of each chapter in the text. The Exercises for Simulation Participants, found at the end of each chapter, provide clear guidance to class members in applying the concepts and analytical tools covered in the chapters to the issues and decisions that they have to wrestle with in managing their simulation company.

Through our experiences as business school faculty members, we also fully understand the assessment demands on faculty teaching strategic management and business policy courses. In many institutions, capstone courses have emerged as the logical home for assessing student achievement of program learning objectives. The fifth edition includes Assurance of Learning Exercises at the end of each chapter that link to the specific Learning Objectives appearing at the beginning of each chapter and highlighted throughout the text. *An important instructional feature of this edition is the linkage of selected chapter-end Assurance of Learning Exercises and cases to the publisher's Connect web-based assignment and assessment platform.* Your students will be able to use the online *Connect* supplement to (1) complete two of the Assurance of Learning Exercises appearing at the end of each of the 10 chapters, (2) complete chapter-end quizzes, and (3) complete case tutorials based upon the suggested assignment questions for all 12 cases in this edition. With the exception of some of the chapter-end Assurance of Learning exercises, all of the *Connect* exercises are automatically graded, thereby enabling you to easily assess the learning that has occurred.

In addition, both of the companion strategy simulations have a built-in Learning Assurance Report that quantifies how well each member of your class performed on nine skills/learning measures *versus tens of thousands of other students worldwide* who completed the simulation in the past 12 months. We believe the chapter-end Assurance of Learning Exercises, the all-new online and automatically graded Connect exercises, and the Learning Assurance Report generated at the conclusion of *The Business Strategy Game* and *GLO-BUS* simulations provide you with easy-to-use, empirical measures of student learning in your course. All can be used in conjunction with other instructor-developed or school-developed scoring rubrics and assessment tools to comprehensively evaluate course or program learning outcomes and measure compliance with AACSB accreditation standards.

Taken together, the various components of the fifth edition package and the supporting set of Instructor Resources provide you with enormous course design flexibility and a powerful kit of teaching/learning tools. We've done our very best to ensure that the elements comprising this edition will work well for you in the classroom, help you economize on the time needed to be well prepared for each class, and cause students to conclude that your course is one of the very best they have ever taken—from the standpoint of both enjoyment and learning.

Differentiation from Other Texts

Five noteworthy traits strongly differentiate this text and the accompanying instructional package from others in the field:

1. *Our integrated coverage of the two most popular perspectives on strategic management positioning theory and resource-based theory is unsurpassed by any other leading strategy text.* Principles and concepts from both the positioning perspective and the resource-based perspective are prominently and comprehensively integrated into our coverage of crafting both single-business and multibusiness strategies. By highlighting the relationship between a firm's resources and capabilities to the activities it conducts along its value chain, we show explicitly how these two perspectives relate to one another. Moreover, in Chapters 3 through 8, it is emphasized repeatedly that a company's strategy must be matched not only to its external market circumstances but also to its internal resources and competitive capabilities.

2. *Our coverage of business ethics, core values, social responsibility, and environmental sustainability is unsurpassed by any other leading strategy text.* Chapter 9, "Ethics, Corporate Social Responsibility, Environmental Sustainability, and Strategy," is embellished with fresh content so that it can better fulfill the important functions of (1) alerting students to the role and importance of ethical and socially responsible decision making and (2) addressing the accreditation requirements that business ethics be visibly and thoroughly embedded in the core curriculum. Moreover, discussions of the roles of values and ethics are integrated into portions of other chapters to further reinforce why and how considerations relating to ethics, values, social responsibility, and sustainability should figure prominently into the managerial task of crafting and executing company strategies.

3. *The caliber of the case collection in the fifth edition is truly unrivaled* from the standpoints of student appeal, teachability, and suitability for drilling students in the use of the concepts and analytical treatments in Chapters 1 through 10. The 12 cases included in this edition are the very latest, the best, and the most on-target that we could find. The ample information about the cases in the Instructor's Manual makes it effortless to select a set of cases each term that will capture the interest of students from start to finish.

4. *The publisher's Connect assignment and assessment platform is tightly linked to the text chapters and case lineup.* The *Connect* package for the fifth edition allows professors to assign autograded quizzes and select chapter-end Assurance of Learning Exercises to assess class members' understanding of chapter concepts. In addition, our texts have pioneered the extension of the *Connect* platform to case analysis. The autograded case exercises for each of the 12 cases in this edition are robust and extensive and will better enable students to make meaningful contributions to class discussions. The autograded *Connect* case exercises may also be used as graded assignments in the course.

5. The two cutting-edge and widely used strategy simulations—*The Business Strategy Game* and *GLO-BUS*—that are optional companions to the fifth edition give you unmatched capability to employ a text-case-simulation model of course delivery.

Organization, Content, and Features of the Fifth Edition Text Chapters

The following rundown summarizes the noteworthy features and topical emphasis in this new edition:

- Chapter 1 serves as a introduction to the topic of strategy, focusing on the managerial actions that will determine why a company matters in the marketplace. We introduce students to the primary approaches to building competitive advantage and the key elements of business-level strategy. Following Henry Mintzberg's pioneering research, we also stress why a company's strategy is partly planned and partly reactive and why this strategy tends to evolve. The chapter also discusses why it is important for a company to have a *viable business model* that outlines the company's customer value proposition and its profit formula.

This brief chapter is the perfect accompaniment to your opening-day lecture on what the course is all about and why it matters.

- Chapter 2 delves more deeply into the managerial process of actually crafting and executing a strategy. It makes a great assignment for the second day of class and provides a smooth transition into the heart of the course. The focal point of the chapter is the five-stage managerial process of crafting and executing strategy: (1) forming a strategic vision of where the company is headed and why, (2) developing strategic as well as financial objectives with which to measure the company's progress, (3) crafting a strategy to achieve these targets and move the company toward its market destination, (4) implementing and executing the strategy, and (5) evaluating a company's situation and performance to identify corrective adjustments that are needed. Students are introduced to such core concepts as strategic visions, mission statements and core values, the balanced scorecard, and business-level versus corporate-level strategies. There's a robust discussion of why *all managers are on a company's strategy-making, strategy-executing team* and why a company's strategic plan is a collection of strategies devised by different managers at different levels in the organizational hierarchy. The chapter winds up with a section on how to exercise good corporate governance and examines the conditions that led to recent high-profile corporate governance failures.

- Chapter 3 sets forth the now-familiar analytical tools and concepts of industry and competitive analysis and demonstrates the importance of tailoring strategy to fit the circumstances of a company's industry and competitive environment. The standout feature of this chapter is a presentation of Michael Porter's "five forces model of competition" *that has long been the clearest, most straightforward discussion of any text in the field.* Chapter revisions include an improved discussion of the macro-environment, focusing on the use of the PESTEL analysis framework for assessing the *p*olitical, *e*conomic, *s*ocial, *t*echnological, *e*nvironmental, and *l*egal factors in a company's macro-environment. New to this edition is a discussion of Michael Porter's Framework for Competitor Analysis used for assessing a rival's likely strategic moves.

- Chapter 4 presents the resource-based view of the firm, showing why resource and capability analysis is such a powerful tool for sizing up a company's competitive assets. It offers a simple framework for identifying a company's resources and capabilities and explains how the VRIN framework can be used to determine whether they can provide the company with a sustainable competitive advantage over its competitors. Other topics covered in this chapter include dynamic capabilities, SWOT analysis, value chain analysis, benchmarking, and competitive strength assessments, thus enabling a solid appraisal of a company's relative cost position and customer value proposition vis-à-vis its rivals.

- Chapter 5 deals with the basic approaches used to compete successfully and gain a competitive advantage over market rivals. This discussion is framed around the five generic competitive strategies—low-cost leadership, differentiation, best-cost provider, focused differentiation, and focused low-cost. It describes when each of these approaches works best and what pitfalls to avoid. It explains the role of *cost drivers* and *uniqueness drivers* in reducing a company's costs and enhancing its differentiation, respectively.

- Chapter 6 deals with the *strategy options* available to complement a company's competitive approach and maximize the power of its overall strategy. These include a variety of offensive or defensive competitive moves, and their timing, such as blue ocean strategy and first-mover advantages and disadvantages. It also includes choices concerning the breadth of a company's activities (or its scope of operations along an industry's entire value chain), ranging from horizontal mergers and acquisitions, to vertical integration, outsourcing, and strategic alliances. This material serves to segue into that covered in the next two chapters on international and diversification strategies.

- Chapter 7 explores the full range of strategy options for competing in international markets: export strategies; licensing; franchising; establishing a subsidiary in a foreign market; and using strategic alliances and joint ventures to build competitive strength in foreign markets. There's also a discussion of how to best tailor a company's international strategy to cross-country differences in market conditions and buyer preferences, how to use international operations to improve overall competitiveness, the choice between multidomestic, global, and transnational strategies, and the unique characteristics of competing in emerging markets.

- Chapter 8 introduces the topic of corporate-level strategy—a topic of concern for multibusiness companies pursuing diversification. This chapter begins by explaining why successful diversification strategies must create shareholder value and lays out the three essential tests that a strategy must pass to achieve this goal (*the industry attractiveness, cost of entry, and better-off tests*). Corporate strategy topics covered in the chapter include methods of entering new businesses, related diversification, unrelated diversification, combined related and unrelated diversification approaches, and strategic options for improving the overall performance of an already diversified company. The chapter's analytical spotlight is trained on the techniques and procedures for assessing a diversified company's business portfolio—the relative attractiveness of the various businesses the company has diversified into, the company's competitive strength in each of its business lines, and the *strategic fit* and *resource fit* among a diversified company's different businesses. The chapter concludes with a brief survey of a company's four main post-diversification strategy alternatives: (1) sticking closely with the existing business lineup, (2) broadening the diversification base, (3) divesting some businesses and retrenching to a narrower diversification base, and (4) restructuring the makeup of the company's business lineup.

- Although the topic of ethics and values comes up at various points in this textbook, Chapter 9 brings more direct attention to such issues and may be used as a stand-alone assignment in either the early, middle, or late part of a course. It concerns the themes of ethical standards in business, approaches to ensuring consistent ethical standards for companies with international operations, corporate social responsibility, and environmental sustainability. The contents of this chapter are sure to give students some things to ponder, rouse lively discussion, and help to make students more ethically aware and conscious of *why all companies should conduct their business in a socially responsible and sustainable manner.*

- Chapter 10 is anchored around a pragmatic, compelling conceptual framework: (1) building dynamic capabilities, core competencies, resources, and structure necessary for proficient strategy execution; (2) allocating ample resources to strategy-critical activities; (3) ensuring that policies and procedures facilitate rather than impede strategy execution; (4) pushing for continuous improvement in how value chain activities are performed; (5) installing information and operating systems that enable company personnel to better carry out essential activities; (6) tying rewards and incentives directly to the achievement of performance targets and good strategy execution; (7) shaping the work environment and corporate culture to fit the strategy; and (8) exerting the internal leadership needed to drive execution forward. The recurring theme throughout the chapter is that implementing and executing strategy entails figuring out the specific actions, behaviors, and conditions that are needed for a smooth strategy-supportive operation—the goal here is to ensure that students understand that the strategy-implementing/strategy executing phase is a make-it-happen-right kind of managerial exercise that leads to operating excellence and good performance.

In this latest edition, we have put our utmost effort into ensuring that the 10 chapters are consistent with the latest and best thinking of academics and practitioners in the field of strategic management and hit the bull's-eye in topical coverage for senior- and MBA-level strategy courses. The ultimate test of the text, of course, is the positive pedagogical impact it has in the classroom. If this edition sets a more effective stage for your lectures and does a better job of helping you persuade students that the discipline of strategy merits their rapt attention, then it will have fulfilled its purpose.

The Case Collection

The 12-case lineup in this edition is flush with interesting companies and valuable lessons for students in the art and science of crafting and executing strategy. There's a good blend of cases from a length perspective—about one-third are under 10 pages, yet offer plenty for students to chew on; about a third are medium-length cases; and the remaining one-third are detail-rich cases that call for sweeping analysis.

At least 11 of the 12 cases involve companies, products, people, or activities that students will have heard of, know about from personal experience, or can easily identify with. The lineup includes at least four cases that will provide students with insight into the special demands of competing in industry environments where technological developments are an everyday event, product life cycles are short, and competitive maneuvering among rivals comes fast and furious. All of the cases involve situations where the role of company resources and competitive capabilities in the strategy formulation, strategy execution scheme is emphasized. Scattered throughout the lineup are six cases concerning non-U.S. companies, globally competitive industries, and/or cross-cultural situations; these cases, in conjunction with the globalized content of the text chapters, provide abundant material for linking the study of strategic management tightly to the ongoing globalization of the world economy. You'll also find three cases dealing with the strategic problems of family-owned or relatively small entrepreneurial businesses and 10 cases involving public companies and situations where students can do further research on the Internet. A number of the cases have accompanying videotape segments.

The Two Strategy Simulation Supplements:
The Business Strategy Game and *GLO-BUS*

The Business Strategy Game and *GLO-BUS: Developing Winning Competitive Strategies*—two competition-based strategy simulations that are delivered online and that feature automated processing and grading of performance—are being marketed by the publisher as companion supplements for use with the fifth edition (and other texts in the field). *The Business Strategy Game* is the world's most popular strategy simulation, having been used by more than 2,500 instructors in courses involving over 750,000 students at 1050+ university campuses in 66 countries. *GLO-BUS*, a somewhat simpler strategy simulation introduced in 2004, has been used by more than 1,450 instructors in courses involving over 180,000 students at 640+ university campuses in 48 countries. Both simulations allow students to apply strategy-making and analysis concepts presented in the text and may be used as part of a comprehensive effort to assess undergraduate or graduate program learning objectives.

The Compelling Case for Incorporating Use of a Strategy Simulation

There are *three exceptionally important benefits* associated with using a competition-based simulation in strategy courses taken by seniors and MBA students:

- *A three-pronged text-case-simulation course model delivers significantly more teaching and learning power than the traditional text-case model.* Using *both* cases and a strategy simulation to drill students in thinking strategically and applying what they read in the text chapters is a stronger, more effective means of helping them connect theory with practice and develop better business judgment. What cases do that a simulation cannot is give class members broad exposure to a variety of companies and industry situations and insight into the kinds of strategy-related problems managers face. But what a competition-based strategy simulation does far better than case analysis is thrust class members squarely into *an active, hands-on managerial role* where they are totally responsible for assessing market conditions, determining how to respond to the actions of competitors, forging a long-term direction and strategy for their company, and making all kinds of operating decisions. Because they are held fully accountable for their decisions and their company's performance, *co-managers are strongly motivated* to dig deeply into company operations, probe for ways to be more cost-efficient and competitive, and ferret out strategic moves and decisions calculated to boost company performance. *Consequently, incorporating both case assignments and a strategy simulation to develop the skills of class members in thinking strategically and applying the concepts and tools of strategic analysis turns out to be more pedagogically powerful than relying solely on case assignments: there's stronger retention of the lessons learned and better achievement of course learning objectives.*

- *The competitive nature of a strategy simulation arouses positive energy and steps up the whole tempo of the course by a notch or two.* Nothing sparks class excitement quicker or better than the concerted efforts on the part of class members during each decision round to achieve a high industry ranking and avoid the perilous consequences of being outcompeted by other class members. Students really enjoy taking on the role of a manager, running their own company, crafting strategies, making all kinds of operating decisions, trying to outcompete rival companies, and getting immediate feedback on the resulting company performance. Co-managers become *emotionally invested* in running their company and figuring out what strategic moves to make to boost their company's performance. All this stimulates learning and causes students to see the practical relevance of the subject matter and the benefits of taking your course.

- *Use of a fully automated online simulation reduces the time instructors spend on course preparation, course administration, and grading.* Since the simulation exercise involves a 20- to 30-hour workload for student-teams (roughly 2 hours per decision round times 10-12 rounds, plus optional assignments), simulation adopters often compensate by trimming the number of assigned cases from, say, 10 to 12 to perhaps 4 to 6. This significantly reduces the time instructors spend reading cases, studying teaching notes, and otherwise getting ready to lead class discussion of a case or grade oral team presentations. Course preparation time is further cut because you can use several class days to have students meet in the computer lab to work on upcoming decision rounds or a three-year strategic plan (in lieu of lecturing on a chapter or covering an additional assigned case). Not only does use of a simulation permit assigning fewer cases, but it also permits you to eliminate at least one assignment that entails considerable grading on your part. Grading one less written case or essay exam or other written assignment saves enormous time. With *BSG* and *GLO-BUS,* grading is effortless and takes only minutes; once you enter percentage weights for each assignment in your online grade book, a suggested overall grade is calculated for you. You'll be pleasantly surprised—and quite pleased—at how little time it takes to gear up for and to administer *The Business Strategy Game* or *GLO-BUS.*

In sum, incorporating use of a strategy simulation turns out to be *a win-win proposition for both students and instructors.* Moreover, a very convincing argument can be made that a competition-based strategy simulation is *the single most effective teaching/learning tool that instructors can employ to teach the discipline of business and competitive strategy, to make learning more enjoyable, and to promote better achievement of course learning objectives.*

Administration and Operating Features of the Two Simulations

The Internet delivery and user-friendly designs of both *BSG* and *GLO-BUS* make them incredibly easy to administer, even for first-time users. And the menus and controls are so similar that you can readily switch between the two simulations or use one in your undergraduate class and the other in a graduate class. If you have not yet used either of the two simulations, you may find the following of particular interest:

- Setting up the simulation for your course is done online and takes about 10 to 15 minutes. Once setup is completed, no other administrative actions are required beyond that of moving participants to a different team (should the need arise) and monitoring the progress of the simulation (to whatever extent desired).

- Participant's Guides are delivered electronically to class members at the website—students can read it on their monitors or print out a copy, as they prefer.

- There are two- to four-minute Video Tutorials scattered throughout the software (including each decision screen and each page of each report) that provide on-demand guidance to class members who may be uncertain about how to proceed.

- Complementing the video tutorials are detailed and clearly written Help sections explaining "all there is to know" about (a) each decision entry and the relevant cause-effect relationships, (b) the information on each page of the Industry Reports, and (c) the numbers presented in the Company Reports. *The Video Tutorials and the Help screens allow company co-managers to figure things out for themselves, thereby curbing the need for students to ask the instructor "how things work."*

- Team members running the same company who are logged-in simultaneously on different computers at different locations can click a button to enter Collaboration Mode, enabling them to work collaboratively from the same screen in viewing reports and making decision entries, and click a second button to enter Audio Mode, letting them talk to one another.

  - When in "Collaboration Mode," each team member sees the same screen at the same time as all other team members who are logged in and have joined Collaboration Mode. If one team member chooses to view a particular decision screen, that same screen appears on the monitors for all team members in Collaboration Mode.

  - Team members each control their own color-coded mouse pointer (with their first-name appearing in a color-coded box linked to their mouse pointer) and can make a decision entry or move the mouse to point to particular on-screen items.

  - A decision entry change made by one team member is seen by all, in real time, and all team members can immediately view the on-screen calculations that result from the new decision entry.

  - If one team member wishes to view a report page and clicks on the menu link to the desired report, that same report page will immediately appear for the other team members engaged in collaboration.

  - Use of Audio Mode capability requires that team members work from a computer with a built-in microphone (if they want to be heard by their team members) and speakers (so they may hear their teammates) or else have a headset with a microphone that they can plug into their desktop or laptop. A headset is recommended for best results, but most laptops now are equipped with a built-in microphone and speakers that will support use of our new voice chat feature.

  - Real-time VoIP audio chat capability among team members who have entered both the Audio Mode and the Collaboration Mode is a tremendous boost in functionality that enables team members to go online simultaneously on computers at different locations and conveniently and effectively collaborate in running their simulation company.

  - In addition, instructors have the capability to join the online session of any company and speak with team members, thus circumventing the need for team members to arrange for and attend a meeting in the instructor's office. Using the standard menu for administering a particular industry, instructors can connect with the company desirous of assistance. Instructors who wish not only to talk but also enter Collaboration (highly recommended because all attendees are then viewing the same screen) have a red-colored mouse pointer linked to a red box labeled Instructor.

Without a doubt, the Collaboration and Voice-Chat capabilities are hugely valuable for students enrolled in online and distance-learning courses where meeting face-to-face is impractical or time-consuming. Likewise, the instructors of online and distance-learning courses will appreciate having the capability to join the online meetings of particular company teams when their advice or assistance is requested.

- Both simulations are quite suitable for use in distance-learning or online courses (and are currently being used in such courses on numerous campuses).

- Participants and instructors are notified via e-mail when the results are ready (usually about 15 to 20 minutes after the decision round deadline specified by the instructor/game administrator).

- Following each decision round, participants are provided with a complete set of reports—a six-page Industry Report, a one-page Competitive Intelligence report for each geographic region that includes strategic group maps and bulleted lists of competitive strengths and weaknesses, and a set of Company Reports (income statement, balance sheet, cash flow statement, and assorted production, marketing, and cost statistics).

- Two "open-book" multiple-choice tests of 20 questions are built into each simulation. The quizzes, which you can require or not as you see fit, are taken online and automatically graded, with scores reported instantaneously to participants and automatically recorded in the instructor's electronic grade book. Students are automatically provided with three sample questions for each test.

- Both simulations contain a three-year strategic plan option that you can assign. Scores on the plan are automatically recorded in the instructor's online grade book.

- At the end of the simulation, you can have students complete online peer evaluations (again, the scores are automatically recorded in your online grade book).

- Both simulations have a Company Presentation feature that enables each team of company co-managers to easily prepare PowerPoint slides for use in describing their strategy and summarizing their company's performance in a presentation to either the class, the instructor, or an "outside" board of directors.

- *A Learning Assurance Report provides you with hard data concerning how well your students performed vis-à-vis students playing the simulation worldwide over the past 12 months.* The report is based on nine measures of student proficiency, business know-how, and decision-making skill and can also be used in evaluating the extent to which your school's academic curriculum produces the desired degree of student learning insofar as accreditation standards are concerned.

For more details on either simulation, please consult Section 2 of the Instructor's Manual accompanying this text or register as an instructor at the simulation websites (www.bsg-online.com and www.globus.com) to access even more comprehensive information. You should also consider signing up for one of the webinars that the simulation authors conduct several times each month (sometimes several times weekly) to demonstrate how the software works, walk you through the various features and menu options, and answer any questions. You have an open invitation to call the senior author of this text at (205) 722-9145 to arrange a personal demonstration or talk about how one of the simulations might work in one of your courses. We think you'll be quite impressed with the cutting-edge capabilities that have been programmed into *The Business Strategy Game* and *GLO-BUS,* the simplicity with which both simulations can be administered, and their exceptionally tight connection to the text chapters, core concepts, and standard analytical tools.

Resources and Support Materials for the Fifth Edition for Students

Key Points Summaries

At the end of each chapter is a synopsis of the core concepts, analytical tools, and other key points discussed in the chapter. These chapter-end synopses, along with the core concept definitions and margin notes scattered through out each chapter, help students focus on basic strategy principles, digest the messages of each chapter, and prepare for tests.

Two Sets of Chapter-End Exercises

Each chapter concludes with two sets of exercises. The Assurance of Learning Exercises can be used as the basis for class discussion, oral presentation assignments, short written reports, and substitutes for case assignments. The Exercises for Simulation Participants are designed expressly for use by adopters who have incorporated use of a simulation and wish to go a step further in tightly and explicitly connecting the chapter content to the simulation company their students are running. The questions in both sets of exercises (along with those Concepts & Connections illustrations that qualify as "mini cases") can be used to round out the rest of a 75-minute class period, should your lecture on a chapter only last for 50 minutes.

The *Connect* Web-Based Assignment and Assessment Platform

The *Essentials of Strategic Management,* Fifth Edition takes full advantage of the publisher's innovative *Connect* assignment and assessment platform. The *Connect* package for this edition includes several robust and valuable features that simplify the task of assigning and grading three types of exercises for students:

- There are autograded chapter tests consisting of 20 multiple-choice questions that students can take to measure their grasp of the material presented in each of the 10 chapters.
- *Connect Management* includes interactive versions of two Assurance of Learning Exercises for each chapter that drill students in the use and application of the concepts and tools of strategic analysis. There is both an autograded and open-ended short-answer interactive exercise for each of the 10 chapters.

- The *Connect Management* platform also includes fully autograded interactive application exercises for each of the 12 cases in this edition. The exercises require students to work through tutorials based upon the analysis set forth in the assignment questions for the case; these exercises have multiple components such as resource and capability analysis, financial ratio analysis, identification of a company's strategy, or analysis of the five competitive forces. The content of these case exercises is tailored to match the circumstances presented in each case, calling upon students to do whatever strategic thinking and strategic analysis is called for to arrive at pragmatic, analysis-based action recommendations for improving company performance. The entire exercise is autograded, allowing instructors to focus on grading only the students' strategic recommendations.

All of the *Connect* exercises are automatically graded (with the exception of a few exercise components that entail student entry of essay answers), thereby simplifying the task of evaluating each class member's performance and monitoring the learning outcomes. The progress-tracking function built into the *Connect* system enables you to

- View scored work immediately and track individual or group performance with assignment and grade reports.
- Access an instant view of student or class performance relative to learning objectives.
- Collect data and generate reports required by many accreditation organizations, such as AACSB International.

For Instructors

Connect Management

Connect's Instructor Resources includes an Instructor's Manual and other support materials. Your McGraw-Hill representative can arrange delivery of instructor support materials in a format-ready Standard Cartridge for Blackboard, WebCT, and other web-based educational platforms.

Instructor's Manual

The accompanying IM contains:

- A section on suggestions for organizing and structuring your course.
- Sample syllabi and course outlines.
- A set of lecture notes on each chapter.
- Answers to the chapter-end Assurance of Learning Exercises.
- A comprehensive case teaching note for each of the 12 cases. These teaching notes are filled with suggestions for using the case effectively, have very thorough, analysis-based answers to the suggested assignment questions for the case, and contain an epilogue detailing any important developments since the case was written.

Test Bank and EZ Test Online

There is a test bank containing over 700 multiple-choice questions and short-answer/essay questions. It has been tagged with AACSB and Bloom's Taxonomy criteria. All of the test bank questions are accessible within Connect. All of the test bank questions are also accessible within a computerized test bank powered by McGraw-Hill's flexible electronic testing program, EZ Test Online (www.eztestonline.com). Using EZ Test Online allows you to create paper or online tests and quizzes. With EZ Test Online, instructors can select questions from multiple McGraw-Hill test banks or author their own and then either print the test for paper distribution or give it online.

PowerPoint Slides

To facilitate delivery preparation of your lectures and to serve as chapter outlines, you'll have access to approximately 350 colorful and professional-looking slides displaying core concepts, analytical procedures, key points, and all the figures in the text chapters.

The Business Strategy Game and *GLO-BUS* Online Simulations

Using one of the two companion simulations is a powerful and constructive way of emotionally connecting students to the subject matter of the course. We know of no more effective way to arouse the competitive energy of students and prepare them for the challenges of real-world business decision making than to have them match strategic wits with classmates in running a company in head-to-head competition for global market leadership.

Acknowledgments

We heartily acknowledge the contributions of the case researchers whose case-writing efforts appear herein and the companies whose cooperation made the cases possible. To each one goes a very special thank-you. We cannot overstate the importance of timely, carefully researched cases in contributing to a substantive study of strategic management issues and practices. From a research standpoint, strategy-related cases are invaluable in exposing the generic kinds of strategic issues that companies face in forming hypotheses about strategic behavior and in drawing experienced-based generalizations about the practice of strategic management. From an instructional standpoint, strategy cases give students essential practice in diagnosing and evaluating the strategic situations of companies and organizations, in applying the concepts and tools of strategic analysis, in weighing strategic options and crafting strategies, and in tackling the challenges of successful strategy execution. Without a continuing stream of fresh, well-researched, and well-conceived cases, the discipline of strategic management would lose its close ties to the very institutions whose strategic actions and behavior it is aimed at explaining. There's no question, therefore, that first-class case research constitutes a valuable scholarly contribution to the theory and practice of strategic management.

A great number of colleagues and students at various universities, business acquaintances, and people at McGraw-Hill provided inspiration, encouragement, and counsel during the course of this project. Like all text authors in the strategy field, we are intellectually indebted to the many academics whose research and writing have blazed new trails and advanced the discipline of strategic management.

We also express our thanks to Todd M. Alessandri, Michael Anderson, Gerald D. Baumgardner, Edith C. Busija, Gerald E. Calvasina, Sam D. Cappel, Richard Churchman, John W. Collis, Connie Daniel, Christine DeLaTorre, Vickie Cox Edmondson, Diane D. Galbraith, Naomi A. Gardberg, Sanjay Goel, Les Jankovich, Jonatan Jelen, William Jiang, Bonnie Johnson, Roy Johnson, John J. Lawrence, Robert E. Ledman, Mark Lehrer, Fred Maidment, Frank Markham, Renata Mayrhofer, Simon Medcalfe, Elouise Mintz, Michael Monahan, Gerry Nkombo Muuka, Cori J. Myers, Jeryl L. Nelson, David Olson, John Perry, L. Jeff Seaton, Charles F. Seifert, Eugene S. Simko, Karen J. Smith, Susan Steiner, Troy V. Sullivan, Elisabeth J. Teal, Lori Tisher, Vincent Weaver, Jim Whitlock, and Beth Woodard. These reviewers provided valuable guidance in steering our efforts to improve earlier editions.

As always, we value your recommendations and thoughts about the book. Your comments regarding coverage and contents will be taken to heart, and we always are grateful for the time you take to call our attention to printing errors, deficiencies, and other shortcomings. Please e-mail us at john.gamble@tamucc.edu, or athompso@cba.ua.edu, or margaret.a.peteraf@tuck.dartmouth.edu.

John E. Gamble
Margaret A. Peteraf
Arthur A. Thompson

Contents

Section B: Core Concepts and Analytical Tools

Chapter 3   Evaluating a Company's External Environment   36

Chapter 4   Evaluating a Company's Resources, Capabilities, and Competitiveness   65

Section C: Crafting a Strategy

Chapter 5 The Five Generic Competitive Strategies 89

Chapter 6 Strengthening a Company's Competitive Position: Strategic Moves, Timing, and Scope of Operations 111

Chapter 9 Ethics, Corporate Social Responsibility, Environmental Sustainability, and Strategy 181

Section D: Executing the Strategy

Chapter 10 Superior Strategy Execution—Another Path to Competitive Advantage 198

PART TWO   CASES IN CRAFTING AND EXECUTING STRATEGY

Cases

Required=Results

McGraw-Hill Connect®
Learn Without Limits

Connect is a teaching and learning platform that is proven to deliver better results for students and instructors.

Connect empowers students by continually adapting to deliver precisely what they need, when they need it, and how they need it, so your class time is more engaging and effective.

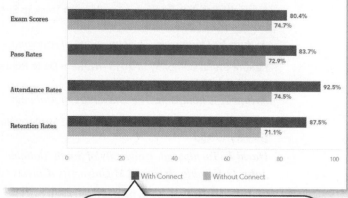

Course outcomes improve with Connect.

	With Connect	Without Connect
Exam Scores	80.4%	74.7%
Pass Rates	83.7%	72.9%
Attendance Rates	92.5%	74.5%
Retention Rates	87.5%	71.1%

Using **Connect** improves passing rates by **10.8%** and retention by **16.4%**.

88% of instructors who use **Connect** require it; instructor satisfaction **increases** by 38% when **Connect** is required.

Analytics

Connect Insight®

Connect Insight is Connect's new one-of-a-kind visual analytics dashboard—now available for both instructors and students—that provides

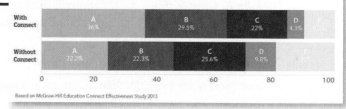

Connect helps students achieve better grades

With Connect	A 36%	B 29.5%	C 22%	D 4.3%
Without Connect	A 22.2%	B 22.3%	C 25.6%	D 9.8%

Based on McGraw-Hill Education Connect Effectiveness Study 2013

at-a-glance information regarding student performance, which is immediately actionable. By presenting assignment, assessment, and topical performance results together with a time metric that is easily visible for aggregate or individual results, Connect Insight gives the user the ability to take a just-in-time approach to teaching and learning, which was never before available. Connect Insight presents data that empowers students and helps instructors improve class performance in a way that is efficient and effective.

Students can view their results for any **Connect** course.

Mobile

Connect's new, intuitive mobile interface gives students and instructors flexible and convenient, anytime–anywhere access to all components of the Connect platform.

Adaptive

THE FIRST AND ONLY **ADAPTIVE READING EXPERIENCE** DESIGNED TO TRANSFORM THE WAY STUDENTS READ

> More students earn **A's** and **B's** when they use McGraw-Hill Education **Adaptive** products.

SmartBook®

Proven to help students improve grades and study more efficiently, SmartBook contains the same content within the print book, but actively tailors that content to the needs of the individual. SmartBook's adaptive technology provides precise, personalized instruction on what the student should do next, guiding the student to master and remember key concepts, targeting gaps in knowledge and offering customized feedback, and driving the student toward comprehension and retention of the subject matter. Available on smartphones and tablets, SmartBook puts learning at the student's fingertips—anywhere, anytime.

> Over **4 billion questions** have been answered, making McGraw-Hill Education products more intelligent, reliable, and precise.

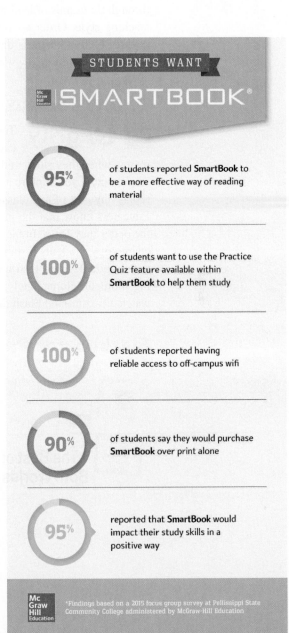

STUDENTS WANT

SMARTBOOK®

95% of students reported **SmartBook** to be a more effective way of reading material

100% of students want to use the Practice Quiz feature available within **SmartBook** to help them study

100% of students reported having reliable access to off-campus wifi

90% of students say they would purchase **SmartBook** over print alone

95% reported that **SmartBook** would impact their study skills in a positive way

Create

Instructors can now tailor their teaching resources to match the way they teach! With McGraw-Hill Create, www.mcgrawhillcreate.com, instructors can easily rearrange chapters, combine material from other content sources, and quickly upload and integrate their own content, such as course syllabi or teaching notes. Find the right content in Create by searching through thousands of leading McGraw-Hill textbooks. Arrange the material to fit your teaching style. Order a Create book and receive a complimentary print review copy in three to five business days or a complimentary electronic review copy via e-mail within one hour. Go to www.mcgrawhillcreate.com today and register.

Tegrity Campus

Tegrity makes class time available 24/7 by automatically capturing every lecture in a searchable format for students to review when they study and complete assignments. With a simple one-click start-and-stop process, you capture all computer screens and corresponding audio. Students can replay any part of any class with easy-to-use browser-based viewing on a PC or Mac. Educators know that the more students can see, hear, and experience class resources, the better they learn. In fact, studies prove it. With patented Tegrity "search anything" technology, students instantly recall key class moments for replay online or on iPods and mobile devices. Instructors can help turn all their students' study time into learning moments immediately supported by their lecture. To learn more about Tegrity, watch a two-minute Flash demo at http://tegritycampus.mhhe.com.

Blackboard® Partnership

McGraw-Hill Education and Blackboard have teamed up to simplify your life. Now you and your students can access Connect and Create right from within your Blackboard course—all with one single sign-on. The grade books are seamless, so when a student completes an integrated Connect assignment, the grade for that assignment automatically (and instantly) feeds your Blackboard grade center. Learn more at www.domorenow.com

Mcgraw-Hill Campus™

Campus McGraw-Hill Campus is a new one-stop teaching and learning experience available to users of any learning management system. This institutional service allows faculty and students to enjoy single sign-on (SSO) access to all McGraw-Hill Higher Education materials, including the award-winning McGraw-Hill Connect platform, from directly within the institution's website. With McGraw-Hill Campus, faculty receive instant access to teaching materials (e.g., eTextbooks, test banks, PowerPoint slides, animations, learning objectives, etc.), allowing them to browse, search, and use any instructor ancillary content in our vast library at no additional cost to instructor or students. In addition, students enjoy SSO access to a variety of free content (e.g., quizzes, flash cards, narrated presentations, etc.) and subscription-based products (e.g., McGraw-Hill Connect). With McGraw-Hill Campus enabled, faculty and students will never need to create another account to access McGraw-Hill products and services. Learn more at www.mhcampus.com.

Strategy, Business Models, and Competitive Advantage

LEARNING OBJECTIVES

LO1   Understand why every company needs a distinctive strategy to compete successfully, manage its business operations, and strengthen its prospects for long-term success.

LO2   Learn why it is important for a company to have a viable business model that outlines the company's customer value proposition and its profit formula.

LO3   Develop an awareness of the five most dependable strategic approaches for setting a company apart from rivals and winning a sustainable competitive advantage.

LO4   Understand that a company's strategy tends to evolve over time because of changing circumstances and ongoing management efforts to improve the company's strategy.

LO5   Learn the three tests of a winning strategy.

In thinking strategically about a company, *managers of all types of businesses must develop a clear understanding of what moves and approaches will be employed to gain advantage in the marketplace.* Advantage over rivals and market-leading performance rarely occur due to happenstance or by merely following routines. Top-performing companies deliberately develop and carry out plans to offer customers value in ways that competitors cannot match. Long-term success in the marketplace is dependent on an action plan for making a company's products or services unique and important in the minds of customers.

> **CORE CONCEPT**
>
> A company's **strategy** explains why the company matters in the marketplace by specifying an approach to creating superior value for customers and determining how capabilities and resources will be utilized to deliver the desired value to customers.

A company's **strategy** spells out why the company matters in the marketplace by defining its approach to creating superior value for customers and how capabilities and resources will be employed to deliver the desired value to customers. In effect, the crafting of a strategy represents a managerial commitment to pursuing an array of choices about how to compete. These include choices about:

- *How* to create products or services that attract and please customers.
- *How* to position the company in the industry.
- *How* to develop and deploy resources to build valuable competitive capabilities.
- *How* each functional piece of the business (R&D, supply chain activities, production, sales and marketing, distribution, finance, and human resources) will be operated.
- *How* to achieve the company's performance targets.

In most industries, companies have considerable freedom in choosing the *hows* of strategy. Thus some rivals strive to create superior value for customers by achieving lower costs than rivals, while others pursue product superiority or personalized customer service or the development of capabilities that rivals cannot match. Some competitors position themselves in only one part of the industry's chain of production/distribution activities, while others are partially or fully integrated, with operations ranging from components production to manufacturing and assembly to wholesale distribution or retailing. Some competitors deliberately confine their operations to local or regional markets; others opt to compete nationally, internationally (several countries), or globally. Some companies decide to operate in only one industry, while others diversify broadly or narrowly, into related or unrelated industries.

The role of this chapter is to define the concepts of strategy and competitive advantage, the relationship between a company's strategy and its business model, why strategies are partly proactive and partly reactive, and why company strategies evolve over time. Particular attention will be paid to what sets a winning strategy apart from a ho-hum or flawed strategy and why the caliber of a company's strategy determines whether it will enjoy a competitive advantage or be burdened by competitive disadvantage. By the end of this chapter, you will have a clear idea of why the tasks of crafting and executing strategy are core management functions and why excellent execution of an excellent strategy is the most reliable recipe for turning a company into a standout performer.

The Importance of a Distinctive Strategy and Competitive Approach

LO1 Understand why every company needs a distinctive strategy to compete successfully, manage its business operations, and strengthen its prospects for long-term success.

For a company to matter in the minds of customers, its strategy needs a distinctive element that sets it apart from rivals and produces a competitive edge. A strategy must tightly fit a company's own particular situation, but there is no shortage of opportunity to fashion a strategy that is discernibly different from the strategies of rivals. In fact, competitive success requires a company's managers to make strategic choices about the key building blocks of its strategy that differ from the choices made by competitors—not 100 percent different but at least different in several important respects. A strategy stands a chance of succeeding only when it is predicated on actions, business approaches, and competitive moves aimed at appealing to buyers *in ways that set a company apart from rivals.* Simply trying to mimic the strategies of the industry's successful companies never works. Rather, every company's strategy needs to have some distinctive element that draws in customers and produces a competitive edge. Strategy, at its essence, is about competing differently—doing what rival firms *don't* do or, better yet, what rival firms *can't* do.[1]

> Mimicking the strategies of successful industry rivals—with either copycat product offerings or efforts to stake out the same market position—rarely works. A creative, distinctive strategy that sets a company apart from rivals and yields a competitive advantage is a company's most reliable ticket for earning above-average profits.

The Relationship Between a Company's Strategy and Business Model

LO2 Learn why it is important for a company to have a viable business model that outlines the company's customer value proposition and its profit formula.

Closely related to the concept of strategy is the concept of a company's **business model**. While the company's strategy sets forth an approach to offering superior value, a company's business model is management's blueprint for delivering a valuable product or service to customers in a manner that will yield an attractive profit.[2] The two elements of a company's business model are (1) its *customer value proposition* and (2) its *profit formula.* The customer value proposition is established by the company's overall strategy and lays out the company's approach to satisfying buyer wants and needs at a price customers will consider a good value. The greater the value provided and the lower the price, the more attractive the value proposition is to customers. The profit formula describes the company's approach to determining a cost structure that will allow for acceptable profits given the pricing tied to its customer value proposition. The lower the costs given the customer value proposition, the greater the ability of the business model to be a moneymaker. The nitty-gritty issue surrounding a company's business model is whether it can execute its customer value proposition profitably. Just because company managers have crafted a strategy for competing and running the business does not automatically mean the strategy will lead to profitability—it may or it may not.[3]

> **CORE CONCEPT**
> A company's **business model** sets forth how its strategy and operating approaches will create value for customers, while at the same time generating ample revenues to cover costs and realizing a profit. The two elements of a company's business model are its (1) customer value proposition and (2) its profit formula.

Cable television providers utilize a business model, keyed to delivering news and entertainment that viewers will find valuable, to secure sufficient revenues from

Concepts Connections 1.1

PANDORA, SIRIUS XM, AND OVER-THE-AIR BROADCAST RADIO: THREE CONTRASTING BUSINESS MODELS

	Pandora	Sirius XM	Over-the-Air Radio Broadcasters
Customer value proposition	• Through free-of-charge Internet radio service, allowed PC, tablet computer, and smartphone users to create up to 100 personalized music and comedy stations • Utilized algorithms to generate playlists based on users' predicted music preferences • Offered programming interrupted by brief, occasional ads; eliminated advertising for Pandora One subscribers	• For a monthly subscription fee, provided satellite-based music, news, sports, national and regional weather, traffic reports in limited areas, and talk radio programming • Also offered subscribers streaming Internet channels and the ability to create personalized, commercial-free stations for online and mobile listening • Offered programming interrupted only by brief, occasional ads	• Provided free-of-charge music, national and local news, local traffic reports, national and local weather, and talk radio programming • Included frequent programming interruption for ads
Profit Formula	Revenue generation: Display, audio, and video ads targeted to different audiences and sold to local and national buyers; subscription revenues generated from an advertising-free option called Pandora One Cost structure: Fixed costs associated with developing software for computers, tablets, and smartphones Fixed and variable costs related to operating data centers to support streaming network content royalties, marketing, and support activities Profit margin: Profitability dependent on generating sufficient advertising revenues and subscription revenues to cover costs and provide attractive profits	Revenue generation: Monthly subscription fees, sales of satellite radio equipment, and advertising revenues Cost structure: Fixed costs associated with operating a satellite-based music delivery service and streaming Internet service Fixed and variable costs related to programming and content royalties, marketing, and support activities Profit margin: Profitability dependent on attracting a sufficiently large number of subscribers to cover costs and provide attractive profits	Revenue generation: Advertising sales to national and local businesses Cost structure: Fixed costs associated with terrestrial broadcasting operations Fixed and variable costs related to local news reporting, advertising sales operations, network affiliate fees, programming and content royalties, commercial production activities, and support activities Profit margin: Profitability dependent on generating sufficient advertising revenues to cover costs and provide attractive profits

Sources: Company documents, 10-Ks, and information posted on their websites.

subscriptions and advertising to cover operating expenses and allow for profits. Aircraft engine manufacturer Rolls Royce employs a "power-by-the-hour" business model that charges airlines leasing fees for engine use, maintenance, and repairs based upon actual hours flown. The company retains ownership of the engines and is able to minimize engine maintenance costs through the use of sophisticated sensors that optimize maintenance and repair schedules. Gillette's business model in razor blades involves achieving economies of scale in the production of its shaving products, selling razors at an attractively low price, and then making money on repeat purchases of razor blades. Concepts & Connections 1.1 discusses three contrasting business models in radio broadcasting.

Strategy and the Quest for Competitive Advantage

The heart and soul of any strategy is the actions and moves in the marketplace that managers are taking to gain a competitive edge over rivals.[4] Five of the most frequently used and dependable strategic approaches to setting a company apart from rivals and winning a sustainable competitive advantage are:

LO3 Develop an awareness of the five most dependable strategic approaches for setting a company apart from rivals and winning a sustainable competitive advantage.

1. *A low-cost provider strategy*—achieving a cost-based advantage over rivals. Walmart and Southwest Airlines have earned strong market positions because of the low-cost advantages they have achieved over their rivals. Low-cost provider strategies can produce a durable competitive edge when rivals find it hard to match the low-cost leader's approach to driving costs out of the business.

2. *A broad differentiation strategy*—seeking to differentiate the company's product or service from rivals' in ways that will appeal to a broad spectrum of buyers. Successful adopters of broad differentiation strategies include Johnson & Johnson in baby products (product reliability) and Apple (innovative products). Differentiation strategies can be powerful so long as a company is sufficiently innovative to thwart rivals' attempts to copy or closely imitate its product offering.

3. *A focused low-cost strategy*—concentrating on a narrow buyer segment (or market niche) and outcompeting rivals by having lower costs than rivals and thus being able to serve niche members at a lower price. Private-label manufacturers of food, health and beauty products, and nutritional supplements use their low-cost advantage to offer supermarket buyers lower prices than those demanded by producers of branded products.

4. *A focused differentiation strategy*—concentrating on a narrow buyer segment (or market niche) and outcompeting rivals by offering niche members customized attributes that meet their tastes and requirements better than rivals' products. Louis Vuitton and Rolex have sustained their advantage in the luxury goods industry through a focus on affluent consumers demanding luxury and prestige.

5. *A best-cost provider strategy*—giving customers more value for the money by satisfying buyers' expectations on key quality/features/performance/service attributes, while beating their price expectations. This approach is a hybrid strategy that blends elements of low-cost provider and differentiation strategies; the aim

Concepts Connections 1.2

STARBUCKS' STRATEGY IN THE SPECIALTY COFFEE MARKET

Since its founding in 1985 as a modest nine-store operation in Seattle, Washington, Starbucks had become the premier roaster and retailer of specialty coffees in the world, with nearly 22,000 store locations in more than 65 countries as of April 2015 and annual sales that were expected to exceed $19 billion in fiscal 2015. The key elements of Starbucks' strategy in specialty coffees included:

- **Train "baristas" to serve a wide variety of specialty coffee drinks that allow customers to satisfy their individual preferences in a customized way.** Starbucks essentially brought specialty coffees, such as cappuccinos, lattes, and macchiatos, to the mass market in the United States, encouraging customers to personalize their coffee drinking habits. Requests for such items as an "Iced Grande Hazelnut Macchiato with Soy Milk and NO Hazelnut Drizzle" could be served up quickly with consistent quality.

- **Emphasis on store ambience and elevating the customer experience at Starbucks stores.** Starbucks management viewed each store as a billboard for the company and as a contributor to building the company's brand and image. Each detail was scrutinized to enhance the mood and ambience of the store to make sure everything signaled "best-of-class" and reflected the personality of the community and the neighborhood. The thesis was "everything mattered." The company went to great lengths to make sure the store fixtures, the merchandise displays, the colors, the artwork, the banners, the music, and the aromas all blended to create a consistent, inviting, stimulating environment that evoked the romance of coffee, that signaled the company's passion for coffee, and that rewarded customers with ceremony, stories, and surprise.

- **Purchase and roast only top-quality coffee beans.** The company purchased only the highest quality arabica beans and carefully roasted coffee to exacting standards of quality

and flavor. Starbucks did not use chemicals or artificial flavors when preparing its roasted coffees.

- **Commitment to corporate responsibility.** Starbucks was protective of the environment and contributed positively to the communities where Starbucks stores were located. In addition, Starbucks promoted fair trade practices and paid above-market prices for coffee beans to provide its growers/suppliers with sufficient funding to sustain their operations and provide for their families.

- **Expansion of the number of Starbucks stores domestically and internationally.** Starbucks operated stores in high-traffic, high-visibility locations in the United States and abroad. The company's ability to vary store size and format made it possible to locate stores in settings such as downtown and suburban shopping areas, office buildings, and university campuses. Starbucks added 317 new company-owned locations in the United States and another 253 company-owned stores internationally in fiscal 2014. Starbucks also added 101 licensed store locations in the United States and 648 licensed stores internationally in 2014. The company planned to open 1,650 new stores globally in fiscal 2015, with 1,000 new units being opened in international markets.

- **Broaden and periodically refresh in-store product offerings.** Noncoffee products offered by Starbucks included teas, fresh pastries and other food items, candy, juice drinks, music CDs, and coffee mugs and coffee accessories.

- **Fully exploit the growing power of the Starbucks name and brand image with out-of-store sales.** Starbucks consumer packaged goods division included domestic and international sales of Frappuccino, coffee ice creams, and Starbucks coffees.

Sources: Company documents, 10-Ks, and information posted on Starbucks' website.

is to have the lowest (best) costs and prices among sellers offering products with comparable differentiating attributes. Target's best-cost advantage allows it to give discount store shoppers more value for the money by offering an attractive product lineup and an appealing shopping ambience at low prices.

In Concepts & Connections 1.2, it's evident that Starbucks has gained a competitive advantage over rivals through its efforts to offer the highest quality coffee-based beverages, create an emotional attachment with customers, expand its global presence, expand the product line, and ensure consistency in store operations. A creative, distinctive strategy such as that used by Starbucks is a company's most reliable ticket for developing a sustainable competitive advantage and earning above-average profits. A **sustainable competitive advantage** allows a company to attract sufficiently large numbers of buyers who have a lasting preference for its products or services over those offered by rivals, despite the efforts of competitors to offset that appeal and overcome the company's advantage. The bigger and more durable the competitive advantage, the better a company's prospects for winning in the marketplace and earning superior long-term profits relative to rivals.

> **CORE CONCEPT**
>
> A company achieves **sustainable competitive advantage** when an attractively large number of buyers develop a durable preference for its products or services over the offerings of competitors, despite the efforts of competitors to overcome or erode its advantage.

The Importance of Capabilities in Building and Sustaining Competitive Advantage

Winning a *sustainable* competitive edge over rivals with any of the above five strategies generally hinges as much on building competitively valuable capabilities that rivals cannot readily match as it does on having a distinctive product offering. Clever rivals can nearly always copy the attributes of a popular product or service, but it is substantially more difficult for rivals to match the know-how and specialized capabilities a company has developed and perfected over a long period. FedEx, for example, has superior capabilities in next-day delivery of small packages. And Hyundai has become the world's fastest-growing automaker as a result of its advanced manufacturing processes and unparalleled quality control system. The capabilities of both of these companies have proven difficult for competitors to imitate or best and have allowed each to build and sustain competitive advantage.

Why a Company's Strategy Evolves over Time

LO4 Understand that a company's strategy tends to evolve over time because of changing circumstances and ongoing management efforts to improve the company's strategy.

The appeal of a strategy that yields a sustainable competitive advantage is that it offers the potential for an enduring edge over rivals. However, managers of every company must be willing and ready to modify the strategy in response to the unexpected moves of competitors, shifting buyer needs and preferences, emerging market opportunities, new ideas for improving the strategy, and mounting evidence that the strategy is not working well. Most of the time, a company's strategy evolves incrementally as management fine-tunes various pieces of the strategy and adjusts the strategy to respond to unfolding events. However, on occasion, major strategy shifts are called for, such as when the strategy is clearly failing or when industry conditions change in dramatic ways.

Regardless of whether a company's strategy changes gradually or swiftly, the important point is that the task of crafting strategy is not a onetime event but is always a work in progress.[5] The evolving nature of a company's strategy means the typical company strategy is a blend of (1) *proactive* moves to improve the company's financial performance and secure a competitive edge and (2) *adaptive* reactions to unanticipated developments and

> Changing circumstances and ongoing management efforts to improve the strategy cause a company's strategy to evolve over time—a condition that makes the task of crafting a strategy a work in progress, not a onetime event.

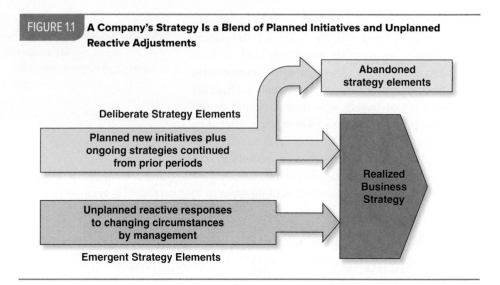

FIGURE 1.1 **A Company's Strategy Is a Blend of Planned Initiatives and Unplanned Reactive Adjustments**

fresh market conditions—see Figure 1.1.[6] The biggest portion of a company's current strategy flows from ongoing actions that have proven themselves in the marketplace and newly launched initiatives aimed at building a larger lead over rivals and further boosting financial performance. This part of management's action plan for running the company is its proactive, **deliberate strategy.**

At times, certain components of a company's deliberate strategy will fail in the marketplace and become **abandoned strategy elements.** Also, managers must always be willing to supplement or modify planned, deliberate strategy elements with as-needed reactions to unanticipated developments. Inevitably, there will be occasions when market and competitive conditions take unexpected turns that call for some kind of strategic reaction. Novel strategic moves on the part of rival firms, unexpected shifts in customer preferences, fast-changing technological developments, and new market opportunities call for unplanned, reactive adjustments that form the company's **emergent strategy.** As shown in Figure 1.1, a company's **realized strategy** tends to be a *combination* of deliberate planned elements and unplanned, emergent elements.

CORE CONCEPT

A company's **realized strategy** is a combination *deliberate planned elements* and *unplanned emergent elements.* Some components of a company's deliberate strategy will fail in the marketplace and become *abandoned strategy elements.*

LO5 Learn the three tests of a winning strategy.

The Three Tests of a Winning Strategy

Three questions can be used to distinguish a winning strategy from a so-so or flawed strategy:

1. *How well does the strategy fit the company's situation?* To qualify as a winner, a strategy has to be well matched to the company's external and internal situations. The strategy must fit competitive conditions in the industry and other aspects of the enterprise's external environment. At the same time, it should be tailored to the company's collection of competitively important resources and

A winning strategy must fit the company's external and internal situation, build sustainable competitive advantage, and improve company performance.

capabilities. It's unwise to build a strategy upon the company's weaknesses or pursue a strategic approach that requires resources that are deficient in the company. Unless a strategy exhibits a tight fit with both the external and internal aspects of a company's overall situation, it is unlikely to produce respectable, first-rate business results.

2. ***Is the strategy helping the company achieve a sustainable competitive advantage?*** Strategies that fail to achieve a durable competitive advantage over rivals are unlikely to produce superior performance for more than a brief period of time. Winning strategies enable a company to achieve a competitive advantage over key rivals that is long lasting. The bigger and more durable the competitive edge that the strategy helps build, the more powerful it is.

3. ***Is the strategy producing good company performance?*** The mark of a winning strategy is strong company performance. Two kinds of performance improvements tell the most about the caliber of a company's strategy: (1) gains in profitability and financial strength and (2) advances in the company's competitive strength and market standing.

Strategies that come up short on one or more of the above tests are plainly less appealing than strategies passing all three tests with flying colors. Managers should use the same questions when evaluating either proposed or existing strategies. New initiatives that don't seem to match the company's internal and external situation should be scrapped before they come to fruition, while existing strategies must be scrutinized on a regular basis to ensure they have a good fit, offer a competitive advantage, and have contributed to above-average performance or performance improvements.

Why Crafting and Executing Strategy Are Important Tasks

High-achieving enterprises are nearly always the product of astute, creative, and proactive strategy making. Companies don't get to the top of the industry rankings or stay there with illogical strategies, copycat strategies, or timid attempts to try to do better. Among all the things managers do, nothing affects a company's ultimate success or failure more fundamentally than how well its management team charts the company's direction, develops competitively effective strategic moves and business approaches, and pursues what needs to be done internally to produce good day-in, day-out strategy execution and operating excellence. Indeed, *good strategy and good strategy execution are the most telling signs of good management.* The rationale for using the twin standards of good strategy making and good strategy execution to determine whether a company is well managed is therefore compelling: *The better conceived a company's strategy and the more competently it is executed, the more likely that the company will be a standout performer in the marketplace.* In stark contrast, a company that lacks clear-cut direction, has a flawed strategy, or can't execute its strategy competently is a company whose financial performance is probably suffering, whose business is at long-term risk, and whose management is sorely lacking.

> How well a company performs is directly attributable to the caliber of its strategy and the proficiency with which the strategy is executed.

The Road Ahead

Throughout the chapters to come and the accompanying case collection, the spotlight is trained on the foremost question in running a business enterprise: *What must managers do, and do well, to make a company a winner in the marketplace?* The answer that emerges is that doing a good job of managing inherently requires good strategic thinking and good management of the strategy-making, strategy-executing process.

The mission of this book is to provide a solid overview of what every business student and aspiring manager needs to know about crafting and executing strategy. We will explore what good strategic thinking entails, describe the core concepts and tools of strategic analysis, and examine the ins and outs of crafting and executing strategy. The accompanying cases will help build your skills in both diagnosing how well the strategy-making, strategy-executing task is being performed and prescribing actions for how the strategy in question or its execution can be improved. The strategic management course that you are enrolled in may also include a strategy simulation exercise where you will run a company in head-to-head competition with companies run by your classmates. Your mastery of the strategic management concepts presented in the following chapters will put you in a strong position to craft a winning strategy for your company and figure out how to execute it in a cost-effective and profitable manner. As you progress through the chapters of the text and the activities assigned during the term, we hope to convince you that first-rate capabilities in crafting and executing strategy are essential to good management.

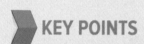 **KEY POINTS**

1. A company's strategy is management's game plan to attract and please customers, compete successfully, conduct operations, and achieve targeted levels of performance. The essence of the strategy explains why the company matters to its customers. It outlines an approach to creating superior customer value and determining how capabilities and resources will be utilized to deliver the desired value to customers.

2. Closely related to the concept of strategy is the concept of a company's business model. A company's business model is management's blueprint for delivering customer value in a manner that will generate revenues sufficient to cover costs and yield an attractive profit. The two elements of a company's business model are its (1) customer value proposition and (2) its profit formula.

3. The central thrust of a company's strategy is undertaking moves to build and strengthen the company's long-term competitive position and financial performance by competing differently from rivals and gaining a sustainable competitive advantage over them.

4. A company's strategy typically evolves over time, arising from a blend of (1) proactive and deliberate actions on the part of company managers and (2) adaptive emergent responses to unanticipated developments and fresh market conditions.

5. A winning strategy fits the circumstances of a company's external and internal situations, builds competitive advantage, and boosts company performance.

ASSURANCE OF LEARNING EXERCISES

1. Based on your experiences as a coffee consumer, does Starbucks' strategy as described in Concepts & Connections 1.2 seem to set it apart from rivals? Does the strategy seem to be keyed to a cost-based advantage, differentiating features, serving the unique needs of a niche, or some combination of these? What is there about Starbucks' strategy that can lead to sustainable competitive advantage?

LO1, LO3

2. Go to investor.siriusxm.com and check whether the SiriusXM's recent financial reports indicate that its business model is working. Are its subscription fees increasing or declining? Is its revenue stream from advertising and equipment sales growing or declining? Does its cost structure allow for acceptable profit margins?

LO2

3. Elements of Google's strategy have evolved in meaningful ways since the company's founding in 1998. After reviewing the company's history at www.google.com/about/company/history/ and all of the links at the company's investor relations site (investor.google.com), prepare a one- to two-page report that discusses how its strategy has evolved. Your report should also assess how well Google's strategy passes the three tests of a winning strategy.

LO4, LO5

EXERCISES FOR SIMULATION PARTICIPANTS

After you have read the Participant's Guide or Player's Manual for the strategy simulation exercise that you will participate in this academic term, you and your co-managers should come up with brief one- or two-paragraph answers to the questions that follow *before* entering your first set of decisions. While your answers to the first of the four questions can be developed from your reading of the manual, the remaining questions will require a collaborative discussion among the members of your company's management team about how you intend to manage the company you have been assigned to run.

1. What is our company's current situation? A substantive answer to this question should cover the following issues:

    • Does your company appear to be in sound financial condition?
    • What problems does your company have that need to be addressed?

    LO5

2. Why will our company matter to customers? A complete answer to this question should say something about each of the following:

    • How will you create customer value?
    • What will be distinctive about the company's products or services?
    • How will capabilities and resources be deployed to deliver customer value?

    LO1, LO3

3. What are the primary elements of your company's business model?

    • Describe your customer value proposition.
    • Discuss the profit formula tied to your business model.
    • What level of revenues is required for your company's business model to become a moneymaker?

    LO2

LO3, LO4, LO5 4. How will you build and sustain competitive advantage?

- Which of the basic strategic and competitive approaches discussed in this chapter do you think makes the most sense to pursue?
- What kind of competitive advantage over rivals will you try to achieve?
- How do you envision that your strategy might evolve as you react to the competitive moves of rival firms?
- Does your strategy have the ability to pass the three tests of a winning strategy? Explain.

ENDNOTES

1. Michael E. Porter, "What Is Strategy?" *Harvard Business Review* 74, no. 6 (November–December 1996).

2. Mark W. Johnson, Clayton M. Christensen, and Henning Kagermann, "Reinventing Your Business Model," *Harvard Business Review* 86, no. 12 (December 2008); Joan Magretta, "Why Business Models Matter," *Harvard Business Review* 80, no. 5 (May 2002).

3. W. Chan Kim and Renée Mauborgne, "How Strategy Shapes Structure," *Harvard Business Review* 87, no. 9 (September 2009).

4. Porter, "What Is Strategy?"

5. Cynthia A. Montgomery, "Putting Leadership Back into Strategy," *Harvard Business Review* 86, no. 1 (January 2008).

6. Henry Mintzberg and Joseph Lampel, "Reflecting on the Strategy Process," *Sloan Management Review* 40, no. 3 (Spring 1999); Henry Mintzberg and J. A. Waters, "Of Strategies, Deliberate and Emergent," *Strategic Management Journal* 6 (1985); Costas Markides, "Strategy as Balance: From 'Either-Or' to 'And,'" *Business Strategy Review* 12, no. 3 (September 2001); Henry Mintzberg, Bruce Ahlstrand, and Joseph Lampel, *Strategy Safari: A Guided Tour Through the Wilds of Strategic Management* (New York: Free Press, 1998); C. K. Prahalad and Gary Hamel, "The Core Competence of the Corporation," *Harvard Business Review* 70, no. 3 (May–June 1990).

Strategy Formulation, Execution, and Governance

LEARNING OBJECTIVES

LO1 Grasp why it is critical for company managers to have a clear strategic vision of where a company needs to head and why.

LO2 Understand the importance of setting both strategic and financial objectives.

LO3 Understand why the strategic initiatives taken at various organizational levels must be tightly coordinated to achieve companywide performance targets.

LO4 Learn what a company must do to achieve operating excellence and to execute its strategy proficiently.

LO5 Become aware of the role and responsibility of a company's board of directors in overseeing the strategic management process.

Crafting and executing strategy are the heart and soul of managing a business enterprise. But exactly what is involved in developing a strategy and executing it proficiently? What are the various components of the strategy formulation, strategy execution process, and to what extent are company personnel—aside from senior management—involved in the process? This chapter presents an overview of the ins and outs of crafting and executing company strategies. Special attention will be given to management's direction-setting responsibilities—charting a strategic course, setting performance targets, and choosing a strategy capable of producing the desired outcomes. We will also explain why strategy formulation is a task for a company's entire management team and discuss which kinds of strategic decisions tend to be made at which levels of management. The chapter concludes with a look at the roles and responsibilities of a company's board of directors and how good corporate governance protects shareholder interests and promotes good management.

The Strategy Formulation, Strategy Execution Process

The managerial process of crafting and executing a company's strategy is an ongoing, continuous process consisting of five integrated stages:

1. *Developing a strategic vision* that charts the company's long-term direction, a *mission statement* that describes the company's business, and a set of *core values* to guide the pursuit of the strategic vision and mission.
2. *Setting objectives* for measuring the company's performance and tracking its progress in moving in the intended long-term direction.
3. *Crafting a strategy* for advancing the company along the path to management's envisioned future and achieving its performance objectives.
4. *Implementing and executing the chosen strategy* efficiently and effectively.
5. *Evaluating and analyzing the external environment and the company's internal situation and performance* to identify corrective adjustments that are needed in the company's long-term direction, objectives, strategy, or approach to strategy execution.

Figure 2.1 displays this five-stage process. The model illustrates the need for management to evaluate a number of external and internal factors in deciding upon a strategic direction, appropriate objectives, and approaches to crafting and executing strategy (see Table 2.1). Management's decisions that are made in the strategic management process must be shaped by the prevailing economic conditions and competitive environment and the company's own internal resources and competitive capabilities. These strategy-shaping conditions will be the focus of Chapters 3 and 4.

The model shown in Figure 2.1 also illustrates the need for management to evaluate the company's performance on an ongoing basis. Any indication that the company is failing to achieve its objectives calls for corrective adjustments in one of the first four stages of the process. The company's implementation efforts might have fallen short, and new tactics must be devised to fully exploit the potential of the company's strategy. If management determines that the company's execution efforts are sufficient, it should challenge the assumptions underlying the company's business strategy

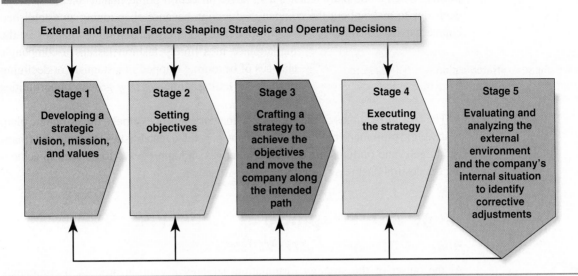

FIGURE 2.1   The Strategy Formulation, Strategy Execution Process

and alter the strategy to better fit competitive conditions and the company's internal capabilities. If the company's strategic approach to competition is rated as sound, then perhaps management set overly ambitious targets for the company's performance.

The evaluation stage of the strategic management process shown in Figure 2.1 also allows for a change in the company's vision, but this should be necessary only when it becomes evident to management that the industry has changed in a significant way that

TABLE 2.1

Factors Shaping Decisions in The Strategy Formulation, Strategy Execution Process

External Considerations

- Does sticking with the company's present strategic course present attractive opportunities for growth and profitability?
- What kind of competitive forces are industry members facing, and are they acting to enhance or weaken the company's prospects for growth and profitability?
- What factors are driving industry change, and what impact on the company's prospects will they have?
- How are industry rivals positioned, and what strategic moves are they likely to make next?
- What are the key factors of future competitive success, and does the industry offer good prospects for attractive profits for companies possessing those capabilities?

Internal Considerations

- Does the company have an appealing customer value proposition?
- What are the company's competitively important resources and capabilities, and are they potent enough to produce a sustainable competitive advantage?
- Does the company have sufficient business and competitive strength to seize market opportunities and nullify external threats?
- Are the company's costs competitive with those of key rivals?
- Is the company competitively stronger or weaker than key rivals?

renders the vision obsolete. Such occasions can be referred to as **strategic inflection points**. When a company reaches a strategic inflection point, management has tough decisions to make about the company's direction because abandoning an established course carries considerable risk. However, responding to unfolding changes in the marketplace in a timely fashion lessens a company's chances of becoming trapped in a stagnant or declining business or letting attractive new growth opportunities slip away.

> A company's **strategic plan** lays out its future direction, performance targets, and strategy.

The first three stages of the strategic management process make up a strategic plan. A **strategic plan** maps out where a company is headed, establishes strategic and financial targets, and outlines the competitive moves and approaches to be used in achieving the desired business results.[1]

Stage 1: Developing a Strategic Vision, a Mission, and Core Values

LO1 Grasp why it is critical for company managers to have a clear strategic vision of where a company needs to head and why.

At the outset of the strategy formulation, strategy execution process, a company's senior managers must wrestle with the issue of what directional path the company should take and whether its market positioning and future performance prospects could be improved by changing the company's product offerings and/or the markets in which it participates and/or the customers it caters to and/or the technologies it employs. Top management's views about the company's direction and future product-customer-market-technology focus constitute a **strategic vision** for the company. A clearly articulated strategic vision communicates management's aspirations to stakeholders about "where we are going" and helps steer the energies of company personnel in a common direction. For instance, Henry Ford's vision of a car in every garage had power because it captured the imagination of others, aided internal efforts to mobilize the Ford Motor Company's resources, and served as a reference point for gauging the merits of the company's strategic actions.

CORE CONCEPT

A **strategic vision** describes "where we are going"—the course and direction management has charted and the company's future product-customer-market-technology focus.

Well-conceived visions are *distinctive* and *specific* to a particular organization; they avoid generic, feel-good statements such as "We will become a global leader and the first choice of customers in every market we choose to serve"—which could apply to any of hundreds of organizations.[2] And they are not the product of a committee charged with coming up with an innocuous but well-meaning one-sentence vision that wins consensus approval from various stakeholders. Nicely worded vision statements with no specifics about the company's product-market-customer-technology focus fall well short of what it takes for a vision to measure up.

For a strategic vision to function as a valuable managerial tool, it must provide understanding of what management wants its business to look like and provide managers with a reference point in making strategic decisions. It must say something definitive about how the company's leaders intend to position the company beyond where it is today. Table 2.2 lists some characteristics of effective vision statements.

A surprising number of the vision statements found on company websites and in annual reports are vague and unrevealing, saying very little about the company's

TABLE 2.2
Characteristics of Effectively Worded Vision Statements

Graphic—Paints a picture of the kind of company that management is trying to create and the market position(s) the company is striving to stake out

Directional—Is forward-looking; describes the strategic course that management has charted and the kinds of product-market-customer-technology changes that will help the company prepare for the future

Focused—Is specific enough to provide managers with guidance in making decisions and allocating resources

Flexible—Is not so focused that it makes it difficult for management to adjust to changing circumstances in markets, customer preferences, or technology

Feasible—Is within the realm of what the company can reasonably expect to achieve

Desirable—Indicates why the directional path makes good business sense

Easy to communicate—Is explainable in 5 to 10 minutes and, ideally, can be reduced to a simple, memorable "slogan" (like Henry Ford's famous vision of "a car in every garage")

Source: Based partly on John P. Kotter, *Leading Change* (Boston: Harvard Business School Press, 1996), p. 72.

TABLE 2.3
Common Shortcomings in Company Vision Statements

Vague or incomplete—Short on specifics about where the company is headed or what the company is doing to prepare for the future

Not forward-looking—Doesn't indicate whether or how management intends to alter the company's current product-market-customer-technology focus

Too broad—So all-inclusive that the company could head in most any direction, pursue most any opportunity, or enter most any business

Bland or uninspiring—Lacks the power to motivate company personnel or inspire shareholder confidence about the company's direction

Not distinctive—Provides no unique company identity; could apply to companies in any of several industries (including rivals operating in the same market arena)

Too reliant on superlatives—Doesn't say anything specific about the company's strategic course beyond the pursuit of such distinctions as being a recognized leader, a global or worldwide leader, or the first choice of customers

Sources: Based on information in Hugh Davidson, *The Committed Enterprise* (Oxford: Butterworth Heinemann, 2002), chap. 2; and Michel Robert, *Strategy Pure and Simple II* (New York: McGraw-Hill, 1998), chaps. 2, 3, and 6.

future product-market-customer-technology focus. Some could apply to most any company in any industry. Many read like a public relations statement—lofty words that someone came up with because it is fashionable for companies to have an official vision statement.[3] Table 2.3 provides a list of the most common shortcomings in company vision statements. Like any tool, vision statements can be used properly or improperly, either clearly conveying a company's strategic course or not. Concepts & Connections 2.1 provides a critique of the strategic visions of several prominent companies.

The Importance of Communicating the Strategic Vision

A strategic vision has little value to the organization unless it's effectively communicated down the line to lower-level managers and employees. It would be difficult for a vision statement to provide direction to decision makers and energize employees toward achieving long-term strategic intent unless they know of the vision and observe management's commitment to that vision. Communicating the vision to organization members nearly always means putting "where we are going and why" in writing, distributing the statement organization-wide, and having executives personally explain the vision and its rationale to as many people as feasible. Ideally, executives should present their vision for the company in a manner that reaches out and grabs people's attention. An engaging and convincing strategic vision has enormous motivational value—for the same reason that a stonemason is inspired by building a great cathedral for the ages. Therefore, an executive's ability to paint a convincing and inspiring picture of a company's journey to a future destination is an important element of effective strategic leadership.[4]

Expressing the Essence of the Vision in a Slogan The task of effectively conveying the vision to company personnel is assisted when management can capture the vision of where to head in a catchy or easily remembered slogan. A number of organizations have summed up their vision in a brief phrase. Nike's vision slogan is "To bring innovation and inspiration to every athlete in the world." The Mayo Clinic's vision is to provide "The best care to every patient every day," while Greenpeace's envisioned future is "To halt environmental abuse and promote environmental solutions." Creating a short slogan to illuminate an organization's direction and then using it repeatedly as a reminder of "where we are headed and why" helps rally organization members to hurdle whatever obstacles lie in the company's path and maintain their focus.

> An effectively communicated vision is a valuable management tool for enlisting the commitment of company personnel to engage in actions that move the company in the intended direction.

Why a Sound, Well-Communicated Strategic Vision Matters A well-thought-out, forcefully communicated strategic vision pays off in several respects: (1) it crystallizes senior executives' own views about the firm's long-term direction; (2) it reduces the risk of rudderless decision making by management at all levels; (3) it is a tool for winning the support of employees to help make the vision a reality; (4) it provides a beacon for lower-level managers in forming departmental missions; and (5) it helps an organization prepare for the future.

Developing a Company Mission Statement

> The distinction between a **strategic vision** and a **mission statement** is fairly clear-cut: A strategic vision portrays a company's *future business scope* ("where we are going"), whereas a company's mission statement typically describes its *present business and purpose* ("who we are, what we do, and why we are here").

The defining characteristic of a well-conceived **strategic vision** is what it says about the company's *future strategic course—"where we are headed and what our future product-customer-market-technology focus will be."* The **mission statements** of most companies say much more about the enterprise's *present* business scope and purpose—"who we are, what we do, and why we are here." Very few mission statements are forward-looking

Concepts & Connections 2.1

EXAMPLES OF STRATEGIC VISIONS—HOW WELL DO THEY MEASURE UP?

Vision Statement	Effective Elements	Shortcomings
Coca-Cola Our vision serves as the framework for our roadmap and guides every aspect of our business by describing what we need to accomplish in order to continue achieving sustainable, quality growth. • People: Be a great place to work where people are inspired to be the best they can be. • Portfolio: Bring to the world a portfolio of quality beverage brands that anticipate and satisfy people's desires and needs. • Partners: Nurture a winning network of customers and suppliers; together we create mutual, enduring value. • Planet: Be a responsible citizen that makes a difference by helping build and support sustainable communities. • Profit: Maximize long-term return to shareowners while being mindful of our overall responsibilities. • Productivity: Be a highly effective, lean and fast-moving organization.	• Focused • Flexible • Feasible • Desirable	• Long • Not forward-looking
UBS We are determined to be the best global financial services company. We focus on wealth and asset management, and on investment banking and securities businesses. We continually earn recognition and trust from clients, shareholders, and staff through our ability to anticipate, learn and shape our future. We share a common ambition to succeed by delivering quality in what we do. Our purpose is to help our clients make financial decisions with confidence. We use our resources to develop effective solutions and services for our clients. We foster a distinctive, meritocratic culture of ambition, performance and learning as this attracts, retains and develops the best talent for our company. By growing both our client and our talent franchises, we add sustainable value for our shareholders.	• Focused • Feasible • Desirable	• Not forward-looking • Bland or uninspiring
Caterpillar Our vision is a world in which all people's basic needs—such as shelter, clean water, sanitation, food and reliable power—are fulfilled in an environmentally sustainable way and a company that improves the quality of the environment and the communities where we live and work.	• Graphic • Desirable	• Too broad • Too reliant on superlatives • Not distinctive
Procter & Gamble We will provide branded products and services of superior quality and value that improve the lives of the world's consumers, now and for generations to come. As a result, consumers will reward us with leadership sales, profit and value creation, allowing our people, our shareholders, and the communities in which we live and work to prosper.	• Directional • Flexible • Desirable	• Too broad • Too reliant on superlatives

Sources: Company documents and websites.

in content or emphasis. Consider, for example, the mission statement of Singapore Airlines, which is consistently rated among the world's best in terms of passenger safety and comfort:

> Singapore Airlines is a global company dedicated to providing air transportation services of the highest quality and to maximizing returns for the benefit of its shareholders and employees.

Note that Singapore Airlines' mission statement does a good job of conveying "who we are, what we do, and why we are here," but it provides no sense of "where we are headed."

An example of a well-stated mission statement with ample specifics about what the organization does is that of St. Jude Children's Research Hospital: "to advance cures, and means of prevention, for pediatric catastrophic diseases through research and treatment. Consistent with the vision of our founder Danny Thomas, no child is denied treatment based on race, religion or a family's ability to pay." Facebook's mission statement, while short, still captures the essence of what the company is about: "to give people the power to share and make the world more open and connected." An example of a not-so-revealing mission statement is that of Microsoft. "To help people and businesses throughout the world realize their full potential" says nothing about its products or business makeup and could apply to many companies in many different industries. A well-conceived mission statement should employ language specific enough to give the company its own identity. A mission statement that provides scant indication of "who we are and what we do" has no apparent value.

> **CORE CONCEPT**
>
> A well-conceived **mission statement** conveys a company's purpose in language specific enough to give the company its own identity.

Ideally, a company mission statement is sufficiently descriptive to:

- Identify the company's products or services.
- Specify the buyer needs it seeks to satisfy.
- Specify the customer groups or markets it is endeavoring to serve.
- Specify its approach to pleasing customers.
- Give the company its own identity.

Occasionally, companies state that their mission is to simply earn a profit. This is misguided. Profit is more correctly an *objective* and a *result* of what a company does. Moreover, earning a profit is the obvious intent of every commercial enterprise. Such companies as BMW, Netflix, Shell Oil, Procter & Gamble, Google, and McDonald's are each striving to earn a profit for shareholders, but the fundamentals of their businesses are substantially different when it comes to "who we are and what we do."

Linking the Strategic Vision and Mission with Company Values

> **CORE CONCEPT**
>
> A company's **values** are the beliefs, traits, and behavioral norms that company personnel are expected to display in conducting the company's business and pursuing its strategic vision and mission.

Many companies have developed a statement of **values** (sometimes called *core values*) to guide the actions and behavior of company personnel in conducting the company's business and pursuing its strategic vision and mission. These values are the designated beliefs and desired ways of doing things at the company and frequently relate to such things as fair treatment, honor and integrity, ethical behavior, innovativeness, teamwork, a passion for excellence, social responsibility, and community citizenship.

Most companies normally have four to eight core values. At Samsung, five core values are linked to its philosophy of devoting its talent and technology to create superior products and services that contribute to a better global society: (1) giving people opportunities to reach their full potential, (2) developing the best products and services on the market, (3) embracing change, (4) operating in an ethical way, and (5) dedication to social and environmental responsibility. Home Depot embraces eight values—entrepreneurial spirit, excellent customer service, giving back to the community, respect for all people, doing the right thing, taking care of people, building strong relationships, and creating shareholder value—in its quest to be the world's leading home improvement retailer.

Do companies practice what they preach when it comes to their professed values? Sometimes no, sometimes yes—it runs the gamut. At one extreme are companies with window-dressing values; the professed values are given lip service by top executives but have little discernible impact on either how company personnel behave or how the company operates. At the other extreme are companies whose executives are committed to grounding company operations on sound values and principled ways of doing business. Executives at these companies deliberately seek to ingrain the designated core values into the corporate culture—the core values thus become an integral part of the company's DNA and what makes it tick. At such values-driven companies, executives "walk the talk" and company personnel are held accountable for displaying the stated values. Concepts & Connections 2.2 describes how core values drive the company's mission at Patagonia, a widely known and quite successful outdoor clothing and gear company.

Stage 2: Setting Objectives

LO2 Understand the importance of setting both strategic and financial objectives.

The managerial purpose of setting **objectives** is to convert the strategic vision into specific performance targets. Objectives reflect management's aspirations for company performance in light of the industry's prevailing economic and competitive conditions and the company's internal capabilities. Well-stated objectives are *quantifiable,* or *measurable,* and contain a *deadline for achievement.* Concrete, measurable objectives are managerially valuable because they serve as yardsticks for tracking a company's performance and progress toward its vision. Vague targets such as "maximize profits," "reduce costs," "become more efficient," or "increase sales," which specify neither how much nor when, offer little value as a management tool to improve company performance. Ideally, managers should develop *challenging,* yet *achievable* objectives that *stretch an organization to perform at its full potential.* As Mitchell Leibovitz, former CEO of the auto parts and service retailer Pep Boys, once said, "If you want to have ho-hum results, have ho-hum objectives."

> **CORE CONCEPT**
>
> **Objectives** are an organization's performance targets—the results management wants to achieve.

What Kinds of Objectives to Set

Two very distinct types of performance yardsticks are required: those relating to financial performance and those relating to strategic performance. **Financial objectives**

Concepts Connections 2.2

PATAGONIA, INC.: A VALUES-DRIVEN COMPANY

PATAGONIA'S MISSION STATEMENT

Build the best product, cause no unnecessary harm, use business to inspire and implement solutions to the environmental crisis.

PATAGONIA'S CORE VALUES

Quality: Pursuit of ever-greater quality in everything we do.

Integrity: Relationships built on integrity and respect.

Environmentalism: Serve as a catalyst for personal and corporate action.

Not Bound by Convention: Our success—and much of the fun—lies in developing innovative ways to do things.

Patagonia, Inc., is an American outdoor clothing and gear company that clearly "walks the talk" with respect to its mission and values. While its mission is relatively vague about the types of products Patagonia offers, it clearly states the foundational "how" and "why" of the company. The four core values individually reinforce the mission in distinct ways, charting a defined path for employees to follow. At the same time, each value is reliant on the others for maximum effect. The values' combined impact on internal operations and public perception has made Patagonia a strong leader in the outdoor gear world.

While many companies espouse the pursuit of **quality** as part of their strategy, at Patagonia quality must come through honorable practices or not at all. Routinely, the company opts for more expensive materials and labor to maintain internal consistency with the mission. Patagonia learned early on that it could not make good products in bad factories, so it holds its manufacturers accountable through a variety of auditing partnerships and alliances. In this way, the company maintains relationships built on **integrity** and respect. In addition to keeping faith with those who make its products, Patagonia relentlessly pursues integrity in sourcing production inputs. Central to its **environmental** mission and core values, it targets for use sustainable and recyclable materials, ethically procured. Demonstrating leadership in environmentalism, Patagonia established foundations to support ecological causes, even **defying convention** by giving 1 percent of profits to conservation causes. These are but a few examples of the ways in which Patagonia's core values fortify each other and support the mission.

For Patagonia, quality would not be possible without integrity, unflinching environmentalism, and the company's unconventional approach. Since its founding in 1973 by rock climber Yvon Chouinard, Patagonia has remained remarkably consistent to the spirit of these values. This has endeared the company to legions of loyal customers while leading other businesses in protecting the environment. More than an apparel and gear company, Patagonia inspires everyone it touches to do their best for the planet and each other, in line with its mission and core values.

Note: Developed with Nicholas J. Ziemba.

Sources: Patagonia, Inc., "Corporate Social Responsibility," *The Footprint Chronicles,* 2007, and "Becoming a Responsible Company," www.patagonia.com/us/patagonia.go?assetid=2329 (accessed February 28, 2014).

communicate management's targets for financial performance. Common financial objectives relate to revenue growth, profitability, and return on investment. **Strategic objectives** are related to a company's marketing standing and competitive vitality. The importance of attaining financial objectives is intuitive. Without adequate profitability and financial strength, a company's long-term health and ultimate survival is jeopardized. Furthermore, subpar earnings and a weak balance sheet alarm shareholders and creditors and put the jobs of senior executives at risk. However, good financial performance, by itself, is not enough.

A company's financial objectives are really *lagging indicators* that reflect the results of past decisions and organizational activities.[5] The results of past decisions and organizational activities are not reliable indicators of a company's future prospects. Companies that have been poor financial performers are sometimes able to turn things around, and good financial performers on occasion fall upon hard times. Hence, the best and most reliable predictors of a company's success in the marketplace and future financial performance are strategic objectives. Strategic outcomes are *leading indicators* of a company's future financial performance and business prospects. The accomplishment of strategic objectives signals the company is well positioned to sustain or improve its performance. For instance, if a company is achieving ambitious strategic objectives, then there's reason to expect that its *future* financial performance will be better than its current or past performance. If a company begins to lose competitive strength and fails to achieve important strategic objectives, then its ability to maintain its present profitability is highly suspect.

Consequently, utilizing a performance measurement system that strikes a *balance* between financial objectives and strategic objectives is optimal.[6] Just tracking a company's financial performance overlooks the fact that what ultimately enables a company to deliver better financial results is the achievement of strategic objectives that improve its competitiveness and market strength. Representative examples of financial and strategic objectives that companies often include in a **balanced scorecard** approach to measuring their performance are displayed in Table 2.4.[7]

> ### CORE CONCEPT
> **Financial objectives** relate to the financial performance targets management has established for the organization to achieve.
>
> **Strategic objectives** relate to target outcomes that indicate a company is strengthening its market standing, competitive vitality, and future business prospects.

> ### CORE CONCEPT
> The **balanced scorecard** is a widely used method for combining the use of both strategic and financial objectives, tracking their achievement, and giving management a more complete and balanced view of how well an organization is performing.

In 2010, nearly 50 percent of global companies used a balanced scorecard approach to measuring strategic and financial performance.[8] Examples of organizations that have adopted a balanced scorecard approach to setting objectives and measuring performance include Siemens AG, Wells Fargo Bank, Ann Taylor Stores, Ford Motor Company, Hilton Hotels, and Ohio State University.[9] Concepts & Connections 2.3 provides selected strategic and financial objectives of three prominent companies.

Short-Term and Long-Term Objectives

A company's set of financial and strategic objectives should include both near-term and long-term performance targets. Short-term objectives focus attention on delivering performance improvements in the current period, whereas long-term targets force the organization to consider how actions currently under way will affect the company later. Specifically, long-term objectives stand as a barrier to an undue focus on short-term results by nearsighted management. When trade-offs have to be made between achieving long-run and short-run objectives, long-run objectives should take precedence (unless the achievement of one or more short-run performance targets has unique importance).

choices for the particular operating unit under their supervision—knowing the prevailing market and competitive conditions, customer requirements and expectations, and all the other relevant aspects affecting the several strategic options available.

A Company's Strategy-Making Hierarchy

The larger and more diverse the operations of an enterprise, the more points of strategic initiative it will have and the more managers at different organizational levels will have a relevant strategy-making role. In diversified companies, where multiple and sometimes strikingly different businesses have to be managed, crafting a full-fledged strategy involves four distinct types of strategic actions and initiatives, each undertaken at different levels of the organization and partially or wholly crafted by managers at different organizational levels, as shown in Figure 2.2. A company's overall strategy is therefore *a collection of strategic initiatives and actions* devised by managers up and down the whole organizational hierarchy. Ideally, the pieces of a company's strategy up and down the strategy hierarchy should be cohesive and mutually reinforcing, fitting together like a jigsaw puzzle.

FIGURE 2.2 **A Company's Strategy-Making Hierarchy**

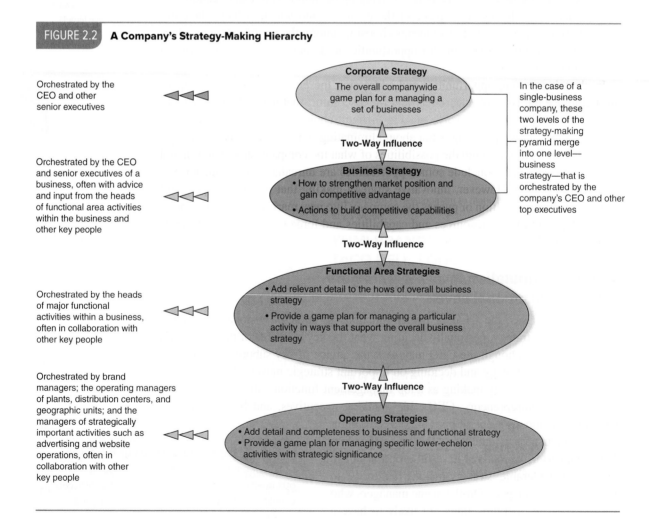

Orchestrated by the CEO and other senior executives

Corporate Strategy
The overall companywide game plan for a managing a set of businesses

In the case of a single-business company, these two levels of the strategy-making pyramid merge into one level—business strategy—that is orchestrated by the company's CEO and other top executives

Two-Way Influence

Orchestrated by the CEO and senior executives of a business, often with advice and input from the heads of functional area activities within the business and other key people

Business Strategy
• How to strengthen market position and gain competitive advantage
• Actions to build competitive capabilities

Two-Way Influence

Orchestrated by the heads of major functional activities within a business, often in collaboration with other key people

Functional Area Strategies
• Add relevant detail to the hows of overall business strategy
• Provide a game plan for managing a particular activity in ways that support the overall business strategy

Two-Way Influence

Orchestrated by brand managers; the operating managers of plants, distribution centers, and geographic units; and the managers of strategically important activities such as advertising and website operations, often in collaboration with other key people

Operating Strategies
• Add detail and completeness to business and functional strategy
• Provide a game plan for managing specific lower-echelon activities with strategic significance

As shown in Figure 2.2, **corporate strategy** is orchestrated by the CEO and other senior executives and establishes an overall game plan for managing a *set of businesses* in a diversified, multibusiness company. Corporate strategy addresses the questions of how to capture cross-business synergies, what businesses to hold or divest, which new markets to enter, and how to best enter new markets—by acquisition, by creation of a strategic alliance, or through internal development. Corporate strategy and business diversification are the subject of Chapter 8, where they are discussed in detail.

> **Corporate strategy** establishes an overall game plan for managing a *set of businesses* in a diversified, multibusiness company.
>
> **Business strategy** is primarily concerned with strengthening the company's market position and building competitive advantage in a single business company or a single business unit of a diversified multibusiness corporation.

Business strategy is primarily concerned with building competitive advantage in a single business unit of a diversified company or strengthening the market position of a nondiversified single business company. Business strategy is also the responsibility of the CEO and other senior executives, but key business-unit heads may also be influential, especially in strategic decisions affecting the businesses they lead. *In single-business companies, the corporate and business levels of the strategy-making hierarchy merge into a single level—business strategy—because the strategy for the entire enterprise involves only one distinct business.* So, a single-business company has three levels of strategy: business strategy, functional-area strategies, and operating strategies.

Functional-area strategies concern the actions related to particular functions or processes within a business. A company's product development strategy, for example, represents the managerial game plan for creating new products that are in tune with what buyers are looking for. Lead responsibility for functional strategies within a business is normally delegated to the heads of the respective functions, with the general manager of the business having final approval over functional strategies. For the overall business strategy to have maximum impact, a company's marketing strategy, production strategy, finance strategy, customer service strategy, product development strategy, and human resources strategy should be compatible and mutually reinforcing rather than each serving its own narrower purpose.

Operating strategies concern the relatively narrow strategic initiatives and approaches for managing key operating units (plants, distribution centers, geographic units) and specific operating activities such as materials purchasing or Internet sales. Operating strategies are limited in scope but add further detail to functional-area strategies and the overall business strategy. Lead responsibility for operating strategies is usually delegated to front line managers, subject to review and approval by higher-ranking managers.

Stage 4: Implementing and Executing the Chosen Strategy

LO4 Learn what a company must do to achieve operating excellence and to execute its strategy proficiently.

Managing the implementation and execution of strategy is easily the most demanding and time-consuming part of the strategic management process. Good strategy execution entails that managers pay careful attention to how key internal business processes are performed and see to it that employees' efforts are directed toward the accomplishment of desired operational outcomes. The task of implementing and executing the strategy also necessitates an ongoing analysis of the efficiency and effectiveness of a company's internal activities and a managerial awareness of new technological developments that might improve business processes. In most situations, managing the strategy execution process includes the following principal aspects:

- Staffing the organization to provide needed skills and expertise.
- Allocating ample resources to activities critical to good strategy execution.
- Ensuring that policies and procedures facilitate rather than impede effective execution.
- Installing information and operating systems that enable company personnel to perform essential activities.
- Pushing for continuous improvement in how value chain activities are performed.
- Tying rewards and incentives directly to the achievement of performance objectives.
- Creating a company culture and work climate conducive to successful strategy execution.
- Exerting the internal leadership needed to propel implementation forward.

Stage 5: Evaluating Performance and Initiating Corrective Adjustments

The fifth stage of the strategy management process—evaluating and analyzing the external environment and the company's internal situation and performance to identify needed corrective adjustments—is the trigger point for deciding whether to continue or change the company's vision, objectives, strategy, and/or strategy execution methods. So long as the company's direction and strategy seem well matched to industry and competitive conditions and performance targets are being met, company executives may well decide to stay the course. Simply fine-tuning the strategic plan and continuing with efforts to improve strategy execution are sufficient.

But whenever a company encounters disruptive changes in its environment, questions need to be raised about the appropriateness of its direction and strategy. If a company experiences a downturn in its market position or persistent shortfalls in performance, then company managers are obligated to ferret out the causes—do they relate to poor strategy, poor strategy execution, or both?—and take timely corrective action. A company's direction, objectives, and strategy have to be revisited any time external or internal conditions warrant.

> A company's vision, objectives, strategy, and approach to strategy execution are never final; managing strategy is an ongoing process, not an every-now-and-then task.

Also, it is not unusual for a company to find that one or more aspects of its strategy implementation and execution are not going as well as intended. Proficient strategy execution is always the product of much organizational learning. It is achieved unevenly—coming quickly in some areas and proving nettlesome in others. Successful strategy execution entails vigilantly searching for ways to improve and then making corrective adjustments whenever and wherever it is useful to do so.

Corporate Governance: The Role of the Board of Directors in the Strategy Formulation, Strategy Execution Process

LO5 Become aware of the role and responsibility of a company's board of directors in overseeing the strategic management process.

Although senior managers have *lead responsibility* for crafting and executing a company's strategy, it is the duty of the board of directors to exercise strong oversight and see that the five tasks of strategic management are done in a manner that benefits shareholders (in the case of investor-owned enterprises) or stakeholders (in the case of not-for-profit organizations). In watching over management's strategy formulation, strategy execution actions, a company's board of directors has four important corporate governance obligations to fulfill:

1. *Oversee the company's financial accounting and financial reporting practices.* While top management, particularly the company's CEO and CFO (chief financial officer), is primarily responsible for seeing that the company's financial statements accurately report the results of the company's operations, board members have a fiduciary duty to protect shareholders by exercising oversight of the company's financial practices. In addition, corporate boards must ensure that generally acceptable accounting principles (GAAP) are properly used in preparing the company's financial statements and determine whether proper financial controls are in place to prevent fraud and misuse of funds. Virtually all boards of directors monitor the financial reporting activities by appointing an audit committee, always composed entirely of *outside directors* (*inside directors* hold management positions in the company and either directly or indirectly report to the CEO). The members of the audit committee have lead responsibility for overseeing the decisions of the company's financial officers and consulting with both internal and external auditors to ensure that financial reports are accurate and adequate financial controls are in place. Faulty oversight of corporate accounting and financial reporting practices by audit committees and corporate boards during the early 2000s resulted in the federal investigation of more than 20 major corporations between 2000 and 2002. The investigations of such well-known companies as AOL Time Warner, Global Crossing, Enron, Qwest Communications, and WorldCom found that upper management had employed fraudulent or unsound accounting practices to artificially inflate revenues, overstate assets, and reduce expenses. The scandals resulted in the conviction of a number of corporate executives and the passage of the Sarbanes-Oxley Act of 2002, which tightened financial reporting standards and created additional compliance requirements for public boards.

2. *Diligently critique and oversee the company's direction, strategy, and business approaches.* Even though board members have a legal obligation to warrant the accuracy of the company's financial reports, directors must set aside time to guide management in choosing a strategic direction and to make independent judgments about the validity and wisdom of management's proposed strategic actions. Many boards have found that meeting agendas become consumed by compliance matters and little time is left to discuss matters of strategic importance. The board of directors and management at Philips Electronics hold annual two- to three-day retreats devoted to evaluating the company's

long-term direction and various strategic proposals. The company's exit from the semiconductor business and its increased focus on medical technology and home health care resulted from management–board discussions during such retreats.[12]

3. *Evaluate the caliber of senior executives' strategy formulation and strategy execution skills.* The board is always responsible for determining whether the current CEO is doing a good job of strategic leadership and whether senior management is actively creating a pool of potential successors to the CEO and other top executives.[13] Evaluation of senior executives' strategy formulation and strategy execution skills is enhanced when outside directors go into the field to personally evaluate how well the strategy is being executed. Independent board members at GE visit operating executives at each major business unit once per year to assess the company's talent pool and stay abreast of emerging strategic and operating issues affecting the company's divisions. Home Depot board members visit a store once per quarter to determine the health of the company's operations.[14]

4. *Institute a compensation plan for top executives that rewards them for actions and results that serve shareholder interests.* A basic principle of corporate governance is that the owners of a corporation delegate operating authority and managerial control to top management in return for compensation. In their role as an *agent* of shareholders, top executives have a clear and unequivocal duty to make decisions and operate the company in accord with shareholder interests (but this does not mean disregarding the interests of other stakeholders, particularly those of employees, with whom they also have an agency relationship). Most boards of directors have a compensation committee, composed entirely of directors from outside the company, to develop a salary and incentive compensation plan that rewards senior executives for boosting the company's *long-term performance* and growing the economic value of the enterprise on behalf of shareholders; the compensation committee's recommendations are presented to the full board for approval.

   But too often, boards of directors have done a poor job of ensuring that executive salary increases, bonuses, and stock option awards are tied tightly to performance measures that are truly in the long-term interests of shareholders. Rather, compensation packages at many companies have rewarded executives for *short-term performance* improvements—most notably, achieving quarterly and annual earnings targets and boosting the stock price by specified percentages. This has had the perverse effect of causing company managers to become preoccupied with actions to improve a company's near-term performance, even if excessively risky and damaging to long-term company performance—witness the huge loss of shareholder wealth that occurred at many financial institutions in 2008–2009 because of executive risk-taking in subprime loans, credit default swaps, and collateralized mortgage securities in 2006–2007. As a consequence, the need to overhaul and reform executive compensation has become a hot topic in both public circles and corporate boardrooms. Concepts & Connections 2.4 discusses how weak governance at Fannie Mae and Freddie Mac allowed opportunistic senior managers to secure exorbitant bonuses, while making decisions that imperiled the futures of the companies they managed.

Concepts & Connections 2.4

CORPORATE GOVERNANCE FAILURES AT FANNIE MAE AND FREDDIE MAC

Executive compensation in the financial services industry during the mid-2000s ranks high among examples of failed corporate governance. Corporate governance at the government-sponsored mortgage giants Fannie Mae and Freddie Mac was particularly weak. The politically appointed boards at both enterprises failed to understand the risks of the subprime loan strategies being employed, did not adequately monitor the decisions of the CEO, did not exercise effective oversight of the accounting principles being employed (which led to inflated earnings), and approved executive compensation systems that allowed management to manipulate earnings to receive lucrative performance bonuses. The audit and compensation committees at Fannie Mae were particularly ineffective in protecting shareholder interests, with the audit committee allowing the government-sponsored enterprise's financial officers to audit reports prepared under their direction and used to determine performance bonuses. Fannie Mae's audit committee also was aware of management's use of questionable accounting practices that reduced losses and recorded onetime gains to achieve earnings per share targets linked to bonuses. In addition, the audit committee failed to investigate formal charges of accounting improprieties filed by a manager in the Office of the Controller.

Fannie Mae's compensation committee was equally ineffective. The committee allowed the company's CEO, Franklin Raines, to select the consultant employed to design the mortgage firm's executive compensation plan and agreed to a tiered bonus plan that would permit Raines and other senior managers to receive maximum bonuses without great difficulty. The compensation plan allowed Raines to earn performance-based bonuses of $52 million and total compensation of $90 million between 1999 and 2004. Raines was forced to resign in December 2004 when the Office of Federal Housing Enterprise Oversight found that Fannie Mae executives had fraudulently inflated earnings to receive bonuses linked to financial performance. Securities and Exchange Commission investigators also found evidence of improper accounting at Fannie Mae and required it to restate its earnings between 2002 and 2004 by $6.3 billion.

Poor governance at Freddie Mac allowed its CEO and senior management to manipulate financial data to receive performance-based compensation as well. Freddie Mac CEO Richard Syron received 2007 compensation of $19.8 million while the mortgage company's share price declined from a high of $70 in 2005 to $25 at year-end 2007. During Syron's tenure as CEO, the company became embroiled in a multibillion-dollar accounting scandal, and Syron personally disregarded internal reports dating to 2004 that warned of an impending financial crisis at the company. Forewarnings within Freddie Mac and by federal regulators and outside industry observers proved to be correct, with loan underwriting policies at Freddie Mac and Fannie Mae leading to combined losses at the two firms in 2008 of more than $100 billion. The price of Freddie Mac's shares had fallen to below $1 by Syron's resignation in September 2008.

Both organizations were placed into a conservatorship under the direction of the U.S. government in September 2008 and were provided bailout funds of nearly $200 billion by 2013. At that point, the U.S. Treasury amended the organization's bailout terms to require that all profits be transferred to the government while downsizing the firms. By 2014, the bailout had finally been fully repaid.

Sources: Chris Isidore, "Fannie, Freddie Bailout: $153 Billion . . . and Counting," *CNNMoney,* February 11, 2011; "Adding Up the Government's Total Bailout Tab," *New York Times Online,* February 4, 2009; Eric Dash, "Fannie Mae to Restate Results by $6.3 Billion Because of Accounting," *New York Times Online,* www.nytimes.com, December 7, 2006; Annys Shin, "Fannie Mae Sets Executive Salaries," *Washington Post,* February 9, 2006, p. D4; and Scott DeCarlo, Eric Weiss, Mark Jickling, and James R. Cristie, *Fannie Mae and Freddie Mac: Scandal in U.S. Housing.* (Hauppauge, NY: Nova Publishers, 2006), pp. 266–86.

Every corporation should have a strong, independent board of directors that (1) is well informed about the company's performance, (2) guides and judges the CEO and other top executives, (3) has the courage to curb management actions it believes are inappropriate or unduly risky, (4) certifies to shareholders that the CEO is doing what the board expects, (5) provides insight and advice to management, and (6) is intensely involved in debating the pros and cons of key decisions and actions.[15] Boards of directors that lack the backbone to challenge a strong-willed or "imperial" CEO or that rubber-stamp most anything the CEO recommends without probing inquiry and debate abandon their duty to represent and protect shareholder interests.

 **KEY POINTS**

The strategic management process consists of five interrelated and integrated stages:

1. *Developing a strategic vision* of where the company needs to head and what its future product-customer-market-technology focus should be. This managerial step provides long-term direction, infuses the organization with a sense of purposeful action, and communicates to stakeholders management's aspirations for the company.

2. *Setting objectives* and using the targeted results as yardsticks for measuring the company's performance. Objectives need to spell out *how much* of *what kind* of performance *by when*. A *balanced scorecard* approach for measuring company performance entails setting both *financial objectives and strategic objectives.*

3. *Crafting a strategy to achieve the objectives* and move the company along the strategic course that management has charted. The total strategy that emerges is really a collection of strategic actions and business approaches initiated partly by senior company executives, partly by the heads of major business divisions, partly by functional-area managers, and partly by operating managers on the front lines. A single business enterprise has three levels of strategy—business strategy for the company as a whole, functional-area strategies for each main area within the business, and operating strategies undertaken by lower-echelon managers. In diversified, multibusiness companies, the strategy-making task involves four distinct types or levels of strategy: corporate strategy for the company as a whole, business strategy (one for each business the company has diversified into), functional-area strategies within each business, and operating strategies. Typically, the strategy-making task is more top-down than bottom-up, with higher-level strategies serving as the guide for developing lower-level strategies.

4. *Implementing and executing the chosen strategy efficiently and effectively.* Managing the implementation and execution of strategy is an operations-oriented, make-things-happen activity aimed at shaping the performance of core business activities in a strategy supportive manner. Management's handling of the strategy implementation process can be considered successful if things go smoothly enough that the company meets or beats its strategic and financial performance targets and shows good progress in achieving management's strategic vision.

5. *Evaluating and analyzing the external environment and the company's internal situation and performance to identify corrective adjustments* in vision, objectives, strategy, or execution. This stage of the strategy management process is the trigger point for deciding whether to continue or change the company's vision, objectives, strategy, and/or strategy execution methods.

The sum of a company's strategic vision, objectives, and strategy constitutes a *strategic plan.*

Boards of directors have a duty to shareholders to play a vigilant role in overseeing management's handling of a company's strategy formulation, strategy execution process. A company's board is obligated to (1) ensure that the company issues accurate financial reports and has adequate financial controls, (2) critically appraise and ultimately approve strategic action plans, (3) evaluate the strategic leadership skills of the CEO, and (4) institute a compensation plan for top executives that rewards them for actions and results that serve stakeholder interests, most especially those of shareholders.

 ASSURANCE OF LEARNING EXERCISES

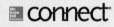

LO1

1. Using the information in Tables 2.2 and 2.3, critique the adequacy and merit of the following vision statements, listing effective elements and shortcomings. Rank the vision statements from best to worst once you complete your evaluation.

VISION STATEMENT

American Express
We work hard every day to make American Express the world's most respected service brand.

Hilton Hotels Corporation
Our vision is to be the first choice of the world's travelers. Hilton intends to build on the rich heritage and strength of our brands by:
- Consistently delighting our customers
- Investing in our team members
- Delivering innovative products and services
- Continuously improving performance
- Increasing shareholder value
- Creating a culture of pride
- Strengthening the loyalty of our constituents

BASF
We are "The Chemical Company" successfully operating in all major markets.
- Our customers view BASF as their partner of choice.
- Our innovative products, intelligent solutions and services make us the most competent worldwide supplier in the chemical industry.
- We generate a high return on assets.
- We strive for sustainable development.
- We welcome change as an opportunity.
- We, the employees of BASF, together ensure our success.

Source: Company websites and annual reports.

2. Go to the company investor relations websites for Starbucks (investor.starbucks.com), Pfizer (www.pfizer.com/investors), and Salesforce (investor.salesforce.com) to find examples of strategic and financial objectives. List four objectives for each company, and indicate which of these are strategic and which are financial.   **LO2**

3. American Airlines' Chapter 11 reorganization plan filed in 2012 involved the company reducing operating expenses by $2 billion, while increasing revenues by $1 billion. The company's strategy to increase revenues included expanding the number of international flights and destinations and increasing daily departures for its five largest markets by 20 percent. The company also intended to upgrade its fleet by spending $2 billion to purchase new aircraft and refurbish the first-class cabins for planes not replaced. A final component of the restructuring plan included a merger with US Airways to create a global airline with more than 56,700 daily flights to 336 destinations in 56 countries. The merger was expected to produce cost savings from synergies of more than $1 billion and result in a stronger airline capable of paying creditors and rewarding employees and shareholders. Explain why the strategic initiatives at various organizational levels and functions require tight coordination to achieve the results desired by American Airlines.   **LO3**

4. Go to the investor relations website for Walmart Stores, Inc., (http://investors.walmartstores.com) and review past presentations it has made during various investor conferences by clicking on the Events option in the navigation bar. Prepare a one- to two-page report that outlines what Walmart has said to investors about its approach to strategy execution. Specifically, what has management discussed concerning staffing, resource allocation, policies and procedures, information and operating systems, continuous improvement, rewards and incentives, corporate culture, and internal leadership at the company?   **LO4**

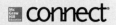

5. Based on the information provided in Concepts & Connections 2.4, explain how corporate governance at Freddie Mac failed the enterprise's shareholders and other stakeholders. Which important obligations to shareholders were fulfilled by Fannie Mae's board of directors? What is your assessment of how well Fannie Mae's compensation committee handled executive compensation at the government-sponsored mortgage giant?

LO5

 EXERCISES FOR SIMULATION PARTICIPANTS

LO1 1. Meet with your co-managers and prepare a strategic vision statement for your company. It should be at least one sentence long and no longer than a brief paragraph. When you are finished, check to see if your vision statement meets the conditions for an effectively worded strategic vision set forth in Table 2.2 and avoids the shortcomings set forth in Table 2.3. If not, then revise it accordingly. What would be a good slogan that captures the essence of your strategic vision and that could be used to help communicate the vision to company personnel, shareholders, and other stakeholders?

LO2 2. What are your company's financial objectives? What are your company's strategic objectives?

LO3 3. What are the three or four key elements of your company's strategy?

 ENDNOTES

1. Gordon Shaw, Robert Brown, and Philip Bromiley, "Strategic Stories: How 3M Is Rewriting Business Planning," *Harvard Business Review* 76, no. 3 (May–June 1998); David J. Collins and Michael G. Rukstad, "Can You Say What Your Strategy Is?" *Harvard Business Review* 86, no. 4 (April 2008).

2. Hugh Davidson, *The Committed Enterprise: How to Make Vision and Values Work* (Oxford: Butterworth Heinemann, 2002); W. Chan Kim and Renée Mauborgne, "Charting Your Company's Future," *Harvard Business Review* 80, no. 6 (June 2002); James C. Collins and Jerry I. Porras, "Building Your Company's Vision," *Harvard Business Review* 74, no. 5 (September–October 1996); Jim Collins and Jerry Porras, *Built to Last: Successful Habits of Visionary Companies* (New York: HarperCollins, 1994); Michel Robert, *Strategy Pure and Simple II: How Winning Companies Dominate Their Competitors* (New York: McGraw-Hill, 1998).

3. Hugh Davidson, *The Committed Enterprise* (Oxford: Butterworth Heinemann, 2002).

4. Ibid.

5. Robert S. Kaplan and David P. Norton, *The Strategy-Focused Organization* (Boston: Harvard Business School Press, 2001).

6. Ibid. Also, see Robert S. Kaplan and David P. Norton, *The Balanced Scorecard: Translating Strategy into Action* (Boston: Harvard Business School Press, 1996); Kevin B.Hendricks, Larry Menor, and Christine Wiedman, "The Balanced Scorecard: To Adopt or Not to Adopt," *Ivey Business Journal* 69, no. 2 (November–December 2004); Sandy Richardson, "The Key Elements of Balanced Scorecard Success," *Ivey Business Journal* 69, no. 2 (November–December 2004).

7. Kaplan and Norton, *The Balanced Scorecard: Translating Strategy into Action,* pp. 25–29. Kaplan and Norton classify strategic objectives under the categories of customer-related, business processes, and learning and growth. In practice, companies using the balanced scorecard may choose categories of strategic objectives that best reflect the organization's value-creating activities and processes.

8. Information posted on the website of Bain and Company, www.bain.com (accessed May 27, 2011).

9. Information posted on the website of Balanced Scorecard Institute (accessed May 27, 2011).

10. Henry Mintzberg, Bruce Ahlstrand, and Joseph Lampel, *Strategy Safari: A Guided Tour Through the Wilds of Strategic Management* (New York: Free Press, 1998); Bruce Barringer and Allen C. Bluedorn, "The Relationship Between Corporate Entrepreneurship and Strategic Management," *Strategic Management Journal* 20 (1999); Jeffrey G. Covin and Morgan P. Miles,

"Corporate Entrepreneurship and the Pursuit of Competitive Advantage," *Entrepreneurship: Theory and Practice* 23, no. 3 (Spring 1999); David A. Garvin and Lynne C. Levesque, "Meeting the Challenge of Corporate Entrepreneurship," *Harvard Business Review* 84, no. 10 (October 2006).

11. Roger L. Martin, "The Big Lie of Strategic Planning," *Harvard Business Review* 92, no. 1/2 (January–February 2014), pp. 78–84.

12. Jay W. Lorsch and Robert C. Clark, "Leading from the Boardroom," *Harvard Business Review* 86, no. 4 (April 2008).

13. Ibid., p. 110.

14. Stephen P. Kaufman, "Evaluating the CEO," *Harvard Business Review* 86, no. 10 (October 2008).

15. David A. Nadler, "Building Better Boards," *Harvard Business Review* 82, no. 5 (May 2004); Cynthia A. Montgomery and Rhonda Kaufman, "The Board's Missing Link," *Harvard Business Review* 81, no. 3 (March 2003); John Carver, "What Continues to Be Wrong with Corporate Governance and How to Fix It," *Ivey Business Journal* 68, no. 1 (September/October 2003); Gordon Donaldson, "A New Tool for Boards: The Strategic Audit," *Harvard Business Review* 73, no. 4 (July–August 1995).

Evaluating a Company's External Environment

LEARNING OBJECTIVES

LO1 Identify factors in a company's broad macro-environment that may have strategic significance.

LO2 Recognize the factors that cause competition in an industry to be fierce, more or less normal, or relatively weak.

LO3 Become adept at mapping the market positions of key groups of industry rivals.

LO4 Learn how to determine whether an industry's outlook presents a company with sufficiently attractive opportunities for growth and profitability.

In Chapter 2, we learned that the strategy formulation, strategy execution process begins with an appraisal of the company's present situation. The company's situation includes two facets: (1) its external environment—most notably, the competitive conditions in the industry in which the company operates; and (2) its internal environment—particularly the company's resources and organizational capabilities.

Charting a company's long-term direction, conceiving its customer value proposition, setting objectives, or crafting a strategy without first gaining an understanding of the company's external and internal environments hamstrings attempts to build competitive advantage and boost company performance. Indeed, the first test of a winning strategy inquires, *"How well does the strategy fit the company's situation?"*

This chapter presents the concepts and analytical tools for zeroing in on a single-business company's external environment. Attention centers on the competitive arena in which the company operates, the drivers of market change, the market positions of rival companies, and the factors that determine competitive success. Chapter 4 explores the methods of evaluating a company's internal circumstances and competitiveness.

Assessing the Company's Industry and Competitive Environment

Thinking strategically about a company's industry and competitive environment entails using some well-validated concepts and analytical tools to get clear answers to seven questions:

1. Do macro-environmental factors and industry characteristics offer sellers opportunities for growth and attractive profits?
2. What kinds of competitive forces are industry members facing, and how strong is each force?
3. What forces are driving industry change, and what impact will these changes have on competitive intensity and industry profitability?
4. What market positions do industry rivals occupy—who is strongly positioned and who is not?
5. What strategic moves are rivals likely to make next?
6. What are the key factors of competitive success?
7. Does the industry outlook offer good prospects for profitability?

Analysis-based answers to these questions are prerequisites for a strategy offering good fit with the external situation. The remainder of this chapter is devoted to describing the methods of obtaining solid answers to these seven questions.

Question 1: What Are the Strategically Relevant Components of the Macro-Environment?

A company's external environment includes the immediate industry and competitive environment and broader macro-environmental factors such as general economic conditions, societal values and cultural norms, political factors, the legal and regulatory

LO1 Identify factors in a company's broad macro-environment that may have strategic significance.

CORE CONCEPT

The **macro-environment** encompasses the broad environmental context in which a company is situated and is comprised of six principal components: political factors, economic conditions, sociocultural forces, technological factors, environmental factors, and legal/regulatory conditions.

PESTEL analysis can be used to assess the strategic relevance of the six principal components of the macro-environment: political, economic, sociocultural, technological, environmental, and legal forces.

environment, ecological considerations, and technological factors. These two levels of a company's external environment—the broad outer ring macro-environment and immediate inner ring industry and competitive environment—are illustrated in Figure 3.1. Strictly speaking, the **macro-environment** encompasses all of the *relevant factors* making up the broad environmental context in which a company operates; by *relevant,* we mean the factors are important enough that they should shape management's decisions regarding the company's long-term direction, objectives, strategy, and business model. The relevance of macro-environmental factors can be evaluated using **PESTEL analysis,** an acronym for the six principal components of the macro-environment: political factors, economic conditions in the firm's general environment, sociocultural forces, technological factors, environmental forces, and legal/regulatory factors. Table 3.1 provides a description of each of the six PESTEL components of the macro-environment.

The impact of outer ring macro-environmental factors on a company's choice of strategy can be big or small. But even if the factors of the macro-environment change slowly or are likely to have a low impact on the company's business situation, they still merit a watchful eye. Changes in sociocultural forces and technological factors have begun to have strategy-shaping effects on companies competing in industries ranging from news and entertainment to taxi services. As company managers scan the external environment, they must be alert for potentially important outer ring developments, assess their impact and influence, and adapt the company's direction and strategy as needed.

FIGURE 3.1 **The Components of a Company's External Environment**

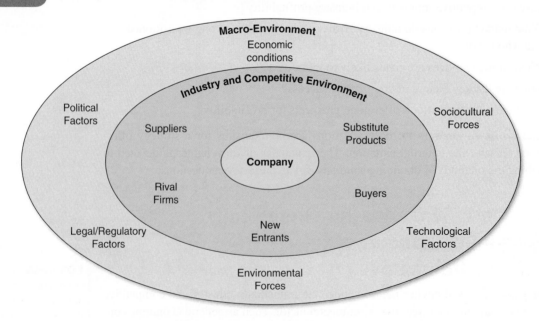

TABLE 3.1

The Six Components of the Macro-Environment Included in a PESTEL Analysis

Component	Description
Political factors	These factors include political policies and processes, including the extent to which a government intervenes in the economy. They include such matters as tax policy, fiscal policy, tariffs, the political climate, and the strength of institutions such as the federal banking system. Some political factors, such as bailouts, are industry-specific. Others, such as energy policy, affect certain types of industries (energy producers and heavy users of energy) more than others.
Economic conditions	Economic conditions include the general economic climate and specific factors such as interest rates, exchange rates, the inflation rate, the unemployment rate, the rate of economic growth, trade deficits or surpluses, savings rates, and per capita domestic product. Economic factors also include conditions in the markets for stocks and bonds, which can affect consumer confidence and discretionary income. Some industries, such as construction, are particularly vulnerable to economic downturns but are positively affected by factors such as low interest rates. Others, such as discount retailing, may benefit when general economic conditions weaken, as consumers become more price-conscious. Economic characteristics of the industry such as market size and growth rate are also important to evaluate when assessing an industry's prospects for growth and attractive profits.
Sociocultural forces	Sociocultural forces include the societal values, attitudes, cultural factors, and lifestyles that impact businesses, as well as demographic factors such as the population size, growth rate, and age distribution. Sociocultural forces vary by locale and change over time. An example is the trend toward healthier lifestyles, which can shift spending toward exercise equipment and health clubs and away from alcohol and snack foods. Population demographics can have large implications for industries such as health care, where costs and service needs vary with demographic factors such as age and income distribution.
Technological factors	Technological factors include the pace of technological change and technical developments that have the potential for wide-ranging effects on society, such as genetic engineering and nanotechnology. They include institutions involved in creating knowledge and controlling the use of technology, such as R&D consortia, university-sponsored technology incubators, patent and copyright laws, and government control over the Internet. Technological change can encourage the birth of new industries, such as those based on nanotechnology, and disrupt others, such as the recording industry.
Environmental forces	These include ecological and environmental forces such as weather, climate, climate change, and associated factors such as water shortages. These factors can directly impact industries such as insurance, farming, energy production, and tourism. They may have an indirect but substantial effect on other industries such as transportation and utilities.
Legal and regulatory factors	These factors include the regulations and laws with which companies must comply such as consumer laws, labor laws, antitrust laws, and occupational health and safety regulations. Some factors, such as banking deregulation, are industry-specific. Others, such as minimum wage legislation, affect certain types of industries (low-wage, labor-intensive industries) more than others.

However, the factors and forces in a company's external environment that have the *biggest* strategy-shaping impact typically pertain to the company's immediate inner ring industry and competitive environment—the competitive pressures brought about by the actions of rival firms, the competitive effects of buyer behavior, supplier-related competitive considerations, the impact of new entrants to the industry, and availability of acceptable or superior substitutes for a company's products or services. The inner ring industry and competitive environment is fully explored in Question 2 of this chapter using Porter's Five-Forces Model of Competition.

Question 2: How Strong Are the Industry's Competitive Forces?

LO2 Recognize the factors that cause competition in an industry to be fierce, more or less normal, or relatively weak.

After an understanding of the industry's general economic characteristics is gained, industry and competitive analysis should focus on the competitive dynamics of the industry. The nature and subtleties of competitive forces are never the same from one industry to another and must be wholly understood to accurately assess the company's current situation. Far and away the most powerful and widely used tool for assessing the strength of the industry's competitive forces is the *five-forces model of competition*.[1] This model, as depicted in Figure 3.2, holds that competitive forces affecting industry attractiveness go beyond rivalry among competing sellers and include pressures stemming from four coexisting sources. The five competitive forces affecting industry attractiveness are listed.

1. Competitive pressures stemming from *buyer* bargaining power.

2. Competitive pressures coming from companies in other industries to win buyers over to *substitute products.*

FIGURE 3.2 **The Five-Forces Model of Competition**

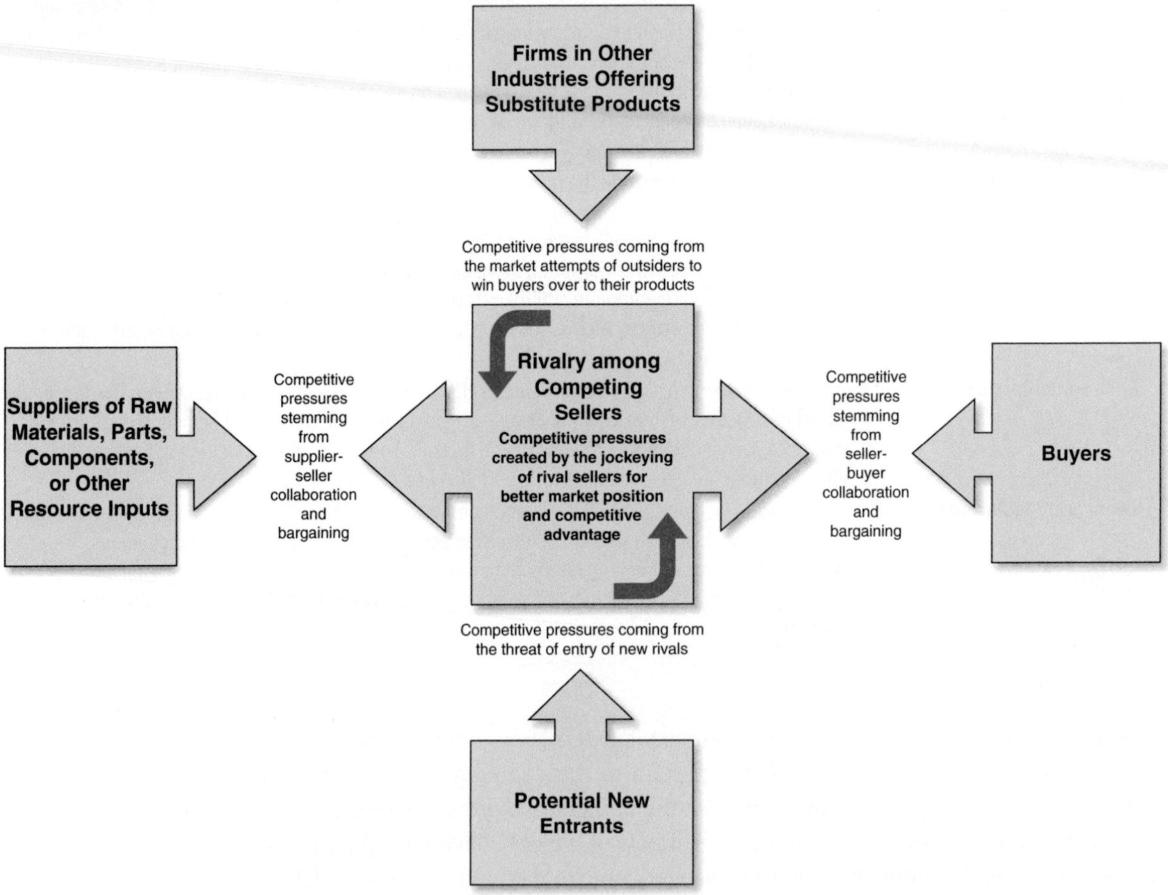

Sources: Based on Michael E. Porter, "How Competitive Forces Shape Strategy," *Harvard Business Review* 57, no. 2 (March–April 1979), pp. 137–45; and Michael E. Porter, "The Five Competitive Forces That Shape Strategy," *Harvard Business Review* 86, no. 1 (January 2008), pp. 80–86.

3. Competitive pressures stemming from *supplier* bargaining power.

4. Competitive pressures associated with the threat of *new entrants* into the market.

5. Competitive pressures associated with *rivalry among competing sellers* to attract customers. This is usually the strongest of the five competitive forces.

The Competitive Force of Buyer Bargaining Power

Whether seller-buyer relationships represent a minor or significant competitive force depends on (1) whether some or many buyers have sufficient bargaining leverage to obtain price concessions and other favorable terms, and (2) the extent to which buyers are price sensitive. Buyers with strong bargaining power can limit industry profitability by demanding price concessions, better payment terms, or additional features and services that increase industry members' costs. Buyer price sensitivity limits the profit potential of industry members by restricting the ability of sellers to raise prices without losing volume or unit sales.

The leverage that buyers have in negotiating favorable terms of the sale can range from weak to strong. Individual consumers, for example, rarely have much bargaining power in negotiating price concessions or other favorable terms with sellers. The primary exceptions involve situations in which price haggling is customary, such as the purchase of new and used motor vehicles, homes, and other big-ticket items such as jewelry and pleasure boats. For most consumer goods and services, individual buyers have no bargaining leverage—their option is to pay the seller's posted price, delay their purchase until prices and terms improve, or take their business elsewhere.

In contrast, large retail chains such as Walmart, Best Buy, Staples, and Home Depot typically have considerable negotiating leverage in purchasing products from manufacturers because retailers usually stock just two or three competing brands of a product and rarely carry all competing brands. In addition, the strong bargaining power of major supermarket chains such as Kroger, Safeway, and Albertsons allows them to demand promotional allowances and lump-sum payments (called slotting fees) from food products manufacturers in return for stocking certain brands or putting them in the best shelf locations. Motor vehicle manufacturers have strong bargaining power in negotiating to buy original equipment tires from Goodyear, Michelin, Bridgestone/Firestone, Continental, and Pirelli not only because they buy in large quantities but also because tire makers have judged original equipment tires to be important contributors to brand awareness and brand loyalty.

Even if buyers do not purchase in large quantities or offer a seller important market exposure or prestige, they gain a degree of bargaining leverage in the following circumstances:

- *If buyers' costs of switching to competing brands or substitutes are relatively low.* Buyers who can readily switch between several sellers have more negotiating leverage than buyers who have high switching costs. When the products of rival sellers are virtually identical, it is relatively easy for buyers to switch from seller to seller at little or no cost. For example, the screws, rivets, steel, and capacitors used in the production of large home appliances such as washers and dryers are all commodity-like and available from many sellers. The potential for buyers to easily switch from one seller to another encourages sellers to make concessions to win or retain a buyer's business.

- *If the number of buyers is small or if a customer is particularly important to a seller.* The smaller the number of buyers, the less easy it is for sellers to find alternative buyers when a customer is lost to a competitor. The prospect of losing a customer who is not easily replaced often makes a seller more willing to grant concessions of one kind or another. Because of the relatively small number of digital camera brands, the sellers of lenses and other components used in the manufacture of digital cameras are in a weak bargaining position in their negotiations with buyers of their components.

- *If buyer demand is weak.* Weak or declining demand creates a "buyers' market"; conversely, strong or rapidly growing demand creates a "sellers' market" and shifts bargaining power to sellers.

- *If buyers are well informed about sellers' products, prices, and costs.* The more information buyers have, the better bargaining position they are in. The mushrooming availability of product information on the Internet is giving added bargaining power to individuals. It has become common for automobile shoppers to arrive at dealerships armed with invoice prices, dealer holdback information, a summary of incentives, and manufacturers' financing terms.

- *If buyers pose a credible threat of integrating backward into the business of sellers.* Companies such as Anheuser-Busch, Coors, and Heinz have integrated backward into metal can manufacturing to gain bargaining power in obtaining the balance of their can requirements from otherwise powerful metal can manufacturers.

Figure 3.3 summarizes factors causing buyer bargaining power to be strong or weak.

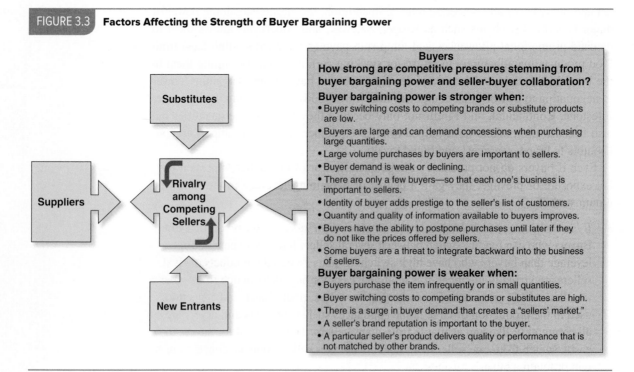

FIGURE 3.3   **Factors Affecting the Strength of Buyer Bargaining Power**

Not all buyers of an industry's product have equal degrees of bargaining power with sellers, and some may be less sensitive than others to price, quality, or service differences. For example, apparel manufacturers confront significant bargaining power when selling to big retailers such as Macy's, T. J. Maxx, or Target, but they can command much better prices selling to small owner-managed apparel boutiques.

The Competitive Force of Substitute Products

Companies in one industry are vulnerable to competitive pressure from the actions of companies in another industry whenever buyers view the products of the two industries as good substitutes. For instance, the producers of sugar experience competitive pressures from the sales and marketing efforts of the makers of Splenda, Truvia, and Sweet'N Low. Newspapers are struggling to maintain their relevance to subscribers who can watch the news on numerous television channels or go to the Internet for updates, blogs, and articles. Similarly, the producers of eyeglasses and contact lenses face competitive pressures from doctors who do corrective laser surgery.

Just how strong the competitive pressures are from the sellers of substitute products depends on three factors:

1. *Whether substitutes are readily available and attractively priced.* The presence of readily available and attractively priced substitutes creates competitive pressure by placing a ceiling on the prices industry members can charge. When substitutes are cheaper than an industry's product, industry members come under heavy competitive pressure to reduce their prices and find ways to absorb the price cuts with cost reductions.

2. *Whether buyers view the substitutes as comparable or better in terms of quality, performance, and other relevant attributes.* Customers are prone to compare performance and other attributes as well as price. For example, consumers have found digital cameras to be a superior substitute to film cameras because of the superior ease of use, the ability to download images to a home computer, and the ability to delete bad shots without paying for film developing.

3. *Whether the costs that buyers incur in switching to the substitutes are high or low.* High switching costs deter switching to substitutes, whereas low switching costs make it easier for the sellers of attractive substitutes to lure buyers to their products. Typical switching costs include the inconvenience of switching to a substitute, the costs of additional equipment, the psychological costs of severing old supplier relationships, and employee retraining costs.

Figure 3.4 summarizes the conditions that determine whether the competitive pressures from substitute products are strong, moderate, or weak. As a rule, the lower the price of substitutes, the higher their quality and performance, and the lower the user's switching costs, the more intense the competitive pressures posed by substitute products.

The Competitive Force of Supplier Bargaining Power

Whether the suppliers of industry members represent a weak or strong competitive force depends on the degree to which suppliers have sufficient *bargaining power* to influence the terms and conditions of supply in their favor. Suppliers with strong bargaining power can erode industry profitability by charging industry members higher

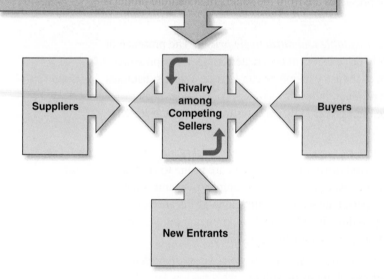

FIGURE 3.4   **Factors Affecting Competition from Substitute Products**

Firms in Other Industries Offering Substitute Products

How strong are competitive pressures coming from substitute products from outside the industry?

Competitive pressures from substitutes are stronger when:
- Good substitutes are readily available or new ones are emerging.
- Substitutes are attractively priced.
- Substitutes have comparable or better performance features.
- End users have low costs in switching to substitutes.
- End users grow more comfortable with using substitutes.

Competitive pressures from substitutes are weaker when:
- Good substitutes are not readily available or don't exist.
- Substitutes are higher priced relative to the performance they deliver.
- End users have high costs in switching to substitutes.

Signs That Competition from Substitutes Is Strong
- Sales of substitutes are growing faster than sales of the industry being analyzed (an indication that the sellers of substitutes are drawing customers away from the industry in question).
- Producers of substitutes are moving to add new capacity.
- Profits of the producers of substitutes are on the rise.

Suppliers

Rivalry among Competing Sellers

Buyers

New Entrants

prices, passing costs on to them, and limiting their opportunities to find better deals. For instance, Microsoft and Intel, both of which supply PC makers with essential components, have been known to use their dominant market status not only to charge PC makers premium prices but also to leverage PC makers in other ways. The bargaining power possessed by Microsoft and Intel when negotiating with customers is so great that both companies have faced antitrust charges on numerous occasions. Before a legal agreement ending the practice, Microsoft pressured PC makers to load only Microsoft products on the PCs they shipped. Intel has also defended against antitrust charges resulting from its bargaining strength but continues to give PC makers that use the biggest percentages of Intel chips in their PC models top priority in filling orders for newly introduced Intel chips. Being on Intel's list of preferred customers helps a PC maker get an early allocation of Intel's latest chips and thus allows a PC maker to get new models to market ahead of rivals.

The factors that determine whether any of the industry suppliers are in a position to exert substantial bargaining power or leverage are fairly clear-cut:

- *If the item being supplied is a commodity that is readily available from many suppliers.* Suppliers have little or no bargaining power or leverage whenever industry members have the ability to source from any of several alternative and eager suppliers.

- *The ability of industry members to switch their purchases from one supplier to another or to switch to attractive substitutes.* High switching costs increase supplier bargaining power, whereas low switching costs and the ready availability of good substitute inputs weaken supplier bargaining power.

- *If certain inputs are in short supply.* Suppliers of items in short supply have some degree of pricing power.

- *If certain suppliers provide a differentiated input that enhances the performance, quality, or image of the industry's product.* The greater the ability of a particular input to enhance a product's performance, quality, or image, the more bargaining leverage its suppliers are likely to possess.

- *Whether certain suppliers provide equipment or services that deliver cost savings to industry members in conducting their operations.* Suppliers who provide cost-saving equipment or services are likely to possess some degree of bargaining leverage.

- *The fraction of the costs of the industry's product accounted for by the cost of a particular input.* The bigger the cost of a specific part or component, the more opportunity for competition in the marketplace to be affected by the actions of suppliers to raise or lower their prices.

- *If industry members are major customers of suppliers.* As a rule, suppliers have less bargaining leverage when their sales to members of this one industry constitute a big percentage of their total sales. In such cases, the well-being of suppliers is closely tied to the well-being of their major customers.

- *Whether it makes good economic sense for industry members to vertically integrate backward.* The make-or-buy decision generally boils down to whether suppliers are able to supply a particular component at a lower cost than industry members could achieve if they were to integrate backward.

Figure 3.5 summarizes the conditions that tend to make supplier bargaining power strong or weak.

The Competitive Force of Potential New Entrants

Several factors determine whether the threat of new companies entering the marketplace presents a significant competitive pressure. One factor relates to the size of the pool of likely entry candidates and the resources at their command. As a rule, the bigger the pool of entry candidates, the stronger the threat of potential entry. This is especially true when some of the likely entry candidates have ample resources to support entry into a new line of business. Frequently, the strongest competitive pressures associated with potential entry come not from outsiders but from current industry participants looking for growth opportunities. *Existing industry members are often strong candidates to enter market segments or geographic areas where they currently do not have a market presence.*

FIGURE 3.5 **Factors Affecting the Strength of Supplier Bargaining Power**

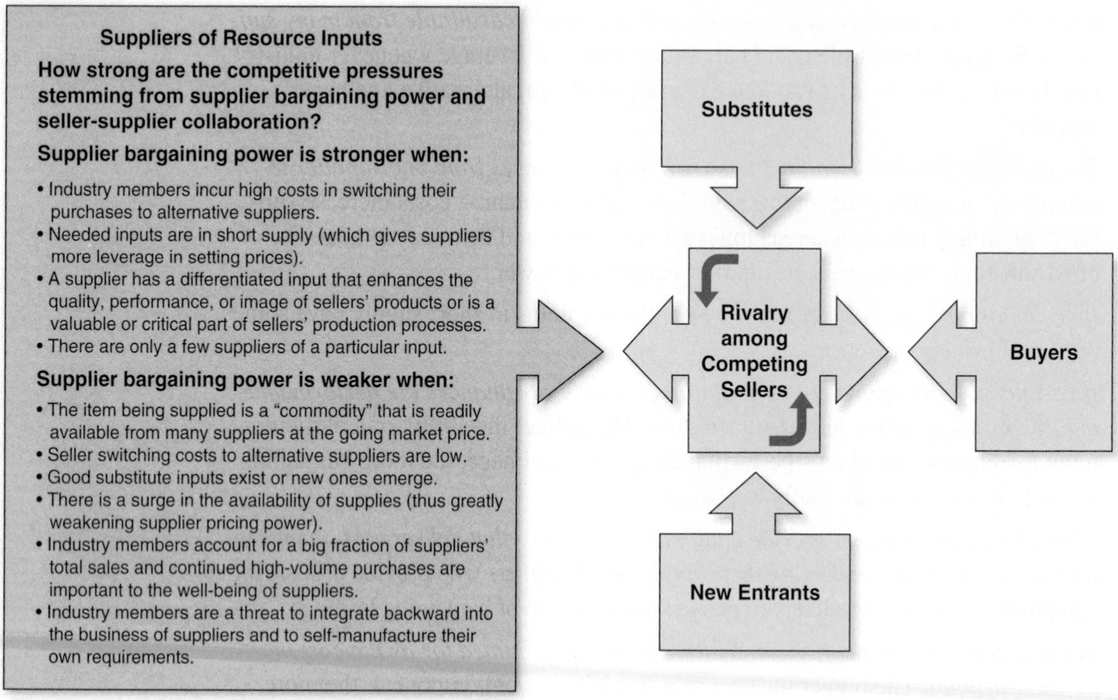

A second factor concerns whether the likely entry candidates face high or low entry barriers. High barriers reduce the competitive threat of potential entry, whereas low barriers make entry more likely, especially if the industry is growing and offers attractive profit opportunities. The most widely encountered barriers that entry candidates must hurdle include:[2]

- *The presence of sizable economies of scale in production or other areas of operation.* When incumbent companies enjoy cost advantages associated with large-scale operations, outsiders must either enter on a large scale (a costly and perhaps risky move) or accept a cost disadvantage and consequently lower profitability.

- *Cost and resource disadvantages not related to scale of operation.* Aside from enjoying economies of scale, industry incumbents can have cost advantages that stem from the possession of proprietary technology, partnerships with the best and cheapest suppliers, low fixed costs (because they have older facilities that have been mostly depreciated), and experience/learning curve effects. The microprocessor industry is an excellent example of how learning/experience curves put new entrants at a substantial cost disadvantage. Manufacturing unit costs for microprocessors tend to decline about 20 percent each time *cumulative* production volume doubles. With a 20 percent experience curve effect, if the first 1 million chips cost $100 each, once production volume reaches 2 million, the unit cost would fall to $80 (80 percent of $100), and by a production volume of 4 million, the unit cost would be $64 (80 percent of $80).[3] The bigger the learning or experience curve effect, the bigger the cost advantage of the company with the largest *cumulative* production volume.

- *Strong brand preferences and high degrees of customer loyalty.* The stronger the attachment of buyers to established brands, the harder it is for a newcomer to break into the marketplace.

- *High capital requirements.* The larger the total dollar investment needed to enter the market successfully, the more limited the pool of potential entrants. The most obvious capital requirements for new entrants relate to manufacturing facilities and equipment, introductory advertising and sales promotion campaigns, working capital to finance inventories and customer credit, and sufficient cash to cover start-up costs.

- *The difficulties of building a network of distributors-retailers and securing adequate space on retailers' shelves.* A potential entrant can face numerous distribution channel challenges. Wholesale distributors may be reluctant to take on a product that lacks buyer recognition. Retailers have to be recruited and convinced to give a new brand ample display space and an adequate trial period. Potential entrants sometimes have to "buy" their way into wholesale or retail channels by cutting their prices to provide dealers and distributors with higher markups and profit margins or by giving them big advertising and promotional allowances.

- *Restrictive regulatory policies.* Government agencies can limit or even bar entry by requiring licenses and permits. Regulated industries such as cable TV, telecommunications, electric and gas utilities, and radio and television broadcasting entail government-controlled entry.

- *Tariffs and international trade restrictions.* National governments commonly use tariffs and trade restrictions (antidumping rules, local content requirements, local ownership requirements, quotas, etc.) to raise entry barriers for foreign firms and protect domestic producers from outside competition.

- *The ability and willingness of industry incumbents to launch vigorous initiatives to block a newcomer's successful entry.* Even if a potential entrant has or can acquire the needed competencies and resources to attempt entry, it must still worry about the reaction of existing firms.[4] Sometimes, there's little that incumbents can do to throw obstacles in an entrant's path. But there are times when incumbents use price cuts, increase advertising, introduce product improvements, and launch legal attacks to prevent the entrant from building a clientele. Taxi-cab companies across the world are aggressively lobbying local governments to impose regulations that would bar ridesharing services such as Uber or Lyft.

Figure 3.6 summarizes conditions making the threat of entry strong or weak.

The Competitive Force of Rivalry Among Competing Sellers

The strongest of the five competitive forces is nearly always the rivalry among competing sellers of a product or service. In effect, *a market is a competitive battlefield* where there's no end to the campaign for buyer patronage. Rival sellers are prone to employ whatever weapons they have in their business arsenal to improve their market positions, strengthen their market position with buyers, and earn good profits. The strategy formulation challenge is to craft a competitive strategy that, at the very least, allows a company to hold its own against rivals and that, ideally, *produces a competitive edge over rivals.* But competitive contests are ongoing and dynamic. When one firm makes a strategic move that produces good results, its rivals typically respond with offensive

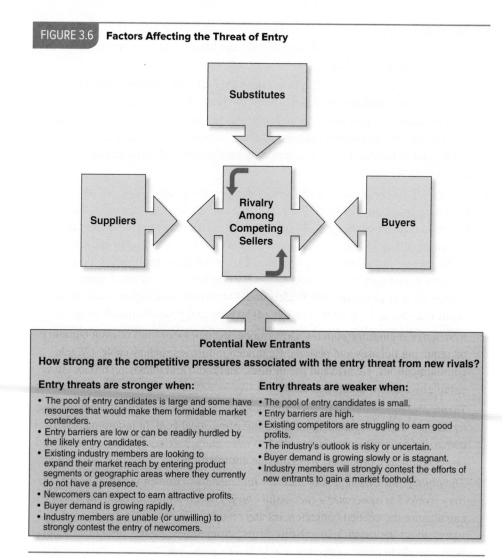

FIGURE 3.6   **Factors Affecting the Threat of Entry**

Potential New Entrants

How strong are the competitive pressures associated with the entry threat from new rivals?

Entry threats are stronger when:

- The pool of entry candidates is large and some have resources that would make them formidable market contenders.
- Entry barriers are low or can be readily hurdled by the likely entry candidates.
- Existing industry members are looking to expand their market reach by entering product segments or geographic areas where they currently do not have a presence.
- Newcomers can expect to earn attractive profits.
- Buyer demand is growing rapidly.
- Industry members are unable (or unwilling) to strongly contest the entry of newcomers.

Entry threats are weaker when:

- The pool of entry candidates is small.
- Entry barriers are high.
- Existing competitors are struggling to earn good profits.
- The industry's outlook is risky or uncertain.
- Buyer demand is growing slowly or is stagnant.
- Industry members will strongly contest the efforts of new entrants to gain a market foothold.

or defensive countermoves of their own. This pattern of action and reaction produces a continually evolving competitive landscape in which the market battle ebbs and flows and produces winners and losers. But the current market leaders have no guarantees of continued leadership. In every industry, the ongoing jockeying of rivals leads to one or more companies gaining or losing momentum in the marketplace according to whether their latest strategic maneuvers succeed or fail.[5]

Figure 3.7 shows a sampling of competitive weapons that firms can deploy in battling rivals and indicates the factors that influence the intensity of their rivalry. Some factors that influence the tempo of rivalry among industry competitors include:

- *Rivalry intensifies when competing sellers regularly launch fresh actions to boost their market standing and business performance.* Normally, competitive jockeying among rival sellers is fairly intense. Indicators of strong competitive rivalry include lively price competition, the rapid introduction of next-generation products, and moves to differentiate products by offering better performance features, higher quality, improved customer service, or a wider product selection. Other

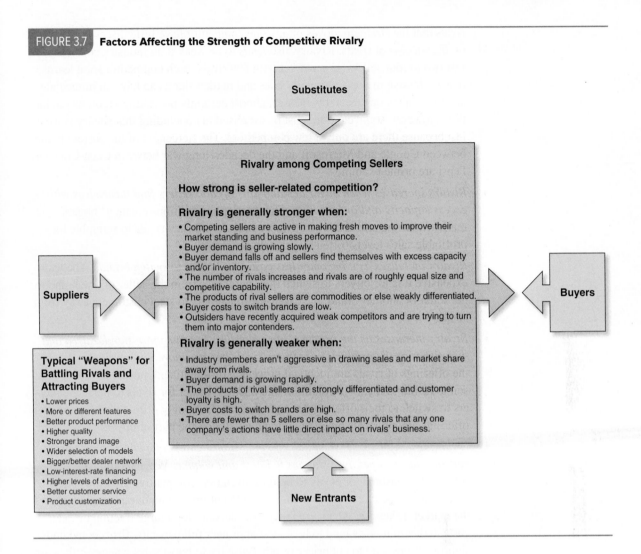

FIGURE 3.7 **Factors Affecting the Strength of Competitive Rivalry**

Substitutes

Rivalry among Competing Sellers

How strong is seller-related competition?

Rivalry is generally stronger when:
- Competing sellers are active in making fresh moves to improve their market standing and business performance.
- Buyer demand is growing slowly.
- Buyer demand falls off and sellers find themselves with excess capacity and/or inventory.
- The number of rivals increases and rivals are of roughly equal size and competitive capability.
- The products of rival sellers are commodities or else weakly differentiated.
- Buyer costs to switch brands are low.
- Outsiders have recently acquired weak competitors and are trying to turn them into major contenders.

Rivalry is generally weaker when:
- Industry members aren't aggressive in drawing sales and market share away from rivals.
- Buyer demand is growing rapidly.
- The products of rival sellers are strongly differentiated and customer loyalty is high.
- Buyer costs to switch brands are high.
- There are fewer than 5 sellers or else so many rivals that any one company's actions have little direct impact on rivals' business.

Suppliers

Buyers

Typical "Weapons" for Battling Rivals and Attracting Buyers
- Lower prices
- More or different features
- Better product performance
- Higher quality
- Stronger brand image
- Wider selection of models
- Bigger/better dealer network
- Low-interest-rate financing
- Higher levels of advertising
- Better customer service
- Product customization

New Entrants

common tactics used to temporarily boost sales include special sales promotions, heavy advertising, rebates, or low-interest-rate financing.

- *Rivalry is stronger in industries where competitors are equal in size and capability.* Competitive rivalry in the quick-service restaurant industry is particularly strong where there are numerous relatively equal-sized hamburger, deli sandwich, chicken, and taco chains. For the most part, McDonald's, Burger King, Taco Bell, Arby's, Chick-fil-A, and other national fast-food chains have comparable capabilities and are required to compete aggressively to hold their own in the industry.

- *Rivalry is usually stronger in slow-growing markets and weaker in fast-growing markets.* Rapidly expanding buyer demand produces enough new business for all industry members to grow. But in markets where growth is sluggish or where buyer demand drops off unexpectedly, it is not uncommon for competitive rivalry to intensify significantly as rivals battle for market share and volume gains.

- *Rivalry is usually weaker in industries comprised of vast numbers of small rivals; likewise, it is often weak when there are fewer than five competitors.* Head-to-head rivalry tends to be weak once an industry becomes populated with so many rivals that the strategic moves of any one competitor have little discernible impact on the success of rivals. Rivalry also *tends* to be weak if an industry consists of just two to four sellers. In a market with few rivals, each competitor soon learns that aggressive moves to grow its sales and market share can have an immediate adverse impact on rivals' businesses, almost certainly provoking vigorous retaliation. However, some caution must be exercised in concluding that rivalry is weak just because there are only a few competitors. The fierceness of the current battle between Google and Microsoft and the decades-long war between Coca-Cola and Pepsi are prime examples.

- *Rivalry increases when buyer demand falls off and sellers find themselves with excess capacity and/or inventory.* Excess supply conditions create a "buyers' market," putting added competitive pressure on industry rivals to scramble for profitable sales levels (often by price discounting).

- *Rivalry increases as it becomes less costly for buyers to switch brands.* The less expensive it is for buyers to switch their purchases from the seller of one brand to the seller of another brand, the easier it is for sellers to steal customers away from rivals.

- *Rivalry increases as the products of rival sellers become more standardized and diminishes as the products of industry rivals become more differentiated.* When the offerings of rivals are identical or weakly differentiated, buyers have less reason to be brand loyal—a condition that makes it easier for rivals to persuade buyers to switch to their offering. On the other hand, strongly differentiated product offerings among rivals breed high brand loyalty on the part of buyers.

- *Rivalry is more intense when industry conditions tempt competitors to use price cuts or other competitive weapons to boost unit volume.* When a product is perishable, seasonal, or costly to hold in inventory, competitive pressures build quickly any time one or more firms decide to cut prices and dump supplies on the market. Likewise, whenever fixed costs account for a large fraction of total cost, so that unit costs tend to be lowest at or near full capacity, firms come under significant pressure to cut prices or otherwise try to boost sales whenever they are operating below full capacity.

- *Rivalry increases when one or more competitors become dissatisfied with their market position.* Firms that are losing ground or are in financial trouble often pursue aggressive (or perhaps desperate) turnaround strategies that can involve price discounts, greater advertising, or merger with other rivals. Such strategies can turn competitive pressures up a notch.

- *Rivalry increases when strong companies outside the industry acquire weak firms in the industry and launch aggressive, well-funded moves to build market share.* A concerted effort to turn a weak rival into a market leader nearly always entails launching well-financed strategic initiatives to dramatically improve the competitor's product offering, excite buyer interest, and win a much bigger market share—actions that, if successful, put added pressure on rivals to counter with fresh strategic moves of their own.

Rivalry can be characterized as *cutthroat* or *brutal* when competitors engage in protracted price wars or habitually employ other aggressive tactics that are mutually destructive to profitability. Rivalry can be considered *fierce* to *strong* when the battle for market share is so vigorous that the profit margins of most industry members are squeezed to bare-bones levels. Rivalry can be characterized as *moderate* or *normal* when the maneuvering among industry members, while lively and healthy, still allows most industry members to earn acceptable profits. Rivalry is *weak* when most companies in the industry are relatively well satisfied with their sales growth and market share and rarely undertake offensives to steal customers away from one another.

The Collective Strengths of the Five Competitive Forces and Industry Profitability

Scrutinizing each of the five competitive forces one by one provides a powerful diagnosis of what competition is like in a given market. Once the strategist has gained an understanding of the competitive pressures associated with each of the five forces, the next step is to evaluate the collective strength of the five forces and determine if companies in this industry should reasonably expect to earn decent profits.

As a rule, the stronger the collective impact of the five competitive forces, the lower the combined profitability of industry participants. The most extreme case of a "competitively unattractive" industry is when all five forces are producing strong competitive pressures: Rivalry among sellers is vigorous, low entry barriers allow new rivals to gain a market foothold, competition from substitutes is intense, and both suppliers and custom-

> The stronger the forces of competition, the harder it becomes for industry members to earn attractive profits.

ers are able to exercise considerable bargaining leverage. Fierce to strong competitive pressures coming from all five directions nearly always drive industry profitability to unacceptably low levels, frequently producing losses for many industry members and forcing some out of business. But an industry can be competitively unattractive without all five competitive forces being strong. Fierce competitive pressures from just one of the five forces, such as brutal price competition among rival sellers, may suffice to destroy the conditions for good profitability.

In contrast, when the collective impact of the five competitive forces is moderate to weak, an industry is competitively attractive in the sense that industry members can reasonably expect to earn good profits and a nice return on investment. The ideal competitive environment for earning superior profits is one in which both suppliers and customers are in weak bargaining positions, there are no good substitutes, high barriers block further entry, and rivalry among present sellers generates only moderate competitive pressures. Weak competition is the best of all possible worlds for companies with mediocre strategies and second-rate implementation because even they can expect a decent profit.

Question 3: What Are the Industry's Driving Forces of Change, and What Impact Will They Have?

The intensity of competitive forces and the level of industry attractiveness are almost always fluid and subject to change. It is essential for strategy makers to understand the current competitive dynamics of the industry, but it is equally important for strategy makers to consider how the industry is changing and the effect of industry changes that are under way. Any strategies devised by management will play out in a dynamic industry environment, so it's imperative that such plans consider what the industry environment might look like during the near term.

The Concept of Industry Driving Forces

Industry and competitive conditions change because forces are enticing or pressuring certain industry participants (competitors, customers, suppliers) to alter their actions in important ways. The most powerful of the change agents are called **driving forces** because they have the biggest influences in reshaping the industry landscape and altering competitive conditions. Some driving forces originate in the outer ring of the company's

macro-environment (see Figure 3.1), but most originate in the company's more immediate industry and competitive environment.

Driving forces analysis has three steps: (1) identifying what the driving forces are, (2) assessing whether the drivers of change are, individually or collectively, acting to make the industry more or less attractive, and (3) determining what strategy changes are needed to prepare for the impact of the driving forces.

Identifying an Industry's Driving Forces

Many developments can affect an industry powerfully enough to qualify as driving forces, but most drivers of industry and competitive change fall into one of the following categories:

- *Changes in an industry's long-term growth rate.* Shifts in industry growth have the potential to affect the balance between industry supply and buyer demand, entry and exit, and the character and strength of competition. An upsurge in buyer demand triggers a race among established firms and newcomers to capture the new sales opportunities. A slowdown in the growth of demand nearly always brings an increase in rivalry and increased efforts by some firms to maintain their high rates of growth by taking sales and market share away from rivals.

- *Increasing globalization.* Competition begins to shift from primarily a regional or national focus to an international or global focus when industry members begin seeking customers in foreign markets or when production activities begin to migrate to countries where costs are lowest. The forces of globalization are sometimes such a strong driver that companies find it highly advantageous, if not necessary, to spread their operating reach into more and more country markets. Globalization is very much a driver of industry change in such industries as energy, mobile phones, steel, social media, and pharmaceuticals.

- *Changes in who buys the product and how they use it.* Shifts in buyer demographics and the ways products are used can alter competition by affecting how customers perceive value, how customers make purchasing decisions, and where customers purchase the product. The burgeoning popularity of streaming video has affected broadband providers, wireless phone carriers, and television broadcasters, and created opportunities for such new entertainment businesses as Hulu and Netflix.

- *Product innovation.* An ongoing stream of product innovations tends to alter the pattern of competition in an industry by attracting more first-time buyers, rejuvenating industry growth, and/or creating wider or narrower product differentiation among rival sellers. Phillips Lighting hue bulbs allow homeowners to use a smartphone app to remotely turn lights on and off and program them to blink if an intruder is detected.

- *Technological change and manufacturing process innovation.* Advances in technology can dramatically alter an industry's landscape, making it possible to produce new and better products at lower cost and opening new industry frontiers. For instance, Corning utilizes a 100 percent mechanized manufacturing process to produce high-quality sheet glass products to customer specifications in widths as thin as 30 microns. The company's Gorilla Glass is 20 times stiffer and 30 times harder than plastic in the same width.

- *Marketing innovation.* When firms are successful in introducing *new ways* to market their products, they can spark a burst of buyer interest, widen industry demand, increase product differentiation, and lower unit costs—any or all of which can alter the competitive positions of rival firms and force strategy revisions.

- *Entry or exit of major firms.* The entry of one or more foreign companies into a geographic market once dominated by domestic firms nearly always shakes up competitive conditions. Likewise, when an established domestic firm from another industry attempts entry either by acquisition or by launching its own start-up venture, it usually pushes competition in new directions.

- *Diffusion of technical know-how across more companies and more countries.* As knowledge about how to perform a particular activity or execute a particular manufacturing technology spreads, the competitive advantage held by firms originally possessing this know-how erodes. Knowledge diffusion can occur through scientific journals, trade publications, on-site plant tours, word of mouth among suppliers and customers, employee migration, and Internet sources.

- *Changes in cost and efficiency.* Widening or shrinking differences in the costs among key competitors tend to dramatically alter the state of competition. Declining costs to produce tablet computers have enabled price cuts and spurred tablet sales by making them more affordable to users.

- *Growing buyer preferences for differentiated products instead of a commodity product (or for a more standardized product instead of strongly differentiated products).* When a shift from standardized to differentiated products occurs, rivals must adopt strategies to outdifferentiate one another. However, buyers sometimes decide that a standardized, budget-priced product suits their requirements as well as a premium-priced product with lots of snappy features and personalized services.

- *Regulatory influences and government policy changes.* Government regulatory actions can often force significant changes in industry practices and strategic approaches. New rules and regulations pertaining to government-sponsored health insurance programs are driving changes in the health care industry. In international markets, host governments can drive competitive changes by opening their domestic markets to foreign participation or closing them.

- *Changing societal concerns, attitudes, and lifestyles.* Emerging social issues and changing attitudes and lifestyles can be powerful instigators of industry change.

Consumer concerns about the use of chemical additives and the nutritional content of food products have forced food producers to revamp food-processing techniques, redirect R&D efforts into the use of healthier ingredients, and compete in developing nutritious, good-tasting products.

While many forces of change may be at work in a given industry, *no more than three or four* are likely to be true driving forces powerful enough to qualify as the *major determinants* of why and how the industry is changing. Thus, company strategists must resist the temptation to label every change they see as a driving force. Table 3.2 lists the most common driving forces.

Assessing the Impact of the Industry Driving Forces

The second step in driving forces analysis is to determine whether the prevailing driving forces are acting to make the industry environment more or less attractive. Getting a handle on the collective impact of the driving forces usually requires looking at the likely effects of each force separately, because the driving forces may not all be pushing change in the same direction. For example, two driving forces may be acting to spur demand for the industry's product, while one driving force may be working to curtail demand. Whether the net effect on industry demand is up or down hinges on which driving forces are the more powerful.

> An important part of driving forces analysis is to determine whether the individual or collective impact of the driving forces will be to increase or decrease market demand, make competition more or less intense, and lead to higher or lower industry profitability.

Determining Strategy Changes Needed to Prepare for the Impact of Driving Forces

The third step of driving forces analysis—where the real payoff for strategy making comes—is for managers to draw some conclusions about what strategy adjustments will be needed to deal with the impact of the driving forces. Without understanding the forces driving industry change and the impacts these forces will have on the industry

TABLE 3.2

Common Driving Forces

1. Changes in the long-term industry growth rate
2. Increasing globalization
3. Emerging new Internet capabilities and applications
4. Changes in who buys the product and how they use it
5. Product innovation
6. Technological change and manufacturing process innovation
7. Marketing innovation
8. Entry or exit of major firms
9. Diffusion of technical know-how across more companies and more countries
10. Changes in cost and efficiency
11. Growing buyer preferences for differentiated products instead of a standardized commodity product (or for a more standardized product instead of strongly differentiated products)
12. Regulatory influences and government policy changes
13. Changing societal concerns, attitudes, and lifestyles

environment over the next one to three years, managers are ill prepared to craft a strategy tightly matched to emerging conditions. Similarly, if managers are uncertain about the implications of one or more driving forces, or if their views are off-base, it will be difficult for them to craft a strategy that is responsive to

> The real payoff of driving forces analysis is to help managers understand what strategy changes are needed to prepare for the impacts of the driving forces.

the consequences of driving forces. So driving forces analysis is not something to take lightly; it has practical value and is basic to the task of thinking strategically about where the industry is headed and how to prepare for the changes ahead.

Question 4: How Are Industry Rivals Positioned?

LO3 Become adept at mapping the market positions of key groups of industry rivals.

The nature of competitive strategy inherently positions companies competing in an industry into strategic groups with diverse price/quality ranges, different distribution channels, varying product features, and different geographic coverages. The best technique for revealing the market positions of industry competitors is **strategic group mapping.** This analytical tool is useful for comparing the market positions of industry competitors or for grouping industry combatants into like positions.

> **CORE CONCEPT**
> **Strategic group mapping** is a technique for displaying the different market or competitive positions that rival firms occupy in the industry.

Using Strategic Group Maps to Assess the Positioning of Key Competitors

A **strategic group** consists of those industry members with similar competitive approaches and positions in the market. Companies in the same strategic group can resemble one another in any of several ways: they may have comparable product-line breadth, sell in the same price/quality range, emphasize the same distribution channels, use essentially the same product attributes to appeal to similar types of buyers, depend on identical technological approaches, or offer buyers similar services and technical assistance.[6] An industry with a commodity-like product may contain only one strategic group whereby all sellers pursue essentially identical strategies and have comparable market positions. But even with commodity products, there is likely some attempt at differentiation occurring in the form of varying delivery times, financing terms, or levels of customer service. Most industries offer a host of competitive approaches that allow companies to find unique industry positioning and avoid fierce competition in a crowded strategic group. Evaluating strategy options entails examining what strategic groups exist, identifying which companies exist within each group, and determining if a competitive "white space" exists where industry competitors are able to create and capture altogether new demand.

> **CORE CONCEPT**
> A **strategic group** is a cluster of industry rivals that have similar competitive approaches and market positions.

The procedure for constructing a *strategic group map* is straightforward:

- Identify the competitive characteristics that delineate strategic approaches used in the industry. Typical variables used in creating strategic group maps are the price/quality range (high, medium, low), geographic coverage (local, regional, national,

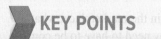

KEY POINTS

Thinking strategically about a company's external situation involves probing for answers to seven questions:

1. *What are the strategically relevant components of the macro-environment?* Industries differ as to how they are affected by conditions in the broad macro-environment. PES-TEL analysis of the political, economic, sociocultural, technological, environmental/ecological, and legal/regulatory factors provides a framework for approaching this issue systematically.

2. *What kinds of competitive forces are industry members facing, and how strong is each force?* The strength of competition is a composite of five forces: (1) competitive pressures stemming from buyer bargaining power and seller-buyer collaboration, (2) competitive pressures associated with the sellers of substitutes, (3) competitive pressures stemming from supplier bargaining power and supplier-seller collaboration, (4) competitive pressures associated with the threat of new entrants into the market, and (5) competitive pressures stemming from the competitive jockeying among industry rivals.

3. *What forces are driving changes in the industry, and what impact will these changes have on competitive intensity and industry profitability?* Industry and competitive conditions change because forces are in motion that create incentives or pressures for change. The first phase is to identify the forces that are driving industry change. The second phase of driving forces analysis is to determine whether the driving forces, taken together, are acting to make the industry environment more or less attractive.

4. *What market positions do industry rivals occupy—who is strongly positioned and who is not?* Strategic group mapping is a valuable tool for understanding the similarities and differences inherent in the market positions of rival companies. Rivals in the same or nearby strategic groups are close competitors, whereas companies in distant strategic groups usually pose little or no immediate threat. Some strategic groups are more favorable than others. The profit potential of different strategic groups may not be the same because industry driving forces and competitive forces likely have varying effects on the industry's distinct strategic groups.

5. *What strategic moves are rivals likely to make next?* Scouting competitors well enough to anticipate their actions can help a company prepare effective countermoves and allows managers to take rivals' probable actions into account in designing their own company's best course of action. Using a Framework for Competitor Analysis that considers rivals' current strategy, objectives, resources and capabilities, and assumptions can be helpful in this regard.

6. *What are the key factors for competitive success?* An industry's key success factors (KSFs) are the particular product attributes, competitive capabilities, and intangible assets that spell the difference between being a strong competitor and a weak competitor—and sometimes between profit and loss. KSFs by their very nature are so important to competitive success that *all firms* in the industry must pay close attention to them or risk being driven out of the industry.

7. *Does the outlook for the industry present the company with sufficiently attractive prospects for profitability?* Conclusions regarding industry attractiveness are a major driver of company strategy. When a company decides an industry is fundamentally attractive and presents good opportunities, a strong case can be made that it should invest aggressively to capture the opportunities it sees. When a strong competitor concludes an industry is relatively unattractive and lacking in opportunity, it may elect to simply protect its present

position, investing cautiously, if at all, and looking for opportunities in other industries. A competitively weak company in an unattractive industry may see its best option as finding a buyer, perhaps a rival, to acquire its business. On occasion, an industry that is unattractive overall is still very attractive to a favorably situated company with the skills and resources to take business away from weaker rivals.

ASSURANCE OF LEARNING EXERCISES

1. Prepare a brief analysis of the organic food industry using the information provided by the Organic Trade Association. Based upon information provided in the *Organic Report* magazine, draw a five-forces diagram for the organic food industry and briefly discuss the nature and strength of each of the five competitive forces.

    connect
   LO2

2. Based on the strategic group map in **Concepts & Connections 3.1**, who are Yuengling & Son's closest competitors? Between which two strategic groups is competition the strongest? Why do you think no beer producers are positioned in the lower-left corner of the map? Which company/strategic group faces the weakest competition from the members of other strategic groups?

   connect
   LO3

3. The National Restaurant Association publishes an annual industry factbook that can be found at www.restaurant.org. Based on information in the latest report, does it appear that macro-environmental factors and the economic characteristics of the industry will present industry participants with attractive opportunities for growth and profitability? Explain.

   LO1, LO4

EXERCISES FOR SIMULATION PARTICIPANTS

1. Which of the five competitive forces is creating the strongest competitive pressures for your company?

   LO1, LO2, LO3, LO4

2. What are the "weapons of competition" that rival companies in your industry can use to gain sales and market share? See Figure 3.7 to help you identify the various competitive factors.

3. What are the factors affecting the intensity of rivalry in the industry in which your company is competing? Use Figure 3.7 and the accompanying discussion to help you in pinpointing the specific factors most affecting competitive intensity. Would you characterize the rivalry and jockeying for better market position, increased sales, and market share among the companies in your industry as fierce, very strong, strong, moderate, or relatively weak? Why?

4. Are there any driving forces in the industry in which your company is competing? What impact will these driving forces have? Will they cause competition to be more or less intense? Will they act to boost or squeeze profit margins? List at least two actions your company should consider taking to combat any negative impacts of the driving forces.

5. Draw a strategic group map showing the market positions of the companies in your industry. Which companies do you believe are in the most attractive position on the map? Which companies are the most weakly positioned? Which companies do you believe are likely to try to move to a different position on the strategic group map?

6. What do you see as the key factors for being a successful competitor in your industry? List at least three.

7. Does your overall assessment of the industry suggest that industry rivals have sufficiently attractive opportunities for growth and profitability? Explain.

ENDNOTES

1. Michael E. Porter, *Competitive Strategy: Techniques for Analyzing Industries and Competitors* (New York: Free Press, 1980), chap. 1; Michael E. Porter, "The Five Competitive Forces That Shape Strategy," *Harvard Business Review* 86, no. 1 (January 2008).

2. J. S. Bain, *Barriers to New Competition* (Cambridge, MA: Harvard University Press, 1956); F. M. Scherer, *Industrial Market Structure and Economic Performance* (Chicago: Rand McNally & Co., 1971).

3. Pankaj Ghemawat, "Building Strategy on the Experience Curve," *Harvard Business Review* 64, no. 2 (March–April 1985).

4. Michael E. Porter, "How Competitive Forces Shape Strategy," *Harvard Business Review* 57, no. 2 (March–April 1979).

5. Pamela J. Derfus, Patrick G. Maggitti, Curtis M. Grimm, and Ken G. Smith, "The Red Queen Effect: Competitive Actions and Firm Performance," *Academy of Management Journal* 51, no. 1 (February 2008).

6. Mary Ellen Gordon and George R. Milne, "Selecting the Dimensions That Define Strategic Groups: A Novel Market-Driven Approach," *Journal of Managerial Issues* 11, no. 2 (Summer 1999).

7. Avi Fiegenbaum and Howard Thomas, "Strategic Groups as Reference Groups: Theory, Modeling and Empirical Examination of Industry and Competitive Strategy," *Strategic Management Journal* 16 (1995); S. Ade Olusoga, Michael P. Mokwa, and Charles H. Noble, "Strategic Groups, Mobility Barriers, and Competitive Advantage," *Journal of Business Research* 33 (1995).

Evaluating a Company's Resources, Capabilities, and Competitiveness

LEARNING OBJECTIVES

LO1   Learn how to assess how well a company's strategy is working.

LO2   Understand why a company's resources and capabilities are central to its strategic approach and how to evaluate their potential for giving the company a competitive edge over rivals.

LO3   Grasp how a company's value chain activities can affect the company's cost structure and customer value proposition.

LO4   Learn how to evaluate a company's competitive strength relative to key rivals.

LO5   Understand how a comprehensive evaluation of a company's external and internal situations can assist managers in making critical decisions about their next strategic moves.

Chapter 3 described how to use the tools of industry and competitive analysis to assess a company's external environment and lay the groundwork for matching a company's strategy to its external situation. This chapter discusses the techniques of evaluating a company's internal situation, including its collection of resources and capabilities, its cost structure and customer value proposition, and its competitive strength versus that of its rivals. The analytical spotlight will be trained on five questions:

1. How well is the company's strategy working?
2. What are the company's competitively important resources and capabilities?
3. Are the company's cost structure and customer value proposition competitive?
4. Is the company competitively stronger or weaker than key rivals?
5. What strategic issues and problems merit front-burner managerial attention?

The answers to these five questions complete management's understanding of the company's overall situation and position the company for a good strategy-situation fit required by the "The Three Tests of a Winning Strategy" (see Chapter 1).

LO1 Learn how to assess how well a company's strategy is working.

Question 1: How Well Is the Company's Strategy Working?

The two best indicators of how well a company's strategy is working are (1) whether the company is recording gains in financial strength and profitability, and (2) whether the company's competitive strength and market standing are improving. Persistent shortfalls in meeting company financial performance targets and weak performance relative to rivals are reliable warning signs that the company suffers from poor strategy making, less-than-competent strategy execution, or both. Other indicators of how well a company's strategy is working include:

- Trends in the company's sales and earnings growth.
- Trends in the company's stock price.
- The company's overall financial strength.
- The company's customer retention rate.
- The rate at which new customers are acquired.
- Changes in the company's image and reputation with customers.
- Evidence of improvement in internal processes such as defect rate, order fulfillment, delivery times, days of inventory, and employee productivity.

The stronger a company's current overall performance, the less likely the need for radical changes in strategy. The weaker a company's financial performance and market standing, the more its current strategy must be questioned. (A compilation of financial ratios most commonly used to evaluate a company's financial performance and balance sheet strength is presented in the Appendix.)

Question 2: What Are the Company's Competitively Important Resources and Capabilities?

LO2 Understand why a company's resources and capabilities are central to its strategic approach and how to evaluate their potential for giving the company a competitive edge over rivals.

As discussed in Chapter 1, a company's business model and strategy must be well matched to its collection of resources and capabilities. An attempt to create and deliver customer value in a manner that depends on resources or capabilities that are deficient and cannot be readily acquired or developed is unwise and positions the company for failure. A company's competitive approach requires a tight fit with a company's internal situation and is strengthened when it exploits resources that are competitively valuable, rare, hard to copy, and not easily trumped by rivals' substitute resources. In addition, long-term competitive advantage requires the ongoing development and expansion of resources and capabilities to pursue emerging market opportunities and defend against future threats to its market standing and profitability.[1]

Sizing up the company's collection of resources and capabilities and determining whether they can provide the foundation for competitive success can be achieved through **resource and capability analysis.** This is a two-step process: (1) identify the company's resources and capabilities, and (2) examine them more closely to ascertain which are the most competitively important and whether they can support a sustainable competitive advantage over rival firms.[2] This second step involves applying the *four tests of a resource's competitive power.*

Identifying Competitively Important Resources and Capabilities

A company's **resources** are competitive assets that are owned or controlled by the company and may either be *tangible resources* such as plants, distribution centers, manufacturing equipment, patents, information systems, and capital reserves or creditworthiness, or *intangible assets* such as a well-known brand or a results-oriented organizational culture. Table 4.1 lists the common types of tangible and intangible resources that a company may possess.

> **CORE CONCEPT**
>
> A **resource** is a competitive asset that is owned or controlled by a company; a **capability** is the capacity of a company to competently perform some internal activity. Capabilities are developed and enabled through the deployment of a company's resources.

A **capability** is the capacity of a firm to competently perform some internal activity. A capability may also be referred to as a **competence.** Capabilities or competences also vary in form, quality, and competitive importance, with some being more competitively valuable than others. *Organizational capabilities are developed and enabled through the deployment of a company's resources or some combination of its resources.*[3] Some capabilities rely heavily on a company's intangible resources such as human assets and intellectual capital. For example, Nestlé's brand management capabilities for its 2,000+ food, beverage, and pet care brands draw upon the knowledge of the company's brand managers, the expertise of its marketing department, and the company's relationships with retailers in nearly 200 countries. W. L. Gore's product innovation capabilities in its fabrics, medical, and industrial products businesses result from the personal initiative, creative talents, and technological expertise of its associates and the company's culture that encourages accountability and creative thinking.

TABLE 4.1

Common Types of Tangible and Intangible Resources

Tangible Resources

- *Physical resources*—state-of-the-art manufacturing plants and equipment, efficient distribution facilities, attractive real estate locations, or ownership of valuable natural resource deposits
- *Financial resources*—cash and cash equivalents, marketable securities, and other financial assets such as a company's credit rating and borrowing capacity
- *Technological assets*—patents, copyrights, superior production technology, and technologies that enable activities
- *Organizational resources*—information and communication systems (servers, workstations, etc.), proven quality control systems, and a strong network of distributors or retail dealers

Intangible Resources

- *Human assets and intellectual capital*—an experienced and capable workforce, talented employees in key areas, collective learning embedded in the organization, or proven managerial know-how
- *Brand, image, and reputational assets*—brand names, trademarks, product or company image, buyer loyalty, and reputation for quality, superior service
- *Relationships*—alliances or joint ventures that provide access to technologies, specialized know-how, or geographic markets, and trust established with various partners
- *Company culture*—the norms of behavior, business principles, and ingrained beliefs within the company

---

Determining the Competitive Power of a Company's Resources and Capabilities

What is most telling about a company's aggregation of resources and capabilities is how powerful they are in the marketplace. The competitive power of a resource or capability is measured by how many of four tests for sustainable competitive advantage it can pass.[4]

The tests are often referred to as the **VRIN tests for sustainable competitive advantage**—an acronym for *valuable, rare, inimitable,* and *nonsubstitutable.* The first two tests determine whether the resource or capability may contribute to a competitive advantage. The last two determine the degree to which the competitive advantage potential can be sustained.

> **CORE CONCEPT**
>
> The **VRIN tests for sustainable competitive advantage** ask if a resource or capability is *valuable, rare, inimitable,* and *nonsubstitutable.*

1. *Is the resource or capability competitively **valuable?*** All companies possess a collection of resources and capabilities—some have the potential to contribute to a competitive advantage, while others may not. Google has failed in converting its technological resources and software innovation capabilities into success for Google Wallet, which has incurred losses of more than $300 million. While these resources and capabilities have made Google the world's number-one search engine, they have proven to be less valuable in the mobile payments industry.

2. *Is the resource or capability **rare**—is it something rivals lack?* Resources and capabilities that are common among firms and widely available cannot be a source of competitive advantage. All makers of branded cookies and sweet snacks have valuable marketing capabilities and brands. Therefore, these skills are not rare or unique in the industry. However, the brand strength of Oreo is uncommon and has provided Kraft Foods with greater market share as well as the opportunity to benefit from brand extensions such as Reese's Peanut Butter Cup Oreo cookies and Mini Oreo cookies.

3. *Is the resource or capability **inimitable** or hard to copy?* The more difficult and more expensive it is to imitate a company's resource or capability, the more likely that it can also provide a *sustainable* competitive advantage. Resources tend to be difficult to copy when they are unique (a fantastic real estate location, patent protection), when they must be built over time (a brand name, a strategy-supportive organizational culture), and when they carry big capital requirements (a cost-effective plant to manufacture cutting-edge microprocessors). Imitation by rivals is most challenging when capabilities reflect a high level of *social complexity* (for example, a stellar team-oriented culture or unique trust-based relationships with employees, suppliers, or customers) and *causal ambiguity,* a term that signifies the hard-to-disentangle nature of complex processes such as the web of intricate activities enabling a new drug discovery.

4. *Is the resource or capability **nonsubstitutable** or is it vulnerable to the threat of substitution from different types of resources and capabilities?* Resources that are competitively valuable, rare, and costly to imitate may lose much of their ability to offer competitive advantage if rivals possess equivalent substitute resources. For example, manufacturers relying on automation to gain a cost-based advantage in production activities may find their technology-based advantage nullified by rivals' use of low-wage offshore manufacturing. Resources can contribute to a competitive advantage only when resource substitutes don't exist.

Very few firms have resources and capabilities that can pass all four tests, but those that do enjoy a sustainable competitive advantage with far greater profit potential. Walmart is a notable example, with capabilities in logistics and supply chain management that have surpassed those of its competitors for over 40 years. Lincoln Electric Company, less well known but no less notable in its achievements, has been the world leader in welding products for over 100 years as a result of its unique piecework incentive system for compensating production workers and the unsurpassed worker productivity and product quality that this system has fostered.[5]

If management determines that the company doesn't possess a resource that independently passes all four tests with high marks, it may have a **bundle of resources** that can pass the tests. Although Nike's resources dedicated to research and development, marketing research, and product design are matched relatively well by rival Adidas, its cross-functional design process allows it to set the pace for innovation in athletic apparel and footwear and consistently outperform Adidas and other rivals in the marketplace. Nike's footwear designers get ideas for new performance features from the professional athletes who endorse its products and then work alongside footwear materials researchers, consumer trend analysts, color designers, and marketers to design new models that are presented to a review committee. Nike's review committee is made up of hundreds of individuals who evaluate prototype details such as shoe proportions and color designs, the size of the swoosh, stitching patterns, sole color and tread pattern, and insole design. About 400 models are approved by the committee each year, which are sourced from contract manufacturers and marketed in more than 180 countries. The bundling of Nike's professional endorsements, R&D activities, marketing research efforts, styling expertise, and managerial know-how has become an important source of the company's competitive advantage and has allowed it to remain number one in the athletic footwear and apparel industry for more than 20 years.

Companies lacking certain resources needed for competitive success in an industry may be able to adopt strategies directed at eroding or at least neutralizing the competitive potency of a particular rival's resources and capabilities by identifying and developing **substitute resources** to accomplish the same purpose. For example, Amazon.com lacked a big network of retail stores such as that operated by rival Barnes & Noble, but its much larger, readily accessible, and searchable book inventory—coupled with its short delivery times and free shipping on orders over $35—has proven to be more attractive to many busy consumers than visiting a big-box bookstore. In other words, Amazon carefully and consciously developed a set of competitively valuable resources that were effective substitutes for the superior tangible resources of Barnes & Noble dedicated to its 1,400 brick-and-mortar retail stores and college book stores.[6]

The Importance of Dynamic Capabilities in Sustaining Competitive Advantage

Resources and capabilities must be continually strengthened and nurtured to sustain their competitive power and, at times, may need to be broadened and deepened to allow the company to position itself to pursue emerging market opportunities.[7] Organizational resources and capabilities that grow stale can impair competitiveness unless they are refreshed, modified, or even phased out and replaced in response to ongoing market changes and shifts in company strategy. In addition, disruptive environmental change may destroy the value of key strategic assets, turning *static* resources and capabilities "from diamonds to rust."[8] Management's organization-building challenge has two elements: (1) attending to ongoing recalibration of existing capabilities and resources, and (2) casting a watchful eye for opportunities to develop totally new capabilities for delivering better customer value and/or outcompeting rivals. Companies that know the importance of recalibrating and upgrading resources and capabilities make it a routine management function to build new resource configurations and capabilities. Such a managerial approach allows a company to prepare for market changes and pursue emerging opportunities. This ability to build and integrate new competitive assets becomes a capability in itself—a **dynamic capability.** A dynamic capability is the ability to modify, deepen, or reconfigure the company's existing resources and capabilities in response to its changing environment or market opportunities.[9]

Management at Toyota has aggressively upgraded the company's capabilities in fuel-efficient hybrid engine technology and constantly fine-tuned the famed Toyota Production System to enhance the company's already proficient capabilities in manufacturing top-quality vehicles at relatively low costs. Likewise, management at BMW developed new organizational capabilities in hybrid engine design that allowed the company to launch its highly touted i3 and i8 plug-in hybrids. Resources and capabilities can also be built and augmented through alliances and acquisitions.[10] Cisco Systems has greatly expanded its engineering capabilities and its ability to enter new product categories through frequent acquisitions. Strategic alliances are a commonly used approach to developing and reconfiguring capabilities in the biotech and pharmaceutical industries.

> **CORE CONCEPT**
>
> A **dynamic capability** is the ability to modify, deepen, or reconfigure the company's existing resources and capabilities in response to its changing environment or market opportunities.

> A company requires a dynamically evolving portfolio of resources and capabilities in order to sustain its competitiveness and position itself to pursue future market opportunities.

Is the Company Able to Seize Market Opportunities and Nullify External Threats?

An essential element in evaluating a company's overall situation entails examining the company's resources and competitive capabilities in terms of the degree to which they enable it to pursue its best market opportunities and defend against the external threats to its future well-being. The simplest and most easily applied tool for conducting this examination is widely known as **SWOT analysis,** so named because it zeros in on a company's internal **S**trengths and **W**eaknesses, market **O**pportunities, and external **T**hreats. *A company's internal strengths should always serve as the basis of its strategy—placing heavy reliance on a company's best competitive assets is the soundest route to attracting customers and competing successfully against rivals.*[11] As a rule, strategies that place heavy demands on areas where the company is weakest or has unproven competencies should be avoided. Plainly, managers must look toward correcting competitive weaknesses that make the company vulnerable, hold down profitability, or disqualify it from pursuing an attractive opportunity. Furthermore, a company's strategy should be aimed squarely at capturing those market opportunities that are most attractive and suited to the company's collection of capabilities. How much attention to devote to defending against external threats to the company's future performance hinges on how vulnerable the company is, whether defensive moves can be taken to lessen their impact, and whether the costs of undertaking such moves represent the best use of company resources. A first-rate SWOT analysis provides the basis for crafting a strategy that capitalizes on the company's strengths, aims squarely at capturing the company's best opportunities, and defends against the threats to its well-being. Table 4.2 lists the kinds of factors to consider in compiling a company's resource strengths and weaknesses.

> **CORE CONCEPT**
>
> **SWOT analysis** is a simple but powerful tool for sizing up a company's internal strengths and competitive deficiencies, its market opportunities, and the external threats to its future well-being.

> Basing a company's strategy on its strengths resulting from most competitively valuable resources and capabilities gives the company its best chance for market success.

TABLE 4.2

Factors to Consider When Identifying a Company's Strengths, Weaknesses, Opportunities, and Threats

Potential Internal Strengths and Competitive Capabilities

- Core competencies in _____
- A strong financial condition; ample financial resources to grow the business
- Strong brand-name image/company reputation
- Economies of scale and/or learning and experience curve advantages over rivals
- Proprietary technology/superior technological skills/important patents
- Cost advantages over rivals
- Product innovation capabilities
- Proven capabilities in improving production processes
- Good supply chain management capabilities
- Good customer service capabilities
- Better product quality relative to rivals
- Wide geographic coverage and/or strong global distribution capability
- Alliances/joint ventures with other firms that provide access to valuable technology, competencies, and/or attractive geographic markets

Potential Internal Weaknesses and Competitive Deficiencies

- No clear strategic direction
- No well-developed or proven core competencies
- A weak balance sheet; burdened with too much debt
- Higher overall unit costs relative to key competitors
- A product/service with features and attributes that are inferior to those of rivals
- Too narrow a product line relative to rivals
- Weak brand image or reputation
- Weaker dealer network than key rivals
- Behind on product quality, R&D, and/or technological know-how
- Lack of management depth
- Short on financial resources to grow the business and pursue promising initiatives

Potential Market Opportunities

- Serving additional customer groups or market segments
- Expanding into new geographic markets
- Expanding the company's product line to meet a broader range of customer needs
- Utilizing existing company skills or technological know-how to enter new product lines or new businesses
- Falling trade barriers in attractive foreign markets
- Acquiring rival firms or companies with attractive technological expertise or capabilities

Potential External Threats to a Company's Future Prospects

- Increasing intensity of competition among industry rivals—may squeeze profit margins
- Slowdowns in market growth
- Likely entry of potent new competitors
- Growing bargaining power of customers or suppliers
- A shift in buyer needs and tastes away from the industry's product
- Adverse demographic changes that threaten to curtail demand for the industry's product
- Vulnerability to unfavorable industry driving forces
- Restrictive trade policies on the part of foreign governments
- Costly new regulatory requirements

The Value of a SWOT Analysis A SWOT analysis involves more than making four lists. The most important parts of SWOT analysis are:

1. Drawing conclusions from the SWOT listings about the company's overall situation.

2. Translating these conclusions into strategic actions to better match the company's strategy to its strengths and market opportunities, correcting problematic weaknesses, and defending against worrisome external threats.

> Simply listing a company's strengths, weaknesses, opportunities, and threats is not enough; the payoff from SWOT analysis comes from the conclusions about a company's situation and the implications for strategy improvement that flow from the four lists.

Question 3: Are the Company's Cost Structure and Customer Value Proposition Competitive?

> **LO3** Grasp how a company's value chain activities can affect the company's cost structure and customer value proposition.

Company managers are often stunned when a competitor cuts its prices to "unbelievably low" levels or when a new market entrant comes on strong with a great new product offered at a surprisingly low price. Such competitors may not, however, be buying market positions with prices that are below costs. They may simply have substantially lower costs and therefore are able to offer prices that result in more appealing customer value propositions. One of the most telling signs of whether a company's business position is strong or precarious is whether its cost structure and customer value proposition are competitive with those of industry rivals.

Cost comparisons are especially critical in industries where price competition is typically the ruling market force. But even in industries where products are differentiated, rival companies have to keep their costs in line with rivals offering value propositions based upon a similar mix of differentiating features. But a company must also remain competitive in terms of its customer value proposition. Tiffany's value proposition, for example, remains attractive to people who want customer service, the assurance of quality, and a high-status brand despite the availability of cut-rate diamond jewelry online. Target's customer value proposition has withstood the Walmart low-price juggernaut by attention to product design, image, and attractive store layouts in addition to efficiency. The key for managers is to keep close track of how *cost effectively* the company can deliver value to customers relative to its competitors. *If the company can deliver the same amount of value with lower expenditures (or more value at a similar cost), it will maintain a competitive edge.* Two analytical tools are particularly useful in determining whether a company's value proposition and costs are competitive: value chain analysis and benchmarking.

> Competitive advantage hinges on how cost effectively a company can execute its customer value proposition.

Company Value Chains

Every company's business consists of a collection of activities undertaken in the course of designing, producing, marketing, delivering, and supporting its product or service. All of the various activities that a company performs internally combine to form a **value chain,** so called because the underlying intent of a company's activities is to do things that ultimately *create value for buyers.*

> **CORE CONCEPT**
>
> A company's **value chain** identifies the primary activities that create customer value and related support activities.

As shown in Figure 4.1, a company's value chain consists of two broad categories of activities that drive costs and create customer value: the *primary activities* that are foremost in creating value for customers and the requisite *support activities* that facilitate and enhance the performance of the primary activities.[12] For example, the primary

FIGURE 4.1 **A Representative Company Value Chain**

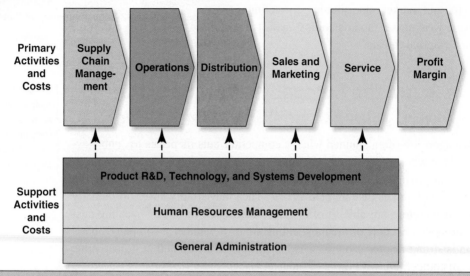

PRIMARY ACTIVITIES

- **Supply Chain Management**—Activities, costs, and assets associated with purchasing fuel, energy, raw materials, parts and components, merchandise, and consumable items from vendors; receiving, storing, and disseminating inputs from suppliers; inspection; and inventory management.

- **Operations**—Activities, costs, and assets associated with converting inputs into final product form (production, assembly, packaging, equipment maintenance, facilities, operations, quality assurance, environmental protection).

- **Distribution**—Activities, costs, and assets dealing with physically distributing the product to buyers (finished goods warehousing, order processing, order picking and packing, shipping, delivery vehicle operations, establishing and maintaining a network of dealers and distributors).

- **Sales and Marketing**—Activities, costs, and assets related to sales force efforts, advertising and promotion, market research and planning, and dealer/distributor support.

- **Service**—Activities, costs, and assets associated with providing assistance to buyers, such as installation, spare parts delivery, maintenance and repair, technical assistance, buyer inquiries, and complaints.

SUPPORT ACTIVITIES

- **Product R&D, Technology, and Systems Development**—Activities, costs, and assets relating to product R&D, process R&D, process design improvement, equipment design, computer software development, telecommunications systems, computer-assisted design and engineering, database capabilities, and development of computerized support systems.

- **Human Resources Management**—Activities, costs, and assets associated with the recruitment, hiring, training, development, and compensation of all types of personnel; labor relations activities; and development of knowledge-based skills and core competencies.

- **General Administration**—Activities, costs, and assets relating to general management, accounting and finance, legal and regulatory affairs, safety and security, management information systems, forming strategic alliances and collaborating with strategic partners, and other "overhead" functions.

Source: Based on the discussion in Michael E. Porter, *Competitive Advantage* (New York: Free Press, 1985), pp. 37–43.

activities and cost drivers for a big-box retailer such as Target include merchandise selection and buying, store layout and product display, advertising, and customer service; its support activities that affect customer value and costs include site selection, hiring and training, store maintenance, plus the usual assortment of administrative activities. A hotel chain's primary activities and costs are mainly comprised of reservations and hotel operations (check-in and check-out, maintenance and housekeeping, dining and room service, and conventions and meetings); principal support activities that drive costs and impact customer value include accounting, hiring and training hotel staff, and general administration. Supply chain management is a crucial activity for Kroger or Amazon.com but is not a value chain component at LinkedIn or DirectTV. Sales and marketing are dominant activities at Procter & Gamble and GAP but have minor roles at oil-drilling companies and natural gas pipeline companies. With its focus on value-creating activities, the value chain is an ideal tool for examining how a company delivers on its customer value proposition. It permits a deep look at the company's cost structure and ability to offer low prices. It reveals the emphasis that a company places on activities that enhance differentiation and support higher prices, such as service and marketing.

The value chain also includes a profit margin component; profits are necessary to compensate the company's owners/shareholders and investors, who bear risks and provide capital. Tracking the profit margin along with the value-creating activities is critical because unless an enterprise succeeds in delivering customer value profitably (with a sufficient return on invested capital), it can't survive for long. Attention to a company's profit formula in addition to its customer value proposition is the essence of a sound business model, as described in Chapter 1. Concepts & Connections 4.1 shows representative costs for various activities performed by American Giant, a maker of high-quality sweatshirts, in its U.S. plants versus the various costs incurred by sweatshirt producers in Asia.

Benchmarking: A Tool for Assessing Whether a Company's Value Chain Activities Are Competitive

Benchmarking entails comparing how different companies perform various value chain activities—how materials are purchased, how inventories are managed, how products are assembled, how customer orders are filled and shipped, and how maintenance is performed—and then making cross-company comparisons of the costs and effectiveness of these activities.[13] The objectives of benchmarking are to identify the best practices in performing an activity and to emulate those best practices when they are possessed by others.

> ### CORE CONCEPT
> **Benchmarking** is a potent tool for learning which companies are best at performing particular activities and then using their techniques (or "best practices") to improve the cost and effectiveness of a company's own internal activities.

Xerox led the way in the use of benchmarking to become more cost-competitive by deciding not to restrict its benchmarking efforts to its office equipment rivals, but by comparing itself to *any company* regarded as "world class" in performing activities relevant to Xerox's business. Other companies quickly picked up on Xerox's approach. Toyota managers got their idea for just-in-time inventory deliveries by studying how U.S. supermarkets replenished their shelves. Southwest Airlines reduced the turnaround time of its aircraft at each scheduled stop by studying pit crews on the

Concepts Connections 4.1

AMERICAN GIANT: USING THE VALUE CHAIN TO COMPARE COSTS OF PRODUCING A HOODIE IN THE UNITED STATES AND ASIA

American Giant Clothing Company claims to make the world's best hooded sweatshirt, and it makes them in American plants, despite the higher cost of U.S production, as shown in the accompanying table. Why is this a good choice for the company? Because costs are not the only thing that matters. American Giant's proximity to its factories allows for better communication and control, better quality monitoring, and faster production cycles. This in turn has led to a much higher-quality product—so much higher that the company is selling far more hoodies than it could if it produced lower-cost, lower-quality products overseas. Demand has soared for its hoodies, and American Giant's reputation has soared along with it, giving the company a strong competitive advantage in the hoodie market.

AMERICAN GIANT'S VALUE CHAIN ACTIVITIES AND COSTS IN PRODUCING AND SELLING A HOODIE SWEATSHIRT: U.S. VERSUS ASIAN PRODUCTION

		U.S.	Asia
1.	Fabric (Highly automated plants make the spinning, knitting, and dyeing of cotton cheaper for American Giant's U.S. suppliers.)	$17.40	$18.40
2.	Trim and hardware	3.20	2.30
3.	Labor (Without highly automated sweatshirt manufacture, U.S. labor costs would be even higher.)	17.00	5.50
4.	Duty	0.00	3.50
5.	Shipping (Shipping from overseas is more expensive and takes longer.)	0.50	1.70
6.	Total company costs	$38.10	$31.40
7.	Wholesale markup over company costs (company operating profit)	41.90	48.60
8.	Retail price (American Giant sells online to keep the price lower by avoiding middlemen and their markups.)	$80.00	$80.00

Source: Stephanie Clifford, "U.S. Textile Plants Return, with Floors Largely Empty of People," *New York Times,* Business Day, September 19, 2013, www.nytimes.com/2013/09/20/business/us-textile-factories-return.html?emc=eta1&_r=0 (accessed February 14, 2014).

auto-racing circuit. More than 80 percent of Fortune 500 companies reportedly use benchmarking for comparing themselves against rivals on cost and other competitively important measures.

The tough part of benchmarking is not whether to do it, but rather how to gain access to information about other companies' practices and costs. Sometimes benchmarking can be accomplished by collecting information from published reports, trade groups, and industry research firms and by talking to knowledgeable industry analysts, customers, and suppliers. Sometimes field trips to the facilities of competing or noncompeting companies can be arranged to observe how things are done, compare practices and processes, and perhaps exchange data on productivity and other cost components. However, such companies, even if they agree to host facilities tours and answer questions, are unlikely to share competitively sensitive cost information. Furthermore, comparing two companies' costs may not involve comparing apples to apples if the two companies employ different cost accounting principles to calculate the costs of particular activities.

However, a fairly reliable source of benchmarking information has emerged. The explosive interest of companies in benchmarking costs and identifying best practices has prompted consulting organizations (e.g., Accenture, A. T. Kearney, Benchnet—The Benchmarking Exchange, Towers Watson, and Best Practices, LLC) and several councils and associations (e.g., the APQC, the Qualserve Benchmarking Clearinghouse, and the Strategic Planning Institute's Council on Benchmarking) to gather benchmarking data, distribute information about best practices, and provide comparative cost data without identifying the names of particular companies. Having an independent group gather the information and report it in a manner that disguises the names of individual companies avoids the disclosure of competitively sensitive data and lessens the potential for unethical behavior on the part of company personnel in gathering their own data about competitors.

The Value Chain System for an Entire Industry

A company's value chain is embedded in a larger system of activities that includes the value chains of its suppliers and the value chains of whatever distribution channel allies it utilizes in getting its product or service to end users. The value chains of forward channel partners are relevant because (1) the costs and margins of a company's distributors and retail dealers are part of the price the consumer ultimately pays, and (2) the activities that distribution allies perform affect the company's customer value proposition. For these reasons, companies normally work closely with their suppliers and forward channel allies to perform value chain activities in mutually beneficial ways. For instance, motor vehicle manufacturers work closely with their forward channel allies (local automobile dealers) to ensure that owners are satisfied with dealers' repair and maintenance services.[14] Also, many automotive parts suppliers have built plants near the auto assembly plants they supply to facilitate just-in-time deliveries, reduce warehousing and shipping costs, and promote close collaboration on parts design and production scheduling. Irrigation equipment companies, suppliers of grape-harvesting and winemaking equipment, and firms making barrels, wine bottles, caps, corks, and labels all have facilities in the California wine country to be close to the nearly 700 winemakers they supply.[15] The lesson here is that a company's value chain activities are often closely linked to the value chains of its suppliers and the forward allies.

> A company's customer value proposition and cost competitiveness depend not only on internally performed activities (its own company value chain), but also on the value chain activities of its suppliers and forward channel allies.

As a consequence, *accurately assessing the competitiveness of a company's cost structure and customer value proposition requires that company managers understand an industry's entire value chain system for delivering a product or service to customers, not just the company's own value chain.* A typical industry value chain that incorporates the value-creating activities, costs, and margins of suppliers and forward channel allies, if any, is shown in Figure 4.2. However, industry value chains vary significantly by industry. For example, the primary value chain activities in the bottled water industry (spring operation or water purification, processing of basic ingredients used in flavored or vitamin-enhanced water, bottling, wholesale distribution, advertising, and retail merchandising) differ from those for the coffee industry (farming, harvesting, exporting, roasting, packaging, marketing, wholesale distribution, and, in some cases, retail store operation). Producers of bathroom and kitchen faucets depend heavily on

FIGURE 4.2 **Representative Value Chain for an Entire Industry**

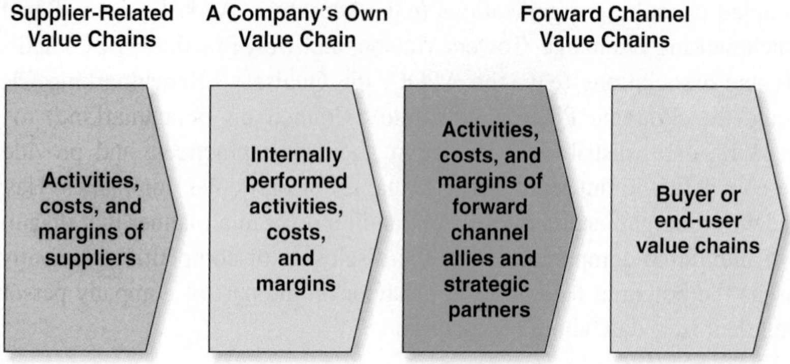

Supplier-Related
Value Chains

A Company's Own
Value Chain

Forward Channel
Value Chains

Activities,
costs, and
margins of
suppliers

Internally
performed
activities,
costs,
and
margins

Activities,
costs, and
margins of
forward
channel
allies and
strategic
partners

Buyer or
end-user
value chains

Source: Based in part on the single-industry value chain displayed in Michael E. Porter, *Competitive Advantage* (New York: Free Press, 1985), p. 35.

the activities of wholesale distributors and building supply retailers in winning sales to home builders and do-it-yourselfers, but producers of papermaking machines internalize their distribution activities by selling directly to the operators of paper plants.

Strategic Options for Remedying a Cost or Value Disadvantage

The results of value chain analysis and benchmarking may disclose cost or value disadvantages relative to key rivals. These competitive disadvantages are likely to lower a company's relative profit margin or weaken its customer value proposition. In such instances, actions to improve a company's value chain are called for to boost profitability or to allow for the addition of new features that drive customer value. There are three main areas in a company's overall value chain where important differences between firms in costs and value can occur: a company's own internal activities, the suppliers' part of the industry value chain, and the forward channel portion of the industry chain.

Improving Internally Performed Value Chain Activities Managers can pursue any of several strategic approaches to reduce the costs of internally performed value chain activities and improve a company's cost competitiveness.

1. *Implement the use of best practices* throughout the company, particularly for high-cost activities.

2. *Try to eliminate some cost-producing activities* by revamping the value chain. Many retailers have found that donating returned items to charitable organizations and taking the appropriate tax deduction results in a smaller loss than incurring the costs of the value chain activities involved in reverse logistics.

3. *Relocate high-cost activities* (such as manufacturing) to geographic areas such as China, Latin America, or Eastern Europe where they can be performed more cheaply.

4. *Outsource certain internally performed activities* to vendors or contractors if they can perform them more cheaply than can be done in-house.

5. *Invest in productivity-enhancing, cost-saving technological improvements* (robotics, flexible manufacturing techniques, state-of-the-art electronic networking).

6. *Find ways to detour around the activities or items where costs are high.* Computer chip makers regularly design around the patents held by others to avoid paying royalties; automakers have substituted lower-cost plastic for metal at many exterior body locations.

7. *Redesign the product* and/or some of its components to facilitate speedier and more economical manufacture or assembly.

8. *Try to make up the internal cost disadvantage* by reducing costs in the supplier or forward channel portions of the industry value chain—usually a last resort.

Rectifying a weakness in a company's customer value proposition can be accomplished by applying one or more of the following approaches:

1. Implement the use of best practices throughout the company, particularly for activities that are important for creating customer value—product design, product quality, or customer service.

2. Adopt best practices for marketing, brand management, and customer relationship management to improve brand image and customer loyalty.

3. Reallocate resources to activities having a significant impact on value delivered to customers—larger R&D budgets, new state-of-the-art production facilities, new distribution centers, modernized service centers, or enhanced budgets for marketing campaigns.

Additional approaches to managing value chain activities that drive costs, uniqueness, and value are discussed in Chapter 5.

Improving Supplier-Related Value Chain Activities Supplier-related cost disadvantages can be attacked by pressuring suppliers for lower prices, switching to lower-priced substitute inputs, and collaborating closely with suppliers to identify mutual cost-saving opportunities.[16] For example, just-in-time deliveries from suppliers can lower a company's inventory and internal logistics costs, eliminate capital expenditures for additional warehouse space, and improve cash flow and financial ratios by reducing accounts payable. In a few instances, companies may find that it is cheaper to integrate backward into the business of high-cost suppliers and make the item in-house instead of buying it from outsiders.

Similarly, a company can enhance its customer value proposition through its supplier relationships. Some approaches include selecting and retaining suppliers that meet higher-quality standards, providing quality-based incentives to suppliers, and integrating suppliers into the design process. When fewer defects exist in components provided by suppliers, this not only improves product quality and reliability, but it can also lower costs because there is less disruption to production processes and lower warranty expenses.

Improving Value Chain Activities of Forward Channel Allies There are three main ways to combat a cost disadvantage in the forward portion of the industry value chain: (1) Pressure dealers-distributors and other forward channel allies to reduce their costs and markups; (2) work closely with forward channel allies to identify win-win opportunities to reduce costs—for example, a chocolate manufacturer learned that by shipping its bulk chocolate in liquid form in tank cars instead of 10-pound molded bars, it could not only save its candy bar manufacturing customers the costs associated with unpacking and melting but also eliminate its own costs of molding bars and packing them; and (3) change to a more economical distribution strategy or perhaps integrate forward into company-owned retail outlets. Dell Computer's direct sales model eliminated all activities, costs, and margins of distributors, dealers, and retailers by allowing buyers to purchase customized PCs directly from Dell.

A company can improve its customer value proposition through the activities of forward channel partners by the use of (1) cooperative advertising and promotions with forward channel allies; (2) training programs for dealers, distributors, or retailers to improve the purchasing experience or customer service; and (3) creating and enforcing operating standards for resellers or franchisees to ensure consistent store operations. Papa John's International, for example, is consistently rated highly by customers for its pizza quality, convenient ordering systems, and responsive customer service across its 4,500 company-owned and franchised units. The company's marketing campaigns and extensive employee training and development programs enhance its value proposition and the unit sales and operating profit for its franchisees in all 50 states and 34 countries.

How Value Chain Activities Relate to Resources and Capabilities

A close relationship exists between the value-creating activities that a company performs and its resources and capabilities. When companies engage in a value-creating activity, they do so by drawing on specific company resources and capabilities that underlie and enable the activity. For example, brand-building activities that enhance a company's customer value proposition can depend on human resources, such as experienced brand managers, as well as organizational capabilities related to developing and executing effective marketing campaigns. Distribution activities that lower costs may derive from organizational capabilities in inventory management and resources such as cutting-edge inventory tracking systems.

Because of the linkage between activities and enabling resources and capabilities, value chain analysis complements resource and capability analysis as another tool for assessing a company's competitive advantage. Resources and capabilities that are *both valuable and rare* provide a company with the *necessary preconditions* for competitive advantage. When these assets are deployed in the form of a value-creating activity, *that potential is realized.* Resource analysis is a valuable tool for assessing the competitive advantage potential of resources and capabilities. But the actual competitive benefit provided by resources and capabilities can only be assessed objectively after they are deployed in the form of activities.

LO4 Learn how to evaluate a company's competitive strength relative to key rivals.

Question 4: What Is the Company's Competitive Strength Relative to Key Rivals?

An additional component of evaluating a company's situation is developing a comprehensive assessment of the company's overall competitive strength. Making this determination requires answers to two questions:

1. How does the company rank relative to competitors on each of the important factors that determine market success?

2. All things considered, does the company have a net competitive advantage or disadvantage versus major competitors?

Step 1 in doing a competitive strength assessment is to list the industry's key success factors and other telling measures of competitive strength or weakness (6 to 10 measures usually suffice). Step 2 is to assign a weight to each measure of competitive strength based on its perceived importance in shaping competitive success. (The sum of the weights for each measure must add up to 1.0.) Step 3 is to calculate weighted strength ratings by scoring each competitor on each strength measure (using a 1-to-10 rating scale where 1 is very weak and 10 is very strong) and multiplying the assigned rating by the assigned weight. Step 4 is to sum the weighted strength ratings on each factor to get an overall measure of competitive strength for each company being rated. Step 5 is to use the overall strength ratings to draw conclusions about the size and extent of the company's net competitive advantage or disadvantage and to take specific note of areas of strength and weakness. Table 4.3 provides an example of a competitive strength assessment using the hypothetical ABC Company against four rivals. ABC's total score of 5.95 signals a net competitive advantage over Rival 3 (with a score of 2.10) and Rival 4 (with a score of 3.70) but indicates a net competitive disadvantage against Rival 1 (with a score of 7. 70) and Rival 2 (with an overall score of 6.85).

Interpreting the Competitive Strength Assessments

Competitive strength assessments provide useful conclusions about a company's competitive situation. The ratings show how a company compares against rivals, factor by factor or capability by capability, thus revealing where it is strongest and weakest. Moreover, the overall competitive strength scores indicate whether the company is at a net competitive advantage or disadvantage against each rival.

> A company's competitive strength scores pinpoint its strengths and weaknesses against rivals and point to offensive and defensive strategies capable of producing first-rate results.

In addition, the strength ratings provide guidelines for designing wise offensive and defensive strategies. For example, consider the ratings and weighted scores in Table 4.3. If ABC Co. wants to go on the offensive to win additional sales and market share, such an offensive probably needs to be aimed directly at winning customers away from Rivals 3 and 4 (which have lower overall strength scores) rather than Rivals 1 and 2 (which have higher overall strength scores). ABC's advantages over Rival 4 tend to be in areas that are moderately important to competitive success in the industry, but ABC outclasses Rival 3 on the two most heavily weighted strength factors—relative cost position and customer service capabilities. Therefore, Rival 3 should be viewed as the primary target of ABC's offensive strategies, with Rival 4 being a secondary target.

A competitively astute company should utilize the strength scores in deciding what strategic moves to make. When a company has important competitive strengths in areas where one or more rivals are weak, it makes sense to consider offensive moves to exploit rivals' competitive weaknesses. When a company has competitive weaknesses in important areas where one or more rivals are strong, it makes sense to consider defensive moves to curtail its vulnerability.

TABLE 4.3

Illustration of a Competitive Strength Assessment

Key Success Factor/ Strength Measure	Importance Weight	ABC CO.		RIVAL 1		RIVAL 2		RIVAL 3		RIVAL 4	
		Strength Rating	Score	Strength Rating	Score	Strength Rating	Score	Strength Rating	Score	Strength Rating	Score
Quality/product performance	0.10	8	0.80	5	0.50	10	1.00	1	0.10	6	0.60
Reputation/image	0.10	8	0.80	7	0.70	10	1.00	1	0.10	6	0.60
Manufacturing capability	0.10	2	0.20	10	1.00	4	0.40	5	0.50	1	0.10
Technological skills	0.05	10	0.50	1	0.05	7	0.35	3	0.15	8	0.40
Dealer network/distribution capability	0.05	9	0.45	4	0.20	10	0.50	5	0.25	1	0.05
New-product innovation capability	0.05	9	0.45	4	0.20	10	0.50	5	0.25	1	0.05
Financial resources	0.10	5	0.50	10	1.00	7	0.70	3	0.30	1	0.10
Relative cost position	0.30	5	1.50	10	3.00	3	0.95	1	0.30	4	1.20
Customer service capabilities	0.15	5	0.75	7	1.05	10	1.50	1	0.15	4	0.60
Sum of importance weights	1.00										
Weighted overall strength rating			**5.95**		**7.70**		**6.85**		**2.10**		**3.70**

(Rating scale: 1 = very weak; 10 = very strong)

Question 5: What Strategic Issues and Problems Must Be Addressed by Management?

LO5 Understand how a comprehensive evaluation of a company's external and internal situations can assist managers in making critical decisions about their next strategic moves.

The final and most important analytical step is to zero in on exactly what strategic issues company managers need to address. This step involves drawing on the results of both industry and competitive analysis and the evaluations of the company's internal situation. The task here is to get a clear fix on exactly what industry and competitive challenges confront the company, which of the company's internal weaknesses need fixing, and what specific problems merit front-burner attention by company managers. *Pinpointing the precise things that management needs to worry about sets the agenda for deciding what actions to take next to improve the company's performance and business outlook.*

If the items on management's "worry list" are relatively minor, which suggests the company's strategy is mostly on track and reasonably well matched to the company's overall situation, company managers seldom need to go much beyond fine-tuning the present strategy. If, however, the issues and problems confronting the company are serious and indicate the present strategy is not well suited for the road ahead, the task of crafting a better strategy has got to go to the top of management's action agenda.

> Compiling a "worry list" of problems and issues creates an agenda for managerial strategy making.

KEY POINTS

In analyzing a company's own particular competitive circumstances and its competitive position vis-à-vis key rivals, consider five key questions:

1. *How well is the present strategy working?* This involves evaluating the strategy in terms of the company's financial performance and competitive strength and market standing. The stronger a company's current overall performance, the less likely the need for radical strategy changes. The weaker a company's performance and/or the faster the changes in its external situation (which can be gleaned from industry and competitive analysis), the more its current strategy must be questioned.

2. *Do the company's resources and capabilities have sufficient competitive power to give it a sustainable advantage over competitors?* The answer to this question comes from conducting the four tests of a resource's competitive power—the VRIN tests. If a company has resources and capabilities that are competitively *valuable* and *rare,* the firm will have the potential for a competitive advantage over market rivals. If its resources and capabilities are also hard to copy (*inimitable*) with no good substitutes (*nonsubstitutable*), then the firm may be able to sustain this advantage even in the face of active efforts by rivals to overcome it.

   SWOT analysis can be used to assess if a company's resources and capabilities are sufficient to seize market opportunities and overcome external threats to its future well-being. The two most important parts of SWOT analysis are (1) drawing conclusions about what story the compilation of strengths, weaknesses, opportunities, and threats tells about the company's overall situation, and (2) acting on the conclusions to better match the company's strategy to its internal strengths and market opportunities, to correct the important internal weaknesses, and to defend against external threats. A company's strengths and competitive assets are strategically relevant because they are the most logical and appealing building blocks for strategy; internal weaknesses are important because they may represent vulnerabilities that need correction. External opportunities and threats come into play because a good strategy necessarily aims at capturing a company's most attractive opportunities and at defending against threats to its well-being.

3. *Are the company's cost structure and customer value proposition competitive?* One telling sign of whether a company's situation is strong or precarious is whether its costs are competitive with those of industry rivals. Another sign is how it compares with rivals in terms of its customer value proposition. Value chain analysis and benchmarking are essential tools in determining whether the company is performing particular functions and activities well, whether its costs are in line with competitors, whether it is able to offer an attractive value proposition to customers, and whether particular internal activities and business processes need improvement. Value chain analysis complements resource and capability analysis because of the tight linkage between activities and enabling resources and capabilities.

4. *Is the company competitively stronger or weaker than key rivals?* The key appraisals here involve how the company matches up against key rivals on industry key success factors and other chief determinants of competitive success and whether and why the company has a competitive advantage or disadvantage. Quantitative competitive strength assessments, using the method presented in Table 4.3, indicate where a company is competitively strong and weak and provide insight into the company's ability to defend or enhance its market position. As a rule, a company's competitive strategy should be built around its competitive strengths and should aim at shoring up areas where it is competitively vulnerable. When a company has important competitive strengths in areas where one or more rivals are weak, it makes sense to consider offensive moves to exploit rivals' competitive weaknesses. When a company has important competitive weaknesses in areas where one or more rivals are strong, it makes sense to consider defensive moves to curtail its vulnerability.

5. *What strategic issues and problems merit front-burner managerial attention?* This analytical step zeros in on the strategic issues and problems that stand in the way of the company's success. It involves using the results of both industry and competitive analysis and company situation analysis to identify a "worry list" of issues to be resolved for the company to be financially and competitively successful in the years ahead. Actually deciding upon a strategy and what specific actions to take comes after the list of strategic issues and problems that merit front-burner management attention has been developed.

Good company situation analysis, like good industry and competitive analysis, is a valuable precondition for good strategy making.

> ## ASSURANCE OF LEARNING EXERCISES

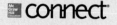

LO1

1. Using the financial ratios provided in the Appendix and the financial statement information for Costco Wholesale Corporation, Inc., below, calculate the following ratios for Costco for both 2013 and 2014.

   1. Gross profit margin
   2. Operating profit margin
   3. Net profit margin
   4. Times interest earned coverage

5. Return on shareholders' equity
6. Return on assets
7. Debt-to-equity ratio
8. Days of inventory
9. Inventory turnover ratio
10. Average collection period

Based on these ratios, did Costco's financial performance improve, weaken, or remain about the same from 2013 to 2014?

Consolidated Statements of Income for Costco Wholesale Corporation, Inc., 2013–2014 (in millions, except per share data)

	2014	2013
Net sales	$110,212	$102,870
Membership fees	2,428	2,286
Total revenue	112,640	105,156
Operating Expenses		
Merchandise costs	98,458	91,948
Selling, general and administrative	10,899	10,104
Operating income	3,220	3,053
Other Income (Expense)		
Interest expense	(113)	(99)
Interest income and other, net	90	97
Income before income taxes	3,197	3,051
Provision for income taxes	1,109	990
Net income including noncontrolling interests	2,088	2,061
Net income attributable to noncontrolling interests	(30)	(22)
Net income	$2,058	$2,039
Basic earnings per share	$ 4.69	$ 4.68
Diluted earnings per share	$ 4.65	$ 4.63

Consolidated Balance Sheets for Costco Wholesale Corporation, 2013–2014 (in millions, except per share data)

ASSETS	AUGUST 31, 2014	SEPTEMBER 1, 2014
Current Assets		
Cash and cash equivalents	$ 5,738	$ 4,644
Short-term investments	1,577	1,480
Receivables, net	1,148	1,201
Merchandise inventories	8,456	7,894
Deferred income taxes and other current assets	669	621
Total current assets	17,588	15,7840
Property and Equipment		
Land	4,716	4,409
Buildings and improvements	12,522	11,556
Equipment and fixtures	4,845	4,472
Construction in progress	592	585
Less accumulated depreciation and amortization	(7,845)	(7,141)
Net property and equipment	14,830	13,881

Consolidated Balance Sheets for Costco Wholesale Corporation, 2013–2014 (in millions, except per share data)

ASSETS	AUGUST 31, 2014	SEPTEMBER 1, 2014
Other assets	606	562
Total assets	$ 33,024	$ 30,283
Liabilities and Equity		
Current Liabilities		
Accounts payable	$8,491	$7,872
Accrued salaries and benefits	2,231	2,037
Accrued member rewards	773	710
Accrued sales and other taxes	442	382
Deferred membership fees	1,254	1,167
Other current liabilities	1,221	1,089
Total current liabilities	14,412	13,257
Long-term debt	5,093	4,998
Deferred income taxes and other liabilities	1,004	1,016
Total liabilities	20,509	19,271
Equity		
Preferred stock $.005 par value; 100,000,000 shares authorized; no shares issued and outstanding	0	0
Common stock $.005 par value; 900,000,000 shares authorized; 437,683,000 and 436,839,000 shares issued and outstanding	2	2
Additional paid-in capital	4,919	4,670
Accumulated other comprehensive loss	(76)	(122)
Retained earnings	7,458	6,283
Total Costco stockholders' equity	12,303	10,833
Noncontrolling interests	212	179
Total equity	12,515	11,012
Total liabilities and equity	$ 33,024	$30,283

Source: Costco Wholesale Corporation, 2014 10-K.

LO2
2. REI operates more than 130 sporting goods and outdoor recreation stores in 34 states. How many of the four tests of the competitive power of a resource does the retail store network pass? Explain your answer.

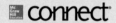

LO3
3. Review the information in Concepts & Connections 4.1 concerning American Giant's average costs of producing and selling a hoodie sweatshirt and compare this with the representative value chain depicted in Figure 4.1. Then answer the following questions:
   (a) Which of the company's costs correspond to the primary value chain activities depicted in Figure 4.1?
   (b) Which of the company's costs correspond to the support activities described in Figure 4.1?
   (c) How would its various costs and activities differ if the company chose to produce its hoodies in Asia?
   (d) What value chain activities might be important in securing or maintaining American Giant's competitive advantage?

LO4
4. Using the methodology illustrated in Table 4.3 and your knowledge as an automobile owner, prepare a competitive strength assessment for General Motors and its rivals Ford,

Chrysler, Toyota, and Honda. Each of the five automobile manufacturers should be evaluated on the key success factors/strength measures of cost competitiveness, product-line breadth, product quality and reliability, financial resources and profitability, and customer service. What does your competitive strength assessment disclose about the overall competitiveness of each automobile manufacturer? What factors account most for Toyota's competitive success? Does Toyota have competitive weaknesses that were disclosed by your analysis? Explain.

 EXERCISES FOR SIMULATION PARTICIPANTS

1. Using the formulas in the Appendix and the data in your company's latest financial statements, calculate the following measures of financial performance for your company: **LO1**

   1. Operating profit margin
   2. Return on total assets
   3. Current ratio
   4. Working capital
   5. Long-term debt-to-capital ratio
   6. Price-earnings ratio

2. Based on your company's latest financial statements and all of the other available data regarding your company's performance that appear in the Industry Report, list the three measures of financial performance on which your company did "best" and the three measures on which your company's financial performance was "worst."   **LO1**

3. What hard evidence can you cite that indicates your company's strategy is working fairly well (or perhaps not working so well, if your company's performance is lagging that of rival companies)?   **LO1**

4. What internal strengths and weaknesses does your company have? What external market opportunities for growth and increased profitability exist for your company? What external threats to your company's future well-being and profitability do you and your co-managers see? What does the preceding SWOT analysis indicate about your company's present situation and future prospects—where on the scale from "exceptionally strong" to "alarmingly weak" does the attractiveness of your company's situation rank?   **LO2**

5. Does your company have any core competencies? If so, what are they?   **LO2**

6. What are the key elements of your company's value chain? Refer to Figure 4.1 in developing your answer.   **LO3**

7. Using the methodology illustrated in Table 4.3, do a weighted competitive strength assessment for your company and two other companies that you and your co-managers consider to be very close competitors.   **LO4**

 ENDNOTES

1. Birger Wernerfelt, "A Resource-Based View of the Firm," *Strategic Management Journal* 5, no. 5 (September– October 1984); Jay Barney, "Firm Resources and Sustained Competitive Advantage," *Journal of Management* 17, no. 1 (1991); Margaret A. Peteraf, "The Cornerstones of Competitive Advantage: A Resource-Based View," *Strategic Management Journal* 14, no. 3 (March 1993).

2. Birger Wernerfelt, "A Resource-Based View of the Firm," *Strategic Management Journal* 5, no. 5 (September– October 1984), pp. 171–80; Jay Barney, "Firm Resources and Sustained Competitive Advantage," *Journal of Management* 17, no. 1 (1991); Margaret A. Peteraf, "The Cornerstones of Competitive Advantage: A Resource-Based View," *Strategic Management Journal* 14, no. 3 (March 1993).

3. R. Amit and P. Schoemaker, "Strategic Assets and Organizational Rent," *Strategic Management Journal* 14, no. 1 (1993).

4. David J. Collis and Cynthia A. Montgomery, "Competing on Resources: Strategy in the 1990s," *Harvard Business Review* 73, no. 4 (July–August 1995).

5. Margaret A. Peteraf and Mark E. Bergen, "Scanning Dynamic Competitive Landscapes: A Market-Based and Resource-Based Framework," *Strategic Management Journal* 24 (2003), pp. 1027–42.

6. George Stalk, Philip Evans, and Lawrence E. Schulman, "Competing on Capabilities: The New Rules of Corporate Strategy," *Harvard Business Review* 70, no. 2 (March–April 1992).

7. David J. Teece, Gary Pisano, and Amy Shuen, "Dynamic Capabilities and Strategic Management," *Strategic Management Journal* 18, no. 7 (1997); Constance E. Helfat and Margaret A. Peteraf, "The Dynamic Resource-Based View: Capability Lifecycles," *Strategic Management Journal* 24, no. 10 (2003).

8. C. Montgomery, "Of Diamonds and Rust: A New Look at Resources," in *Resource-Based and Evolutionary Theories of the Firm*, ed. C. Montgomery (Boston: Kluwer Academic Publishers, 1995), pp. 251–68.

9. D. Teece, G. Pisano, and A. Shuen, "Dynamic Capabilities and Strategic Management," *Strategic Management Journal* 18, no. 7 (1997); K. Eisenhardt and J. Martin, "Dynamic Capabilities: What Are They?" *Strategic Management Journal* 21, nos. 10–11 (2000); M. Zollo and S. Winter, "Deliberate Learning and the Evolution of Dynamic Capabilities," *Organization Science* 13 (2002); C. Helfat et al., *Dynamic Capabilities: Understanding Strategic Change in Organizations* (Malden, MA: Blackwell, 2007).

10. W. Powell, K. Koput, and L. Smith-Doerr, "Interorganizational Collaboration and the Locus of Innovation," *Administrative Science Quarterly* 41, no. 1 (1996).

11. M. Peteraf, "The Cornerstones of Competitive Advantage: A Resource-Based View," *Strategic Management Journal*, March 1993, pp. 179–91.

12. Michael E. Porter, *Competitive Advantage* (New York: Free Press, 1985).

13. Gregory H. Watson, *Strategic Benchmarking: How to Rate Your Company's Performance Against the World's Best* (New York: John Wiley & Sons, 1993); Robert C. Camp, *Benchmarking: The Search for Industry Best Practices That Lead to Superior Performance* (Milwaukee: ASQC Quality Press, 1989); Christopher E. Bogan and Michael J. English, *Benchmarking for Best Practices: Winning Through Innovative Adaptation* (New York: McGraw-Hill, 1994); Dawn Iacobucci and Christie Nordhielm, "Creative Benchmarking," *Harvard Business Review* 78, no. 6 (November–December 2000).

14. M. Hegert and D. Morris, "Accounting Data for Value Chain Analysis," *Strategic Management Journal* 10 (1989); Robin Cooper and Robert S. Kaplan, "Measure Costs Right: Make the Right Decisions," *Harvard Business Review* 66, no. 5 (September–October 1988); John K. Shank and Vijay Govindarajan, *Strategic Cost Management* (New York: Free Press, 1993).

15. Michael E. Porter, "Clusters and the New Economics of Competition," *Harvard Business Review* 76, no. 6 (November–December 1998).

16. Reuben E. Stone, "Leading a Supply Chain Turnaround," *Harvard Business Review* 82, no. 10 (October 2004).

The Five Generic Competitive Strategies

LEARNING OBJECTIVES

LO1   Understand what distinguishes each of the five generic strategies and why some of these strategies work better in certain kinds of industry and competitive conditions than in others.

LO2   Learn the major avenues for achieving a competitive advantage based on lower costs.

LO3   Gain command of the major avenues for developing a competitive advantage based on differentiating a company's product or service offering from the offerings of rivals.

LO4   Recognize the required conditions for delivering superior value to customers through the use of a hybrid of low-cost provider and differentiation strategies.

2. *Incorporate tangible features that improve product performance.* Commercial buyers and consumers alike value higher levels of performance in many types of products. Product reliability, output, durability, convenience, and ease of use are aspects of product performance that differentiate products offered to buyers. Tablet computer manufacturers are currently in a race to develop next-generation tablets with the functionality and processing power to capturing market share from rivals and cannibalize the laptop computer market.

3. *Incorporate intangible features that enhance buyer satisfaction in noneconomic ways.* Toyota's Prius appeals to environmentally conscious motorists who wish to help reduce global carbon dioxide emissions. Bentley, Ralph Lauren, Louis Vuitton, Tiffany, Cartier, and Rolex have differentiation-based competitive advantages linked to buyer desires for status, image, prestige, upscale fashion, superior craftsmanship, and the finer things in life.

> Differentiation can be based on *tangible* or *intangible* features and attributes.

Perceived Value and the Importance of Signaling Value

The price premium commanded by a differentiation strategy reflects *the value actually delivered* to the buyer and *the value perceived* by the buyer. The value of certain differentiating features is rather easy for buyers to detect, but in some instances, buyers may have trouble assessing what their experience with the product will be. Successful differentiators go to great lengths to make buyers knowledgeable about a product's value and incorporate signals of value such as attractive packaging, extensive ad campaigns, the quality of brochures and sales presentations, the seller's list of customers, the length of time the firm has been in business, and the professionalism, appearance, and personality of the seller's employees. Such signals of value may be as important as actual value (1) when the nature of differentiation is subjective or hard to quantify, (2) when buyers are making a first-time purchase, (3) when repurchase is infrequent, and (4) when buyers are unsophisticated.

Concepts & Connections 5.2 describes key elements of BMW's differentiation strategy that has allowed it to become the number-one luxury automobile brand in the United States.

When a Differentiation Strategy Works Best

Differentiation strategies tend to work best in market circumstances where:

1. *Buyer needs and uses of the product are diverse.* Diverse buyer preferences allow industry rivals to set themselves apart with product attributes that appeal to particular buyers. For instance, the diversity of consumer preferences for menu selection, ambience, pricing, and customer service gives restaurants exceptionally wide latitude in creating differentiated concepts. Other industries offering opportunities for differentiation based upon diverse buyer needs and uses include magazine publishing, automobile manufacturing, footwear, kitchen appliances, and computers.

2. *There are many ways to differentiate the product or service that have value to buyers.* Industries that allow competitors to add features to product attributes are well suited to differentiation strategies. For example, hotel chains can differentiate on such features as location, size of room, range of guest services, in-hotel

Concepts Connections 5.2

HOW BMW'S DIFFERENTIATION STRATEGY ALLOWED IT TO BECOME THE NUMBER-ONE LUXURY CAR BRAND

BMW entered the U.S. market for automobiles in 1975 with a model line comprised of the two-door 2002 and 3.0 CSL models and the four-door 530i. The BMW brand was so poorly known in the United States that most Americans assumed that BMW meant "British Motor Works." The company set about building brand recognition through its BMW Motorsport program that emblazoned "Bavarian Motor Works" across the upper windshields of its 3.0 CSL cars competing in races at Sebring, Laguna Seca, Riverside, and Talladega. BMW's success on the race track and the instant popularity of its 320i introduced in the United States in 1977 helped build one of the strongest luxury brands in the country by the mid-1980s. The 320i was wildly popular with young professionals, and with each new generation of the 3-series, BMW attracted new young buyers and increased demand for its larger, more expensive models such as the 5-series, 6-series, and 7-series as its repeat buyers moved up in their careers.

BMW's customer value proposition was also keyed to state-of-the-art engineering that resulted in high-performing engines, innovative features, and responsive handling. The company's "Ultimate Driving Machine" tagline signaled its commitment to sports performance along with luxury. Through the late 2000s, the average pricing for BMW models was at the upper end of the industry, which limited its market share and solidified its reputation as an aspirational luxury brand focused on high-income consumers. However, the introduction of the BMW 1-series in 2008 that carried a sticker price of $28,600 vastly expanded the market for BMWs and allowed the company overtake Lexus as the number-one luxury car brand in the United States that same year.

The company also expanded its product line to include a six sedan models, five sports activity vehicle models, seven two-door coupes and convertible models, three hybrid models, the plug-in hybrid i8 sports car, and an all-electric i3 by 2015. The base pricing for BMW's product line in 2015 ranged from $32,100 for the 2-series coupe to $136,500 for the i8.

Sources: www.bmwusa.com; and *BMW Magazine*, Spring/Summer 2015.

dining, and the quality and luxuriousness of bedding and furnishings. Similarly, cosmetics producers are able to differentiate based upon prestige and image, formulations that fight the signs of aging, UV light protection, exclusivity of retail locations, the inclusion of antioxidants and natural ingredients, or prohibitions against animal testing.

3. *Few rival firms are following a similar differentiation approach.* The best differentiation approaches involve trying to appeal to buyers on the basis of attributes that rivals are not emphasizing. A differentiator encounters less head-to-head rivalry when it goes its own separate way to create uniqueness and does not try to outdifferentiate rivals on the very same attributes. When many rivals are all claiming "ours tastes better than theirs" or "ours gets your clothes cleaner than theirs," competitors tend to end up chasing the same buyers with very similar product offerings.

4. *Technological change is fast-paced and competition revolves around rapidly evolving product features.* Rapid product innovation and frequent introductions of next-version products heighten buyer interest and provide space for companies to pursue distinct differentiating paths. In HD TVs, mobile phones, and automobile backup, parking, and lane detection sensors, competitors are locked into an ongoing battle to set themselves apart by introducing the best next-generation products; companies that fail to come up with new and improved products and distinctive performance features quickly lose out in the marketplace.

Pitfalls to Avoid in Pursuing a Differentiation Strategy

Differentiation strategies can fail for any of several reasons. *A differentiation strategy keyed to product or service attributes that are easily and quickly copied is always suspect.* Rapid imitation means that no rival achieves meaningful differentiation, because whatever new feature one firm introduces that strikes the fancy of buyers is almost immediately added by rivals. This is why a firm must search out sources of uniqueness that are time-consuming or burdensome for rivals to match if it hopes to use differentiation to win a sustainable competitive edge over rivals.

Differentiation strategies can also falter when buyers see little value in the unique attributes of a company's product. Thus, even if a company sets the attributes of its brand apart from its rivals' brands, its strategy can fail because of trying to differentiate on the basis of something that does not deliver adequate value to buyers. Any time many potential buyers look at a company's differentiated product offering and conclude "so what," the company's differentiation strategy is in deep trouble; buyers will likely decide the product is not worth the extra price, and sales will be disappointingly low.

Overspending on efforts to differentiate is a strategy flaw that can erode profitability. Company efforts to achieve differentiation nearly always raise costs. The trick to profitable differentiation is either to keep the costs of achieving differentiation below the price premium the differentiating attributes can command in the marketplace or to offset thinner profit margins by selling enough additional units to increase total profits. If a company goes overboard in pursuing costly differentiation, it could be saddled with unacceptably thin profit margins or even losses. The need to contain differentiation costs is why many companies add little touches of differentiation that add to buyer satisfaction but are inexpensive to institute.

Other common pitfalls and mistakes in crafting a differentiation strategy include:

- *Overdifferentiating so that product quality or service levels exceed buyers' needs.* Buyers are unlikely to pay extra for features and attributes that will go unused. For example, consumers are unlikely to purchase programmable large appliances such as washers, dryers, and ovens if they are satisfied with manually controlled appliances.

- *Trying to charge too high a price premium.* Even if buyers view certain extras or deluxe features as "nice to have," they may still conclude that the added benefit or luxury is not worth the price differential over that of lesser differentiated products.

- *Being timid and not striving to open up meaningful gaps in quality or service or performance features vis-à-vis the products of rivals.* Tiny differences between rivals' product offerings may not be visible or important to buyers.

A low-cost provider strategy can always defeat a differentiation strategy when buyers are satisfied with a basic product and don't think "extra" attributes are worth a higher price.

Focused (or Market Niche) Strategies

What sets focused strategies apart from low-cost leadership or broad differentiation strategies is a concentration on a narrow piece of the total market. The targeted segment, or niche, can be defined by geographic uniqueness or by special product attributes that appeal only to niche members. The advantages of focusing a company's entire competitive effort on a single market niche are considerable, especially for smaller and medium-sized companies that may lack the breadth and depth of resources to tackle going after a national customer base with a "something for everyone" lineup of models, styles, and product selection. Lagunitas Brewing Company is a craft brewery with a geographic focus on California, Colorado, Texas, Florida, New York, and Illinois. Lagunitas' sales of about 250,000 barrels is a small percentage of total U.S. craft beer sales of about 22 million barrels, but it has become the sixth largest craft brewer in the United States and 13th largest U.S. beer producer with annual sales in excess of $100 million. Examples of firms that concentrate on a well-defined market niche keyed to a particular product or buyer segment include Discovery Channel and Comedy Central (in cable TV), Google (in Internet search engines), Porsche (in sports cars), and CGA, Inc. (a specialist in providing insurance to cover the cost of lucrative hole-in-one prizes at golf tournaments). Local bakeries and cupcake shops, bed-and-breakfast inns, and local owner-managed retail boutiques are all good examples of enterprises that have scaled their operations to serve narrow or local customer segments.

A Focused Low-Cost Strategy

A focused strategy based on low cost aims at securing a competitive advantage by serving buyers in the target market niche at a lower cost and a lower price than rival competitors. This strategy has considerable attraction when a firm can lower costs significantly by limiting its customer base to a well-defined buyer segment. The avenues to achieving a cost advantage over rivals also serving the target market niche are the same as for low-cost leadership—outmanage rivals in keeping the costs to a bare minimum and searching for innovative ways to bypass or reduce non-essential activities. The only real difference between a low-cost provider strategy and a focused low-cost strategy is the size of the buyer group to which a company is appealing.

Focused low-cost strategies are fairly common. Producers of private-label goods are able to achieve low costs in product development, marketing, distribution, and advertising by concentrating on making generic items similar to name-brand merchandise and selling directly to retail chains wanting a low-priced store brand. The Perrigo Company has become a leading manufacturer of over-the-counter health care products with 2014 sales of more than $4.1 billion by focusing on producing private-label brands for retailers such as Walmart, CVS, Walgreens, Rite Aid, and Safeway. Even though Perrigo doesn't make branded products, a focused low-cost strategy is appropriate for the makers of branded products as well. Concepts & Connections 5.3 describes how Aravind's focus on lowering the costs of cataract removal allowed the company to address the needs of the "bottom of the pyramid" in India's population where blindness due to cataracts is an endemic problem.

A Focused Differentiation Strategy

Focused differentiation strategies are keyed to offering carefully designed products or services to appeal to the unique preferences and needs of a narrow, well-defined group of buyers (as opposed to a broad differentiation strategy aimed at many buyer groups and market segments). Companies such as Four Seasons Hotels and Resorts, Chanel, Gucci, and Louis Vuitton employ successful differentiation-based focused strategies

Concepts Connections 5.3

ARAVIND EYE CARE SYSTEM'S FOCUSED LOW-COST STRATEGY

Cataracts, the largest cause of preventable blindness, can be treated with a quick surgical procedure that restores sight; however, poverty and limited access to care prevent millions worldwide from obtaining surgery. The Aravind Eye Care System has found a way to address this problem with a focused low-cost strategy that has made cataract surgery not only affordable for more people in India but also free for the very poorest. On the basis of this strategy, Aravind has achieved world renown and become the largest provider of eye care in the world.

High volume and high efficiency are at the cornerstone of Aravind's strategy. The Aravind network of five eye hospitals in India has become one of the most productive systems in the world, conducting about 350,000 surgeries a year in addition to seeing more than 2.8 million outpatients each year. Using the unique model of screenings at camps all over the country, Aravind reaches a broad cross-section of the market for surgical treatment. Additionally, Aravind attains very high staff productivity with each surgeon performing more than 2,500 surgeries annually, compared to 125 for a comparable American surgeon.

This level of productivity (with no loss in quality of care) was achieved through the development of a standardized system of surgical treatment, capitalizing on the fact that cataract removal is a fairly routine process. Aravind streamlined as much of the process as possible, reducing discretionary elements to a minimum and tracking outcomes to ensure continuous process improvement. At Aravind's hospitals, no time is wasted between surgeries as different teams of support staff prepare patients for surgery and bring them to the operating theater; surgeons simply turn from one table to another to perform surgery on the next prepared patient. Aravind also drove costs down through the creation of its own manufacturing division, Aurolab, to produce intraocular lenses, suture needles, pharmaceuticals, and surgical blades in India.

Aravind's low costs allow it to keep prices for cataract surgery very low—about $10 per patient, compared to an average cost of $1,500 in the United States. Nevertheless, the system provides surgical outcomes and quality comparable to those of clinics in the United States. As a result of its unique fee system and effective management, Aravind is also able to provide free eye care to 60 percent of its patients from the revenue generated from paying patients.

Sources: Developed with Avni V. Patel. G. Natchiar, A. L. Robin, R. Thulasiraj, et al., "Attacking the Backlog of India's Curable Blind; The Aravind Eye Hospital Model," *Archives of Ophthalmology* 112, no. 7 (July 1994), pp. 987–93; D. F. Chang, "Tackling the Greatest Challenge in Cataract Surgery," *British Journal of Ophthalmology* 89, no. 9 (September 2005), pp. 1073–77; and McKinsey & Co., "Driving Down the Cost of High-Quality Care," *Health International*, December 2011.

targeted at affluent buyers wanting products and services with world-class attributes. Indeed, most markets contain a buyer segment willing to pay a price premium for the very finest items available, thus opening the strategic window for some competitors to pursue differentiation-based focused strategies aimed at the very top of the market pyramid.

Another successful focused differentiator is "fashion food retailer" Trader Joe's, a 457-store, 42-state chain that is a combination gourmet deli and food warehouse. Customers shop Trader Joe's as much for entertainment as for conventional grocery items; the store stocks out-of-the-ordinary culinary treats such as raspberry salsa, salmon burgers, and jasmine fried rice, as well as the standard goods normally found in supermarkets. What sets Trader Joe's apart is not just its unique combination of food novelties and competitively priced grocery items but also its capability to turn an otherwise mundane grocery excursion into a whimsical treasure hunt that is just plain fun.

When a Focused Low-Cost or Focused Differentiation Strategy Is Viable

A focused strategy aimed at securing a competitive edge based on either low cost or differentiation becomes increasingly attractive as more of the following conditions are met:

- The target market niche is big enough to be profitable and offers good growth potential.
- Industry leaders have chosen not to compete in the niche—focusers can avoid battling head-to-head against the industry's biggest and strongest competitors.
- It is costly or difficult for multisegment competitors to meet the specialized needs of niche buyers and at the same time satisfy the expectations of mainstream customers.
- The industry has many different niches and segments, thereby allowing a focuser to pick a niche suited to its resource strengths and capabilities.
- Few, if any, rivals are attempting to specialize in the same target segment.

The Risks of a Focused Low-Cost or Focused Differentiation Strategy

Focusing carries several risks. The *first major risk* is the chance that competitors will find effective ways to match the focused firm's capabilities in serving the target niche. In the lodging business, large chains such as Marriott and Hilton have launched multibrand strategies that allow them to compete effectively in several lodging segments simultaneously. Marriott has flagship hotels with a full complement of services and amenities that allow it to attract travelers and vacationers going to major resorts; it has J.W. Marriott, Ritz-Carlton, and Renaissance hotels that provide deluxe comfort and service to business and leisure travelers; it has Courtyard by Marriott and SpringHill Suites brands for business travelers looking for moderately priced lodging; it has Marriott Residence Inns and TownePlace Suites designed as a "home away from home" for travelers staying five or more nights; and it has more than 700 Fairfield Inn locations that cater to travelers looking for quality lodging at an "affordable" price. Marriott has also added Edition, AC Hotels by Marriott, and Autograph Collection hotels that offer stylish, distinctive decors and personalized services that appeal to young professionals seeking distinctive lodging alternatives. Multibrand strategies are attractive to large companies such as Marriott precisely because they enable a company to enter a market niche and siphon business away from companies that employ a focus strategy.

A *second risk* of employing a focus strategy is the potential for the preferences and needs of niche members to shift over time toward the product attributes desired by the majority of buyers. An erosion of the differences across buyer segments lowers entry barriers into a focuser's market niche and provides an open invitation for rivals in adjacent segments to begin competing for the focuser's customers. A *third risk* is that the segment may become so attractive it is soon inundated with competitors, intensifying rivalry and splintering segment profits.

LO4 Recognize the required conditions for delivering superior value to customers through the use of a hybrid of low-cost provider and differentiation strategies.

Best-Cost Provider Strategies

As Figure 5.1 indicates, **best-cost provider strategies** are a *hybrid* of low-cost provider and differentiation strategies that aim at satisfying buyer expectations on key quality/features/performance/service attributes and beating customer expectations on price. Companies pursuing best-cost strategies aim squarely at the sometimes great mass of value-conscious buyers looking for a good-to-very-good product or service at an economical price. The essence of a best-cost provider strategy is giving customers *more value for the money* by satisfying buyer desires for appealing features/performance/quality/service and charging a lower price for these attributes compared to that of rivals with similar-caliber product offerings.[3]

> **CORE CONCEPT**
>
> **Best-cost provider strategies** are a *hybrid* of low-cost provider and differentiation strategies that aim at satisfying buyer expectations on key quality/features/performance/ service attributes and beating customer expectations on price.

To profitably employ a best-cost provider strategy, a company *must have the capability to incorporate attractive or upscale attributes at a lower cost than rivals.* This capability is contingent on (1) a superior value chain configuration that eliminates or minimizes activities that do not add value, (2) unmatched efficiency in managing essential value chain activities, and (3) core competencies that allow differentiating attributes to be incorporated at a low cost. When a company can incorporate appealing features, good-to-excellent product performance or quality, or more satisfying customer service into its product offering *at a lower cost than that of rivals,* then it enjoys "best-cost" status—it is the low-cost provider of a product or service with *upscale attributes.* A best-cost provider can use its low-cost advantage to underprice rivals whose products or services have similar upscale attributes and still earn attractive profits.

Concepts & Connections 5.4 describes how American Giant has applied the principles of a best-cost provider strategy in producing and marketing its hoodie sweatshirts.

When a Best-Cost Provider Strategy Works Best

A best-cost provider strategy works best in markets where product differentiation is the norm and attractively large numbers of value-conscious buyers can be induced to purchase midrange products rather than the basic products of low-cost producers or the expensive products of top-of-the-line differentiators. A best-cost provider usually needs to position itself near the middle of the market with either a medium-quality product at a below-average price or a high-quality product at an average or slightly higher-than-average price. Best-cost provider strategies also work well in recessionary times when great masses of buyers become value-conscious and are attracted to economically priced products and services with especially appealing attributes.

The Danger of an Unsound Best-Cost Provider Strategy

A company's biggest vulnerability in employing a best-cost provider strategy is not having the requisite core competencies and efficiencies in managing value chain activities to support the addition of differentiating features without significantly increasing costs. A company with a modest degree of differentiation and no real cost advantage will most likely find itself squeezed between the firms using low-cost strategies and those using differentiation strategies. Low-cost providers may be able to siphon customers away with the appeal of a lower price (despite having marginally less appealing

Concepts & Connections 5.4

AMERICAN GIANT'S BEST-COST PROVIDER STRATEGY

Bayard Winthrop, founder and owner of American Giant, set out to make a hoodie like the soft, ultra-thick Navy sweatshirts his dad used to wear in the 1950s. But he also had two other aims: He wanted it to have a more updated look with a tailored fit, and he wanted it produced cost-effectively so that it could be sold at a great price. To accomplish these aims, he designed the sweatshirt with the help of a former industrial engineer from Apple and an internationally renowned pattern maker, rethinking every aspect of sweatshirt design and production along the way. The result was a hoodie differentiated from others on the basis of extreme attention to fabric, fit, construction, and durability. The hoodie is made from heavy-duty cotton that is run through a machine that carefully picks loops of thread out of the fabric to create a thick, combed, ring-spun fleece fabric that feels three times thicker than most sweatshirts. A small amount of spandex paneling along the shoulders and sides creates the fitted look and maintains the shape, keeping the sweatshirt from looking slouchy or sloppy. It has double stitching with strong thread on critical seams to avoid deterioration and boost durability. The zippers and draw cord are customized to match the sweatshirt's color—an uncommon practice in the business.

American Giant sources yarn from Parkdale, South Carolina, and turns it into cloth at the nearby Carolina Cotton Works. This reduces transport costs, creates a more dependable, durable product that American Giant can easily quality-check, and shortens product turnaround to about a month, lowering inventory costs. This process also enables the company to use a genuine "Made in the U.S.A" label, a perceived quality driver.

American Giant disrupts the traditional, expensive distribution models by having no stores or resellers. Instead, it sells

directly to customers from its website, with free two-day shipping and returns. Much of the company's growth comes from word of mouth and a strong public relations effort that promotes the brand in magazines, newspapers, and key business-oriented television programs. American Giant has a robust refer-a-friend program that offers a discount to friends of, and a credit to, current owners. Articles in popular media proclaiming its product "the greatest hoodie ever made" have made demand for its sweatshirts skyrocket.

At $79 for the original men's hoodie, American Giant is not cheap but offers customers value in terms of both price and quality. The price is higher than what one would pay at The Gap or American Apparel and comparable to Levi's, J.Crew, or Banana Republic. But its quality is more on par with high-priced designer brands, while its price is far more affordable.

Note: Developed with Sarah Boole.
Sources: www.nytimes.com/2013/09/20/business/us-textile-factories-return.html?emc=eta1&_r=0; www.american-giant.com; www.slate.com/articles/technology/technology/2012/12/american_giant_hoodie_this_is_the_greatest_sweatshirt_known_to_man.html; www.businessinsider.com/this-hoodie-is-so-insanely-popular-you-have-to-wait-months-to-get-it-2013-12.

product attributes). High-end differentiators may be able to steal customers away with the appeal of appreciably better product attributes (even though their products carry a somewhat higher price tag). Thus, a successful best-cost provider must offer buyers *significantly* better product attributes to justify a price above what low-cost leaders are charging. Likewise, it has to achieve significantly lower costs in providing upscale features so that it can outcompete high-end differentiators on the basis of a *significantly* lower price.

Successful Competitive Strategies Are Resource Based

For a company's competitive strategy to succeed in delivering good performance and the intended competitive edge over rivals, it has to be well matched to a company's internal situation and underpinned by an appropriate set of resources, know-how, and competitive capabilities. To succeed in employing a low-cost provider strategy, a company has to have the resources and capabilities to keep its costs below those of its competitors; this means having the expertise to cost-effectively manage value chain activities better than rivals and/or the innovative capability to bypass certain value chain activities being performed by rivals. To succeed in strongly differentiating its product in ways that are appealing to buyers, a company must have the resources and capabilities (such as better technology, strong skills in product innovation, expertise in customer service) to incorporate unique attributes into its product offering that a broad range of buyers will find appealing and worth paying for. Strategies focusing on a narrow segment of the market require the capability to do an outstanding job of satisfying the needs and expectations of niche buyers. Success in employing a strategy keyed to a best-value offering requires the resources and capabilities to incorporate upscale product or service attributes at a lower cost than that of rivals.

> A company's competitive strategy should be well matched to its internal situation and predicated on leveraging its collection of competitively valuable resources and competencies.

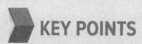

KEY POINTS

1. Early in the process of crafting a strategy, company managers have to decide which of the five basic competitive strategies to employ: overall low-cost, broad differentiation, focused low-cost, focused differentiation, or best-cost provider.

2. In employing a low-cost provider strategy, a company must do a better job than rivals of cost-effectively managing internal activities, and/or it must find innovative ways to eliminate or bypass cost-producing activities. Particular attention should be paid to cost drivers, which are factors having a strong effect on the cost of a company's value chain activities and cost structure. Low-cost provider strategies work particularly well when price competition is strong and the products of rival sellers are very weakly differentiated. Other conditions favoring a low-cost provider strategy are when supplies are readily available from eager sellers, when there are not many ways to differentiate that have value to buyers, when the majority of industry sales are made to a few large buyers, when buyer switching costs are low, and when industry newcomers are likely to use a low introductory price to build market share.

3. Broad differentiation strategies seek to produce a competitive edge by incorporating attributes and features that set a company's product/service offering apart from rivals in ways that buyers consider valuable and worth paying for. Such features and attributes are best integrated through the systematic management of uniqueness—value chain activities or factors that can have a strong effect on customer value and creating differentiation. Successful differentiation allows a firm to (1) command a premium price for its product, (2) increase unit sales (because additional buyers are won over by the differentiating features),

and/or (3) gain buyer loyalty to its brand (because some buyers are strongly attracted to the differentiating features and bond with the company and its products). Differentiation strategies work best in markets with diverse buyer preferences where there are big windows of opportunity to strongly differentiate a company's product offering from those of rival brands, in situations where few other rivals are pursuing a similar differentiation approach, and in circumstances where technological change is fast-paced and competition centers on rapidly evolving product features. A differentiation strategy is doomed when competitors are able to quickly copy most or all of the appealing product attributes a company comes up with, when a company's differentiation efforts meet with a ho-hum or so-what market reception, or when a company erodes profitability by overspending on efforts to differentiate its product offering.

4. A focused strategy delivers competitive advantage either by achieving lower costs than rivals' in serving buyers comprising the target market niche or by offering niche buyers an appealingly differentiated product or service that meets their needs better than rival brands. A focused strategy becomes increasingly attractive when the target market niche is big enough to be profitable and offers good growth potential, when it is costly or difficult for multisegment competitors to put capabilities in place to meet the specialized needs of the target market niche and at the same time satisfy the expectations of their mainstream customers, when there are one or more niches that present a good match with a focuser's resource strengths and capabilities, and when few other rivals are attempting to specialize in the same target segment.

5. Best-cost provider strategies stake out a middle ground between pursuing a low-cost advantage and a differentiation-based advantage and between appealing to the broad market as a whole and a narrow market niche. The aim is to create competitive advantage by giving buyers more value for the money—satisfying buyer expectations on key quality/features/performance/service attributes while beating customer expectations on price. To profitably employ a best-cost provider strategy, a company *must have the capability to incorporate attractive or upscale attributes at a lower cost than that of rivals.* This capability is contingent on (1) a superior value chain configuration, (2) unmatched efficiency in managing essential value chain activities, and (3) resource strengths and core competencies that allow differentiating attributes to be incorporated at a low cost. A best-cost provider strategy works best in markets where opportunities to differentiate exist and where many buyers are sensitive to price and value.

6. Deciding which generic strategy to employ is perhaps the most important strategic commitment a company makes—it tends to drive the rest of the strategic actions a company decides to undertake, and it sets the whole tone for the pursuit of a competitive advantage over rivals.

▶ ASSURANCE OF LEARNING EXERCISES

1. Best Buy is the largest consumer electronics retailer in the United States with 2015 sales of more than $40 billion. The company competes aggressively on price with rivals such as Costco Wholesale, Sam's Club, Walmart, and Target but is also known by consumers for its first-rate customer service. Best Buy customers have commented that the retailer's sales staff is exceptionally knowledgeable about products and can direct them to the exact location of difficult-to-find items. Best Buy customers also appreciate that demonstration models of PC monitors, digital media players, and other electronics are fully powered and ready for in-store use. Best Buy's Geek Squad tech support and installation services are additional customer service features valued by many customers.

LO1, LO2, LO3, LO4

How would you characterize Best Buy's competitive strategy? Should it be classified as a low-cost provider strategy? A differentiation strategy? A best-cost strategy? Explain your answer.

LO2

2. Concepts & Connections 5.1 discusses Walmart's low-cost advantage in the supermarket industry. Based on information provided in the illustration, explain how Walmart has built its low-cost advantage in the supermarket industry and why a low-cost provider strategy is well suited to the industry.

LO1, LO2, LO3, LO4

3. USAA is a Fortune 500 insurance and financial services company with 2014 annual sales exceeding $24 billion. The company was founded in 1922 by 25 Army officers who decided to insure each other's vehicles and continues to limit its membership to active-duty and retired military members, officer candidates, and adult children and spouses of military-affiliated USAA members. The company has received countless awards, including being listed among *Fortune*'s World's Most Admired Companies in 2014 and 2015 and 100 Best Companies to Work For in 2010 through 2015. USAA was also ranked as the number-one Bank, Credit Card and Insurance Company by Forrester Research from 2013 to 2015. You can read more about the company's history and strategy at www.usaa.com. How would you characterize USAA's competitive strategy? Should it be classified as a low-cost provider strategy? A differentiation strategy? A best-cost strategy? Also, has the company chosen to focus on a narrow piece of the market, or does it appear to pursue a broad market approach? Explain your answer.

LO3

4. Explore lululemon athletica's website at info.lululemon.com and see if you can identify at least three ways in which the company seeks to differentiate itself from rival athletic apparel firms. Is there reason to believe that lululemon's differentiation strategy has been successful in producing a competitive advantage? Why or why not?

▶ EXERCISES FOR SIMULATION PARTICIPANTS

LO1, LO2, LO3, LO4

1. Which one of the five generic competitive strategies best characterizes your company's strategic approach to competing successfully?

2. Which rival companies appear to be employing a low-cost provider strategy?

3. Which rival companies appear to be employing a broad differentiation strategy?

4. Which rival companies appear to be employing a best-cost provider strategy?

5. Which rival companies appear to be employing some type of focus strategy?

6. What is your company's action plan to achieve a sustainable competitive advantage over rival companies? List at least three (preferably, more than three) specific kinds of decision entries on specific decision screens that your company has made or intends to make to win this kind of competitive edge over rivals.

▶ ENDNOTES

1. Michael E. Porter, *Competitive Strategy: Techniques for Analyzing Industries and Competitors* (New York: Free Press, 1980), chap. 2, and Michael E. Porter, "What Is Strategy?" *Harvard Business Review* 74, no. 6 (November–December 1996).

2. Michael E. Porter, *Competitive Advantage* (New York: Free Press, 1985).

3. Peter J. Williamson and Ming Zeng, "Value-for-Money Strategies for Recessionary Times," *Harvard Business Review* 87, no. 3 (March 2009).

Strengthening a Company's Competitive Position: Strategic Moves, Timing, and Scope of Operations

LEARNING OBJECTIVES

LO1   Learn whether and when to pursue offensive or defensive strategic moves to improve a company's market position.

LO2   Recognize when being a first mover or a fast follower or a late mover can lead to competitive advantage.

LO3   Become aware of the strategic benefits and risks of expanding a company's horizontal scope through mergers and acquisitions.

LO4   Learn the advantages and disadvantages of extending a company's scope of operations via vertical integration.

LO5   Understand the conditions that favor farming out certain value chain activities to outside parties.

LO6   Gain an understanding of how strategic alliances and collaborative partnerships can bolster a company's collection of resources and capabilities.

Once a company has settled on which of the five generic competitive strategies to employ, attention turns to what *other strategic actions* it can take to complement its competitive approach and maximize the power of its overall strategy. Several decisions regarding the company's operating scope and how to best strengthen its market standing must be made:

- Whether and when to go on the offensive and initiate aggressive strategic moves to improve the company's market position
- Whether and when to employ defensive strategies to protect the company's market position
- When to undertake strategic moves based upon whether it is advantageous to be a first mover or a fast follower or a late mover
- Whether to integrate backward or forward into more stages of the industry value chain
- Which value chain activities, if any, should be outsourced
- Whether to enter into strategic alliances or partnership arrangements with other enterprises
- Whether to bolster the company's market position by merging with or acquiring another company in the same industry

This chapter presents the pros and cons of each of these measures that round out a company's overall strategy.

LO1 Learn whether and when to pursue offensive or defensive strategic moves to improve a company's market position.

Launching Strategic Offensives to Improve a Company's Market Position

No matter which of the five generic competitive strategies a company employs, there are times when a company *should be aggressive and go on the offensive.* Strategic offensives are called for when a company spots opportunities to gain profitable market share at the expense of rivals or when a company has no choice but to try to whittle away at a strong rival's competitive advantage. Companies such as Samsung, Amazon, Autonation, and Google play hardball, aggressively pursuing competitive advantage and trying to reap the benefits a competitive edge offers—a leading market share, excellent profit margins, and rapid growth.[1]

Choosing the Basis for Competitive Attack

Generally, strategic offensives should be grounded in a company's competitive assets and strong points and should be aimed at exploiting competitor weaknesses.[2] Ignoring the need to tie a strategic offensive to a company's competitive strengths is like going to war with a popgun—the prospects for success are dim. For instance, it is foolish for a company with relatively high costs to employ a price-cutting offensive. Likewise, it is ill advised to pursue a product innovation offensive without having proven expertise in R&D, new-product development, and speeding new or improved products to market.

The best offensives use a company's most competitively potent resources to attack rivals in those competitive areas where they are weakest.

The principal offensive strategy options include:

1. *Offering an equally good or better product at a lower price.* Lower prices can produce market share gains if competitors offering similarly performing products don't respond with price cuts of their own. Price-cutting offensives are best initiated by companies that have *first achieved a cost advantage.*[3]

2. *Leapfrogging competitors by being the first to market with next-generation technology or products.* Microsoft got its next-generation Xbox 360 to market 12 months ahead of Sony's PlayStation 3 and Nintendo's Wii, helping it build a sizable market share and develop a reputation for cutting-edge innovation in the video game industry.

3. *Pursuing continuous product innovation to draw sales and market share away from less innovative rivals.* Ongoing introductions of new or improved products can put rivals under tremendous competitive pressure, especially when rivals' new-product development capabilities are weak.

4. *Pursuing disruptive product innovations to create new markets.* While this strategy can be riskier and more costly than a strategy of continuous innovation, it can be a game changer if successful. Disruptive innovation involves perfecting new products or services that offer an altogether new and better value proposition. Examples include Facebook, Tumblr, Twitter, Priceline.com, Square (mobile credit card processing), and Amazon's Kindle.

5. *Adopting and improving on the good ideas of other companies (rivals or otherwise).* The idea of warehouse-type home improvement centers did not originate with Home Depot co-founders Arthur Blank and Bernie Marcus; they got the "big box" concept from their former employer, Handy Dan Home Improvement. But they were quick to improve on Handy Dan's business model and strategy and take Home Depot to a higher plateau in terms of product-line breadth and customer service.

6. *Using hit-and-run or guerrilla warfare tactics to grab sales and market share from complacent or distracted rivals.* Options for "guerrilla offensives" include occasional lowballing on price (to win a big order or steal a key account from a rival) or surprising key rivals with sporadic but intense bursts of promotional activity (offering a 20 percent discount for one week to draw customers away from rival brands).[4] Guerrilla offensives are particularly well suited to small challengers who have neither the resources nor the market visibility to mount a full-fledged attack on industry leaders.

7. *Launching a preemptive strike to capture a rare opportunity or secure an industry's limited resources.*[5] What makes a move preemptive is its one-of-a-kind nature—whoever strikes first stands to acquire competitive assets that rivals can't readily match. Examples of preemptive moves include (1) securing the best distributors in a particular geographic region or country; (2) moving to obtain the most favorable site at a new interchange or intersection, in a new shopping mall, and so on; and (3) tying up the most reliable, high-quality suppliers via exclusive partnerships, long-term contracts, or even acquisition. To be successful, a preemptive move doesn't have to totally block rivals from following or copying; it merely needs to give a firm a prime position that is not easily circumvented.

Choosing Which Rivals to Attack

Offensive-minded firms need to analyze which of their rivals to challenge as well as how to mount that challenge. The best targets for offensive attacks are:

- *Market leaders that are vulnerable.* Offensive attacks make good sense when a company that leads in terms of size and market share is not a true leader in terms of serving the market well. Signs of leader vulnerability include unhappy buyers, an inferior product line, a weak competitive strategy with regard to low-cost leadership or differentiation, a preoccupation with diversification into other industries, and mediocre or declining profitability.

- *Runner-up firms with weaknesses in areas where the challenger is strong.* Runner-up firms are an especially attractive target when a challenger's resource strengths and competitive capabilities are well suited to exploiting their weaknesses.

- *Struggling enterprises that are on the verge of going under.* Challenging a hard-pressed rival in ways that further sap its financial strength and competitive position can hasten its exit from the market.

- *Small local and regional firms with limited capabilities.* Because small firms typically have limited expertise and resources, a challenger with broader capabilities is well positioned to raid their biggest and best customers.

Blue Ocean Strategy—A Special Kind of Offensive

A **blue ocean strategy** seeks to gain a dramatic and durable competitive advantage *by abandoning efforts to beat out competitors in existing markets and, instead, inventing a new industry or distinctive market segment that renders existing competitors largely irrelevant and allows a company to create and capture altogether new demand.*[6] This strategy views the business universe as consisting of two distinct types of market space. One is where industry boundaries are defined and accepted, the competitive rules of the game are well understood by all industry members, and companies try to outperform rivals by capturing a bigger share of existing demand; in such markets, lively competition constrains a company's prospects for rapid growth and superior profitability since rivals move quickly to either imitate or counter the successes of competitors. The second type of market space is a "blue ocean" where the industry does not really exist yet, is untainted by competition, and offers wide-open opportunity for profitable and rapid growth if a company can come up with a product offering and strategy that allows it to create new demand rather than fight over existing demand. A terrific example of such wide-open or blue ocean market space is the online auction industry that eBay created and now dominates.

> **CORE CONCEPT**
>
> **Blue ocean strategies** offer growth in revenues and profits by discovering or inventing new industry segments that create altogether new demand.

Other examples of companies that have achieved competitive advantages by creating blue ocean market spaces include Starbucks in the coffee shop industry, Amazon's Kindle in eBooks, FedEx in overnight package delivery, Uber in ride sharing services, and Cirque du Soleil in live entertainment. Cirque du Soleil "reinvented the circus" by creating a distinctively different market space for its performances (Las Vegas nightclubs and theater-type settings) and pulling in a whole new group of customers—adults and corporate clients—who were willing to pay several times more than the price of a conventional circus ticket to have an "entertainment experience" featuring sophisticated clowns and star-quality acrobatic acts in a comfortable atmosphere.

Blue ocean strategies provide a company with a great opportunity in the short run. But they don't guarantee a company's long-term success, which depends more on whether a company can protect the market position it opened up. Concepts & Connections 6.1 discusses how Gilt Groupe used a blue ocean strategy to open a new competitive space in online luxury retailing.

Using Defensive Strategies to Protect a Company's Market Position and Competitive Advantage

In a competitive market, all firms are subject to offensive challenges from rivals. The purposes of defensive strategies are to lower the risk of being attacked, weaken the impact of any attack that occurs, and influence challengers to aim their efforts at other rivals. While defensive strategies usually don't enhance a firm's competitive advantage, they can definitely help fortify its competitive position. Defensive strategies can take either of two forms: actions to block challengers and actions signaling the likelihood of strong retaliation.

> Good defensive strategies can help protect competitive advantage but rarely are the basis for creating it.

Blocking the Avenues Open to Challengers

The most frequently employed approach to defending a company's present position involves actions to restrict a competitive attack by a challenger. A number of obstacles can be put in the path of would-be challengers.[7] A defender can introduce new features, add new models, or broaden its product line to close vacant niches to opportunity-seeking challengers. It can thwart the efforts of rivals to attack with a lower price by maintaining economy-priced options of its own. It can try to discourage buyers from trying competitors' brands by making early announcements about upcoming new products or planned price changes. Finally, a defender can grant volume discounts or better financing terms to dealers and distributors to discourage them from experimenting with other suppliers.

Signaling Challengers That Retaliation Is Likely

The goal of signaling challengers that strong retaliation is likely in the event of an attack is either to dissuade challengers from attacking or to divert them to less threatening options. Either goal can be achieved by letting challengers know the battle will cost more than it is worth. Would-be challengers can be signaled by:

- Publicly announcing management's commitment to maintain the firm's present market share.
- Publicly committing the company to a policy of matching competitors' terms or prices.
- Maintaining a war chest of cash and marketable securities.
- Making an occasional strong counterresponse to the moves of weak competitors to enhance the firm's image as a tough defender.

Concepts Connections 6.1

GILT GROUPE'S BLUE OCEAN STRATEGY IN THE U.S. FLASH SALE INDUSTRY

Luxury fashion flash sales exploded onto the U.S. e-commerce scene when Gilt Groupe launched its business in 2007. Flash sales offer limited quantities of high-end designer brands at steep discounts to site members over a very narrow time frame: The opportunity to snap up an incredible bargain is over in a "flash." The concept of online time-limited, designer-brand sale events, available to members only, had been invented six years earlier by the French company Vente Privée. But since Vente Privée operated in Europe and the United Kingdom, the U.S. market represented a wide-open, blue ocean of uncontested opportunity. Gilt Groupe's only rival was Ideeli, another U.S. start-up that had launched in the same year.

Gilt Groupe grew rapidly in the calm waters of the early days of the U.S. industry. Its tremendous growth stemmed from its recognition of an underserved segment of the population—the web-savvy, value-conscious fashionista—and also from fortuitous timing. The Great Recession hit the United States in December 2007, causing a sharp decline in consumer buying and leaving designers with unforeseen quantities of luxury items they could not sell. The fledgling flash sale industry was the perfect channel to off-load excess inventory, while it still maintained the cachet of exclusivity through members-only sales and limited-time availability.

Gilt's revenue grew exponentially from $25 million in 2008 to upward of $700 million by 2012. But the company's success prompted an influx of fast followers into the luxury flash sale industry, including HauteLook and Rue La La, which entered the market in December 2007 and April 2008, respectively. Competition among rival sites became especially strong since memberships were free and online customers could switch easily from site to site. Competition also heightened as larger retailers entered the luxury flash sale industry, with Nordstrom acquiring HauteLook, eBay purchasing Rue La La, and Amazon acquiring MyHabit.com. In late 2011, Vente Privée announced the launch of its U.S. online site, via a joint venture with American Express.

As the competitive waters roiled and turned increasingly red, Gilt Groupe began looking for new ways to compete, expanding into a variety of online luxury product and services niches and venturing overseas. While the company is not yet profitable, its operating performance has improved, and it attracted an additional $50 million in investor funding in 2015. The flash sale site has received more than $300 million in angel investments and venture capital since its launch in 2007. Can Gilt Groupe survive in a more crowded competitive space and provide its investors with a strong return? Only time will tell.

Developed with Judith H. Lin.
Sources: Matthew Carroll, "The Rise of Gilt Groupe," Forbes.com, January 2012, www.forbes.com (accessed February 26, 2012);
Mark   "Launching Gilt Groupe, A Fashionable Enterprise," *Wall Street Journal,* October 2010, www.wsj.com (accessed February 26, 2012);
http://about.americanexpress.com/news/pr/2011/vente_usa.aspx, accessed March 3, 2012.

LO2 Recognize when being a first mover or a fast follower or a late mover can lead to competitive advantage.

Timing a Company's Offensive and Defensive Strategic Moves

When to make a strategic move is often as crucial as *what* move to make. Timing is especially important when **first-mover advantages or disadvantages** exist. Being first to initiate a strategic move can have a high payoff when (1) pioneering helps build a firm's image and reputation with buyers; (2) early commitments to new technologies, new-style components, new or emerging distribution channels, and so on can produce an absolute cost advantage over rivals; (3) first-time customers remain strongly loyal to pioneering firms in making repeat purchases; and (4) moving first constitutes a preemptive strike, making imitation extra hard or unlikely. The bigger the first-mover advantages, the more attractive making the first move becomes.[8]

CORE CONCEPT

Because of **first-mover advantages and disadvantages**, competitive advantage can spring from *when* a move is made as well as from *what* move is made.

Sometimes, though, markets are slow to accept the innovative product offering of a first mover, in which case a fast follower with substantial resources and marketing muscle can overtake a first mover. CNN had enjoyed a powerful first mover advantage in cable news until 2002, when it was surpassed by Fox News as the number-one cable news network. Fox has used innovative programming and intriguing hosts to expand its demographic appeal to retain its number-one ranking for 15 consecutive years. Sometimes furious technological change or product innovation makes a first mover vulnerable to quickly appearing next-generation technology or products. For instance, former market leaders in mobile phones Nokia and BlackBerry have been victimized by far more innovative iPhone and Android models. Hence, there are no guarantees that a first mover will win sustainable competitive advantage.[9]

To sustain any advantage that may initially accrue to a pioneer, a first mover needs to be a fast learner and continue to move aggressively to capitalize on any initial pioneering advantage. If a first mover's skills, know-how, and actions are easily copied or even surpassed, then followers and even late movers can catch or overtake the first mover in a relatively short period. What makes being a first mover strategically important is not being the first company to do something but rather being the first competitor to put together the precise combination of features, customer value, and sound revenue/cost/profit economics that gives it an edge over rivals in the battle for market leadership.[10] If the marketplace quickly takes to a first mover's innovative product offering, a first mover must have large-scale production, marketing, and distribution capabilities if it is to stave off fast followers that possess similar resources capabilities. If technology is advancing at a torrid pace, a first mover cannot hope to sustain its lead without having strong capabilities in R&D, design, and new-product development, along with the financial strength to fund these activities.

The Potential for Late-Mover Advantages or First-Mover Disadvantages

There are instances when there are actually *advantages* to being an adept follower rather than a first mover. Late-mover advantages (or *first-mover disadvantages*) arise in four instances:

- When pioneering leadership is more costly than followership and only negligible experience or learning curve benefits accrue to the leader—a condition that allows a follower to end up with lower costs than the first mover.
- When the products of an innovator are somewhat primitive and do not live up to buyer expectations, thus allowing a clever follower to win disenchanted buyers away from the leader with better-performing products.
- When potential buyers are skeptical about the benefits of a new technology or product being pioneered by a first mover.
- When rapid market evolution (due to fast-paced changes in either technology or buyer needs and expectations) gives fast followers and maybe even cautious late movers the opening to leapfrog a first mover's products with more attractive next-version products.

Concepts & Connections 6.2 describes how Amazon.com achieved a first-mover advantage in online retailing.

Deciding Whether to Be an Early Mover or Late Mover

In weighing the pros and cons of being a first mover versus a fast follower versus a slow mover, it matters whether the race to market leadership in a particular industry is a marathon or a sprint. In marathons, a slow mover is not unduly penalized—first-mover advantages can be fleeting, and there's ample time for fast followers and sometimes even late movers to catch up.[11] Thus the speed at which the pioneering innovation is likely to catch on matters considerably as companies struggle with whether to pursue a particular emerging market opportunity aggressively or cautiously. For instance, it took 5.5 years for worldwide mobile phone use to grow from 10 million to 100 million worldwide and close to 10 years for the number of at-home broadband subscribers to grow to 100 million worldwide. The lesson here is that there is a market-penetration curve for every emerging opportunity; typically, the curve has an inflection point at which all the pieces of the business model fall into place, buyer demand explodes, and the market takes off. The inflection point can come early on a fast-rising curve (as with the use of e-mail) or farther on up a slow-rising curve (such as the use of broadband). Any company that seeks competitive advantage by being a first mover thus needs to ask some hard questions:

- Does market takeoff depend on the development of complementary products or services that currently are not available?
- Is new infrastructure required before buyer demand can surge?
- Will buyers need to learn new skills or adopt new behaviors? Will buyers encounter high switching costs?
- Are there influential competitors in a position to delay or derail the efforts of a first mover?

When the answers to any of these questions are yes, then a company must be careful not to pour too many resources into getting ahead of the market opportunity—the race is likely going to be more of a 10-year marathon than a 2-year sprint.

Strengthening a Company's Market Position via Its Scope of Operations

Apart from considerations of offensive and defensive competitive moves and their timing, another set of managerial decisions can affect the strength of a company's market position. These decisions concern the **scope of the firm**—the breadth of a company's activities and the extent of its market reach. For example, Ralph Lauren Corporation designs, markets, and distributes fashionable apparel and other merchandise to more than 10,000 major department stores and specialty retailers around the world, plus it also operates nearly 400 Ralph Lauren retail stores, 200-plus factory stores, and seven e-commerce sites. Scope decisions also concern which segments of the market to serve—decisions that can include geographic market segments as well as product and service segments. Almost 40 percent of Ralph Lauren's sales are made outside the United States, and its product line includes apparel, fragrances, home furnishings,

CORE CONCEPT

The **scope of the firm** refers to the range of activities the firm performs internally, the breadth of its product and service offerings, the extent of its geographic market presence, and its mix of businesses.

eyewear, watches and jewelry, and handbags and other leather goods. The company has also expanded its brand lineup through the acquisitions of Chaps menswear and casual retailer Club Monaco.

> **CORE CONCEPT**
> **Horizontal scope** is the range of product and service segments that a firm serves within its focal market.

Four dimensions of firm scope have the capacity to strengthen a company's position in a given market: the breadth of its product and service offerings, the range of activities the firm performs internally, the extent of its geographic market presence, and its mix of businesses. In this chapter, we discuss horizontal and vertical scope decisions in relation to its breadth of offerings and range of internally performed activities. A company's **horizontal scope,** which is the range of product and service segments that it serves, can be expanded through new-business development or mergers and acquisitions of other companies in the marketplace. The company's **vertical scope** is the extent to which it engages in the various activities that make up the industry's entire value chain system—from raw-material or component production all the way to retailing and after-sales service. Expanding a company's vertical scope by means of vertical integration can also affect the strength of a company's market position.

> **CORE CONCEPT**
> **Vertical scope** is the extent to which a firm's internal activities encompass one, some, many, or all of the activities that make up an industry's entire value chain system, ranging from raw-material production to final sales and service activities.

Additional dimensions of a firm's scope are discussed in Chapter 7, which focuses on the company's geographic scope and expansion into foreign markets, and Chapter 8, which takes up the topic of business diversification and corporate strategy.

Horizontal Merger and Acquisition Strategies

Mergers and acquisitions are much-used strategic options to strengthen a company's market position. A *merger* is the combining of two or more companies into a single corporate entity, with the newly created company often taking on a new name. An *acquisition* is a combination in which one company, the acquirer, purchases and absorbs the operations of another, the acquired. The difference between a merger and an acquisition relates more to the details of ownership, management control, and financial arrangements than to strategy and competitive advantage. The resources and competitive capabilities of the newly created enterprise end up much the same whether the combination is the result of an acquisition or merger.

Horizontal mergers and acquisitions, which involve combining the operations of companies within the same product or service market, allow companies to rapidly increase scale and horizontal scope. For example, the merger of AMR Corporation (parent of American Airlines) with US Airways has increased the airlines' scale of operations and their reach geographically to create the world's largest airline.

> Combining the operations of two companies, via merger or acquisition, is an attractive strategic option for achieving operating economies, strengthening the resulting company's competencies and competitiveness, and opening avenues of new market opportunity.

Merger and acquisition strategies typically set sights on achieving any of five objectives:[12]

1. *Extending the company's business into new product categories.* Many times a company has gaps in its product line that need to be filled. Acquisition can be a quicker and more potent way to broaden a company's product line than going

through the exercise of introducing a company's own new product to fill the gap. Coca-Cola has expanded its offerings by acquiring Minute Maid, Glacéau VitaminWater, and Hi-C.

2. *Creating a more cost-efficient operation out of the combined companies.* When a company acquires another company in the same industry, there's usually enough overlap in operations that certain inefficient plants can be closed or distribution and sales activities can be partly combined and downsized. The combined companies may also be able to reduce supply chain costs through buying in greater volume from common suppliers. Likewise, it is usually feasible to squeeze out cost savings in administrative activities, again by combining and downsizing such activities as finance and accounting, information technology, human resources, and so on.

3. *Expanding a company's geographic coverage.* One of the best and quickest ways to expand a company's geographic coverage is to acquire rivals with operations in the desired locations. Food products companies such as Nestlé, Kraft, Unilever, and Procter & Gamble have made acquisitions an integral part of their strategies to expand internationally.

4. *Gaining quick access to new technologies or complementary resources and capabilities.* Making acquisitions to bolster a company's technological know-how or to expand its skills and capabilities allows a company to bypass a time-consuming and expensive internal effort to build desirable new resources and capabilities. From 2000 through June 2015, Cisco Systems purchased 121 companies to give it more technological reach and product breadth, thereby enhancing its standing as the world's largest provider of hardware, software, and services for building and operating Internet networks.

5. *Leading the convergence of industries whose boundaries are being blurred by changing technologies and new market opportunities.* Such acquisitions are the result of a company's management betting that two or more distinct industries are converging into one and deciding to establish a strong position in the consolidating markets by bringing together the resources and products of several different companies. News Corporation has prepared for the convergence of media services with the purchase of satellite TV companies to complement its media holdings in TV broadcasting (the Fox network and TV stations in various countries), cable TV (Fox News, Fox Sports, and FX), filmed entertainment (Twentieth Century Fox and Fox Studios), newspapers, magazines, and book publishing.

Why Mergers and Acquisitions Sometimes Fail to Produce Anticipated Results

Despite many successes, mergers and acquisitions do not always produce the hoped-for outcomes.[13] Cost savings may prove smaller than expected. Gains in competitive capabilities may take substantially longer to realize or, worse, may never materialize. Efforts to mesh the corporate cultures can stall due to formidable resistance from organization members. Key employees at the acquired company can quickly become disenchanted and leave; the morale of company personnel who remain can drop to disturbingly low levels because they disagree with newly instituted changes. Differences in management styles and operating procedures can prove hard to resolve. In addition,

Concepts Connections 6.2

AMAZON.COM'S FIRST-MOVER ADVANTAGE IN ONLINE RETAILING

Amazon.com's path to becoming the world's largest online retailer began in 1994 when Jeff Bezos, a Manhattan hedge fund analyst at the time, noticed that the number of Internet users was increasing by 2,300 percent annually. Bezos saw the tremendous growth as an opportunity to sell products online that would be demanded by a large number of Internet users and could be easily shipped. Bezos launched the online bookseller Amazon.com in 1995. The startup's revenues soared to $148 million in 1997, $610 million in 1998, and $1.6 billion in 1999. Bezos's business plan—hatched while on a cross-country trip with his wife in 1994—made him *Time* magazine's Person of the Year in 1999.

The volume-based and reputational benefits of Amazon.com's early entry into online retailing had delivered a first-mover advantage, but between 2000 and 2013, Bezos undertook a series of additional strategic initiatives to solidify the company's number-one ranking in the industry. Bezos undertook a massive building program in the late-1990s that added five new warehouses and fulfillment centers at a total cost of $300 million. The additional warehouse capacity was added years before it was needed, but Bezos wanted to move preemptively against potential rivals and ensure that, as demand continued to grow, the company could continue to offer its customers the best selection, the lowest prices, and the cheapest and most convenient delivery. The company also expanded its product line to include sporting goods, tools, toys, grocery items, electronics, and digital music downloads, giving it another means of maintaining its experience and scale-based advantages. Amazon.com's 2013 revenues of $74.5 billion not

only made it the world's leading Internet retailer but made it larger than its 12 biggest competitors combined. As a result, Jeff Bezos's shares in Amazon.com made him the 12th wealthiest person in the United States, with an estimated net worth of $27.2 billion.

Moving down the learning curve in Internet retailing was not an entirely straightforward process for Amazon.com. Bezos commented in a *Fortune* article profiling the company, "We were investors in every bankrupt, 1999-vintage e-commerce startup: Pets.com, living.com, kozmo.com. We invested in a lot of high-profile flameouts." He went on to specify that although the ventures were a "waste of money," they "didn't take us off our own mission." Bezos also suggested that gaining advantage as a first mover is "taking a million tiny steps—and learning quickly from your missteps."

Sources: Mark Brohan, "The Top 500 Guide,"*Internet Retailer,* June 2009, www.internetretailer.com (accessed June 17, 2009); Josh Quittner, "How Jeff Bezos Rules the Retail Space," *Fortune,* May 5, 2008, pp. 126–134; S. Banjo and P. Ziobro, "After Decades of Toil, Web Sales Remain Small for Many Retailers," *Wall Street Journal Online,* August 27, 2013 (accessed March 2014); Company Snapshot, Bloomberg *Businessweek Online* (accessed March 28, 2014); Forbes.com; and company website.

the managers appointed to oversee the integration of a newly acquired company can make mistakes in deciding which activities to leave alone and which activities to meld into their own operations and systems.

A number of mergers/acquisitions have been notably unsuccessful. The 2008 merger of Arby's and Wendy's is a prime example. After only three years, Wendy's decided to sell Arby's due to the roast beef sandwich chain's continued poor profit performance. The jury is still out as to whether Microsoft's 2011 acquisition of Skype for $8.5 billion or the $3 billion merger of United Airlines and Continental Airlines in 2010 will prove to be moneymakers or money losers.

Vertical Integration Strategies

Vertical integration extends a firm's competitive and operating scope within the same industry. It involves expanding the firm's range of value chain activities backward into sources of supply and/or forward toward end users. Thus, if a manufacturer invests in facilities to produce certain component parts that it formerly purchased from outside suppliers or if it opens its own chain of retail stores to market its products to consumers, it is engaging in vertical integration. For example, paint manufacturer Sherwin-Williams remains in the paint business even though it has integrated forward into retailing by operating more than 4,000 retail stores that market its paint products directly to consumers.

> **CORE CONCEPT**
>
> A **vertically integrated** firm is one that performs value chain activities along more than one stage of an industry's overall value chain

A firm can pursue vertical integration by starting its own operations in other stages of the vertical activity chain, by acquiring a company already performing the activities it wants to bring in-house, or by means of a strategic alliance or joint venture. Vertical integration strategies can aim at *full integration* (participating in all stages of the vertical chain) or *partial integration* (building positions in selected stages of the vertical chain). Companies may choose to pursue *tapered integration,* a strategy that involves both outsourcing and performing the activity internally. Oil companies' practice of supplying their refineries with both crude oil produced from their own wells and crude oil supplied by third-party operators and well owners is an example of tapered backward integration. Coach, Inc., the maker of Coach handbags and accessories, engages in tapered forward integration since it operates full-price and factory outlet stores but also sells its products through third-party department store outlets.

> **CORE CONCEPT**
>
> **Backward integration** involves performing industry value chain activities previously performed by suppliers or other enterprises engaged in earlier stages of the industry value chain; **forward integration** involves performing industry value chain activities closer to the end user.

The Advantages of a Vertical Integration Strategy

The two best reasons for investing company resources in vertical integration are to strengthen the firm's competitive position and/or to boost its profitability.[14] Vertical integration has no real payoff unless it produces sufficient cost savings to justify the extra investment, adds materially to a company's technological and competitive strengths, and/or helps differentiate the company's product offering.

Integrating Backward to Achieve Greater Competitiveness It is harder than one might think to generate cost savings or boost profitability by integrating backward into activities such as parts and components manufacture. For backward integration to be a viable and profitable strategy, a company must be able to (1) achieve the same scale economies as outside suppliers and (2) match or beat suppliers' production efficiency with no decline in quality. Neither outcome is easily achieved. To begin with, a company's in-house requirements are often too small to reach the optimum size for low-cost operation; for instance, if it takes a minimum production volume of 1 million units to achieve scale economies and a company's in-house requirements are just 250,000 units, then it falls way short of being able to match the costs of outside suppliers (who may readily find buyers for 1 million or more units).

But that said, there are still occasions when a company can improve its cost position and competitiveness by performing a broader range of value chain activities in-house rather than having these activities performed by outside suppliers. The best potential for being able to reduce costs via a backward integration strategy exists in situations where suppliers have very large profit margins, where the item being supplied is a major cost component, and where the requisite technological skills are easily mastered or acquired. Backward vertical integration can produce a differentiation-based competitive advantage when performing activities internally contributes to a better-quality product/service offering, improves the caliber of customer service, or in other ways enhances the performance of a final product. Other potential advantages of backward integration include sparing a company the uncertainty of being dependent on suppliers for crucial components or support services and lessening a company's vulnerability to powerful suppliers inclined to raise prices at every opportunity. Spanish clothing maker Inditex has backward integrated into fabric making, as well as garment design and manufacture, for its successful Zara chain of clothing stores. By tightly controlling the design and production processes, it can quickly respond to changes in fashion trends to keep its stores stocked with the hottest new items and lines.

Integrating Forward to Enhance Competitiveness Vertical integration into forward stages of the industry value chain allows manufacturers to gain better access to end users, improve market visibility, and include the end user's purchasing experience as a differentiating feature. For example, Harley-Davidson's company-owned retail stores bolster the company's image and appeal through personalized selling, attractive displays, and riding classes that create new motorcycle riders and build brand loyalty. Insurance companies and brokerages such as Allstate and Edward Jones have the ability to make consumers' interactions with local agents and office personnel a differentiating feature by focusing on building relationships.

Most consumer goods companies have opted to integrate forward into retailing by selling direct to consumers via their websites. Bypassing regular wholesale/retail channels in favor of direct sales and Internet retailing can have appeal if it lowers distribution costs, produces a relative cost advantage over certain rivals, offers higher margins, or results in lower selling prices to end users. In addition, sellers are compelled to include the Internet as a retail channel when a sufficiently large number of buyers in an industry prefer to make purchases online. However, a company that is vigorously pursuing online sales to consumers at the same time that it is also heavily promoting sales to consumers through its network of wholesalers and retailers *is competing directly against its distribution allies.* Such actions constitute *channel conflict* and create a tricky route to negotiate. A company that is actively trying to grow online sales to consumers is signaling *a weak strategic commitment to its dealers* and *a willingness to cannibalize dealers' sales and growth potential.* The likely result is angry dealers and loss of dealer goodwill. Quite possibly, a company may stand to lose more sales by offending its dealers than it gains from its own online sales effort. Consequently, in industries where the strong support and goodwill of dealer networks are essential, companies may conclude that it is important to avoid channel conflict and that *their website should be designed to partner with dealers rather than compete with them.*

- *It improves organizational flexibility and speeds time to market.* Outsourcing gives a company the flexibility to switch suppliers in the event that its present supplier falls behind competing suppliers. Also, to the extent that its suppliers can speedily get next-generation parts and components into production, a company can get its own next-generation product offerings into the marketplace quicker.

- *It reduces the company's risk exposure to changing technology and/or buyer preferences.* When a company outsources certain parts, components, and services, its suppliers must bear the burden of incorporating state-of-the-art technologies and/or undertaking redesigns and upgrades to accommodate a company's plans to introduce next-generation products.

- *It allows a company to concentrate on its core business, leverage its key resources and core competencies, and do even better what it already does best.* A company is better able to build and develop its own competitively valuable competencies and capabilities when it concentrates its full resources and energies on performing those activities. Nike, for example, devotes its energy to designing, marketing, and distributing athletic footwear, sports apparel, and sports equipment, while outsourcing the manufacture of all its products to some 785 contract factories in nearly 50 countries. Apple also outsources production of its iPod, iPhone, and iPad models to Chinese contract manufacturer Foxconn. Hewlett-Packard and others have sold some of their manufacturing plants to outsiders and contracted to repurchase the output from the new owners.

> A company should guard against outsourcing activities that hollow out the resources and capabilities that it needs to be a master of its own destiny.

The Big Risk of an Outsourcing Strategy The biggest danger of outsourcing is that a company will farm out the wrong types of activities and thereby hollow out its own capabilities.[16] In such cases, a company loses touch with the very activities and expertise that over the long run determine its success. But most companies are alert to this danger and take actions to protect against being held hostage by outside suppliers. Cisco Systems guards against loss of control and protects its manufacturing expertise by designing the production methods that its contract manufacturers must use. Cisco keeps the source code for its designs proprietary, thereby controlling the initiation of all improvements and safeguarding its innovations from imitation. Further, Cisco uses the Internet to monitor the factory operations of contract manufacturers around the clock and can know immediately when problems arise and decide whether to get involved.

LO6 Gain an understanding of how strategic alliances and collaborative partnerships can bolster a company's collection of resources and capabilities.

Strategic Alliances and Partnerships

Companies in all types of industries have elected to form strategic alliances and partnerships to complement their accumulation of resources and capabilities and strengthen their competitiveness in domestic and international markets. A **strategic alliance** is a formal agreement between two or more separate companies in which there is strategically relevant collaboration of some sort, joint contribution of resources, shared risk, shared control, and mutual dependence. Collaborative relationships between partners may entail a contractual agreement, but they commonly stop short of formal ownership ties between the partners (although there are a few strategic alliances where one or more allies have minority ownership in certain of the other alliance members). Collaborative arrangements involving shared ownership are called joint ventures. A **joint venture** is a partnership involving the establishment of an independent corporate entity that is jointly owned and controlled by two or more companies. Since joint ventures involve setting up a mutually owned business, they tend to be more durable but also riskier than other arrangements.

> **CORE CONCEPT**
>
> A **strategic alliance** is a formal agreement between two or more companies to work cooperatively toward some common objective.

The most common reasons companies enter into strategic alliances are to expedite the development of promising new technologies or products, to overcome deficits in their own technical and manufacturing expertise, to bring together the personnel and expertise needed to create desirable new skill sets and capabilities, to improve supply chain efficiency, to gain economies of scale in production and/or marketing, and to acquire or improve market access through joint marketing agreements.[17] Shell Oil Company and Mexico's Pemex have found that joint ownership of their Deer Park Refinery in Texas lowers their investment costs and risks in comparison to going it alone. In 2013, Ford Motor Company joined Daimler AG and Renault-Nissan in an effort to develop affordable, mass-market hydrogen fuel cell vehicles by 2017.

Because of the varied benefits of strategic alliances, many large corporations have become involved in 30 to 50 alliances, and a number have formed hundreds of alliances. Genentech, a leader in biotechnology and human genetics, has formed R&D alliances with over 30 companies to boost its prospects for developing new cures for various diseases and ailments. Companies that have formed a host of alliances need to manage their alliances like a portfolio—terminating those that no longer serve a useful purpose or that have produced meager results, forming promising new alliances, and restructuring existing alliances to correct performance problems and/or redirect the collaborative effort.

> **CORE CONCEPT**
>
> A **joint venture** is a type of strategic alliance that involves the establishment of an independent corporate entity that is jointly owned and controlled by the two partners.

Failed Strategic Alliances and Cooperative Partnerships

Most alliances with an objective of technology sharing or providing market access turn out to be temporary, fulfilling their purpose after a few years because the benefits of mutual learning have occurred. Although long-term alliances sometimes prove mutually beneficial, most partners don't hesitate to terminate the alliance and go it alone when the payoffs run out. Alliances are more likely to be long lasting when (1) they involve collaboration with partners that do not compete directly, (2) a trusting relationship has been established, and (3) both parties conclude that continued collaboration is in their mutual interest, perhaps because new opportunities for learning are emerging.

A surprisingly large number of alliances never live up to expectations, with estimates that as many as 60 to 70 percent of alliances fail each year. The high "divorce rate" among strategic allies has several causes, the most common of which are:[18]

- Diverging objectives and priorities.
- An inability to work well together.
- Changing conditions that make the purpose of the alliance obsolete.

- The emergence of more attractive technological paths.
- Marketplace rivalry between one or more allies.

Experience indicates that *alliances stand a reasonable chance of helping a company reduce competitive disadvantage, but very rarely have they proved a strategic option for gaining a durable competitive edge over rivals.*

The Strategic Dangers of Relying on Alliances for Essential Resources and Capabilities

The Achilles' heel of alliances and cooperative strategies is becoming dependent on other companies for *essential* expertise and capabilities. To be a market leader (and perhaps even a serious market contender), a company must ultimately develop its own resources and capabilities in areas where internal strategic control is pivotal to protecting its competitiveness and building competitive advantage. Moreover, some alliances hold only limited potential because the partner guards its most valuable skills and expertise; in such instances, acquiring or merging with a company possessing the desired know-how and resources is a better solution.

 KEY POINTS

Once a company has selected which of the five basic competitive strategies to employ in its quest for competitive advantage, then it must decide whether and how to supplement its choice of a basic competitive strategy approach.

1. Companies have a number of offensive strategy options for improving their market positions and trying to secure a competitive advantage: (1) attacking competitors' weaknesses, (2) offering an equal or better product at a lower price, (3) pursuing sustained product innovation, (4) leapfrogging competitors by being first to adopt next-generation technologies or the first to introduce next-generation products, (5) adopting and improving on the good ideas of other companies, (6) deliberately attacking those market segments where key rivals make big profits, (7) going after less contested or unoccupied market territory, (8) using hit-and-run tactics to steal sales away from unsuspecting rivals, and (9) launching preemptive strikes. A blue ocean offensive strategy seeks to gain a dramatic and durable competitive advantage by abandoning efforts to beat out competitors in existing markets and, instead, inventing a new industry or distinctive market segment that renders existing competitors largely irrelevant and allows a company to create and capture altogether new demand.

2. Defensive strategies to protect a company's position usually take the form of making moves that put obstacles in the path of would-be challengers and fortify the company's present position while undertaking actions to dissuade rivals from even trying to attack (by signaling that the resulting battle will be more costly to the challenger than it is worth).

3. The timing of strategic moves also has relevance in the quest for competitive advantage. Company managers are obligated to carefully consider the advantages or disadvantages that attach to being a first mover versus a fast follower versus a wait-and-see late mover.

4. Decisions concerning the scope of a company's operations can also affect the strength of a company's market position. The scope of the firm refers to the range of its activities,

the breadth of its product and service offerings, the extent of its geographic market presence, and its mix of businesses. Companies can expand their scope horizontally (more broadly within their focal market) or vertically (up or down the industry value chain system that starts with raw-materials production and ends with sales and service to the end consumer). Horizontal mergers and acquisitions (combinations of market rivals) provide a means for a company to expand its horizontal scope. Vertical integration expands a firm's vertical scope.

5. Horizontal mergers and acquisitions can be an attractive strategic option for strengthening a firm's competitiveness. When the operations of two companies are combined via merger or acquisition, the new company's competitiveness can be enhanced in any of several ways—lower costs; stronger technological skills; more or better competitive capabilities; a more attractive lineup of products and services; wider geographic coverage; and/or greater financial resources with which to invest in R&D, add capacity, or expand into new areas.

6. Vertically integrating forward or backward makes strategic sense only if it strengthens a company's position via either cost reduction or creation of a differentiation-based advantage. Otherwise, the drawbacks of vertical integration (increased investment, greater business risk, increased vulnerability to technological changes, and less flexibility in making product changes) are likely to outweigh any advantages.

7. Outsourcing pieces of the value chain formerly performed in-house can enhance a company's competitiveness whenever (1) an activity can be performed better or more cheaply by outside specialists; (2) the activity is not crucial to the firm's ability to achieve sustainable competitive advantage and won't hollow out its core competencies, capabilities, or technical know-how; (3) it improves a company's ability to innovate; and/or (4) it allows a company to concentrate on its core business and do what it does best.

8. Many companies are using strategic alliances and collaborative partnerships to help them in the race to build a global market presence or be a leader in the industries of the future. Strategic alliances are an attractive, flexible, and often cost-effective means by which companies can gain access to missing technology, expertise, and business capabilities.

ASSURANCE OF LEARNING EXERCISES

1. Live Nation operates music venues, provides management services to music artists, and promotes more than 22,000 live music events annually. The company merged with Ticketmaster and acquired concert and festival promoters in the United States, Australia, and Great Britain. How has the company used horizontal mergers and acquisitions to strengthen its competitive position? Are these moves primarily offensive or defensive? Has either Live Nation or Ticketmaster achieved any type of advantage based on the timing of its strategic moves?

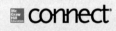

LO1, LO2, LO3

2. Kaiser Permanente, a standout among managed health care systems, has become a model for how to deliver good health care cost-effectively. Concepts & Connections 6.3 describes how Kaiser Permanente has made vertical integration a central part of its strategy. What value chain segments has Kaiser Permanente chosen to enter and perform internally? How has vertical integration aided the company in building competitive advantage? Has vertical integration strengthened its market position? Explain why or why not.

LO4

LO5   3.   Perform an Internet search to identify at least two companies in different industries that have entered into outsourcing agreements with firms with specialized services. In addition, describe what value chain activities the companies have chosen to outsource. Do any of these outsourcing agreements seem likely to threaten any of the companies' competitive capabilities?

LO6   4.   Using your university library's subscription to Lexis-Nexis, EBSCO, or a similar database, find two examples of how companies have relied on strategic alliances or joint ventures to substitute for horizontal or vertical integration.

 EXERCISES FOR SIMULATION PARTICIPANTS

LO1, LO2   1.   Has your company relied more on offensive or defensive strategies to achieve your rank in the industry? What options for being a first mover does your company have? Do any of these first-mover options hold competitive advantage potential?

LO3   2.   Does your company have the option to merge with or acquire other companies? If so, which rival companies would you like to acquire or merge with?

LO4   3.   Is your company vertically integrated? Explain.

LO5   4.   Is your company able to engage in outsourcing? If so, what do you see as the pros and cons of outsourcing?

 ENDNOTES

1.   GeorgeStalk, Jr., and Rob Lachenauer, "Hardball: Five Killer Strategies for Trouncing the Competition," *Harvard Business Review* 82, no. 4 (April 2004); Richard D'Aveni, "The Empire Strikes Back: Counterrevolutionary Strategies for Industry Leaders," *Harvard Business Review* 80, no. 11 (November 2002); David J. Bryce and Jeffrey H. Dyer, "Strategies to Crack Well-Guarded Markets," *Harvard Business Review* 85, no. 5 (May 2007).

2.   David B. Yoffie and Mary Kwak, "Mastering Balance: How to Meet and Beat a Stronger Opponent," *California Management Review* 44, no. 2 (Winter 2002).

3.   Ian C. MacMillan, Alexander B. van Putten, and Rita Gunther McGrath, "Global Gamesmanship," *Harvard Business Review* 81, no. 5 (May 2003); Askay R. Rao, Mark E. Bergen, and Scott Davis, "How to Fight a Price War," *Harvard Business Review* 78, no. 2 (March–April 2000).

4.   Ming-Jer Chen and Donald C. Hambrick, "Speed, Stealth, and Selective Attack: How Small Firms Differ from Large Firms in Competitive Behavior," *Academy of Management Journal* 38, no. 2 (April 1995); Ian MacMillan, "How Business Strategists Can Use Guerrilla Warfare Tactics," *Journal of Business Strategy* 1, no. 2 (Fall 1980); William E. Rothschild, "Surprise and the Competitive Advantage," *Journal of Business Strategy* 4, no. 3 (Winter 1984); Kathryn R. Harrigan, *Strategic Flexibility* (Lexington, MA: Lexington Books, 1985); Liam Fahey, "Guerrilla Strategy: The Hit-and-Run Attack," in *The Strategic Management Planning Reader*, ed. Liam Fahey (Englewood Cliffs, NJ: Prentice Hall, 1989).

5.   Ian MacMillan, "Preemptive Strategies," *Journal of Business Strategy* 14, no. 2 (Fall 1983).

6.   W. Chan Kim and Renée Mauborgne, "Blue Ocean Strategy," *Harvard Business Review* 82, no. 10 (October 2004).

7.   Michael E. Porter, *Competitive Advantage* (New York: Free Press, 1985).

8.   Jeffrey G. Covin, Dennis P. Slevin, and Michael B. Heeley, "Pioneers and Followers: Competitive Tactics, Environment, and Growth," *Journal of Business Venturing* 15, no. 2 (March 1999); Christopher A. Bartlett and Sumantra Ghoshal, "Going Global: Lessons from Late-Movers," *Harvard Business Review* 78, no. 2 (March–April 2000).

9.   Fernando Suarez and Gianvito Lanzolla, "The Half-Truth of First-Mover Advantage," *Harvard Business Review* 83 no. 4 (April 2005).

10.   Gary Hamel, "Smart Mover, Dumb Mover," *Fortune,* September 3, 2001.

11.   Costas Markides and Paul A. Geroski, "Racing to Be 2nd: Conquering the Industries of the Future," *Business Strategy Review* 15, no. 4 (Winter 2004).

12.   Joseph L. Bower, "Not All M&As Are Alike—and That Matters," *Harvard Business Review* 79, no. 3 (March 2001); O. Chatain and P. Zemsky, "The Horizontal Scope of the Firm: Organizational Tradeoffs vs. Buyer–Supplier Relationships," *Management Science* 53, no. 4 (April 2007), pp. 550–65.

13.   Jeffrey H. Dyer, Prashant Kale, and Harbir Singh, "When to Ally and When to Acquire," *Harvard Business Review* 82, no. 4 (July–August 2004), pp. 109–10.

14. Kathryn R. Harrigan, "Matching Vertical Integration Strategies to Competitive Conditions," *Strategic Management Journal* 7, no. 6 (November–December 1986); John Stuckey and David White, "When and When Not to Vertically Integrate," *Sloan Management Review,* Spring 1993.

15. Thomas Osegowitsch and Anoop Madhok, "Vertical Integration Is Dead, or Is It?" *Business Horizons* 46, no. 2 (March–April 2003).

16. Jérôme Barthélemy, "The Seven Deadly Sins of Outsourcing," *Academy of Management Executive* 17, no. 2 (May 2003); Gary P. Pisano and Willy C. Shih, "Restoring American Competitiveness," *Harvard Business Review* 87, no. 7/8 (July–August 2009); Ronan McIvor, "What Is the Right Outsourcing Strategy for Your Process?" *European Management Journal* 26, no. 1 (February 2008).

17. Michael E. Porter, *The Competitive Advantage of Nations* (New York: Free Press, 1990); K. M. Eisenhardt and C. B. Schoonhoven, "Resource-Based View of Strategic Alliance Formation: Strategic and Social Effects in Entrepreneurial Firms," *Organization Science* 7, no. 2 (March–April 1996); Nancy J. Kaplan and Jonathan Hurd, "Realizing the Promise of Partnerships," *Journal of Business Strategy* 23, no. 3 (May–June 2002); Salvatore Parise and Lisa Sasson, "Leveraging Knowledge Management across Strategic Alliances," *Ivey Business Journal* 66, no. 4 (March–April 2002); David Ernst and James Bamford, "Your Alliances Are Too Stable," *Harvard Business Review* 83, no. 6 (June 2005).

18. Yves L. Doz and Gary Hamel, *Alliance Advantage; The Art of Creating Value Through Partnering* (Boston: Harvard Business School Press, 1998).

7 Strategies for Competing in International Markets

LEARNING OBJECTIVES

LO1 Develop an understanding of the primary reasons companies choose to compete in international markets.

LO2 Learn why and how differing market conditions across countries influence a company's strategy choices in international markets.

LO3 Gain familiarity with the five general modes of entry into foreign markets.

LO4 Learn the three main options for tailoring a company's international strategy to cross-country differences in market conditions and buyer preferences.

LO5 Understand how multinational companies are able to use international operations to improve overall competitiveness.

LO6 Gain an understanding of the unique characteristics of competing in developing-country markets.

Any company that aspires to industry leadership in the 21st century must think in terms of global, not domestic, market leadership. The world economy is globalizing at an accelerating pace as countries previously closed to foreign companies open their markets, as countries with previously planned economies embrace market or mixed economies, as information technology shrinks the importance of geographic distance, and as ambitious, growth-minded companies race to build stronger competitive positions in the markets of more and more countries. The forces of globalization are changing the competitive landscape in many industries, offering companies attractive new opportunities but at the same time introducing new competitive threats. Companies in industries where these forces are greatest are under considerable pressure to develop strategies for competing successfully in international markets.

This chapter focuses on strategy options for expanding beyond domestic boundaries and competing in the markets of either a few or many countries. We will discuss the factors that shape the choice of strategy in international markets and the specific market circumstances that support the adoption of multidomestic, transnational, and global strategies. The chapter also includes sections on strategy options for entering foreign markets; how international operations may be used to improve overall competitiveness; and the special circumstances of competing in such emerging markets as China, India, Brazil, Russia, and Eastern Europe.

Why Companies Expand into International Markets

A company may opt to expand outside its domestic market for any of five major reasons:

LO1 Develop an understanding of the primary reasons companies choose to compete in international markets.

1. *To gain access to new customers.* Expanding into foreign markets offers potential for increased revenues, profits, and long-term growth, and becomes an especially attractive option when a company's home markets are mature. Honda has done this with its classic 50-cc motorcycle, the Honda Cub, which is still selling well in developing markets, more than 50 years after it was introduced in Japan.

2. *To achieve lower costs and enhance the firm's competitiveness.* Many companies are driven to sell in more than one country because domestic sales volume alone is not large enough to fully capture manufacturing economies of scale or learning curve effects. The relatively small size of country markets in Europe explains why companies such as Michelin, BMW, and Nestlé long ago began selling their products all across Europe and then moved into markets in North America and Latin America.

3. *To further exploit its core competencies.* A company may be able to leverage its competencies and capabilities into a position of competitive advantage in foreign markets as well as domestic markets. Walmart is capitalizing on its considerable expertise in discount retailing to expand into the United Kingdom, Japan, China, and Latin America. Walmart executives are particularly excited about the company's growth opportunities in China.

4. *To gain access to resources and capabilities located in foreign markets.* An increasingly important motive for entering foreign markets is to acquire resources and capabilities that cannot be accessed as readily in a company's home market.

Companies often enter into cross-border alliances, make acquisitions abroad, or establish operations in foreign countries to access local resources such as distribution networks, low-cost labor, natural resources, or specialized technical knowledge.[1]

5. *To spread its business risk across a wider market base.* A company spreads business risk by operating in a number of foreign countries rather than depending entirely on operations in its domestic market. Thus, if the economies of North American countries turn down for a period of time, a company with operations across much of the world may be sustained by buoyant sales in Latin America, Asia, or Europe.

Factors That Shape Strategy Choices in International Markets

LO2 Learn why and how differing market conditions across countries influence a company's strategy choices in international markets.

Four important factors shape a company's strategic approach to competing in foreign markets: (1) the degree to which there are important cross-country differences in demographic, cultural, and market conditions; (2) whether opportunities exist to gain a location-based advantage based on wage rates, worker productivity, inflation rates, energy costs, tax rates, and other factors that impact cost structure; (3) the risks of adverse shifts in currency exchange rates; and (4) the extent to which governmental policies affect the local business climate.

Cross-Country Differences in Demographic, Cultural, and Market Conditions

Buyer tastes for a particular product or service sometimes differ substantially from country to country. For example, ice cream flavors such as eel, shark fin, and dried shrimp appeal to Japanese customers, whereas fruit-based flavors have more appeal in the United States and Europe. In France, top-loading washing machines are very popular with consumers, whereas in most other European countries, consumers prefer front-loading machines. Consequently, companies operating in a global marketplace must wrestle with *whether and how much to customize their offerings in each different country market to match the tastes and preferences of local buyers or whether to pursue a strategy of offering a mostly standardized product worldwide.* While making products that are closely matched to local tastes makes them more appealing to local buyers, customizing a company's products country by country may raise production and distribution costs. Greater standardization of a global company's product offering, on the other hand, can lead to scale economies and learning curve effects, thus contributing to the achievement of a low-cost advantage. *The tension between the market pressures to localize a company's product offerings country by country and the competitive pressures to lower costs is one of the big strategic issues that participants in foreign markets have to resolve.*

Understandably, differing population sizes, income levels, and other demographic factors give rise to considerable differences in market size and growth rates from country to country. In emerging markets such as India, China, Brazil, and Malaysia, market growth potential is far higher for such products as mobile phones, steel, credit cards, and electric energy than in the more mature economies of Britain, Canada, and Japan.

The potential for market growth in automobiles is explosive in China, where 2013 sales of new vehicles amounted to 18 million, surpassing U.S. sales of 15.6 million and making China the world's largest market for the second year in a row.[2] Owing to widely differing population demographics and income levels, there is a far bigger market for luxury automobiles in the United States and Germany than in Argentina, India, Mexico, and Thailand. Cultural influences can also affect consumer demand for a product. For instance, in China, many parents are reluctant to purchase PCs even when they can afford them because of concerns that their children will be distracted from their schoolwork by surfing the web, playing PC-based video games, and downloading and listening to pop music.

Market growth can be limited by the lack of infrastructure or established distribution and retail networks in emerging markets. India has well-developed national channels for distribution of goods to the nation's 3 million retailers, whereas in China distribution is primarily local. Also, the competitive rivalry in some country marketplaces is only moderate, whereas others are characterized by strong or fierce competition. The managerial challenge at companies with international or global operations is how best to tailor a company's strategy to take all these cross-country differences into account.

Opportunities for Location-Based Cost Advantages

Differences from country to country in wage rates, worker productivity, energy costs, environmental regulations, tax rates, inflation rates, and the like are often so big that *a company's operating costs and profitability are significantly impacted by where its production, distribution, and customer service activities are located.* Wage rates, in particular, vary enormously from country to country. For example, in 2013, hourly compensation for manufacturing workers averaged about $3.07 in China, $6.82 in Mexico, $9.37 in Taiwan, $9.44 in Hungary, $10.69 in Brazil, $12.90 in Portugal, $21.96 in South Korea, $29.13 in Japan, $36.33 in Canada, $36.34 in the United States, $48.98 in Germany, and $65.86 in Norway.[3] Not surprisingly, China has emerged as the manufacturing capital of the world—virtually all of the world's major manufacturing companies now have facilities in China. A manufacturer can also gain cost advantages by locating its manufacturing and assembly plants in countries with less costly government regulations, low taxes, low energy costs, and cheaper access to essential natural resources.

The Risks of Adverse Exchange Rate Shifts

When companies produce and market their products and services in many different countries, they are subject to the impacts of sometimes favorable and sometimes unfavorable changes in currency exchange rates. The rates of exchange between different currencies can vary by as much as 20 to 40 percent annually, with the changes occurring sometimes gradually and sometimes swiftly. Sizable shifts in exchange rates, which tend to be hard to predict because of the variety of factors involved and the uncertainties surrounding when and by how much these factors will change, *shuffle the global cards of which countries represent the low-cost manufacturing location* and *which rivals have the upper hand in the marketplace.*

To illustrate the competitive risks associated with fluctuating exchange rates, consider the case of a U.S. company that has located manufacturing facilities in Brazil (where the currency is reals—pronounced *ray-alls*) and that exports most of its

Brazilian-made goods to markets in the European Union (where the currency is euros). To keep the numbers simple, assume the exchange rate is 4 Brazilian reals for 1 euro and that the product being made in Brazil has a manufacturing cost of 4 Brazilian reals (or 1 euro). Now suppose that for some reason the exchange rate shifts from 4 reals per euro to 5 reals per euro (meaning the real has declined in value and the euro is stronger). Making the product in Brazil is now more cost-competitive because a Brazilian good costing 4 reals to produce has fallen to only 0.8 euro at the new exchange rate (4 reals divided by 5 reals per euro = 0.8 euro). On the other hand, should the value of the Brazilian real grow stronger in relation to the euro—resulting in an exchange rate of 3 reals to 1 euro—the same Brazilian-made good formerly costing 4 reals to produce now has a cost of 1.33 euros (4 reals divided by 3 reals per euro = 1.33). This increase in the value of the real has eroded the cost advantage of the Brazilian manufacturing facility for goods shipped to Europe and affects the ability of the U.S. company to underprice European producers of similar goods. Thus, *the lesson of fluctuating exchange rates is that companies that export goods to foreign countries always gain in competitiveness when the currency of the country in which the goods are manufactured is weak. Exporters are disadvantaged when the currency of the country where goods are being manufactured grows stronger.*

The Impact of Government Policies on the Business Climate in Host Countries

National governments enact all kinds of measures affecting business conditions and the operation of foreign companies in their markets. It matters whether these measures create a favorable or unfavorable business climate. Governments of countries eager to spur economic growth, create more jobs, and raise living standards for their citizens usually make a special effort to create a business climate that outsiders will view favorably. They may provide such incentives as reduced taxes, low-cost loans, and site-development assistance to companies agreeing to construct or expand production and distribution facilities in the host country.

On the other hand, governments sometimes enact policies that, from a business perspective, make locating facilities within a country's borders less attractive. For example, the nature of a company's operations may make it particularly costly to achieve compliance with environmental regulations in certain countries. Some governments, wishing to discourage foreign imports, may enact deliberately burdensome customs procedures and requirements or impose tariffs or quotas on imported goods. Host-country governments may also specify that products contain a certain percentage of locally produced parts and components, require prior approval of capital spending projects, limit withdrawal of funds from the country, and require local ownership stakes in foreign-company operations in the host country. Such governmental actions make a country's business climate unattractive and in some cases may be sufficiently onerous as to discourage a company from locating facilities in that country or selling its products there.

A country's business climate is also a function of the political and economic risks associated with operating within its borders. **Political risks** have to do with the instability of weak governments, the likelihood of

CORE CONCEPT

Political risks stem from instability or weakness in national governments and hostility to foreign business; **economic risks** stem from the stability of a country's monetary system, economic and regulatory policies, and the lack of property rights protections.

new onerous legislation or regulations on foreign-owned businesses, or the potential for future elections to produce government leaders hostile to foreign-owned businesses. In a growing number of emerging markets, governments are pursuing state capitalism in industries deemed to be of national importance. Financial services, information technology, telecommunications, and food sectors have become politicized in some emerging markets and are tightly controlled by government. In 2012, for example, Argentina nationalized the country's top oil producer, YPF, which was owned by Spanish oil major Repsol. China has established very low price ceilings on as many as 500 prescription drugs, which helps boost the profitability of its state-owned hospitals but makes it challenging for global pharmaceutical companies to do business in China.

Economic risks have to do with the threat of piracy and lack of protection for the company's intellectual property and the stability of a country's economy—whether inflation rates might skyrocket or whether uncontrolled deficit spending on the part of government could lead to a breakdown of the country's monetary system and prolonged economic distress.

Strategy Options for Entering Foreign Markets

A company choosing to expand outside its domestic market may elect one of the following five general modes of entry into a foreign market:

LO3 Gain familiarity with the five general modes of entry into foreign markets.

1. Maintain a national (one-country) production base and export goods to foreign markets.
2. License foreign firms to produce and distribute the company's products abroad.
3. Employ a franchising strategy.
4. Establish a subsidiary in a foreign market via acquisition or internal development.
5. Rely on strategic alliances or joint ventures with foreign partners to enter new country markets.

This section of the chapter discusses the five general options in more detail.

Export Strategies

Using domestic plants as a production base for exporting goods to foreign markets is an excellent initial strategy for pursuing international sales. It is a conservative way to test the international waters. The amount of capital needed to begin exporting is often quite minimal, and existing production capacity may be sufficient to make goods for export. With an export-based entry strategy, a manufacturer can limit its involvement in foreign markets by contracting with foreign wholesalers experienced in importing to handle the entire distribution and marketing function in their countries or regions of the world. If it is more advantageous to maintain control over these functions, however, a manufacturer can establish its own distribution and sales organizations in some or all of the target foreign markets. Either way, a home-based production and export strategy helps the firm minimize its direct investments in foreign countries.

An export strategy is vulnerable when (1) manufacturing costs in the home country are substantially higher than in foreign countries where rivals have plants, (2) the costs of shipping the product to distant foreign markets are relatively high, or (3) adverse shifts occur in currency exchange rates. Unless an exporter can both keep its production and shipping costs competitive with rivals and successfully hedge against unfavorable changes in currency exchange rates, its success will be limited.

Licensing Strategies

Licensing as an entry strategy makes sense when a firm with valuable technical know-how or a unique patented product has neither the internal organizational capability nor the resources to enter foreign markets. Licensing also has the advantage of avoiding the risks of committing resources to country markets that are unfamiliar, politically volatile, economically unstable, or otherwise risky. By licensing the technology or the production rights to foreign-based firms, the firm does not have to bear the costs and risks of entering foreign markets on its own, yet it is able to generate income from royalties. The big disadvantage of licensing is the risk of providing valuable technological know-how to foreign companies and thereby losing some degree of control over its use. Also, monitoring licensees and safeguarding the company's proprietary know-how can prove quite difficult in some circumstances. But if the royalty potential is considerable and the companies to which the licenses are being granted are both trustworthy and reputable, then licensing can be a very attractive option. Many software and pharmaceutical companies use licensing strategies.

Franchising Strategies

While licensing works well for manufacturers and owners of proprietary technology, franchising is often better suited to the global expansion efforts of service and retailing enterprises. McDonald's, Yum! Brands (the parent of Pizza Hut, KFC, and Taco Bell), the UPS Store, 7-Eleven, and Hilton Hotels have all used franchising to build a presence in international markets. Franchising has much the same advantages as licensing. The franchisee bears most of the costs and risks of establishing foreign locations, so a franchisor has to expend only the resources to recruit, train, support, and monitor franchisees. The big problem a franchisor faces is maintaining quality control. In many cases, foreign franchisees do not always exhibit strong commitment to consistency and standardization, especially when the local culture does not stress the same kinds of quality concerns. Another problem that can arise is whether to allow foreign franchisees to modify the franchisor's product offering to better satisfy the tastes and expectations of local buyers. Should McDonald's allow its franchised units in Japan to modify Big Macs slightly to suit Japanese tastes? Should the franchised KFC units in China be permitted to substitute spices that appeal to Chinese consumers? Or should the same menu offerings be rigorously and unvaryingly required of all franchisees worldwide?

Foreign Subsidiary Strategies

While exporting, licensing, and franchising rely upon the resources and capabilities of allies in international markets to deliver goods or services to buyers, companies pursuing international expansion may elect to take responsibility for the performance of all essential value chain activities in foreign markets. Companies that prefer direct control over all aspects of operating in a foreign market can establish a wholly owned subsidiary, either by acquiring a foreign company or by establishing operations from the ground up via internal development.

Acquisition is the quicker of the two options, and it may be the least risky and cost-efficient means of hurdling such entry barriers as gaining access to local distribution channels, building supplier relationships, and establishing working relationships with key government officials and other constituencies. Buying an ongoing operation allows the acquirer to move directly to the tasks of transferring resources and personnel to the newly acquired business, integrating and redirecting the activities of the acquired business into its own operation, putting its own strategy into place, and accelerating efforts to build a strong market position.[4]

The big issue an acquisition-minded firm must consider is whether to pay a premium price for a successful local company or to buy a struggling competitor at a bargain price. If the buying firm has little knowledge of the local market but ample capital, it is often better off purchasing a capable, strongly positioned firm—unless the acquisition price is prohibitive. However, when the acquirer sees promising ways to transform a weak firm into a strong one and has the resources and managerial know-how to do it, a struggling company can be the better long-term investment.

Entering a new foreign country via internal development and building a foreign subsidiary from scratch makes sense when a company already operates in a number of countries, has experience in getting new subsidiaries up and running and overseeing their operations, and has a sufficiently large pool of resources and competencies to rapidly equip a new subsidiary with the personnel and capabilities it needs to compete successfully and profitably. Four other conditions make an internal start-up strategy appealing:

- When creating an internal start-up is cheaper than making an acquisition
- When adding new production capacity will not adversely impact the supply–demand balance in the local market
- When a start-up subsidiary has the ability to gain good distribution access (perhaps because of the company's recognized brand name)
- When a start-up subsidiary will have the size, cost structure, and resources to compete head-to-head against local rivals

Alliance and Joint Venture Strategies

Strategic alliances, joint ventures, and other cooperative agreements with foreign companies are a favorite and potentially fruitful means for entering a foreign market or strengthening a firm's competitiveness in world markets.[5] Historically, export-minded firms in industrialized nations sought alliances with firms in less-developed countries to import and market their products locally; such arrangements were often necessary to win approval for entry from the host country's government. Both Japanese and American companies are actively forming alliances with European companies to strengthen their ability to compete in the 28-nation European Union (and the five countries that are candidates to become EU members) and to capitalize on the opening of Eastern European markets. Many U.S. and European companies are allying with Asian companies in their efforts to enter markets in China, India, Malaysia, Thailand, and other Asian countries. Many foreign companies, of course, are particularly interested in strategic partnerships that will strengthen their ability to gain a foothold in the U.S. market.

However, cooperative arrangements between domestic and foreign companies have strategic appeal for reasons besides gaining better access to attractive country markets.[6] A second big appeal of cross-border alliances is to capture economies of scale in production and/or marketing. By joining forces in producing components, assembling models, and marketing their products, companies can realize cost savings not achievable with their own small volumes. A third motivation for entering into a cross-border alliance is to fill gaps in technical expertise and/or knowledge of local markets (buying habits and product preferences of consumers, local customs, and so on). A fourth motivation for cross-border alliances is to share distribution facilities and dealer networks, and to mutually strengthen each partner's access to buyers.

A fifth benefit is that cross-border allies can direct their competitive energies more toward mutual rivals and less toward one another; teaming up may help them close the gap on leading companies. A sixth driver of cross-border alliances comes into play when companies wanting to enter a new foreign market conclude that alliances with local companies are an effective way to establish working relationships with key officials in the host-country government.[7] And, finally, alliances can be a particularly useful way for companies across the world to gain agreement on important technical standards—they have been used to arrive at standards for assorted PC devices, Internet-related technologies, high-definition televisions, and mobile phones.

What makes cross-border alliances an attractive strategic means of gaining the aforementioned types of benefits (as compared to acquiring or merging with foreign-based companies) is that entering into alliances and strategic partnerships allows a company to preserve its independence and avoid using perhaps scarce financial resources to fund acquisitions. Furthermore, an alliance offers the flexibility to readily disengage once its purpose has been served or if the benefits prove elusive, whereas an acquisition is a more permanent sort of arrangement.[8] Concepts & Connections 7.1 discusses how California-based Solazyme, a maker of biofuels and other green products, has used cross-border strategic alliances to fuel its growth.

The Risks of Strategic Alliances with Foreign Partners Alliances and joint ventures with foreign partners have their pitfalls, however. Cross-border allies typically have to overcome language and cultural barriers and figure out how to deal with diverse (or perhaps conflicting) operating practices. The communication, trust-building, and coordination costs are high in terms of management time.[9] It is not unusual for partners to discover they have conflicting objectives and strategies, deep differences of opinion about how to proceed, or important differences in corporate values and ethical standards. Tensions build, working relationships cool, and the hoped-for benefits never materialize. The recipe for successful alliances requires many meetings of many people working in good faith over a period of time to iron out what is to be shared, what is to remain proprietary, and how the cooperative arrangements will work.[10]

Even if the alliance becomes a win-win proposition for both parties, there is the danger of becoming overly dependent on foreign partners for essential expertise and competitive capabilities. If a company is aiming for global market leadership and needs to develop capabilities of its own, then at some juncture cross-border merger or acquisition may have to be substituted for cross-border alliances and joint ventures. One of the lessons about cross-border alliances is that they are more effective in helping a company establish a beachhead of new opportunity in world markets than they are in enabling a company to achieve and sustain global market leadership.

Concepts & Connections 7.1

SOLAZYME'S CROSS-BORDER ALLIANCES WITH UNILEVER, SEPHORA, QANTAS, AND ROQUETTE

Solazyme, a California-based company that produces oils from algae for nutritional, cosmetic, and biofuel products, was named "America's Fastest-Growing Manufacturing Company" by *Inc.* magazine in 2011. The company has fueled its rapid growth through a variety of cross-border strategic alliances with much larger partners. These partnerships have not only facilitated Solazyme's entry into new markets, but they have also created value through resource sharing and risk spreading.

Its partnership with Unilever, a British–Dutch consumer goods company, has focused on collaborative R&D. Projects under way are aimed at meeting the growing demand for completely renewable, natural, and sustainable personal care products through the use of algal oils. By further developing Solazyme's technology platform, the partnership will enable the production of Solazyme's oils and other biomaterials efficiently and at large scale.

Solazyme has entered into a variety of marketing and distribution agreements with French cosmetics company Sephora (now part of LVMH). In March 2011, Solazyme launched its luxury skin care brand, Algenist, with Sephora's help. Sephora has also agreed to distribute Solazyme's antiaging skin care line, making it available in Sephora stores and at Sephora.com.

In 2011, Solazyme also signed a contract with Australian airline Qantas to supply, test, and refine Solazyme's jet fuel product, SolaJet. Solazyme stands to gain valuable input on how to design and distribute its product while receiving media attention and the

marketing advantage of a well-known customer. On the other hand, Qantas hopes to better understand how it will achieve its sustainability goals while building its reputation as a sustainability leader in the airline industry.

However, not every partnership ends successfully, regardless of the strength of the initial motivations and relationship. Because its algae require sugar to produce oil, Solazyme developed an interest in securing a stable supply of this feedstock. For this purpose, Solazyme created a 50/50 joint venture with French starch processor Roquette to develop, produce, and market food products globally. By working with Roquette to source feedstock and manufacture final food products, Solazyme hoped to lower its exposure to sugar price fluctuations, trading the use of its innovative technological resources in return for Roquette's manufacturing infrastructure and expertise. But in 2013, the joint venture dissolved; both parties felt that after the exchange of ideas, technologies, and goals, they would be better off going it alone on the algal food product frontier.

Developed with John L. Gardner.

Sources: Company website; http://gigaom.com/cleantech/solazyme-draws-richard-branson-unilever-to-algae/; www.businessgreen.com/bg/news/2026103/qantas-inks-solazyme-algae-biofuel-deal; www.reuters.com/article/2012/02/22/us-smallbiz-solazyme-feb-idUSTRE81L1ZO20120222; www.foodnavigator-usa.com/Business/Solazyme-Roquette-JV-prepares-for-January-2012-launch-of-unique-algal-flour, accessed March 4, 2012.

International Strategy: The Three Principal Options

LO4 Learn the three main options for tailoring a company's international strategy to cross-country differences in market conditions and buyer preferences.

Broadly speaking, a company's **international strategy** is simply its strategy for competing in two or more countries simultaneously. Typically, a company will start to compete internationally by entering just one or perhaps a select few foreign markets, selling its products or services in countries where there is a ready market for them. But as it expands further internationally, it will have to confront head-on the conflicting pressures of local responsiveness versus efficiency gains from standardizing its product offering globally. As discussed earlier in the chapter, deciding upon the degree to vary its competitive approach to fit the specific market conditions and buyer preferences in each host country is perhaps the foremost strategic issue

CORE CONCEPT

A company's **international strategy** is its strategy for competing in two or more countries simultaneously.

FIGURE 7.1	**A Company's Three Principal Strategic Options for Competing Internationally**

Strategic Posturing Options	Ways to Deal with National Variations in Buyer Preferences and Market Conditions
Multidomestic Strategy **(Think Local, Act Local)**	**Employ localized strategies—one for each country market** ■ Tailor the company's competitive approach and product offering to fit specific market conditions and buyer preferences in each host country. ■ Delegate strategy making to local managers with firsthand knowledge of local conditions.
Global Strategy **(Think Global, Act Global)**	**Employ same strategy worldwide** ■ Pursue *the same basic competitive strategy theme* (low-cost, differentiation, best-cost, or focused) *in all country markets*—a global strategy. ■ Offer the same products worldwide, with only very minor deviations from one country to another when local market conditions so dictate. ■ Utilize the same capabilities, distribution channels, and marketing approaches worldwide. ■ Coordinate strategic actions from central headquarters.
Transnational Strategy **(Think Global, Act Local)**	**Employ a combination global-local strategy** ■ Employ essentially *the same basic competitive strategy theme* (low-cost, differentiation, best-cost, or focused) in *all country markets.* ■ Develop the capability to customize product offerings and sell different product versions in different countries (perhaps even under different brand names). ■ Give local managers the latitude to adapt the global approach as needed to accommodate local buyer preferences and be responsive to local market and competitive conditions.

that must be addressed when operating in two or more foreign markets.[11] Figure 7.1 shows a company's three strategic approaches for competing internationally and resolving this issue.

Multidomestic Strategy—A Think Local, Act Local Approach to Strategy Making

A **multidomestic strategy** or **think local, act local** approach to strategy making is essential when there are significant country-to-country differences in customer preferences and buying habits, when there are significant cross-country differences in distribution channels and marketing methods, when host governments enact regulations requiring that products sold locally meet strict manufacturing specifications or performance standards, and when the trade restrictions of host governments are so diverse and complicated that they preclude a uniform, coordinated worldwide market approach. With localized strategies, a company often has different product versions for different countries and sometimes sells the products under different brand names. Government requirements for gasoline additives that help reduce carbon monoxide, smog, and other emissions are almost never the same from country to country. BP utilizes localized strategies in its gasoline and service station business segment because of these cross-country formulation differences and because of customer familiarity with local brand names. For example, the company markets gasoline in the United States under its BP and Arco brands, but markets gasoline in Germany, Belgium, Poland, Hungary, and the Czech Republic under the Aral brand. Companies in the food products industry often vary the ingredients in their products and sell the localized versions under local brand names to cater to country-specific tastes and eating preferences. The strength of employing a set of localized or multidomestic strategies is that the company's actions and business approaches are deliberately crafted to appeal to the tastes and expectations of buyers in each country and to stake out the most attractive market positions vis-à-vis local competitors.[12]

However, think local, act local strategies have two big drawbacks: (1) They hinder transfer of a company's competencies and resources across country boundaries because the strategies in different host countries can be grounded in varying competencies and capabilities; and (2) they do not promote building a single, unified competitive advantage, especially one based on low cost. Companies employing highly localized or multidomestic strategies face big hurdles in achieving low-cost leadership *unless* they find ways to customize their products and *still* be in a position to capture scale economies and learning curve effects. Toyota's unique mass customization production capability has been key to its ability to effectively adapt product offerings to local buyer tastes, while maintaining low-cost leadership.

Global Strategy—A Think Global, Act Global Approach to Strategy Making

While multidomestic strategies are best suited for industries where a fairly high degree of local responsiveness is important, global strategies are best suited for globally standardized industries. A **global strategy** is one in which the company's approach is predominantly the same in all countries: it sells the same products under the same brand names everywhere, utilizes much the same distribution channels in all countries, and competes on the basis of the same capabilities and marketing approaches worldwide. Although the company's strategy or product offering may be adapted in very minor ways to accommodate specific situations in a few host countries, the company's fundamental competitive approach (low-cost, differentiation, or focused) remains very much intact worldwide, and local managers stick close to the global strategy. A **think global, act global** strategic theme prompts company managers to integrate and coordinate the company's strategic moves worldwide and to expand into most, if not all, nations where

> **CORE CONCEPT**
>
> **Global strategies** employ the same basic competitive approach in all countries where a company operates and are best suited to industries that are globally standardized in terms of customer preferences, buyer purchasing habits, distribution channels, or marketing methods. This is the **think global, act global** strategic theme.

there is significant buyer demand. It puts considerable strategic emphasis on building a *global* brand name and aggressively pursuing opportunities to transfer ideas, new products, and capabilities from one country to another.

Ford's global design strategy is a move toward a think global, act global strategy by the company and involves the development and production of standardized models with country-specific modifications limited primarily to what is required to meet local country emission and safety standards. The 2010 Ford Fiesta and 2011 Ford Focus were the company's first global design models to be marketed in Europe, North America, Asia, and Australia. Whenever country-to-country differences are small enough to be accommodated within the framework of a global strategy, a global strategy is preferable to localized strategies because a company can more readily unify its operations and focus on establishing a brand image and reputation that is uniform from country to country. Moreover, with a global strategy, a company is better able to focus its full resources on securing a sustainable low-cost or differentiation-based competitive advantage over both domestic rivals and global rivals.

Transnational Strategy—A Think Global, Act Local Approach to Strategy Making

A **transnational strategy** is a **think global, act local** approach to developing strategy that accommodates cross-country variations in buyer tastes, local customs, and market conditions while also striving for the benefits of standardization. This middle-ground approach entails utilizing the same basic competitive theme (low-cost, differentiation, or focused) in each country but allows local managers the latitude to (1) incorporate whatever country-specific variations in product attributes are needed to best satisfy local buyers and (2) make whatever adjustments in production, distribution, and marketing are needed to respond to local market conditions and compete successfully against local rivals. Both McDonald's and KFC have discovered ways to customize their menu offerings in various countries without compromising costs, product quality, and operating effectiveness. Otis Elevator found that a transnational strategy delivers better results than a global strategy when competing in countries such as China where local needs are highly differentiated. By switching from its customary single-brand approach to a multibrand strategy aimed at serving different segments of the market, Otis was able to double its market share in China and increased its revenues sixfold over a nine-year period.[13]

Concepts & Connections 7.2 explains how Four Seasons Hotels has been able to compete successfully on the basis of a transnational strategy.

As a rule, most companies that operate multinationally endeavor to employ as global a strategy as customer needs and market conditions permit. Electronic Arts has two major design studios—one in Vancouver, British Columbia, and one in Los Angeles—and smaller design studios in San Francisco, Orlando, London, and Tokyo. This dispersion of design studios helps EA to design games that are specific to different cultures: for example, the London studio took the lead in designing the popular FIFA Soccer game to suit European tastes and to replicate the stadiums, signage, and team rosters; the U.S. studio took the lead in designing games involving NFL football, NBA basketball, and NASCAR racing.

> **CORE CONCEPT**
>
> A **transnational strategy** is a **think global, act local** approach to strategy making that involves employing essentially the same strategic theme (low-cost, differentiation, focused, best-cost) in all country markets, while allowing some country-to-country customization to fit local market conditions.

Concepts & Connections 7.2

FOUR SEASONS HOTELS: LOCAL CHARACTER, GLOBAL SERVICE

Four Seasons Hotels is a Toronto, Canada–based manager of luxury hotel properties. With 92 properties located in many of the world's most popular tourist destinations and business centers, Four Seasons commands a following of many of the world's most discerning travelers. In contrast to its key competitor, Ritz-Carlton, which strives to create one uniform experience globally, Four Seasons Hotels has gained market share by deftly combining local architectural and cultural experiences with globally consistent luxury service.

When moving into a new market, Four Seasons always seeks out a local capital partner. The understanding of local custom and business relationships this financier brings is critical to the process of developing a new Four Seasons hotel. Four Seasons also insists on hiring a local architect and design consultant for each property, as opposed to using architects or designers it's worked with in other locations. While this can be a challenge, particularly in emerging markets, Four Seasons has found it is worth it in the long run to have a truly local team.

The specific layout and programming of each hotel are also unique. For instance, when Four Seasons opened its hotel in Mumbai, India, it prioritized space for large banquet halls to target the Indian wedding market. In India, weddings often draw guests numbering in the thousands. When moving into the Middle East, Four Seasons designed its hotels with separate prayer rooms for men and women. In Bali, where destination weddings are common, the hotel employs a "weather shaman" who, for some guests, provides reassurance that the weather will cooperate for their special day. In all cases, the objective is to provide a truly local experience.

When staffing its hotels, Four Seasons seeks to strike a fine balance between employing locals who have an innate understanding of the local culture alongside expatriate staff or "culture carriers" who understand the DNA of Four Seasons. It also

uses global systems to track customer preferences and employs globally consistent service standards. Four Seasons claims that its guests experience the same high level of service globally but that no two experiences are the same.

While it is much more expensive and time-consuming to design unique architectural and programming experiences, doing so is a strategic trade-off Four Seasons has made to achieve the local experience demanded by its high-level clientele. Likewise, it has recognized that maintaining globally consistent operation processes and service standards is important too. Four Seasons has struck the right balance between thinking globally and acting locally—the marker of a truly transnational strategy. As a result, the company has been rewarded with an international reputation for superior service and a leading market share in the luxury hospitality segment.

Note: Developed with Brian R. McKenzie.

Sources: Four Seasons annual report and corporate website; and interview with Scott Woroch, Executive Vice President of Development, Four Seasons Hotels, February 22, 2014.

Using International Operations to Improve Overall Competitiveness

A firm can gain competitive advantage by expanding outside its domestic market in two important ways. One, it can use location to lower costs or help achieve greater product differentiation. And two, it can use cross-border coordination in ways that a domestic-only competitor cannot.

LO5 Understand how multinational companies are able to use international operations to improve overall competitiveness.

Using Location to Build Competitive Advantage

To use location to build competitive advantage, a company must consider two issues: (1) whether to concentrate each internal process in a few countries or to disperse performance of each process to many nations, and (2) in which countries to locate particular activities.

When to Concentrate Internal Processes in a Few Locations   Companies tend to concentrate their activities in a limited number of locations in the following circumstances:

- *When the costs of manufacturing or other activities are significantly lower in some geographic locations than in others.* For example, much of the world's athletic footwear is manufactured in Asia (China and Korea) because of low labor costs; much of the production of circuit boards for PCs is located in Taiwan because of both low costs and the high-caliber technical skills of the Taiwanese labor force.

- *When there are significant scale economies.* The presence of significant economies of scale in components production or final assembly means a company can gain major cost savings from operating a few superefficient plants as opposed to a host of small plants scattered across the world. Makers of digital cameras and LED TVs located in Japan, South Korea, and Taiwan have used their scale economies to establish a low-cost advantage.

- *When there is a steep learning curve associated with performing an activity.* In some industries, learning curve effects in parts manufacture or assembly are so great that a company establishes one or two large plants from which it serves the world market. The key to riding down the learning curve is to concentrate production in a few locations to increase the accumulated volume at a plant (and thus the experience of the plant's workforce) as rapidly as possible.

- *When certain locations have superior resources, allow better coordination of related activities, or offer other valuable advantages.* A research unit or a sophisticated production facility may be situated in a particular nation because of its pool of technically trained personnel. Samsung became a leader in memory chip technology by establishing a major R&D facility in Silicon Valley and transferring the know-how it gained back to headquarters and its plants in South Korea.

> Companies that compete multinationally can pursue competitive advantage in world markets by locating their value chain activities in whichever nations prove most advantageous.

When to Disperse Internal Processes Across Many Locations   There are several instances when dispersing a process is more advantageous than concentrating it in a single location. Buyer-related activities, such as distribution to dealers, sales and advertising, and after-sale service, usually must take place close to buyers. This makes it necessary to physically locate the capability to perform such activities in every country market where a global firm has major customers. For example, large public accounting firms have numerous international offices to service the foreign operations of their multinational corporate clients. Dispersing activities to many locations is also competitively important when high transportation costs, diseconomies of large size, and trade barriers make it too expensive to operate from a central location. In addition, it is strategically advantageous to disperse activities to hedge against the risks of fluctuating exchange rates and adverse political developments.

Using Cross-Border Coordination to Build Competitive Advantage

Multinational and global competitors are able to coordinate activities across different countries to build competitive advantage.[14] If a firm learns how to assemble its product more efficiently at, say, its Brazilian plant, the accumulated expertise and knowledge can be shared with assembly plants in other world locations. Also, knowledge gained in marketing a company's product in Great Britain, for instance, can readily be exchanged with company personnel in New Zealand or Australia. Other examples of cross-border coordination include shifting production from a plant in one country to a plant in another to take advantage of exchange rate fluctuations and to respond to changing wage rates, energy costs, or changes in tariffs and quotas.

Efficiencies can also be achieved by shifting workloads from where they are unusually heavy to locations where personnel are underutilized. Whirlpool's efforts to link its product R&D and manufacturing operations in North America, Latin America, Europe, and Asia allowed it to accelerate the discovery of innovative appliance features, coordinate the introduction of these features in the appliance products marketed in different countries, and create a cost-efficient worldwide supply chain. Whirlpool's conscious efforts to integrate and coordinate its various operations around the world have helped it become a low-cost producer and speed product innovations to market, thereby giving Whirlpool an edge over rivals worldwide.

Strategies for Competing in the Markets of Developing Countries

Companies racing for global leadership have to consider competing in developing-economy markets such as China, India, Brazil, Indonesia, Thailand, Poland, Russia, and Mexico—countries where the business risks are considerable but where the opportunities for growth are huge, especially as their economies develop and living standards climb toward levels in the industrialized world.[15] For example, in 2014 China was the world's second-largest economy (behind the United States) based upon purchasing power, and its population of 1.3 billion people made it the world's largest market for many commodities and types of consumer goods. China's growth in demand for consumer goods has made it the fifth largest market for luxury goods, with sales greater than those in developed markets such as Germany, Spain, and the United Kingdom.[16] Thus, no company pursuing global market leadership can afford to ignore the strategic importance of establishing competitive market positions in China, India, other parts of the Asian-Pacific region, Latin America, and Eastern Europe.

Tailoring products to fit conditions in an emerging country market such as China, however, often involves more than making minor product changes and becoming more familiar with local cultures. McDonald's has had to offer vegetable burgers in parts of Asia and to rethink its prices, which are often high by local standards and affordable only by the well-to-do. Kellogg has struggled to introduce its cereals successfully because consumers in many less-developed countries do not eat cereal for breakfast—changing habits is difficult and expensive. Single-serving packages of detergents, shampoos, pickles, cough syrup, and cooking oils are very popular in India because they allow buyers to conserve cash by purchasing only what they need immediately.

LO6 Gain an understanding of the unique characteristics of competing in developing-country markets.

Thus, many companies find that trying to employ a strategy akin to that used in the markets of developed countries is hazardous.[17] Experimenting with some, perhaps many, local twists is usually necessary to find a strategy combination that works.

Strategy Options for Competing in Developing-Country Markets

Several strategy options for tailoring a company's strategy to fit the sometimes unusual or challenging circumstances presented in developing-country markets include:

- *Prepare to compete on the basis of low price.* Consumers in emerging markets are often highly focused on price, which can give low-cost local competitors the edge unless a company can find ways to attract buyers with bargain prices as well as better products. For example, when Unilever entered the market for laundry detergents in India, it developed a low-cost detergent (named Wheel) that was not harsh to the skin, constructed new superefficient production facilities, distributed the product to local merchants by handcarts, and crafted an economical marketing campaign that included painted signs on buildings and demonstrations near stores. The new brand quickly captured $100 million in sales and was the top detergent brand in India in 2014 based on dollar sales. Unilever later replicated the strategy with low-price shampoos and deodorants in India and in South America with a detergent brand named Ala.

- *Modify aspects of the company's business model or strategy to accommodate local circumstances (but not so much that the company loses the advantage of global scale and global branding).* For instance, Honeywell had sold industrial products and services for more than 100 years outside the United States and Europe using a foreign subsidiary model that focused international activities on sales only. When Honeywell entered China, it discovered that industrial customers in that country considered how many key jobs foreign companies created in China in addition to the quality and price of the product or service when making purchasing decisions. Honeywell added about 150 engineers, strategists, and marketers in China to demonstrate its commitment to bolstering the Chinese economy. Honeywell replicated its "East for East" strategy when it entered the market for industrial products and services in India. Within 10 years of Honeywell establishing operations in China and three years of expanding into India, the two emerging markets accounted for 30 percent of the firm's worldwide growth.

- *Try to change the local market to better match the way the company does business elsewhere.* A multinational company often has enough market clout to drive major changes in the way a local country market operates. When Japan's Suzuki entered India, it triggered a quality revolution among Indian auto parts manufacturers. Local parts and components suppliers teamed up with Suzuki's vendors in Japan and worked with Japanese experts to produce higher-quality products. Over the next two decades, Indian companies became very proficient in making top-notch parts and components for vehicles, won more prizes for quality than companies in any country other than Japan, and broke into the global market as suppliers to many automakers in Asia and other parts of the world. Mahindra and Mahindra, one of India's premier automobile manufacturers, has been recognized by a number of organizations for its product quality. Among its most noteworthy awards was its number-one ranking by J. D. Power Asia Pacific for new-vehicle overall quality.

- *Stay away from those emerging markets where it is impractical or uneconomical to modify the company's business model to accommodate local circumstances.* Home Depot expanded into Mexico in 2001 and China in 2006 but has avoided entry into other emerging countries because its value proposition of good quality, low prices, and attentive customer service relies on (1) good highways and logistical systems to minimize store inventory costs, (2) employee stock ownership to help motivate store personnel to provide good customer service, and (3) high labor costs for housing construction and home repairs to encourage homeowners to engage in do-it-yourself projects. Relying on these factors in the U.S. and Canadian markets has worked spectacularly for Home Depot, but Home Depot has found that it cannot count on these factors in nearby Latin America.

Company experiences in entering developing markets such as China, India, Russia, and Brazil indicate that profitability seldom comes quickly or easily. Building a market for the company's products can often turn into a long-term process that involves reeducation of consumers, sizable investments in advertising and promotion to alter tastes and buying habits, and upgrades of the local infrastructure (the supplier base, transportation systems, distribution channels, labor markets, and capital markets). In such cases, a company must be patient, work within the system to improve the infrastructure, and lay the foundation for generating sizable revenues and profits once conditions are ripe for market takeoff.

> Profitability in emerging markets rarely comes quickly or easily. New entrants have to adapt their business models and strategies to local conditions and be patient in earning a profit.

KEY POINTS

1. Competing in international markets allows multinational companies to (1) gain access to new customers, (2) achieve lower costs and enhance the firm's competitiveness by more easily capturing scale economies or learning curve effects, (3) leverage core competencies refined domestically in additional country markets, (4) gain access to resources and capabilities located in foreign markets, and (5) spread business risk across a wider market base.

2. Companies electing to expand into international markets must consider cross-country differences in buyer tastes, market sizes, and growth potential; location-based cost drivers; adverse exchange rates; and host-government policies when evaluating strategy options.

3. Options for entering foreign markets include maintaining a national (one-country) production base and exporting goods to foreign markets, licensing foreign firms to use the company's technology or produce and distribute the company's products, employing a franchising strategy, establishing a foreign subsidiary, and using strategic alliances or other collaborative partnerships.

4. In posturing to compete in foreign markets, a company has three basic options: (1) a multidomestic or think local, act local approach to crafting a strategy, (2) a global or

Diversifying into Related Businesses

CORE CONCEPT

Strategic fit exists when value chains of different businesses present opportunities for cross-business skills transfer, cost sharing, or brand sharing.

A related diversification strategy involves building the company around businesses whose value chains possess competitively valuable strategic fit, as shown in Figure 8.2. **Strategic fit** exists whenever one or more activities comprising the value chains of different businesses are sufficiently similar to present opportunities for:[5]

- *Transferring competitively valuable resources, expertise, technological know-how, or other capabilities from one business to another.* Google's technological know-how and innovation capabilities refined in its Internet search business have aided considerably in the development of its Android mobile operating system and Chrome operating system for computers. After acquiring Marvel Comics in 2009, Walt Disney Company shared Marvel's iconic characters such as Spider-Man, Iron Man, and the Black Widow with many of the other Disney businesses, including its theme parks, retail stores, motion picture division, and video game business.

- *Cost sharing between separate businesses where value chain activities can be combined.* For instance, it is often feasible to manufacture the products of different businesses in a single plant or have a single sales force for the products of different businesses if they are marketed to the same types of customers.

FIGURE 8.2 **Related Diversification Is Built upon Competitively Valuable Strategic Fit in Value Chain Activities**

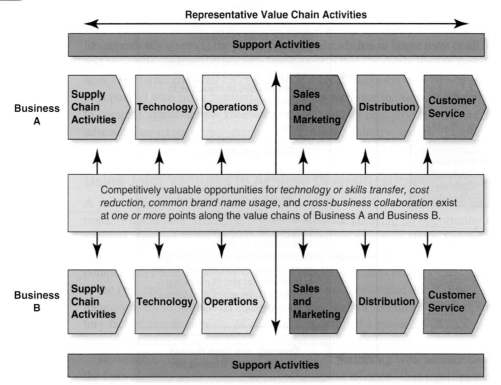

- *Brand sharing between business units that have common customers or that draw upon common core competencies.* For example, Apple's reputation for producing easy-to-operate computers and stylish designs were competitive assets that facilitated the company's diversification into digital music players, smartphones, tablet computers, and wearable technology.

Cross-business strategic fit can exist anywhere along the value chain: in R&D and technology activities, in supply chain activities, in manufacturing, in sales and marketing, or in distribution activities. Likewise, different businesses can often use the same administrative and customer service infrastructure. For instance, a cable operator that diversifies as a broadband provider can use the same customer data network, the same customer call centers and local offices, the same billing and customer accounting systems, and the same customer service infrastructure to support all its products and services.[6]

Strategic Fit and Economies of Scope

Strategic fit in the value chain activities of a diversified corporation's different businesses opens up opportunities for economies of scope—a concept distinct from *economies of scale*. Economies of *scale* are cost savings that accrue directly from a larger operation; for example, unit costs may be lower in a large plant than in a small plant. **Economies of scope,** however, stem directly from cost-saving strategic fit along the value chains of related businesses. Such economies are open only to a multibusiness enterprise and are the result of a related diversification strategy that allows sibling businesses to share technology, perform R&D together, use common manufacturing

> **CORE CONCEPT**
>
> **Economies of scope** are cost reductions stemming from strategic fit along the value chains of related businesses (thereby, a larger scope of operations), whereas *economies of scale* accrue from a larger operation.

or distribution facilities, share a common sales force or distributor/dealer network, and/or share the same administrative infrastructure. *The greater the cross-business economies associated with cost-saving strategic fit, the greater the potential for a related diversification strategy to yield a competitive advantage based on lower costs than rivals.*

The Ability of Related Diversification to Deliver Competitive Advantage and Gains in Shareholder Value

Economies of scope and the other strategic-fit benefits provide a dependable basis for earning higher profits and returns than what a diversified company's businesses could earn as stand-alone enterprises. Converting the competitive advantage potential into greater profitability is what fuels $1 + 1 = 3$ gains in shareholder value—the necessary outcome for satisfying the *better-off test.* There are three things to bear in mind here: (1) Capturing cross-business strategic fit via related diversification builds shareholder value in ways that shareholders cannot replicate by simply owning a diversified portfolio of stocks; (2) the capture of cross-business strategic-fit benefits is possible only through related diversification; and (3) the benefits of cross-business strategic fit are not automatically realized—*the benefits materialize only after management has successfully pursued internal actions to capture them.*[7]

Diversifying into Unrelated Businesses

LO3 Become aware of the merits and risks of corporate strategies keyed to unrelated diversification.

An unrelated diversification strategy discounts the importance of pursuing cross-business strategic fit and, instead, focuses squarely on entering and operating businesses in industries that allow the company as a whole to increase its earnings. Companies that pursue a strategy of unrelated diversification generally exhibit a willingness to diversify into *any industry* where senior managers see opportunity to realize improved financial results. Such companies are frequently labeled *conglomerates* because their business interests range broadly across diverse industries.

Companies that pursue unrelated diversification nearly always enter new businesses by acquiring an established company rather than by internal development. The premise of acquisition-minded corporations is that growth by acquisition can deliver enhanced shareholder value through upward-trending corporate revenues and earnings and a stock price that *on average* rises enough year after year to amply reward and please shareholders. Three types of acquisition candidates are usually of particular interest: (1) businesses that have bright growth prospects but are short on investment capital, (2) undervalued companies that can be acquired at a bargain price, and (3) struggling companies whose operations can be turned around with the aid of the parent company's financial resources and managerial know-how.

Building Shareholder Value Through Unrelated Diversification

Given the absence of cross-business strategic fit with which to capture added competitive advantage, the task of building shareholder value via unrelated diversification ultimately hinges on the ability of the parent company to improve its businesses via other means. To succeed with a corporate strategy keyed to unrelated diversification, corporate executives must:

- Do a superior job of identifying and acquiring new businesses that can produce consistently good earnings and returns on investment.
- Do an excellent job of negotiating favorable acquisition prices.
- Do such a good job *overseeing* and *parenting* the firm's businesses that they perform at a higher level than they would otherwise be able to do through their own efforts alone. The parenting activities of corporate executives can take the form of providing expert problem-solving skills, creative strategy suggestions, and first-rate advice and guidance on how to improve competitiveness and financial performance to the heads of the various business subsidiaries.[8] The outstanding leadership of Royal Little, the founder of Textron, was a major reason that the company became an exemplar of the unrelated diversification strategy while he was CEO. Little's bold moves transformed the company from its origins as a small textile manufacturer into a global powerhouse known for its Bell helicopters, Cessna aircraft, and host of other strong brands in an array of industries.

The Pitfalls of Unrelated Diversification

Unrelated diversification strategies have two important negatives that undercut the pluses: very demanding managerial requirements and limited competitive advantage potential.

Demanding Managerial Requirements   Successfully managing a set of fundamentally different businesses operating in fundamentally different industry and competitive environments is an exceptionally difficult proposition for corporate-level managers. The greater the number of businesses a company is in and the more diverse they are, the more difficult it is for corporate managers to:

1. Stay abreast of what's happening in each industry and each subsidiary.

2. Pick business-unit heads having the requisite combination of managerial skills and know-how to drive gains in performance.

3. Tell the difference between those strategic proposals of business-unit managers that are prudent and those that are risky or unlikely to succeed.

4. Know what to do if a business unit stumbles and its results suddenly head downhill.[9]

As a rule, the more unrelated businesses that a company has diversified into, the more corporate executives are forced to "manage by the numbers"—that is, keep a close track on the financial and operating results of each subsidiary and assume that the heads of the various subsidiaries have most everything under control so long as the latest key financial and operating measures look good. Managing by the numbers works if the heads of the various business units are quite capable and consistently meet their numbers. But problems arise when things start to go awry and corporate management has to get deeply involved in turning around a business it does not know much about.

> Unrelated diversification requires that corporate executives rely on the skills and expertise of business-level managers to build competitive advantage and boost the performance of individual businesses.

Limited Competitive Advantage Potential   The second big negative associated with unrelated diversification is that such a strategy *offers limited potential for competitive advantage beyond what each individual business can generate on its own.* Unlike a related diversification strategy, there is no cross-business strategic fit to draw on for reducing costs; transferring capabilities, skills, and technology; or leveraging use of a powerful brand name and thereby adding to the competitive advantage possessed by individual businesses. *Without the competitive advantage potential of strategic fit, consolidated performance of an unrelated group of businesses is unlikely to be better than the sum of what the individual business units could achieve independently in most instances.*

Misguided Reasons for Pursuing Unrelated Diversification

Competently overseeing a set of widely diverse businesses can turn out to be much harder than it sounds. In practice, comparatively few companies have proved that they have top management capabilities that are up to the task. Far more corporate executives have failed than have been successful at delivering consistently good financial results with an unrelated diversification strategy.[10] Odds are that the result of unrelated diversification will be 1 + 1 = 2 or less. In addition, management sometimes undertakes a strategy of unrelated diversification for the wrong reasons.

- *Risk reduction.* Managers sometimes pursue unrelated diversification to reduce risk by spreading the company's investments over a set of diverse industries. But this cannot create long-term shareholder value alone since the company's shareholders can more efficiently reduce their exposure to risk by investing in a diversified portfolio of stocks and bonds.

- *Growth.* While unrelated diversification may enable a company to achieve rapid or continuous growth in revenues, only profitable growth can bring about increases in shareholder value and justify a strategy of unrelated diversification.

- *Earnings stabilization.* In a broadly diversified company, there's a chance that market downtrends in some of the company's businesses will be partially offset by cyclical upswings in its other businesses, thus producing somewhat less earnings volatility. In actual practice, however, there's no convincing evidence that the consolidated profits of firms with unrelated diversification strategies are more stable than the profits of firms with related diversification strategies.

- *Managerial motives.* Unrelated diversification can provide benefits to managers such as higher compensation, which tends to increase with firm size and degree of diversification. Diversification for this reason alone is far more likely to reduce shareholder value than to increase it.

Diversifying into Both Related and Unrelated Businesses

There's nothing to preclude a company from diversifying into both related and unrelated businesses. Indeed, the business makeup of diversified companies varies considerably. Some diversified companies are really *dominant-business enterprises*—one major "core" business accounts for 50 to 80 percent of total revenues, and a collection of small related or unrelated businesses accounts for the remainder. Some diversified companies are *narrowly diversified* around a few (two to five) related or unrelated businesses. Others are *broadly diversified* around a wide-ranging collection of related businesses, unrelated businesses, or a mixture of both. And a number of multibusiness enterprises have diversified into *several unrelated groups of related businesses.* There's ample room for companies to customize their diversification strategies to incorporate elements of both related and unrelated diversification.

Evaluating the Strategy of a Diversified Company

LO4 Gain command of the analytical tools for evaluating a company's diversification strategy.

Strategic analysis of diversified companies builds on the methodology used for single-business companies discussed in Chapters 3 and 4 but utilizes tools that streamline the overall process. The procedure for evaluating the pluses and minuses of a diversified company's strategy and deciding what actions to take to improve the company's performance involves six steps:

1. Assessing the attractiveness of the industries the company has diversified into.

2. Assessing the competitive strength of the company's business units.

3. Evaluating the extent of cross-business strategic fit along the value chains of the company's various business units.

4. Checking whether the firm's resources fit the requirements of its present business lineup.

5. Ranking the performance prospects of the businesses from best to worst and determining a priority for allocating resources.

6. Crafting new strategic moves to improve overall corporate performance.

The core concepts and analytical techniques underlying each of these steps are discussed further in this section of the chapter.

Step 1: Evaluating Industry Attractiveness

A principal consideration in evaluating the caliber of a diversified company's strategy is the attractiveness of the industries in which it has business operations. The more attractive the industries (both individually and as a group) a diversified company is in, the better its prospects for good long-term performance. A simple and reliable analytical tool for gauging industry attractiveness involves calculating quantitative industry attractiveness scores based upon the following measures:

- *Market size and projected growth rate.* Big industries are more attractive than small industries, and fast-growing industries tend to be more attractive than slow-growing industries, other things being equal.

- *The intensity of competition.* Industries in which competitive pressures are relatively weak are more attractive than industries with strong competitive pressures.

- *Emerging opportunities and threats.* Industries with promising opportunities and minimal threats on the near horizon are more attractive than industries with modest opportunities and imposing threats.

- *The presence of cross-industry strategic fit.* The more the industry's value chain and resource requirements match up well with the value chain activities of other industries in which the company has operations, the more attractive the industry is to a firm pursuing related diversification. However, cross-industry strategic fit may be of no consequence to a company committed to a strategy of unrelated diversification.

- *Resource requirements.* Industries having resource requirements within the company's reach are more attractive than industries where capital and other resource requirements could strain corporate financial resources and organizational capabilities.

- *Seasonal and cyclical factors.* Industries where buyer demand is relatively steady year-round and not unduly vulnerable to economic ups and downs tend to be more attractive than industries with wide seasonal or cyclical swings in buyer demand.

- *Social, political, regulatory, and environmental factors.* Industries with significant problems in such areas as consumer health, safety, or environmental pollution or that are subject to intense regulation are less attractive than industries where such problems are not burning issues.

- *Industry profitability.* Industries with healthy profit margins are generally more attractive than industries where profits have historically been low or unstable.

- *Industry uncertainty and business risk.* Industries with less uncertainty on the horizon and lower overall business risk are more attractive than industries whose prospects for one reason or another are quite uncertain.

Each attractiveness measure should be assigned a weight reflecting its relative importance in determining an industry's attractiveness; it is weak methodology to assume that the various attractiveness measures are equally important. The intensity of competition in an industry should nearly always carry a high weight (say, 0.20 to 0.30). Strategic-fit considerations should be assigned a high weight in the case of companies with related diversification strategies; but for companies with an unrelated diversification strategy, strategic fit with other industries may be given a low weight or even dropped from the list of attractiveness measures. Seasonal and cyclical factors generally are assigned a low weight (or maybe even eliminated from the analysis) unless a company has diversified into industries strongly characterized by seasonal demand and/or heavy vulnerability to cyclical upswings and downswings. The importance weights must add up to 1.0.

Next, each industry is rated on each of the chosen industry attractiveness measures, using a rating scale of 1 to 10 (where 10 signifies *high* attractiveness and 1 signifies *low* attractiveness). Weighted attractiveness scores are then calculated by multiplying the industry's rating on each measure by the corresponding weight. For example, a rating of 8 times a weight of 0.25 gives a weighted attractiveness score of 2.00. The sum of the weighted scores for all the attractiveness measures provides an overall industry attractiveness score. This procedure is illustrated in Table 8.1.

Calculating Industry Attractiveness Scores Two conditions are necessary for producing valid industry attractiveness scores using this method. One is deciding on appropriate weights for the industry attractiveness measures. This is not always easy because different analysts have different views about which weights are most appropriate. Also, different weightings may be appropriate for different companies—based on their

TABLE 8.1

Calculating Weighted Industry Attractiveness Scores

Rating scale: 1 = Very unattractive to company; 10 = Very attractive to company

Industry Attractiveness Measure	Importance Weight	Industry A Rating/Score	Industry B Rating/Score	Industry C Rating/Score	Industry D Rating/Score
Market size and projected growth rate	0.10	8/0.80	5/0.50	2/0.20	3/0.30
Intensity of competition	0.25	8/2.00	7/1.75	3/0.75	2/0.50
Emerging opportunities and threats	0.10	2/0.20	9/0.90	4/0.40	5/0.50
Cross-industry strategic fit	0.20	8/1.60	4/0.80	8/1.60	2/0.40
Resource requirements	0.10	9/0.90	7/0.70	5/0.50	5/0.50
Seasonal and cyclical influences	0.05	9/0.45	8/0.40	10/0.50	5/0.25
Societal, political, regulatory, and environmental factors	0.05	10/0.50	7/0.35	7/0.35	3/0.15
Industry profitability	0.10	5/0.50	10/1.00	3/0.30	3/0.30
Industry uncertainty and business risk	0.05	5/0.25	7/0.35	10/0.50	1/0.05
Sum of the assigned weights	1.00				
Overall weighted industry attractiveness scores		**7.20**	**6.75**	**5.10**	**2.95**

strategies, performance targets, and financial circumstances. For instance, placing a low weight on financial resource requirements may be justifiable for a cash-rich company, whereas a high weight may be more appropriate for a financially strapped company.

The second requirement for creating accurate attractiveness scores is to have sufficient knowledge to rate the industry on each attractiveness measure. It's usually rather easy to locate statistical data needed to compare industries on market size, growth rate, seasonal and cyclical influences, and industry profitability. Cross-industry fit and resource requirements are also fairly easy to judge. But the attractiveness measure that is toughest to rate is that of intensity of competition. It is not always easy to conclude whether competition in one industry is stronger or weaker than in another industry. In the event that the available information is too skimpy to confidently assign a rating value to an industry on a particular attractiveness measure, then it is usually best to use a score of 5, which avoids biasing the overall attractiveness score either up or down.

Despite the hurdles, calculating industry attractiveness scores is a systematic and reasonably reliable method for ranking a diversified company's industries from most to least attractive.

Step 2: Evaluating Business-Unit Competitive Strength

The second step in evaluating a diversified company is to determine how strongly positioned its business units are in their respective industries. Doing an appraisal of each business unit's strength and competitive position in its industry not only reveals its chances for industry success but also provides a basis for ranking the units from competitively strongest to weakest. Quantitative measures of each business unit's competitive strength can be calculated using a procedure similar to that for measuring industry attractiveness. The following factors may be used in quantifying the competitive strengths of a diversified company's business subsidiaries:

- *Relative market share.* A business unit's *relative market share* is defined as the ratio of its market share to the market share held by the largest rival firm in the industry, with market share measured in unit volume, not dollars. For instance, if business A has a market-leading share of 40 percent and its largest rival has 30 percent, A's relative market share is 1.33. If business B has a 15 percent market share and B's largest rival has 30 percent, B's relative market share is 0.5.

- *Costs relative to competitors' costs.* There's reason to expect that business units with higher relative market shares have lower unit costs than competitors with lower relative market shares because of the possibility of scale economies and experience or learning curve effects. Another indicator of low cost can be a business unit's supply chain management capabilities.

- *Products or services that satisfy buyer expectations.* A company's competitiveness depends in part on being able to offer buyers appealing features, performance, reliability, and service attributes.

- *Ability to benefit from strategic fit with sibling businesses.* Strategic fit with other businesses within the company enhances a business unit's competitive strength and may provide a competitive edge.

- *Number and caliber of strategic alliances and collaborative partnerships.* Well-functioning alliances and partnerships may be a source of potential competitive advantage and thus add to a business's competitive strength.

- *Brand image and reputation.* A strong brand name is a valuable competitive asset in most industries.
- *Competitively valuable capabilities.* All industries contain a variety of important competitive capabilities related to product innovation, production capabilities, distribution capabilities, or marketing prowess.
- *Profitability relative to competitors.* Above-average returns on investment and large profit margins relative to rivals are usually accurate indicators of competitive advantage.

After settling on a set of competitive strength measures that are well matched to the circumstances of the various business units, weights indicating each measure's importance need to be assigned. As in the assignment of weights to industry attractiveness measures, the importance weights must add up to 1.0. Each business unit is then rated on each of the chosen strength measures, using a rating scale of 1 to 10 (where 10 signifies competitive *strength* and a rating of 1 signifies competitive *weakness*). If the available information is too skimpy to confidently assign a rating value to a business unit on a particular strength measure, then it is usually best to use a score of 5. Weighted strength ratings are calculated by multiplying the business unit's rating on each strength measure by the assigned weight. For example, a strength score of 6 times a weight of 0.15 gives a weighted strength rating of 0.90. The sum of weighted ratings across all the strength measures provides a quantitative measure of a business unit's overall market strength and competitive standing. Table 8.2 provides sample calculations of competitive strength ratings for four businesses.

TABLE 8.2

Calculating Weighted Competitive Strength Scores for a Diversified Company's Business Units

Rating scale: 1 = Very weak; 10 = Very strong

Competitive Strength Measure	Importance Weight	Business A in Industry A Rating/Score	Business B in Industry B Rating/Score	Business C in Industry C Rating/Score	Business D in Industry D Rating/Score
Relative market share	0.15	10/1.50	1/0.15	6/0.90	2/0.30
Costs relative to competitors' costs	0.20	7/1.40	2/0.40	5/1.00	3/0.60
Ability to match or beat rivals on key product attributes	0.05	9/0.45	4/0.20	8/0.40	4/0.20
Ability to benefit from strategic fit with sister businesses	0.20	8/1.60	4/0.80	4/0.80	2/0.60
Bargaining leverage with suppliers/buyers; caliber of alliances	0.05	9/0.45	3/0.15	6/0.30	2/0.10
Brand image and reputation	0.10	9/0.90	2/0.20	7/0.70	5/0.50
Competitively valuable capabilities	0.15	7/1.05	2/0.30	5/0.75	3/0.45
Profitability relative to competitors	0.10	5/0.50	1/0.10	4/0.40	4/0.40
Sum of the assigned weights	1.00				
Overall weighted competitive strength scores		**7.85**	**2.30**	**5.25**	**3.15**

Using a Nine-Cell Matrix to Evaluate the Strength of a Diversified Company's Business Lineup

The industry attractiveness and business strength scores can be used to portray the strategic positions of each business in a diversified company. Industry attractiveness is plotted on the vertical axis and competitive strength on the horizontal axis. A nine-cell grid emerges from dividing the vertical axis into three regions (high, medium, and low attractiveness) and the horizontal axis into three regions (strong, average, and weak competitive strength). As shown in Figure 8.3, high attractiveness is associated with scores of 6.7 or greater on a rating scale of 1 to 10, medium attractiveness with scores of 3.3 to 6.7, and low attractiveness with scores below 3.3. Likewise,

FIGURE 8.3   **A Nine-Cell Industry Attractiveness–Competitive Strength Matrix**

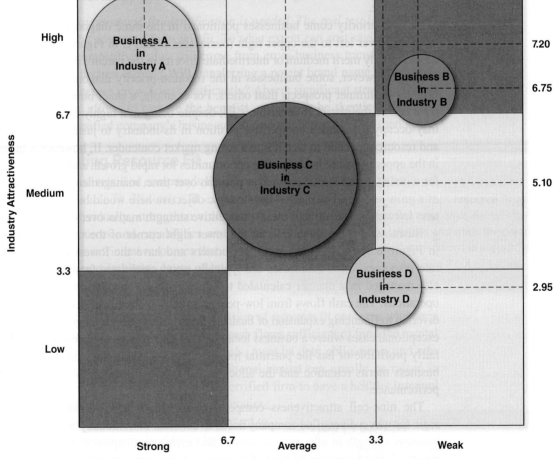

Note: Circle sizes are scaled to reflect the percentage of companywide revenues generated by the business unit.

High priority for resource allocation
Medium priority for resource allocation
Low priority for resource allocation

to the present parent; in such cases, shareholders would be well served if the company were to sell the business and collect a premium price from the buyer for whom the business is a valuable fit.[15]

Broadly Restructuring the Business Lineup Through a Mix of Divestitures and New Acquisitions Corporate restructuring strategies involve divesting some businesses and acquiring others so as to put a new face on the company's business lineup. Performing radical surgery on a company's group of businesses is an appealing corporate strategy when its financial performance is squeezed or eroded by:

- Too many businesses in slow-growth, declining, low-margin, or otherwise unattractive industries.
- Too many competitively weak businesses.
- An excessive debt burden with interest costs that eat deeply into profitability.
- Ill-chosen acquisitions that haven't lived up to expectations.

Candidates for divestiture in a corporate restructuring effort typically include not only weak or up-and-down performers or those in unattractive industries but also business units that lack strategic fit with the businesses to be retained, businesses that are cash hogs or that lack other types of resource fit, and businesses incompatible with the company's revised diversification strategy (even though they may be profitable or in an attractive industry). As businesses are divested, corporate restructuring generally involves aligning the remaining business units into groups with the best strategic fit and then redeploying the cash flows from the divested business to either pay down debt or make new acquisitions.

Over the past decade, corporate restructuring has become a popular strategy at many diversified companies, especially those that had diversified broadly into many different industries and lines of business. VF Corporation, maker of North Face and other popular "lifestyle" apparel brands, has used a restructuring strategy to provide its shareholders with returns that are more than five times greater than shareholder returns for competing apparel makers. Since its acquisition and turnaround of North Face in 2000, VF has spent nearly $5 billion to acquire 19 additional businesses, including about $2 billion in 2011 for Timberland. New apparel brands acquired by VF Corporation include 7 For All Mankind sportswear, Vans skateboard shoes, Nautica, John Varvatos, Reef surf wear, and Lucy athletic wear. By 2015, VF Corporation had become an $12 billion powerhouse—one of the largest and most profitable apparel and footwear companies ion the world. It was listed as number 241 on *Fortune*'s 2014 list of the 500 largest U.S. companies.

1. The purpose of diversification is to build shareholder value. Diversification builds shareholder value when a diversified group of businesses can perform better under the auspices of a single corporate parent than they would as independent, stand-alone businesses—the goal is to achieve not just a $1 + 1 = 2$ result but rather to realize important $1 + 1 = 3$ performance benefits. Whether getting into a new business has potential to enhance shareholder value hinges on whether a company's entry into that business can pass the attractiveness test, the cost-of-entry test, and the better-off test.

2. Entry into new businesses can take any of three forms: acquisition, internal development, or joint venture/strategic partnership. Each has its pros and cons, but acquisition usually provides the quickest entry into a new entry; internal development takes the longest to produce home-run results; and joint venture/strategic partnership tends to be the least durable.

3. There are two fundamental approaches to diversification: into related businesses and into unrelated businesses. The rationale for *related* diversification is based on cross-business *strategic fit:* Diversify into businesses with strategic fit along their respective value chains, capitalize on strategic-fit relationships to gain competitive advantage, and then use competitive advantage to achieve the desired $1 + 1 = 3$ impact on shareholder value.

4. *Unrelated diversification* strategies surrender the competitive advantage potential of strategic fit. Given the absence of cross-business strategic fit, the task of building shareholder value through a strategy of unrelated diversification hinges on the ability of the parent company to (1) do a superior job of identifying and acquiring new businesses that can produce consistently good earnings and returns on investment; (2) do an excellent job of negotiating favorable acquisition prices; and (3) do such a good job of overseeing and parenting the collection of businesses that they perform at a higher level than they would on their own efforts. The greater the number of businesses a company has diversified into and the more diverse these businesses are, the harder it is for corporate executives to select capable managers to run each business, know when the major strategic proposals of business units are sound, or decide on a wise course of recovery when a business unit stumbles.

5. Evaluating a company's diversification strategy is a six-step process:

   - Step 1: *Evaluate the long-term attractiveness of the industries into which the firm has diversified.* Determining industry attractiveness involves developing a list of industry attractiveness measures, each of which might have a different importance weight.

   - Step 2: *Evaluate the relative competitive strength of each of the company's business units.* The purpose of rating each business's competitive strength is to gain clear understanding of which businesses are strong contenders in their industries, which are weak contenders, and the underlying reasons for their strength or weakness. The conclusions about industry attractiveness can be joined with the conclusions about competitive strength by drawing an industry attractiveness–competitive strength matrix that helps identify the prospects of each business and what priority each business should be given in allocating corporate resources and investment capital.

   - Step 3: *Check for cross-business strategic fit.* A business is more attractive strategically when it has value chain relationships with sibling business units that offer the potential to (1) realize economies of scope or cost-saving efficiencies; (2) transfer technology, skills, know-how, or other resources and capabilities from one business to another; and/or (3) leverage use of a well-known and trusted brand name.

LO1, LO2 2. What specific resources and capabilities does your company possess that would make it attractive to diversify into related businesses? Indicate what kinds of strategic fit benefits could be captured by transferring these resources and competitive capabilities to newly acquired related businesses.

LO1, LO2 3. If your company opted to pursue a strategy of related diversification, what industries or product categories could your company diversify into that would allow it to achieve economies of scope? Name at least two or three such industries/product categories, and indicate the specific kinds of cost savings that might accrue from entry into each of these businesses/product categories.

LO1, LO2, LO3, LO4, LO5 4. If your company opted to pursue a strategy of related diversification, what industries or product categories could your company diversify into that would allow your company to capitalize on using your company's present brand name and corporate image to good advantage in these newly entered businesses or product categories? Name at least two or three such industries or product categories, and indicate *the specific benefits* that might be captured by transferring your company's brand name to each of these other businesses/product categories.

Would you prefer to pursue a strategy of related or unrelated diversification? Why?

ENDNOTES

1. Constantinos C. Markides, "To Diversify or Not to Diversify," *Harvard Business Review* 75, no. 6 (November–December 1997).

2. Michael E. Porter, "From Competitive Advantage to Corporate Strategy," *Harvard Business Review* 45, no. 3 (May–June 1987).

3. Michael E. Porter, *Competitive Strategy: Techniques for Analyzing Industries and Competitors* (New York: Free Press, 1980).

4. Yves L. Doz and Gary Hamel, *Alliance Advantage: The Art of Creating Value Through Partnering* (Boston: Harvard Business School Press, 1998).

5. Michael E. Porter, *Competitive Advantage* (New York: Free Press, 1985); Constantinos C. Markides and Peter J. Williamson, "Corporate Diversification and Organization Structure: A Resource-Based View," *Academy of Management Journal* 39, no. 2 (April 1996).

6. Jeanne M. Liedtka, "Collaboration Across Lines of Business for Competitive Advantage," *Academy of Management Executive* 10, no. 2 (May 1996).

7. Kathleen M. Eisenhardt and D. Charles Galunic, "Coevolving: At Last, a Way to Make Synergies Work," *Harvard Business Review* 78, no. 1 (January–February 2000); Constantinos C. Markides and Peter J. Williamson, "Related Diversification, Core Competencies and Corporate Performance," *Strategic Management Journal* 15 (Summer 1994).

8. A. Campbell, M. Goold, and M. Alexander, "Corporate Strategy: The Quest for Parenting Advantage," *Harvard Business Review* 73, no. 2 (March–April 1995); Cynthia A. Montgomery and Birger Wernerfelt, "Diversification, Ricardian Rents, and Tobin-Q," *RAND Journal of Economics* 19, no. 4 (1988).

9. Patricia L. Anslinger and Thomas E. Copeland, "Growth Through Acquisitions: A Fresh Look," *Harvard Business Review* 74, no. 1 (January–February 1996).

10. Lawrence G. Franko, "The Death of Diversification? The Focusing of the World's Industrial Firms, 1980–2000," *Business Horizons* 47, no. 4 (July–August 2004).

11. Andrew Campbell, Michael Gould, and Marcus Alexander, "Corporate Strategy: The Quest for Parenting Advantage," *Harvard Business Review* 73, no. 2 (March–April 1995).

12. Constantinos C. Markides, "Diversification, Restructuring, and Economic Performance," *Strategic Management Journal* 16 (February 1995).

13. Lee Dranikoff, Tim Koller, and Antoon Schneider, "Divestiture: Strategy's Missing Link," *Harvard Business Review* 80, no. 5 (May 2002).

14. Peter F. Drucker, *Management: Tasks, Responsibilities, Practices* (New York: Harper & Row, 1974).

15. David J. Collis and Cynthia A. Montgomery, "Creating Corporate Advantage," *Harvard Business Review* 76, no. 3 (May–June 1998).

Ethics, Corporate Social Responsibility, Environmental Sustainability, and Strategy

LEARNING OBJECTIVES

LO1 Understand why the standards of ethical behavior in business are no different from ethical standards in general.

LO2 Recognize conditions that give rise to unethical business strategies and behavior.

LO3 Gain an understanding of the costs of business ethics failures.

LO4 Learn the concepts of corporate social responsibility and environmental sustainability and how companies balance these duties with economic responsibilities to shareholders.

Clearly, a company has a responsibility to make a profit and grow the business, but just as clearly, a company and its personnel also have a duty to obey the law and play by the rules of fair competition. But does a company have a duty to go beyond legal requirements and operate according to the ethical norms of the societies in which it operates? And does it have a duty or obligation to contribute to the betterment of society independent of the needs and preferences of the customers it serves? Should a company display a social conscience and devote a portion of its resources to bettering society? Should its strategic initiatives be screened for possible negative effects on future generations of the world's population?

This chapter focuses on whether a company, in the course of trying to craft and execute a strategy that delivers value to both customers and shareholders, also has a duty to (1) act in an ethical manner, (2) demonstrate socially responsible behavior by being a committed corporate citizen, and (3) adopt business practices that conserve natural resources, protect the interest of future generations, and preserve the well-being of the planet.

What Do We Mean by Business Ethics?

LO1 Understand why the standards of ethical behavior in business are no different from ethical standards in general.

Business ethics is the application of ethical principles and standards to the actions and decisions of business organizations and the conduct of their personnel.[1] Ethical principles in business are not materially different from ethical principles in general because business actions have to be judged in the context of society's standards of right and wrong. There is not a special set of rules that businesspeople decide to apply to their own conduct. If dishonesty is considered unethical and immoral, then dishonest behavior in business—whether it relates to customers, suppliers, employees, or shareholders—qualifies as equally unethical and immoral. If being ethical entails adhering to generally accepted norms about conduct that is right and wrong, then managers must consider such norms when crafting and executing strategy.

CORE CONCEPT

Business ethics involves the application of general ethical principles to the actions and decisions of businesses and the conduct of their personnel.

While most company managers are careful to ensure that a company's strategy is within the bounds of what is legal, evidence indicates they are not always so careful to ensure that their strategies are within the bounds of what is considered ethical. In recent years, there have been revelations of ethical misconduct on the part of managers at such companies as casino giant Las Vegas Sands, Hewlett-Packard, GlaxoSmithKline, Marathon Oil Corporation, Kraft Foods Inc., Motorola Solutions, Pfizer, Oracle Corporation, several leading investment banking firms, and a host of mortgage lenders. The consequences of crafting strategies that cannot pass the test of moral scrutiny are manifested in sharp drops in stock price that cost shareholders billions of dollars, devastating public relations hits, sizable fines, and criminal indictments and convictions of company executives.

Drivers of Unethical Strategies and Business Behavior

LO2 Recognize conditions that give rise to unethical business strategies and behavior.

Apart from "the business of business is business, not ethics" kind of thinking apparent in recent high-profile business scandals, three other main drivers of unethical business behavior also stand out:[2]

- *Faulty oversight, enabling the unscrupulous pursuit of personal gain and other selfish interests.* People who are obsessed with wealth accumulation, greed, power, status, and other selfish interests often push ethical principles aside in their quest for self-gain. Driven by their ambitions, they exhibit few qualms in skirting the rules or doing whatever is necessary to achieve their goals. A general disregard for business ethics can prompt all kinds of unethical strategic maneuvers and behaviors at companies.

The U.S. government has been conducting a multiyear investigation of insider trading, the illegal practice of exchanging confidential information to gain an advantage in the stock market. Focusing on the hedge fund industry and nicknamed "Operation Perfect Hedge," the investigation has brought to light scores of violations and led to more than 79 guilty pleas or convictions by early 2014. Among the most prominent of those convicted was Raj Rajaratnam, the former head of Galleon Group, who was sentenced to 11 years in prison and fined $10 million. At SAC Capital, a $14 billion hedge fund, eight hedge fund mangers were convicted of insider trading in what has been called the most lucrative insider trading scheme in U.S. history. The company has agreed to pay $1.8 billion in penalties and has been forced to stop managing money for outside investors.[3]

- *Heavy pressures on company managers to meet or beat performance targets.* When key personnel find themselves scrambling to meet the quarterly and annual sales and profit expectations of investors and financial analysts or to hit other ambitious performance targets, they often feel enormous pressure to *do whatever it takes* to protect their reputation for delivering good results. As the pressure builds, they start stretching the rules further and further, until the limits of ethical conduct are overlooked.[4] Once people cross ethical boundaries to "meet or beat their numbers," the threshold for making more extreme ethical compromises becomes lower. In 2014, the U.S. Securities and Exchange Commission charged Diamond Foods (maker of Pop Secret and Emerald Nuts) with accounting fraud, alleging that the company falsified costs in order to boost earnings and stock prices. The company has agreed to pay $5 million, while its (now ousted) CEO must pay $125,000 to settle a separate charge of negligence and return $4 million in bonuses to the company. The real blow for the company was that its pending acquisition of potato chip giant Pringles fell apart as a result of the scandal, thwarting the company's dreams of becoming the second largest snack company in the world.[5]

- *A company culture that puts profitability and good business performance ahead of ethical behavior.* When a company's culture spawns an ethically corrupt or amoral work climate, people have a company-approved license to ignore "what's right" and engage in most any behavior or employ most any strategy they think they can get away with. Such cultural norms as "everyone else does it" and "it is OK to bend the rules to get the job done" permeate the work environment. At such companies, ethically immoral or amoral people are certain to play down observance of ethical strategic actions and business conduct. Moreover, cultural pressures to utilize unethical means if circumstances become challenging can prompt otherwise honorable people to behave unethically. Enron's leaders created a culture that pressured company personnel to be innovative and aggressive in figuring out how to grow current earnings—regardless of the methods. Enron's annual "rank and yank" performance evaluation process, in which the lowest-ranking 15 to 20 percent of employees were let go, made it abundantly clear that bottom-line results were what mattered most. The name of the game at Enron became devising clever ways to boost revenues and earnings, even if this sometimes meant operating outside established policies. In fact, outside-the-lines behavior was celebrated if it generated profitable new business.

The Business Case for Ethical Strategies

LO3 Gain an understanding of the costs of business ethics failures.

While it is undoubtedly true that unethical business behavior may sometimes contribute to higher company profits (*so long as such behavior escapes public scrutiny*), deliberate pursuit of unethical strategies and tolerance of unethical conduct are risky practices from both a shareholder perspective and a reputational standpoint. Figure 9.1 shows the wide-ranging costs a company can incur when unethical behavior is discovered and it is forced to make amends for its behavior. The more egregious a company's ethical violations, the higher are the costs and the bigger the damage to its reputation (and to the reputations of the company personnel involved). In high-profile instances, the costs of ethical misconduct can easily run into the hundreds of millions and even billions of dollars, especially if they provoke widespread public outrage and many people were harmed.

The fallout of ethical misconduct on the part of a company goes well beyond just the costs of making amends for the misdeeds. Buyers shun companies known for their shady behavior. Companies known to have engaged in unethical conduct have difficulty recruiting and retaining talented employees.[6] Most ethically upstanding people don't want to get entrapped in a compromising situation, nor do they want their

---

FIGURE 9.1   **The Costs Companies Incur When Ethical Wrongdoing Is Discovered and Punished**

Visible Costs	Internal Administrative Costs	Intangible or Less Visible Costs
• Government fines and penalties • Civil penalties arising from class-action lawsuits and other litigation aimed at punishing the company for its offense and the harm done to others • The costs to shareholders in the form of a lower stock price (and possibly lower dividends)	• Legal and investigative costs incurred by the company • The costs of providing remedial education and ethics training to company personnel • Costs of taking corrective actions • Administration costs associated with ensuring future compliance	• Customer defections • Loss of reputation • Lost employee morale and higher degrees of employee cynicism • Higher employee turnover • Higher recruiting costs and difficulty in attracting employees • Adverse effects on employee productivity • The costs of complying with often harsher government regulation

Source: Adapted from Terry Thomas, John R. Schermerhorn, and John W. Dienhart, "Strategic Leadership of Ethical Behavior," *Academy of Management Executive* 18, no. 2 (May 2004), p. 58.

personal reputations tarnished by the actions of an unsavory employer. A company's unethical behavior risks considerable damage to shareholders in the form of lost revenues, higher costs, lower profits, lower stock prices, and a diminished business reputation. To a significant degree, therefore, ethical strategies and ethical conduct are *good business.*

> Shareholders suffer major damage when a company's unethical behavior is discovered and punished. Making amends for unethical business conduct is costly, and it takes years to rehabilitate a tarnished company reputation.

Ensuring a Strong Commitment to Business Ethics in Companies with International Operations

Notions of right and wrong, fair and unfair, moral and immoral, ethical and unethical are present in all societies, organizations, and individuals. But there are three schools of thought about the extent to which the ethical standards travel across cultures and whether multinational companies can apply the same set of ethical standards in all of the locations where they operate. Concepts & Connections 9.1 describes how IKEA enforces its ethical principles regarding child labor across its vast international supplier network.

The School of Ethical Universalism

According to the school of **ethical universalism,** some concepts of what is right and what is wrong are *universal* and transcend most all cultures, societies, and religions.[7] For instance, being truthful strikes a chord of what's right in the peoples of all nations. Ethical norms considered universal by many ethicists include honesty, trustworthiness, respecting the rights of others, practicing the Golden Rule, and avoiding unnecessary harm to workers or to the users of the

> **CORE CONCEPT**
>
> According to the school of **ethical universalism**, the same standards of what's ethical and what's unethical resonate with peoples of most societies, regardless of local traditions and cultural norms; hence, common ethical standards can be used to judge employee conduct in a variety of country markets and cultural circumstances.

company's product or service.[8] *To the extent there is common moral agreement about right and wrong actions and behaviors across multiple cultures and countries, there exists a set of universal ethical standards to which all societies, companies, and individuals can be held accountable.* The strength of ethical universalism is that it draws upon the collective views of multiple societies and cultures to put some clear boundaries on what constitutes ethical business behavior no matter what country market its personnel are operating in. This means that in those instances in which basic moral standards really do not vary significantly according to local cultural beliefs, traditions, or religious convictions, a multinational company can develop a code of ethics that it applies more or less evenly across its worldwide operations.

The School of Ethical Relativism

Beyond widely accepted ethical norms, many ethical standards likely vary from one country to another because of divergent religious beliefs, social customs, and prevailing political and economic doctrines (whether a country leans more toward a capitalistic market economy or one heavily dominated by socialistic or state-directed capitalism

Concepts Connections 9.1

IKEA'S GLOBAL SUPPLIER STANDARDS: MAINTAINING LOW COSTS WHILE FIGHTING THE ROOT CAUSES OF CHILD LABOR

Known for its stylish, ready-to-assemble home furnishings, IKEA has long relied on an extensive supplier network to manufacture its products and support its rapid global expansion. It has worked hard to develop a successful approach to encourage high ethical standards among its suppliers, including standards concerning the notoriously difficult issue of child labor.

IKEA's initial plan to combat the use of child labor by its suppliers involved (1) contracts that threatened immediate cancellation and (2) random audits by a third-party partner. Despite these safeguards, the company discovered that some of its Indian suppliers were still employing children. IKEA realized that this issue would crop up again and again if it continued to use low-cost suppliers in developing countries—a critical element in its cost-containment strategy.

To address this problem, IKEA developed and introduced its new code for suppliers, IWAY, that addresses social, safety, and environmental issues across its purchasing model. When faced with a supplier slip-up, IKEA works with the company to figure out and tackle the root cause of violations. Using child labor, for example, can signal bigger problems: production inefficiencies that require the lowest-cost labor, lack of alternative options for children such as school or supervised community centers, family health or income challenges that mean children need to become breadwinners, and so on. IKEA takes action to provide technical expertise to improve working conditions and processes, offer financing help at reasonable rates, run training programs onsite, and help develop resources and infrastructure in areas where its suppliers are based. The IKEA foundation also began focusing on these issues through partnerships with UNICEF and Save the Children aimed at funding long-term community programs that support

access to education, health care, and sustainable family incomes. It expects the programs will reach 15 million children by 2017.

IKEA's proactive approach has reduced some of the risks involved in relying on suppliers in developing countries. Through its approach, IKEA has been able to maintain its core strategic principles even when they seem to be at odds: low costs, great design, adherence to its ethical principles, and a commitment to a better world.

Note: Developed with Kiera O'Brien.

Sources: IKEA, "About the Company: This is IKEA," www.ikea.com/ms/en_US/this-is-ikea/people-and-planet/people-and-communities/ (accessed January 24, 2014); and Elain Cohen, "Banning Child Labor: The Symptom or the Cause?" CSR Newswire, www.csrwire.com/blog/posts/547-banning-child-labor-the-symptom-or-the-cause (accessed January 24, 2014).

CORE CONCEPT

According to the school of **ethical relativism**, different societal cultures and customs create divergent standards of right and wrong; thus, what is ethical or unethical must be judged in the light of local customs and social mores, and can vary from one culture or nation to another.

principles). The school of **ethical relativism** holds that when there are national or cross-cultural differences in what is deemed an ethical or unethical business situation, it is appropriate for local moral standards to take precedence over what the ethical standards may be in a company's home market. The thesis is that whatever a culture thinks is right or wrong really is right or wrong for that culture.[9]

A company that adopts the principle of ethical relativism and holds company personnel to local ethical standards necessarily assumes that what prevails as local morality is an adequate guide to ethical behavior. This can be ethically dangerous; it leads to the conclusion that if a country's culture generally accepts bribery or environmental degradation or exposing workers to dangerous conditions, then managers working in that country are free to engage in such activities. Adopting such a position places a company in a perilous position if it is required to defend these activities to its stakeholders in countries with higher ethical expectations. Moreover, from a global markets perspective, ethical relativism results in a maze of conflicting ethical standards for multinational companies. Imagine, for example, that a multinational company in the name of ethical relativism takes the position that it is acceptable for company personnel to pay bribes and kickbacks in countries where such payments are customary but forbids company personnel from making such payments in those countries where bribes and kickbacks are considered unethical or illegal. Having thus adopted conflicting ethical standards for operating in different countries, company managers have little moral basis for enforcing ethical standards companywide. Rather, the clear message to employees would be that the company has no ethical standards or principles of its own, preferring to let its practices be governed by the countries in which it operates.

> Codes of conduct based upon ethical relativism can be *ethically dangerous* by creating a maze of conflicting ethical standards for multinational companies.

Integrative Social Contracts Theory

Integrative social contracts theory provides a middle position between the opposing views of universalism and relativism.[10] According to **integrative social contracts theory,** the ethical standards a company should try to uphold are governed both by (1) a limited number of universal ethical principles that are widely recognized as putting legitimate ethical boundaries on actions and behavior in *all* situations and (2) the circumstances of local cultures, traditions, and shared values that further prescribe what constitutes ethically permissible behavior and what does not. This "social contract" by which managers in all situations have a duty to serve provides that *"first-order" universal ethical norms always take precedence over "second-order" local ethical norms in circumstances in which local ethical norms are more permissive.* Integrative social contracts theory offers managers in multinational companies clear guidance in resolving cross-country ethical differences: Those parts of the company's code of ethics that involve universal ethical norms must be enforced worldwide, but within these boundaries, there is room for ethical diversity and opportunity for host-country cultures to exert *some* influence in setting their own moral and ethical standards.

CORE CONCEPT

According to **integrative social contracts theory,** universal ethical principles based on collective views of multiple cultures combine to form a "social contract" that all employees in all country markets have a duty to observe. Within the boundaries of this social contract, there is room for host-country cultures to exert *some* influence in setting their own moral and ethical standards. However, *"first-order"* universal ethical norms always take precedence over *"second-order"* local ethical norms in circumstances in which local ethical norms are more permissive

A good example of the application of integrative social contracts theory involves the payment of bribes and kickbacks. Bribes and kickbacks seem to be common in some countries, but does this justify paying them? Just because bribery flourishes in a country does not mean that it is an authentic or legitimate ethical norm. Virtually all of the world's major religions (Buddhism, Christianity, Confucianism, Hinduism, Islam, Judaism, Sikhism, and Taoism) and all moral schools of thought condemn bribery and corruption.[11] Therefore, a multinational company might reasonably conclude that the right ethical standard is one of refusing to condone bribery and kickbacks on the part of company personnel no matter what the second-order local norm is and no matter what the sales consequences are.

Strategy, Corporate Social Responsibility, and Environmental Sustainability

LO4 Learn the concepts of corporate social responsibility and environmental sustainability and how companies balance these duties with economic responsibilities to shareholders.

The idea that businesses have an obligation to foster social betterment, a much-debated topic in the past 50 years, took root in the 19th century when progressive companies in the aftermath of the industrial revolution began to provide workers with housing and other amenities. The notion that corporate executives should balance the interests of all stakeholders—shareholders, employees, customers, suppliers, the communities in which they operated, and society at large—began to blossom in the 1960s.

What Do We Mean by Corporate Social Responsibility?

The essence of socially responsible business behavior is that a company should balance strategic actions to benefit shareholders against the *duty* to be a good corporate citizen. The underlying thesis is that company managers should display a *social conscience* in operating the business and specifically consider how management decisions and company actions affect the well-being of employees, local communities, the environment, and society at large.[12] Acting in a socially responsible manner thus encompasses more than just participating in community service projects and donating monies to charities and other worthy social causes. Demonstrating **corporate social responsibility (CSR)** also entails undertaking actions that earn trust and respect from all stakeholders—operating in an honorable and ethical manner, striving to make the company a great place to work, demonstrating genuine respect for the environment, and trying to make a difference in bettering society. Corporate social responsibility programs commonly involve:

> **CORE CONCEPT**
>
> **Corporate social responsibility (CSR)** refers to a company's *duty* to operate in an honorable manner, provide good working conditions for employees, encourage workforce diversity, be a good steward of the environment, and actively work to better the quality of life in the local communities in which it operates and in society at large.

- *Efforts to employ an ethical strategy and observe ethical principles in operating the business.* A sincere commitment to observing ethical principles is a necessary component of a CSR strategy simply because unethical conduct is incompatible with the concept of good corporate citizenship and socially responsible business behavior.

- *Making charitable contributions, supporting community service endeavors, engaging in broader philanthropic initiatives, and reaching out to make a difference in the lives of the disadvantaged.* Some companies fulfill their philanthropic obligations by spreading their efforts over a multitude of charitable and community activities; for instance, Microsoft and Johnson & Johnson support a broad variety of community, art, and social welfare programs. Others prefer to focus their energies more narrowly. McDonald's, for example, concentrates on sponsoring the Ronald McDonald House program (which provides a home away from home for the families of seriously ill children receiving treatment at nearby hospitals).

British Telecom gives 1 percent of its profits directly to communities, largely for education—teacher training, in-school workshops, and digital technology. Leading prescription drug maker GlaxoSmithKline and other pharmaceutical companies either donate or heavily discount medicines for distribution in the least-developed nations. Companies frequently reinforce their philanthropic efforts by encouraging employees to support charitable causes and participate in community affairs, often through programs that match employee contributions.

- *Actions to protect the environment and, in particular, to minimize or eliminate any adverse impact on the environment stemming from the company's own business activities.* Corporate social responsibility as it applies to environmental protection entails actively striving to be good stewards of the environment. This means using the best available science and technology to reduce environmentally harmful aspects of its operations *below the levels required by prevailing environmental regulations.* It also means putting time and money into improving the environment in ways that extend past a company's own industry boundaries—such as participating in recycling projects, adopting energy conservation practices, and supporting efforts to clean up local water supplies.

- *Actions to create a work environment that enhances the quality of life for employees.* Numerous companies exert extra effort to enhance the quality of life for their employees, both at work and at home. This can include onsite day care, flexible work schedules, workplace exercise facilities, special leaves to care for sick family members, work-at-home opportunities, career development programs and education opportunities, special safety programs, and the like.

- *Actions to build a workforce that is diverse with respect to gender, race, national origin, and other aspects that different people bring to the workplace.* Most large companies in the United States have established workforce diversity programs, and some go the extra mile to ensure that their workplaces are attractive to ethnic minorities and inclusive of all groups and perspectives.

The particular combination of socially responsible endeavors a company elects to pursue defines its **corporate social responsibility strategy.** Concepts & Connections 9.2 describes Burt's Bees' approach to corporate social responsibility. But the specific components emphasized in a CSR strategy vary from company to company and are typically linked to a company's core values. General Mills, for example, builds its CSR strategy around the theme of "nourishing lives" to emphasize its commitment to good nutrition as well as philanthropy, community building, and environmental protection.[13] Starbucks's CSR strategy includes four main elements (ethical sourcing, community service, environmental stewardship, and farmer support), all of which have touch points with the way that the company procures its coffee—a key aspect of its product differentiation strategy.[14]

> **CORE CONCEPT**
>
> A company's **corporate social responsibility strategy** is defined by the specific combination of socially beneficial activities it opts to support with its contributions of time, money, and other resources.

Corporate Social Responsibility and the Triple Bottom Line   CSR initiatives undertaken by companies are frequently directed at improving the company's "triple bottom line"—a reference to three types of performance metrics: *economic, social,*

Concepts & Connections 9.2

BURT'S BEES: A STRATEGY BASED ON CORPORATE SOCIAL RESPONSIBILITY

Burt's Bees is a leading company in natural personal care, offering nearly 200 products, including its popular beeswax lip balms and skin care creams. The brand has enjoyed tremendous success as consumers have begun to embrace all-natural, environmentally friendly products, boosting Burt's Bees' revenues to more than $160 million in 2012. Much of Burt's Bees' success can be attributed to its skillful use of corporate social responsibility (CSR) as a strategic tool to engage customers and differentiate itself from competitors.

While many companies have embraced corporate social responsibility, few companies have managed to integrate CSR as fully and seamlessly throughout their organizations as Burt's Bees. The company's business model is centered on a principle referred to as "The Greater Good," which specifies that all company practices must be socially responsible. The execution of this strategy is managed by a special committee dedicated to leading the organization to attain its CSR goals with respect to three primary areas: natural well-being, humanitarian responsibility, and environmental sustainability.

Natural well-being is focused on the ingredients used to create Burt's Bees products. Today, the average Burt's Bees product contains over 99 percent natural ingredients; by 2020, the brand expects to produce only 100 percent natural products.

Burt's Bees' humanitarian focus is centered on its relationships with employees and suppliers. A key part of this effort involves a mandatory employee training program that focuses on four key areas: outreach, wellness, world-class leadership, and the environment. Another is the company's responsible sourcing mission, which lays out a carefully prescribed set of guidelines for sourcing responsible suppliers and managing supplier relationships.

A focus on caring for the environment is clearly interwoven into all aspects of Burt's Bees. By focusing on environmentally efficient processes, the company uses its in-house manufacturing capability as a point of strategic differentiation.

Burt's Bees faced some consumer backlash when it was purchased by The Clorox Company, whose traditional image is viewed in sharp contrast to Burt's Bees' values. But while Burt's Bees is still only a small part of Clorox's total revenue, it has become its fastest-growing division.

Developed with Ross M. Templeton.

Sources: Company websites; Louise Story, "Can Burt's Bees Turn Clorox Green?" *New York Times,* January 6, 2008; Bill Chameides, "Burt's Bees Are Busy on the Sustainability Front," *Huffington Post,* June 25, 2010; Katie Bird, "Burt's Bees' International Performance Weaker Than Expected," CosmeticsDesign.com, January 6, 2011; "Burt's Bees, Marks & Spencer Share Staff Engagement Tactics," *EnvironmentalLeader.com,* May 31, 2011; http://blogs.newsobserver.com/business/investor-icahn-pushes-for-sale-of-burts-bees-parent-clorox#storylink=cpy (accessed March 1, 2012).

environmental. The goal is for a company to succeed simultaneously in all three dimensions.[15] The three dimensions of performance are often referred to in terms of the three pillars of "people, planet, and profit." The term *people* refers to the various social initiatives that make up CSR strategies, such as corporate giving and community involvement. *Planet* refers to a firm's ecological impact and environmental practices. The term *profit* has a broader meaning with respect to the triple bottom line than it does otherwise. It encompasses not only the profit a firm earns for its shareholders but also the economic impact the company has on society more generally. Triple-bottom-line (TBL) reporting is emerging as an increasingly important way for companies to make the results of their CSR strategies apparent to stakeholders.

What Do We Mean by Sustainability and Sustainable Business Practices?

The term *sustainability* is used in a variety of ways. In many firms, it is synonymous with corporate social responsibility; it is seen by some as a term that is gradually replacing CSR in the business lexicon. Indeed, sustainability reporting and TBL reporting are often one and the same. More often, however, the term takes on a more focused meaning, concerned with the relationship of a company to its *environment* and its use of *natural resources,* including land, water, air, minerals, and fossil fuels. Since corporations are the biggest users of finite natural resources, managing and maintaining these resources is critical for the long-term economic interests of corporations.

For some companies, this issue has direct and obvious implications for the continued viability of their business model and strategy. Pacific Gas and Electric has begun measuring the full carbon footprint of its supply chain to become not only "greener" but also a more efficient energy producer.[16] For other companies, the connection is less direct, but all companies are part of a business ecosystem whose economic health depends on the availability of natural resources. In response, most major companies have begun to change *how* they do business, emphasizing the use of **sustainable business practices,** defined as those capable of meeting the needs of the present without compromising the ability to meet the needs of the future.[17] Many have also begun to incorporate a consideration of environmental sustainability into their strategy-making activities.

Environmental sustainability strategies entail deliberate and concerted actions to operate businesses in a manner that protects and maybe even enhances natural resources and ecological support systems, guards against outcomes that will ultimately endanger the planet, and is therefore sustainable for centuries.[18] Sustainability initiatives undertaken by companies are directed at improving the company's triple bottom line—its performance on economic, environment, and social metrics.[19]

> **CORE CONCEPT**
>
> **Sustainable business practices** are those that meet the needs of the present without compromising the ability to meet the needs of the future.

> **CORE CONCEPT**
>
> **Environmental sustainability** involves deliberate actions to protect the environment, provide for the longevity of natural resources, maintain ecological support systems for future generations, and guard against the ultimate endangerment of the planet.

Unilever, a diversified producer of processed foods, personal care, and home cleaning products, is among the most committed corporations pursuing environmentally sustainable business practices. The company tracks 11 sustainable agricultural indicators in its processed-foods business and has launched a variety of programs to improve the environmental performance of its suppliers. Examples of such programs include special low-rate financing for tomato suppliers choosing to switch to water-conserving irrigation systems and training programs in India that have allowed contract cucumber growers to reduce pesticide use by 90 percent, while improving yields by 78 percent.

Unilever has also reengineered many internal processes to improve the company's overall performance on sustainability measures. For example, the company's factories have reduced water usage by 50 percent and manufacturing waste by 14 percent through the implementation of sustainability initiatives. Unilever has also redesigned packaging for many of its products to conserve natural resources and reduce the volume of consumer waste. The company's Suave shampoo bottles in the United States were reshaped to save almost 150 tons of plastic resin per year, which is the equivalent of 15 million fewer empty bottles. As the producer of Lipton Tea, Unilever is the world's largest purchaser of tea leaves; the company has committed to sourcing all of its tea from Rainforest Alliance Certified farms by 2015, due to Unilever's comprehensive triple-bottom-line approach toward sustainable farm management. Because 40 percent of Unilever's sales are made to consumers in developing countries, the company also is committed to addressing societal needs of consumers in those countries. Examples of the company's social performance include free laundries in poor neighborhoods in developing countries, start-up assistance for women-owned micro businesses in India, and free drinking water provided to villages in Ghana.

Sometimes cost savings and improved profitability are drivers of corporate sustainability strategies. Nike's sustainability initiatives have reduced energy consumption by 24 percent, emissions by 21 percent, water consumption by 13 percent, waste by 35 percent, and chemical usage by 20 percent between 2010 and 2015. Procter & Gamble's Swiffer cleaning system, one of the company's best-selling products, was developed as a sustainable product; not only does the Swiffer system have an earth-friendly design, but it also outperforms less ecologically friendly alternatives. Although most consumers probably aren't aware that the Swiffer mop reduces demands on municipal water sources, saves electricity that would be needed to heat water, and doesn't add to the amount of detergent making its way into waterways and waste treatment facilities, they are attracted to purchasing Swiffer mops because they prefer Swiffer's disposable cleaning sheets to filling and refilling a mop bucket and wringing out a wet mop until the floor is clean.

Crafting Corporate Social Responsibility and Sustainability Strategies

While striving to be socially responsible and to engage in environmentally sustainable business practices, there's plenty of room for every company to make its own statement about what charitable contributions to make, what kinds of community service projects to emphasize, what environmental actions to support, how to make the company a good place to work, where and how workforce diversity fits into the picture, and what else it will do to support worthy causes and projects that benefit society. A company may choose to focus its social responsibility strategy on generic social issues, but social responsibility strategies linked to its customer value proposition or key value chain activities may also help build competitive advantage.[20]

At Whole Foods Market, a $14.2 billion supermarket chain specializing in organic and natural foods, its environmental sustainability strategy is evident in almost every segment of its company value chain and is a big part of its differentiation strategy. The company's procurement policies encourage stores to purchase fresh fruits and vegetables from local farmers and screen processed-food items for more than 400 common ingredients that the company considers unhealthy or environmentally unsound. Spoiled food items are sent to regional composting centers rather than landfills, and all cleaning products used in its stores are biodegradable. The company also has created the Animal Compassion Foundation to develop natural and humane ways of raising farm animals and has converted all of its vehicles to run on biofuels.

CSR strategies that have the effect of both providing valuable social benefits and fulfilling customer needs in a superior fashion can lead to competitive advantage. Corporate social agendas that address generic social issues may help boost a company's reputation but are unlikely to improve its competitive strength in the marketplace.

The Business Case for Socially Responsible Behavior

It has long been recognized that it is in the enlightened self-interest of companies to be good citizens and devote some of their energies and resources to the betterment of employees, the communities in which they operate, and society in general.

In short, there are several reasons the exercise of corporate social responsibility is good business:

- *Such actions can lead to increased buyer patronage.* A strong, visible social responsibility strategy gives a company an edge in differentiating itself from rivals and in appealing to those consumers who prefer to do business with companies that are good corporate citizens. Whole Foods Market, TOMS, Green Mountain Coffee Roasters, and Patagonia have definitely expanded their customer bases because of their visible and well-publicized activities as socially conscious companies.

- *A strong commitment to socially responsible behavior reduces the risk of reputation-damaging incidents.* Companies that place little importance on operating in a socially responsible manner are more prone to scandal and embarrassment. Consumer, environmental, and human rights activist groups are quick to criticize businesses whose behavior they consider to be out of line, and they are adept at getting their message into the media and onto the Internet. For many years, Nike received stinging criticism for not policing sweatshop conditions in the Asian factories that produced Nike footwear, causing Nike co-founder and former CEO Phil Knight to observe, "Nike has become synonymous with slave wages, forced overtime, and arbitrary abuse."[21] Nike began an extensive effort to monitor conditions in the 800 factories of the contract manufacturers that produced Nike shoes. As Knight said, "Good shoes come from good factories and good factories have good labor relations." Nonetheless, Nike has continually been plagued by complaints from human rights activists that its monitoring procedures are flawed and that it is not doing enough to correct the plight of factory workers.

- *Socially responsible actions yield internal benefits (particularly for employee recruiting, workforce retention, and training costs) and can improve operational efficiency.* Companies with deservedly good reputations for contributing time and money to the betterment of society are better able to attract and retain employees compared to companies with tarnished reputations. Some employees just feel better about working for a company committed to improving society.[22] This can contribute to lower turnover and better worker productivity. Other direct and indirect economic benefits include lower costs for staff recruitment and training. For example, Starbucks is said to enjoy much lower rates of employee turnover because of its full benefits package for both full-time and part-time employees, management efforts to make Starbucks a great place to work, and the company's socially responsible practices. When a U.S. manufacturer of recycled paper, taking eco-efficiency to heart, discovered how to increase its fiber recovery rate, it saved the equivalent of 20,000 tons of waste paper—a factor that helped the company become the industry's lowest-cost producer. By helping two-thirds of its employees stop smoking and investing in a number of wellness programs for employees, Johnson & Johnson has saved $250 million on its health care costs over the past decade.[23]

- *Well-conceived social responsibility strategies work to the advantage of shareholders.* A two-year study of leading companies found that improving environmental compliance and developing environmentally friendly products can enhance earnings per share, profitability, and the likelihood of winning contracts. The stock prices of companies that rate high on social and environmental performance criteria have been found to perform 35 to 45 percent better than the average of the 2,500 companies comprising the Dow Jones Global Index.[24] A review of some 135 studies indicated there is a positive, but small, correlation between good corporate behavior and good financial performance; only 2 percent of the studies showed that dedicating corporate resources to social responsibility harmed the interests of shareholders.[25]

In sum, companies that take social responsibility seriously can improve their business reputations and operational efficiency while also reducing their risk exposure and encouraging loyalty and innovation. Overall, companies that take special pains to protect the environment (beyond what is required by law), are active in community affairs, and are generous supporters of charitable causes and projects that benefit society are more likely to be seen as good investments and as good companies to work for or do business with. Shareholders are likely to view the business case for social responsibility as a strong one, even though they certainly have a right to be concerned about whether the time and money their company spends to carry out its social responsibility strategy outweigh the benefits and reduce the bottom line by an unjustified amount.

 KEY POINTS

1. Business ethics concerns the application of ethical principles and standards to the actions and decisions of business organizations and the conduct of their personnel. Ethical principles in business are not materially different from ethical principles in general.

2. The three main drivers of unethical business behavior stand out:

   - Overzealous or obsessive pursuit of personal gain, wealth, and other selfish interests
   - Heavy pressures on company managers to meet or beat earnings targets
   - A company culture that puts profitability and good business performance ahead of ethical behavior

3. Business ethics failures can result in visible costs (fines, penalties, civil penalties arising from lawsuits, stock price declines), the internal administrative or "cleanup" costs, and intangible or less visible costs (customer defections, loss of reputation, higher turnover, harsher government regulations).

4. There are three schools of thought about ethical standards for companies with international operations:

   - According to the *school of ethical universalism,* the same standards of what's ethical and unethical resonate with peoples of most societies, regardless of local traditions and cultural norms; hence, common ethical standards can be used to judge the conduct of personnel at companies operating in a variety of international markets and cultural circumstances.
   - According to the *school of ethical relativism,* different societal cultures and customs have divergent values and standards of right and wrong; thus, what is ethical or unethical must be judged in the light of local customs and social mores and can vary from one culture or nation to another.

- According to *integrative social contracts theory,* universal ethical principles or norms based on the collective views of multiple cultures and societies combine to form a "social contract" that all individuals in all situations have a duty to observe. Within the boundaries of this social contract, local cultures can specify other impermissible actions; however, universal ethical norms always take precedence over local ethical norms.

5. The term *corporate social responsibility* concerns a company's *duty* to operate in an honorable manner, provide good working conditions for employees, encourage workforce diversity, be a good steward of the environment, and support philanthropic endeavors in local communities in which it operates and in society at large. The particular combination of socially responsible endeavors a company elects to pursue defines its corporate social responsibility (CSR) strategy.

6. The triple bottom line refers to company performance in three realms: economic, social, environmental. Increasingly, companies are reporting their performance with respect to all three performance dimensions.

7. *Sustainability* is a term that is used variously, but most often, it concerns a firm's relationship to the environment and its use of natural resources. Environmentally sustainable business practices are those capable of meeting the needs of the present without compromising the world's ability to meet future needs. A company's environmental sustainability strategy consists of its deliberate actions to protect the environment, provide for the longevity of natural resources, maintain ecological support systems for future generations, and guard against ultimate endangerment of the planet.

8. There are also solid reasons CSR and environmental sustainability strategies may be good business: they can be conducive to greater buyer patronage, reduce the risk of reputation-damaging incidents, provide opportunities for revenue enhancement, and lower costs. Well-crafted CSR and environmental sustainability strategies are in the best long-term interest of shareholders for the reasons above and because they can avoid or preempt costly legal or regulatory actions.

ASSURANCE OF LEARNING EXERCISES

1. Dell is widely known as an ethical company and has recently committed itself to becoming a more environmentally sustainable business. After reviewing the Corporate Social Responsibility section of Dell's website (www.dell.com/learn/us/en/uscorp1/cr?~ck=mn), prepare a list of 10 specific policies and programs that help the company bring about social and environmental change while still remaining innovative and profitable.

   LO1, LO4

2. Prepare a one- to two-page analysis of a recent ethics scandal using your university library's access to LexisNexis or other Internet resources. Your report should *(a)* discuss the conditions that gave rise to unethical business strategies and behavior and *(b)* provide an overview of the costs resulting from the company's business ethics failure.

   LO2, LO3

3. Based on the information provided in Concepts & Connections 9.2, explain how Burt's Bees' CSR strategy has contributed to its success in the marketplace. How are its various stakeholder groups affected by its commitment to social responsibility? How would you evaluate its triple-bottom-line performance?

   connect

   LO4

4. Go to www.google.com/green/ and read the company's latest sustainability initiatives. What are Google's key policies and actions that help it reduce its environmental footprint? How does the company integrate the idea of creating a "better web that's better for the environment" with its strategies for crating value and profits? How doe these initiatives help build competitive advantage?

   connect

   LO4

EXERCISES FOR SIMULATION PARTICIPANTS

LO1 1. Is your company's strategy ethical? Why or why not? Is there anything that your company has done or is now doing that could legitimately be considered as "shady" by your competitors?

LO4 2. In what ways, if any, is your company exercising corporate social responsibility? What are the elements of your company's CSR strategy? What changes to this strategy would you suggest?

LO3, LO4 3. If some shareholders complained that you and your co-managers have been spending too little or too much on corporate social responsibility, what would you tell them?

LO4 4. Is your company striving to conduct its business in an environmentally sustainable manner? What specific *additional* actions could your company take that would make an even greater contribution to environmental sustainability?

LO4 5. In what ways is your company's environmental sustainability strategy in the best long-term interest of shareholders? Does it contribute to your company's competitive advantage or profitability?

 ENDNOTES

1. James E. Post, Anne T. Lawrence, and James Weber, *Business and Society: Corporate Strategy, Public Policy, Ethics,* 10th ed. (New York: McGraw-Hill Irwin, 2002).

2. John F. Veiga, Timothy D. Golden, and Kathleen Dechant, "Why Managers Bend Company Rules," *Academy of Management Executive* 18, no. 2 (May 2004).

3. Jason M. Breslow, "Isn't This Illegal," *Frontline*, January 6, 2014, http://www.pbs.org/wgbh/pages/frontline/business-economy-financial-crisis/to-catch-a-trader/isnt-this-illegal/ (accessed July 13, 2015).

4. Ronald R. Sims and Johannes Brinkmann, "Enron Ethics (Or: Culture Matters More Than Codes)," *Journal of Business Ethics* 45, no. 3 (July 2003).

5. Andrew Ross, "SEC Charges Diamond Foods with Accounting Fraud," *SFGate*, January 13, 2014, http://www.sfgate.com/business/bottomline/article/SEC-charges-Diamond-Foods-with-accounting-fraud-5129129.php (accessed July 13, 2015).

6. Archie B. Carroll, "The Four Faces of Corporate Citizenship," *Business and Society Review* 100/101 (September 1998).

7. Mark S. Schwartz, "Universal Moral Values for Corporate Codes of Ethics," *Journal of Business Ethics* 59, no. 1 (June 2005).

8. Mark S. Schwartz, "A Code of Ethics for Corporate Codes of Ethics," *Journal of Business Ethics* 41, nos. 1–2 (November–December 2002).

9. T. L. Beauchamp and N. E. Bowie, *Ethical Theory and Business* (Upper Saddle River, NJ: Prentice Hall, 2001).

10. Thomas Donaldson and Thomas W. Dunfee, "Towards a Unified Conception of Business Ethics: Integrative Social Contracts Theory," *Academy of Management Review* 19, no. 2 (April 1994); Thomas Donaldson and Thomas W. Dunfee, *Ties That Bind: A Social Contracts Approach to Business Ethics* (Boston: Harvard Business School Press, 1999); Andrew Spicer, Thomas W. Dunfee, and Wendy J. Bailey, "Does National Context Matter in Ethical Decision Making? An Empirical Test of Integrative Social Contracts Theory," *Academy of Management Journal* 47, no. 4 (August 2004).

11. P. M. Nichols, "Outlawing Transnational Bribery Through the World Trade Organization," *Law and Policy in International Business* 28, no. 2 (1997).

12. Timothy M. Devinney, "Is the Socially Responsible Corporation a Myth? The Good, the Bad, and the Ugly of Corporate Social Responsibility," *Academy of Management Perspectives* 23, no. 2 (May 2009).

13. "General Mills' 2010 Corporate Social Responsibility Report Highlights New and Longstanding Achievements in the Areas of Health, Community, and Environment," CSRwire, April 15, 2010, www.csrwire.com/press_releases/29347-General-Mills-2010-Corporate-Social Responsibility-report-now-available.html.

14. Arthur A. Thompson and Amit J. Shah, "Starbucks' Strategy and Internal Initiatives to Return to Profitable Growth," *Crafting & Executing Strategy: The Quest for Competitive Advantage,* 18th ed. (New York: McGraw-Hill Irwin, 2012).

15. Gerald I.J.M. Zwetsloot and Marcel N. A. van Marrewijk, "From Quality to Sustainability," *Journal of Business Ethics* 55 (December 2004), pp. 79–82.

16. Tilde Herrera, "PG&E Claims Industry First with Supply Chain Footprint Project," *GreenBiz.com*, June 30, 2010, www.greenbiz.com/news/2010/06/30/pge-claims-industry-first-supply-chain-carbon-footprint-project.

17. This definition is based on the Brundt-land Commission's report, which described sustainable development in a like manner: United Nations General Assembly, "Report of the World Commission on Environment and Development: Our Common Future," 1987, www.un-documents.net/wced-ocf.htm, transmitted to the General Assembly as an annex to document A/42/427—"Development and International Cooperation: Environment" (accessed February 15, 2009).

18. Robert Goodland, "The Concept of Environmental Sustainability," *Annual Review of Ecology and Systematics* 26 (1995); J. G. Speth, *The Bridge at the End of the World: Capitalism, the Environment, and Crossing from Crisis to Sustainability* (New Haven, CT: Yale University Press, 2008).

19. Gerald I. J. M. Zwetsloot and Marcel N. A. van Marrewijk, "From Quality to Sustainability," *Journal of Business Ethics* 55 (December 2004); John B. Elkington, *Cannibals with Forks: The Triple Bottom Line of 21st Century Business* (Oxford: Capstone Publishing, 1997).

20. Michael E. Porter and Mark R. Kramer, "Strategy & Society: The Link Between Competitive Advantage and Corporate Social Responsibility," *Harvard Business Review* 84, no. 12 (December 2006).

21. Tom McCawley, "Racing to Improve Its Reputation: Nike Has Fought to Shed Its Image as an Exploiter of Third-World Labor Yet It Is Still a Target of Activists," *Financial Times,* December 2000.

22. N. Craig Smith, "Corporate Responsibility: Whether and How" *California Management Review* 45, no. 4 (Summer 2003), p. 63; see also World Economic Forum, "Findings of a Survey on Global Corporate Leadership," www.weforum.org/ corporatecitizenship (accessed October 11, 2003).

23. Michael E. Porter and Mark Kramer, "Creating Shared Value," *Harvard Business Review* 89, nos. 1–2 (January–February 2011).

24. James C. Collins and Jerry I. Porras, *Built to Last: Successful Habits of Visionary Companies,* 3rd ed. (London: HarperBusiness, 2002).

25. Joshua D. Margolis and Hillary A. Elfenbein, "Doing Well by Doing Good: Don't Count on It," *Harvard Business Review* 86, no. 1 (January 2008); Lee E. Preston and Douglas P. O'Bannon, "The Corporate Social-Financial Performance Relationship," *Business and Society* 36, no. 4 (December 1997); Ronald M. Roman, Sefa Hayibor, and Bradley R. Agle, "The Relationship Between Social and Financial Performance: Repainting a Portrait," *Business and Society* 38, no. 1 (March 1999); Joshua D. Margolis and James P. Walsh, *People and Profits* (Mahwah, NJ: Lawrence Erlbaum, 2001).

Superior Strategy Execution— Another Path to Competitive Advantage

LEARNING OBJECTIVES

LO1 Gain command of what managers must do to build an organization capable of good strategy execution.

LO2 Learn why resource allocation should always be based on strategic priorities.

LO3 Understand why policies and procedures should be designed to facilitate good strategy execution.

LO4 Understand how process management programs that drive continuous improvement help an organization achieve operating excellence.

LO5 Recognize the role of information and operating systems in enabling company personnel to carry out their strategic roles proficiently.

LO6 Learn how and why the use of well-designed incentives and rewards can be management's single most powerful tool for promoting operating excellence.

LO7 Gain an understanding of how and why a company's culture can aid the drive for proficient strategy execution.

LO8 Understand what constitutes effective managerial leadership in achieving superior strategy execution.

Once managers have decided on a strategy, the emphasis turns to converting it into actions and good results. Putting the strategy into place and getting the organization to execute it well call for different sets of managerial skills. Whereas crafting strategy is largely a market-driven and resource-driven activity, strategy implementation is an operations-driven activity primarily involving the management of people and business processes. Successful strategy execution depends on management's ability to direct organizational change and do a good job of allocating resources, building and strengthening competitive capabilities, instituting strategy-supportive policies, improving processes and systems, motivating and rewarding people, creating and nurturing a strategy-supportive culture, and consistently meeting or beating performance targets. While an organization's chief executive officer and other senior managers are ultimately responsible for ensuring that the strategy is executed successfully, it is middle and lower-level managers who must see to it that front line employees and work groups competently perform the strategy-critical activities that allow companywide performance targets to be met. *Hence, strategy execution requires every manager to think through the answer to the question "What does my area have to do to implement its part of the strategic plan, and what should I do to get these things accomplished effectively and efficiently?"*

> **CORE CONCEPT**
>
> Good strategy execution requires a *team effort.* All managers have strategy execution responsibility in their areas of authority, and all employees are active participants in the strategy execution.

The Principal Managerial Components of Strategy Execution

Executing strategy entails figuring out the specific techniques, actions, and behaviors that are needed to get things done and deliver results. The exact items that need to be placed on management's action agenda always have to be customized to fit the particulars of a company's situation. The hot buttons for successfully executing a low-cost provider strategy are different from those in executing a differentiation strategy. Implementing a new strategy for a struggling company in the midst of a financial crisis is different from improving strategy execution in a company where the execution is already pretty good. While there's no definitive managerial recipe for successful strategy execution that cuts across all company situations and all types of strategies, certain managerial bases have to be covered no matter what the circumstances. Eight managerial tasks crop up repeatedly in company efforts to execute strategy (see Figure 10.1):

1. Building an organization with the capabilities, people, and structure needed to execute the strategy successfully

2. Allocating ample resources to strategy-critical activities

3. Ensuring that policies and procedures facilitate rather than impede effective strategy execution

4. Adopting process management programs that drive continuous improvement in how strategy execution activities are performed

5. Installing information and operating systems that enable company personnel to perform essential activities

3. *Administer the reward system with scrupulous objectivity and fairness.* If performance standards are set unrealistically high or if individual/group performance evaluations are not accurate and well documented, dissatisfaction with the system will overcome any positive benefits.

4. *Tie incentives to performance outcomes directly linked to good strategy execution and financial performance.* Incentives should never be paid just because people are thought to be "doing a good job" or because they "work hard." An argument can be presented that exceptions should be made in giving rewards to people who've come up short because of circumstances beyond their control. The problem with making exceptions for unknowable, uncontrollable, or unforeseeable circumstances is that once good excuses start to creep into justifying rewards for subpar results, the door is open for all kinds of reasons actual performance has failed to match targeted performance.

5. *Make sure the performance targets that each individual or team is expected to achieve involve outcomes that the individual or team can personally affect.* The role of incentives is to enhance individual commitment and channel behavior in beneficial directions.

6. *Keep the time between achieving the target performance outcome and the payment of the reward as short as possible.* Weekly or monthly payments for good performance work much better than annual payments for employees in most job categories. Annual bonus payouts work best for higher-level managers and for situations in which target outcome relates to overall company profitability or stock price performance.

Once the incentives are designed, they have to be communicated and explained. Everybody needs to understand how their incentive compensation is calculated and how individual/group performance targets contribute to organizational performance targets.

Nonmonetary Rewards

Financial incentives generally head the list of motivating tools for trying to gain wholehearted employee commitment to good strategy execution and operating excellence. But most successful companies also make extensive use of nonmonetary incentives. Some of the most important nonmonetary approaches used to enhance motivation are listed here:[23]

- *Provide attractive perks and fringe benefits.* The various options include full coverage of health insurance premiums; college tuition reimbursement; paid vacation time; onsite child care; onsite fitness centers; telecommuting; and compressed workweeks (four 10-hour days instead of five 8-hour days).

- *Adopt promotion-from-within policies.* This practice helps bind workers to their employers and employers to their workers, plus it is an incentive for good performance.

- *Act on suggestions from employees.* Research indicates that the moves of many companies to push decision making down the line and empower employees increase employee motivation and satisfaction, as well as boost productivity.

- *Create a work atmosphere in which there is genuine sincerity, caring, and mutual respect among workers and between management and employees.* A "family" work environment in which people are on a first-name basis and there is strong camaraderie promotes teamwork and cross-unit collaboration.

- *Share information with employees about financial performance, strategy, operational measures, market conditions, and competitors' actions.* Broad disclosure and prompt communication send the message that managers trust their workers.

- *Have attractive office spaces and facilities.* A workplace environment with appealing features and amenities usually has decidedly positive effects on employee morale and productivity.

Concepts & Connections 10.3 presents specific examples of the motivational tactics employed by several prominent companies that have appeared on *Fortune*'s list of the "100 Best Companies to Work For" in America.

Instilling a Corporate Culture That Promotes Good Strategy Execution

Every company has its own unique culture. The character of a company's culture or work climate defines "how we do things around here," its approach to people management, and the "chemistry" that permeates its work environment. The meshing of shared core values, beliefs, ingrained behaviors and attitudes, and business principles constitutes a company's **corporate culture**. A company's culture is important because it influences the organization's actions and approaches to conducting business—in a very real sense, the culture is the company's organizational DNA.[24]

LO7 Gain an understanding of how and why a company's culture can aid the drive for proficient strategy execution.

> **CORE CONCEPT**
>
> **Corporate culture** is a company's internal work climate and is shaped by its core values, beliefs, and business principles. A company's culture is important because it influences its traditions, work practices, and style of operating

The psyche of corporate cultures varies widely. For instance, the bedrock of Walmart's culture is dedication to customer satisfaction, zealous pursuit of low costs and frugal operating practices, a strong work ethic, ritualistic Saturday-morning headquarters meetings to exchange ideas and review problems, and company executives' commitment to visiting stores, listening to customers, and soliciting suggestions from employees. At Nordstrom, the corporate culture is centered on delivering exceptional service to customers, where the company's motto is "Respond to unreasonable customer requests," and each out-of-the-ordinary request is seen as an opportunity for a "heroic" act by an employee that can further the company's reputation for unparalleled customer service. Nordstrom makes a point of promoting employees noted for their heroic acts and dedication to outstanding service. The company motivates its salespeople with a commission-based compensation system that enables Nordstrom's best salespeople to earn more than double what other department stores pay. Concepts & Connections 10.4 describes the corporate culture at W. L. Gore & Associates, the inventor of Gore-Tex.

High-Performance Cultures

Some companies have so-called "high-performance" cultures in which the standout cultural traits are a "can-do" spirit, pride in doing things right, no-excuses accountability, and a pervasive results-oriented work climate in which people go the extra mile to meet or beat stretch objectives. In high-performance cultures, there's a strong sense

Concepts & Connections 10.3

HOW THE BEST COMPANIES TO WORK FOR MOTIVATE AND REWARD EMPLOYEES

Companies design a variety of motivational and reward practices to create a work environment that energizes employees and promotes better strategy execution. Other benefits of a successful recognition system include high job satisfaction, high retention rates, and increased output. Here's a sampling of what some of the best companies to work for in America are doing to motivate their employees:

- Software developer SAS prioritizes work-life balance and mental health for its workforce of 7,000. The onsite health center it hosts for families of all employees maintains a staff of 53 medical and support personnel, including nurses, registered dietitians, lab technicians, and clinical psychologists. The sprawling headquarters also has a Frisbee golf course, indoor swimming pool, and walking and biking trails decorated with sculptures from the company's 4,000-item art collection. With such an environment, it should come as no surprise that 95 percent of employees report looking forward to heading to the office every day.

- Salesforce.com Inc., a global cloud-computing company based in San Francisco, has been listed by *Forbes* magazine as the most innovative company in America. Doubling its workforce from 5,000 to 10,000 in the past two years, Salesforce.com incentivizes new hires to work cooperatively with existing teams. The company's recognition programs include rewards for achievement both in the office and in the larger community. For example, in 2013, top sellers were awarded two-week trips to Bhutan for their dedication and results.

- DPR Construction is one of the nation's top-50 general contractors, serving such clients as Facebook, Pixar, and Genentech. The company fosters teamwork and equality across levels with features such as open-office floor plans, business cards with no titles, and a bonus plan for employees. DPR also prioritizes safety for its employees. In 1999, a craftsperson

who reached 30,000 consecutive safe work hours was rewarded with a new Ford F-150 truck. Management created a new safety award in his name that includes a plaque, a $2,000 trip, a 40-hour week off with pay, and a safety jacket with hours printed on it. In 2013, 13 craftspeople received this generous award for their dedication to safety.

- Hilcorp, an oil and gas exploration company, made headlines in 2011 for its shocking generosity. After reaching its five-year goal to double in size, the company gave every employee a $50,000 dream car voucher (or $35,000 in cash). Building on this success, later that year, Hilcorp announced an incentive program called Dream 2015. This plan promises to award every person in the company $100,000 in 2015 if certain goals are met.

Note: Developed with Meghan L. Cooney.

Sources: "100 Best Companies to Work For, 2014," *Fortune,* money. cnn.com/magazines/fortune/best-companies/ (accessed February 15, 2014); and company profiles, GreatRated! us.greatrated.com/sas (accessed February 24, 2014).

of involvement on the part of company personnel and emphasis on individual initiative and creativity. Performance expectations are clearly stated for the company as a whole, for each organizational unit, and for each individual. Issues and problems are promptly addressed—there's a razor-sharp focus on what needs to be done. A high-performance culture in which there's constructive pressure to achieve good results is a valuable contributor to good strategy execution and operating excellence. Results-oriented cultures are permeated with a spirit of achievement and have a good track record in meeting or beating performance targets.[25]

Concepts Connections 10.4

THE CULTURE THAT DRIVES INNOVATION AT W. L. GORE & ASSOCIATES

W. L. Gore & Associates is best known for Gore-Tex, the waterproof/breathable fabric so highly prized by outdoor enthusiasts. But the company has developed a wide variety of other revolutionary products, including Elixir guitar strings, Ride-On bike cables, and a host of medical devices such as cardiovascular patches and synthetic blood vessels. As a result, it is now one of the largest privately held companies in the United States, with roughly $3 billion in revenue and more than 10,000 employees in 30 countries worldwide.

When the company developed the core technology on which most of its more than 2,000 worldwide patents are based, its unique culture played a crucial role in allowing it to pursue multiple end-market applications simultaneously, enabling rapid growth from a niche business into a diversified multinational company. The company's culture is team-based and designed to foster personal initiative. It is described on the company's website as follows:

> There are no traditional organizational charts, no chains of command, nor predetermined channels of communication. Instead, we communicate directly with each other and are accountable to fellow members of our multi-disciplines teams. We encourage hands-on innovation, involving those closest to a project in decision making. Teams organize around opportunities and leaders emerge.

Personal stories posted on the website describe the discovery process behind a number of breakthrough products developed by particular teams at W. L. Gore & Associates. Employees are encouraged to use 10 percent of their time to tinker with new ideas and to take the long view regarding the idea's development. Promising ideas attract more people who are willing to work on them without orders from higher-ups. Instead, self-managing associates operating in self-developed teams are simply encouraged to pursue novel applications of Gore technology until they are fully commercialized or have had their potential exhausted. The encouragement comes from both the culture (norms and practices) of the organization and from a profit-sharing arrangement that allows employees to benefit directly from their successes.

This approach makes Gore a great place to work and has helped it attract, retain, and motivate top talent globally. Gore has been on *Fortune* magazine's list of the "100 Best Companies to Work For" in America for the past 15 years. It places similarly on the lists of other countries in which it operates, including the United Kingdom, Germany, France, Italy, and Sweden.

Developed with Kenneth P. Fraser.

Sources: Company websites; www.gore.com/en_xx/news/FORTUNE-2011.html; www.director.co.uk/magazine/2010/2_Feb/WLGore_63_06.html; www.fastcompany.com/magazine/89/open_gore.html.

The challenge in creating a high-performance culture is to inspire high loyalty and dedication on the part of employees such that they are energized to put forth their very best efforts to do things right. Managers have to take pains to reinforce constructive behavior, reward top performers, and purge habits and behaviors that stand in the way of good results. They must work at knowing the strengths and weaknesses of their subordinates so as to better match talent with task. In sum, there has to be an overall disciplined, performance-focused approach to managing the organization.

Adaptive Cultures

The hallmark of adaptive corporate cultures is willingness on the part of organizational members to accept change and take on the challenge of introducing and executing new strategies. In direct contrast to change-resistant cultures, **adaptive cultures** are very supportive of managers and employees at all ranks who propose or help initiate useful change. Internal entrepreneurship on the part of individuals and groups is encouraged and rewarded. Senior executives seek out, support, and promote individuals who

> As a company's strategy evolves, an adaptive culture is a definite ally in the strategy execution process.

exercise initiative, spot opportunities for improvement, and display the skills to take advantage of them. As in high-performance cultures, the company exhibits a proactive approach to identifying issues, evaluating the implications and options, and quickly moving ahead with workable solutions.

Technology companies, software companies, and Internet-based companies are good illustrations of organizations with adaptive cultures. Such companies thrive on change—driving it, leading it, and capitalizing on it (but sometimes also succumbing to change when they make the wrong move or are swamped by better technologies or the superior business models of rivals). Companies such as Twitter, Groupon, Apple, Google, and Intel cultivate the capability to act and react rapidly. They are avid practitioners of entrepreneurship and innovation, with a demonstrated willingness to take bold risks to create new products, new businesses, and new industries. To create and nurture a culture that can adapt rapidly to changing or shifting business conditions, they staff their organizations with people who are proactive, who rise to the challenge of change, and who have an aptitude for adapting.

In fast-changing business environments, a corporate culture that is receptive to altering organizational practices and behaviors is a virtual necessity. However, adaptive cultures work to the advantage of all companies, not just those in rapid-change environments. Every company operates in a market and business climate that is changing to one degree or another. *As a company's strategy evolves, an adaptive culture is a definite ally in the strategy implementation, strategy execution process as compared to cultures that have to be coaxed and cajoled to change.*

Unhealthy Corporate Cultures

The distinctive characteristic of an unhealthy corporate culture is the presence of counterproductive cultural traits that adversely impact the work climate and company performance.[26] Five particularly unhealthy cultural traits are a heavily politicized internal environment, hostility to change, an insular "not invented here" mind-set, a disregard for high ethical standards, and the presence of incompatible, clashing subcultures.

Politicized Cultures A politicized internal environment is unhealthy because political infighting consumes a great deal of organizational energy and often results in the company's strategic agenda taking a backseat to political maneuvering. In companies in which internal politics pervades the work climate, empire-building managers pursue their own agendas, and the positions they take on issues are usually aimed at protecting or expanding their turf. The support or opposition of politically influential executives and/or coalitions among departments with vested interests in a particular outcome typically weighs heavily in deciding what actions the company takes. All this maneuvering detracts from efforts to execute strategy with real proficiency and frustrates company personnel who are less political and more inclined to do what is in the company's best interests.

Change-Resistant Cultures Change-resistant cultures encourage a number of undesirable or unhealthy behaviors—avoiding risks, hesitation in pursuing emerging opportunities, and widespread aversion to continuous improvement in performing value chain activities. Change-resistant companies have little appetite for being first movers or fast followers, believing that being in the forefront of change is too risky and that acting too quickly increases vulnerability to costly mistakes. They are more inclined to adopt a wait-and-see posture, learn from the missteps of early movers, and then move forward cautiously with initiatives that are deemed safe. Hostility to change is most often found in companies with multilayered management bureaucracies that have enjoyed considerable market success in years past and that are wedded to the "We have done it this way for years" syndrome.

General Motors, IBM, Sears, and Eastman Kodak are classic examples of companies whose change-resistant bureaucracies have damaged their market standings and financial performance; clinging to what made them successful, they were reluctant to alter operating practices and modify their business approaches when signals of market change first sounded. As strategies of gradual change won out over bold innovation, all four lost market share to rivals that quickly moved to institute changes more in tune with evolving market conditions and buyer preferences. While IBM has made strides in building a culture needed for market success, Sears, GM, and Kodak are still struggling to recoup lost ground.

Insular, Inwardly Focused Cultures Sometimes a company reigns as an industry leader or enjoys great market success for so long that its personnel start to believe they have all the answers or can develop them on their own. Such confidence breeds arrogance—company personnel discount the merits of what outsiders are doing and what can be learned by studying best-in-class performers. Benchmarking and a search for the best practices of outsiders are seen as offering little payoff. The big risk of a must-be-invented-here mind-set and insular cultural thinking is that the company can underestimate the competencies and accomplishments of rival companies and overestimate its own progress—with a resulting loss of competitive advantage over time.

Unethical and Greed-Driven Cultures Companies that have little regard for ethical standards or that are run by executives driven by greed and ego gratification are scandals waiting to happen. Executives exude the negatives of arrogance, ego, greed, and an "ends-justify-the-means" mentality in pursuing overambitious revenue and profitability targets.[27] Senior managers wink at unethical behavior and may cross the line to unethical (and sometimes criminal) behavior themselves. They are prone to adopt accounting principles that make financial performance look better than it really is. Legions of companies have fallen prey to unethical behavior and greed, most notably Enron, Countrywide Financial, World Savings Bank, Stanford Financial Group, Rite Aid, and Marsh & McLennan, with executives being indicted and/or convicted of criminal behavior.

Incompatible Subcultures It is not unusual for companies to have multiple subcultures with values, beliefs, and ingrained behaviors and attitudes varying to some extent by department, geographic location, division, or business unit. These subcultures within a company don't pose a problem as long as the subcultures don't conflict with the overarching corporate work climate and are supportive of the strategy execution effort. Multiple subcultures become unhealthy when they are incompatible with each other or the overall corporate culture. The existence of conflicting business philosophies and values eventually leads to inconsistent strategy execution. Incompatible subcultures arise most commonly because of important cultural differences between a company's culture and those of a recently acquired company or because of a merger between companies with cultural differences. Cultural due diligence is often as important as financial due diligence in deciding whether to go forward on an acquisition or merger. On a number of occasions, companies have decided to pass on acquiring particular companies because of culture conflicts they believed would be hard to resolve.

Changing a Problem Culture

Changing a company culture that impedes proficient strategy execution is among the toughest management tasks. It is natural for company personnel to cling to familiar practices and to be wary, if not hostile, to new approaches toward how things are to be done. Consequently, it takes concerted management action over a period of time to root out certain unwanted behaviors and replace an out-of-sync culture with more effective ways of doing things. *The single most visible factor that distinguishes successful culture-change efforts from failed attempts is competent leadership at the top.* Great power is needed to force major cultural change and overcome the unremitting resistance of entrenched cultures—and great power is possessed only by the most senior executives, especially the CEO. However, while top management must lead the culture-change effort, instilling new cultural behaviors is a job for the whole management team. Middle managers and front line supervisors play a key role in implementing the new work practices and operating approaches, helping win rank-and-file acceptance of and support for the changes, and instilling the desired behavioral norms.

As shown in Figure 10.2, the first step in fixing a problem culture is for top management to identify those facets of the present culture that pose obstacles to executing new strategic initiatives. Second, managers have to clearly define the desired new behaviors and features of the culture they want to create. Third, managers have to convince company personnel why the present culture poses problems and why and how new behaviors and operating approaches will improve company performance. Finally, all the talk about remodeling the present culture has to be followed swiftly by visible, forceful actions on the part of management to promote the desired new behaviors and work practices.

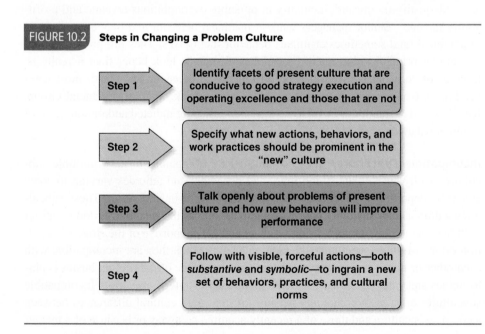

FIGURE 10.2   **Steps in Changing a Problem Culture**

Step 1 Identify facets of present culture that are conducive to good strategy execution and operating excellence and those that are not

Step 2 Specify what new actions, behaviors, and work practices should be prominent in the "new" culture

Step 3 Talk openly about problems of present culture and how new behaviors will improve performance

Step 4 Follow with visible, forceful actions—both *substantive* and *symbolic*—to ingrain a new set of behaviors, practices, and cultural norms

Making a Compelling Case for a Culture Change The place for management to begin a major remodeling of the corporate culture is by selling company personnel on the need for new-style behaviors and work practices. This means making a compelling case for why the company's new strategic direction and culture-remodeling efforts are in the organization's best interests and why company personnel should wholeheartedly join the effort to do things somewhat differently. This can be done by:

- Citing reasons the current strategy has to be modified and why new strategic initiatives are being undertaken. The case for altering the old strategy usually needs to be predicated on its shortcomings—why sales are growing slowly, why too many customers are opting to go with the products of rivals, why costs are too high, and so on. There may be merit in holding events where managers and other key personnel are forced to listen to dissatisfied customers or the complaints of strategic allies.

- Citing why and how certain behavioral norms and work practices in the current culture pose obstacles to good execution of new strategic initiatives.

- Explaining why new behaviors and work practices have important roles in the new culture and will produce better results.

Management's efforts to make a persuasive case for changing what is deemed to be a problem culture must be *quickly followed* by forceful, high-profile actions across several fronts. The actions to implant the new culture must be both substantive and symbolic.

Substantive Culture-Changing Actions No culture-change effort can get very far when leaders merely talk about the need for different actions, behaviors, and work practices. Company executives have to give the culture-change effort some teeth by initiating *a series of actions* that company personnel will see as *unmistakable support* for the change program. The strongest signs that management is truly committed to instilling a new culture include:

1. Replacing key executives who stonewall needed organizational and cultural changes.

2. Promoting individuals who have stepped forward to advocate the shift to a different culture and who can serve as role models for the desired cultural behavior.

3. Appointing outsiders with the desired cultural attributes to high-profile positions—bringing in new-breed managers sends an unambiguous message that a new era is dawning.

4. Screening all candidates for new positions carefully, hiring only those who appear to fit in with the new culture.

5. Mandating that all company personnel attend culture-training programs to better understand the culture-related actions and behaviors that are expected.

6. Designing compensation incentives that boost the pay of teams and individuals who display the desired cultural behaviors, while hitting change-resisters in the pocketbook.

7. Revising policies and procedures in ways that will help drive cultural change.

Symbolic Culture-Changing Actions There's also an important place for symbolic managerial actions to alter a problem culture and tighten the strategy–culture fit. The most important symbolic actions are those that top executives take to *lead by example.*

For instance, if the organization's strategy involves a drive to become the industry's low-cost producer, senior managers must display frugality in their own actions and decisions: inexpensive decorations in the executive suite, conservative expense accounts and entertainment allowances, a lean staff in the corporate office, few executive perks, and so on. At Walmart, all the executive offices are simply decorated; executives are habitually frugal in their own actions, and they are zealous in their own efforts to control costs and promote greater efficiency. At Nucor, one of the world's low-cost producers of steel products, executives fly coach class and use taxis at airports rather than limousines. Top executives must be alert to the fact that company personnel will be watching their actions and decisions to see if they are walking the talk.[28]

Another category of symbolic actions includes holding ceremonial events to single out and honor people whose actions and performance exemplify what is called for in the new culture. A point is made of holding events to celebrate each culture-change success. Executives sensitive to their role in promoting the strategy–culture fit make a habit of appearing at ceremonial functions to praise individuals and groups that get with the program. They show up at employee training programs to stress strategic priorities, values, ethical principles, and cultural norms. Every group gathering is seen as an opportunity to repeat and ingrain values, praise good deeds, and cite instances of how the new work practices and operating approaches have led to improved results.

Leading the Strategy Execution Process

LO8 Understand what constitutes effective managerial leadership in achieving superior strategy execution.

For an enterprise to execute its strategy in truly proficient fashion and approach operating excellence, top executives have to take the lead in the implementation/execution process and personally drive the pace of progress. They have to be out in the field, seeing for themselves how well operations are going, gathering information firsthand, and gauging the progress being made. Proficient strategy execution requires company managers to be diligent and adept in spotting problems, learning what obstacles lie in the path of good execution, and then clearing the way for progress: the goal must be to produce better results speedily and productively.[29] In general, leading the drive for good strategy execution and operating excellence calls for three actions on the part of the manager:

- Staying on top of what is happening and closely monitoring progress
- Putting constructive pressure on the organization to execute the strategy well and achieve operating excellence
- Initiating corrective actions to improve strategy execution and achieve the targeted performance results

Staying on Top of How Well Things Are Going

One of the best ways for executives to stay on top of strategy execution is by regularly visiting the field and talking with many different people at many different levels—a technique often labeled *managing by walking around* (MBWA). Walmart executives have had a long-standing practice of spending two to three days every week visiting stores and talking with store managers and employees. Jeff Bezos, Amazon.com's CEO, is noted for his frequent facilities visits and his insistence that other Amazon managers spend time in the trenches with their people to prevent overly abstract thinking and getting disconnected from the reality of what's happening.[30]

Most managers practice MBWA, attaching great importance to gathering information from people at different organizational levels about how well various aspects of the strategy execution are going. They believe facilities visits and face-to-face contacts give them a good feel for what progress is being made, what problems are being encountered, and whether additional resources or different approaches may be needed. Just as important, MBWA provides opportunities to give encouragement, lift spirits, shift attention from old to new priorities, and create excitement—all of which help mobilize organizational efforts behind strategy execution.

Putting Constructive Pressure on Organizational Units to Achieve Good Results and Operating Excellence

Managers have to be out front in mobilizing the effort for good strategy execution and operating excellence. Part of the leadership requirement here entails fostering a results-oriented work climate in which performance standards are high and a spirit of achievement is pervasive. Successfully leading the effort to foster a results-oriented, high-performance culture generally entails such leadership actions and managerial practices as:

- *Treating employees with dignity and respect.*
- *Encouraging employees to use initiative and creativity in performing their work.*
- *Setting stretch objectives* and clearly communicating an expectation that company personnel are to give their best in achieving performance targets.
- *Focusing attention on continuous improvement.*
- *Using the full range of motivational techniques and compensation incentives to reward high performance.*
- *Celebrating individual, group, and company successes.* Top management should miss no opportunity to express respect for individual employees and show appreciation of extraordinary individual and group effort.[31]

While leadership efforts to instill a spirit of high achievement into the culture usually accentuate the positive, there are negative reinforcers too. Low-performing workers and people who reject the results-oriented cultural emphasis have to be weeded out or at least moved to out-of-the-way positions. Average performers have to be candidly counseled that they have limited career potential unless they show more progress in the form of additional effort, better skills, and improved ability to deliver good results. In addition, managers whose units consistently perform poorly have to be replaced.

Initiating Corrective Actions to Improve Both the Company's Strategy and Its Execution

The leadership challenge of making corrective adjustments is twofold: deciding when adjustments are needed and deciding what adjustments to make. Both decisions are a normal and necessary part of managing the strategic management process, since no scheme for implementing and executing strategy can foresee all the events and problems that will arise.[32] There comes a time at every company when managers have to fine-tune or overhaul the company's strategy or its approaches to strategy execution and push for better results. Clearly, when a company's strategy or its execution efforts are not delivering good results, it is the leader's responsibility to step forward and push corrective actions.

KEY POINTS

Implementing and executing strategy is an operations-driven activity revolving around the management of people and business processes. The managerial emphasis is on converting strategic plans into actions and good results. *Management's handling of the process of implementing and executing the chosen strategy can be considered successful if and when the company achieves the targeted strategic and financial performance and shows good progress in making its strategic vision a reality.*

Like crafting strategy, executing strategy is a job for a company's whole management team, not just a few senior managers. Top-level managers have to rely on the active support and cooperation of middle and lower-level managers to push strategy changes into functional areas and operating units, and to see that the organization actually operates in accordance with the strategy on a daily basis.

Eight managerial tasks crop up repeatedly in company efforts to execute strategy:

1. *Building an organization capable of executing the strategy successfully.* Building an organization capable of good strategy execution entails three types of organization-building actions: *(a)* s*taffing the organization*—assembling a talented, can-do management team, and recruiting and retaining employees with the needed experience, technical skills, and intellectual capital, *(b) acquiring, developing, and strengthening key resources and capabilities* that will enable good strategy execution, and *(c) structuring the organization and work effort*—organizing value chain activities and business processes and deciding how much decision-making authority to push down to lower-level managers and front line employees.

2. *Allocating ample resources to strategy-critical activities.* Managers implementing and executing a new or different strategy must identify the resource requirements of each new strategic initiative and then consider whether the current pattern of resource allocation and the budgets of the various subunits are suitable.

3. *Ensuring that policies and procedures facilitate rather than impede effective strategy execution.* Anytime a company alters its strategy, managers should review existing policies and operating procedures, proactively revise or discard those that are out of sync, and formulate new ones to facilitate execution of new strategic initiatives.

4. *Adopting business processes that drive continuous improvement in how strategy execution activities are performed.* Reengineering core business processes and continuous improvement initiatives such as total quality management (TQM) or Six Sigma programs all aim at improved efficiency, lower costs, better product quality, and greater customer satisfaction.

5. *Installing information and operating systems that enable company personnel to perform essential activities.* Well-conceived, state-of-the-art support systems not only facilitate better strategy execution but also strengthen organizational capabilities enough to provide a competitive edge over rivals.

6. *Tying rewards directly to the achievement of performance objectives.* For an incentive compensation system to work well, *(a)* the monetary payoff should be a major piece of the compensation package, *(b)* the use of incentives should extend to all managers and workers, *(c)* the system should be administered with care and fairness, *(d)* the incentives should be linked to performance targets spelled out in the strategic plan, *(e)* each individual's performance targets should involve outcomes the person can personally affect, *(f)* rewards should promptly follow the determination of good performance, and *(g)* monetary rewards should be supplemented with liberal use of nonmonetary rewards.

7. *Fostering a corporate culture that promotes good strategy execution.* The psyche of corporate cultures varies widely. There are five types of unhealthy cultures: *(a)* those that are highly political and characterized by empire-building, *(b)* those that are change resistant, *(c)* those that are insular and inwardly focused, *(d)* those that are ethically unprincipled and are driven by greed, and *(e)* those that possess clashing subcultures that prevent a company from coordinating its strategy execution efforts. High-performance cultures and adaptive cultures both have positive features that are conducive to good strategy execution.

8. *Exerting the internal leadership needed to propel implementation forward.* Leading the drive for good strategy execution and operating excellence calls for three actions on the part of the manager: *(a)* staying on top of what is happening, closely monitoring progress, and learning what obstacles lie in the path of good execution; *(b)* putting constructive pressure on the organization to achieve good results and operating excellence; and *(c)* pushing corrective actions to improve strategy execution and achieve the targeted results.

▶ ASSURANCE OF LEARNING EXERCISES

1. The heart of Zara's strategy in the apparel industry is to outcompete rivals by putting fashionable clothes in stores quickly and maximizing the frequency of customer visits. Concepts & Connections 10.1 discusses the capabilities that the company has developed in the execution of its strategy. How do its capabilities lead to a quick production process and new apparel introductions? How do these capabilities encourage customers to visit its stores every few weeks? Does the execution of the company's site selection capability also contribute to its competitive advantage? Explain.   **LO1**

2. Implementing and executing a new or different strategy call for new resource allocations. Using your university's access to LexisNexis or EBSCO, search for recent articles that discuss how a company has revised its pattern of resource allocation and divisional budgets to support new strategic initiatives.   **LO2**

3. Netflix avoids the use of formal policies and procedures to better empower its employees to maximize innovation and productivity. The company goes to great lengths to hire, reward, and tolerate only what it considers mature, "A" player employees. How does the company's selection process affect its ability to operate without formal travel and expense policies, a fixed number of vacation days for employees, or a formal employee performance evaluation system?   **LO3**

4. Concepts & Connections 10.2 discusses Whirlpool Corporation's Operational Excellence initiative and its use of Six Sigma practices. How did the implementation of the program change the culture and mind-set of the company's personnel? List three tangible benefits provided by the program. Explain why a commitment to quality control is important in the appliance industry.   **LO4**

5. Company strategies can't be implemented or executed well without a number of information systems to carry on business operations. Using your university's access to LexisNexis or EBSCO, search for recent articles that discuss how a company has used real-time information systems and control systems to aid the cause of good strategy execution.   **LO5**

6. Concepts & Connections 10.3 provides a sampling of motivational tactics employed by several companies (many of which appear on *Fortune*'s list of the "100 Best Companies to Work For" in America). Discuss how rewards at SAS, Salesforce.com, DPR Construction, and Hilcorp aid in the strategy execution of each company.   McGraw Hill Education **connect**

     LO6

 **connect**

LO7

7. Go to the company website for REI (www.rei.com). Click on the Stewardship tab, and then click on some of the tabs below to learn more about the company's culture and values. What are the key features of its culture? Do features of REI's culture influence the company's ethical practices? If so, how?

LO8

8. Leading the strategy execution process involves staying on top of the situation and monitoring progress, putting constructive pressure on the organization to achieve operating excellence, and initiating corrective actions to improve the execution effort. Using your university's access to business periodicals, discuss a recent example of how a company's managers have demonstrated the kind of effective internal leadership needed for superior strategy execution.

EXERCISES FOR SIMULATION PARTICIPANTS

LO1

1. How would you describe the organization of your company's top management team? Is some decision making decentralized and delegated to individual managers? If so, explain how the decentralization works. Or are decisions made more by consensus, with all co-managers having input? What do you see as the advantages and disadvantages of the decision-making approach your company is employing?

LO2

2. Have you and your co-managers allocated ample resources to strategy-critical areas? If so, explain how these investments have contributed to good strategy execution and improved company performance.

LO6

3. Does your company have opportunities to use incentive compensation techniques? If so, explain your company's approach to incentive compensation. Is there any hard evidence you can cite that indicates your company's use of incentive compensation techniques has worked? For example, have your company's compensation incentives actually boosted productivity? Can you cite evidence indicating the productivity gains have resulted in lower labor costs? If the productivity gains have *not* translated into lower labor costs, then is it fair to say that your company's use of incentive compensation is a failure?

LO7

4. If you were making a speech to company personnel, what would you tell them about the kind of corporate culture you would like to have at your company? What specific cultural traits would you like your company to exhibit? Explain.

LO8

5. Following each decision round, do you and your co-managers make corrective adjustments in either your company's strategy or how well the strategy is being executed? List at least three such adjustments you made in the most recent decision round. What hard evidence (in the form of results relating to your company's performance in the most recent year) can you cite that indicates the various corrective adjustments you made either succeeded or failed to improve your company's performance?

ENDNOTES

1. Christopher A. Bartlett and Sumantra Ghoshal, "Building Competitive Advantage Through People," *MIT Sloan Management Review* 43, no. 2 (Winter 2002).

2. Justin Menkes, "Hiring for Smarts," *Harvard Business Review* 83, no. 11 (November 2005); Justin Menkes,

Executive Intelligence (New York: HarperCollins, 2005).

3. Larry Bossidy and Ram Charan, *Execution: The Discipline of Getting Things Done* (New York: Crown Business, 2002).

4. Jim Collins, *Good to Great* (New York: HarperBusiness, 2001).

5. C. Helfat et al., *Dynamic Capabilities: Understanding Strategic Change in Organizations* (Malden, MA: Blackwell, 2007); R. Grant, *Contemporary Strategy Analysis,* 6th ed. (Malden, MA: Blackwell, 2008).

6. G. Dosi, R. Nelson, and S. Winter, eds., *The Nature and Dynamics of*

Organizational Capabilities (Oxford, England: Oxford University Press, 2001).

7. B. Kogut and U. Zander, "Knowledge of the Firm, Combinative Capabilities, and the Replication of Technology," *Organization Science* 3, no. 3 (August 1992), pp. 383–97.

8. S. Karim and W. Mitchell, "Path-Dependent and Path-Breaking Change: Reconfiguring Business Resources Following Business," *Strategic Management Journal* 21, nos. 10–11 (October–November 2000), pp. 1061–82; L. Capron, P. Dussauge, and W. Mitchell, "Resource Redeployment Following Horizontal Acquisitions in Europe and North America, 1988–1992," *Strategic Management Journal* 19, no. 7 (July 1998), pp. 631–62.

9. Alfred Chandler, *Strategy and Structure* (Cambridge, MA: MIT Press, 1962).

10. Stanley E. Fawcett, Gary K. Rhoads, and Phillip Burnah, "People as the Bridge to Competitiveness: Benchmarking the 'ABCs' of an Empowered Workforce," *Benchmarking: An International Journal* 11, no. 4 (2004).

11. Rosabeth Moss Kanter, "Collaborative Advantage: The Art of the Alliance," *Harvard Business Review* 72, no. 4 (July–August 1994), pp. 96–108.

12. Michael Hammer and James Champy, *Reengineering the Corporation* (New York: HarperBusiness, 1993).

13. Gene Hall, Jim Rosenthal, and Judy Wade, "How to Make Reengineering Really Work," *Harvard Business Review* 71, no. 6 (November–December 1993).

14. M. Walton, *The Deming Management Method* (New York: Pedigree, 1986); J. Juran, *Juran on Quality by Design* (New York: Free Press, 1992); Philip Crosby, *Quality Is Free: The Act of Making Quality Certain* (New York: McGraw-Hill, 1979); S. George, *The Baldrige Quality System* (New York: John Wiley & Sons, 1992); Mark J. Zbaracki, "The Rhetoric and Reality of Total Quality Management," *Administrative Science Quarterly* 43, no. 3 (September 1998).

15. Robert T. Amsden, Thomas W. Ferratt, and Davida M. Amsden, "TQM: Core Paradigm Changes," *Business Horizons* 39, no. 6 (November–December 1996).

16. Peter S. Pande and Larry Holpp, *What Is Six Sigma?* (New York: McGraw-Hill, 2002); Jiju Antony, "Some Pros and Cons of Six Sigma: An Academic Perspective," *The TQM Magazine* 16, no. 4 (2004); Peter S. Pande, Robert P. Neuman, and Roland R. Cavanagh, *The Six Sigma Way: How GE, Motorola and Other Top Companies Are Honing Their Performance* (New York: McGraw-Hill, 2000); Joseph Gordon and M. Joseph Gordon, Jr., *Six Sigma Quality for Business and Manufacture* (New York: Elsevier, 2002); Godecke Wessel and Peter Burcher, "Six Sigma for Small and Medium-Sized Enterprises," *The TQM Magazine* 16, no. 4 (2004).

17. Based on information posted at www.sixsigma.com, November 4, 2002.

18. Kennedy Smith, "Six Sigma for the Service Sector," *Quality Digest Magazine,* May 2003, www.qualitydigest.com (accessed September 28, 2003).

19. Del Jones, "Taking the Six Sigma Approach," *USA Today,* October 31, 2002.

20. As quoted in "A Dark Art No More," *The Economist* 385, no. 8550 (October 13, 2007).

21. Charles A. O'Reilly and Michael L. Tushman, "The Ambidextrous Organization," *Harvard Business Review* 82, no. 4 (April 2004).

22. See Steven Kerr, "On the Folly of Rewarding A while Hoping for B," *Academy of Management Executive* 9, no. 1 (February 1995); Steven Kerr, "Risky Business: The New Pay Game," *Fortune,* July 22, 1996; Doran Twer, "Linking Pay to Business Objectives," *Journal of Business Strategy* 15, no. 4 (July–August 1994).

23. Jeffrey Pfeffer and John F. Veiga, "Putting People First for Organizational Success," *Academy of Management Executive* 13, no. 2 (May 1999); Linda K. Stroh and Paula M. Caligiuri, "Increasing Global Competitiveness Through Effective People Management," *Journal of World Business* 33, no. 1 (Spring 1998); articles in *Fortune* on the 100 best companies to work for (various issues).

24. Joanne Reid and Victoria Hubbell, "Creating a Performance Culture," *Ivey Business Journal* 69, no. 4 (March–April 2005).

25. Jay B. Barney and Delwyn N. Clark, *Resource-Based Theory: Creating and Sustaining Competitive Advantage* (New York: Oxford University Press, 2007).

26. John P. Kotter and James L. Heskett, *Corporate Culture and Performance* (New York: Free Press, 1992).

27. Kurt Eichenwald, *Conspiracy of Fools: A True Story* (New York:Broadway Books, 2005).

28. Judy D. Olian and Sara L. Rynes, "Making Total Quality Work: Aligning Organizational Processes, Performance Measures, and Stakeholders," *Human Resource Management* 30, no. 3 (Fall 1991).

29. Larry Bossidy and Ram Charan, *Confronting Reality: Doing What Matters to Get Things Right* (New York: Crown Business, 2004); Larry Bossidy and Ram Charan, *Execution: The Discipline of Getting Things Done* (New York: Crown Business, 2002); John P. Kotter, "Leading Change: Why Transformation Efforts Fail," *Harvard Business Review* 73, no. 2 (March–April 1995); Thomas M. Hout and John C. Carter, "Getting It Done: New Roles for Senior Executives," *Harvard Business Review* 73, no. 6 (November–December 1995); Sumantra Ghoshal and Christopher A. Bartlett, "Changing the Role of Top Management: Beyond Structure to Processes," *Harvard Business Review* 73, no. 1 (January–February 1995).

30. Fred Vogelstein, "Winning the Amazon Way," *Fortune,* May 26, 2003.

31. Jeffrey Pfeffer, "Producing Sustainable Competitive Advantage Through the Effective Management of People," *Academy of Management Executive* 9, no. 1 (February 1995).

32. Cynthia A. Montgomery, "Putting Leadership Back into Strategy," *Harvard Business Review* 86, no. 1 (January 2008).

APPENDIX

Ratio	How Calculated	What It Shows
Profitability Ratios		
1. Gross profit margin	$\dfrac{\text{Sales revenues} - \text{Cost of goods sold}}{\text{Sales revenues}}$	Shows the percentage of revenues available to cover operating expenses and yield a profit. Higher is better, and the trend should be upward.
2. Operating profit margin (or return on sales)	$\dfrac{\text{Sales revenues} - \text{Operating expenses}}{\text{Sales revenues}}$ or $\dfrac{\text{Operating income}}{\text{Sales revenues}}$	Shows the profitability of current operations without regard to interest charges and income taxes. Higher is better, and the trend should be upward.
3. Net profit margin (or net return on sales)	$\dfrac{\text{Profits after taxes}}{\text{Sales revenues}}$	Shows after-tax profits per dollar of sales. Higher is better, and the trend should be upward.
4. Total return on assets	$\dfrac{\text{Profits after taxes} + \text{Interest}}{\text{Total assets}}$	A measure of the return on total monetary investment in the enterprise. Interest is added to after-tax profits to form the numerator since total assets are financed by creditors as well as by stockholders. Higher is better, and the trend should be upward.
5. Net return on total assets (ROA)	$\dfrac{\text{Profits after taxes}}{\text{Total assets}}$	A measure of the return earned by stockholders on the firm's total assets. Higher is better, and the trend should be upward.
6. Return on stockholder's equity	$\dfrac{\text{Profits after taxes}}{\text{Total stockholders' equity}}$	Shows the return stockholders are earning on their capital investment in the enterprise. A return in the 12–15% range is "average," and the trend should be upward.
7. Return on invested capital (ROIC) – sometimes referred to as return on capital (ROCE)	$\dfrac{\text{Profits after taxes}}{\text{Long term debt} + \text{Total stockholders' equity}}$	A measure of the return shareholders are earning on the long-term monetary capital invested in the enterprise. Higher is better, and the trend should be upward.
8. Earnings per share (EPS)	$\dfrac{\text{Profits after taxes}}{\text{Number of shares of common stock outstanding}}$	Shows the earnings for each share of common stock outstanding. The trend should be upward, and the bigger the annual percentage gains, the better.
Liquidity Ratios		
1. Current ratio	$\dfrac{\text{Current assets}}{\text{Current liabilities}}$	Shows a firm's ability to pay current liabilities using assets that can be converted to cash in the near term. Ratio should definitely be higher than 1.0; ratios of 2 or higher are better still.
2. Working capital	$\text{Current assets} - \text{Current liabilities}$	Bigger amounts are better because the company has more internal funds available to (1) pay its current liabilities on a timely basis and (2) finance inventory expansion, additional accounts receivable, and a larger base of operations without resorting to borrowing or raising more equity capital.
Leverage Ratios		
1. Total debt-to-assets ratio	$\dfrac{\text{Total debt}}{\text{Total assets}}$	Measures the extent to which borrowed funds (both short-term loans and long-term debt) have been used to finance the firm's operations. A low fraction or ratio is better—a high fraction indicates overuse of debt and greater risk of bankruptcy.

Ratio	How Calculated	What It Shows
2. Long-term debt-to-capital ratio	$\dfrac{\text{Long-term debt}}{\text{Long-term debt} + \text{Total stockholders' equity}}$	An important measure of creditworthiness and balance sheet strength. It indicates the percentage of capital investment in the enterprise that has been financed by both long-term lenders and stockholders. A ratio below 0.25 is usually preferable since monies invested by stockholders account for 75% or more of the company's total capital. The lower the ratio, the greater the capacity to borrow additional funds. Debt-to-capital ratios above 0.50 and certainly above 0.75 indicate a heavy and perhaps excessive reliance on long-term borrowing, lower creditworthiness, and weak balance sheet strength.
3. Debt-to-equity ratio	$\dfrac{\text{Total debt}}{\text{Total stockholders' equity}}$	Shows the balance between debt (funds borrowed both short-term and long-term) and the amount that stockholders have invested in the enterprise. The farther the ratio is below 1.0, the greater the firm's ability to borrow additional funds. Ratios above 1.0 and definitely above 2.0 put creditors at greater risk, signal weaker balance sheet strength, and often result in lower credit ratings.
4. Long-term debt-to-equity ratio	$\dfrac{\text{Long-term debt}}{\text{Total stockholders' equity}}$	Shows the balance between long-term debt and stockholders' equity in the firm's *long-term* capital structure. Low ratios indicate greater capacity to borrow additional funds if needed.
5. Times-interest-earned (or coverage) ratio	$\dfrac{\text{Operating income}}{\text{Interest expenses}}$	Measures the ability to pay annual interest charges. Lenders usually insist on a minimum ratio of 2.0, but ratios progressively above 3.0 signal progressively better creditworthiness.

Activity Ratios

Ratio	How Calculated	What It Shows
1. Days of inventory	$\dfrac{\text{Inventory}}{\text{Cost of goods sold} \div 365}$	Measures inventory management efficiency. Fewer days of inventory are usually better.
2. Inventory turnover	$\dfrac{\text{Cost of goods sold}}{\text{Inventory}}$	Measures the number of inventory turns per year. Higher is better.
3. Average collection period	$\dfrac{\text{Accounts receivable}}{\text{Total sales} \div 365}$ or $\dfrac{\text{Accounts receivable}}{\text{Average daily sales}}$	Indicates the average length of time the firm must wait after making a sale to receive cash payment. A shorter collection time is better.

Other Important Measures of Financial Performance

Ratio	How Calculated	What It Shows
1. Dividend yield on common stock	$\dfrac{\text{Annual dividends per share}}{\text{Current market price per share}}$	A measure of the return that shareholders receive in the form of dividends. A "typical" dividend yield is 2–3%. The dividend yield for fast-growth companies is often below 1% (maybe even 0); the dividend yield for slow-growth companies can run 4–5%.
2. Price-earnings ratio	$\dfrac{\text{Current market price per share}}{\text{Earnings per share}}$	P-E ratios above 20 indicate strong investor confidence in a firm's outlook and earnings growth; firms whose future earnings are at risk or likely to grow slowly typically have ratios below 12.
3. Dividend payout ratio	$\dfrac{\text{Annual dividends per share}}{\text{Earnings per share}}$	Indicates the percentage of after-tax profits paid out as dividends.
4. Internal cash flow	After tax profits + Depreciation	A quick and rough estimate of the cash a company's business is generating after payment of operating expenses, interest, and taxes. Such amounts can be used for dividend payments or funding capital expenditures.
5. Free cash flow	After tax profits + Depreciation − Capital expenditures − Dividends	A quick and rough estimate of the cash a company's business is generating after payment of operating expenses, interest, taxes, dividends, and desirable reinvestments in the business. The larger a company's free cash flow, the greater is its ability to internally fund new strategic initiatives, repay debt, make new acquisitions, repurchase shares of stock, or increase dividend payments.

BillCutterz.com: Business Model, Strategy, and the Challenges of Exponential Growth

connect

JOHN E. GAMBLE Texas A&M University–Corpus Christi

RANDALL D. HARRIS Texas A&M University–Corpus Christi

Barry Gross, founder and president of BillCutterz.com, celebrated his birthday on January 21, 2014, by inviting friends and family to his Corpus Christi, Texas, home to watch the airing of his previously taped interview with Diane Sawyer on *ABC World News Tonight*. His four-year-old bill negotiation company, BillCutterz.com, was being featured on that evening's "Real Money" segment, which explained how his company was saving its customers hundreds or thousands of dollars each year on their monthly bills. The segment described how BillCutterz.com negotiated on behalf of its enrolled customers to reduce the amounts of their cable, Internet, mobile phone, and other service provider bills by as much as 50 percent. BillCutterz.com's negotiation tactic centered on convincing the provider that it was less costly to lower the customer's monthly bill than to go through the expense of acquiring a new customer to replace a dissatisfied customer. The segment also featured interviews with BillCutterz.com customers who discussed how the company's bill negotiation service had saved them $1,500 or more per year on their monthly expenses.

Those gathered to celebrate Gross's birthday marveled at how much his customers benefited from the service provided by his company, and many asked about how they could enroll to have their bills lowered as well. Gross explained that customers could enroll at BillCutterz.com and upload copies of their most recent bills to begin the process. After telling his guests more about his business and enjoying the evening, he received a call from an employee telling him that 6,500 new customers had enrolled and 19,500 bills had been uploaded in the first one-and-a-half hours since the segment aired. Gross expected the segment to boost enrollees, but he was not prepared for such a spike in new business.

Within days of the *ABC World News Tonight* segment, Gross also appeared live on *Fox Business News* to discuss his company's approach to saving money for its customers on their monthly bills. The exposure from the two news segments brought in more than 30,000 new enrollees by February 2014. The vast increase in enrollees immediately focused Gross's activities on recruiting, selecting, and training new employees and ensuring that the bills of its new customers were properly negotiated to receive the greatest possible savings. At the end of its first quarter in 2014, BillCutterz.com was adding 20 to 30 new enrollments every day and had seen its revenues increase by more than 400 percent over the same period in 2013. However, it was far too early to tell if the company's business model, strategy, and operating approaches could withstand the challenges of exponential growth.

Company History

BillCutterz.com was launched in May 2009 when Barry Gross decided to pursue a business opportunity presented to him by a close friend. During a visit with long-time friend and mortgage banker Mindy Niles, Gross asked if she could give him advice for lowering his mortgage payment. Niles told Gross he should request that his lender eliminate his PMI insurance requirement since the equity in his home had grown since the time of purchase. Gross called his lender and was able to save $180 per month.

volume, BillCutterz.com could enter into prenegotiated savings agreements with high-volume service providers such as Verizon, T-Mobile, Time Warner Cable, and AT&T. Such agreements would eliminate the need for individual negotiations unless an account involved a large amount needing nonroutine negotiation.

Until Gross was able to modify the company's business model and strategy to better accommodate scale, much of his daily effort would be put into selecting and training new employees. In addition, the company had grown to such a size that it would soon become a graduate of the Coastal Bend Business Innovation Center. Ample office space was available in the community for the growing company, but relocating to a new space would be another task that would take away from Barry's time and would alter the company's cost structure. The company's meteoric growth had made it a standout among entrepreneurial startups, but its rise had also created a need for new strategies and operating practices to flourish as an established business.

ENDNOTES

[1] M. Kon, "Customer Churn: Stop It Before It Starts," *Mercer Management Journal* 17 (2005), pp. 53–60.

[2] Ibid.

[3] Ibid.

[4] Ibid.

Whole Foods Market in 2014: Vision, Core Values, and Strategy

ARTHUR A. THOMPSON   The University of Alabama

Founded in 1980, Whole Foods Market had evolved from a local supermarket for natural and health foods in Austin, Texas, into the most visible and best-known leader of the natural and organic food movement across the United States, helping the industry gain acceptance among growing numbers of consumers concerned about the food they ate. The company had 2013 sales revenues of $12.9 billion and in spring 2014 had 379 stores in the United States, Canada, and Great Britain. Over the past 22 years, sales had grown at a compound annual rate of 25.2 percent, and profits had grown at a compound average rate of 30.4 percent. In 2013, Whole Foods was the eighth-largest food and drug retailer in the United States (up from 21st in 2009) and ranked 232nd on *Fortune* magazine's 2013 list of the 500 largest companies in the United States. Over 7 million customers visited Whole Foods stores in 41 U.S. states, Canada, and the United Kingdom each week, and Whole Foods was the number-two retail brand on Twitter, with 4 million followers.

Whole Foods' mission was "to promote the vitality and well-being of all individuals by supplying the highest quality, most wholesome foods available." The core of the mission involved promoting organically grown foods, healthy eating, and the sustainability of the world's entire ecosystem. For many years, the company used the slogan "Whole Foods, Whole People, Whole Planet" to capture the essence of its mission. John Mackey, the company's cofounder and co-CEO, was convinced that Whole Foods' rapid growth and market success had much to do with its having "remained a uniquely mission-driven company—highly selective about what we sell, dedicated to our core values and stringent quality standards, and committed to sustainable agriculture."

Mackey's vision was for Whole Foods to become an international brand synonymous with carrying the highest-quality natural and organic foods available and being the best food retailer in every community in which a Whole Foods store was located. The company sought to offer the highest-quality, least processed, most flavorful and naturally preserved foods available, and it marketed them in appealing store environments that made shopping at Whole Foods interesting and enjoyable. Mackey believed that marketing high-quality natural and organic foods to more and more customers in more and more communities would, over time, gradually transform the diets of individuals in a manner that would help them live longer, healthier, more pleasurable lives.

The Natural and Organic Foods Industry

The retail grocery industry in the United States—which included conventional supermarkets, supercenters, and limited-assortment and natural/gourmet-positioned supermarkets—had sales of approximately $603 billion in 2012, up 3 percent over 2011.[1] Within this broader category, retail sales of food products labeled "natural" were approximately $81 billion, a 10 percent increase over the prior year.[2]

Foods labeled "organic" generated estimated retail sales across North America approaching $35 billion in 2013, up from $9 billion in 2002. *Natural foods* were (1) minimally processed, (2) largely or completely free of artificial ingredients, preservatives, and other non-naturally occurring chemicals, and (3) as near to their whole, natural state as possible. The U.S. Department of Agriculture's Food and Safety Inspection Service defined *natural food* as "a product containing no artificial ingredient or added color and that is minimally processed." *Organic foods* were a special subset of the natural food category and had to be grown and processed without the use of pesticides, antibiotics, hormones, synthetic chemicals, artificial fertilizers, preservatives, dyes or additives, or genetic engineering. Organic foods included fresh fruits and vegetables, meats, and processed foods that had been produced using:

1. Agricultural management practices that promoted a healthy and renewable ecosystem and that used no genetically engineered seeds or crops, petroleumbased fertilizers, fertilizers made from sewage sludge, or long-lasting pesticides, herbicides, and fungicides.

2. Livestock management practices that involved organically grown feed, fresh air and outdoor access for the animals, and no use of antibiotics or growth hormones.

3. Food processing practices that protected the integrity of the organic product and disallowed the use of radiation, genetically modified ingredients, or synthetic preservatives.

Organic food sales accounted for 5 to 6 percent of total U.S. retail sales of food and beverages in 2013.

In 1990, passage of the Organic Food Production Act started the process of establishing national standards for organically grown products in the United States, a movement that included farmers, food activists, conventional food producers, and consumer groups. In October 2002, the U.S. Department of Agriculture (USDA) officially established labeling standards for organic products, overriding both the patchwork of inconsistent state regulations for what could be labeled as organic and the different rules of some 43 agencies for certifying organic products. The new USDA regulations established four categories of food with organic ingredients, with varying levels of organic purity:

1. *100 percent organic products.* Such products were usually whole foods, such as fresh fruits and vegetables, grown by organic methods— which meant that the product had been grown without the use of synthetic pesticides or sewage-based fertilizers, had not been subjected to irradiation, and had not been genetically modified or injected with bioengineered organisms, growth hormones, or antibiotics. Products that were 100 percent organic could carry the green USDA organic certification seal provided the merchant could document that the food product had been organically grown (usually by a certified-organic producer).

2. *Organic products.* Such products, often processed, had to have at least 95 percent organically certified ingredients. These could also carry the green USDA organic certification seal.

3. *Made with organic ingredients.* Such products had to have at least 70 percent organic ingredients; they could be labeled "made with organic ingredients" but could not display the USDA seal.

4. *All other products with organic ingredients.* Products with less than 70 percent organic ingredients could not use the word *organic* on the front of a package, but organic ingredients could be listed among other ingredients in a less prominent part of the package.

The USDA's labeling standards were intended to enable shoppers who were ingredient-conscious or wanted to buy pesticide-free or support sustainable agricultural practices to evaluate product labels on which the word *organic* appeared. The standards were not meant to imply anything about the health or safety of organic products (because there was no credible scientific evidence that organic products were more nutritious or safer to eat than conventionally grown products). The USDA also issued regulations requiring documentation on the part of growers, processors, exporters, importers, shippers, and merchants to verify that they were certified to grow, process, or handle organic products carrying the USDA's organic seal. In 2003, Whole Foods was designated as the first national "Certified Organic" grocer by Quality Assurance International, a federally recognized independent third-party certification organization.

Major food processing companies such as Kraft, General Mills, Danone (the parent of Dannon Yogurt), Dean Foods, and Kellogg had all purchased organic food producers in an effort to capitalize on growing consumer interest in purchasing organic products. Heinz had introduced an organic ketchup and bought a 19 percent stake in Hain Celestial Group, one of the largest organic and natural food producers. Campbell Soup had introduced organic tomato juice. Starbucks, Green Mountain Coffee, and several other premium coffee marketers were marketing organically grown coffees; Coca-Cola's Odwalla juices were organic; Del Monte and Hunt's were marketing organic canned tomatoes; and Tyson Foods and several other chicken producers had introduced organic chicken products. Producers of organically grown beef were selling all they could produce in 2011–2013, with demand growing an estimated 20 to 25 percent annually; headed into 2014, the market share of natural, organic, and grass-fed beef was estimated to be 5 percent based on dollars and 3 percent based on volume.

According to the most recent data from the U.S. Department of Agriculture, U.S. producers dedicated approximately 5.4 million acres of farmland—3.1 million acres of cropland and 2.3 million acres of rangeland and pasture—to certified-organic production systems in 2011, up from a total of 2.1 million acres in 2001.[3] Only about 0.8 percent of all U.S. cropland and 0.5 percent of all U.S. pasture were certified-organic in 2011. There were approximately 13,000 certified-organic producers in the United States in 2011 and perhaps another 9,000 small farmers growing organic products. All 50 states had some certified-organic farmland, with California, Oregon, New York, North Dakota, Montana, Minnesota, Wisconsin, and Texas having the most acres of certified-organic cropland.

Farmers were becoming increasingly interested in and attracted to organic farming, chiefly because of the substantially higher prices they could get for organically grown fruits, vegetables, and meats. Since 2005, health-conscious chefs at many fine-dining restaurants had begun sourcing ingredients for their dishes from local organic farmers and touting the use of organically grown products on their menus. Growing restaurant use of organically grown herbs, lettuces, vegetables, and fruits, as well as organic cheeses and organic meats, was spurring the growth of organic farming (since supplying local restaurants gave organic producers a ready market for their crops). Likewise, there was growing demand for locally grown organic fruits and vegetables on the part of many supermarkets—growing numbers had begun promoting fresh, locally grown organic produce in their stores. Organic farmers were also experiencing strong demand for their products among consumers who shopped at local farmers' markets.

Retailing of Organic Foods

Organic foods and beverages were available in nearly every food category in 2014 and were available in over 90 percent of U.S. retail food stores. Increasingly, the vast majority of retail sales of organic products in 2013–2014 were made through mainstream supermarkets and grocery stores and through leading organic and natural food supermarket chains such as Whole Foods, Trader Joe's, and Fresh Market. Only a small portion of organic sales occurred through independent, small-chain natural grocery stores.

Over the past decade, mainstream supermarkets had gradually expanded their offerings of natural and organic products for two reasons. One was because mounting consumer enthusiasm for organic products allowed retailers to earn attractively high profit margins on organics (compared to other grocery items, for which intense price competition among rival supermarket chains on general food products limited profit margins). The other was because consumer demand for organics was growing two to three times faster than the demand for traditional grocery products. Several factors had combined to transform organic food retailing, once a niche market, into the fastest-growing segment of U.S. food sales:

- A "wellness," or health-consciousness, trend among people of many ages and ethnic groups.

- Heightened awareness of the role that food, nutrition, and good eating patterns played in long-term health. Among those most interested in organic products were aging, affluent people concerned about maintaining their health and eating better-for-you foods.

- Increasing consumer concerns over the purity and safety of food due to the presence of pesticide residues, growth hormones, artificial ingredients and other chemicals, and genetically engineered ingredients.

- The growing belief that organic farming had positive environmental effects, particularly in contributing to healthier soil and water conditions and to sustainable agricultural practices.

Organic food products were between 10 and 40 percent more expensive than nonorganic foods, chiefly because of the higher production, distribution, and marketing costs for organic products. Such higher prices were the primary barrier for most consumers in trying or using organic products.

As of 2014, most supermarket chains stocked a selection of natural and organic food items—including fresh produce, canned and frozen fruits and vegetables, milk, cheeses, yogurt, vinegars, salad dressings, cereals, pastas, and meats—and the number and variety of organic items on supermarket shelves were growing. Fresh fruits and vegetables accounted for close to 40 percent of total organic food sales, with organic lettuces, spinach, broccoli, cauliflower, celery, carrots, and apples among the biggest sellers. Meat, dairy, grains, and snack foods were among the fastest-growing organic product categories.

Leading supermarket chains such as Walmart, Kroger, Safeway, Supervalu/Save-a-Lot, and Publix had created special "organic and health food" sections for nonperishable natural foods and organics in most of their stores. Kroger, Publix, and several other chains also had special sections for fresh organic fruits and vegetables in their produce cases in almost all of their stores. Walmart, Target, Safeway, Publix, and Kroger were stocking organic chicken and organic, pasture-raised beef at most of their stores.

Whole Foods Market

Whole Foods Market was founded in Austin, Texas, when John Mackey, the current co-CEO, and three other local natural food grocers in Austin decided

the natural food industry was ready for a supermarket format. The original Whole Foods Market opened in 1980 with a staff of only 19. It was an immediate success. At the time, there were less than half a dozen natural food supermarkets in the United States. By 1991, the company had 10 stores, revenues of $92.5 million, and net income of $1.6 million. Whole Foods became a public company in 1992, with its stock trading on the NASDAQ. In February 2014, Whole Foods operated 358 stores in 41 U.S. states and the District of Columbia, 8 stores in Canada, and 7 in Great Britain. Its stores averaged 38,000 square feet in size and $37.4 million in sales annually. More than 50 Whole Foods stores had average sales volumes of more than $1 million per week in fiscal 2013, up from just 6 stores in 2005; several Whole Foods stores averaged sales of over $2 million per week. Exhibit 1 presents highlights of the company's financial performance for fiscal years 2009–2013 (Whole Foods' fiscal year ended the last Sunday in September).

Core Values

In 1997, when Whole Foods developed the "Whole Foods, Whole People, Whole Planet" slogan to characterize its mission, John Mackey, known as a go-getter with a "cowboy way of doing things," said:

> This slogan taps into perhaps the deepest purpose of Whole Foods Market. It's a purpose we seldom talk about because it seems pretentious, but a purpose nevertheless felt by many of our Team Members and by many of our customers (and hopefully many of our shareholders too). Our deepest purpose as an organization is helping support the health, well-being, and healing of both people (customers and Team Members) and of the planet (sustainable agriculture, organic production and environmental sensitivity). When I peel away the onion of my personal consciousness down to its core in trying to understand what has driven me to create and grow this company, I come to my desire to promote the general well-being of everyone on earth as well as the earth itself. This is my personal greater purpose with the company and the slogan perfectly reflects it.

Complementing the "Whole Foods, Whole People, Whole Planet" mission was a statement of eight

EXHIBIT 1

Select Financial Information, Whole Foods Market, Fiscal Years 2009—2013 (in millions, except per share amounts)

	Fiscal Year Ending				
	Sept. 29, 2013	Sept. 30, 2012	Sept. 25, 2011	Sept. 26, 2010	Sept. 27, 2009
Income statement data					
Sales	$12,917	$11,699	$10,108	$9,006	$8,032
Cost of goods sold and occupancy costs	8,288	7,543	6,571	5,870	5,277
Gross profit	4,629	4,156	3,537	3,136	2,754
Direct store expenses	3,285	2,983	2,629	2,377	2,146
Store contribution[1]	1,344	1,173	908	759	608
General and administrative expenses	397	372	311	272	244
Preopening and relocation costs	52	47	41	38	49
Relocation, store closure, and lease termination costs	12	10	8	11	31
Operating income	883	743	548	438	284
Interest expense, net	—	—	(4)	(33)	(37)
Investment and other income	11	8	8	7	4
Income before income taxes	894	752	552	412	251
Provision for income taxes	343	286	209	166	104147
Net income	551	466	343	246	
Preferred stock dividends	—	—	—	6	28
Net income available to common shareholders	$ 551	$ 466	$ 343	$ 240	$ 119
Basic earnings per share	$1.48	$1.28	$0.98	$0.72	$0.42
Weighted average shares outstanding	371.2	364.8	350.5	332.5	280.8
Diluted earnings per share	$1.47	$1.26	$0.97	$0.72	$0.42
Weighted-average shares outstanding, diluted basis	374.5	368.9	354.6	343.4	280.8
Dividends declared per share	$1.40	$0.28	$0.20	—	—
Balance sheet data					
Net working capital[2]	$ 892	$ 1,126	$ 574	$ 414	$ 371
Total assets	5,538	5,294	4,292	3,987	3,783
Long-term debt (including current maturities)	27	24	18	509	739
Shareholders' equity	3,878	3,802	2,991	2,373	1,628
Cash flow data					
Net cash provided by operating activities	$ 1,009	$ 920	$ 759	$ 585	$ 588
Development costs of new locations	(339)	(262)	(203)	(171)	(288)
Other property and equipment expenditures	(67)	(85)	(162)	(194)	(198)
Free cash flow	$ 273	$ 328	$ 390	$ 464	$ 472

Note: Whole Foods' fiscal year ends the last Sunday in September.
[1] Store contribution is defined as gross profit less direct store expenses.
[2] Net working capital is defined as total current assets minus total current liabilities.

Source: 2013 10-K report, pp. 20 and 40; and 2011 10-K report, p. 36.

core values that governed how the company endeavored to conduct its business (see Exhibit 2). Whole Foods' managers and employees (referred to as *team members*) took pride in "walking the talk" when it came to the company's core values. The prevailing philosophy at Whole Foods was that the company's success and long-term profitability depended on its ability to simultaneously satisfy the needs and desires of its customers, team members, investors, and suppliers while also demonstrating a genuine concern for the communities in which it operated and for the environment.

Growth Strategy

Since going public in 1991, Whole Foods' growth strategy had been to expand via a combination of opening its own new stores and acquiring small,

owner-managed chains that had capable personnel and were located in desirable markets. During 1992–2001, Whole Foods' most significant acquisitions consisted of seven small chains with a total of 45 stores ranging in size from 5,000 to 20,000 square feet. The company entered the Atlanta market in 2001 by acquiring Harry's Market, which operated three 55,000-square-foot supermarkets. Starting in 2002, Whole Foods' management decided to drive growth by opening 10 to 15 decidedly bigger stores in metropolitan areas each year—stores that ranged from 40,000 square feet to as much as 80,000 square feet and were on the same scale as or larger than the conventional supermarkets operated by Kroger, Safeway, Publix, and other chains. However, the company did opt to enter Great Britain in 2004 by purchasing Fresh and Wild, an operator of seven small stores in the London area.

EXHIBIT 2

Whole Foods Market's Eight Core Values

Our Core Values

The following list of core values reflects what is truly important to us as an organization. These are not values that change from time to time, situation to situation or person to person, but rather they are the underpinning of our company culture.

1. **We Sell the Highest Quality Natural and Organic Products Available**
   - **Passion for Food**—We appreciate and celebrate the difference natural and organic products can make in the quality of one's life.
   - **Quality Standards**—We have high standards and our goal is to sell the highest quality products we possibly can. We define quality by evaluating the ingredients, freshness, safety, taste, nutritive value and appearance of all of the products we carry. We are buying agents for our customers and not the selling agents for the manufacturers.

2. **We Satisfy, Delight and Nourish Our Customers**
   - **Our Customers**—They are our most important stakeholders in our business and the lifeblood of our business. Only by satisfying our customers first do we have the opportunity to satisfy the needs of our other stakeholders.
   - **Extraordinary Customer Service**—We go to extraordinary lengths to satisfy and delight our customers. We want to meet or exceed their expectations on every shopping trip. We know that by doing so we turn customers into advocates for our business. Advocates do more than shop with us, they talk about Whole Foods to their friends and others. We want to serve our customers competently, efficiently, knowledgeably and with flair.
   - **Education**—We can generate greater appreciation and loyalty from all of our stakeholders by educating them about natural and organic foods, health, nutrition and the environment.
   - **Meaningful Value**—We offer value to our customers by providing them with high quality products, extraordinary service and a competitive price. We are constantly challenged to improve the value proposition to our customers.
   - **Retail Innovation**—We value retail experiments. Friendly competition within the company helps us to continually improve our stores. We constantly innovate and raise our retail standards and are not afraid to try new ideas and concepts.
   - **Inviting Store Environments**—We create store environments that are inviting and fun, and reflect the communities they serve. We want our stores to become community meeting places where our customers meet their friends and make new ones.

3. **We Support Team Member Happiness and Excellence**
   - **Empowering Work Environments**—Our success is dependent upon the collective energy and intelligence of all of our Team Members. We strive to create a work environment where motivated Team Members can flourish and succeed to their highest potential. We appreciate effort and reward results.
   - **Self-Responsibility**—We take responsibility for our own success and failures. We celebrate success and see failures as opportunities for growth. We recognize that we are responsible for our own happiness and success.
   - **Self-Directed Teams**—The fundamental work unit of the company is the self-directed team. Teams meet regularly to discuss issues, solve problems and appreciate each others' contributions. Every Team Member belongs to a team.
   - **Open & Timely Information**—We believe knowledge is power and we support our Team Members' right to access information that impacts their jobs. Our books are open to our Team Members, including our annual individual compensation report. We also recognize everyone's right to be listened to and heard regardless of their point of view.
   - **Incremental Progress**—Our company continually improves through unleashing the collective creativity and intelligence of all of our Team Members. We recognize that everyone has a contribution to make. We keep getting better at what we do.
   - **Shared Fate**—We recognize there is a community of interest among all of our stakeholders. There are no entitlements; we share together in our collective fate. To that end we have a salary cap that limits the compensation (wages plus profit incentive bonuses) of any Team Member to nineteen times the average total compensation of all full-time Team Members in the company.

4. **We Create Wealth through Profits & Growth**
   - **Stewardship**—We are stewards of our shareholders' investments and we take that responsibility very seriously. We are committed to increasing long term shareholder value.
   - **Profits**—We earn our profits everyday through voluntary exchange with our customers. We recognize that profits Satisfaction and job security are essential to creating capital for growth, prosperity, opportunity, job.

5. **We Serve and Support Our Local and Global Communities**
   Our business is intimately tied to the neighborhood and larger community that we serve and in which we live. Caring for the communities in which we reside is hugely important to our organization.
   - **Local**—First off, it's a given that each store donates food to area food banks and shelters. We have food; they know how to get it to people who need it. Done. Then, several times a year, our stores hold community-giving days (otherwise known as "5% Days") where five percent of that day's net sales are donated to a local nonprofit or educational organization. The groups that benefit from these "5% Days" are as varied as the communities themselves. Last but not least, Team Members are constantly volunteering their time and expertise to an assortment of local non-profits.
   - **Global**—While our store donations provide the backbone of our community giving, we also give back to the larger national and global community.
   Whole Planet Foundation works toward poverty alleviation in developing-world communities where Whole Foods Market sources product. Through microcredit, Whole Planet Foundation seeks to unleash the energy and creativity of every human being they work with in order to create wealth and prosperity in emerging economies.

   Whole Kids Foundation supports schools and inspires families to improve children's nutrition and wellness.

   Through partnerships with innovative organizations, schools and educators they work to provide children access to fresh, nutritious meals.

   Our Local Producer Loan Program provides up to $10 million in low-interest loans to small, local producers.

   Why? Because we believe in supporting local farmers and producers.

6. **We Practice and Advance Environmental Stewardship**
   - **Sustainable Agriculture**—We support organic farmers, growers and the environment through our commitment to sustainable agriculture and by expanding the market for organic products.
   - **Wise Environmental Practices**—We respect our environment and recycle, reuse, and reduce our waste wherever and whenever we can.

7. **We Create Ongoing Win-Win Partnerships with Our Suppliers**
   - **Integrity in All Business Dealings**—Our supplier partners are our allies in serving the interests of our other stakeholders in bringing to market the safest highest quality products available. We treat them with respect, fairness and integrity at all times and expect the same in return. We seek supplier partnerships that share our concern for social responsibility and the environment.
   - **Honesty and Communication**—We are committed to honesty, timeliness and clarity in communicating with our suppliers and we expect the same in return.

online chat activities and took no actions against Mackey or Whole Foods.

A second controversy-stirring incident involved a Mackey-authored blog entitled "Whole Foods, Wild Oats and the FTC" that was posted on the company's website on June 19, 2007. Mackey, who objected strenuously to the grounds on which the Federal Trade Commission was trying to block Whole Foods' acquisition of Wild Oats, authored a blog that was dedicated to providing updates and information regarding the FTC proceeding and to making the case for why the company's acquisition of Wild Oats Market should be allowed to go forward. Mackey explained the basis for the blog posting:

> My blog posting provides a detailed look into Whole Foods Market's decision-making process regarding the merger, as well as our company's experience interacting with the FTC staff assigned to this merger. I provide explanations of how I think the FTC, to date, has neglected to do its homework appropriately, especially given the statements made regarding prices, quality, and service levels in its complaint. I also provide a glimpse into the bullying tactics used against Whole Foods Market by this taxpayer-funded agency. Finally, I provide answers in my FAQ section to many of the questions that various Team Members have fielded from both the media and company stakeholders. As previously announced, we set an intention as a company to be as transparent as possible throughout this legal process, and this blog entry is my first detailed effort at transparency.

The blog posting by Mackey addressed:

- Why Whole Foods Market wants to buy Wild Oats.
- Whole Foods Market's objections to the FTC's investigation.
- What the FTC is claiming in its objections to the merger.
- FAQs.

Critics of the Mackey blog posting said it was inappropriate for a CEO to publicly air the company's position, to take issue with the FTC, and to make the company's case for why the acquisition should be allowed to proceed. At the least, some critics opined, the blog should be toned down.[22] When the SEC announced on July 17, 2007, that it would investigate John Mackey's financial message board postings, Mackey put a hold on further blog postings regarding the FTC's actions to try to block the Wild Oats acquisition.

In 2010, Ethisphere Institute named Whole Foods as one of the world's most ethical companies; Ethisphere is a leading research-based international think tank dedicated to the creation, advancement, and sharing of best practices in business ethics, corporate social responsibility, anticorruption, and environmental sustainability.

Whole Foods Market's Outlook for Fiscal Year 2014

In February 2014, Whole Foods provided the following guidance for fiscal year 2014, ending September 28:[23]

- Sales growth of 11 to 12 percent
- Comparable-store sales growth in the range of 5.5 to 6.2 percent
- Diluted earnings per share in the range of $1.58 to $1.65
- New openings of 33 to 38 stores (followed by the opening of 38 to 45 new stores in fiscal 2015)
- Percentage of total sales contributed by new stores of about 6 percent
- Capital expenditures in the range of $600 million to $650 million

Competitors

The food retailing business was intensely competitive. The degree of competition Whole Foods faced varied from locality to locality and to some extent from store location to store location within a given locale, depending on the proximity of stores of its two closest competitors in the natural food and organic segment of the food retailing industry, Fresh Market and Trader Joe's. Other competitors included local supermarkets, small chains, local independent retailers of natural and health foods, regional and national supermarkets (most of which had begun stocking a growing and more diverse selection of natural and organic products), and national superstores (Walmart and Target). Whole Foods also faced competition in parts of its product line from specialty grocery stores (with upscale delicatessen offerings and prepared foods), small-scale health food stores, retailers of vitamins and nutritional supplements, local farmers' markets, and warehouse clubs (Costco and Sam's Club). Whole Foods' executives had said it was to the company's benefit for conventional supermarkets to offer natural and organic foods for two reasons: First, it helped fulfill the company's mission of improving the health and well-being of people and the planet, and, second, it helped create new customers for Whole Foods by providing a gateway experience. They contended that as more people were exposed to natural and organic products, they were more likely to become a Whole Foods customer because Whole Foods was the category leader for natural and organic products, offered the largest selection at competitive prices, and provided the most informed customer service.

The Fresh Market

The Fresh Market, headquartered in Greensboro, North Carolina, operated over 150 stores in 26 states in the Southeast, Midwest, Mid-Atlantic, Northeast, and West; the company opened 22 new stores in fiscal 2013 and had signed leases for 25 future store locations to be opened in 2014. Founded by Ray Berry, a former vice president with Southland Corporation who had responsibility over some 3,600 7-Eleven stores, the first Fresh Market store opened in 1982 in Greensboro. Berry's concept was to deliver a differentiated food shopping experience—a small, rustically decorated, neighborhood store with a warm, inviting atmosphere that featured friendly, knowledgeable service and a focus on premium perishable goods. The Greensboro store, which had low-level lighting and classical music playing in the background, was a hit with customers, and Berry began to open similar stores in other locales. Between 1982 and 2010, The Fresh Market steadily expanded its geographic presence into additional states, and as sales approached $1 billion in late 2010, the company opted to become a public company via an initial public offering of its common stock. The company had sales of $1.51 billion (up 13.7 percent over the prior year) and net income of $50.8 million (down 20.8 percent) for fiscal year 2013, ending January 26, 2014.

Fresh Market stores were typically in the 17,000- to 22,000-square-foot range (the average was 21,190 square feet) and were located mostly in high-traffic and/or upscale neighborhood shopping areas. Fresh Market stores were organized around distinct departments with engaging merchandise displays. Accent lighting, classical background music, terra-cotta–colored tiles, and colorful product presentations made Fresh Market stores a cozier, more inviting place to shop than a typical supermarket. The atmosphere was meant to encourage customers to slow down, interact with employees, and have an enjoyable shopping experience.

Fresh Market's product line consisted of 9,000 to 10,000 items that included meats, seafood, fresh fruits and vegetables, fresh baked goods, prepared foods, premium coffees and teas, a small selection of grocery and dairy items, bulk products, more than 200 varieties of domestic and imported cheeses, deli items (including rotisserie meats, sandwiches, wraps, soups, and sandwiches), wine and beer, and a small assortment of cookbooks, candles, kitchen items, and seasonal gift baskets. The emphasis was on variety, freshness, and quality. Management characterized the company as a specialty food retailer, with a store atmosphere and product selection that were distinct from those of competitors. Based on operating experience and market research, management believed that the market in the United States could support at least 500 Fresh Market stores operating under the current format.

The typical Fresh Market store was staffed with approximately 70 to 80 full- and part-time employees including a store manager, two to three assistant store managers, and five department heads. The store management team was responsible for all aspects of store execution including managing inventory and cash, maintaining a clean and engaging store environment, and hiring, training, and supervising store employees. Store employees, especially store managers, were encouraged to engage regularly with customers. To facilitate interaction between staff and customers, store managers were stationed on the selling floor, near the service counters. Special efforts were devoted to hiring, training, retaining, developing, and promoting qualified and enthusiastic employees who displayed a passion for delivering an extraordinary food shopping experience.

Because Fresh Market was opening new stores at a rapid pace, management believed it was important to maintain a sufficient pipeline of people qualified to be store managers and assistant store managers. Nearly all store managers and district managers were promoted from within.

After 60 days, all full-time employees who worked at least 30 hours per week were eligible to enroll in plans providing medical, prescription medication, dental, life, and disability coverage; coverage could be extended to spouses or domestic partners and children. In addition, there were employee discounts on most products, a paid annual-leave program, a 401(k) plan with 50 percent company matching of employee contributions, an employee assistance program, and a discounted stock purchase plan.

Trader Joe's

Founded in 1967 and headquartered in Monrovia, California, Trader Joe's was a specialty supermarket chain with 408 stores in 31 states and Washington, D.C.; about half of the stores were in California. Owned by Germany's Albrecht family, Trader Joe's sales in 2013 were an estimated $10.5 billion. Trader Joe's was ranked number 21 on the *Supermarket News* 2013 list of the top-75 retailers. The company had an ongoing strategy to open additional stores.

The company's mission and business were described on its website as follows:[24]

> At Trader Joe's, our mission is to bring our customers the best food and beverage values and the information to make informed buying decisions. There are more than 2000 unique grocery items in our label, all at honest everyday low prices. We work hard at buying things right: Our buyers travel the world searching for new items and we work with a variety of suppliers who make interesting products for us, many of them exclusive to Trader Joe's. All our private label products have their own "angle," i.e., vegetarian, Kosher, organic or just plain decadent, and all have minimally processed ingredients.
>
> Customers tell us, "I never knew food shopping could be so much fun!" Some even call us "The home of cheap thrills!" We like to be part of our neighborhoods and get to know our customers. And where else do you shop that even the CEO, Dan Bane, wears a loud Hawaiian shirt.

> Our tasting panel tastes every product before we buy it. If we don't like it, we don't buy it. If customers don't like it, they can bring it back for a no-hassle refund.
>
> We stick to the business we know: good food at the best prices! Whenever possible we buy direct from our suppliers, in large volume. We bargain hard and manage our costs carefully. We pay in cash, and on time, so our suppliers like to do business with us.
>
> Trader Joe's Crew Members are friendly, knowledgeable and happy to see their customers. They taste our items too, so they can discuss them with their customers. All our stores regularly cook up new and interesting products for our customers to sample.

Trader Joe's stores had open layouts, with wide aisles, appealing displays, cedar plank walls, a nautical decor, and crew members wearing colorful Hawaiian shirts; store sizes ranged from 8,000 to 12,000 square feet. Prices and product offerings varied somewhat by region and state. There were no weekly specials or cents-off coupons or glitzy promotional discounts. Customers could choose from an eclectic and somewhat upscale variety of baked goods, organic foods, fresh fruits and vegetables, imported and domestic cheeses, gourmet chocolates and candies, coffees, fresh salads, meatless entrees and other vegan products, low-fat and low-carbohydrate foods, frozen fish and seafood, heat-and-serve entrees, packaged meats, juices, wine and beer, snack foods, energy bars, vitamins, nuts and trail mixes, and whatever other exotic items the company's buyers had come upon. About 20 to 25 percent of Trader Joe's products were imported. There were very few brand-name items; more than 2,000 items carried the Trader Joe's label and the company's other quirky labels for particular foods: Trader Jose's (Mexican food), Trader Ming's (Chinese food), Trader Giotto's (Italian food), Pilgrim Joe's (seafood), Trader Jacques' (imported French soaps), Joe's Diner (certain frozen entrees), and Joe's Kids (children's food); these items accounted for about 70 percent of total sales. Items with a Trader Joe's logo contained no artificial flavors, colors, or preservatives and no trans fats, monosodium glutamate (MSG), or genetically modified ingredients. About 10 to 15 new, seasonal, or one-time-buy items were introduced each week. Products that weren't selling well were dropped. Trader Joe's was the exclusive retailer of Charles Shaw wine, popularly known as "Two Buck Chuck" because of its $1.99 price tag in California—raised to $2.49 in 2013; outside California, the price ranged as high as $3.79 because of higher liquor taxes and transportation costs.

The appealingly low prices at Trader Joe's enabled the company to draw large numbers of bargain-hunting shoppers, as well as upscale shoppers intrigued by the quirky product offerings. Because of its combination of low everyday prices, emporium-like atmosphere, intriguing selections, friendly service, and fast checkout lanes, customers viewed shopping at Trader Joe's as an enjoyable experience. The company was able to keep the prices of its unique products low because of (1) discount buying (its buyers were always on the lookout for exotic items they could buy at a discount—all products had to pass a taste test and a cost test), (2) less expensive store locations and decor, (3) lower labor costs (it had fewer employees per store compared with competitors), (4) the very high percentage of products sold under labels exclusive to Trader Joe's, and (5) high sales volumes per square foot of store space (reputed to be in excess of $1,000 per square foot).

Most cities and towns that did not have a Trader Joe's were anxious to get one, particularly those with residents who had shopped at Trader Joe's regularly when they lived in places with a Trader Joe's store. Trader Joe's owed much of its reputation to the glowing word-of-mouth experiences of highly satisfied customers. However, Trader Joe's revealed scant information about its operations and plans—the locations and opening dates of soon-to-be-opened stores were closely guarded secrets. Many sizable markets, such as Tampa–St. Petersburg, Houston, Denver, Kansas City, and Milwaukee typically had only one or two stores, making shopping at Trader Joe's more of a destination trip for loyal customers.

Sprouts Farmers Market

Founded in 2002, Sprouts Farmers Market had grown into a regional chain with 170 stores in Arizona, California, Colorado, Kansas, Nevada, New Mexico, Oklahoma, Texas, and Utah. A total of 19 new stores were opened in 2013. Sprouts had 2013 sales of $2.4 billion and net income of $51.3 million. The company completed an initial public offering of common stock in August 2013. It used $340 million of the net proceeds of $344 million to repay a portion of its outstanding debt.

Management viewed Sprouts Farmers Market as a fast-growing differentiated specialty retailer of natural and organic food, offering a complete shopping experience that included fresh produce, bulk foods, vitamins and supplements, grocery items, meat and seafood, bakery goods, dairy items, frozen foods, body care products, and natural household items catering to consumers' growing interest in eating and living healthier. Sprouts mission was "Healthy Living for Less." The foundation of the company's value proposition was fresh, high-quality produce offered at prices significantly below those of conventional food retailers and even further below high-end natural and organic food retailers.

In 2014, Sprouts management was pursuing a number of strategies designed to continue the company's growth, including expanding the store base, driving comparable-store sales growth, enhancing operating margins, and building the Sprouts brand. The strategy to expand the store base included opening new stores in existing markets, expanding into adjacent markets, and penetrating new markets. The plan was to expand the store base primarily through new store openings, but management expected the company to grow through strategic acquisitions if it identified suitable targets and was able to negotiate acceptable terms and conditions for acquisition.

The strategic objective was to achieve 12 percent or more annual new store growth for at least the next five years.

Independent and Small-Chain Retailers of Natural and Organic Products

In 2014, there were approximately 12,000 to 13,000 independent and small-chain retailers of natural and organic foods, vitamins and supplements, and natural personal care products. While there were a few regional chains such as Natural Grocers by Vitamin Cottage (70 stores in 13 states) and several hundred multistore retailers, the majority were single-store, owner-managed enterprises serving small to medium-sized communities and particular neighborhoods in metropolitan areas. Product lines and range of selection at the stores of independent natural and health food retailers varied from narrow to moderately broad, depending on a store's size and market focus and the shopper traffic it was able to generate.

Over half of the independent stores had less than 2,500 square feet of retail sales space and generated revenues of less than $1 million annually; the core product offerings of these retailers were vitamins and mineral and herbal supplements, complemented by a limited selection of organic and natural foods and some prepared foods, as many as 5,000 items in total. But there were roughly 1,000 natural and health food retailers with store sizes exceeding 6,000 square feet and sales per store of about $10 million annually. Sales of vitamins and supplements at many small independent stores were beginning to flatten, chiefly because conventional supermarket chains and most large drugstore chains had begun to carry a sizable selection of vitamins and supplements. Sales at small retailers of natural and organic foods were also under pressure because conventional supermarkets had a growing selection of organic and natural foods, while chains such as Whole Foods and Trader Joe's had a far wider selection of organic and natural products of all types. As one industry expert noted, "Shoppers can pick up a bag of mixed organic salad greens, a half-gallon of organic milk, some hormone-free chicken, trans-fat-free cookies and crackers, non-dairy beverages and—brace yourself—even gluten-free foods, right in the aisles of their regular supermarkets." [25]

Walmart

Over the past decade or so, Walmart had opened hundreds of new Walmart Supercenters that included a full-line supermarket; food items were also sold at Walmart Discount Stores and Walmart Neighborhood Markets. As of 2014, Walmart was far and away the biggest seller of food, grocery, and household products in the United States, with sales of such products exceeding $150 billion. In April 2014,

Walmart announced that it had struck a deal with Yuciapa Companies, a private investment firm that owned the Wild Oats trademarks, to begin selling 100 mostly organic Wild Oats–branded products in the food sections of its 3,290 Supercenters and 346 Neighborhood Markets and in the pantry sections of its 508 Discount Stores. Because of concerns about adequate supplies, the Wild Oats products would initially be introduced in about 2,000 stores and then gradually rolled out to the more than 2,100 remaining stores.[26] Walmart said it would enter into long-term agreements with suppliers to lock in the large-volume requirements of Wild Oats products it expected it would need to supply its network of stores in the United States.

The lines of Wild Oats products to be offered at Walmart's stores included:

- *Wild Oats Marketplace Organic*—a selection of items that adhered to USDA guidelines for organic certification and included everything from canned vegetables (15 ounces) at $0.88 to spices such as paprika and curry powder (2 ounces) starting at $2.48. This Wild Oats line of organic items represented nearly 90 percent of the 100 Wild Oats products that Walmart would initially offer its customers.
- *Wild Oats Marketplace*—a selection of items with simple and natural ingredients such as ready-to-prepare skillet meals (5.8 ounces) at $1.50.
- *Wild Oats Marketplace Originals*—a selection of new and uniquely formulated items that Walmart expected to introduce in late 2014.

Walmart indicated that it planned to sell the Wild Oats–branded items at prices that would undercut national brand-name organic competitors by 25 percent or more—see Exhibit 7. Walmart said that its internal research found that 91 percent of Walmart shoppers would consider purchasing products from an affordable organic brand at the company's stores.

EXHIBIT 7

Expected Price Savings for Walmart Consumers on Select Wild Oats Marketplace Organic Products

Wild Oats' Product	Wild Oats' Price at Walmart	Price of Comparable National-Brand Organic Item	Price Difference
Organic Tomato Paste (6 oz.)	$0.58	$0.98	41%
Organic Chicken Broth (32 oz.)	1.98	3.47	43
Organic Cinnamon Applesauce Cups (24 oz.)	1.98	2.78	29
Organic Tomato Sauce (15 oz.)	0.88	1.38	36

Source: Walmart press release, April 10, 2014.

ENDNOTES

[1]According to Nielsen's TDLinx and *Progressive Grocer,* as cited by Whole Foods Market in its 2013 10-K report, p. 1.

[2]According to *Natural Foods Merchandiser,* a leading trade publication for the natural foods industry, as cited by Whole Foods Market in its 2013 10-K report, p. 1.

[3]Economic Research Service, U.S. Department of Agriculture, www.ers.usda.gov, September 27, 2013 (accessed February 14, 2014).

[4]2009 10-K report, p. 51.

[5]2009 10-K report, p. 10.

[6]Company press releases, February 19, 2008, and February 16, 2010.

[7]Letter to Shareholders, 2003 annual report.

[8]Hollie Shaw, "Retail-Savvy Whole Foods Opens in Canada," *National Post,* May 1, 2002, p. FP9.

[9]See Karin Schill Rives, "Texas-Based Whole Foods Market Makes Changes to Cary, N.C. Grocery Store," *News and Observer,* March 7, 2002.

[10]Letter to Stakeholders, 2009 annual report.

[11]As quoted in Marilyn Much, "Whole Foods Markets: Austin, Texas Green Grocer Relishes Atypical Sales," *Investors Business Daily,* September 10, 2002.

[12]As quoted in "Whole Foods Market to Open in Albuquerque, N.M.," *Santa Fe New Mexican,* September 10, 2002.

[13]Information contained in John R. Wells and Travis Haglock, "Whole Foods Market, Inc.," Harvard Business School case 9-705-476.

[14]Company 2009 10-K report, p. 14; company press release, January 21, 2010.

[15]As quoted in John K. Wilson, "Going Whole Hog with Whole Foods," *Bankrate.com*, December 23, 1999 (accessed March 21, 2010). Mackey made the statement in 1991 when efforts were being made to unionize the company's store in Berkeley, California.

[16]Company 2013 annual report.

[17]"Frank Talk from Whole Foods' John Mackey," *Wall Street Journal,* August 4, 2009, online.wsj.com (accessed March 13, 2010).

[18]David Kesmodel and John. R. Wilke, "Whole Foods Is Hot, Wild Oats a Dud— So Said Rahodeb," *Wall Street Journal,* July 12, 2007, online.wsj .com/article/SB118418782959963745.html (accessed April 7, 2007).

[19]Andrew Martin, "Whole Foods Executive Used Alias," *New York Times,* July 12, 2007, www.nytimes.com/2007/07/12/business/12foods.html (accessed April 7, 2008).

[20]Ibid.

[21]Company press release, October 5, 2007.

[22]According to a July 13, 2007, posting on a *Business Week* message board, www.businessweek.com/careers/ managementiq/archives/2007/07/who_advises_joh.html(accessed March 26, 2010).

[23]Company press release, February 12, 2014.

[24]Information posted at www.traderjoes.com (accessed December 1, 2005).

[25]Jay Jacobwitz, "Independent Retailers Need New Customers: The New 'Integrated' Foods Shopper," *Merchandising Insights,* November 2009, wfcgreen book.com (accessed March 30, 2010).

[26]Walmart press release, April 10, 2014.

connect

JOHN E. GAMBLE   Texas A&M University—Corpus Christi

JOHN D. VARLARO   Johnson & Wales University

Since the death of Steve Jobs on October 5, 2011, critics had questioned Tim Cook's ability to lead Apple. Much of the criticism centered on Apple's lack of innovation since Jobs, citing how Cook may not possess the same product vision. Further, many wondered whether Apple could sustain its success. Yet, despite the economic conditions in the United States post-recession, Apple Inc. had been able to sustain its impressive growth, resulting in a 275 percent growth in net sales between 2010 and 2014. The company set record quarterly revenues and profits during its second quarter of 2012, which resulted in its stock price catapulting to a level that made it the world's most valuable company—a title it continued to hold in early 2015 with market capitalization of nearly $760 billion. Some analysts speculated that Apple might eventually become the world's first trillion-dollar company.

Despite the company's tremendous successes, new challenges faced Cook and his chief managers in 2015. The company had yet to reverse the general decline in iPod unit sales and was facing a serious competitive threat in both the smartphone and tablet markets. Samsung had surged to the top of the smartphone market in late 2011 by introducing the Galaxy and other models that utilized Google's Android operating system to match the key features of the iPhone. In 2015, Android maintained its status as the most widely used operating system platform for smartphones worldwide with a 24.5 percent share of the market at year-end 2014. Dell, HP, and other computer manufacturers had also released tablet computers, furthering pressure on the iPad.

Apple's record growth in revenues and profits in previous years came primarily from volume increases in the sale of iPhones and iPads. Still critical to the company's financial performance, iPhone sales accounted for $102 billion of the company's 2014 revenues of $182.8 billion, and Apple's iPad tablet computers were the company's second-largest contributor to total revenues with sales of more than $30.2 billion during 2014. Although iPhone sales increased by 12 percent in 2014, sales of the iPhone had experienced a 16 percent year-over-year increase from 2012 to 2013. In addition, iPad sales had decreased by 5 percent from 2013 to 2014. Disappointing sales continued for the iPod, with a 48 percent year-over-year decline in sales in 2014.

With competitive rivalry continuing in the smartphone and tablet market, Cook and his chief managers would need to consider different avenues for growth. The single largest growth in sales was within Apple's iTunes, App, Mac, and iBookstore, where revenues increased by 40 percent between 2012 and 2014. Also, the rising popularity among consumers to seek alternatives to cable television had fueled sales of Apple TV in 2014. And it was still undetermined how Cook's unveiling of the Apple Watch in September 2014 would impact the company's prospects for growth in revenues.

Steve Jobs' Strategic Leadership at Apple

Stephen Wozniak and Steve Jobs founded Apple Computer in 1976 when they began selling a crudely designed personal computer called the Apple I to

Silicon Valley computer enthusiasts. Two years later, the partners introduced the first mass-produced personal computer (PC), the Apple II, which eventually sold more than 10,000 units. While the Apple II was relatively successful, the next revision of the product line, the Macintosh (Mac), would dramatically change personal computing through its user-friendly graphical user interface (GUI), which allowed users to interact with screen images rather than merely type text commands.

The Macintosh that was introduced in 1984 was hailed as a breakthrough in personal computing, but it did not have the speed, power, or software availability to compete with the PC that IBM had introduced in 1981. One of the reasons the Macintosh lacked the necessary software was that Apple put very strict restrictions on the Apple Certified Developer Program, which made it difficult for software developers to obtain Macs at a discount and receive informational materials about the operating system.

With the Mac faring poorly in the market, founder Steve Jobs became highly critical of the company's president and CEO, John Sculley, who had been hired by the board in 1983. Finally, in 1985, as Sculley was preparing to visit China, Jobs devised a boardroom coup to replace him. Sculley found out about the plan and canceled his trip. After Apple's board voted unanimously to keep Sculley in his position, Jobs, who was retained as chairman of the company but stripped of all decision-making authority, soon resigned. During the remainder of 1985, Apple continued to encounter problems and laid off one-fifth of its employees while posting its first ever quarterly loss.

Despite these setbacks, Apple kept bringing innovative products to the market, while closely guarding the secrets behind its technology. In 1987, Apple released a revamped Macintosh computer that proved to be a favorite in K–12 schools and with graphic artists and other users needing excellent graphics capabilities. However, by 1990, PCs running Windows 3.0 and Word for Windows were preferred by businesses and consumers and held a commanding 97+ percent share of the market for personal computers.

In 1991, Apple released its first-generation notebook computer, the PowerBook and, in 1993, Apple's board of directors opted to remove Sculley from the position of CEO. The board chose to place the chief operating officer, Michael Spindler, in the vacated spot. Under Spindler, Apple released the PowerMac family of PCs in 1994, the first Macs to incorporate the PowerPC chip, a very fast processor co-developed with Motorola and IBM. Even though the PowerMac family received excellent reviews by technology analysts, Microsoft's Windows 95 matched many of the capabilities of the Mac OS and prevented the PowerMac from gaining significant market share. In January 1996, Apple asked Spindler to resign and chose Gil Amelio, former president of National Semiconductor, to take his place.

During his first 100 days in office, Amelio announced many sweeping changes for the company. He split Apple into seven distinct divisions, each responsible for its own profit or loss, and he tried to better inform the developers and consumers of Apple's products and projects. Amelio acquired NeXT, the company Steve Jobs had founded upon his resignation from Apple in 1985. Steve Jobs was rehired by Apple as part of the acquisition. In 1997, after recording additional quarterly losses, Apple's board terminated Amelio's employment with the company and named Steve Jobs interim CEO.

Under Jobs' leadership, Apple introduced the limited-feature iMac in 1998 and the company's iBook line of notebook computers in 1999. The company was profitable in every quarter during 1998 and 1999, and its share price reached an all-time high in the upper $70 range. Jobs was named permanent CEO of Apple in 2000 and, in 2001, oversaw the release of the iPod. The iPod recorded modest sales until the 2003 launch of iTunes, the online retail store where consumers could legally purchase individual songs. By July 2004, 100 million songs had been sold, and iTunes had a 70 percent market share among all legal online music download services. The tremendous success of the iPod helped transform Apple from a struggling computer company into a powerful consumer electronics company.

By 2005, consumers' satisfaction with the iPod had helped renew interest in Apple computers, with its market share in personal computers growing from a negligible share to 4 percent. The company also exploited consumer loyalty and satisfaction with the iPod to enter the market for smartphones with the 2007 launch of the iPhone. The brand loyalty developed through the first iPod and then the iPhone made the company's 2010 launch of the iPad a roaring success with 3.3 million units sold during its first three months on the market. Much of Apple's turnaround could be credited to Steve Jobs, who had idea after idea for how to improve the company and turn its performance around. He not only consistently pushed for innovative new ideas and products but also enforced several structural changes, including ridding the company of unprofitable segments and divisions.

The success of the turnaround could also be attributed to the efforts of Tim Cook, Apple's chief operating officer, who oversaw the company's operations at various times between 2004 and 2011. Cook was first asked to act as the company's chief manager in 2004 when Steve Jobs was recovering from pancreatic cancer surgery, later in 2009 when Jobs

took a six-month medical leave for a liver transplant, and again in early 2011 when Jobs left the company for another medical leave. Jobs' illness eventually forced his resignation shortly before his death on October 5, 2011. While Jobs had been the inspiration for the company's hottest new products such as the iPhone, iPad, and iPod, analysts and key Apple managers viewed Cook as an "operational genius." While COO and acting CEO, Tim Cook was responsible for overhauling Apple's supply chain system and transforming it into one of the lowest cost electronics manufacturers.[1] Prior to coming to Apple in 1998, Cook was a rising star in Compaq Computer's management team.

A summary of Apple's financial performance for fiscal years 2010 through 2014 is provided in Exhibit 1. The company's net sales by operating segment and product line and unit sales by product line for 2012 through 2014 are provided in Exhibit 2.

EXHIBIT 1

Summary of Apple Inc.'s Financial Performance, 2010–2014 ($ in millions, except share amounts)

	2014	2013	2012	2011	2010
Net sales	$182,795	$170,910	$156,508	$108,249	$65,225
Costs and expenses					
Cost of sales	112,258	106,606	87,846	64,431	39,541
Research and development	6,041	4,475	3,381	2,429	1,782
Selling, general and administrative	11,993	10,830	10,040	7,599	5,517
Total operating expenses	18,034	15,305	13,421	10,028	7,299
Operating income	52,503	48,999	55,241	33,790	18,385
Other income and expenses	980	1,156	522	415	155
Income before provision for income taxes	53,483	50,155	55,763	34,205	18,540
Provision for income taxes	13,973	13,118	14,030	8,283	4,527
Net income	$39,510	$37,037	$41,733	$25,922	$14,013
Earnings per common share					
Basic	$6.49	$40.03	$44.64	$28.05	$15.41
Diluted	$6.45	$39.75	$44.15	$27.68	$15.15
Cash dividends declared per common share	$1.82	$11.40	$2.65	$0.00	$0.00
Shares used in computing earnings per share					
Basic	6,085,572	925,331	934,818	924,258	909,461
Diluted	6,122,663	931,662	945,355	936,645	924,712
Total cash, cash equivalents, and marketable securities	$155,239	$146,761	$121,251	$81,570	$51,011
Total assets	231,839	207,000	176,064	116,371	75,183
Total long-term obligations	24,826	20,208	16,664	10,100	5,531
Total liabilities	120,292	83,451	57,854	39,756	27,392
Total shareholders' equity	111,547	123,549	118,210	76,615	47,791

Sources: Apple Inc., 2012, 2013 and 2014 10-K reports.
*A seven-for-one stock split occurred on June 6, 2014.

Apple, Inc.'s Net Sales by Operating Segment, Net Sales by Product, and Unit Sales by Product, 2012–2014 ($ in millions; unit sales in thousands)

Net Sales by Operating Segment:	2014	Change	2013	Change	2012
Americas net sales	$65,232	4%	$62,739	9%	$57,512
Europe net sales	40,929	8%	37,883	4%	36,323
Greater Chine net sales	29,846	17%	25,417	13%	22,533
Japan net sales	14,982	11%	13,462	27%	10,571
Rest of Asia Pacific net sales	10,344	(7)%	11,181	4%	10,741
Retail net sales	21,462	6%	20,228	7%	18,828
Total net sales	$182,795	7%	$170,910	9%	$156,508
Net Sales by Product:					
iPhone[1]	$101,991	12%	$91,279	16%	$78,692
iPad[1]	30,283	(5)%	31,980	3%	30,945
Mac[1]	24,079	12%	21,483	(7)%	23,221
iPod[1]	2,286	(48)%	4,411	(21)%	5,615
iTunes, Software and Services[2]	18,063	13%	16,051	25%	12,890
Accessories[3]	6,093	7%	5,706	11%	5,145
Total net sales	$182,795	7%	$170,910	9%	$156,508
Unit Sales by Product:					
iPhone	169,219	13%	150,257	20%	125,046
iPad	67,977	(4)%	71,033	22%	58,310
Mac	18,906	16%	16,341	(10)%	18,158
iPod	14,377	(45)%	26,379	(25)%	35,165

Source: Apple Inc., 2014 10-K report.

[1] Deferrals and amortizations of related nonsoftware services and software upgrade rights included.

[2] Revenues from the iTunes Store, the App Store, the Mac App Store, the iBooks Store, AppleCare, licensing, and other services are included in figures.

[3] Sales of Apple-branded and third-party iPod, iPad, Mac, and iPhone accessories are included.

Overview of the Personal Computer Industry

The personal computer industry was relatively consolidated, with five sellers accounting for 81.3 percent of the U.S. shipments and 65.3 percent of worldwide shipments in 2014 (see Exhibit 3). Worldwide PC shipments had declined since 2011 with total global PC demand projected to erode by as much as 30 percent by 2018. The downward trend was partly due to the rise in popularity of tablet computers for home and business use. Tablet computers, such as the iPad, were becoming replacements for laptops and PCs primarily among consumers but were increasingly becoming a viable substitute for PCs within the business setting as business apps and cloud computing expanded. The market for tablet computers increased from 219.9 million units in 2013 to 229.6 million units in 2014, which represented 4.4 percent year-over-year growth.

Apple's Competitive Position in the Personal Computer Industry

Apple's proprietary operating system, strong graphics-handling capabilities, and sleek designs differentiated Macs from PCs, but many consumers and business users who owned PCs were hesitant to purchase a Mac because of Apple's premium pricing and because of the learning curve involved with mastering its proprietary operating system. Since the introduction of the first Macintosh computer in

EXHIBIT 3

U.S. and Global Market Shares of Leading PC Vendors, 2010-2014

A. U.S. Market Shares of the Leading PC Vendors, 2010-2014

2014 Rank	Vendor	2014 Shipments (in 000s)	2014 Market Share	2013 Shipments (in 000s)	2013 Market Share	2012 Shipments (in 000s)	2012 Market Share	2011 Shipments (in 000s)	2011 Market Share	2010 Shipments (in 000s)	2010 Market Share
1	Hewlett-Packard	18,332	27.6%	16,160	25.5%	17,845	27.0%	18,595	26.1%	19,488	25.9%
2	Dell	16,158	24.3	14,055	22.1	14,062	21.3	15,898	22.3	17,352	23.1
3	Apple	8,085	12.2	7,255	11.4	7,182	10.9	7,649	10.7	6,586	8.8
4	Lenovo	7,100	10.7	6,195	9.8	5,277	8.0	n.a	n.a	n.a	n.a
5	Toshiba	4,299	6.5	4,647	7.3	4,664	7.1	6,695	9.4	6,624	8.8
	Others	12,396	18.7	15,151	23.9	15,008	21.5	22,472	31.5	25,050	33.4
	All vendors	71,309	100.0%	75,101	100.0%	69,829	100.0%	71,309	100.0%	75,101	100.0%

B. Global Market Shares of the Leading PC Vendors, 2010-2014

2014 Rank	Vendor	2014 Shipments (in 000s)	2014 Market Share	2013 Shipments (in 000s)	2013 Market Share	2012 Shipments (in 000s)	2012 Market Share	2011 Shipments (in 000s)	2011 Market Share	2010 Shipments (in 000s)	2010 Market Share
1	Lenovo	59,233	19.2%	53,804	17.1%	52,348	15.0%	44,007	12.5%	34,182	9.9%
2	Hewlett-Packard	56,849	18.4	52,188	16.6	58,129	16.6	62,334	17.7	64,213	18.5
3	Dell	41,665	13.5	37,787	12.0	38,719	11.1	44,282	12.6	43,403	12.5
4	Acer Group	24,104	7.8	24,508	7.8	33,588	9.6	37,169	10.6	42,430	12.3
5	Apple	19,822	6.4	17,132	5.4	n.a.	n.a.	n.a.	n.a.	n.a.	n.a.
	Others	106,952	34.7	129,702	41.2	143,386	41.0	164,6034	46.64	142,874	41.3
	All vendors	308,625	100.0%	315,121	100.0%	349,383	100.0%	352,395	100.0%	346,198	100.0%

1984, the company had been unable to achieve a 5 percent market share in the United States. However, the company's market share in the United States had improved from 4.7 percent in 2006 to 8.8 percent in 2010, primarily because of the success of the iPod and iPhone. These products created a halo effect whereby some consumers (but not business users) switched to Apple computers after purchasing an iPod, iPhone, or iPad. This trend continued as more consumers adopted Apple computers due to their experience with other Apple products and how each product seamlessly integrates with the other. By 2014, Apple's market share in the United States had grown to 12.2 percent—giving it a number-three ranking in the U.S. PC market. Apple was also ranked fifth in the world for the first time in 2013.

Apple's computer product line consisted of several models in various configurations. Its desktop lines included the Mac Pro (aimed at professional and business users); the iMac (targeted toward consumer, educational, and business use); and Mac mini (made specifically for consumer use). Apple had two notebook product lines: MacBook Pro (for professional and advanced consumer users) and MacBook Air (designed for education users and consumers). All Apple computers were priced at a steep premium compared to PCs and laptops offered by Dell, HP, and other rivals. In January 2015, Mac Pro pricing started at $2,999, representing a $500 increase since 2012. iMac and MacBook Pro pricing began at $1,099, the MacBook Air was offered from $899, and Mac mini pricing started at $499, representing a $100 decrease in each from the 2012 prices.

Apple and Tablet Computers

Apple entered the market for tablet computers with its April 3, 2010, launch of the iPad. Tablet computers had been on the market since the late 1990s, but only Apple's version had gained any significant interest from consumers and business users. Previous-generation tablet computers required the use of a stylus to launch applications and enter information. Most users found the stylus interface to be an annoyance and preferred to use a smartphone or laptop when portability was required. Dell, Acer, and Hewlett-Packard had all raced to get touch-screen tablet computers to market but were unable to do so until very late 2010 and early 2011 because of the

technological differences between tablet computers and PCs. Tablet computers were technologically similar to smartphones and shared almost no components with PCs. HP acquired Palm for $1.2 billion in May 2010 to accelerate its entry into tablet computers. However, most PC manufacturers chose to utilize smartphone microprocessors and Google's Android operating system in their tablet computer models.

By mid-2012, Apple held a 68 percent share of the market for tablet computers. However, competitive pressures had dramatically reduced Apple's market share. In 2013, Apple was responsible for 33.8 percent of all shipments, but by 2014, the company's share of shipments had decreased to 27.6 percent. Its chief rival in the smartphone market, Samsung, had captured a 17.5 percent market share by 2014. Yet, the most significant impact may be due to an increase in the overall number of competitors. Only 60 percent of the total shipments in 2014 were accounted for by the top five vendors.

Apple's iPad 2, launched in March 2011, contained a dual-core processor that was far more powerful than the first-generation iPad and most competing tablet computers. Apple reduced the size and thickness of its iPad models and launched the iPad Air in late 2013 to address consumer criticism over weight and comfort of use. The iPad Air was approximately 22 percent lighter than standard iPad models and weighed about one pound. Apple launched the iPad Mini in direct response to smaller "phablets" offered by competitors. Although the same width as the iPad Air, the iPad Mini was approximately 1.5 inches shorter and weighed 25 percent less. The original iPad was discontinued in 2014.

In 2015, iPad Air and iPad Air 2 models retailed from $399 to $499 for the 16GB, respectively. The 128GB iPad Air 2 model retailed for $699. The iPad Mini model was $249. Apple's tablet computer pricing had dropped dramatically since 2012, when its 64GB iPad 2 retailed for $829.

Apple's Rivals in the Personal Computer Industry
Hewlett-Packard

Hewlett-Packard (HP) was broadly diversified across segments of the computer industry with business divisions focused on information technology consulting services, large enterprise systems, software, personal computers, printers and other imaging devices, and financial services. The company's Printing and Personal Systems Group (PSS), which manufactured and marketed HP and Compaq desktop computers and portable computers, was its largest division, accounting for revenues over 34 billion in 2014. HP recorded total net revenues of $111 billion in 2014, with its enterprise group and enterprise services accounting for 26.7 billion and 21.2 billion, respectively. The company's software business units accounted for sales of nearly $3.6 billion and its financial services unit contributed net revenue of about $3.4 billion in 2014.

PSS revenues remained the same between 2013 and 2014. Previous decreases in net revenue may be attributed to a decrease in the overall PC market; however, PSS revenues increased slightly from 2013 to 2014 due to an increase in commercial PC purchases.

In October 2014, HP announced its intent to split into two independent, publicly traded companies. The PSS segment, currently the printing and personal systems business units, would form HP Inc. The other segments, such as the enterprise systems and financial businesses, would be renamed Hewlett-Packard Enterprise. This division was expected to be completed by the end of 2015. Exhibit 4 provides the revenue contribution by PSS business unit for 2010 through 2014.

Dell Inc.

Dell Inc. had been the leading producer of PCs in the United States from 2001 through 2006. Tough economic conditions, declining demand for PCs by consumers, and growing price competition in the PC industry had significantly affected Dell's financial performance later in the 2000s, with its revenues declining from $62 billion in fiscal 2012 to $56.9 billion in fiscal 2013. In addition, Dell's net earnings fell from $3.5 billion in fiscal 2012 to $2.4 billion in fiscal 2013.

In 2013, Dell's stockholders approved the acquisition of the company by its founder, Michael Dell, and technology investment firm, Silver Lake Partners. The acquisition was aimed at refocusing the company on its core business and allow it to restore its formally impressive financial performance.

The company offered a wide range of desktop computers and portables, ranging from low-end, low-priced models to state-of-the-art, high-priced models. The company also offered servers; workstations; peripherals such as printers, monitors, and projectors; and Wi-Fi products. The company's shipments of PCs, however, declined from 62 billion in 2011 to 56.7 billion in 2014. Lenovo's deep price discounts had yielded a 34 percent increase in worldwide shipments over the same period, resulting in its rise to the top and Dell's fall to third worldwide for 2014. See Exhibit 5.

Apple's Competitive Position in the Market for Smartphones

The first version of the iPhone was released on June 29, 2007, with more than 270,000 first-generation iPhones being sold during the first 30 hours of the product's launch. The iPhone was named *Time*

EXHIBIT 4					
Hewlett-Packard Personal Systems Group, Net Revenue, 2010–2014 ($ millions)					
Product	2014	2013	2012	2011	2010
Notebooks	$17,540	$16,029	$18,830	$21,824	$22,545
Desktop PCs	13,197	12,844	13,888	15,370	15,478
Workstations	2,218	2,147	2,148	1,805	1,786
Other	1,348	1,159	977	575	932
Total	$34,303	$ 32,179	$35,843	$39,574	$ 40,741

Sources: Hewlett-Packard, 2011 and, 2014 10-K reports.

Dell's Revenues by Product Category, Fiscal 2010 – Fiscal 2013 ($ millions)

Product Category	Fiscal 2013	Fiscal 2012	Fiscal 2011	Fiscal 2010
Servers and networking	$9,294	$8,336	$7,609	$6,032
Storage	1,699	1,943	2,295	2,192
Services	8,396	8,322	7,673	5,622
Software and peripherals	9,257	10,222	10,261	9,499
Mobility	15,303	19,104	18,971	16,610
Desktop PCs	12,991	14,144	14,685	12,947
Total net revenue	$56,940	$62,071	$61,494	$52,904

Source: Dell Inc., 2011, 2012 and 2013 10-K reports.

magazine's Invention of the Year in 2007. The iPhone 3G was released in 70 countries on July 11, 2008, and was available in the United States exclusively through AT&T Mobility. The iPhone 3G allowed users to access the Internet wirelessly at twice the speed of the previous version of the iPhone and featured a built-in global positioning system (GPS), and, in an effort to increase adoption by corporate users, was compatible with Microsoft Exchange. The iPhone 3GS was introduced on June 19, 2009, and included all of the 3G features, and again doubled the Internet speeds over the 3G.

The iPhone 4 was launched on June 24, 2010, and included video-calling capabilities (only over a Wi-Fi network), a 5-megapixel camera including flash and zoom, 720p video recording, a longer-lasting battery, and a gyroscopic motion sensor to enable an improved gaming experience. The iPhone 4 sold more than 1.7 million units within three days of its launch. The iPhone 4S sold more than 4 million units within the first three days of its October 14, 2011, launch. The iPhone 4S also possessed the first significant innovation in the iPhone series with the addition of Siri, Apple's intelligent assistant and voice control feature. By 2011, Apple had expanded its carrier network beyond AT&T to include Verizon, Sprint, and C-Spire in the United States and a variety of carriers in Europe and Asia.

The iPhone 5 represented several shifts in Apple's strategy with its iPhone product. Mirroring Apple's approach to consumer trends in size preference, the iPhone 5 was increased to 4 inches from the previous 3.5-inch size. It also featured the first change in the connector, an all-digital "lighting connector." One of the more dramatic shifts, it changed how the phone interfaced with other products and rendered many peripherals obsolete.

The release of both the iPhone 5S and 5C demonstrated Apple's change in approach to segmenting the market. Both were still the larger, 4-inch format; however, the 5C maintained many of the previous features found in the iPhone 5 and was less expensive. The 5S, however, extended many of the current capabilities, while introducing a new feature, Touch ID. The Touch ID was a fingerprint scanner in the home button meant to increase security. This would also lay the foundation for another new feature found in the iPhone 5S: the Apple Pay mobile payment system.

The iPhone 6 and 6 Plus continued Apple's changing strategy regarding phone size. While the iPhone 6 increased to 4.7 inches, the iPhone 6 Plus was 5.5 inches, furthering Apple's move into the phablet market and mirroring the strategy with the iPad Mini. The price of the iPhone 6 and 6Plus in 2015 were $199 and $299, respectively, for the 16GB models.

Demand and Competition in the Smartphone Market

Since 2012, worldwide shipments of smartphones had almost doubled, from 725 million units in 2012 to 1.3 billion in 2014. For the first time, shipments of smartphones were more than 50 percent of all mobile phone shipments in 2013, demonstrating a dramatic change in how consumers used mobile technology to access the Internet and multimedia content. Driving this increase in smartphone shipments was the steady decrease in overall manufacturing costs and increased competition, leading to a decrease in the price paid by the consumer.

Countries such as China and South Korea and regions such as the Middle East and Africa offered the greatest growth opportunities but also presented challenges to smartphone producers. For example, in 2014, there were over 1 billion mobile phone users in China, approximately 700 million of whom were smartphone users. Apple began selling the iPhone 4 in China in 2010 through its partnership with China Telecom, the country's second-largest wireless provider and its network of 25 flagship stores located in the country's largest cities. The iPhone 4S became available in China in January 2012—making it available in 90 countries within three months of its initial launch. However, intellectual property protection and counterfeit products, including counterfeit Apple Stores, posed significant problems.

In South Korea, smartphone usage surpassed PC usage in 2014, where 84 percent of the population used a smartphone to access the Internet, compared to 78 percent that used a PC. Yet, strong brand loyalty for Korea-based Samsung can be found not only in Korea but also in the United States, helping Samsung capture nearly 25 percent of the global market share for smartphone shipments in 2014.

The Middle East and Africa experienced 83 percent growth in 2014. This growth was due to less expensive smartphones, as 20 percent of all smartphones in the region were priced at $100 or less. This growing market was a challenge due to Apple's pricing strategy. Competitors such as Lenovo successfully targeted this market and built large market shares in the region.

With the market for smartphones growing rapidly, competition was becoming stronger. Google's entry into the market with its Android operating system had allowed vendors such as LG, Motorola, and Samsung to offer models that matched many of the features of the iPhone. In fact, Android's strong capabilities had made it the number-one smartphone platform worldwide, with 76.6 percent of shipments running on Android in the fourth quarter of 2014. Exhibit 6 presents shipments and market shares for the leading smartphone producers between 2012 and 2014.

Apple's Competitive Position in the Personal Media Player Industry

Although Apple didn't introduce the first portable digital music player, the company has consistently possessed over 70 percent of the market, and the

EXHIBIT 6

Top Five Worldwide Smartphone Vendors, Shipment Volumes and Market Shares, 2012-2014

Rank	Vendor	2014		2013		2012	
		Shipments (in millions)	Market Share	Shipments (in millions)	Market Share	Shipments (in millions)	Market Share
1	Samsung	318.2	24.5%	316.4	31.0%	219.7	30.3%
2	Apple	192.7	14.8	153.4	15.1	135.9	18.7
3	Huawei	73.6	5.7	49.0	4.8	29.1	4.0
4	Lenovo	70.0	5.4	45.5	4.5	23.7	3.3
5	LG	59.2	4.6	47.8	4.7	26.3	3.6
	Others	587.3	45.1	407.4	40.0	290.5	40.1
	All vendors	1,301.1	100.0%	1019.4	100.0%	725.3	100.0%

Source: International Data Corporation.

name iPod had become a generic term used to describe digital media players. When Apple launched its first iPod in 2001, many critics did not give the product much of a chance for success, given its fairly hefty price tag of $399. However, the iPod's sleek styling, ease of use, and integration with iTunes and digital music purchases, coupled with the eventual price decreases and differing models, allowed it to develop such high levels of customer satisfaction and loyalty that rivals found it difficult to gain traction in the marketplace. Even though many competing MP3 players compared favorably to Apple's iPod models, none of Apple's key rivals in the media player industry had been able to achieve a market share greater than 5 percent since 2004. Most consumers did not find many convincing reasons to consider any brand of media player other than Apple.

While the original iPod only played music, the most popular portable players in 2015 not only played music but also could be connected to Wi-Fi networks to play videos, access the Internet, view photos, or listen to FM high-definition radio. The iPod Touch had remained the best-selling media player since its introduction in 2012 with more than 350 million units sold by year-end 2014. However, the wide-scale adoption of smartphones had cannibalized the portable media player market with iPod sales declining by 45 percent between 2013 and 2014 and Apple formally discontinuing the iPod Classic in September 2014. Apple continued to sell the iPod touch, iPod nano, and iPod Shuffle in 2015 with prices beginning at $199, $149, and $49, respectively.

App Store and iTunes

iTunes was Apple's software for managing digital music, movies, and other content on its PCs, tablets, and smartphones. Further, iTunes was its online marketplace to sell music, as well as movies and TV shows. In the early 2000s, when Napster and other free music sharing sites were encountering legal issues, Apple was able to gain widespread acceptance in both the marketplace and from the music industry through the ease of use and copyright protection afforded by iTunes. As of 2015, over 43 million songs were available for consumers to choose

from, and the iTunes Store had expanded to offer consumers the ability to purchase and download videos, movies, and television shows that could be played on iPods, iPhones, or Apple TV devices.

Users of Apple's iPods, iPhones, iPads, or Macs could also use the company's iMatch or iCloud services that integrated apps, iBooks, and iTunes purchased at the App Store to all devices owned by the individual. The iCloud service also allowed users to share calendars and contacts, wirelessly push photographs to all devices, and back up data from Apple devices.

Finally, the growth in popularity of cable-alternative devices such as Apple TV had further contributed to sales on iTunes. Consumers increasingly cancelled traditional cable services and began consuming TV and movie content through streaming services. Netflix, Amazon, and Hulu, for example, provided monthly subscription services allowing consumers to access movies and TV seasons. Full NBA, MLS, and other sports seasons are also available through subscriptions. In 2015, HBO announced a cable-free subscription service available to Apple TV owners. While Apple TV provided users with the ability to access Apple's content, other media companies were selling their services through Apple as well.

Apple's Performance in 2015 and the Launch of the Apple Watch

As of 2015, Apple's outstanding performance had not been impeded by the loss of Steve Jobs as CEO, who had been the inspiration of its most important and innovative products. Since 2011, Apple had almost tripled its net sales and had become ranked in the top five of global PC shipments. Yet, as Mac sales had increased to 19 million units and iPhone sales to 170 million units, the iPod had been discontinued, and iPad sales had stagnated around 70 million units.

The biggest concerns for the company in 2015 were how to handle the shrinking market for PCs and the increased competition in the smartphone and tablet markets. Clearly, iPad and iPhone sales were the largest contributors to the company's financial performance. Even though Tim Cook was successfully leading the company after the death of Steve Jobs, it was Jobs who had been widely recognized as the visionary force behind the development of the iPod, iPhone, and iPad. With the launch of the Apple Watch, however, industry observers would learn whether Cook would also be able to lead the development of products that would disrupt technology markets.

ENDNOTES

[1] Yukari Iwatani Kane and Nick Wingfield, "Apple's Deep Bench Faces Challenges," *Wall Street Journal Online,* August 24, 2011.

Sirius XM Satellite Radio, Inc., in 2014: On Track to Succeed After a Near-Death Experience?

ARTHUR A. THOMPSON   The University of Alabama

In February 2009, the outlook for Sirius XM Satellite Radio was grim. Despite having 2008 revenues of nearly $1.7 billion and some 19 million subscribers, the company's stock price had dropped to a low of $0.05 per share, and the company was mired in a deep financial crisis, with debts totaling more than $3 billion. Years of big spending and annual losses in the hundreds of billions had depleted the company's ability to secure additional credit to pay its bills, and the company lacked the cash to make a scheduled debt payment of $171.6 million due on February 17. But hours before filing for Chapter 11 bankruptcy (to avoid defaulting on the scheduled debt payment), Sirius XM got a lifeline from Liberty Media, a $2 billion company with business interests in the media, communications, and entertainment industries; Liberty was headed by cable TV pioneer and financial tycoon John Malone, who not only owned a controlling interest in Liberty Media but also was known for making big investments in troubled or undervalued companies having what he believed were good prospects for long-term profitability. Liberty agreed to provide an aggregate of $530 million in loans to Sirius in return for (1) 12.5 million shares of Sirius XM preferred stock convertible into 40 percent of common stock of Sirius XM and (2) seats on the Sirius XM board of directors proportional to its equity ownership. Two of these seats were to be occupied by John Malone, Liberty's chairman, and Greg Maffei, Liberty's CEO. Many outsiders viewed the terms to be a sweetheart deal for Liberty Media.

Headed into 2014, Sirius XM had 25.6 million subscribers, 2013 revenues of $3.8 billion, operating income of $1 billion, net income of $377 million, and cash flows from operations of $1.1 billion. The company's stock price had rebounded nicely and traded mostly in the $3.50 to $4 range during the last three months of 2013, equal to a market capitalization of $21 billion to $24 billion.

Company Background

Sirius XM Satellite Radio was the product of a 2008 merger of Sirius Satellite Radio and XM Satellite Radio. The two predecessor companies had begun operations in 2001–2002, spending hundreds of millions to launch satellites for broadcasting signals, arrange for the manufacture of satellite radio receivers and other equipment, install terrestrial signal repeaters and other necessary networking equipment, develop programming, conduct market research, and attract subscribers. The primary target market for satellite radio service included the owners of the more than 230 million registered vehicles in North America and, secondarily, the over 120 million households in the United States and Canada.

Market research done in 2000–2001 indicated that as many as 49 million people might subscribe to satellite radio service by 2012, assuming a monthly fee of $9.95 and radio receiver prices of $150 to $399, depending on the car or home model chosen. A 2002 market research study conducted for XM concluded there would be a total of about 15 million satellite radio subscribers by the end of 2006. Considering that in spring 2005 both XM and Sirius raised their subscription rates to $12.95 monthly, the forecast turned out to be fairly close to the actual 13.6 million satellite radio subscribers in the United States reported at year-end 2006.

Both Sirius and XM employed a subscription-based business model to generate revenues. Subscribers received discounts if they had multiple XM or Sirius satellite radios (for different vehicles or for home and office use) or if they signed up for prepaid plans of two to three years. Both companies did not expect to cover the high startup costs and become profitable until acquiring at least 8 million to 10 million subscribers.

Competition Between XM and Sirius Quickly Becomes Spirited and Expensive

Early on, the two companies became embroiled in a fierce market battle waged on multiple fronts:

- Creating a programming lineup that was more attractive than its rival's programming lineup
- Convincing automakers to factory-install its brand of satellite radio (the radios of the two rivals were incompatible—XM radios could not receive signals broadcast by Sirius, and vice versa)
- Gaining broad retail distribution of its various satellite radio models and equipment for use at home or in used vehicles
- Building brand awareness and stimulating consumer demand for satellite radio service

The Race to Differentiate Programming Content While each company's programming strategy was to offer a diverse, appealing selection of digital-quality radio programs that would attract listeners willing to subscribe to mostly commercial-free programming, each company recognized that the key to gaining a competitive edge was having differentiated programming content capable of attracting and retaining the greatest number of subscribers. Each company quickly moved to create one or more channels for almost every music genre and a big assortment of channels devoted to news and commentary, sports, comedy and entertainment, family and health, religion, politics, traffic, and weather. By

2007, XM had a programming lineup of over 170 channels that included 69 commercial-free music channels; 5 commercial music channels; 37 news, talk, and commentary channels; 38 sports channels; and 21 instant traffic and weather channels. Sirius was broadcasting on 133 channels that included 69 channels of 100 percent commercial-free music and 64 channels providing sports programming, news, talk, information, entertainment, traffic, and weather. To achieve differentiation, both companies spent large, sometimes lavish, sums for contracts to:

- Obtain broadcast rights for the audio portions of programs on National Public Radio and such cable TV channels as Fox News, CNN, CNBC, MSNBC, ESPN News, and ESPN Radio.
- Gain *exclusive* rights to air live play-by-play broadcasts of various sporting events (Major League Baseball games, National Football League games, National Basketball Association games, National Hockey League games, college football and basketball games for all major conferences, professional golf and tennis tournaments, NASCAR races, horse races, FIFA World Cup soccer games, etc.). As an example of the large amounts spent to acquire exclusive rights for high-profile programming, XM paid $60 million annually for a six-year agreement to broadcast Major League Baseball games live nationwide for the years 2007 through 2012.
- Secure the services of well-known personalities and brands (such as Howard Stern, Oprah Winfrey, and Martha Stewart Living) and create special channels featuring their shows and content. In 2004, Sirius signed a five-year contractual agreement with Howard Stern said to be worth $400 million to $500 million in salaries for Stern and his staff plus stock bonuses for Stern and his agent that were based on exceeding specified subscriber targets; Howard Stern broadcasts began on two Sirius channels in January 2006.

At XM, expenditures for programming and content were $101 million in 2005, $165.2 million in 2006, and $183.9 million in 2007. Sirius Satellite Radio's expenditures for programming were $100.8 million in 2005, $520.4 million in 2006, and $236.1 million in 2007. Apart from battling to achieve differentiated programming content, the two competitors also strived to attain overall product differentiation by offering greater geographic coverage, more commercial-free programming choices, and digital sound quality.

Partnering with Automakers and Gaining Broad Distribution in the Retail Marketplace

Simultaneously, both XM and Sirius aggressively launched well-funded strategic initiatives to gain broad distribution of their satellite radios via partnerships with motor vehicle manufacturers, making satellite radios available at national and regional consumer electronics retailers and mass merchandisers (Best Buy, Walmart, and Target), and selling radios at their websites—all were sources of new subscribers. The battle was particularly fierce in the automobile segment for three reasons:

1. A big majority of the new subscribers for satellite radio service were the owners of newly purchased vehicles equipped with a satellite radio.

2. A majority of the satellite radios for new vehicles were factory-installed, although automobile dealers could install satellite radios in some models.

3. The incompatibility of XM and Sirius radios forced vehicle manufacturers to choose which brand to install in factory-assembled vehicles.

Each of the competitors lobbied hard for vehicle manufacturers to sign contractual agreements to exclusively install only its brand of satellite radio in vehicles scheduled to be equipped with a satellite radio. Both XM and Sirius used liberal subsidies and commissions to induce manufacturers to sign exclusivity agreements: Each rival paid automakers a subsidy if its brand of satellite radio and a prepaid trial subscription (usually for three months but sometimes for six months) was included in the sale or lease price of a new vehicle. As a further incentive, each paid automakers either a commission or a share of the subscription revenues to purchase, install, and activate its brand of satellite radio. There were also revenue-sharing payments on subsequent subscriptions by new vehicle owners after the trial period expired. For instance, XM had a long-term distribution agreement with General Motors whereby GM agreed to exclusively install only XM's brand of satellite radios in return for GM being paid a portion of

the revenues derived from all subscribers using GM vehicles equipped to receive XM's service; this was in addition to the incentives XM paid to GM to subsidize a portion of the costs of installing XM radios in GM vehicles. Indeed, it was common practice for XM and Sirius to reimburse automakers for certain hardware-related costs, tooling expenses, and promotional and advertising expenses directly related to including a satellite radio as a vehicle option.

For the 2007 model year, Sirius radios were available as a factory-installed option in 89 vehicle models and as a dealer-installed option in 19 vehicle models; Sirius service was also offered to renters of Hertz vehicles at 55 airport locations nationwide. For the same model year, XM's satellite radios were available as original equipment in over 140 vehicle models.

In addition to offering subsidies and incentives to automakers, XM and Sirius also offered subsidies and incentives to (1) the manufacturers of their satellite radios, (2) the makers of chip sets and other components used in manufacturing satellite radios, (3) the various distributors and retailers of satellite radio devices and equipment, and (4) automotive dealers that installed satellite radios on vehicles not having a factory-installed satellite radio. Moreover, there were device royalties for certain types of satellite radios, subsidies for handling product warranty obligations, price protection for distributor inventories, and provisions for inventory allowances.

All of these expenses (except for revenue-sharing payments) were incurred in advance of acquiring a subscriber and were classified as subscriber acquisition costs. For XM, subscriber acquisition costs were $245.6 million in 2005, $224.9 million in 2006, and $259.1 million in 2007; Sirius incurred subscriber acquisition costs of $399.4 million in 2005, $451.6 million in 2006, and $407.6 million in 2007.

In 2006, the Federal Communications Commission, which had jurisdiction for satellite radio communications and had regulatory authority for issuing operating licenses for satellite radio enterprises, responded to growing numbers of consumer complaints about being locked into subscribing to the service of one company or the other, depending on the brand of satellite radio they had purchased. The FCC brought pressure on XM and Sirius to resolve the signal reception incompatibility and issued rules requiring the interoperability of both licensed satellite radio systems. Late in 2006, XM and Sirius signed an agreement to develop a unified standard for satellite radios to enable consumers to purchase one radio capable of receiving either company's broadcast signal and thus subscribe to whichever company's service they wished. The agreement called for the technology relating to this unified standard to be developed, jointly funded, and jointly owned by the two companies. Satellite radio manufacturers began including both XM and Sirius chip sets in their satellite radios to enable dual-signal reception in 2008; within months, all satellite radios were being manufactured with dual-reception capability.

Building Brand Awareness and Stimulating Demand for Satellite Radio Service Both XM and Sirius pursued aggressive marketing strategies, spending heavily on a variety of sizable sales, marketing, and promotional activities calculated to build brand awareness, communicate the appealing features of satellite radio service compared to traditional radio, and attract, first, hundreds of thousands and, then, millions of new subscribers annually. Advertising and promotional activities were conducted via television, radio, print, and the Internet; brochures illustrating the array of available channels and programs, along with other satellite radio features, were distributed at retail outlets, concert venues, and motor sports events and on the Internet to generate consumer interest; some major retailers participated in jointly funded local advertising campaigns. In-store promotions typically included displays at electronics and music stores, car audio retailers and other retailers that stocked and promoted sales of satellite radios, automobile dealerships, and rental car agencies with vehicles equipped with a satellite radio.

At XM, expenses for marketing and advertising were $182.4 million in 2005, $164.4 million in 2006, and $178.7 million in 2007. Sirius had sales and marketing expenses of $197.7 million in 2005, $203.7 million in 2006, and $173.6 million in 2007.

The Competitive Battle Between XM and Sirius Inflicted Major Financial Damage

The heavy expenses incurred by the efforts of the two rivals as each tried to gain an edge over the other produced gigantic losses every year of their existence, despite having attracted millions of subscribers. Comparative performance statistics for 2005–2007 are shown in Exhibit 1.

With both companies burdened by sizable negative cash flows from operations, balance sheets that were becoming precariously weaker as long-term borrowings and stockholders' deficits mounted, waning ability to raise additional equity capital from increasingly anxious investors, and growing concerns about the viability of their business models, there was much speculation in 2006–2007 about whether either XM or Sirius could obtain the financing needed to survive for much longer. Executives at both companies concluded that after six years of battling for subscribers and bidding up programming costs, the only long-term solution was to merge and bring a halt to the destructive competitive battle that was unlikely to end short of bankruptcy. The executives and boards of directors of the two companies hammered out a planned merger agreement that was announced on February 19, 2007.

But there were significant hurdles to overcome because the merger, if approved by the FCC and the Antitrust Division of the U.S. Department of Justice, would create a satellite radio monopoly, although the merged company would still face competition for listeners from multiple sources, including terrestrial AM/FM radio, both free and paid Internet streaming services (from Clear Channel, CBS Radio, Pandora, and others), the music channels offered by cable TV providers, digital music devices such as iPods and MP3 players, and the music and other programming that could be stored on or streamed to smartphones. Traditional AM/FM radio enterprises offered free broadcast reception paid for by commercial advertising rather than by a subscription fee. Sirius and XM argued that the free broadcast programs of AM/FM enterprises (as well as all the other free and paid music programming that was widely available) not only reduced the likelihood that customers would be willing to pay for satellite radio subscription service but also imposed limits on what a merged XM-Sirius could charge for its service. Thus, XM and Sirius alleged that competitive forces would be adequate to protect consumers from any "monopoly pricing" or other monopolistically abusive practices stemming from an XM-Sirius merger. However, many AM/FM

EXHIBIT 1

Comparative Performance, XM Satellite Radio and Sirius Satellite Radio, 2005–2007 (dollar amounts in thousands, except per-subscriber data)

	2005	2006	2007
XM Radio			
Number of subscribers, year-end	5,933,000	7,629,000	9,027,000
Gross subscriber additions	4,130,000	3,866,000	3,891,000
Deactivated subscribers	1,427,000	2,170,000	2,493,000
Net subscriber additions	2,703,000	1,696,000	1,398,000
Subscriber revenues	$ 502,612	$ 825,626	$ 1,005,479
Total revenues	558,266	933,417	1,136,542
Operating expenses	1,113,801	1,336,515	1,647,979
Loss from operations	(555,535)	(403,098)	(511,437)
Net loss	(666,715)	(718,872)	(682,381)
Long-term debt	1,035,584	1,286,179	1,480,639
Total stockholders' (deficit) equity	80,948	(397,880)	(984,303)
Cash flows from operations	$(166,717)	$(462,091)	$(154,730)
Average monthly revenue per subscriber	$10.57	$11.41	$11.48
Subscriber acquisition costs per gross subscriber addition*	$109	$108	$121
Sirius Satellite Radio			
Number of subscribers, year-end	3,316,560	6,024,555	8,321,785
Gross subscriber additions	2,519,301	3,758,163	4,183,901
Deactivated subscribers	345,999	1,050,168	1,886,671
Net subscriber additions	2,173,302	2,707,995	2,297,230
Subscriber revenues	$ 223,615	$ 575,404	$ 854,933
Total revenues	242,245	637,235	922,066
Operating expenses	1,071,385	1,704,959	1,435,156
Loss from operations	(829,140)	(1,067,724)	(513,090)
Net loss	(862,997)	(1,104,867)	(562,252)
Long-term debt	1,084,437	1,068,249	1,278,617
Total stockholders' (deficit) equity	324,968	(389,071)	(792,737)
Cash flows from operations	$(269,994)	$(421,702)	$(148,766)
Average monthly revenue per subscriber	$10.34	$11.01	$10.46
Subscriber acquisition costs per gross subscriber addition*	$139	$114	$101

*Subscriber acquisition costs include hardware subsidies paid to radio manufacturers, distributors, and automakers, including subsidies paid to automakers that included a satellite radio and subscription to Sirius or XM service in the sale or lease price of a new vehicle; subsidies paid for chip sets and certain other components used in manufacturing satellite radios; device royalties for certain radios and chip sets; commissions paid to automakers as incentives to purchase, install, and activate satellite radios; payments for handling product warranty obligations; freight; and provisions for inventory allowances associated with factory-installations of satellite radios by automakers and the orders and sales of satellite radio equipment by distributors and retailers.

Source: Company 10-K report for 2007.

enterprises, along with consumer interest groups and other interested parties, expressed opposition to the merger, largely on grounds that it would be anticompetitive and injurious to satellite radio subscribers.

After 17 months of regulatory scrutiny and despite the objections of various concerned parties, the proposed merger won approval from the FCC and the Department of Justice's Antitrust Division in July 2008 after XM and Sirius voluntarily agreed to:

1. Pay a $20 million fine for failure to previously comply with certain FCC regulations.

2. Sign a consent decree to cease such practices and bring their operating activities into full compliance with FCC regulations.

Assorted subscriber metrics are shown in Exhibit 3. Sirius XM Radio had a 38 percent equity interest in Sirius XM Canada, which offered satellite radio services in Canada and had 2 million subscribers in early 2014. However, subscribers to the Sirius XM Canada service were not included in Sirius XM's subscriber count.

Programming Strategy

Since the 2008 merger, the programming strategy had centered on three key elements:

1. *Bargaining hard for lower prices on programming content so as to reduce the company's overall programming costs.* Sirius XM

executives were acutely aware that the fierce rivalry between XM and Sirius during 2002–2007 had led to significant "overbidding" for content. The overbidding resulted from trying to match or beat the content recently acquired by one's rival and/or sometimes agreeing to pay a big price premium to keep the other firm from winning exclusive rights to high-profile content with considerable listener appeal (such as Howard Stern or play-by-play sporting events). Hence, as the contracts expired for programming content negotiated prior to the merger, the central objective during contract renegotiation was to reduce the premium prices the company was paying for high-profile broadcast rights,

EXHIBIT 3

Comparative Performance, XM Satellite Radio and Sirius Satellite Radio, 2010–2013 (dollar amounts in thousands, except per-subscriber data)

	2010	2011	2012	2013
Subscriber data				
Beginning subscribers	18,772,758	20,190,964	21,892,824	23,900,336
Gross subscriber additions	7,768,827	8,696,020	9,617,771	10,136,391
Deactivated subscribers	(6,350,621)	(6,994,160)	(7,610,259)	(8,477,407)
Net additions	1,418,206	1,701,860	2,007,512	1,658,974
Self-pay	982,867	1,221,943	1,661,532	1,511,543
Paid promotional (trial)	435,339	479,917	345,980	147,431
Ending subscribers	20,190,964	21,892,824	23,900,336	25,559,310
Self-pay	16,686,799	17,908,742	19,570,274	21,081,817
Paid promotional (trial)	3,504,165	3,984,082	4,330,062	4,477,493
Subscriber metrics				
Daily weighted-average number of subscribers	19,385,055	20,903,908	22,794,170	24,886,300
Average self-pay monthly churn*	1.9%	1.9%	1.9%	1.8%
New-vehicle conversion rate from trial to self-pay	46%	45%	45%	44%
Average revenue per subscriber	$11.53	$11.73	$12.00	$12.27
Subscriber acquisition cost, per gross subscriber addition	$59	$55	$54	$50
Customer service and billing expense per average subscriber	$1.03	$1.03	$1.07	$1.07

*Derived from the average of the quarterly average self-pay monthly churn during the year. The average self-pay monthly churn for a quarter is calculated by dividing the monthly average of self-pay deactivations for a quarter by the average self-pay subscriber balance for a quarter.

Source: Company 10-K report, 2012, pp. 30 and 32; and company 10-K report, 2013, pp. 31 and 33.

most particularly for sporting events and talk-show personalities (such as Howard Stern).

2. *Curbing the costs of duplicate programming,* particularly in the case of music channels where both XM and Sirius were incurring the costs of programming "look-alike" channels and each operated as an individual station in every music genre. For example, XM had four country-music channels, each with its own format, style, mix of recordings, and branding, that were programmed and hosted by a team of country-music experts, while Sirius also had four country-music channels, each with its own slightly different format, style, recordings mix, and branding, that were programmed and hosted by a different set of country-music experts. The same sort of duplication and overlap existed for the rock, pop, hip-hop, gospel, dance, jazz, Latin, and classical channels the two companies were broadcasting. Sirius XM executives promptly began a multiyear initiative to consolidate the roughly 70 music channels broadcast by XM and the 70 or so music channels broadcast by Sirius into a new set of about 70 music channels that were jointly broadcast to XM subscribers and to Sirius subscribers.

3. *Refreshing and expanding the company's programming lineup.* Sirius executives viewed programming as the foundation of the company's business. To complement and strengthen Sirius XM's broad channel lineup and offering of exclusive programs, management continuously looked for new and unique brands and personalities to collaborate with and develop content that was unavailable to terrestrial radio and online competitors. The strategic objective was to continue to build record numbers of subscribers by producing innovative and appealing content.

Company efforts to cut programming costs had been successful. When interviewed by a *Barron's* reporter in fall 2013, Sirius XM CEO Jim Meyer was quoted as saying:[1]

> Before we merged, our programming cost was $450 million for everything besides music. Now, it's under $300 million. And that's not going to change a lot.

One industry analyst estimated that Sirius XM's monthly programming costs were $0.96 per subscriber in 2013 and would likely fall to $0.76 per subscriber by 2016 because of flat programming costs and growing numbers of subscribers.[2]

Music Programming Sirius XM's music offerings were regularly adjusted and fine-tuned to remain in step with the ongoing changes in the tastes and preferences of music listeners and the shifting popularity of music artists. The channels created by the company were broadcast commercial-free, but certain music channels were programmed by third parties and aired commercials. The 2013 channel lineup also featured interviews and performances of some of the biggest names in music, a *Town Hall* series that featured concerts and interviews before a live audience, and several "pop-up" channels featuring the music of particular artists.

In 2013, music programming accounted for about 60 percent of the company's total programming costs.[3] Sirius XM had to pay royalties to the music publishers, recording studios and record companies, songwriters, and performing artists whose musical works were broadcast on its channels. In some cases, the royalty rate was negotiated directly with the copyright owners or their representatives; but if no agreements were reached, the laws in the United States governing copyrights called for the royalty rates to be determined by the Copyright Royalty Board (CRB) of the Library of Congress. In December 2012, the CRB determined that the royalties paid on sound recordings broadcast over satellite radio for the five-year period starting January 1, 2013, and ending December 31, 2017, would be based on subscription revenue from U.S. satellite digital audio radio subscribers and advertising revenue from channels other than those channels that make only incidental performances of sound recordings and that the royalty rates would be 9 percent for 2013, 9.5 percent for 2014, 10 percent for 2015, 10.5 percent for 2016, and 11 percent for 2017. The rate for 2012 was 8 percent. However, revenues derived from the following were not subject to CRB-mandated royalty payments: (1) channels, programming, and products or other services offered for a separate charge when such channels make only incidental performances of sound recordings,

(2) equipment sales, (3) current and future data services, and (4) certain other services and activities. In addition, the regulations allowed Sirius XM to reduce its monthly royalty fee in proportion to the percentage of its music performances that featured pre-1972 recordings (which were not subject to federal copyright protection), as well as those that were licensed directly from the copyright holder, rather than through a statutory license. Sirius XM charged all U.S. subscribers a U.S. music royalty fee, as an add-on to the regular subscription price, to cover the music royalty payments required by the CRB.

Sports Programming   Live play-by-play sports were an important part of Sirius XM's programming strategy. In 2013–2014, Sirius XM was the Official Satellite Radio Partner of the National Football League (NFL), the National Hockey League (NHL), and the PGA TOUR, and it broadcast most major college sports, including NCAA Division I regular-season football and basketball games, over 30 college football bowl games, and all tournament games of the NCAA Division 1 Men's Basketball Championship. There were broadcasts of soccer matches from the Barclays Premier League, FIS Alpine Skiing events, FIFA World Cup events, and horse racing. In addition, the sports lineup included a number of exclusive talk channels and programs such as MLB Network Radio, SiriusXM NASCAR Radio, Sirius XM NFL Radio, College Sports Nation, and Chris "Mad Dog" Russo's *Mad Dog Unleashed* on Mad Dog Radio, as well as two ESPN channels (ESPN Radio and ESPN Xtra). Simulcasts of select ESPN television shows, including *Sports-Center,* were broadcast on the company's ESPN Xtra channel.

Sirius XM's contract to broadcast every Major League Baseball game ran through 2021. Its agreement with the National Football League was up for renewal at the end of 2015.

Talk and Entertainment Programming   Sirius XM's channel lineup included about 30 talk and entertainment channels that were designed for a broad variety of audiences and thus differentiated the company's programming from terrestrial radio and other audio entertainment providers. The talk-radio listening options featured a multitude of popular talk personalities, some with their own radio shows that aired exclusively on Sirius XM, including Howard Stern, Oprah Winfrey, Dr. Laura Schlessinger, Opie and Anthony, Bob Edwards, former senator Bill Bradley, and doctors from the NYU Langone Medical Center. Subscribers could listen to a range of humor on Sirius XM's comedy channels, including Jamie Foxx's The Foxxhole, Laugh USA, Blue Collar Comedy, and Raw Dog Comedy. Other talk and entertainment channels included a full-time channel devoted to business and management, SiriusXM Book Radio, Kids Place Live, Radio Disney, Rural Radio, Cosmo Radio, OutQ, Road Dog Trucking, and Playboy Radio. Religious programming included The Catholic Channel (programmed with the archdiocese of New York), EWTN (Catholic programming and news programming from around the world), and Family Talk.

The company's contract with Howard Stern was up for renewal at the end of 2015. According to media reports, the five-year contract Sirius XM and Howard Stern signed in December 2010 called for Sirius XM to pay an estimated $80 million annually for Howard Stern programming, down 20 percent from the approximately $100 million annual payments (including bonuses) for the initial five-year contract signed in 2004. Some observers had speculated that Stern's declining popularity and listener base might give Sirius XM greater leverage in negotiating to renew its contract with Stern in 2015. Sirius had already made some progress in reducing the prices of its highest-paid radio personalities—both Martha Stewart and Bubba the Love Sponge Clem had already agreed to reduced compensation.

News and Information Programming   There was a wide range of national, international, and financial news, including news from CNBC, CNN, Fox News, HLN, Bloomberg Radio, MSNBC, NPR, BBC World Service News, and World Radio Network, plus several political call-in talk shows on a variety of channels and Sirius XM's exclusive channel, POTUS. Subscribers could get local traffic reports for 22 metropolitan markets throughout the United States.

Internet Radio   Sirius XM streamed music channels and select nonmusic channels over the Internet, including several channels and features that were not available to satellite radio subscribers. Access to the company's Internet services was offered to satellite radio subscribers for an additional fee. Sirius XM marketed devices that enabled access to its Internet services without the need for a personal computer. It had also developed apps that allowed consumers to access the company's Internet services on certain smartphones and tablet computers.

In 2012, the company launched SiriusXM On Demand, which gave Internet subscribers listening on the company's online media player and on smartphones the ability to choose their favorite episodes from a library of more than 300 shows and over 3,000 hours of content that included regularly updated feature content, commercial-free music from many genres, *Town Hall* specials, music specials, interviews with a wide range of celebrities, *The Howard Stern Show,* Dr. Laura, Jimmy Buffett concerts, Coach K, *Bob Dylan's Theme Time Radio Hour,* and selected shows from the company's lineup of sports, comedy, and exclusive talk and entertainment channels.

More recently, Sirius had introduced MySXM that permitted listeners to personalize the company's existing commercial-free music and comedy channels to create a more tailored listening experience. Channel-specific sliders allowed users to create over 100 variations of each of more than 50 channels by adjusting characteristics such as library depth, familiarity, music style, tempo, region, and multiple other channel-specific attributes. SiriusXM On Demand and MySXM were offered to Internet subscribers at no extra charge.

In 2013, Sirius expanded its online offering to further enhance the appeal of subscribing to Sirius XM Internet Radio. Top management believed that coordinating the content and programming attractions across its satellite and streaming platforms would allow the company to provide subscribers with an "unparalleled experience."[4]

Dynamic Programming Content and Channel Content Sirius XM monitored the popularity of the content on each channel and the size of the audience listening to each channel. Channels with uneconomically low listener appeal either were dropped or had their content revised. Programming of existing channels was periodically refreshed. From time to time,

new channels with altogether new content were added to the lineup of channel offerings. In 2012, the company launched a Comedy Central Radio channel and added Michael Smerconish, a nationally syndicated terrestrial talk-radio star, to its lineup in its ongoing campaign to bring the best audio entertainment to subscribers. In 2013, prominent programming additions included numerous *Town Hall* special events with high-profile personalities, dozens of new weekly programs and special events on existing channels, and the launch of a David Bowie channel, an expanded Pink Floyd channel, a Just for Laughs comedy channel, a Tom Petty Radio channel, an Entertainment Weekly channel (in partnership with *Entertainment Weekly,* which was the content provider), The Girls' Room channel, and a Bon Jovi channel.

Several times each month, the company sent e-mails to subscribers calling attention to upcoming programs, shows, and events of interest scheduled for broadcast across its entire channel lineup. The e-mails also announced the launch of new shows on particular channels, temporary switches to seasonal music on particular channels, and any other noteworthy items (contests to win tickets to live performances and major sporting events, the appearance of special guests and/or the discussion of particular topics on regularly scheduled talk and entertainment shows, and the availability of certain videos that could be watched on the company's website or streamed to subscribers' tablets or smartphones). The e-mails served to heighten subscriber interest in satellite radio and build awareness of the dynamic and unique nature of Sirius XM's programming and how its diverse channel lineup and content offered "something for everyone and every mood."

Programming Studios Sirius XM's programming activities were conducted principally in studio facilities occupying a full floor at the company's corporate headquarters building in midtown Manhattan and at studios in Washington, D.C. The company also operated smaller studio facilities in Cleveland, Los Angeles, Memphis, Nashville, and Austin. Both the New York City and Washington, D.C., offices housed facilities for programming origination, programming personnel, and programming transmission to the company's 140-plus channels.

cooperative marketing activities. The company was also using telemarketing to promote Sirius XM to nonsubscribing owners of satellite radio–equipped used vehicles.

The strategic target was to convert some of the 30 million vehicles on the road with inactive satellite radios into vehicles with active subscriptions to Sirius XM's service. At the end of the 2013 third quarter, Sirius was on track to gain 1.5 million in gross subscriber additions in the used-vehicle segment in 2013 (up from 1 million in 2012); the used-vehicle conversion rate from trial subscriptions to paid subscriptions was running above 30 percent.

Subsidies and Incentives for the Retailers of Satellite Radios Subsidies and incentives were also used to induce retailers to stock satellite radios and promote Sirius XM's satellite radio service. They included hardware subsidies paid to retail distributors, inventory allowances, in-store merchandising materials, sales force training for large-volume retailers, the handling of product warranty obligations on radios sold, loyalty payments, commissions (or some other sort of revenue-sharing arrangement) on subsequent subscriptions, and payments to reimburse retailers for the cost of advertising and other product awareness activities performed on Sirius XM's behalf.

Share-based payments of subscription revenues to automakers, franchised dealers, independent used-car dealers, and the retailers of satellite radios totaled $68.9 million in 2013, $63.8 million in 2012, $53.4 million in 2011, and $63.3 million in 2010. These payments appeared on the company's income statement in the operating expense category labeled "Royalty and revenue-sharing payments" (see Exhibit 2).

A Variety of Subscription Plans and Subscription Packages Sirius marketers had created a variety of subscription plans for customers to choose from; Exhibit 4 shows the three most popular plans. Most customers, especially newer subscribers, opted for annual, semiannual, quarterly, or sometimes monthly subscription plans. To entice customers whose subscriptions were expiring to sign up for a longer term, Sirius offered discounts for prepaid subscriptions and for automatic-renewal plans that ran for terms of two or three years. There were also

discounts for customers who subscribed for service for two or more vehicles or had multiple radios for home and/or office use—roughly 80 percent of car-owning households in the United States owned two or more vehicles. The percentages of subscribers taking advantage of the discounts for longer-term plans and multiple-vehicle service were rising. From time to time, Sirius ran special promotions offering slightly deeper discounts on these plans.

Subscribers having an à la carte–capable radio (Sirius Starmate 8) could customize the programming they received; there were two à la carte subscription plans—one allowed subscribers to pick their 50 favorite channels within the Select package for a monthly price of $7.99, and the other allowed subscribers to choose 100 channels (not including live sports broadcast channels) for a monthly price of $15.99. There were also two family-friendly packages that did not contain adult-themed channels and had $1-per-month cheaper subscription prices, a 50+–channel news-sports-talk package priced at $9.99 per month, and a 155-channel Internet-only plan (for people who preferred to listen on a computer, tablet, smartphone, or other Internet-enabled device) priced at $14.99 per month—people who signed up for the Internet-only plan got a 30-day free trial. Because a substantial number of subscribers were driving older motor vehicles equipped with XM or Sirius radios that did not permit dual-signal reception, the company still had to broadcast both XM signals and Sirius signals rather than just a single signal. But the subscription plan packages and prices for customers with either XM or Sirius radios were identical.

Sales and Marketing Expenses Sirius XM's costs for sales and marketing activities are shown in Exhibit 2. These expenses included (1) expenditures for advertising, promotional events, and sponsorships; (2) reimbursement payments to automakers and retailers for advertising costs, certain cooperative marketing activities, and other product awareness activities performed on Sirius XM's behalf; (3) expenses related to direct mail, outbound telemarketing, and e-mail; and (4) personnel costs. Management anticipated that future sales and marketing expenses would increase as the company launched seasonal advertising, expanded promotional

EXHIBIT 4

Sirius XM's Most Popular Subscription Plans, February 2014

	Sirius or XM Select	Sirius or XM All Access	Sirius or XM Mostly Music
Monthly subscription	$14.99	$18.99	$9.99
Quarterly subscription	$44.97	$56.97	$27.97
	($14.99 per month)	($18.99 per month)	($9.99 per month)
Annual subscription	$164.89	$199.00	$119.88
	($13.74 per month)	($16.58 per month)	($9.99 per month)
	1 free month	1 free month	
2-year subscription	$314.79	$398.00	$239.76
	($13.12 per month)	($16.58 per month)	($9.99 per month)
	3 free months	3 free months	
3-year subscription	$464.69	$588.69	$359.64
	($12.91 per month)	($16.35 per month)	($9.99 per month)
	5 free months	5 free months	
Addition of a second radio	$9.99 per month	$13.99 per month	$9.99 per month
Number of channels	Over 140 channels	Over 150 channels plus online listening	Over 80 channels
Internet Radio	Add $4 per month	Included	Add $4 per month
Howard Stern	√	√	x
Oprah Radio, Opie and Anthony, Bob Edwards	x	√	x
Every NFL game	√	√	x
Every NASCAR race	√	√	x
Every MLB game	x	√	x
NBA and NHL games and PGA Tour coverage	x	√	x
Up-to-the-minute traffic and weather coverage for 22 locations	√	√	x

Source: Company website (accessed February 4, 2014).

initiatives to attract new subscribers, and boosted efforts to retain existing subscribers and win back former subscribers.

Customer Service and Customer Care Strategy

One of Sirius XM's top strategic priorities was to help boost subscriber retention rates through improvements in customer service and overall customer satisfaction. To improve customer retention and customer satisfaction metrics by making it easier and more satisfying to be a Sirius XM subscriber, the company had:

- Made significant investments in customer care and assembled a team of experienced customer

service personnel to perform an assortment of customer support activities.

- Increased its capabilities to "chat" with online customers—a function that online customers liked and used when trying to manage their accounts, purchase equipment, and resolve other questions or issues they had.

- Expanded the customer self-service options that enabled subscribers to perform more transactions online.

- Integrated its subscriber management systems to enable Sirius radios and XM radios to exist on a single consolidated account.

- Launched a mobile service app to allow transactions and account management from a subscriber's smartphone.

Satellite Systems and Operations Strategies

In 2014, Sirius had a fleet of 10 orbiting satellites, costing an average of $300 million each; four were manufactured by Boeing Satellite Systems and six were manufactured by Space Systems/Loral. The company used launch and in-orbit insurance to mitigate the potential financial impact of satellite launch and in-orbit failures unless the premium costs were considered to be uneconomical relative to the risk of satellite failure. The satellite fleet provided clear reception in most areas despite terrain variations, buildings, and other obstructions. Subscribers could receive transmissions at all outdoor locations in the continental United States where the satellite radio had an unobstructed line of sight with one of the satellites or was within range of one of the company's 700 terrestrial repeaters to supplement satellite coverage.

Sirius controlled and communicated with the satellites from facilities in North America and maintained earth stations in Panama and Ecuador to control and communicate with several satellites. The satellites were monitored, tracked, and controlled by a third-party satellite operator.

Satellite Radios   Sirius did not manufacture satellite radios. Rather, it designed the radios, established their specifications, either sourced or specified the needed parts and components, and managed various aspects of the logistics and production of its satellite and Internet radios. It had authorized manufacturers and distributors to produce and distribute radios, and it had licensed the company's technology to various electronics manufacturers to develop, manufacture, and distribute radios under brands other than Sirius XM. It also was responsible for obtaining FCC certification of its radios. Sirius purchased radios from these manufacturers for distribution through the company's website. To facilitate the sale of its radios, Sirius typically subsidized a portion of the radio manufacturing costs to reduce the hardware price to consumers; the majority of these subsidies were paid to the makers of the chip sets (microprocessors) used in its radios and to the suppliers of certain other parts and components.

Radios were manufactured in four principal configurations: in-dash radios for new and used motor vehicles, Dock & Play radios, home or commercial units, and portable radios. In 2011, Sirius introduced the Sirius XM Edge, a Dock & Play radio featuring a technology that expanded the company's available channel lineup and data bandwidth. At the time, the Edge was the only Sirius XM radio able to access Sirius XM's new 2.0 technology; it was sold at retail locations and on the Sirius XM website for $139.99. Later, Sirius XM introduced the Lynx model, a portable radio with Sirius XM 2.0 satellite and Internet radio capability. In addition, there was an interoperable radio, MiRGE, which had a unified control interface allowing for easy switching between the XM and Sirius satellite radio networks. Sirius' other important radio model was the XM SkyDock, which connected to an Apple iPhone and iPod touch and provided live XM satellite radio using the control capability of the iPhone or iPod touch. A new model, the Sirius XM Onyx Plus Dock & Play radio, priced at $99.99, was introduced in November 2013. The Onyx Plus had the capability to receive all of the channels of the company's previous satellite radios plus Sirius XM's expanded channel lineup and SiriusXM Latino, a suite of Spanish-language channels, and was packed with advanced features. With Onyx Plus, the listener was able to:

- Store up to 20 channels for one-touch access, including 18 Smart Favorite channels.
- Automatically start songs from the beginning when tuned to a Smart Favorite music channel with TuneStart.
- Create a customized music channel that was a blend of the Smart Favorite music channels with TuneMix.
- Scan and select songs that had already played on the Smart Favorite music channels with TuneScan.
- Pause, rewind, and replay live satellite radio plus go back and replay music, news, talk, or sports segments on all Smart Favorite channels.
- Browse what was playing on other channels while listening to the current one.
- Get alerts so that the listener wouldn't miss any favorite artists, songs, and games.
- Get score alerts when scores occurred in games that involved the user's favorite teams.

- Catch up on the latest sports scores with Sports Ticker.
- Jump back to the previous channel with One-Touch Jump.
- Lock and unlock channels with mature content.

Onyx Plus also boasted a large color graphic display for viewing album art and channel logos, program and channel information, and song and show titles.

New Technology and Expanded Online and Two-Way Wireless Capabilities

In 2013, Sirius introduced the SiriusXM Internet Radio app for smartphones and other Internet-connected devices to make Sirius XM programming more widely available. In 2013–2014, Sirius accelerated efforts to develop and deliver in-vehicle technology and systems with greater capabilities and connectivity. It was participating in an initiative with Nissan to provide a comprehensive suite of services that would allow for crash notification, stolen or parked vehicle locator service, remote vehicle diagnostics, roadside assistance, monitoring of vehicle emissions, and other safety and convenience measures. In November 2013, Sirius completed the acquisition of the connected-vehicle services business of Agero, Inc., giving it significantly greater capability to develop a connected-vehicle platform and begin delivering connected-vehicle services to a host of major automotive manufacturers. Agreements had already been negotiated with Acura, BMW, Honda, Hyundai, Infiniti, Lexus, Nissan, and Toyota, with several others in the pipeline, making Sirius the current leader in providing connected-vehicle services to automakers. Sirius XM's offerings included safety, security, and convenience services for drivers and end-to-end, turnkey solutions for automakers. The company expected to earn revenues of $100 million from providing these services in 2014 and expected these revenues to reach $200 million in the next three years.

Competition

Despite being the monopoly provider of satellite radio service in the United States, Sirius XM nonetheless faced significant competition for both listeners and advertisers from a number of diverse sources, in addition to prerecorded, disc-based music entertainment that consumers could purchase and play in cars and homes and on various portable devices.

Broadcasters of Analog and Digital AM/FM Radio Programs

The broadcasters of AM/FM programs had a loyal listener base numbering in the tens of millions and long-standing demand for their product offerings They utilized an advertising-based business model that provided free broadcast reception paid for by commercial advertising. Stations chose one of several basic programming formats (music, talk, sports, religious, news, educational, ethnic), put their own differentiating spin on the selected programming format, and then tried to make money by selling a sufficient number of advertising spots at rates commensurate with their audience ratings to produce a profitable revenue stream. Radio stations competed for listeners and advertising revenues with other radio stations in their geographic listening area based on such factors as program content, on-air talent, transmitter power, and audience demographics; these factors, along with audience size and the number and characteristics of other radio stations in the area, affected the rates they were able to charge for advertising. Some AM/FM radio stations had reduced the number of commercials per hour, expanded the range of music played on the air, and experimented with new formats in order to lure customers away from satellite radio.

In recent years, most AM/FM radio stations had begun broadcasting digital signals as well as the older analog signals. Digital signals had clarity similar to Sirius XM signals but made a difference only to listeners with a digital or HD radio. Many AM/FM broadcasters were also complementing their HD radio efforts by aggressively pursuing Internet radio, wireless Internet-based distribution arrangements, and data services. Several automakers had installed HD radio equipment as factory standard equipment in select models, and more were planning to shift from installing analog radios as standard equipment to installing digital radios.

Internet Radio Broadcasters and Internet-Enabled Smartphones

Internet radio broadcasts typically had no geographic limitations and provided listeners with radio programming from across the country and around the world. Major media companies and online-only providers, including Clear Channel, CBS and Pandora, made high-fidelity digital streams available through the Internet for free or, in some cases, for a fraction of the cost of a satellite radio subscription. Pandora, for example, had 70 million listeners and 3 million paying subscribers. Online broadcasters competed directly with Sirius XM's services in automobiles, at home, on mobile devices, and wherever audio entertainment was consumed. Internet-enabled smartphones, most of which had the capability of interfacing with vehicles, could play recorded or cached content and access Internet radio via dedicated applications or browsers. These applications were often free to the user and offered music and talk content as long as the user had subscribed to a sufficiently large mobile data plan. Leading audio smartphone radio applications included Pandora, last.fm, Slacker, iheartradio, and Stitcher. Certain of these applications also included advanced functionality, such as personalization, and allowed the user to access large libraries of content and podcasts on demand.

Spotify had launched a music-streaming service in the United States that allowed its users unlimited, on-demand access to a large library of song tracks, enabling the sharing of playlists with other listeners through the Facebook platform. Other similar services had launched Facebook integration, including MOG and Rdio. These services, which usually required a monthly subscription fee, were currently available on smartphones but were likely to become integrated into connected vehicles in the future.

Third-generation (G3) and fourth-generation (G4) mobile networks had enabled a steady increase in the audio quality and reliability of mobile Internet radio streaming, and this was expected to further increase as G4 networks became standard. Sirius executives expected that improvements from higher bandwidths, wider programming selection, and advancements in functionality would continue making Internet radio and smartphone applications an increasingly significant competitor, particularly in vehicles.

Because the audio entertainment marketplace was evolving rapidly and new media platforms and portable devices emerged periodically, it was likely that new companies would enter the marketplace and begin to compete with Sirius XM's programming and services.

Advanced In-Dash Infotainment Systems

In 2014, nearly all automakers had deployed or were in the process of installing integrated multimedia systems in the dashboards of their models. These systems could combine control of audio entertainment from a variety of sources, including AM/FM/HD radio broadcasts, satellite radio, Internet radio, smartphone applications, and stored audio, with navigation and other advanced applications such as restaurant bookings, movie show times, and stock-trading information. Internet radio and other data were typically connected to the system via a Bluetooth link to an Internet-enabled smartphone, and the entire system could be controlled via dashboard touchscreens or voice recognition. These systems significantly enhanced the attractiveness of the services of Sirius XM's Internet-based competitors by making such applications more prominent, easier to access, and safer to use in the car. Similar systems were also available in the aftermarket for automobile accessories and were being sold by retailers.

Direct Broadcast Satellite and Cable Audio

Such providers of TV programming as DirecTV, Dish, Comcast, Time Warner, Charter, and others typically included a package of audio programs (mostly music) as part of their packages of video programming services. Customers generally did not pay an additional monthly charge for the audio channels, and such programming was accessible only at the fixed locations where customers' TVs were connected.

Providers of Traffic News Services

A number of providers competed with Sirius XM's traffic news services. Clear Channel and Tele Atlas had partnered to deliver nationwide traffic information for the top-50 markets to in-vehicle navigation systems with RDS-TMC traffic reception capability; RDS-TMC was the radio broadcast standard technology for delivering traffic and travel information to drivers. Moreover, the market for in-dash navigation systems was being invaded by increasingly capable smartphones that provided advanced navigation functionality, including live traffic information. Android, BlackBerry, and Apple iOS-based smartphones all included GPS mapping and navigation functionality, often with turn-by-turn navigation.

Government Regulation

As an operator of a privately owned satellite system, Sirius XM was regulated by the Federal Communications Commission under the Communications Act of 1934. Any assignment or transfer of control of the company's FCC licenses had to be approved by the FCC. Sirius XM's licenses for its five Sirius satellites expired in 2017; its FCC licenses for several XM satellites expired in 2014 and 2018. Management anticipated that, absent significant misconduct, the FCC would renew the licenses to permit operation of these satellites for their useful lives and would grant a license for any replacement satellites. The FCC had established rules governing terrestrial repeaters and had granted Sirius XM a license to operate its repeater network. Sirius had to obtain FCC certification for all of its satellite radios.

Sirius XM was required to obtain export licenses from the U.S. government to export certain ground control equipment, satellite communications and control services, and technical data related to its satellites and their operations. The delivery of such equipment, services, and technical data to destinations outside the United States and to foreign persons was subject to strict export control and prior approval requirements.

Important New Developments

In October 2013, Sirius XM announced that its board of directors had approved an additional $2 billion common stock repurchase program to be funded by cash on hand, future cash flow from operations, and future borrowings. The company also announced that it had agreed to repurchase $500 million of common stock from Liberty Media and its affiliates in three installments, in November 2013, January 2014, and April 2014. These purchases were in addition to Sirius XM's recent repurchases of 476.5 million shares of common stock at an aggregate cost of approximately $1.6 billion.

Meanwhile, Liberty Media brought its ownership of Sirius XM common stock to about 53 percent of the shares outstanding, and three new directors chosen by Liberty Media were added to Sirius XM's board. This resulted in a "change of control" at the corporate level since Liberty Media became the controlling owner. On January 3, 2014, Sirius XM's board of directors received a nonbinding letter from Liberty Media Corporation proposing a tax-free transaction whereby all outstanding shares of Sirius XM's common stock not owned by Liberty Media would be converted into the right to receive 0.0760 share of Liberty Series C common stock, which would have no voting rights. Liberty Media indicated that immediately prior to the conversion, it intended to distribute, on a 2-to-1 basis, shares of its Series C common stock to all holders of record of Liberty Media's Series A and B common stock. Liberty Media also indicated that it expected that upon the completion of the proposed transaction, Sirius XM's public stockholders would own approximately 39 percent of Liberty Media's then-outstanding common stock. Sirius XM's board of directors formed a special committee of independent directors to consider Liberty Media's proposal.

In addition to its 53 percent ownership of Sirius XM, Liberty Media owned interests in a broad range of media, communications, and entertainment businesses, including:

- 100 percent ownership of the Atlanta National League Baseball Club and TruePosition, Inc., a global leader in location determination and intelligence solutions that help protect citizens, combat crime, and save lives.
- 67 percent ownership of MacNeil/Lehrer Productions, producer of *The PBS NewsHour,* documentaries, interactive DVDs, civic engagement projects, and educational programs.

- Minority interests in Charter Communications (27 percent); Live Nation Entertainment (26 percent), the largest live entertainment company in the world; Barnes & Noble (17 percent); Mobile Streams (16 percent), a global mobile content retailer of full-track downloads, ringtones, videos, graphics, and games; Kroenke Arena Co. (7 percent), the owner of the Pepsi Center, a sports and entertainment facility in Denver, Colorado; and Crown Media Holdings (3 percent), the owner-operator of the Hallmark Channel and the Hallmark Movie Channel.
- Small common stock investments (generally 1 percent or less) in CenturyLink, Time Warner Cable, and media companies Time Warner, Inc., and Viacom.

Analysts speculated that Liberty Media's offer to Sirius XM shareholders—which they valued at $3.67 per share based on then-prevailing conditions—was predicated on strengthening its balance sheet and gaining access to Sirius XM's $1.1 billion in annual cash flows from operations, cash that it could use to join forces with Charter Communications in a bid to acquire Time Warner Cable (TWC). Charter had offered to buy Time Warner Cable for $127 in October 2013 and had upped its offer to $132.50 in January 2014; TWC had rejected both offers as grossly inadequate. Then in mid-February 2014, TWC agreed to be acquired by Comcast in an all-stock deal worth about $155 per share to Time Warner shareholders. Shortly thereafter, Liberty Media turned its attention to making some acquisitions in Europe and, on March 13, 2014, officially announced it was abandoning its offer to acquire all of the outstanding shares of Sirius XM. A day later, Sirius XM issued a press release saying that it was resuming the common stock repurchase program previously announced in October 2013.

Decline in the Number of Subscribers, Fourth Quarter 2013

On February 4, 2014, Sirius XM announced its financial and operating performance for both full-year 2013 and the fourth quarter of 2013. While the company's performance was on the whole positive, Sirius XM's reported decline in the number of subscribers from the third quarter to the fourth quarter was a red flag that quickly caught the attention of stockholders and industry analysts. Gross subscriber additions of 2,409,804 in Q4 of 2013 were about 155,000 below the gross subscriber additions of 2,561,175 in Q3 of 2013, but a big jump in subscriber deactivations to an all-time record high (up 384,493 over the prior quarter) led to a net decline of 22,756 subscribers in the 2013 fourth quarter; recent quarterly subscriber data for Sirius XM are presented in Exhibit 5.

Several factors contributed to the negative subscriber growth in 2013's last quarter:

- Sirius XM began paying automakers lower subsidy rates per satellite radio–equipped vehicle. Indeed, the lower subsidy payments resulted in subscriber acquisition costs of $124 million in the fourth quarter, or just 12 percent of revenue, the lowest percentage in the company's history. And subscriber acquisition cost per gross subscriber addition was a record low $44, which was 18.5 percent below the $54 average for the fourth quarter of 2012.
- A major automaker shifted to unpaid trial subscriptions in Q4 of 2013, accounting for most of the 434,240 decline in paid promotional (trial) subscriptions from Q3 to Q4.
- The new vehicle conversion rate from trial to self-pay was only 42 percent in Q4, as compared to the normal 45 to 46 percent rates that prevailed during 2010–2012 (see Exhibit 3).

It was unclear whether the jump in deactivations reflected resistance to the costs of subscribing to one of the company's numerous subscription plans. Subscription prices, which ranged from $6.99 to $16.99 per month until mid-2011, were increased shortly after the agreement with the FCC to not raise prices expired in July 2011: the base rate was increased by an average of $1.54. Another $0.50 increase went into effect in January 2014, resulting in subscription plan prices ranging from $9.99 to $18.99 per month. But many new vehicles had in-dash connections that enabled drivers to plug in smartphones and other mobile devices and listen to downloaded or streamed music from sources other than Sirius. However, the data plans that drivers had for their

EXHIBIT 5

Quarterly Gross Subscriber Additions, Deactivated Subscribers, and Net Subscriber Additions, Sirius XM Satellite Radio, 2011–2013

	Gross Subscriber Additions	Deactivated Subscribers	Net Subscriber Additions
2011			
Quarter 1	2,052,367	1,679,303	373,064
Quarter 2	2,179,348	1,727,201	452,147
Quarter 3	2,138,131	1,804,448	333,683
Quarter 4	2,326,174	1,783,208	542,966
2012			
Quarter 1	2,161,693	1,757,097	404,596
Quarter 2	2,481,004	1,858,962	622,042
Quarter 3	2,421,586	1,975,665	445,921
Quarter 4	2,553,489	2,018,536	534,953
2013			
Quarter 1	2,509,914	2,057,024	452,890
Quarter 2	2,655,488	1,939,726	715,762
Quarter 3	2,561,175	2,048,067	513,078
Quarter 4	2,409,804	2,432,560	(22,756)

Source: Company 10-Q reports; and company press releases of fourth-quarter and full-year results, February 5, 2013, and February 4, 2014.

connected devices could often result in higher costs to listen to streamed programs than the cost of a Sirius subscription, especially if they listened to a lot of hours of streamed programming in their vehicles each month.

The performance of Sirius XM's stock price in the first three months of 2014 was disappointing. After jumping to $3.86 per share in the days following Liberty Media's offer on January 3, 2014, to acquire all of the remaining shares of Sirius XM's common stock that it did not already own, Sirius XM's stock price drifted down to $3.43 the day after the company announced its fourth-quarter and full-year results for 2013. On March 31, 2014, the company's stock price closed at $3.20 per share.

Sirius XM's Guidance for 2014

In announcing the company's full-year 2013 financial and operating results on February 4, 2014, Sirius' management reiterated its guidance for the company's performance for 2014:

- Revenue of over $4 billion
- Net subscriber additions of approximately 1.25 million
- Income from operations of approximately $1.30 billion
- Free cash flow approaching $1.1 billion

This guidance was reaffirmed in an April 24, 2014, press release.

ENDNOTES

[1] Alexander Eule, "Sound of Success," *Barron's,* November 25, 2013, p. 26.

[2] Ibid.

[3] Ibid.

[4] Letter to Shareholders, 2012 annual report.

[5] Eule, "Sound of Success."

Panera's Line of Fresh-Baked Breads, March 2015

Artisan Breads	Specialty Breads
Country	**Sourdough**
A crisp crust and nutty flavor. *Available in loaf.*	Panera's signature sourdough bread with no fat, oil, sugar, or cholesterol. *Available in loaf.*
French	**Asiago Cheese**
Slightly blistered crust, wine-like aroma. *Available in baguette, miche.*	Standard sourdough recipe with Asiago cheese baked in and sprinkled on top. *Available in demi, loaf.*
Ciabatta	**Honey Wheat**
A moist, chewy crumb with a thin crust and light olive oil flavor. *Available in loaf.*	Sweet and hearty with honey and molasses. *Available in loaf.*
Focaccia	**All-Natural White Bread**
Italian flatbread baked with olive oil and topped with either asiago cheese or sea salt. *Available in loaf.*	Soft and tender white sandwich bread. *Available in loaf.*
Rye	**Tomato Basil**
With chopped rye kernels and caraway seeds. *Available in loaf.*	Sourdough bread made with tomatoes and basil, and sweet streusel topping. *Available in XL loaf.*
Three Cheese	**Cinnamon Raisin Swirl**
Made with parmesan, romano, and asiago cheeses. *Available in loaf.*	Fresh dough made with flour, whole butter, and eggs, swirled with Vietnamese and Indonesian cinnamons, raisins, and brown sugar, topped with Panera's cinnamon crunch topping. *Available in loaf.*
Three Seed	
Sesame, poppy, and fennel seeds. *Available in demi.*	
Whole Grain	**Sprouted Whole Grain Roll**
Moist and hearty, sweetened with honey. *Available in loaf.*	*Available as single or pack of 6.*
Sesame Semolina	**Soft Dinner Roll**
Delicate, moist, and topped with sesame seeds. *Available in loaf.*	*Available as single or pack of 6.*

Source: www.panerabread.com, accessed March 17, 2015.

recent health-related changes included using organic and all-natural ingredients in selected items, using unbleached flours in its breads, adding a yogurt-granola-fruit parfait and reduced-fat spreads for bagels to the menu, introducing fruit smoothies, increasing the use of fresh ingredients (such as fresh-from-the-farm lettuces and tomatoes), and revising ingredients and preparation methods to yield zero grams of artificial trans fat per serving. All of the menu boards and printed menus at company-owned Panera bakery-cafés included the calories for each food item. Also, Panera's website had a nutritional calculator showing detailed nutritional information for each individual menu item or combination of menu selections.

Off-Premises Catering In 2004–2005, Panera Bread introduced a catering program to extend its market reach into the workplace, schools, and parties and gatherings held in homes, and grow their break-fast-, lunch-, and dinner-hour sales without making capital investments in additional physical facilities. The first menu consisted of items appearing on the regular menu and was posted for viewing at the company's website. A catering coordinator was available to help customers make menu selections, choose between assortments or boxed meals, determine appropriate order quantities, and arrange pick-up or delivery times. Orders came complete with plates, napkins, and utensils, all packaged and presented in convenient, ready-to-serve-from packaging.

EXHIBIT 5

Panera Bread's Menu Selections, March 2015

Bakery
Artisan and specialty breads (17 varieties), bagels (11 varieties), scones (4 varieties), sweet rolls (3 varieties), muffins and "muffies" (6 varieties), artisan pastries (7 varieties), brownies, cookies (7 varieties)

Bagels and cream cheese spreads (11 varieties of bagels, 8 varieties of spreads)

Hot breakfast
Breakfast sandwiches (10 varieties), baked egg soufflés (4 varieties)

Strawberry Granola Parfait

Steel-Cut Oatmeal

Power Almond Quinoa Oatmeal

Fruit smoothies (5 varieties)

Fresh fruit cup

Signature hot paninis
Frontega Chicken, Chipotle Chicken, Smokehouse Turkey, Steak and White Cheddar

Signature sandwiches
Napa Almond, Chicken Salad, Asiago Steak, Italian Combo, Bacon Turkey Bravo

Café sandwiches
Smoked Ham and Swiss, Roasted Turkey and Avocado BLT, Tuna Salad, Mediterranean Veggie, Sierra Turkey, Fontina Grilled Cheese, Classic Grilled Cheese, Smoked Turkey

Flatbread sandwiches
Turkey Cranberry, Mediterranean Chicken, Southwestern Chicken, Tomato Mozzarella

Signature pastas
Chicken Sorrentina, Chicken Tortellini Alfredo, Mac & Cheese, Pesto Sacchettini, Tortellini Alfredo, Pasta Primavera

Soups (5 selections varying daily, plus seasonal specialties)
Options include: Broccoli Cheddar, Bistro French Onion, Baked Potato, Low-Fat All-Natural Chicken Noodle, Cream of Chicken and Wild Rice, New England Clam Chowder, Low-Fat Vegetarian Garden Vegetable with Pesto, Low-Fat Vegetarian Black Bean, Vegetarian Creamy Tomato, All-Natural Turkey Chili

Café salads
Caesar, Classic, Greek

Signature salads
Chicken Cobb, Chicken Cobb with Avocado, Chicken Caesar, Asian Sesame Chicken, Fuji Apple Chicken, Thai Chicken, BBQ Chicken, Mediterranean Shrimp Couscous, Greek with Shrimp, Classic with Chicken, Greek with Chicken, Power Chicken Hummus Bowl, Steak and Blue Cheese

Broth bowls
Soba Noodle with Chicken, Soba Noodle with Edamame, Lentil Quinoa with Chicken, Lentil Quinoa with Cage-Free Egg

Panera Kids
Grilled Cheese Sandwich, Peanut Butter and Jelly Sandwich, Smoked Ham Sandwich, Smoked Turkey Sandwich, Mac & Cheese, Buttered Ribbon Noodles, 10 varieties of regular and seasonal soups, 3 salads

Beverages
Coffee (hot or iced), hot teas, iced tea, iced green tea, Pepsi beverages, Dr. Pepper, bottled water, San Pellegrino, organic milk, chocolate milk, orange juice, organic apple juice, lemonade, fruit punch, Sierra Mist fountain soda

Frozen drinks
Frozen Caramel, Frozen Mocha

Espresso Bar
Espresso, cappuccino, Caffe Latte, Caffe Mocha, Vanilla Latte, Caramel Latte, Skinny Caffe Mocha, Chai Tea Latte (hot or iced), Signature Hot Chocolate

Source: Menu posted at www.panerabread.com, accessed March 18, 2015.

In 2010, Panera boosted the size of its catering sales staff and introduced sales training programs and other tools—factors that helped drive a 26 percent increase in catering sales in 2010. In 2011, Panera introduced an online catering system that catering customers could use to view the catering menu, place orders, specify whether the order was to be picked up or delivered to a specified location, and pay for purchases. The 65-item catering menu in 2015 included breakfast assortments, bagels and spreads, sandwiches and boxed lunches, salads, soups, pasta dishes, pastries and sweets, and a selection of beverages. In large geographic locations with multiple bakery-cafés, Panera operated catering-only "delivery hubs" to expedite deliveries of customer orders. Going forward, top executives at Panera believed that off-premise catering was an important revenue growth opportunity for both company-operated and franchised locations.

The MyPanera Loyalty Program In 2010, Panera initiated a loyalty program to reward customers who dined frequently at Panera Bread locations. The introduction of the MyPanera program was completed systemwide in November, and by the end of December, some 4.5 million customers had signed up and become registered card members. Members presented their MyPanera card when ordering. When the card was swiped, the specific items being purchased were automatically recorded to learn what items a member liked. As Panera got an idea of a member's preferences over the course of several visits, a member's card was "loaded" with such "surprises" as complimentary bakery-café items, exclusive previews and tastings, cooking and baking tips, invitations to special events, ideas for entertaining, or recipe books. On a member's next visit, when an order was placed and the card swiped, order-taking personnel informed the member of the surprise award. Members could also go online at www.MyPanera.com and see if a reward was waiting on their next visit. In March 2015, the company's MyPanera program had over 19 million members, and in both 2013 and 2014, approximately 50 percent of the transactions at Panera Bread bakery-cafés were attached to a MyPanera loyalty card.

Management believed that the loyalty program had two primary benefits. One was to entice members to dine at Panera more frequently and thereby deepen the bond between Panera Bread and its most loyal customers. The second was to provide Panera management with better marketing research data on the purchasing behavior of customers and enable Panera to refine its menu selections and market messages.

The Panera 2.0 Marketing Initiative In 2012, Panera began testing a newly developed Panera 2.0 app that enabled digital ordering and payment by customers and that included capabilities store employees and managers could use to perform an assortment of internal operating activities. The app was adaptable to the differentiated needs of dine-in, to-go, and large-order delivery customers The tests in 14 bakery-cafés were such a huge success that Panera began rolling out the full Panera 2.0 experience to its entire network of company-operated and franchised bakery cafés in 2013, a process that management expected to complete in 2016. Introduction of the "Rapid Pickup" component of Panera 2.0, which featured mobile ordering and payment for customers picking up orders at a particular bakery-café, was completed systemwide in early 2015. Management expected the Panera 2.0 technology to enhance the guest experience, aid the introduction of marketing innovations, permit cost-efficient handling of a growing number of customer transactions volumes, and pave the way for greater operating efficiencies in its bakery-cafés.

Panera's Nonprofit Pay-What-You-Want Bakery-Café Locations In May 2010, Panera Bread converted one of its restaurants in a wealthy St. Louis suburb into a nonprofit pay-what-you-want Saint Louis Bread Cares bakery-café with the idea of helping to feed the needy and raising money for charitable work. A sign in the bakery-café said, "We encourage those with the means to leave the requested amount or more if you're able. And we encourage those with a real need to take a discount." The menu board listed "suggested funding levels," not prices. Payments went into a donation box, with the cashiers providing change and handling credit card payments. The hope was that enough generous customers would donate money above and beyond the menu's suggested funding levels to subsidize discounted meals for those who were experiencing economic hardship and needed help. The restaurant was operated by Panera's charitable Panera Bread Foundation; all profits from the store were donated to community programs.

After several months of operation, the Saint Louis Bread Cares store was judged to be successful enough that Ron Shaich, who headed the Panera Bread Foundation, opted to open two similar Panera Cares cafés—one in the Detroit suburb of Dearborn, Michigan, and one in Portland, Oregon. At one juncture, Panera statistics indicated that roughly 60 percent of store patrons left the suggested amount; 20 percent left more, and 20 percent less.[5] Of course, there were occasional instances in which a patron tried to game the system. Ron Shaich cited the case of a college student who ordered more than $40 worth of food and charged only $3 to his father's credit card; Shaich, who happened to be working in the store behind the counter, had to restrain himself, saying "I wanted to jump over the counter."[6] One person paid $500 for a meal, the largest single payment. Although in May 2011, Panera had intentions to open a new pay-what-you-want store every three months or so, the company still had only three pay-what-you-want café locations as of April 2012, but two locations were added in the next nine months—one in Chicago and one in Boston. Panera expected to serve over 1 million people at the five pay-what-you-can locations in 2013.[7] Statistics showed that in 2013, about 60 percent of store patrons left the suggested amount, 20 percent left more, and 20 percent less, often significantly less.[8]

In March 2013, Panera introduced a special "Meal of Shared Responsibility"—turkey chili in a bread bowl—at a suggested retail price of $5.89 (tax included) at 48 locations in the St. Louis area. The idea was that the needy could get a nutritious 850-calorie meal for whatever they could afford to pay, while those who pay above the company's cost make up the difference.[9] The program was supported by heavy media coverage at launch, extensive in-store signage, and employees explaining how the meal worked. For the first three weeks, customers on average paid above the retail value, but then payments dropped off to an average of around 75 percent of retail value. After six weeks, in-store signage was taken down to promote other meal options and the conversation about the "Meal of Shared Responsibility" faded into the background. Then in July 2013, after serving about 15,000 of the turkey chili meals, Panera canceled the program, chiefly because few needy people were participating—an outcome attributed largely to most Panera locations in the St. Louis area being located in middle-class and affluent neighborhoods. Management indicated it would rethink its approach to social responsibility and possibly retool the program. Later in 2014, the Chicago location of Panera Cares was closed, but the other four locations were still open in March 2015.

Marketing

In the company's early years, marketing had played only a small role in Panera's success. Brand awareness had been built on customers' satisfaction with

their dining experience at Panera and their tendency to share their positive experiences with friends and neighbors. From time to time, Panera had utilized focus groups to determine customer food and drink preferences and price points. In 2006, Panera's marketing research indicated that about 85 percent of consumers who were aware that there was a Panera Bread bakery-café in their community or neighborhood had dined at Panera on at least one occasion; 57 percent of consumers who had "ever tried" dining at Panera Bread had been customers in the past 30 days.[10] Panera's research also showed that people who dined at Panera Bread very frequently or moderately frequently typically did so for only one part of the day, although 81 percent indicated "considerable willingness" to try dining at Panera Bread at other parts of the day.

This data prompted management to pursue three marketing initiatives during 2006–2007. One aimed at raising the quality of awareness about Panera by continuing to feature the caliber and appeal of its breads and baked goods, by hammering home the theme "food you crave, food you can trust," and by enhancing the appeal of its bakery-cafés as a neighborhood gathering place. A second initiative sought to raise awareness and boost customer trials of dining at Panera Bread at multiple meal times (breakfast, lunch, "chill out" times, and dinner). The third initiative was to increase perception of Panera Bread as a viable evening meal option by introducing a number of new entrée menu selections. Panera avoided hard-sell or "in your face" marketing approaches, preferring instead to employ a range of ways to softly drop the Panera Bread name into the midst of consumers as they moved through their lives and let them "gently collide" with the brand. The idea was to let consumers "discover" Panera Bread and then convert them into loyal repeat customers by providing a very satisfying dining experience when they tried Panera bakery-cafés for the first time or opted to try dining at Panera at a different part of the day, particularly during breakfast or dinner as opposed to the busier lunchtime hours. These initiatives were only partially successful, partly because of the difficult economic environment that emerged in 2008–2009 and partly because the new dinner entrées that were introduced did not prove popular enough to significantly boost dinner-hour traffic and were dropped from the menu; in 2011–2012, the only hot entrée on the menu was Mac & Cheese. But in 2013–2014, new entrees appeared in growing numbers during the five annual celebration periods.

Panera management was committed to growing sales at existing and new unit locations, continuously improving the customer experience at its restaurants, and encouraging frequent customer visits via the new menu items featured during the periodic celebrations, increased enrollment of patrons in the MyPanera loyalty programs, and efforts to strengthen relationships with customers who, management believed, would then recommend dining at Panera to their friends and acquaintances. Panera hired a new chief marketing officer and a new vice president of marketing in 2010; both had considerable consumer marketing experience and were playing an important role in crafting the company's long-term marketing strategy to increase awareness of the Panera brand, develop and promote appealing new menu selections, expand customer participation in the MyPanera loyalty program, and otherwise make dining at Panera bakery-cafés a pleasant and satisfying experience.

To promote the Panera brand and menu offerings to target customer groups, Panera employed a mix of radio, billboards, social networking, the Internet, and periodic cable television advertising campaigns. In recent years, Panera had put considerable effort into (a) improving its advertising messages to better capture the points of difference and the soul of the Panera concept and (b) doing a better job of optimizing the media mix in each geographic market.

Whereas it was the practice at many national restaurant chains to spend 3 to 5 percent of revenues on media advertising, Panera's advertising expenses had typically been substantially lower, running as low as 0.6 percent of systemwide sales at company-owned and franchised bakery-cafés in 2008. But in the past five years, Panera had started upping its advertising effort to help spur sales growth. Advertising expenses totaled $33.2 million in 2011 (1.00 percent of systemwide bakery-café sales), $44.5 million in 2012 (1.15 percent of systemwide bakery-café sales), $55.6 million in 2013 (1.30 percent of systemwide bakery-café sales), and $65.5 million in 2014 (1.45 percent of systemwide bakery-café

sales). The increased advertising expenses in 2014 were to support Panera's first-ever national television advertising campaign, an initiative that was financed by both Panera and its franchisees.

Panera's franchise agreements required franchisees to contribute a specified percentage of their net sales to advertising. In 2013, Panera's franchise-operated bakery-cafés were required to contribute 1.8 percent of their sales to a national advertising fund and to pay Panera a marketing administration fee equal to 0.4 percent of their sales; Panera contributed the same net sales percentages from company-owned bakery-cafés toward the national advertising fund and the marketing administration fee. Franchisees were also required in 2013 to spend amounts equal to 1.6 percent of their net sales on advertising in their local markets. Over the past eight years, Panera had raised the contribution of both company-owned and franchised bakery cafés to the national advertising fund—from 0.4 percent of net sales prior to 2006 to 0.7 percent beginning January 2006 to 1.2 percent beginning July 2010 to 1.6 percent starting April 2012. However, to help offset these increases, the amounts franchisees were expected to spend for local advertising had been reduced from 2.0 percent of net sales beginning July 2010 to 1.6 percent of net sales beginning April 2012. Under the terms of its franchise agreements, Panera had the right to increase national advertising fund contributions to a maximum of 2.6 percent of net sales.

To support the new national advertising campaign beginning in 2014, Panera exercised its right to require franchisees to pay the maximum 2.6 percent of net sales to the company's national advertising fund. However, the marketing administration fee of 0.4 percent of net sales remained unchanged and the required percentage franchisees had to spend on advertising in their respective local market areas was reduced from 1.6 percent to 0.8 percent beginning January 2014.

Franchise Operations

Opening additional franchised bakery-cafés was a core element of Panera Bread's strategy and management's initiatives to achieve the company's revenue growth and earnings targets. Panera Bread did not grant single-unit franchises, so a prospective franchisee could not open just one bakery-café. Rather, Panera Bread's franchising strategy was to enter into franchise agreements that required the franchise developer to open a number of units, typically 15 bakery-cafés in a period of six years. Franchisee candidates had to be well-capitalized, have a proven track record as excellent multi-unit restaurant operators, and agree to meet an aggressive development schedule. Applicants had to meet eight stringent criteria to gain consideration for a Panera Bread franchise:

- Experience as a multi-unit restaurant operator
- Recognition as a top restaurant operator
- Net worth of $7.5 million
- Liquid assets of $3 million
- Infrastructure and resources to meet Panera's development schedule for the market area the franchisee was applying to develop
- Real estate experience in the market to be developed
- Total commitment to the development of the Panera Bread brand
- Cultural fit and a passion for fresh bread

Exhibit 6 shows estimated costs of opening a new franchised Panera Bread bakery-café. The franchise agreement typically required the payment of a $5,000 development fee for each bakery-café contracted for in a franchisee's "area development agreement," a franchise fee of $30,000 per bakery-café (payable in a lump sum at least 30 days prior to the scheduled opening of a new bakery-café), and continuing royalties of 5 percent on gross sales at each franchised bakery-café. Franchise-operated bakery-cafés followed the same standards for in-store operating standards, product quality, menu, site selection, and bakery-café construction as did company-owned bakery-cafés. Franchisees were required to purchase all of their dough products from sources approved by Panera Bread. Panera's fresh dough facility system supplied fresh dough products to substantially all franchise-operated bakery-cafés. Panera did not finance franchisee construction or area development agreement payments, or hold an equity interest in any of the franchise-operated bakery-cafés. All area development agreements executed after March 2003 included a clause allowing Panera Bread the right to

purchase all bakery-cafés opened by the franchisee at a defined purchase price at any time five years after the execution of the franchise agreement. In 2010, Panera purchased 37 bakery-cafés from the franchisee in the New Jersey market and sold 3 bakery-cafés in the Mobile, Alabama, market to an existing franchisee. In 2011, Panera completed the purchase of 25 bakery-cafés owned by its Milwaukee franchisee and 5 bakery-cafés owned by an Indiana franchisee; also in 2011, Panera sold 2 Paradise Bakery & Café units to a Texas franchisee and terminated the franchise agreements for 13 Paradise bakery-cafes that were subsequently rebranded by the former franchisee. In 2012, Panera acquired 16 bakery-cafés from a North Carolina franchisee, and in 2013, it acquired 1 bakery-café from a Florida franchisee.

As of January 2015, Panera Bread had agreements with 37 franchise groups that operated 955 bakery-cafés. Panera's largest franchisee operated nearly 200 bakery-cafés in Ohio, Pennsylvania, West Virginia, Kentucky, and Florida. The company's franchise groups had committed to opening an additional 106 bakery-cafés. If a franchisee failed to develop bakery-cafés on schedule, Panera had the right to terminate the franchise agreement and develop its own company-operated locations or develop locations through new franchisees in that market. However, Panera from time to time agreed to modify the commitments of franchisees to open new locations when unfavorable market conditions or other circumstances warranted the postponement or cancellation of new unit openings.

Panera provided its franchisees with support in a number of areas: market analysis and site selection assistance, lease review, design services and new store opening assistance, a comprehensive 10-week initial training program, a training program for hourly employees, manager and baker certification, bakery-café certification, continuing education classes, benchmarking data regarding costs and profit margins, access to company-developed marketing and advertising programs, neighborhood marketing assistance, and calendar planning assistance.

Site Selection and Café Environment

Bakery-cafés were typically located in suburban, strip mall, and regional mall locations. In evaluating

Estimated Initial Investment for a Franchised Panera Bread Bakery-Café, 2012

Investment Category	Actual or Estimated Amount	To Whom Paid
Development fee	$5,000 per bakery-café contracted for in the franchisee's Area Development Agreement	Panera
Franchise fee	$35,000 ($5,000 of the development fee was applied to the $35,000 franchise fee when a new bakery-café was opened)	Panera
Real property	Varies according to site and local real estate market conditions	
Leasehold improvements	$334,000 to $938,500	Contractors
Equipment	$198,000 to $310,000	Equipment vendors, Panera
Fixtures	$32,000 to $54,000	Vendors
Furniture	$28,500 to $62,000	Vendors
Consultant fees and municipal impact fees (if any)	$51,500 to $200,250	Architect, engineer, expeditor, others
Supplies and inventory	$19,150 to $24,350	Panera, other suppliers
Smallwares	$24,000 to $29,000	Suppliers
Signage	$15,000 to $84,000	Suppliers
Additional funds (for working capital and general operating expenses for 3 months)	$175,000 to $245,000	Vendors, suppliers, employees, utilities, landlord, others
Total	**$917,150 to $1,984,100, plus real estate and related costs**	

Source: www.panerabread.com, accessed April 5, 2012.

a potential location, Panera studied the surrounding trade area, demographic information within that area, and information on nearby competitors. Based on analysis of this information, including utilization of predictive modeling using proprietary software, Panera developed projections of sales and return on investment for candidate sites. Cafés had proven successful as free-standing units and as both in-line and end-cap locations in strip malls and large regional malls.

The average Panera bakery-café size was approximately 4,500 square feet. Most all company-operated locations were leased. Lease terms were typically for 10 years, with one, two, or three 5-year renewal option periods. Leases typically entailed charges for minimum base occupancy, a proportionate share of building and common area operating expenses and real estate taxes, and a contingent percentage rent based on sales above a stipulated amount. Some lease agreements provided for scheduled rent increases during the lease term. The average construction, equipment, furniture and fixture, and signage cost

for the 65 company-owned bakery-cafés opened in 2014 was $1,400,000 (excluding capitalized development overhead expenses), compared to average costs of $750,000 for 42 company-owned bakery-cafés opened in 2010 and $920,000 for 66 company-owned bakery-cafés opened in 2005.

Each bakery-café sought to provide a distinctive and engaging environment (what management referred to as "Panera Warmth"), in many cases using fixtures and materials complementary to the neighborhood location of the bakery-café. All Panera cafés used real china and stainless silverware, instead of paper plates and plastic utensils. In 2005–2006, the company had introduced a new café design aimed at further refining and enhancing the appeal of Panera bakery-cafés as a warm and appealing neighborhood gathering place. The design incorporated higher-quality furniture, cozier seating, comfortable gathering areas, and relaxing décor. A number of locations had fireplaces to further create an alluring and hospitable atmosphere that patrons would flock to on a regular basis, sometimes for a meal with or without friends and acquaintances and sometimes to take a break for a light snack or beverage. Many locations had outdoor seating, and all company-operated and most franchised locations had free wireless Internet to help make the bakery-cafés community gathering places where people could catch up on some work, hang out with friends, read the paper, or just relax (a strategy that Starbucks had used with great success).

In 2006, Panera began working on store designs and operating systems that would enable free-standing and end-cap locations to incorporate a drive-thru window. In 2010–2011, increasing numbers of newly opened locations, both company-owned and franchised, featured drive-thru windows. Some existing units had undergone renovation to add a drive-thru window. Going into 2012, about 50 Panera Bread locations had drive-thru windows. Sales at these locations ran about 20 percent higher on average than units without drive-thru capability.

Bakery-Café Operations

Panera's top executives believed that operating excellence was the most important element of Panera Warmth and that without strong execution and operational skills and energized café personnel who were motivated to provide pleasing service, it would be difficult to build and maintain a strong relationship with the customers patronizing its bakery-cafés. Additionally, top management believed high-quality restaurant management was critical to the company's long-term success. Bakery-café managers were provided with detailed operations manuals, and all café personnel received hands-on training, both in small group and individual settings. The company had created systems to educate and prepare café personnel to respond to a customer's questions and do their part to create a better dining experience. Management strived to maintain adequate staffing at each café and had instituted competitive compensation for café managers and both full-time and part-time café personnel (who were called associates).

Panera executives had established a "Joint Venture Program," whereby selected general managers and multi-unit managers of company-operated bakery cafés could participate in a bonus program based upon a percentage of the store profit of the bakery-cafés they operated. The bonuses were based on store profit percentages generally covering a period of five years, and the percentages were subject to annual minimums and maximums. Panera management believed the program's multiyear approach (a) improved operator quality and management retention, (b) created team stability that generally resulted in a higher level of operating consistency and customer service for a particular bakery-café, (c) fostered a low rate management turnover, and (d) helped drive operating improvements at the company's bakery-cafés. In 2013–2014, approximately 45 percent of the bakery-café operators Panera's company-owned locations participated in the Joint Venture Program.

Going into 2014, Panera Bread had approximately 45,400 employees. Approximately 42,700 were employed in Panera's bakery-cafe operations as bakers, managers, and associates, approximately 1,400 were employed in the fresh dough facility operations, and approximately 1,300 were employed in general or administrative functions, principally in the company's support centers. Roughly 25,500 employees worked, on average, at least 25 hours per week. Panera had no collective bargaining agreements with its associates and considered its employee relations to be good.

Panera's Bakery-Café Supply Chain

Panera operated a network of 24 facilities (22 company-owned and 2 franchise-operated) to supply fresh dough for breads and bagels on a daily basis to almost all of its company-owned and franchised bakery-cafés; one of the company's 22 facilities was a limited production operation co-located at a company-owned bakery-café in Ontario, Canada, that supplied dough to 12 Panera bakery-cafés in that market. All of the company's facilities were leased. Most of the 1,400 employees at these facilities were engaged in preparing dough for breads and bagels, a process that took about 48 hours. The dough-making process began with the preparation and mixing of starter dough, which then was given time to rise; other all-natural ingredients were then added to create the dough for each of the different bread and bagel varieties (no chemicals or preservatives were used). Another period of rising then took place. Next, the dough was cut into pieces, shaped into loaves or bagels, and readied for shipment in fresh dough form. There was no freezing of the dough, and no partial baking was done at the fresh dough facilities. Trained bakers at each bakery-café performed all of the baking activities, using the fresh doughs delivered daily.

Distribution of the fresh bread and bagel doughs (along with tuna, cream cheese spreads, and certain fresh fruits and vegetables) was accomplished through a leased fleet of about 225 temperature-controlled trucks operated by Panera personnel. The optimal maximum distribution route was approximately 300 miles; however, routes as long as 500 miles were sometimes necessary to supply cafés in outlying locations. In 2013–2014, the various distribution routes for regional facilities entailed making daily deliveries to eight to nine bakery-cafés.

Panera obtained ingredients for its doughs and other products manufactured at its regional facilities. While a few ingredients used at these facilities were sourced from a single supplier, there were numerous suppliers of each ingredient needed for fresh dough and cheese spreads. Panera contracted externally for the manufacture and distribution of sweet goods to its bakery-cafés. After delivery, sweet good products were finished with fresh toppings and other ingredients (based on Panera's own recipes) and baked to Panera's artisan standards by professionally trained bakers at each café location.

Panera had arrangements with several independent distributors to handle the delivery of sweet goods products and other items to its bakery-cafés, but the company had contracted with a single supplier to deliver the majority of ingredients and other products to its bakery-cafés two or three times weekly. Virtually all other food products and supplies for their bakery-cafés, including paper goods, coffee, and smallwares, were contracted for by Panera and delivered by the vendors to designated independent distributors for delivery to the bakery-cafés. Individual bakery-cafés placed orders for the needed supplies directly with a distributor; distributors made deliveries to bakery-cafés two or three times per week. Panera maintained a list of approved suppliers and distributors that all company-owned and franchised cafés could select from in obtaining food products and other supplies not sourced

from the company's regional facilities or delivered directly by contract suppliers.

Although many of the ingredients and menu items sourced from outside vendors were prepared to Panera's specifications, the ingredients for a big majority of menu selections were generally available and could be obtained from alternative sources when necessary. In a number of instances, Panera had entered into annual and multiyear contracts for certain ingredients in order to decrease the risks of supply interruptions and cost fluctuation. However, Panera had only a limited number of suppliers of antibiotic-free chicken; because there were relatively few producers of meat products raised without antibiotics—as well as certain other organically grown items—it was difficult or more costly for Panera to find alternative suppliers.

Management believed the company's fresh dough-making capability provided a competitive advantage by ensuring consistent quality and dough-making efficiency (it was more economical to concentrate the dough-making operations in a few facilities dedicated to that function than it was to have each bakery-café equipped and staffed to do all of its baking from scratch). Management also believed that the company's growing size and scale of operations gave it increased bargaining power and leverage with suppliers to improve ingredient quality and cost, and that its various supply-chain arrangements entailed little risk that its bakery-cafés would experience significant delivery interruptions from weather conditions or other factors that would adversely affect café operations.

The fresh dough made at the regional facilities was sold to both company-owned and franchised bakery-cafés at a delivered cost not to exceed 27 percent of the retail value of the product. Exhibit 7 provides financial data relating to each of Panera's three business segments: company-operated bakery-cafés, franchise operations, and the operations of the regional facilities that supplied fresh dough and other products. The sales and operating profits of the fresh dough and other products segment shown in Exhibit 7 represent only those transactions with franchised bakery-cafés. The company classified any operating profit of the regional facilities stemming from supplying fresh dough and other products to company-owned bakery-cafés as a reduction

EXHIBIT 7

Business Segment Information, Panera Bread Company, 2009–2014 (in thousands of dollars)

	2014	2013	2012	2011	2009
Segment revenues:					
Company bakery-café operations	$2,230,370	$2,108,908	$1,879,280	$1,592,951	$1,153,255
Franchise operations	123,686	112,641	102,076	92,793	78,367
Fresh dough and other product operations at regional facilities	370,004	347,922	312,308	275,096	216,116
Intercompany sales eliminations	(194,865)	(184,469)	(163,607)	(138,808)	(94,244)
Total revenues	$2,529,195	$2,385,002	$2,130,057	$1,822,032	$1,353,494
Segment operating profit:					
Company bakery-café operations	$400,261	$413,474	$380,432	$307,012	$193,669
Franchise operations	117,770	106,395	95,420	86,148	72,381
Fresh dough and other product operations at regional facilities	22,872	21,293	17,695	20,021	21,643
Total segment operating profit	$540,903	$541,162	$493,547	$413,181	$287,693
Depreciation and amortization:					
Company bakery-café operations	$103,239	$ 90,872	$78,198	$68,651	$55,726
Fresh dough and other product operations at regional facilities	8,613	8,239	6,793	6,777	7,620
Corporate administration	12,257	7,412	5,948	4,471	3,816
Total	$124,109	$106,523	$90,939	$79,899	$67,162
Capital expenditures:					
Company bakery-café operations	$167,856	$153,584	$122,868	$ 94,873	$46,408
Fresh dough and other product operations at regional facilities	12,178	11,461	13,434	6,483	3,681
Corporate administration	44,183	26,965	16,026	6,576	4,595
Total capital expenditures	$224,217	$192,010	$152,328	$107,932	$54,684
Segment assets:					
Company bakery-café operations	$953,896	$867,093	$807,681	$682,246	$498,806
Franchise operations	13,145	10,156	10,285	7,502	3,850
Fresh dough and other product operations at regional facilities	65,219	62,854	60,069	47,710	48,616
Total segment assets	$1,390,902	$940,103	$878,035	$737,458	$551,272

Source: Panera Bread's 2014 10-K Report, p. 66; 2013 10-K Report, p. 67; and 2011 10-K Report, p. 69.

in the cost of food and paper products. The costs of food and paper products for company-operated bakery-cafés are shown in Exhibit 1.

Panera Bread's Management Information Systems

Each company-owned bakery-café had programmed point-of-sale registers that collected transaction data used to generate transaction counts, product mix, average check size, and other pertinent statistics.

The prices of menu selections at all company-owned bakery-cafés were programmed into the point-of-sale registers from the company's data support centers. Franchisees were allowed access to certain parts of Panera's proprietary bakery-café systems and systems support; they were responsible for providing the appropriate menu prices, discount rates, and tax rates for system programming.

The company used in-store enterprise application tools and the capabilities of the Panera 2.0 app to (1) assist café managers in scheduling work hours for café personnel and controlling food costs in order to provide corporate and retail operations management with quick access to retail data, (2) enable café managers to place online orders with distributors, and (3) reduce the time café managers spent on administrative activities. The information collected electronically at café registers was used to generate daily and weekly consolidated reports regarding sales, transaction counts, average check size, product mix, sales trends, and other operating metrics, as well as detailed profit-and-loss statements for company-owned bakery-cafés. This data was incorporated into the company's "exception-based reporting" tools.

Panera's regional facilities had software that accepted electronic orders from bakery-cafés and monitored delivery of the ordered products back to the bakery-cafés. Panera also had developed proprietary digital software to provide online training to employees at bakery-cafés and online baking instructions for the baking personnel at each café.

Most of Panera's bakery-cafés provided customers with free Internet access through a managed WiFi network that was among the largest free public WiFi networks in the United States.

New Developments at Panera Bread, April 2015

In mid-April 2015, following a "constructive dialogue" with activist shareholder Luxor Capital Group, Panera Bread announced that it would (a) expand its share-repurchase plan from $600 million to $750 million, (b) sell 73 of its 925 company-owned bakery-cafés to franchisees to raise money to help fund the added expenditures on repurchasing outstanding shares of the company's common stock, and (c) borrow $500 million to help fund the share-buyback plan. Panera's stock price jumped nearly 12 percent on the day of the announcement. In February 2015, Panera had warned that it expected earnings per share in 2015 would, at best, be flat in comparison to the $6.64 the company earned in 2014.

Luxor, a hedge fund based in New York, had previously been a part of an activist shareholder group that had prodded another restaurant chain to make operating improvements and repurchase shares of stock, partly using debt to fund the share buyback.

Analysts said the pressure Luxor put on Panera could spur management to increase its efforts to make needed operating improvements in its stores: some diners and Panera's bakery cafés had complained about long lines to pay for food and slow delivery of orders to diners' tables. While Panera's rollout of Panera 2.0 was intended to speed service and checkout, as well as enable other operating efficiencies, some investors were concerned that Panera 2.0 was being implemented too slowly and were skeptical whether the new software would actually improve internal operating efficiency and boost customer traffic outside the lunch hour by as much as Panera executives hoped.

The Restaurant Industry in the United States

According to the National Restaurant Association, total food-and-drink sales at some 1 million food service locations of all types in the United States were projected to reach a record $709 billion in 2014, up 3.8 percent over 2014 and up from $379 billion in 2000 and $239 billion in 1990.[11] Of the projected $709 billion in food-and-drink sales industry-wide in 2014, about $471 billion were expected to occur in commercial restaurants, with the remainder divided among bars and taverns, lodging place restaurants, managed food service locations, military restaurants, and other types of retail, vending, recreational, and mobile operations with food service capability. In 2012, unit sales averaged $875,000 at full-service restaurants and $803,000 at quick-service restaurants; however, very popular restaurant locations achieved annual sales volumes in the $2.5 million to $5 million range.

Restaurants were the nation's second largest private employer in 2014 with almost 14 million employees. Nearly half of all adults in the United States had worked in the restaurant industry at some point in their lives, and close to one out of three adults got their first job experience in a restaurant. More than 90 percent of all eating-and-drinking place businesses had fewer than 50 employees, and more than 70 percent of these places were single-unit operations.

Even though the average U.S. consumer ate 76 percent of their meals at home, on a typical day, about 130 million U.S. consumers were food service patrons at an eating establishment. Sales at commercial eating places were projected to average about $1.9 billion daily in 2015. Average household expenditures for food away from home in 2013 were $2,625, equal to about 40 percent of total household expenditures for food.[12]

The restaurant business was labor-intensive, extremely competitive, and risky. Industry members pursued differentiation strategies of one variety of another, seeking to set themselves apart from rivals via pricing, food quality, menu theme, signature menu selections, dining ambiance and atmosphere, service, convenience, and location. To further enhance their appeal, some restaurants tried to promote greater customer traffic via happy hours, lunch and dinner specials, children's menus, innovative or trendy dishes, diet-conscious menu selections, and beverage/appetizer specials during televised sporting events (important at restaurants/bars with big-screen TVs). Most restaurants were quick to adapt their menu offerings to changing consumer tastes and eating preferences, frequently featuring heart-healthy, vegetarian, organic, low-calorie, and/or low-carb items on their menus. Research conducted by the National Restaurant Industry in 2014 indicated that:[13]

- 64 percent of consumers considered themselves to be more adventurous in their restaurant food choices than they were two years ago.

- 76 percent of consumers were more likely to visit a restaurant that offered healthy menu options.

- 79 percent of consumers say restaurant technology increases convenience.

It was the norm at many restaurants to rotate some menu selections seasonally and to periodically introduce creative dishes in an effort to keep regular patrons coming back, attract more patrons, and remain competitive.

The profitability of a restaurant location ranged from exceptional to good to average to marginal to money-losing. Consumers (especially those that ate out often) were prone to give newly opened eating establishments a trial, and if they were pleased with their experience, they might return, sometimes frequently; loyalty to existing restaurants was low when consumers perceived there were better dining alternatives. It was also common for a once-hot restaurant to lose favor and confront the stark realities of a dwindling clientele, forcing it to either reconceive its menu and dining environment or go out of business. Many restaurants had fairly short lives. There were multiple causes for a restaurant's failure: a lack of enthusiasm for the menu or dining experience, inconsistent food quality, poor service, a poor location, meal prices that patrons deemed too high, and being outcompeted by rivals with comparable menu offerings.

ENDNOTES

[1] Harris Interactive press releases, March 16, 2011 and May 10, 2012, and information posted at www.harrisinteractive.com (accessed March 7, 2014).

[2] "Zagat Announces 2012 Fast-Food Survey Results," www.prnewswire.com, September 27, 2012 (accessed March 7, 2014).

[3] Sandelman and Associates Quick-Track surveys and Fast-Food Awards of Excellence Winners, and information included in "Press Kit" posted at www.panerabread.com (accessed March 7, 2014).

[4] As stated in a presentation to securities analysts, May 5, 2006.

[5] Ron Ruggless, "Panera Cares: One Year Later," *Nation's Restaurant News,* May 16, 2011, posted at www.nrn.com (accessed July 19, 2011).

[6] Sean Gregory-Clayton, "Sandwich Philanthropy," *Time,* August 2, 2010, posted at www.time.com. (accessed July 19, 2011).

[7] Annie Gasparro, "A New Test for Panera's Pay-What-You-Can," *Wall Street Journal,* June 4, 2013, posted at www.wsj.com (accessed March 7, 2014).

[8] Ibid.

[9] Jim Salter, "Panera Suspends Latest Pay-What-You-Can Experiment in Stores," www.huffingtonpost.com, July 10, 2013 (accessed March 7, 2014).

[10] As cited in Panera Bread's presentation to securities analysts on May 5, 2006.

[11] The statistical data in this section is based on information posted at www.restaurant.org (accessed July 26, 2011, April 8, 2012, and March 18, 2015).

[12] Bureau of Labor Statistics, news release, September 9, 2014 (accessed at www.bls.gov, March 18, 2015).

[13] National Restaurant Industry, "2015 Restaurant Industry Pocket Factbook," posted at www.restaurant.org (accessed March 18, 2015).v

Vera Bradley in 2015: Can Its Turnaround Strategy Reverse Its Continuing Decline?

connect

DAVID L. TURNIPSEED University of South Alabama

JOHN E. GAMBLE Texas A&M University–Corpus Christi

Vera Bradley had grown rapidly since the mid-2000s with a strategy keyed to offering a distinctive line of colorful, patterned women's luggage, handbags, and accessories sold in department stores, in company-owned full-price retail stores and factory outlet stores, and over the Internet. As the mid-2010s approached, the company's standing seemed less certain as competition intensified in the market for ladies' handbags and accessories. Its meteoric growth had stalled in fiscal 2014, with revenues slipping by only 1 percent but net income declining by nearly 15 percent. This decline in revenues and profits came on the heels of the company's rollout of its new strategic plan in early 2014 that would focus the company on a product line of a limited assortment of the highest-quality ladies' handbags and accessories, expanded distribution channels with an emphasis on outlets and e-commerce, and an enhanced marketing approach.

By 2015, the company's strategic plan had failed to produce the desired results, with fiscal 2015 net revenues slipping 4.1 percent, from $530.9 million in fiscal 2014 to $509 million in fiscal 2015. In addition, operating income had fallen by 33 percent, and net income dropped 35 percent, from $58.8 million in fiscal 2014 to $38.4 million in fiscal 2015.

The strategic plan appeared to match the company's external market conditions and internal situation, but it provided little uniqueness since Vera Bradley's rivals were all competing with similar strategies. Vera Bradley's management believed that the quality of the plan, coupled with the company's management expertise, would yield a competitive advantage. Robert Wallstrom, Vera Bradley's chief executive officer, commented shortly after the new strategic plan was announced that the company's strategies and talented and seasoned team of retail executives would reverse the company's recent decline in revenue and profits and return it to an impressive growth trajectory.[1]

Company History

The inspiration for Vera Bradley occurred in 1982 when two traveling friends, Barbara Bradley Baekgaard and Patricia Miller, observed that passersby in the Hartsfield Atlanta International Airport all had similar, bland luggage and that a market for colorful, stylish luggage might exist. Almost immediately upon their return to Fort Wayne, Indiana, the two women began creating colorful, quilted fabric duffle bags from their homes. They named the company after Barbara Baekgaard's mother, Vera Bradley, and initially focused only on duffle bags, handbags, and sports bags.

As consumer interest in the brand grew, the company developed additional assortments of patterns and products to reach a broader range of customers. The focus of the company's merchandising was changed to highlight Vera Bradley as a lifestyle brand. The company enhanced its marketing function to work collaboratively with the design group in 2012 to improve the product development to market process. In 2014, the company designed, manufactured, marketed, and retailed accessories for women, including luggage, purses, wallets, cell phone and computer covers, jewelry, a wide variety of bags, lunch sacks, scarves, beach accessories, and baby clothing.

As the company grew, Vera Bradley's management realized the importance of a strong infrastructure and began strengthening its supply chain capabilities and IT systems early on. These improvements resulted in significant cost savings and a more flexible and scalable operating structure. In 2005, the company shifted its production from primarily domestic manufacturing to global sourcing, which was substantially more cost-effective. A new state-of-the-art distribution facility was built in Roanoke, Indiana, in 2007 and was expanded in 2013 to approximately 400,000 square feet, which was double its original size.

Vera Bradley's products were initially sold wholesale to department stores and other retailers specializing in women's accessories. The company also maintained specialty retailer accounts that marketed Vera Bradley bags and other distinctive items as corporate gifts. By 2014, the company's products were sold through indirect department store and specialty retailer channels and through direct channels that included the Internet, full-price retail stores, and factory outlet stores. As of February 2014, the company had about 3,100 indirect retail partners, with about 30 percent of the indirect retailers accounting for over 70 percent of the indirect revenue in 2013. The company entered into direct sales in 2006 with the launch of an e-commerce site in the United States, and in 2007 it opened its first retail store. Vera Bradley launched an e-commerce site in Japan in 2012. The company operated 96 full-price retail stores in the United States in 2015. Vera Bradley retail stores were about 1,800 square feet in size and were designed to reflect the casual comfort of a home. The company also operated 29 factory outlet stores in the United States. Its seven retail stores in Japan had been closed by 2015.

Vera Bradley executed its initial public offering in October 2010 and was listed on the NASDAQ with the symbol "VRA." According to Vera Bradley's management, the company's direct competitors were manufacturers and marketers of handbags and accessories, such as Coach, Michael Kors, and Kate Spade. Miller and Baekgaard had been honored by the U.S. Small Business Administration

as "Outstanding Women Entrepreneurs" and by the Indiana Historical Society as "Indiana Living Legends." The Vera Bradley Foundation for Breast Cancer had pledged over $35 million to the Indiana University Melvin and Bren Simon Cancer Center to support cancer research. Exhibit 1 presents a financial summary for Vera Bradley for fiscal 2011 through fiscal 2015. The company's balance sheets for fiscal 2014 and fiscal 2015 are presented in Exhibit 2.

Overview of the Handbag and Leather Accessories Market in 2015

The handbag and leather accessories market was estimated at approximately $96 billion in 2013, with the largest markets being the United States with 36 percent of industry sales, Europe with 21 percent of industry sales, Japan with 16 percent of industry sales, and China with 11 percent of industry sales. The retail market for global luxury goods was affected significantly by general economic conditions, with consumers curtailing expenditures for luxury goods in general during recessions and economic slowdowns. For example, the poor general economic conditions between 2006 and 2010 contributed to a 0.6 percent annual decline in industry sales during those years. Continued growth in China and other emerging markets was expected to increase the sales of luxury goods by 7.8 percent annually through 2015.

Euromonitor predicted that by 2018, the Asia-Pacific region would be the largest market in the world for luxury goods. This growth was due primarily to China but also to other emerging Asian markets such as Indonesia, Malaysia, and India. Emerging markets, especially China and India, were expected to provide a major boost to the luxury goods market because of rapidly increasing wealth levels and standard-of-living gains. China surpassed Japan in 2010 as the third-largest luxury market, with sales of luxury goods approaching $32 billion. The Chinese market for luxury goods was predicted to increase substantially over the next several years, which would make it possibly the world's largest market for luxury goods.

Financial Summary for Vera Bradley, Inc., Fiscal 2011–Fiscal 2015 (dollar amounts in thousands, except per share and store data)

	Fiscal Year Ended				
	January 31, 2015	February 1, 2014	February 2, 2013	January 28, 2012	January 29, 2011
Consolidated statement of income data					
Net revenues	$ 508,990	$ 536,021	$ 541,148	$ 460,843	$ 366,057
Cost of sales	239,981	240,589	232,867	203,220	156,910
Gross profit	269,009	295,432	308,281	257,623	209,147
Selling, general, and administrative expenses	208,675	205,957	204,412	169,427	163,053
Other income	3,736	4,776	6,277	7,975	7,225
Operating income	64,070	94,251	110,146	96,171	53,319
Interest expense, net	407	382	679	1,147	1,625
Income before income taxes	63,663	93,869	109,467	95,024	51,694
Income tax expense	22,828	35,057	40,597	37,103	5,496
Net income	$ 38,449	$ 58,812	$ 68,870	$ 57,921	$ 46,198
Basic weighted-average shares outstanding	40,568	40,599	40,536	40,507	36,813
Diluted weighted-average shares outstanding	40,632	40,648	40,571	40,542	36,851
Basic net income per share	$0.95	$1.45	$1.70	$1.43	$1.25
Diluted net income per share	$0.95	$1.45	$1.70	$1.43	$1.25
Net revenues by segment					
Direct	$ 335,602	$ 326,217	$ 292,564	$ 225,287	$ 151,118
Indirect	173,388	209,804	248,584	235,556	214,939
Total	$ 508,990	$ 536,021	$ 541,148	$ 460,843	$ 366,057
Store data					
Total stores open at end of year	125	99	76	56	39
Comparable-store sales (decrease) increase	(7.6)%	(1.3)%	9.8%	24.9%	34.8%
Total gross square footage at end of year	278,779	207,096	156,310	113,504	74,426
Average net revenues per gross square foot	$ 760	$887	$1,083	$1,042	$851
Consolidated balance sheet data					
Cash and cash equivalents	$ 112,292	$ 59,215	$ 9,603	$ 4,922	$ 13,953
Working capital	204,648	186,543	145,641	106,234	91,919
Total assets	377,284	332,927	277,319	219,513	206,039
Long-term debt, including current portion	—	—	15,095	25,184	67,017
Shareholders' equity	284,471	255,147	194,255	124,007	64,322

Source: Vera Bradley, Inc., 10-K report, 2014, 2015.

The most valuable luxury leather-goods brands in terms of annual revenues were Louis Vuitton, Gucci, Hermès, and Cartier. Luxury brands, in general, relied on creative designs, high quality, and brand reputation to attract customers and build brand loyalty. Price sensitivity for luxury goods was driven by brand exclusivity, customer-centric marketing, and, to a large extent, some emotional sense of status and value. The market for luxury goods was divided into three main categories: haute couture, traditional luxury, and the growing submarket "accessible luxury." The apex of the market was haute couture with its very high-end "custom" product offering that catered to the extremely wealthy. Leading brands in the traditional-luxury category included such fashion design houses as Prada, Burberry, Hermès, Gucci, Polo Ralph Lauren, Calvin Klein, and Louis Vuitton. Some of these luxury goods makers also

EXHIBIT 2

Vera Bradley, Inc.'s Balance Sheets, Fiscal 2014–Fiscal 2015 (in thousands)

	Fiscal Year Ended	
	January 31, 2015	February 1, 2014
Assets		
Current assets:		
Cash and cash equivalents	$112,292	$ 59,215
Accounts receivable, net	31,374	27,718
Inventories	98,403	136,923
Prepaid expenses and other current assets	9,100	9,952
Deferred income taxes	13,320	13,094
Total current assets	267,697	246,902
Property, plant, and equipment, net	109,003	84,940
Other assets	584	1,085
Total assets	$377,284	$332,927
Liabilities and shareholders' equity		
Current liabilities:		
Accounts payable	$32,906	$ 27,745
Accrued employment costs	14,595	10,586
Other accrued liabilities	15,548	20,403
Income taxes payable	–	1,625
Total current liabilities	63,049	60,359
Long-term debt	–	–
Deferred income taxes	5,297	4,643
Other long-term liabilities	24,467	12,778
Total liabilities	92,813	77,780
Commitments and contingencies		
Shareholders' equity:		
Preferred stock; 5,000 shares authorized, no shares issued or outstanding	–	–
Common stock; without par value; 200,000 shares authorized, 40,695 and 40,607 shares issued and outstanding, respectively	–	–
Additional paid-in capital	80,992	78,153
Retained earnings	216,451	178,002
Accumulated other comprehensive loss	(15)	(1,008)
Treasury stock	(12,957)	–
Total shareholders' equity	284,471	255,147
Total liabilities and shareholders' equity	$277,284	$332,927

Source: Vera Bradley, Inc., 10-K report, 2014, 2015.

broadened their appeal with diffusion lines in the accessible-luxury market to compete with Coach, DKNY, and other lesser luxury brands. For example, while Dolce & Gabbana (D&G) dresses sold for $1,000 to $1,500, dresses of similar appearance under the D&G affordable luxury brand were priced at $400 to $600. Giorgio Armani's Emporio Armani line and Gianni Versace's Versus lines typically sold for about 50 percent less than similar-looking items carrying the marquee labels.

Profit margins on marquee brands approximated 40 to 50 percent, while most diffusion brands carried profit margins of about 20 percent. Luxury goods manufacturers believed that the diffusion brands' lower profit margins were offset by the opportunity for increased sales volume, the growing size of the accessible-luxury market, and the protected margins available on such products by sourcing production to low-wage countries. In 2013, Bain & Company reported that online sales were continuing to grow faster than the rest of the market, with 28 percent annual growth for the year, reaching almost $14 billion. Online sales were about 5 percent of total luxury sales.

Industry sales in the United States had become more dependent on the success of diffusion lines in the accessible-luxury category. Although primary traditional-luxury consumers in the United States were among the top 1 percent of wage earners, with household incomes of $300,000 or more, consumers who earned substantially less also aspired to own products with higher levels of quality and styling. The growing desire for luxury goods among middle-income consumers was thought to be a result of a wide range of factors, including effective advertising and television programming that promoted conspicuous consumption. The demanding day-to-day rigor of a two-income household was another factor, suggested as urging middle-income consumers to reward themselves with luxuries. An additional factor contributing to rising sales of luxury goods in the United States was the "trade up, trade down"[2] shopping strategy, whereby consumers would balance their spending by offsetting gains made with lower-priced necessities purchased at major retailers (e.g., Walmart and Target) to enable more discretionary spending for luxury goods.

Vera Bradley's Strategic Plan for 2015–2019

In March 2014, Vera Bradley announced a comprehensive five-year strategic plan designed to improve the company's competitive standing, financial performance, and long-term shareholder value. The company's plan focused on three key areas: product, distribution channels, and marketing.

Product Strategy

Vera Bradley's major product categories in 2014 were handbags; accessories such as wallets, wristlets, eyeglass cases, cosmetics cases, and paper and gifts; and travel and leisure items such as duffle bags, garment bags, rolling luggage, and travel cosmetics cases. The company's new strategic emphasis was on improving its product assortment by focusing on its core designs, with "halo" products used to

expand price points without creating an overly broad product line. The strategy would put the greatest focus on the company's strongest product categories such as travel items, backpacks, bags, and accessories. However, the company planned to invest in emerging growth and brand-enhancing opportunities that would strengthen the future product core, such as scarves and jewelry. Management also intended to add products targeted to career-focused women to expand the customer base.

Vera Bradley planned to limit the number of signature patterns launched each year and add more solids to the pattern assortment to better showcase the signature patterns. The company's product release strategy involved the introduction of two to four patterns per season that were used in each of its key product categories. Production of poor-selling patterns was to be quickly discontinued, with remaining inventory sold through the company's website, outlet stores, and annual outlet sale. Also, management decided to develop new products with a predetermined life cycle in mind and alter product launch campaigns based on the potential of the product. In prior years, all products utilized a similar launch strategy and were intended to be marketed as long as demand permitted. The percentage of Vera Bradley's net revenues accounted for by each major product category is presented in Exhibit 3.

Distribution Channels

Vera Bradley's strategic plan intended to utilize a tightly integrated multichannel distribution strategy that included department stores and specialty retailers, full-line stores, factory outlet stores, and e-commerce. The company believed that its legacy gift channel would remain important, but it planned to reduce the product assortment in the channel. Vera Bradley's long-term strategic objective was to expand to 300 full-price retail stores and 100 factory outlet stores. Vera Bradley planned to add approximately 20 to 25 new stores per year for between 2016 and 2020. By 2019, the company expected that approximately 40 percent of the products sold in factory outlet stores would be designed specifically for the outlet channel. Management expected that 70 percent of the factory outlet items would be unique to the factory outlet channel by 2019. The company

EXHIBIT 3

Vera Bradley's Net Revenue Contributions by Major Product Category, Fiscal 2013–Fiscal 2015

	Fiscal Year Ended		
Net Revenues:	**January 31, 2015**	**February 1, 2014**	**February 2, 2013**
Handbags	$230,978	$223,699	$222,984
Accessories	116,031	133,605	143,946
Travel	109,112	116,251	116,576
Home	17,721	20,270	18,162
Other*	35,148	37,071	33,999
Total†	$508,990	$530,896	$535,667

*Includes primarily home, merchandising, freight, and licensing revenues.

†Excludes net revenues generated by the annual outlet sale.

Source: Vera Bradley, Inc., 10-K report, 2015.

believed this made-for-outlet (MFO) strategy would boost gross margins in the factory outlet channel.

E-commerce was also intended to be a key distribution channel and provide support for the Vera Bradley brand and marketing strategies. The goal was for the e-commerce experience to mirror the in-store shopping experience by segregating the full-line and factory outlet products onto different sites. Vera Bradley's website was upgraded in 2013, which allowed the company to ship to 15 countries. Additional enhancements made to the website in 2015 resulted in over 73 million hits in fiscal 2015.

The company placed greater focus on department store relationships and continued to explore other expansion opportunities in department store space, especially since department stores were the largest handbag channel for career professionals. As of January 2015, Vera Bradley products were sold in about 2,700 specialty retail outlets. The top 30 percent of those outlets accounted for approximately 70 percent of revenue from the indirect segment.

Marketing

The marketing objective for the company was to make Vera Bradley an aspirational brand for consumers, convey the Vera Bradley brand personality, and generate excitement around new product launches.

In 2015, the company used retention advertising to keep the brand fresh in the minds of its present customers and to provide them with news of the season product launches and new products. New customer acquisition advertising—primarily print (*Vogue, Seventeen, Elle, InStyle, Better Homes and Gardens,* and *Real Simple*) and digital—was designed to increase brand awareness and attract new customers. Vera Bradley intended for its marketing approach to expand its customer base while strengthening its connections with loyal customers. The majority of its advertising expenditures were to be allocated to fresh, new products and halo assortments building upon the brand equity of established lines. The company believed its iconic products and styles needed little reinforcement with consumers through additional advertising expenditures.

Vera Bradley's Competitive Resources and Capabilities

Vera Bradley's new strategy was based on competencies that were closely related to success in the markets for handbags, luggage, and women's accessories. The company believed it had a well-developed ability to understand the needs and wants of its customers, valuable product design skills, marketing and brand-building expertise, and strong distribution capabilities. Other capabilities that enabled the company's strategy included site-location expertise and manufacturing efficiencies.

Product Development

Vera Bradley had implemented a fully integrated, cross-functional product development process that aligned its design, market research, merchandise management, sales, marketing, and sourcing functions. The company's product development teams in New York City and Roanoke, Indiana, combined an understanding of target customers' needs with knowledge of approaching color and fashion trends to design new collections as well as totally new product categories that would fit well in their markets. The development cycle for new products for the Vera Bradley portfolio began about 12 to 18 months in advance of their release. Each new pattern included the design of an overall print, a fabric backing that complemented the pattern, and three sizes of coordinating trim materials.

Vera Bradley also collaborated with independent designers to create unique patterns for each season, but the company retained final approval of all patterns and designs. All new patterns, including the print, fabric backing, and coordinating trim, were protected by a copyright. The company believed that great designs were fundamental to its product development and were a central part of its brand development and growth strategies. Vera Bradley routinely updated its classic styles and actively pursued new lines and brand extensions to increase its product offerings.

Vera Bradley's product development group attended major trend shows in Europe and the United States, subscribed to trend-monitoring services, and engaged in comparison shopping to monitor fashion trends and customer needs. Product development personnel were also responsible for assortment planning, pricing, forecasting, promotional development, and product life-cycle management. Forecasting was based on seasonal market research and in-store testing. Seasonal market data were obtained through seasonal in-store testing by releasing test products in full-price stores and evaluating their success in the marketplace prior to introducing the product on a larger scale.

Product Launch Process

Vera Bradley introduced two to three new patterns each season that were incorporated into the designs of a wide range of products, including handbags, accessories, and travel and leisure items. Products were manufactured from cotton-quilted fabric, micro-leather, faux leather, and leather. The seasonal product assortments could be classic styles, updates of older designs, or totally new product introductions. Patterns were discontinued at regular intervals to keep the assortment current and fresh and to focus the inventory investment on top-performing patterns. The remaining inventory of retired products was sold primarily through the company's website, factory outlet stores, and annual outlet sale.

Site Location

Vera Bradley's management believed that ample opportunity for expansion existed since none of its geographic markets had been saturated. The company saw expansion of company-operated full-price and factory outlet stores as complementary to its indirect channels since the visibility of Vera Bradley retail stores increased brand awareness and bolstered its brand image. The site-location process involved analyzing area economic conditions, the specific location within a shopping center, the size and shape of the space, and the presence of desirable co-tenants. Management attempted to achieve a balanced mix of moderate and high-end retailers and co-tenants that shared Vera Bradley's target customers to encourage high levels of traffic. The ideal full-price store size was about 1,800 square feet, but the company could work with spaces as small as 1,000 square feet. Depending on the market strategy and relevant economic factors, spaces as large as 2,800 square feet could be used.

Opening expenses for new locations averaged about $400,000 to provide for space renovation costs, initial inventory, and preopening expenses. New full-price stores generated, on average, $1 million in net revenues during the first 12 months. New factory outlet stores produced an average of $2.6 million in net revenue during the first 12 months. The typical payback period for recovering the company's initial investment in a new location was approximately 12 months.

Profiles of Vera Bradley's Chief Rivals

Coach, Inc.

In 2014, Coach operated 332 full-price stores and 207 factory outlet stores in North America and maintained over 1,000 wholesale department store accounts. The company operated 198 stores in Japan and 277 stores in other Asian nations. Coach products were also available in 183 locations in other international markets. Coach also operated e-commerce websites in the United States, Canada, Japan, and China, and had informational websites in over 20 other countries. Coach viewed its websites as a key communication vehicle for promoting traffic in Coach's retail stores and department store locations and for building brand awareness. With approximately 76 million online visits to its e-commerce websites in fiscal 2014, Coach's online store provided a virtual showcase environment where customers could browse selected offerings of the latest styles and colors. Coach's e-commerce strategy also included invitation-only factory flash sites and third-party flash sites. In addition to its direct retail businesses, Coach had built a strong presence globally through Coach boutiques located within select department stores and specialty retailer locations in North America and through 280 distributor-operated shops in Asia, Latin America, the Middle East, Australia, and Europe.

Coach was one of the most recognized fine-accessories brands in the United States and in its targeted international markets. The company offered attractively priced, premium lifestyle accessories to a loyal and growing customer base, and it provided consumers with well-made, appealing, and innovative products. Coach's product offerings of fine accessories and gifts for women and men included handbags, men's bags, women's and men's small leather goods, footwear, outerwear, watches, weekend and travel accessories, scarves, sunwear, fragrances, jewelry, and related accessories. Continuing development of new categories had further established the signature style and distinctive identity of the Coach brand. With its licensing partners, the company offered watches, footwear, eyewear, and fragrances bearing the Coach brand name in select department stores and specialty retailer locations.

Coach's Strategic Initiatives in 2015 Coach's strategic plan was to sustain growth in the global business by focusing on four key strategic initiatives. The company planned to move from a leading international accessories company to a global lifestyle brand encompassing a wide range of accessories for men and women. Coach management believed that men's products, particularly in North America and Asia, created a unique growth opportunity. Coach capitalized on men's products by opening new stand-alone and dual-gender stores and broadening the men's assortment in existing stores. The company also intended to raise brand awareness and market share in markets where Coach was underpenetrated, most notably in Europe, Asia, and Central and South America. Finally, the company planned to accelerate the development of its digital programs and capabilities in North America and worldwide, reflecting the changing global consumer shopping behavior.

In addition to the four key initiatives underway in late-2014, Coach announced its Transformational Plan to bolster its brand equity and restore its former growth and profit margins. Coach's execution of this plan required $500 million in capital improvements for store locations in 2015 and 2016. In addition, the plan would close about 70 underperforming stores in the United States in 2015, realign inventory levels, and increase annual advertising by $50 million. A summary of the company's financial performance for fiscal 2010 through fiscal 2014 is presented in Exhibit 4.

Michael Kors Holdings

In 2015, Michael Kors was among the leading American luxury lifestyle brands, with sales in 74 countries and a product line focused on handbags, accessories, footwear, and apparel. The company's design team was personally led by Michael Kors, who directed the team in conceptualizing and designing all of the company's products. Michael Kors had been recognized with numerous awards, including the Council of Fashion Designers (CFDA) Women's Fashion Designer of the Year (1999), the CFDA Men's Fashion Designer of the Year (2003), the Accessories Council Excellence (ACE) Accessory Designer of the Year (2006), and the CFDA Lifetime Achievement (2010) awards.

Michael Kors's strategy involved the design, manufacturing, and marketing of two primary

operating losses had grown in size every year since 2009. Nonetheless, investors were bullish on Solar-City's future prospects; the company's stock price ranged from a low of $46 to a high of $85 from January 1, 2014, to March 31, 2015, and traded in the range $48–$58 range for the first three months of 2015. Elon Musk was the Chairman of SolarCity's board of directors and owned 22.9 percent of the outstanding shares of the company as of April 4, 2014.

On August 12, 2013, Musk published a blog post detailing his design for a solar-powered, city-to-city elevated transit system called the Hyperloop that could take passengers and cars from Los Angeles to San Francisco (a distance of 380 miles) in 30 minutes. He then held a press call to go over the details. In Musk's vision, the Hyperloop would transport people via aluminum pods enclosed inside of steel tubes. He described the design as looking like a shotgun with the tubes running side by side for most of the route and closing the loop at either end.[19] The tubes would be mounted on columns 50 to 100 yards apart, and the pods inside would travel up to 800 miles per hour. The pods could be small to carry just people or enlarged to allow people to drive a car into a pod. Musk estimated that a Los Angeles-to-San Francisco Hyperloop could be built for $6 billion with people-only pods or $10 billion for the larger pods capable of holding cars with people inside. Musk claimed his Hyperloop alternative would be four times as fast as California's proposed $70 billion high-speed train, with ticket costs being "much cheaper" than a plane ride. While pods would be equipped with an emergency brake for safety reasons, Musk said the safe distance between the pods would be about 5 miles, so you could have about 70 pods between Los Angeles and San Francisco that departed every 30 seconds. Musk stated that riding on the Hyperloop would be pleasant and super-smooth, with less lateral acceleration—which is what tends to make people feel motion sickness—than a subway ride and no sudden movements due to turbulence (as is the case with airplanes). Musk said travel via a Hyperloop system between cities fewer than 1,000 miles apart would be quicker than flying because of the time it took to board and deplane airline passengers and the time it took for planes to take off and land at busy airports. Musk announced that he would not form a company to build Hyperloop

systems; rather, he was releasing his design in hopes that others would take on such projects.

Since 2008, many business articles had been written about Musk's brilliant entrepreneurship in creating companies with revolutionary products that either spawned new industries or disruptively transformed existing industries. In a 2012 *Success* magazine article, Musk indicated that his commitments to his spacecraft, electric car, and solar panel businesses were long-term and deeply felt.[20] The author quoted Musk as saying, "I never expect to sort of sell them off and do something else. I expect to be with those companies as far into the future as I can imagine." Musk indicated he was involved in SolarCity and Tesla Motors "because I'm concerned about the environment," while "SpaceX is about trying to help us work toward extending life beyond Earth on a permanent basis and becoming a multiplanetary species." The same writer described Musk's approach to a business as one of rallying employees and investors without creating false hope.[21] The article quoted Musk as saying:

> You've got to communicate, particularly within the company, the true state of the company. When people really understand it's do or die but if we work hard and pull through, there's going to be a great outcome, people will give it everything they've got.

Asked if he relied more on information or instinct in making key decisions, Musk said he makes no bright-line distinction between the two.[22]

> Data informs the instinct. Generally, I wait until the data and my instincts are in alignment. And if either the data or my instincts are out of alignment, then I sort of keep working the issue until they are in alignment, either positive or negative.

Musk was widely regarded as being an inspiring and visionary entrepreneur with astronomical ambition and willingness to invest his own money in risky and highly problematic business ventures; on several occasions, Musk's ventures had approached the brink of failure in 2008-2009, and then unexpectedly emerged with seemingly bright prospects. He set stretch performance targets and high product quality standards, and he pushed hard for their achievement. He exhibited perseverance, dedication, and an exceptionally strong work ethic, typically working 85 to 90 hours a week. Most weeks, Musk split his time between SpaceX and Tesla. He was at SpaceX's Los Angeles-based headquarters on Monday and Thursday, and at various Tesla facilities in the San Francisco Bay area on Tuesday and Wednesday.[23] On Friday, he split his time between both companies. Tesla Design had offices in the same office park in a southern Los Angeles suburb as SpaceX; Musk's personal residence was about 18 miles away in a northern Los Angeles suburb.

However, Musk got mixed marks on his management style. He was praised for his grand vision of what his companies could become and his ability to shape the culture of his start-up companies but criticized for being hard to work with, partly because of his impatience for action and results, his intensity and sometimes hands-on micro-management of certain operational and product design issues, and the frequency with which he overruled others and imposed his wishes when big decisions had to be made. In 2000, while on vacation, he was forced out as CEO at PayPal after seven months.[24] Several lawsuits had been filed against him by disgruntled former colleagues and employees. A number of articles had made mention of assorted minor annoyances and criticisms of the ways he did things and his frequent prickly manner when responding to probing or unpleasant questions from reporters. But virtually no one had disparaged his brilliant intellect, inventive aptitude, and exceptional entrepreneurial abilities. In 2015, it was hard to dispute that Musk—at the age of 44—had already made a name for himself in two ways:[25]

- He had envisioned the transformative possibilities of the Internet, a migration from fossil fuels to sustainable energy, and expanding life beyond Earth.

- His companies (Tesla, SpaceX, and SolarCity) had put him in position to personally affect the path the world would take in migrating from fossil fuels to sustainable energy and to expanding life beyond Earth. Musk won the 2010 Automotive Executive of the Year Innovator Award for expediting the development of electric vehicles throughout the global automotive industry. *Fortune* magazine named Elon Musk its 2013 Businessperson of the Year.

In 2015, Elon Musk's base salary as Tesla's CEO was $33,280, an amount required by California's minimum wage law; however, he was accepting only $1 in salary. Musk controlled over 33 million shares of common stock in Tesla Motors (worth some $6.6 billion in March 2015) and had been granted options for an additional 89 million shares, 78 million shares of which were subject to Tesla Motors achieving specified increases in market capitalization and 10 designated performance milestones by 2023.[26]

Recent Financial Performance and Financing Activities

Exhibits 2 and 3 present recent financial statement data for Tesla Motors.

In May 2013, Tesla raised over $1 billion by issuing 4.5 million shares of common stock at a price of $92.24 per share and $660 million of 1.50% convertible senior notes. Elon Musk personally purchased 1.08 million

EXHIBIT 2

Consolidated Statement of Operations, Tesla Motors, 2010–2014 (in thousands, except share and per share data)

	Fiscal Year Ending December 31				
	2014	2013	2012	2011	2010
Income statement data:					
Revenues:					
Sales of vehicles, options and accessories, vehicle service, and regulatory credits	$3,079,415	$1,952,684	$ 354,344	$ 101,748	$ 75,459
Sales of power train components, battery packs, and drive units to other vehicle manufacturers	113,308	45,102	31,355	46,860	21,619

Development of power train components and systems for other vehicle manufacturers	5,633	15,710	27,557	55,674	19,666
Total revenues	3,198,356	2,013,496	413,256	204,242	116,744
Cost of revenues:					
Vehicle sales and sales of , power train components, and related systems to other manufacturers	2,310,011	1,543,878	371,658	115,482	79,982
Development of power train systems and components for other vehicle manufacturers	6,674	13,356	11,531	27,165	6,031
Total cost of revenues	2,316,615	1,557,234	383,189	142,647	86,013
Gross profit (loss)	881,671	456,262	30,067	61,595	30,731
Operating expenses:					
Research and development	464,700	231,976	273,978	208,981	92,996
Selling, general, and administrative	603,660	285,569	150,372	104,102	84,573
Total operating expenses	1,068,360	517,545	424,350	313,083	177,569
Loss from operations	(186,689)	961,283)	(394,283)	(251,488)	(146,838)
Interest income	1,126	189	288	255	258
Interest expense	(100,886)	(32,934)	(254)	(43)	(992)
Other income (expense), net	1,813	22,602	(1,828)	(2,646)	(6,583)
Loss before income taxes	(284,636)	(71,426)	(396,077)	(253,922)	(154,155)
Provision for income taxes	9,404	2,588	136	489	173
Net loss	$(294,040)	$ (74,014)	$(396,213)	$(254,411)	$(154,328)
Net loss per share of common stock, basic and diluted	$(2.36)	$ (0.62)	$(3.69)	$(2.53)	$(3.04)
Weighted average shares used in computing net loss per share of common stock, basic and diluted	124,539,343	119,421,414	107,349,188	100,388,815	50,718,302

Balance Sheet Data:

Cash and cash equivalents	$1,905,713	$845,889	$ 201,890	$ 255,266	$ 99,558
Inventory	953,675	340,355	268,504	50,082	45,182
Total current assets	3,198,657	1,265,939	524,768	372,838	235,886
Property, plant, and equipment, net	1,829,267	738,494	552,229	298,414	114,636
Total assets	5,849,251	2,416,930	1,114,190	713,448	386,082
Total current liabilities	2,107,166	675,160	539,108	191,339	85,565
Long-term debt, less current portion	1,806,518*	—	401,495	268,335	71,828
Total stockholders' equity	911,710	667,121	124,700	224,045	207,048

Cash Flow Data:

Cash flows from operating activities	$ (57,337)	$257,994	$(266,081)	$(128,034)	$(127,817)
Proceeds from issuance of common stock in public offerings	—	(360,000)	221,496	172,410	188,842
Purchases of property and equipment excluding capital leases	(969,885)	(264,224)	(239,228)	(184,226)	(40,203)
Net cash used in investing activities	(990,444)	(249,417)	(206,930)	(162,258)	(180,297)
Net cash provided by financing activities	2,143,130	635,422	419,635	446,000	338,045

Sources: Company 10-K reports for years 2011-2014.

EXHIBIT 3

Tesla's Financial Performance by Quarter, GAAP Versus Non-GAAP, Quarter 4, 2013-Quarter 1, 2015

	Q4, 2013	Q1, 2014	Q2, 2014	Q3, 2014	Q4, 2014	Q1, 2015
Revenues (GAAP)	$615,219	$620,542	$769,349	$851,804	$956,661	$939,880
Model S revenues deferred due to lease accounting	146,125	92,506	88,162	80,544	138,973	163,676
Revenues (Non-GAAP)	761,344	$713,048	857,511	932,348	1,095,634	$1,103,556
Gross profit (loss) (GAAP)	156,590	155,128	212,995	251,851	261,697	260,073
Model S gross profit deferred due to lease accounting	29,796	21,384	18,607	16,564	26,072	46,396
Stock-based compensation expense	3,455	3,106	3,912	5,383	5,053	4,601
Gross profit (loss) (Non-GAAP)	189,641	179,618	235,514	273,798	292,822	311,070
Research and development expenses (GAAP)	68,454	81,544	107,717	135,873	139,565	167,154
Stock-based compensation expense	(10,578)	(13,545)	(14,822)	(16,639)	(17,595)	(19,792)
Research and development expenses (Non-GAAP)	57,876	67,999	92,895	119,234	121,970	147,362
Selling, general, and administrative expenses (GAAP)	101,489	117,551	134,031	155,107	196,970	195,365
Stock-based compensation expense	(14,056)	(20,387)	(17,049)	(17,136)	(21,869)	(18,633)
Selling, general and administrative expenses (Non-GAAP)	87,443	97,164	116,982	137,971	175,101	176,732
Net loss (GAAP)	(16,264)	(49,800)	$(61,902)	(74,708)	(107,629)	$(154,181)
Stock-based compensation expense	(28,089	(37,038	(35,783	(39,158	(44,517	(43,026)
Change in fair value of warrant liability	–	–	–	–	–	–
Noncash interest expense related to convertible notes	4,299	8,393	23,639	22,160	20,826	19,510
Model S gross profit deferred due to lease accounting	29,796	21,384	18,607	16,564	26,072	46,396
Net income (loss) (Non-GAAP)	$45,920	$17,015	$16,127	$3,174	$(16,214)	$(45,249)
Net income (loss) per common share, basic (GAAP)	$(0.32)	$(0.40)	$(0.50)	$(0.60)	$(0.86)	$(1.22)
Net income (loss) per common share, basic (Non-GAAP)	0.37	0.14	0.13	0.02	(0.13)	(0.36)
Shares (in 000s) used in per share calculation, basic (GAAP and Non-GAAP)	122,802	123,473	124,520	124,911	125,497	125,947
Net loss per share, diluted (GAAP)	$(0.12)	$(0.36)	$(0.44)	$(0.52)	$(0.86)	$(1.22)
Net income (loss) per share, diluted (Non-GAAP)	0.33	0.12	0.11	0.02	(0.13)	(0.36)
Shares (in 000s) used in per share calculation, diluted (Non-GAAP)	137,784	140,221	140,948	142,747	125,497	125,947

Special note on GAAP versus non-GAAP treatments: Under generally accepted accounting principles (GAAP), revenues and costs of leased vehicles must be recorded and apportioned across the life of the lease; with non-GAAP lease accounting, all revenues and costs of a leased vehicle are recorded at the time the lease is finalized. Under GAAP, stock compensation must be expensed and allocated to the associated cost category; non-GAAP excludes stock compensation as a cost because it is a noncash item. Many companies, including Tesla Motors, believe non-GAAP treatments are useful in understanding company operations and actual cash flows. In Tesla's case, the non-GAAP treatments exclude such noncash items as stock-based compensation, the change in fair value related to Tesla's warrant liability, and noncash interest expense related to Tesla's 1.5 percent convertible senior notes.

Sources: Tesla Motors' Shareholder Letters, Q4 2013, Q1 2014, Q2, 2014, Q3 2014, Q4 2014, and Q1 2015.

of these shares at the public offering price, boosting his investment in Tesla by another $100 million. Tesla used about $450 million of the offering proceeds to fully pay off its 2009 loan from the U.S. Department of Energy, including an $11 million fee for early payment.

Tesla ended 2013 with $848.9 million in cash and cash equivalents, and current restricted cash, an increase of $52.5 million from the end of the third quarter. Executive management expected that the current level of liquidity, coupled with projected future cash flows from operating activities, was likely to provide adequate liquidity based on current plans. However, if market conditions proved favorable, management said would evaluate the merits of opportunistically pursuing actions to further boost the company's cash balances and overall liquidity.

Tesla had capital expenditures of $264 million in 2013, aimed chiefly at expanding its factory production capabilities and opening additional sales galleries, service centers, and Supercharger stations. Capital expenditures rose sharply to $970 million in 2014 to further expand production capacity, continue development of the Model X and Model 3, and open more sales galleries, service centers, and Supercharger stations. Management expected 2015 capital expenditures would rise to about $1.5 billion to further expand production capacity, get the Model X ready to go into production, continue work on the Model 3, fund construction work on a large-scale factory to build batteries and battery packs for its vehicles, and expand its geographic network of sales galleries, service centers, and Supercharger stations.

Tesla's Strategy to Become the World's Biggest and Most Highly Regarded Producer of Electric Vehicles

In 2015, Tesla's strategy was focused on broadening the company's model line-up, expanding the company's production capacity, stepping up the pace of constructing a new $5 billion plant to produce batteries and battery packs for Tesla's vehicles, and adding sales galleries, service centers, and Supercharger stations in the United States, much of Europe, China, and Australia.

Product Line Strategy

So far, Tesla had introduced two models—the Tesla Roadster and the Model S—but the Model X and Model 3 were rapidly advancing through the pipeline. Management intended to broaden the company's customer base by offering not only a bigger model variety but also by introducing substantially cheaper models. Because the lithium-ion battery pack in the Model S reputedly cost upwards of $25,000 and was far and away the biggest cost component, the speed with which Tesla could profitably introduce new vehicles with prices of $35,000 to $50,000 depended largely on how fast and how far it was able to drive down the costs of its battery pack via greater scale economies in battery production and cost-saving advances in battery technology.

Tesla's First Vehicle—The Tesla Roadster

Following Tesla's initial funding in 2004, Musk took an active role within the company. Although he was not involved in day-to-day business operations, he nonetheless exerted strong influence in the design of the company's first model, the Tesla Roadster, a two-seat convertible that could accelerate from zero to 60 miles per hour in as little as 3.7 seconds, had a maximum speed of about 120 miles per hour, could travel about 245 miles on a single charge, and had a base price of $109,000. Musk insisted from the beginning that the Roadster have a lightweight, high-strength carbon fiber body, and he influenced the design of components of the Roadster ranging from the power electronics module to the headlamps and other styling features.[27] Prototypes of the Roadster were introduced to the public in July 2006, and the first "Signature One Hundred" set of fully equipped Roadsters sold out in less than three weeks and the second hundred sold out by October 2007. General production began on March 17, 2008. New models of the Roadster were introduced in July 2009 (including the Roadster Sport with a base price of $128,500) and in July 2010.[28] Sales of Roadster models to countries in Europe and Asia began in 2010. From 2008 through 2012, Tesla sold more than 2,450 Roadsters in 31 countries. Sales of Roadster models ended in December 2012 so that the company could concentrate exclusively on producing and marketing the Model S. However, Tesla announced that in early

2015, Roadster owners would be able to obtain a Roadster 3.0 package that enabled a 40–50 percent improvement in driving range to as much as 400 miles on a single charge; management expected to introduce additional Roadster updates in future years.

Tesla's Second Vehicle—The Model S Customer deliveries of Tesla's second vehicle, the Model S sedan (see Exhibit 4), began in July 2012. In Q2 of 2013, Tesla introduced several new options for the

Model S, including a subzero weather package, parking sensors, upgraded leather interior, several new wheel options, and a yacht-style floor center console. Xenon headlights and a high-definition backup camera were made standard equipment on all Model S cars. Originally, buyers had a choice of three power trains, but in 2014, an all-wheel drive power train was introduced, and then in April 2015, the power train lineup was again modified to that shown in Exhibit 5. The Tesla Model S provided best-in-class storage space of 63.4 cubic feet, including storage inside the cabin (58.1 cubic feet) and under the hood (5.3 cubic feet): this compared quite favorably with the 14.0 cubic-foot trunk capacity of BMW's large 7-series sedan, the 16.3 cubic-foot capacity of a Mercedes S-class sedan, and the 18.0 cubic-foot trunk capacity of the large Lexus 460 sedan.

In early 2015, Tesla announced that the availability of an autopilot feature on new orders of the Model S. The autopilot option included a forward-looking camera, radar, and 360-degree sonar sensors with real-time traffic updates. An autopilot-equipped Model S could be automatically driven on the open road and in dense stop-and-go traffic. Changing lanes was as simple as a tap of the turn signal. Upon arriving at the destination, the autopilot control could detect a parking spot and automatically park the vehicle. Standard equipment safety features constantly monitored stop signs, traffic signals, and pedestrians, as well as unintentional lane changes. The autopilot features of the Model S were progressively enabled over time with software updates. As of mid-2015, the current 6.2 autopilot software version enabled variable speed cruise control (to match the flow of traffic), automatic lane centering (including around curves), camera-enabled automatic high/low beam headlights, self-parking, automatic self-braking, and blind spot warning; future autopilot software updates were expected to enable forward collision warning and other capabilities (potentially including self-driving). The autopilot parking feature included locating a vacant parallel parking spot and smoothing backing into it, automatically parking in an open stall when pulling into a Tesla Supercharger station, automatically parking in an owner's garage at home, and—when calendar syncing was engaged—checking current traffic conditions to determine how

EXHIBIT 4

Tesla's Model S Sedan

Black Tesla Model S

Tesla interior seats

Tesla interior dashboard

EXHIBIT 5

| **Features, Performance and Pricing of Tesla's Four Model S Versions, 2015** |

	70D All-Wheel Drive	**85 Rear-Wheel Drive**	**85D All-Wheel Drive**	**P85D All-Wheel Drive**
EPA certified range	240 miles	265 miles	270 miles	253 miles
0 to 60 mph	5.2 seconds	5.4 seconds	4.4 seconds	3.2 seconds
Top speed	140 mph	140 mph	155 mph	155 mph
Peak motor power	329 horsepower	380 horsepower	422 horsepower	691 horsepower (221 hp front, 470 hp rear)
Power train	Dual motors (front axle and rear axle)	Single motor (rear axle)	Dual motors (front axle and rear axle)	High-performance, dual motors (front axle and rear axle), smart-air suspension
Battery	70 kwh microprocessor controlled lithium-ion battery	85 kwh microprocessor controlled lithium-ion battery	85 kwh microprocessor controlled lithium-ion battery	85 kwh microprocessor controlled lithium-ion battery
Base price (including destination charge)	$76,200	$81,200	$86,200	$106,200
New vehicle limited warranty	4 years or 50,000 miles, whichever comes first	4 years or 50,000 miles, whichever comes first	4 years or 50,000 miles, whichever comes first	4 years or 50,000 miles, whichever comes first
Battery and drive unit warranty	8 years, unlimited miles	8 years, unlimited miles	8 years, unlimited miles	8 years, unlimited miles
Tesla Supercharger	Standard	Standard	Standard	Standard
Autopilot features	$2,500 (optional)	$2,500 (optional)	$2,500 (optional)	$2,500 (optional)
Supercharging capability				
Standard 110-volt wall outlets	Complete recharge overnight	Complete recharge overnight	Complete recharge overnight	Complete recharge overnight
240-volt outlet, with a single on-board charger	29 miles of range per hour	29 miles of range per hour	29 miles of range per hour	29 miles of range per hour
240-volt outlet, with twin on-board chargers	58 miles of range per hour	58 miles of range per hour	58 miles of range per hour	58 miles of range per hour
Tesla Supercharger enabled	50% in 20 minutes 80% in 40 minutes 100% in 75 minutes	50% in 20 minutes 80% in 40 minutes 100% in 75 minutes	50% in 20 minutes 80% in 40 minutes 100% in 75 minutes	50% in 20 minutes 80% in 40 minutes 100% in 75 minutes
Airbags	8	8	8	8
Overall length	196.0"	196.0"	196.0"	196.0"
Overall width (mirrors extended)	86.2"	86.2"	86.2"	86.2"
Height	56.5"	56.5"	56.5"	56.5"
Ground clearance	5.65"	5.65"	5.65"	5.65"
Total cargo volume	31.6 cubic feet	31.6 cubic feet	31.6 cubic feet	31.6 cubic feet

Sources: Information posted at www.teslamotors.com and www.edmunds.com, accessed April 9, 2015. and .

---

much time was needed to make the driver's first appointment, starting the motor and turning on the climate control, opening the garage door, pulling out of the garage, and meeting the driver at the curb.

Customers who purchased any of the four Model S versions were eligible for a federal tax credit of $7,500; a number of states also offered rebates on electric vehicle purchases, with states such as California and

New York offering rebates as high as $7,500. Customers who leased a Model S were not entitled to rebates.

Tesla's Third Vehicle—The Model X Crossover SUV

To reduce the development costs of the Model X, Tesla had designed the Model X so that it could share about 60 percent of the Model S platform. The Model X had seating for seven adults, dual electric motors that powered an all-wheel drive system, and an expected driving range of about 260 miles per charge. The Model X's distinctive "falcon-wing doors" provided easy access to the second and third seating rows, resulting in a profile that resembled a sedan more than an SUV (see Exhibit 6).

EXHIBIT 6
Model X Crossover

Tesla Model X-Silver with doors up

Tesla Model X-Silver

Initial production of the Model X began in the third quarter of 2015. The base price of the Tesla Model X crossover was similar to a dual-motor, all-wheel drive Model S with autopilot (~$106,000).

In April 2015, Tesla sent software updates to all Model S vehicles previously delivered to customers that included a new "Range Assurance" feature, an always-running application within the car's navigation system that kept tabs on the vehicle's battery charge-level and the locations of Tesla Supercharging stations and parking-spot chargers in the vicinity; when the vehicle's battery began running low, an alert appeared on the navigation screen, along with a list of nearby Tesla Supercharger stations and public charging facilities. A second warning appeared when the vehicle was about to go beyond the radius of nearby chargers without enough juice to get to the next facility, at which point drivers were directed to the nearest charge point.

A few weeks later, a second software update with a Trip Planner feature was sent out. Trip Planner consisted of a GPS navigation tweak that enabled drivers to plan long-distance trips based on the best charging options both en route and at the destination. The software displayed the fastest, most convenient route to the destination on the console screen, indicating where drivers needed to stop and how long they would need to plug in along the way to maintain sufficient battery power. The software was programmed to pull in new data about every 30 seconds, updating to show which charging facilities were vacant so the vehicle would not end up waiting in line for a plug.

Tesla's Fourth Vehicle—The Model 3

Tesla expected to introduce its fourth model, called the Model 3, in 2017. The Model 3 was intended to be a high-volume vehicle with much lower base price—perhaps as low as $35,000, provided Tesla was able to achieve the targeted cost reductions. Headed into 2016, work on the design, styling, and specifications for the Model 3 was nearing the final stages.

Distribution Strategy: A Company-Owned and Operated Network of Retail Stores and Service Centers

Tesla sold its vehicles directly to buyers and provided them with after-sale service through a network of company-owned sales galleries and service centers. This contrasted sharply with the strategy of rival motor vehicle manufacturers, all of whom sold vehicles and replacement parts at wholesale prices to their networks of franchised dealerships that in turn handled retail sales, maintenance and service, and warranty repairs. Management believed that integrating forward into the business of traditional automobile dealers and operating its own retail sales and service network had three important advantages:

1. *The ability to create and control its own version of a compelling buying customer experience,* one that was differentiated from the buying experience consumers had with sales and service locations of franchised automobile dealers. Having customers deal directly with Tesla-employed sales and service personnel enabled Tesla to (a) engage and inform potential customers about electric vehicles in general and the advantages of owning a Tesla in particular and (b) build a more personal relationship with customers and, hopefully, instill a lasting and favorable impression of Tesla Motors, its mission, and the caliber and performance of its vehicles.

2. *The ability to achieve greater operating economies in performing sales and service activities.* Management believed that a company-operated sales and service network offered substantial opportunities to better control inventory costs of both vehicles and replacement parts, manage warranty service and pricing, maintain and strengthen the Tesla brand, and obtain rapid customer feedback.

3. *The opportunity to capture the sales and service revenues of traditional automobile dealerships.* Rival motor vehicle manufacturers sold vehicles and replacement parts at wholesale prices to their networks of franchised dealerships that in turn handled retail sales, maintenance and service, and warranty repairs. But when Tesla buyers purchased a vehicle at a Tesla-owned sales gallery, Tesla captured the full retail sales price, roughly 10 percent greater than the wholesale price realized by vehicle manufacturers selling through franchised dealers. And by operating its own service centers, it captured service revenues not available to vehicle manufacturers that relied upon their franchised dealers to provide

need maintenance and repairs. Furthermore, Tesla management believed that company-owned service centers avoided the conflict of interest between vehicle manufacturers and their franchised dealers where the sale of warranty parts and repairs by a dealer were a key source of revenue and profit for the dealer but where warranty-related costs were typically a substantial expense for the vehicle manufacturer.

Tesla Sales Galleries and Showrooms Currently, all of Tesla's sales galleries and showrooms were in or near major metropolitan areas; some were in prominent regional shopping malls, and others were on highly visible sites along busy thoroughfares. Most sales locations had only several vehicles in stock. While some customers purchased their vehicles from the available inventory, most preferred to order a custom-equipped car in their preferred color.

Tesla was aggressively expanding its network of sales galleries and service centers to broaden its geographical presence and to provide better maintenance and repair service in areas with a high concentration of Model S customers. In 2013, Tesla began combining its sales and service activities at a single location (rather than having separate locations, as earlier had been the case); experience indicated that combination sales and service locations were more cost-efficient and facilitated faster expansion of the company's retail footprint. At the end of 2014, Tesla had 159 sales and service locations around the world and planned to open more stores, galleries, and service centers in all of the company's geographic markets in 2015. Tesla's strategy was to have sufficient service locations to ensure that after-sale services were available to owners when and where needed.

However, in the United States, there was a lurking problem with Tesla's strategy to bypass distributing through franchised Tesla dealers and sell directly to consumers. Going back many years, franchised automobile dealers in the United States had feared that automotive manufacturers might one day decide to integrate forward into selling and servicing the vehicles they produced. To foreclose any attempts by manufacturers to compete directly against their franchised dealers, automobile dealers in every state in the United States had formed statewide franchised dealer associations to lobby for legislation blocking motor vehicle manufacturers from becoming retailers of new and used cars and providing maintenance and repair services to vehicle owners. Legislation either forbidding or severely restricting the ability of automakers to sell vehicles directly to the public had been passed in 48 states; these laws had been in effect for many years, and franchised dealer associations were diligent in pushing for strict enforcement of these laws.

As sales of the Model S rose briskly in 2013 and Tesla continued opening more sales galleries and service centers, both franchised dealers and statewide dealer associations became increasingly anxious about "the Tesla problem" and what actions might need to be taken. Dealers and dealer trade associations in a number of states were openly vocal about their concerns and actively began lobbying state legislatures to consider either enforcement actions against Tesla or amendments to existing legislation that would bring a halt to Tesla's efforts to sell vehicles at company-owned showrooms. A Tesla spokesperson told an *Automotive News* reporter in September 2013 that dealerships around the country "object to the fact that we're trying to educate our consumers directly, sell them cars directly, and service their vehicles directly because this runs entirely counter to the virtual monopoly they have in most states."[29] Tesla had also asserted it was not violating state franchising laws because it did not have any franchises. In the opinion of a senior editor at Edmunds.com, the real fear of automobile dealers was not Tesla but rather that other automakers would follow in Tesla's footsteps.[30]

In mid-December 2013, a group of Ohio car dealers filed a lawsuit against Tesla, the Ohio Bureau of Motor Vehicles, and the Ohio Department of Public Safety in a Franklin County court, alleging violations of Ohio law in granting Tesla a license to sell new cars and asking for an injunction to immediately rescind Tesla's license and prevent the Bureau of Motor Vehicles from issuing additional licenses to Tesla for other new locations. However, a settlement was reached in March 2014 that allowed Tesla to own and operate a maximum of three sales galleries in Ohio as long as it produced only all-electric cars and was not acquired by another company.

In March 2014, the New Jersey Motor Vehicle Commission announced that it would enforce New Jersey's state law forbidding automotive manufacturers from selling cars directly to consumers; at the time, Tesla had two showrooms in New Jersey. A controversy ensued, with some New Jersey lawmakers introducing legislation that would exempt Tesla and other electric car makers from the rule. In March 2015, legislation allowing Tesla to sell vehicles directly to consumers in New Jersey was signed into law. In June 2014, legislation was passed in New York state allowing Tesla to sell its vehicles at five already-established locations in New York; however, the legislation prevented Tesla from opening additional sales locations within New York. In Georgia, legislation passed in 2015 allowing Tesla to operate up to five sales outlets in the state. West Virginia passed a bill in 2015 that prevents any automaker from exhibiting cars to the public unless they do so through a franchised dealership. In Virginia, as of mid-2015, Tesla had been granted the right to open only a single sales location (near Washington, D.C.).

As of 2015, automobile dealers and statewide dealer associations in Texas, Arizona, and Michigan had succeeded in gaining enforcement of existing legislation banning direct sales to consumers and effectively blocking Tesla from taking orders for the Model S at Tesla showrooms in their states, but legislation to reverse the ban had been introduced in both the Texas and Arizona legislatures. Elon Musk had announced that Tesla would be willing to cap its sales locations in Texas at seven.

However, in most states where manufacturer direct sales to consumers were expressly prohibited, Tesla could still have sales galleries, service centers, and Supercharger locations; what it could not do at its sales galleries was sell cars, deliver cars, or discuss pricing with potential buyers. Buyers in these states could place an order for a Tesla online at www.teslamotors.com (usually in about 5 to 10 minutes), specify when they wanted the car to arrive, and then either have it delivered to a nearby Tesla service center for pickup or have it delivered directly to their home or business location.

Tesla Service Centers   Tesla's strategy was to have sufficient service locations to ensure that after-sale services were available to owners when and where needed. The company had over 70 service locations as of February 2014 and was rapidly adding new locations to serve Tesla owners in a growing number of geographic locations.

Tesla Roadster owners could upload data from their vehicle and send it to a service center on a memory card; Model S owners had an on-board system that could communicate directly with a service center, allowing service technicians to diagnose and remedy many problems before ever looking at the vehicle. When maintenance or service was required, a customer could schedule service by contacting a Tesla service center. Some service locations offered valet service, in which the owner's car was picked up, replaced with a very well-equipped Model S loaner car, and then returned when the service was completed; there was no additional charge for valet service. In some locations, owners could opt to have service performed at their home, office, or other remote location by a Tesla Ranger mobile technician who had the capability to perform a variety of services that did not require a vehicle lift. Tesla Rangers could perform most warranty repairs, but the cost of their visit was not covered under the New Vehicle Limited Warranty. Ranger service pricing was based on a per visit, per vehicle basis; there was a $100 minimum charge per Ranger visit.

Prepaid Maintenance Program

Tesla offered a prepaid maintenance program to Model S buyers, which included plans covering maintenance for one year or 12,500 miles ($600), four years or up to 50,000 miles ($1,900), or eight years or up to 100,000 miles ($3,800). Ranger service for all of the prepaid maintenance plans involved a $100 minimum charge per Ranger visit. These plans covered annual inspections and the replacement of wear-and-tear parts, 24-hour roadside assistance, system monitoring, system upgrades, and service-related hardware upgrades.

Tesla's Supercharger Network: Providing Recharging Services to Owners on Long-Distance Trips

A major component of Tesla's strategy to build rapidly growing long-term demand for its vehicles was to make battery-recharging while driving long distances convenient and worry-free for all Tesla vehicle owners. Tesla's solution to providing owners with ample and convenient recharging opportunities was to establish an extensive geographic network of recharging stations. Tesla's Supercharger stations were strategically placed along major

highways connecting city centers, usually at locations with such nearby amenities as roadside diners, cafes, and shopping centers that enabled owners to have a brief rest stop or get a quick meal during the recharging process—about 90 percent of Model S buyers opted to have their vehicle equipped with supercharging capability when they ordered their vehicle. All Model S owners were entitled to use the free supercharging service at any of Tesla's Supercharging stations to get a 50 percent recharge in 20 minutes, an 80 percent recent recharge in 40 minutes, or a 100 percent recharge in 75 minutes. As of April 2015, Tesla had 400 Supercharger stations open worldwide.

Exhibit 7 shows Tesla's planned network of Supercharger stations in the United States by year-end 2016. Exhibit 8 shows a Tesla Supercharger Station and selected Tesla Sales Galleries and Service Centers.

Tesla executives expected that the company's planned Supercharger network would relieve much of the "range anxiety" associated with driving on a long distance trip. However, even with many Supercharger locations strategically positioned along major travel routes, it was likely that Tesla owners in China, Canada, and parts of Europe would still be inconvenienced by having to deviate from the shortest direct route and detour to the closest Supercharger station for needed recharging. The degree to which range anxiety and "detour frustration" might prompt future vehicle shoppers to steer away from buying a Tesla was a risk that Tesla still had to prove it could hurdle.

Battery Swap Service—An Even Faster Battery Replenishment Option.

The design of the Model S permitted the entire battery pack to be lowered from the bottom of the vehicle chassis and swapped out within a span of five minutes or less. In 2015, Tesla began testing a battery swap program at a custom-built California location whereby Model S owners could pay a fee of about $80 to exchange their vehicle's partially discharged battery pack for a fully charged battery pack. The purpose of the pilot program was to test the technology, confirm how fast a battery pack could be swapped out, and assess the strength of market demand for battery swapping. Initially, the battery swap was by appointment and had a cost of about $80.

Tesla's Planned Network of Supercharger Locations in North America, Year-End 2016

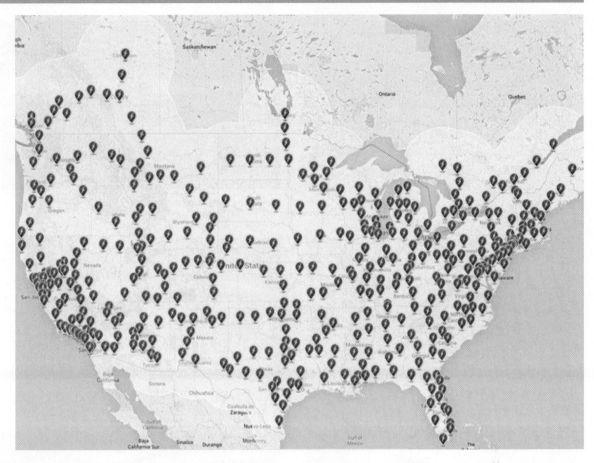

Source: www.teslamotors.com, accessed April 1, 2015.

Technology and Product Development Strategy

Headed into 2015, Tesla had spent almost $1.4 billion on research and development (R&D) activities to design, develop, test, and refine the components and systems needed to produce top-quality electric vehicles and, further, to design and develop prototypes of the Tesla Roadster, Model S, Model X, and Model 3 vehicles (see Exhibit 1 for R&D spending during 2010–2014). In 2014, the company doubled its R&D spending to support engineering and product development efforts on dual-motor power train and right-hand drive features for the Model S, the

introduction of new software with autopilot capabilities for the Model S and forthcoming Model X, engineering and prototyping for the Model X, and design and engineering for the Model 3.

Tesla executives believed the company had developed core competencies in power train and vehicle engineering and innovative manufacturing techniques. The company's core intellectual property was contained in its electric power train technology—the battery pack, power electronics, induction motor, gearbox, and control software that enabled these key components to operate as a system. Tesla personnel had designed each of these major elements for the Tesla Roadster and Model S; much of this

EXHIBIT 8

A Tesla Supercharger Station and Selected Tesla Sales Galleries and Service Centers

Supercharger station, outdoor, Washington state

Supercharger station, indoor

Tesla Sales Gallery, Austin, TX

Tesla Sales Gallery, Newport Beach, CA

Tesla Service center, Denver, Colorado

Tesla Service center, interior, San Diego, California

technology was being used in the power train components that Tesla built for other manufacturers and was scheduled for use in the Model X, Model 3, and future Tesla vehicles.

Tesla's power train was a compact, modular system with far fewer moving parts than the power trains of traditional gasoline-powered vehicles, a feature that enabled Tesla to implement power train enhancements and improvements as fast as they could be identified, designed, and tested. Tesla had incorporated its latest power train technology into the Model S and into the power train components that it built and sold to other makers of electric vehicles; plus, it was planning to use much of this technology in its forthcoming electric vehicles.

As of year-end 2013, Tesla had been issued 203 patents and had more than 280 pending patent applications domestically and internationally in a broad range of areas. However, in 2014, Tesla announced a patent policy whereby it irrevocably pledged the company would not initiate a lawsuit against any party for infringing Tesla's patents through activity relating to electric vehicles or related equipment so long as the party was acting in good faith. Elon Musk said the company made this pledge in order to encourage the advancement of a common, rapidly evolving platform for electric vehicles, thereby benefiting itself, other companies making electric vehicles, and the world. Investor reaction to this announcement was largely negative on grounds that it would negate any technology-based competitive advantage over rival manufacturers of electric vehicles—which many investors viewed as being considerable.

Battery Pack   Over the years, Tesla had tested hundreds of battery cells of different chemistries and performance features. It had an internal battery cell testing lab and had assembled an extensive performance database of the many available lithium-ion cell vendors and chemistry types. Based on this evaluation, it had elected to use "18650 form factor" lithium-ion battery cells, chiefly because a battery pack containing 18650 cells offered two to three times the driving range of the lithium-ion cells used by other makers of electric vehicles (see Exhibit 9). Moreover, Tesla had been able to obtain large quantities of the 18650 lithium-ion cells for its battery

EXHIBIT 9

Comparative Miles per Charge of Selected Electric Vehicles, 2014–2015

Vehicle	Miles per Charge (based on EPA 5-cycle test)
Tesla Model S (85 kWh battery pack)	265 miles
Tesla Model S (60 kWh battery pack)	208 miles
Toyota RAV4 EV	103 miles
Fiat 500e	87 miles
Mercedes B-Class Electric Drive	85 miles
Nissan Leaf	84 miles
Volkswagen e-Golf	83 miles
Honda Fit EV	82 miles
Chevrolet Spark	82 miles
BMW i3	81 miles
Ford Focus EV	76 miles
Mitsubishi 1-MiEV	62 miles

Source: Tesla Motors Investor Presentation, September 14, 2013, posted at www.teslamotors.com (accessed December 1, 2013) and www.cheatsheet.com, posted January 16, 2015 (accessed March 30, 2015).

pack (each pack had about 7,000 of the 18650 cells) at attractive prices because global lithium-ion battery manufacturers were suffering from a huge capacity glut, having overbuilt production capacity in anticipation of a fast-growing buyer demand for electric vehicles that so far had failed to materialize.

Management believed that the company's accumulated experience and expertise had produced a core competence in battery pack design and safety, putting Tesla in position to capitalize on the substantial battery cell investments and advancements being made globally by battery cell manufacturers and to benefit from ongoing improvements in the energy storage capacity, longevity, power delivery, and costs per kilowatt-hour of the battery packs used in its current and forthcoming models. Tesla's battery pack design gave it the ability to change battery cell chemistries and vendors, while retaining the company's existing investments in software, electronics, testing, and other power train components. Going forward, Tesla intended to maintain the flexibility to quickly incorporate the latest advancements in battery technology, change battery cell chemistries if needed, and thereby optimize battery pack system performance and cost for its current and future vehicles.

The driving range of Tesla's vehicles on a single charge declined over the life of the battery, based on a customer's use of their Tesla vehicle and the frequency with which they charged the battery. Tesla estimated that the Tesla Roadster battery pack would retain approximately 60–65 percent of its ability to hold its initial charge after approximately 100,000 miles or seven years, which will result in a decrease to the vehicle's initial range. In addition, based on internal testing, the company estimated that the Tesla Roadster would have a 5–10 percent reduction in range when operated in -20°C temperatures. The battery charge deterioration for Model S battery packs was expected to be less than for the Roadster.

Power Electronics The power electronics in Tesla's power train system had two primary functions, the control of torque generation in the motor while driving and the control of energy delivery back into the battery pack while charging. The first function was accomplished through the drive inverter, which was directly responsible for the performance, energy-use efficiency, and overall driving experience of the vehicle. The second function, charging the battery pack, was accomplished by the vehicle's charger, which converted alternating current (usually from a wall outlet or other electricity source) into direct current that could be accepted by the battery. Most Model S owners ordered vehicles equipped with twin chargers in order to cut the charging time in half. Owners could use any available source of power to charge their vehicle. A standard 12 amp/110 volt wall outlet could charge the battery pack to full capacity in about 42 hours for vehicles equipped with a single charger or 21 hours with a twin charger. Tesla recommended that owners install *at least* a 24 amp/240 volt outlet in their garage or carport (the same voltage used by many electric ovens and clothes dryers), which permitted charging at the rate of 34 miles of range per hour of charging time on vehicles equipped with a twin charger. But Tesla strongly recommended the installation of a more powerful 40-amp/240 volt outlet that charged at the rate of 58 miles of range per hour

of charge when a Model S was equipped with twin chargers. Model S vehicles came standard with three adapters: a 12 amp/110 volt adapter, a 40 amp/ 240 volt adapter, and a J1772 public charging station adapter; other adapters could be purchased online.

Control Software The battery pack and the performance and safety systems of Tesla vehicles required the use of numerous microprocessors and sophisticated software. For example, computer-driven software monitored the charge state of each of the cells of the battery pack and managed all of the safety systems. The flow of electricity between the battery pack and the motor had to be tightly controlled in order to deliver the performance and behavior expected in the vehicle. There were software algorithms that enabled the vehicle to mimic the "creep" feeling that drivers expected from an internal combustion engine vehicle without having to apply pressure on the accelerator. Other algorithms controlled traction, vehicle stability, and the sustained acceleration and regenerative braking of the vehicle. Drivers used the vehicle's information systems to optimize performance and charging modes and times. In addition to the vehicle control software, Tesla had developed software for the infotainment system of Model S. Almost all of the software programs had been developed and written by Tesla personnel. In 2014–2015, Tesla was developing its expertise in building software for vehicle autopilot systems, including road tracking, lane changing, automated parking, driver warning systems, and automated braking functions.

Tesla routinely enhanced the performance of its Model S vehicles by sending wireless software updates to the microprocessors on board each Model S it had sold.

Vehicle Design and Engineering

Tesla had devoted considerable effort to creating significant in-house capabilities related to designing and engineering portions of its vehicles, and it had become knowledgeable about the design and engineering of those parts, components, and systems that it purchased from suppliers. Tesla personnel had designed and engineered the body, chassis, and interior of the Model S and were working on the designs and engineering of these same components for the Model X and Gen III. As a matter of necessity, Tesla was forced to redesign the heating, cooling, and ventilation system for its vehicles to operate without the energy generated from an internal combustion engine and to integrate with its own battery-powered thermal management system. In addition, the low-voltage electric system that powered such features the radio, power windows, and heated seats had to be designed specifically for use in an electric vehicle. Tesla had developed expertise in integrating these components with the high-voltage power source in the Model S and in designing components that significantly reduced their load on the vehicle's battery pack, so as to maximize the available driving range.

Tesla personnel had accumulated considerable expertise in lightweight materials, since an electric vehicle's driving range was heavily impacted by the vehicle's weight and mass. The Tesla Roadster had been built with an in-house designed carbon fiber body to provide a good balance of strength and mass. The Model S was being built with a lightweight aluminum body and a chassis that incorporated a variety of materials and production methods to help optimize vehicle weight, strength, safety, and performance. In addition, top management believed that the company's design and engineering team had core competencies in computer-aided design and crash test simulations; this expertise was expected to reduce the product development time of new models.

Manufacturing Strategy

Tesla contracted with Lotus Cars, Ltd., to produce Tesla Roadster "gliders" (a complete vehicle minus the electric power train) at a Lotus factory in Hethel, England. The Tesla gliders were then shipped to a Tesla facility in Menlo Park, California, where the battery pack, induction motors, and other power train components were installed as part of the final assembly process. The production of Roadster gliders ceased in January 2012.

In May 2010, Tesla purchased the major portion of a recently closed automobile plant in Fremont, California, for $42 million; months later, Tesla purchased some of the plant's equipment for $17 million. The facility—formerly a General Motors manufacturing plant (1960–1982), then operated as joint venture between General Motors and Toyota (1984–2010) to showcase Toyota's famed production system and

produce Toyota Corolla and Tacoma vehicles—was closed in 2010 when GM pulled out of the joint venture and Toyota elected to cease its production of several thousand vehicles per week and permanently layoff about 4,700 workers. Tesla executives viewed the facility as one of the largest, most advanced, and cleanest automotive production plants in the world, and the space inside the 5.5 million square-foot main building was deemed sufficient for Tesla to produce about 500,000 vehicles annually (approximately 1 percent of the total worldwide car production), thus giving Tesla plenty of room to grow its output of electric vehicles. Elon Musk felt the Fremont plant was superior to two other Southern California sites being considered because Fremont's location in the northern section of Silicon Valley facilitated hiring talented engineers already residing nearby and because the short distance between Fremont and Tesla's Palo Alto headquarters ensured "a tight feedback loop between vehicle engineering, manufacturing, and other divisions within the company."[31] Tesla officially took possession of the 350-acre site in October 2010, renamed it the Tesla Factory, and immediately launched efforts to get a portion of the massive facility ready to begin manufacturing components and assembling the Model S in 2012.

In December 2012, Tesla opened a new 60,000 square-foot facility in Tilburg, Netherlands, about 50 miles from the port of Rotterdam, to serve as the final assembly and distribution point for all Model S vehicles sold in Europe and Scandinavia. The facility, called the Tilburg Assembly Plant, received nearly complete Model S units shipped from the Tesla Factory, performed certain final assembly activities, conducted final vehicle testing, and handled the delivery to customers throughout the European market. It also functioned as Tesla's European service and parts headquarters. Tilburg's central location and its excellent rail and highway network to all major markets on the European continent allowed Tesla to distribute to anywhere across the continent in about 12 hours. By fall 2013, the Tilburg operation had been expanded to over 200,000 square feet—including facilities for technical training, parts remanufacturing, and collision repair activities for Tesla's European operations—and was receiving about 200 Model S vehicles weekly for final assembly, testing, and customer delivery.

Tesla's manufacturing strategy was to source a number of parts and components from outside suppliers but to design, develop, and manufacture in-house those key components where it had considerable intellectual property and core competencies (namely lithium-ion battery packs, electric motors, gearboxes, and other power train components) and to perform all assembly-related activities itself. In 2015, the Tesla Factory contained several production-related activities, including stamping, machining, casting, plastics molding, robotics-assisted body assembly, paint operations, final vehicle assembly, and end-of-line quality testing (see Exhibit 10). In addition, the Tesla Factory manufactured lithium-ion battery packs, electric motors, gearboxes, and certain other components for its vehicles and for the power trains sold to various other manufacturers of electric vehicles. In 2014, Tesla began producing and machining various aluminum components at a facility in Lathrop, California. In 2015, Tesla expected to complete construction of a new high-volume paint shop and a new body shop line, both to be used for Model S, Model X, and Model 3 vehicles. During 2014 and 2015, installations of new equipment boosted the annual production capacity of the Tesla Factory from about 21,500 vehicles in 2013 to nearly 60,000 vehicles at year-end 2015.

Initially, production costs for the Model S were high due to an assortment of start-up costs at the Tesla Factory, manufacturing inefficiencies associated with inexperience and low-volume production, higher prices for component parts during the first several months of production runs, and higher logistics costs associated with the immaturity of Tesla's supply chain. However, as Tesla engineers redesigned various elements of the Model S for greater ease of manufacturing, supply chain improvements were instituted, and production volumes approached 1,000 vehicles per week in 2014, manufacturing efficiency rose, the costs of some parts decreased, and overall production costs per vehicle trended downward, enabling the company to achieve a gross margin of 27.6 percent in 2014, up from 22.7 percent in 2013. Management expected that further cost-saving initiatives being undertaken by both Tesla and its suppliers, together with further boosts in production volume, would result in still lower production costs per vehicle at least until mid-2014. Elon Musk

expected that Tesla to achieve could achieve a gross margin of 26 percent or better in 2015, despite the impact of a stronger U.S. dollar, manufacturing inefficiencies associated with production startup of the Model X, and expenditures for greater autopilot functionality.

Tesla's Decision to Build a "Gigafactory" to Produce Battery Packs

In February 2014, Tesla announced that it and unnamed partners would invest $4–5 billion through 2020 in a "gigafactory" capable of producing enough lithium-ion batteries to make battery packs for 500,000 vehicles (plus stationary storage applications for solar-powered generating facilities): the planned output of the battery factory in 2020 exceeded the *total global production of lithium batteries in 2013*. Tesla said its direct investment in the project would be $2 billion. Tesla indicated the new plant (named the Tesla Gigafactory) would reduce the company's battery pack cost by more than 30 percent—to around $200 per kWh by some estimates (from the current estimated level of about $300 per kWh). The schedule called for facility construction in 2014–2015, equipment installation in 2016, and initial production in 2017. Plans called for the plant to be built on a 500–1,000 acre site, employ about 6,500 workers, have about 10 million square feet of space on two levels, and be powered by wind and solar generating facilities located nearby.

Evaluation of finalist plant sites in five states (Nevada, Arizona, New Mexico, Texas, and California) began immediately; competition among the five states to win the plant was fierce, but in September 2014, Tesla announced that a site in an industrial park east of Reno, Nevada, would be the location of the Tesla Gigafactory. It was speculated that the Nevada site was chosen, partly because the state of Nevada offered Tesla a lucrative incentive package said to be worth $1.25 billion over 20 years and partly because the only commercially active lithium mining operation in the United States was in a nearby Nevada county (this county was reputed to have the fifth-largest deposits of lithium in the world). In early 2015, construction of the Tesla Gigafactory was underway and proceeding at a rapid clip.

Less than a month after announcing its intent to build the Gigafactory, Tesla sold $920 million of convertible senior notes due 2019 carrying an interest

EXHIBIT 10

Scenes of Assembly Operations at the Tesla Factory

Tesla factory

rate of 0.25 percent and $1.38 billion in convertible senior notes due 2021 carrying an interest rate of 1.25 percent. The senior notes due 2019 were convertible into cash, shares of Tesla's common stock, or a combination thereof, at Tesla's election. The convertible senior notes due 2021 were convertible into cash and, if applicable, shares of Tesla's common stock (subject to Tesla's right to deliver cash in lieu of shares of common stock). Both bonds had an equity conversion premium of 42.5 percent above the last reported sale price of Tesla's common stock price ($252.54) at the time of the debt issue (which equated to almost $360 per share); in other words, Tesla's stock had to be trading above $360 per share for the holders of the convertible bonds to be eligible to receive 2.8 shares of Tesla common stock for every $1,000 of bonds they choose to convert (but again that was subject to Tesla's right to deliver cash in lieu of common stock). Moreover, to further protect existing shareholders against ownership dilution that might result from the senior notes being converted into additional shares of Tesla stock, Tesla immediately entered into convertible note hedge transactions and warrant transactions at an approximate cost of $186 million that management expected would reduce potential dilution of existing shareholder interests and/or offset cash payments that Tesla was required to make in excess of the principal amounts upon any conversion of the 2019 notes and 2021 notes.

Supply Chain Strategy The Model S contained over 2,000 parts and components that Tesla was sourcing globally from over 300 direct suppliers, the majority of whom were currently single-source suppliers. It was the company's practice to obtain the needed parts and components from multiple sources whenever feasible, and Tesla management expected able to secure alternate sources of supply for most single-sourced components within a year or two. However, qualifying alternate suppliers for certain highly customized components—or producing them internally—was thought to be both time-consuming and costly, perhaps even requiring modifications to a vehicle's design. Tesla had developed close relationships with the suppliers of lithium-ion battery cells and certain other key system parts, but it did not maintain long-term agreements with many of its suppliers.

Marketing Strategy

In 2014–2015, Tesla's principal marketing goals and functions were to:

- Generate demand for the company's vehicles and drive sales leads to personnel in the Tesla's showrooms and sales galleries.
- Build long-term brand awareness and manage the company's image and reputation.
- Manage the existing customer base to create brand loyalty and generate customer referrals.
- Obtain feedback from the owners of Tesla vehicles and make sure their experiences and suggestions for improvement were communicated to Tesla personnel engaged in designing, developing, and/or improving the company's current and future vehicles.

As the first company to commercially produce a federally compliant, fully electric vehicle that achieved market-leading range on a single charge, Tesla had been able to generate significant media coverage of the company and its vehicles. Management expected this would continue to be the case for some time to come. So far, the extensive media coverage, glowing praise from both new Model S owners and admiring car enthusiasts (which effectively enlarged Tesla's sales force at zero cost), and the decisions of many green-minded affluent individuals to help lead the movement away from gasoline-powered vehicles had combined to drive good traffic flows at Tesla's sales galleries and create a backlog of orders for the Model S. As a consequence, going into 2016, the company had achieved a growing volume of sales without traditional advertising and at relatively low marketing costs. Nonetheless, Tesla did make use of pay-per-click advertisements on websites and mobile applications relevant to its target clientele. It also displayed and demonstrated its vehicles at such widely attended public events as the Detroit, Los Angeles, and Frankfurt auto shows and at a few small private events attended by people who were likely to be intrigued by its vehicles.

Tesla's Innovative Resale Guarantee Program for New Vehicle Purchases

During the second quarter of 2013, Tesla instituted its first big internal marketing and sales promotion campaign to spur demand for its Model S vehicles and give owners complete peace of mind about the long-term value of the product. In partnership with Wells Fargo Bank and US Bank, Model S customers in the United States were offered unique financing terms that included giving buyers the option of selling their vehicle back to Tesla within a window of 36 to 39 months after delivery for a guaranteed 50 percent of the base vehicle selling price and 43 percent of the price of any vehicle options. The buyback option enabled customers to enjoy the benefits of Model S ownership without concern for its resale value. During the fourth quarter of 2013, approximately 48 percent of Model S buyers in North America financed their purchase using the innovative buyback guarantee program, an increase from 44 percent in the third quarter and 31 percent in the second quarter.[32] The buyback option was extended to include buyers in selected European countries in 2014. Tesla's liabilities for repurchasing vehicles carrying a resale value guarantee totaled $236.3 million in 2013 and $249.5 million in 2014.

In the event the guaranteed buyback value of 50 percent of the base vehicle selling price plus 43 percent of the price of any vehicle options turned out to be less than the top resale value of any of these vehicles, Elon Musk had personally guaranteed to pay the difference to owners choosing to sell their three-year-old vehicle back to Tesla. Tesla's analysis indicated that the benchmarked premium luxury sedans (Mercedes, BMW, Audi, Jaguar, and Lexus) tended to retain *on average* about 43 percent of their original value after three years. In October 2014, Tesla announced that customers who leased a Model S through would be able to return it in the first three months with no penalties and the remaining payments waived—a feature that Tesla called "the happiness guarantee." Tesla delivered 5,179 vehicles in 2013 and another 5,224 vehicles in 2014 that carried resale value guarantees.

In 2015, Tesla was not only offering loans and leases in North America, Europe, and Asia through its various partner financial institutions, but it was also offering leases directly through its own captive finance company in 37 states, the District of Columbia, and four provinces in Canada. Typically, the amount due at signing of a lease included the first month's payment, a downpayment of $5,000, a $700

acquisition fee, and applicable taxes; a $300 disposition fee was due at lease end. Tesla management intended to broaden its financial services offerings over the next several years.

Tesla's offer to buy back Model S cars from customers using its lease-buyback financing option had the potential to provide Tesla with another profitable revenue stream: selling used Tesla vehicles at prices above the buyback price. According to one analyst, "Buying back three-year-old cars at a set price means Tesla to a great extent can control the secondary market for Model S and other cars it brings out. The company's going to be the main buyer and get a chance to earn a second gross profit on the same car."[33] The analyst estimated that sales of used Model S vehicles in 2016 could mean an added $350–$370 million in revenues for Tesla in 2016 and perhaps an added $40 million in annual gross profit.

Even though Tesla received full upfront payment for the vehicles sold under the resale guarantee financing program, generally accepted accounting principles (GAAP) required Tesla to treat transactions under the resale guarantee program as leased vehicles and to spread the recognition of revenue and cost over the contractual term of the resale value guarantee (36 to 39 months). If a Model S owner decided not to sell their vehicle back to Tesla by the end of the resale value guarantee term, any deferred revenue and the vehicle's undepreciated book value were then recognized as revenues from automotive sales and as a cost of automotive sales, respectively.

The resale guarantee program exposed Tesla to the risk that the vehicles' resale value could be lower than its estimates and to the risk that the volume of vehicles sold back to Tesla at the guaranteed resale price might be higher than the company's estimates. GAAP required such risks to be accounted for on Tesla's financial statements by establishing a reserves account (a contingent liability in the current liabilities section of the balance sheet) deemed sufficient to cover these risks.

Sales of Regulatory Credits to Other Automotive Manufacturers

Because Tesla's electric vehicles had no tailpipe emissions of greenhouse gases or other pollutants,

Tesla earned zero emission vehicle (ZEV) and greenhouse gas (GHG) credits on each vehicle sold in the United States. Moreover, it also earned corporate average fuel economy (CAFE) credits on its sales of vehicles because of their high equivalent miles per gallon ratings. All three of these types of regulatory credits had significant market value because the manufacturers of traditional gasoline-powered vehicles were subject to assorted emission and mileage requirements set by the U.S. Environmental Protection Agency (EPA) and by certain state agencies charged with protecting the environment within their borders; automotive manufacturers whose vehicle sales did not meet prevailing emission and mileage requirements were allowed to achieve compliance by purchasing credits earned by other automotive manufacturers. Tesla had entered into contracts for the sale of ZEV and GHG credits with several automotive manufacturers, and it routinely sold its CAFE credits. Tesla's sales of ZEV, GHG, and CAFE credits produced revenues of $2.8 million in 2010, $2.7 million in 2011, $40.5 million in 2012, $194.4 million in 2013—the proceeds were included on Tesla's income statement as part of item labeled "Sales of vehicles, options and accessories, vehicle service, and regulatory credits" (see Exhibit 1).

Wall Street analysts attributed a large portion of the company's improving financial performance to the revenues earned from the sales of regulatory credits. Without these revenues, their argument went, Tesla's bottom line would look significantly worse in 2013 and 2014. While Tesla planned to pursue opportunities to sell regulatory credits earned from future sales of its vehicles, the company repeatedly asserted in its 10-K and 10-Q reports to the Securities and Exchange Commission that it was not relying on these sales to be a significant contributor to the company's gross margin and that the long-term viability and profitability of Tesla's business model was not predicated on revenues from the sale of regulatory credits.

Strategic Partnerships

In 2015, Tesla had entered into long-term strategic partnerships with Panasonic Corp., Daimler AG (the parent of Mercedes-Benz), and Toyota Motor Corp.

The Panasonic Partnership In 2010, Tesla began collaborating with Panasonic on the development of next-generation battery cells for electric vehicles that were based on the 18650 form factor and nickel-based lithium ion chemistry. In November 2010, Tesla sold 1,418,573 shares of its common stock to an entity affiliated with Panasonic at a price of $21.15, producing $30 million in new investor capital. In October 2011, Tesla and Panasonic finalized an agreement whereby Panasonic would supply Tesla with sufficient battery cells to build more than 80,000 vehicles over the next four years. In October 2013, Tesla and Panasonic agreed to extend the supply agreement though the end of 2017, with Tesla agreeing to purchase a minimum of 1.8 billion lithium-ion battery cells and Panasonic agreeing to provide Tesla with preferential prices.

In July 2014, Panasonic agreed to partner with Tesla in building and operating the Tesla Gigafactory. According to the agreement, Tesla had responsibility for preparing, providing, and managing the land, buildings, and utilities, with Panasonic having responsibility for investing in the equipment and manufacturing the batteries. A network of supplier partners was being created to make sure all the needed materials were available. Plans called for half of the floor space to be devoted to Panasonic's battery-making activities, with the activities of suppliers and Tesla's battery pack operations taking up the other half. To meet its projected demand for battery cells, Tesla agreed to continue to purchase battery cells produced in Panasonic's factories in Japan.

The Daimler Partnership Shortly after Daimler purchased an ownership stake in Tesla for $50 million in 2009, the two companies began working out an arrangement in which Tesla would provide certain research and development services for a battery pack and charger to Daimler for its Smart fortwo electric vehicle. When this development work was completed at the end of 2009, Tesla began supplying battery packs and chargers for the Smart fortwo vehicle—some 2,100 battery packs and chargers were sold to Daimler through December 2011. In early 2010, Daimler engaged Tesla to assist with the development and production of a battery pack and charger for a pilot fleet of A-Class Mercedes electric vehicles to be introduced in Europe during

2011. When the development work was completed in October 2010, Tesla began shipping production parts in February 2010; through December 2011, Tesla sold Daimler over 500 battery packs and chargers for Mercedes A-Class electric vehicles. In early 2010, Tesla also completed the development and sale of modular battery packs for electric delivery vans for Freightliner, an affiliate of Daimler; Freightliner tested use of these electric vans with a limited number of customers.

During the fourth quarter of 2011, Daimler engaged Tesla to assist with the development of a full electric power train for a Daimler Mercedes B-Class electric vehicle; in 2012, formal arrangements were established for Daimler to pay Tesla for the successful completion of certain at-risk development milestones and the delivery of prototype samples. During 2013, Tesla completed various milestones, delivered prototype samples, and recognized $15.7 million in development services revenues for its work on Daimler's A-Class and B-Class electric vehicle programs. Tesla began supplying production parts for Daimler's B-Class electric vehicle program in 2014 and expected to continue to supply parts under this program for the next few years (Mercedes began selling its B-Class electric vehicle models in 2014).

The Toyota Partnership In May 2010, Tesla and Toyota announced their intention to cooperate on the development of electric vehicles and for Tesla to receive Toyota's support with sourcing parts and production and engineering expertise for the Model S. In July 2010, Tesla and Toyota entered into an early phase agreement to develop an electric power train system for Toyota's popular compact RAV4 sports utility vehicle and to provide prototype samples. Also in July 2010, Tesla sold 2,941,176 shares of Tesla's common stock to Toyota at its IPO price of $17.00 per share, which provided Tesla with new investor capital of $50 million.

Tesla began developing and delivering electric power trains for the RAV4 for Toyota's evaluation in September 2010 and the following month entered into a $60.1 million contract services agreement with Toyota for the development of a validated RAV4 power train system (including a battery pack, charging system, inverter, motor, gearbox, and associated software). In July 2011, Tesla contracted with

Toyota to supply an electric power train system for the RAV4 model. All of the development services for the RAV4 electric vehicle were completed in the first quarter of 2012, and Tesla began producing and delivering RAV4 power train systems to Toyota in the first half of 2012, along with providing Toyota with certain services related to the supply of the RAV4 electric power train system. In 2013, Tesla recorded revenues of $45.1 million from power rain system sales to Toyota. During 2014, Tesla's work on the RAV4 electric vehicle program ceased when Toyota elected to halt production of the electric version of RAV4 due to disappointing sales.

Tesla performed its electric power train component and systems activities principally out of a company facility in Palo Alto. This facility, which also served as Tesla's corporate headquarters, housed the company's research and development services, including battery cell and component testing and power train components manufacturing.

Problems for Tesla Emerge in the China Market

Despite enthusiasm and interest in the Model S in Tesla's sales galleries in China in early 2014, sales of the Model S in China for full-year 2014 turned out to be disappointingly small. Tesla opened its first showroom in China in Beijing in November 2013; deliveries to customers in China began in mid-April 2014. Elon Musk expected that Model S deliveries to Chinese customers in 2014 would total about 5,000 vehicles and that Tesla might even begin building vehicles in China in three to four years. Indeed, Tesla Model S reservations reported reached about 4,000 in China by mid-2014, despite the fact that Model S buyers in China were asked to make an initial payment of about $2,450 to make a reservation, followed by a $40,700 deposit to begin the building process and ship the vehicle. The Model S cost quite a bit more in China due to customs duties and taxes ($19,000), a value-added tax of ($17,700), and shipping and handling ($3,600), pushing the base price of a Model S with an 85kWh battery pack to about $121,000 before adding optional equipment.[34] In September 2014, the *Los Angeles Times* reported that Tesla had shipped perhaps as many as 2,800 vehicles to China but that so far only 432

Model S vehicles had been registered to receive license plates, thus raising questions about the big discrepancy between shipments and registrations by buyers. Tesla acknowledged the discrepancy to the reporter; the article went on to speculate that the problem could be due to many vehicles still being in transit, a lag in reported registrations, and possibly to the "scalpers" buying up new Model S sedans and stockpiling them to resell. However, one media outlet in China reported that Tesla China personnel had created a new sales team to make bulk or fleet sales of Model S vehicles to corporate customers (which accounted for the large run-up of orders) and that these bulk/fleet sales had been agreed to without requiring any deposit payments, all of which was done without the knowledge of Tesla headquarters.[35]

Tesla didn't report how many deliveries it made to customers in China, but reports in the Chinese media claimed that Tesla China delivered 2,499 vehicles to Chinese buyers in 2014 and ended 2014 with an inventory of 2,301 vehicles.[36] An anonymous source, quoted by Chinese media, said the huge inventory was partly caused by many cancellations of orders by Chinese buyers.[37] The cancellations went up in October 2014 shortly after Tesla announced the new P85D of the Model S, because many customers decided they preferred to own the P85D version rather than the Model S version they had ordered. But in many cases, according to the source, their originally ordered cars were already shipped and underway. While Tesla's official policy was to collect the second $40,700 deposit before shipment (to preclude last-minute cancellations), in reality Tesla China only collected the first deposit because, according to another anonymous "Tesla insider," collecting the second deposit was "too difficult," thereby enabling customers who had ordered the 60kWh or 85kWh versions to refuse delivery when their previously ordered vehicle arrived and in effect cancel their order.[38] In late 2014, Tesla's U.S. headquarters learned about Tesla China's failure to collect payment of the second deposit and immediately upped the size of the first deposit to $8,000 without consulting Tesla China, although Tesla China later warned against such an increase because it would hurt sales.[39] The higher deposit was indeed viewed as too high by many prospective Chinese buyers, resulting in China sales of about

150 vehicles in December 2014 and about 120 vehicles in January 2015.

Tesla China suggested two ways to deal with the unsold cars: 1) sell the inventory cars with a 20% discount, or 2) use third-party sellers, such as large dealer groups, to get rid of the inventory, as Tesla still has very few stores in China. Both suggestions were rejected by Tesla's headquarters in the United States.[40] In December 2014, Tesla China's president resigned, just nine months after replacing the former president who left in March 2014. In February 2015, the chief marketing officer for Tesla China left the company; the general manager left the organization on April 1. In March 2015, Elon Musk announced that about 30 percent of the Tesla China workforce would be laid off; Musk visited the Tesla China operations in April 2015 and met with Chinese officials to reiterate Tesla's long-term commitment to selling its vehicles in China.

To help stimulate sales in China and get Tesla China back on track, Musk indicated that because many Chinese customers perceived that home charging was difficult and had extreme "range anxiety" (due to heavy traffic and the lack of an extensive public charging network), Tesla would immediately begin installing chargers at the homes of Chinese buyers before their Model S vehicle was delivered. To further improve the appeal of the Model S to wealthy Chinese buyers who were often driven by chauffeurs, Tesla announced that it would begin adding comfortable executive seating and a second-row center console on vehicles shipped to China. Wealthy Chinese vehicle owners considered the big discrepancy in the rear seat comfort of the Model S compared to most other luxury sedans (such as the Mercedes S-Class and the BMW 7 series) to be a major negative. But these changes still left Tesla at a competitive disadvantage in selling luxury sedans in China because of its tiny, albeit growing, network of Supercharger stations. To eliminate this disadvantage, Tesla announced in May 2015 that it was modifying the battery charging technology on its models shipped to China to fit China's national charging standards and thereby enable Tesla owners in China to charge their vehicles at facilities built by China's State Grid—a move that not only relieved much of the range anxiety of electric car owners in China but also eliminated much of Tesla's need to build out its own network of Tesla charging stations.

Why China Was an Important Market for Tesla.
China's automobile market was the world's largest. Annual vehicle sales in China had risen from 6 million units in 2005 to nearly 20 million units in 2014, and China was expected to remain the largest market for motor vehicles worldwide for the coming decades. Moreover, the market for luxury vehicles in China was exceptionally strong because of rapid growth in the number of wealthy people in China: the number of multimillionaires in China was expected to hit 1.09 million in 2015. Registrations of luxury vehicles grew more than four-fold between 2009 and 2013, and the growth rate of luxury vehicle sales was projected to be between 10 and 15 percent for many years to come. Furthermore, China's national and city governments had recently launched a barrage of incentives aimed at getting people to purchase cleaner plug-in cars to help combat China's massive air pollution problems, especially in large metropolitan cities. The incentives included offering free license plates (valued at over $15,000 in many places), no taxes, and no wait to register. The government was also investing $16 billion in a new electric vehicle charging infrastructure to further increase to appeal of plug-in vehicles.[41] For its part, Tesla was committed to rapidly expanding the number of Supercharger stations in all metropolitan areas where it had sales galleries; moreover, these stations would use solar power. As of 2015, there were Tesla sales galleries in just two locations, Beijing and Shanghai, although orders for the Model S had been placed by people residing in other locations in China.

The Launch of Tesla Energy, May 2015

In spring 2015, Tesla announced the formation and launch of Tesla Energy, a new subsidiary that would begin producing and selling two energy storage products in the second half of 2015: Powerwall for homeowners and Powerpack for industrial/commercial customers. Powerwall was a lithium-ion battery charged either by electricity generated from a home's solar panels or from power company sources when electric rates were low; Powerwall came in two models, a 10 kWh model for $3,500 and a 7 kWh model for $3,000. Tesla saw Powerwall as principally a product that energy-conscious homeowners with a rooftop solar system could use to lower their monthly electric bills by programming Powerwall to power their homes during certain hours when the rates of some power companies were high and then recharging the battery during the late-night hours when rates were low. However, Powerwall home batteries could also be used as a backup power source in case of unexpected power company outages. Homeowners with energy needs greater than 7 kWh or 10 kWh or for periods longer than the life of a single battery charge (about two hours) could install multiple models. Both Powerwall models were guaranteed for 10 years.

Powerpack models were 100kW lithium-ion batteries that industrial and commercial enterprises could use for a variety of purposes, with most installations using a minimum of 10 Powerpack batteries and perhaps as many as 20 to 30 batteries. Elon Musk saw Powerpack also being used by utilities for energy storage.

In the first week after the announcement introducing Powerwall and Powerpack, Tesla received 38,000 reservations for Powerwall (although residential buyers could place a reservation with no money down) and requests from 2,500 companies indicating interest in installing or distributing Powerpack batteries. In May 2015, Musk said that Tesla was preparing its supply chain and production teams to begin volume builds on both new products in the July–September 2015 time frame, with production to begin at the Tesla Factory in Fremont and then shift to the Gigafactory in Q1 2016, where it would accelerate significantly. Musk said that the total addressable market size for Tesla Energy products was enormous and much easier to scale globally than vehicle sales. Tesla personnel were pursuing product certification in multiple markets simultaneously; plans called for deliveries to customers in the United States, the European Union, and Australia to begin in Q4 2015. Musk commented that if buyer demand proved to be as strong as the first week of orders signaled, the company would need to begin efforts in early 2016 to expand the battery-making capacity of the Gigafactory well beyond the amount currently planned.

The Electric Vehicle Segment of the Global Automotive Industry

Global sales of passenger cars totaled 65.0 million in 2014, accounting for 73.7 percent of the world's total annual sales of 88.2 million motor vehicles. The remaining 26.3 percent, 23.2 million vehicles, consisted of light trucks (commonly termed pickup trucks), heavy or cargo-carrying trucks, recreational vehicles, buses, and minibuses. In 2014, global sales of plug-in electric vehicles totaled 320,700 units, just under 0.4 percent of global vehicle sales; plug-in vehicles included both battery-only vehicles and so-called plug-in hybrid electric vehicles equipped with a gasoline or diesel engine for use when the vehicle's battery pack (rechargeable only from an external plug-in source) was depleted, usually after a distance of 10 to 40 miles for current models. In 2014, global sales of hybrid electric vehicles were roughly 1.6 million units (equal to 1.8 percent of

global vehicle sales). Hybrid vehicles were jointly powered by an internal combustion engine and an electric motor that ran on batteries charged by "regenerative braking"[42] and the internal combustion engine; the batteries in a hybrid vehicle could not be restored to a full charge by connecting a plug to an external power source.

Total motor vehicle sales in the United States in 2014 were 16.8 million units, of which 7. 7 million were passenger cars (46 percent); the forecast for 2015 was for sales of 17.0 million vehicles. Sales of plug-in electric vehicles in the United States in 2014 totaled over 123,000 units; the three best-selling electric vehicles in the United States in both 2013 and 2014 were the Chevrolet Volt, Nissan LEAF, and Tesla Model S (Exhibit 11). Sales of hybrid vehicles in the United States totaled 434,500 units in 2012 (a 3.0 share of total vehicle sales), 495,800 units in 2013 (a 3.2 percent market share), and 452,200 units in 2014 (a market share of 2.75 percent).

Worldwide production of battery-powered electric vehicles in 2015 was projected to be about

---

EXHIBIT 11

Sales of Plug-in Electric Vehicles in the United States, 2013–2014

Best-Selling Models	2013					2014					2015	
	Q1	Q2	Q3	Q4	Total	Q1	Q2	Q3	Q4	Total	Q1	Q2
Tesla Model S	4,900	5,150	4,100	3,500	**17,650**	3,500	3,900	3,900	6,000	**17,300**	4,700	6,900
Leaf	3,359	6,300	6,237	6,534	**22,610**	5,184	7,552	9,086	8,378	**30,200**	4,085	5,731
Chevrolet Volt	4,244	5,611	6,905	6,334	**23,094**	3,606	5,009	5,925	4,265	**18,805**	1,874	3,748
Toyota Prius Plug-in Hybrid	2,353	1,861	3,760	4,114	**12,088**	3,296	6,004	2,542	1,422	**13,264**	1,271	1,169
Ford Fusion Energi	306	1,170	1,757	2,748	**6,089**	2,211	4,024	3,088	2,227	**11,550**	1,866	2,428
Ford C-Max Energi	1,166	1,316	1,812	2,860	**7,154**	1,633	2,295	2,558	1,947	**8,433**	1,608	1,935
BMW i3	0	0	0	0	**0**	0	694	2,410	2,988	**6,092**	2,681	1,775
Fiat 500e	0	0	1,010	1,300	**2,310**	1,290	1,554	1,581	707	**5,132**	1,884	1,500
All others	375	599	1,361	1,925	**4,260**	1,951	2,558	3,245	4,489	**12,243**	3,370	5,322
U.S. total	17,963	22,884	26,942	29,315	**95,642**	22,671	33,620	34,335	32,423	**123,049**	23,339	30,958
Worldwide	n.a.	n.a.	n.a.	n.a.	n.a.	57,307	79,331	90,719	93,356	**320,713**	90,060	115,362

Note: The falloff in quarterly Tesla sales in the United States beginning in Q3 2013 and continuing into 2014 was the result of Tesla shipping a big fraction of the Model S units assembled at the Tesla Factory in Fremont, California, to fill customer orders throughout Europe and in China.

n.a.: Not available.

Source: Inside EVs, "Monthly Plug-in Sales Scorecard," posted at www.insideevs.com (accessed May 19, 2015 and October 9, 2015).

830,000 vehicles (just under 1 percent of expected total motor vehicle production): some 236,000 of these vehicles were expected to be manufactured in the United States. But with gasoline prices drifting around $2.00–$2.30 per gallon in late 2014 and early 2015 in the United States, the vehicle models posting the biggest sales gains in the United States were pricey pickup trucks, SUVs, and luxury passenger cars rather than smaller, more fuel-efficient, and plug-in vehicles. Nonetheless, over 10 new electric vehicle models had been introduced in 2014–2015 with many more expected in 2016–2017; virtually all of the world's motor vehicle manufacturers were expected to have multiple battery-powered and hybrid vehicles on the market no later than 2017. In mid-2013, Volkswagen announced its intentions to become the world's largest seller of electric vehicles by 2018. Volkswagen introduced a fully electric e-Golf in 2014; combined sales in the United States in the e-Golf's first five months on the market were 863 units.

Headed into 2016, developmental efforts on next-generation battery-powered electric vehicles were aimed chiefly at extending the distance electric car battery packs would go on a single charge and keeping production costs low enough to make a profit selling large quantities of compact electric vehicles for prices of about $30,000.

Toyota Motor Corp. was the global leader in sales of hybrids and plug-ins, with cumulative sales exceeding 7 million units at the end of 2014 and expected sales in excess of 1.3 million units annually in 2015 and 2016 (the big majority of which were hybrid vehicles).[43] In 2014, Toyota sold 27 hybrid models and 1 plug-in model in approximately 90 countries around the world and planned to introduce 15 new hybrid models in 2015.

But despite the comparatively low sales volumes and market shares for plug-in electric vehicles and hybrids in the United States and other countries, executives at automotive companies across the world were closely watching the strategic moves that Elon Musk was making and the waves that Tesla's Model S was making in the marketplace. The publicity that Tesla's Model S received and the rapid climb of the company stock price in 2013 prompted the CEO of General Motors not only to closely monitor what Tesla was doing but also to set up a special team to study how Tesla products might disrupt the automotive industry in upcoming years. Executives at GM were acutely aware that cures were needed for the disappointingly small sales volume of the much ballyhooed Chevrolet Volt and that the Volt had failed to spark consumer interest in electric vehicles: sales totaled only 23,100 units in 2013 (Exhibit 10). To boost sales of the Volt, GM reduced the Volt's 2013 base price of $39,995 to a base price of $34,995 for the 2014 Volt, but 2014 sales of the Volt were a disappointing 18,805 units. GM was rumored to be working on a next-generation compact electric car that could go 200 miles on a charge and that would be equipped with a generator for battery charging; supposedly, the car would be introduced in 2016 and have a base price close to $30,000.

In late 2013, BMW began selling its all-new i3 series electric car models that had a lightweight, carbon fiber–reinforced plastic body, lithium-ion batteries with a driving range of 80–100 miles on a single charge, a 170 horsepower electric motor, and a base price of $41,350; customers could also get the BMW i3 with a range extender package (base price of $45,200) that included a 34 horsepower motor used only to maintain the charge of the of the lithium-ion battery at an approximate 5 percent charge and extend the driving range to 160–180 miles per charge. BMW sold more than 16,000 i3s in 2014 and expected global sales of the i3 to be approximately 22,500 units in 2015. In mid-2014, BMW began selling a super-premium sporty, high-tech electric vehicle called the i8 that had a three-cylinder electric motor, a supplemental gasoline engine for higher speeds, scissor doors, flamboyant aerodynamic flourishes, and an electric-only driving range of about 22 miles. Global sales of the i8 were 1,741 units in 2014, with forecasted sales of 5,100 units in 2015; the 2015 base price of BMW's i8 was $137,450.

Mercedes-Benz launched sales of its premium compact B-Class electric vehicle in the United States in mid-2014; the fpur-door, five-passenger vehicle (base price of $41,450) was built on an entirely new platform compared to other B-Class models with traditional gasoline engines, had an estimated driving range of 115 miles on a single charge, accelerated

from zero to 60 miles per hour in less than 10 seconds, delivered 174 horsepower, had a top speed of
100 miles per hour, utilized an electric power train
system custom-designed and produced by Tesla, and
was loaded with safety features. Mercedes B-Class
electric vehicles with a range extender package were
also available. The new electric B-Class models
competed directly with BMW's i3 series electric car.
While Mercedes and BMW had a near-term focus on
hybrids with a very short battery-only range, media
reports indicated that they, along with Porsche and
Audi, were working on producing fully electric
vehicles with a 300+ mile driving range on a single
charge by 2018.

In late 2015, both Cadillac and Audi introduced
new plug-in hybrid luxury sedans (the Cadillac CT6
and the Audi A6L eTron) that were being produced
in China; initially, both models were only being sold
in China. Both models had an electric-only range
of just over 60 miles on a single charge. However,
Cadillac began marketing three gasoline-only versions of the CT6 luxury sedan in North America and
selected other countries in 2016; there were expectations that Cadillac would begin selling the hybrid
plug-in version of the CT6 in North America and
elsewhere in late 2016 or early 2017. The Cadillac CT6 sedan—the highest-end Cadillac model
introduced in several decades—was designed and
equipped to compete head-to-head against the BMW
7-series, Mercedes S-Class, Audi A8, Jaguar XJ,
Lexus LS, and others. In 2016–2017, the plug-in
hybrid market was expected to include luxury models produced and marketed by Cadillac, Audi, BMW,
Mercedes, and Jaguar Land Rover—each offering an
"electric experience" without the range anxiety and
hassle of recharging.

Exhibit 12 shows how the expected price of
Tesla's forthcoming Model 3 mid-priced sedan
(2016–2017) compared against the price and electric-only driving range of other similarly priced
electric vehicles on the market in 2015.

Hydrogen Fuel Cells: An Alternative to Electric Batteries

Many of the world's major automotive manufacturers, while actively working on next-generation

---

EXHIBIT 12

Comparative Prices and Driving Ranges of Tesla's Forthcoming Model 3 Sedan and Other 2014 Model Electric Vehicles

Low- and Mid-Priced Electric Vehicles	Manufacturer's Suggested Retail Price (base model, no options, including destination fee)
2015 Nissan Leaf Hatchback	$29,860
2015 Chevrolet Spark EV	$27,495
2015 Chevrolet Volt	$34,995
2015 Ford Focus-electric	$31,125
2015 Ford C-Max Energi	$34,270
2015 Fiat 500e	$35,490
2015 Volkswagen e-Golf	$35,090
2015 Honda Fit EV	$37,415
2015 BMW i3 Hatchback	$48,150
2015 Mercedes B-Class	$41,450
2016–2017 Tesla Model 3s	~$35,000-$40,000

Sources: www.edmunds.com, www.kbb.com, and company websites
(accessed April 10, 2015).

---

battery-powered electric vehicles, were nonetheless hedging their bets by also pursuing the development of hydrogen fuel cells as an alternative
means of powering future vehicles. Toyota was
considered the leader in developing hydrogen fuel
cells and, in 2015, was sharing some of its fuel
cell technology patents for free with other automotive companies in an effort to spur determining
whether there was merit in installing fuel cells and
building out a hydrogen charging network. Madza,
Nissan, Honda, and Hyundai were also actively
exploring hydrogen fuel technology. German
automakers had formed a group to support efforts
to build out a hydrogen charging network in Germany and sell both electric and fuel cell models
at the same time. General Motors, Ford, Fiat-
Chrysler, and Tesla were viewed as betting most
heavily on battery-powered vehicles being the
wave of the future.

ENDNOTES

[1] Company press release, August 19, 2013.

[2] *Consumer Reports,* April 2014, p. 10.

[3] Jessica Caldwell, "Drive by Numbers—Tesla Model S Is the Vehicle of Choice in Many of America's Wealthiest Zip Codes," posted at www.edmunds.com, October 31, 2013 (accessed November 18, 2013).

[4] EVObession, "Top Large Luxury Cars in USA," http://evobsession.com/top-large-luxury-cars-usa-2014-sales (accessed March 26, 2015).

[5] Ibid.

[6] Jeff Evanson, Tesla Motors Investor Presentation, September 14, 2013, posted at www.teslamotors.com (accessed November 29, 2013).

[7] Ibid.

[8] John Reed, "Elon Musk's Groundbreaking Electric Car," *FT Magazine,* July 24, 2009, posted at www.ft.com (accessed September 26, 2013).

[9] Reed, "Elon Musk's Groundbreaking Electric Car."

[10] Tesla press release, May 19, 2009, and Michael Arrington, "Tesla Worth More Than Half a Billion After Daimler Investment," posted at www.techcrunch.com, May 19, 2009 (accessed September 30, 2013).

[11] According to an article titled "Abu Dhabi Takes Part of Daimler's Investment Stake," posted at www.marketwatch.com, July 13, 2009.

[12] Chris Morrison, "Tesla's Layoffs: Bad Blood, a Bloodbath, or Business as Usual?" January 11, 2008, posted at www.venturebeat.com (accessed September 24, 2013).

[13] Josh Friedman, "Entrepreneur Tries His Midas Touch in Space," *Los Angeles Times,* April 23, 2003, accessed at www.latimes.com (September 16, 2013).

[14] David Kestenbaum, "Making a Mark with Rockets and Roadsters," *National Public Radio,* August 9, 2007, accessed at www.npr.org (September 17, 2013).

[15] Ibid.

[16] Ibid.

[17] Video interview with Alan Murray, "Elon Musk: I'll Put a Man on Mars in 10 Years," *Market Watch* (*Wall Street Journal*), December 1, 2011 (accessed September 16, 2013).

[18] William Harwood, "SpaceX Dragon Returns to Earth, Ends Historic Trip," CNET, May 31, 2012, accessed at www.cbsnews.com (September 16, 2013).

[19] Ashlee Vance, "Revealed: Elon Musk Explains the Hyperloop, the Solar-Powered High-Speed Future of Inter-City Transportation," *Bloomberg BusinessWeek,* August 12, 2013, posted at www.businessweek.com (accessed September 25, 2013).

[20] Mike Seemuth, "From the Corner Office—Elon Musk," *Success,* April 10, 2011, posted at www.success.com (accessed September 25, 2013).

[21] Ibid.

[22] Ibid.

[23] Jay Yarow, "A Day in the Life of Elon Musk, the Most Inspiring Entrepreneur in the World," *Business Insider,* July 24, 2012, posted at www.businessinsider.com (accessed September 25, 2013).

[24] April Dembosky, "The Entrepreneur with Astronomical Ambition," *Financial Times,* May 25, 2012, posted at www.ft.com (accessed September 25, 2013).

[25] Terry Dawes, "Why Critics Love to Hate Elon Musk," *Cantech Letter,* June 10, 2013, posted at www.cantechletter.com/2013/06/why-critics-love-to-hate-elon-musk0610/.

[26] According to information in the company's Proxy Statement issued April 17, 2013; see pp. 28-30.

[27] According to information in Martin Eberhard's blog titled "Lotus Position," July 25, 2006, posted at www.teslamotors.com/blog/lotus-position (accessed September 17, 2013).

[28] 2013 10-K Report, p. 4

[29] See Vince Bond, Jr., "Tesla's Plan to Sell in Ohio Dodges Bullet," *Automotive News,* posted at www.autonews.com on December 4, 2013 (accessed December 27, 2013).

[30] Dan Gearino, "Ohio Car Dealers Sue to Block Tesla Dealership," *Columbus Dispatch,* December 19, 2013, accessed at www.dispatch.com (December 27, 2013).

[31] Company press release, May 20, 2010.

[32] Calculated by the case author from information on total fourth-quarter Model S sales in the United States in Exhibit 10 and the number of Model S vehicles delivered in the United States in Q4 2013 with a resale value guarantee, as cited in Tesla's press release of February 19, 2014.

[33] As quoted in Alan Ohnsman, "Tesla Model S Buyback Offer May Generate More Revenue," posted at www.bloomberg.com, September 10, 2013 (accessed December 10, 2013).

[34] Tesla Blog, "A Fair Price," posted at www.teslamotors.com on January 22, 2014 (accessed April 15, 2015).

[35] "The Chaos of Tesla China," posted at http://en.pingwest.com, June 11, 2014 (accessed April 17, 2015).

[36] Tycho De Feijter, "Tesla China Has a Record Unsold Inventory of 2301 Cars," www.carnewschina.com, March 16, 2015 (accessed April 16, 2015).

[37] Ibid.

[38] Ibid.

[39] Ibid.

[40] Ibid.

[41] Christopher DeMorro, "Plug-In Car Sales Up 350% in China," http://evobession.com, January 16, 2015 (accessed April 16, 2015).

[42] Regenerative braking involved capturing the energy lost during braking by using the electric motor as a generator and storing the captured energy in the battery. Hybrids could not use off-board sources of electricity to charge the batteries; hybrids could only use regenerative braking and the internal combustion engine to charge. The extra power provided by the electric motor in a hybrid vehicle enabled faster acceleration and allowed for use of a smaller internal combustion engine.

[43] Toyota press release, October 24, 2014, accessed at www.corporatenews pressroom.toyota.com (April 6, 2015).

Deere & Company in 2015: Striving for Growth in a Weakening Global Agricultural Sector

connect

ALEN BADAL Author and Researcher

JOHN E. GAMBLE Texas A&M University–Corpus Christi

DAVID L. TURNIPSEED University of South Alabama

Deere & Company recorded its best-ever year in fiscal 2013, with sales and earnings of $37.8 billion and $3.5 billion, respectively. The company's revenues and earnings declined to $36.1 billion and $3.2 billion in fiscal 2014, but the company's global strategy keyed to product innovation and quality, operating excellence, and best-in-industry customer service protected the company from slowing demand for agricultural equipment. Deere & Company achieved its record-setting year in 2013 and an impressive year in 2014, despite a slowdown in the construction industry, where it also competed with a line of tractors, articulating dump trucks, backhoe loaders, motor graders, excavators, and bulldozers. The company also manufactured and marketed forestry equipment, turf equipment, and diesel engines for marine and construction equipment uses. Deere had introduced dozens of technologically advanced agricultural and construction products that helped boost productivity and lower the costs of its customers in farming and construction.

An increasing world population and the consequential global increase in the demand for grain and grain-dependent foods, as well as the increasing need for construction, turf, and forestry equipment, were all factors that would benefit the company in the long-term. International markets such as China, Brazil, and Russia already accounted for more than 35 percent of the company's revenues in 2013, and they would likely make up a much larger percentage of sales in the long-term as living standards in emerging markets improved. Deere & Company had recognized the importance of international expansion as early as 1956, when it first established operations outside the United States, but it was accelerating its efforts to prepare for rapid increases in the demand for food in international markets. The company built or acquired new plant capacity in Brazil, Germany, and China in 2013. In 2014, new construction equipment factories were opened in Brazil.

The company's prospects for stronger performance in 2015 were challenged, however, by a sudden and significant overall weakness in the global agricultural sector. In 2014 and 2015, the weakening farm economy resulted in lower agriculture sales, which more than offset the increase in construction and forestry sales, resulting in a 5 percent drop in new sales. Reuter's reported that Deere's sales had suffered in 2014 and 2015, as bumper corn harvests drove down prices, leaving farmers with less cash to spend on equipment. Corn prices fell about 15 percent in 2014, on top of a decline of nearly 40 percent in 2013. The company's primary challenge in 2015 was the continuing declining demand for agricultural equipment, which was resulting in significant reductions in sales and earnings. Deere's CFO commented in 2015 that the company was facing the deepest downturn in the North American agricultural sector in 25 years. Nonetheless, John Deere's management expected to have a profitable year despite the prospect of lower sales.

Company History

Deere & Company began manufacturing and marketing farming equipment in 1837, when John Deere, a blacksmith and inventor, began forging steel plows for mule-drawn walking plows. The company added corn planters, wheeled sulky plows, and cultivators during the late 1800s, but its walking plow accounted for the majority of its business until the company acquired motorized tractor producer Waterloo Boy in 1918. The company's acquisition of Waterloo Boy dramatically changed the company's business model and scope of operations, but it was a necessity since Ford Motor Company was revolutionizing agriculture with the manufacture and sale of Fordson farm tractors. Ford sold more than 34,000 farm tractors in 1918, as farmers across the United States easily recognized how machinery could boost productivity in agriculture.

Deere's shift in strategy began with disastrous results, with the Waterloo Boy brand selling only 79 tractors in 1921. The first John Deere–branded tractor, the Model D, was launched in 1923 and was so popular that it remained in the company's product line for 30 years. Deere added more models to the product line throughout the 1920s. The appeal of the company's Model D, GP, Model 1, and Model 2 tractors allowed its revenues to soar until the depths of the Great Depression in 1932, when its revenues plunged to $8.7 million. However, even though Deere & Company was losing money, the company's management chose not to repossess farm equipment owned by farmers unable to make payments during the Depression—a decision that would solidify its bond with farmers for generations.

The company expanded internationally in 1956, when it opened an assembly plant in Mexico and acquired a German tractor manufacturer and a Spanish harvester manufacturer. Deere & Company expanded further internationally when it constructed a tractor and implement manufacturing plant in Argentina in 1958, built a plant in France in 1961, and acquired a cultivator manufacturer in South Africa in 1962. By 1963, John Deere was the world's largest producer of farm and industrial tractors and equipment. The company also began selling lawn and garden tractors that year. In 2015, with its world headquarters in Moline, Illinois, Deere & Company remained the largest agricultural equipment and machinery manufacturer in the world, with operations in more than 26 countries. In May 2015, *Forbes* reported that John Deere was ranked 70th of the World's Most Valuable Brands. The company's

income statements for fiscal 2012 through fiscal 2014 are presented in Exhibit 1. Deere & Company's balance sheets for fiscal 2013 through fiscal 2014 are presented in Exhibit 2.

Overview of the Tractor and Agricultural Equipment Industry

The tractor and agricultural equipment industry was projected to grow at an attractive rate for decades because of increasing urbanization and rising standards of living in many countries around the world. By 2050, the global population was expected to exceed 9.5 billion, up from approximately 7 billion in 2014, with Asia and Africa experiencing the greatest increases. It was also expected that a growing middle class would emerge in Latin America, China, and India, among other developing economies. Thus, agricultural output was projected to double by 2050 in order to maintain pace with the increase in global population, which would require the rate of production to grow. Also, an increase in urbanization would stir a need for infrastructure development, with the percentage of the world's population living in urban areas increasing from 50 percent in 2014 to 70 percent by 2050. The increase in urbanization was expected to result in increases in the demand for construction services and equipment.

The long-term macro-economic trends were favorable for the $41.6 billion tractor and agricultural industry, which had grown annually by 3.9 percent between 2009 and 2013, but had turned down sharply in 2014. The industry consisted of dairy farm equipment and sprayers, dusters, blowers, and attachments, with harvesting machinery representing the largest segment (see Exhibit 3).

The steady growth in the industry since 2009 until 2013 was brought about by favorable sociocultural forces and economic conditions that included farm interest rates supported by the U.S. government and subsidies of various sorts in countries outside the United States. Also, the weakening U.S. dollar and a rising demand for exporting helped rebuild the farming industry. However, in 2014, this favorable scenario reversed, with a strengthening dollar leading to weakening overseas sales. In addition, falling

EXHIBIT 1

Deere & Company Income Statements, 2012–2014 (in thousands, except per share amounts)

	2014	2013	2012
Net Sales and Revenues			
Net sales	$32,960.6	$34,997.9	$33,500.9
Finance and interest income	2,282.1	2,115.1	1,981.3
Other income	824.2	682.4	674.9
Total	36,066.9	37,795.4	36,157.1
Costs and Expenses			
Cost of sales	24,775.8	25,667.3	25,007.8
Research and development expenses	1,452.0	1,477.3	1,433.6
Selling, administrative and general expenses	3,284.4	3,605.5	3,417.0
Interest expense	664.0	741.3	782.8
Other operating expenses	1,093.3	820.6	781.5
Total	31,269.5	32,312.0	31,422.7
Income of Consolidated Group Before Income Taxes	4,797.4	5,483.4	4,734.4
Provision for income taxes	1,626.5	1,945.9	1,659.4
Income of Consolidated Group	3,170.9	3,537.5	3,075.0
Equity in income (loss) of unconsolidated affiliates	(7.6)	.1	(3.4)
Net Income	3,163.3	3,537.6	3,071.6
Less: Net income attributable to noncontrolling interests	1.6	.3	6.9
Net Income Attributable to Deere & Company	$ 3,161.7	$ 3,537.3	$ 3,064.7
Per Share Data			
Basic	$ 8.71	$ 9.18	$ 7.72
Diluted	$ 8.63	$ 9.09	$ 7.63
Dividends declared	$ 2.22	$ 1.99	$ 1.79
Average Shares Outstanding			
Basic	363.0	385.3	397.1
Diluted	366.1	389.2	401.5

Source: Deere & Company 2014 Annual Report.

EXHIBIT 2

Deere & Company Balance Sheets, Fiscal 2011–Fiscal 2013 (in thousands)

	2014	2013
ASSETS		
Cash and cash equivalents	$3,787.0	$3,504.0
Marketable securities	1,215.1	1,624.8
Receivables from unconsolidated affiliates	30.2	31.2
Trade accounts and notes receivable—net	3,277.6	3,758.2
Financing receivables—net	27,422.2	25,632.7
Financing receivables securitized—net	4,602.3	4,153.1
Other receivables	1,500.3	1,464.0
Equipment on operating leases—net	4,015.5	3,152.2
Inventories	4,209.7	4,934.7
Property and equipment—net	5,577.8	5,466.9
Investments in unconsolidated affiliates	303.2	221.4
Goodwill	791.2	844.8
Other intangible assets—net	68.8	77.1

Retirement benefits	262.0	551.1
Deferred income taxes	2,776.6	2,325.4
Other assets	1,496.9	1,274.7
Assets held for sale	—	505.0
Total assets	$61,336.4	$59,521.3
LIABILITIES AND STOCKHOLDERS' EQUITY		
LIABILITIES		
Short-term borrowings	$8,019.2	$8,788.9
Short-term securitization borrowings	4,558.5	4,109.1
Payables to unconsolidated affiliates	101.0	106.9
Accounts payable and accrued expenses	8,554.1	8,973.6
Deferred income taxes	160.9	160.3
Long-term borrowings	24,380.7	21,577.7
Retirement benefits and other liabilities	6,496.5	5,416.7
Liabilities held for sale		120.4
Total liabilities	52,270.9	49,253.6
STOCKHOLDERS' EQUITY		
Common stock, $1 par value (authorized, 1,200,000,000 shares; issued, 536,431,204 shares in 2014 and 2013), at paid-in amount	3,675.4	3,524.2
Common stock in treasury, 190,926,805 shares in 2014 and 162,628,440 shares in 2013, at cost	(12,834.2)	(10,210.9)
Retained earnings	22,004.4	19,645.6
Accumulated other comprehensive income (loss)	(3,783.0)	(2,693.1)
Total Deere & Company stockholders' equity	9,062.6	10,265.8
Noncontrolling interests	2.9	1.9
Total stockholders' equity	9,065.5	10,267.7
Total Liabilities and Stockholders' Equity	$61,336.4	$59,521.3

Source: Deere & Company 2014 Annual Report.

EXHIBIT 3

Product Segmentation of the Tractor and Agricultural Equipment Industry, 2013

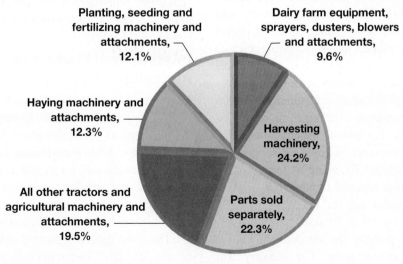

Planting, seeding and fertilizing machinery and attachments, 12.1%

Dairy farm equipment, sprayers, dusters, blowers and attachments, 9.6%

Haying machinery and attachments, 12.3%

Harvesting machinery, 24.2%

All other tractors and agricultural machinery and attachments, 19.5%

Parts sold separately, 22.3%

Total: $41.6 billion

Source: Adapted from *IBISWorld*, February 2014.

crop prices and the curtailment of U.S. incentives had further dampened demand for farm equipment, particularly for large models in the United States and Canada, where Deere dominated the market. According to Reuter's, the U.S. Department of Agriculture expected net farm income to fall 32 percent to $73.6 billion in 2015, the lowest since 2009 and a drop of nearly 43 percent from the record high of $129 billion in 2013.

The farming industry was consolidating as large conglomerates took over smaller farms. As a result, total volume increases and economies of scale were taking place in the industry, along with more vertical integration across supply chains. A demand for better optimization of farming also resulted in reliance on technology to reduce operating costs and increase farming output. Precision agriculture was a growing trend in the industry that allowed farmers to spot-treat fields using aerial photography and GIS technology to precisely water, seed, and harvest in less time.

Industry Competition

The tractor and agricultural equipment industry comprised more than 1,000 companies, with the top four generating half of all revenues. Industry production was concentrated primarily among Deere & Company, CNH Industrial N.V., and AGCO Corporation. Mergers affected the industry, with CNH Industrial N.V. having gone through a merger with KamAZ in 2010 and Fiat Industrial in 2013. The adoption of more stringent emission standards in many countries had an impact on industry competition. Quality control, research and development, and adoption of new technological advances were all strategic factors in the industry.

Agricultural equipment manufacturers were driving the use of technology with larger, more sophisticated equipment. Equipment manufacturers also recognized the importance of customer service and support, and equipment financing as farming consolidated to a smaller group of farming corporations.

The average useful age for farming equipment was estimated to be 10 to 20 years. A preference of farmers was to prolong the life of equipment by purchasing replacement parts. The industry was expected to continue production of replacement parts for equipment and reap the profits of the segment. Interest rates on farm equipment loans had a

direct impact on sales; lower rates and incentives helped boost sales of higher-end equipment.

Industry profits had increased over the five-year 2009–2013 period, with revenues increasing and rising steel costs passed on to buyers. The weakened U.S. dollar had increased export sales for U.S. companies, but in mid-2014, the dollar began to strengthen, which dampened U.S. exports. The dollar was almost at parity with the euro in April 2015, down from a euro-to-dollar exchange rate of $1.39 in May 2014. An average industry profit of 6.2 percent of revenue was projected for 2015. Wages in the industry had decreased as a result of the increased automation of the manufacturing process, which lessened dependence on labor. Because of technological advances in manufacturing, depreciation costs as a percentage of industry revenue had increased for manufacturers. Product quality, innovation, customer service, branding, and performance were essential areas on which rivals competed. Generally, price competition among the three rivals was low; as a result, competitive rivalry centered on factors such as value instead of price.

Globalization had a significant effect on functions within the industry. Between 2009 and 2014, both AGCO and Deere & Company increased their percentage of revenue generated internationally; CNH's tractor sales increased 25 percent in Latin America during 2011, with combined sales growth of 30 percent. Four years later, CNH forecasted tractor sales in Latin America to drop by 5 percent to 10 percent.

International Markets for Agricultural Equipment

The strengthening U.S. dollar made it less affordable to export equipment from the United States. In 2013, total imports to the United States were estimated at $10.5 billion, while exports were estimated at $11.8 billion. Canada was the largest U.S export market, with a 34 percent share of exports, while Mexico, Australia, and Brazil were the next-largest export markets for U.S. agricultural equipment manufacturers. However, the strengthening dollar in 2014, continuing into 2015, began to erode the export market for the U.S. manufactures of agricultural equipment. Germany was the largest exporter of farm equipment to the United States, accounting for 16 percent of U.S. imports. Canada, China, and Japan were also significant exporters of farm equipment to the United States (see Exhibit 4).

Deere & Company's Strategy in 2015

Deere & Company's farming equipment product lines were aimed at supporting the farming of every owner of Deere equipment and compelling the thought of "should've got a John Deere" among those who farmed with rival equipment. Farming was arguably the most time-sensitive industry since harvesting windows could be limited to a matter of a few days. In addition, farming seasons were limited to specific months when weather was favorable to various types of crops. Deere's strategy of producing the highest-quality, most reliable farm equipment and offering farmers the highest level of customer service resulted in fiscal 2013 being the company's best financial year ever.

Deere & Company's strategic intent was to achieve $50 billion in sales by fiscal 2018 and 12 percent profit margins by fiscal 2015. The profit margin goal was not attained (profit margin in fiscal 2014 was less than 9 percent), and the 2018 sales goal was highly doubtful.

Deere's strategy was also keyed to expanding its business globally and enhancing its complementary business. In doing so, the company believed its critical business factors (CBFs) consisted of better understanding consumers at a root level, delivering value, offering a world-class distribution system, and grooming and hiring extraordinary international associates. The CBFs were predicated on building from the foundation already in place, consisting of Deere's exceptional business performance, optimal shareholder value-added growth, and aligned high-performing, team-oriented associates. The company measured the "health and performance" of its operations, as necessary, for possible adjustments. Ultimately, the overarching goal was to offer consumers farming products that were representative of a company with integrity and commitment to manufacturing innovative products of the highest quality.

Deere's purpose was to be fully committed to those "linked to the land." The company's managers believed that many opportunities existed for the company, such as an increase in the global population and income growth, which would require infrastructural needs on a global basis. Additional opportunities included new consumer segmentation and advances in technology.

EXHIBIT 4

Leading U.S. International Trade Partners for Agricultural Products, 2013

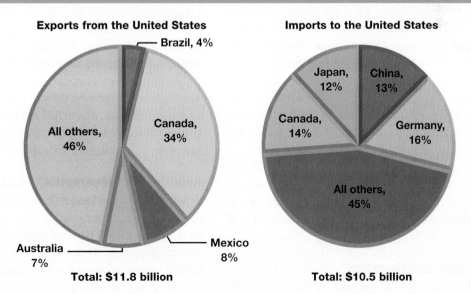

Exports from the United States
- Brazil, 4%
- Canada, 34%
- All others, 46%
- Australia 7%
- Mexico 8%

Total: $11.8 billion

Imports to the United States
- Japan, 12%
- China, 13%
- Canada, 14%
- Germany, 16%
- All others, 45%

Total: $10.5 billion

Source: Adapted from *IBISWorld*, February 2014.

The company identified challenges moving forward. Specifically, Deere foresaw capturing more customers across six identified key regions (United States/Canada, European Union, Brazil, Commonwealth of Independent States/Russia, China, and India), with a focus on meeting each country's local farming and agricultural equipment needs, while leveraging global economies of scale. The company was strategizing forward progress without encountering any headwind. The company planned to increase its market share in developed markets. At the time, Deere was number two in market share in North America, a ranking it hoped to strengthen and increase. Perhaps a continuous focus on technology and increased customer services, coupled with competitive pricing, would help the company increase its market share. Alternatively, maybe the solution was to focus on additional research and development, and enhance its domestic manufacturing plants and products while also focusing on manufacturing equipment to meet the specific country demands of farming abroad. The lackluster 5 percent forecast for Deere's domestic market suggested that an international focus was the only solution for continued growth.

Deere & Company's Business Divisions

In 2015, the company had three primary businesses: Agriculture and Turf Equipment, Construction and Forestry Equipment, and the Financial Services/Power Systems/Global Parts/Intelligent Solutions Group. Deere's strategy in each of its two heavy-equipment divisions was to learn more about its customers' local needs and translate the knowledge into products and services that delivered superior customer value. The Agriculture and Turf division was Deere's largest division and was the focus of its new product development activities. The Construction and Forestry division remained profitable in spite of a slowing demand for construction machines. Deere's Financial Services division also experienced financial success. In 2013, the division achieved net income of $565 billion. The loan and lease portfolio of Deere & Company grew by approximately $5 billion.

Dealership Collaboration

Deere & Company attributed much of its success to its relationship with its dealers throughout the world. It emphasized the necessity of having an effective distribution and aftermarket support system. In the Commonwealth of Independent States, the number of dealerships increased by 50 percent between 2011 and 2013. The company also added new parts distribution centers in South Africa and Argentina, and had additional expansion plans to begin operations in India and Brazil. Deere established cooperative banking relationships in seven African nations where additional sales opportunities were projected. Also, the company had a retailing-financing presence in over 40 countries that accounted for more than 90 percent of its sales.

Product Innovation

Deere & Company focused on the use of technology to better assist end users with managing and using their equipment. This was achieved via the MyJohnDeere platform. This wireless data transmission system enabled the collection of data that was used for analysis by John Deere in regard to the mechanical performance of equipment and by customers in regard to production metrics. In addition, Deere focused on manufacturing dozens of equipment attachments, such as those utilized for demolition and landscaping.

Increases in product lines also helped the company with its goal of continued growth and profitability. In 2013, Deere introduced nine advanced agricultural equipment models, as well as flex-fuel premium lawn tractors, commercial mowers, and Deere's first hybrid-electric construction equipment. The company focused particularly on increasing efficiency and incorporating technology while reducing emissions and meeting consumers' requirements for power, reliability, and fluid and fuel efficiency. In a highly notable achievement, Deere's larger engines were certified as meeting the strict U.S. and European emission standards. Deere had reduced the emissions level of all its engines by over 99 percent since 1996 as a result of redesigning virtually all of its engines.

Awards, Achievements, and Corporate Responsibility

Deere & Company was named one of the top-100 innovators by a leading business media group on the basis of its patents and technology developments. The company received additional awards and recognition from organizations throughout the world, including special recognition for its new Chinese-made combine, which took top honors at China's largest machinery venue.

In 2013, Deere focused on identifying solutions to world hunger, improving educational opportunities, and helping to develop better communities in the locations where it operated. In most cases, Deere & Company employees volunteered to assist in the execution of its social initiatives. For example, to further the company's social mission, more than 3,000 U.S. employees prepared approximately 960,000 packaged meals for those in need in 2013, and 20 employees spent a week in northwest India training small farmers in new farming methods. In 2014, Deere & Company was named for the sixth time to *Fortune*'s "Most Admired Companies" list, and in 2015, it was named as the 38th best employer among the 500 companies included in the ranking by *Forbes*magazine.

Domestic Manufacturing Operations   Deere's manufacturing plants in the United States were located in seven states (Iowa, Illinois, North Dakota, Georgia, Louisiana, Missouri, and Wisconsin). Deere manufactured tractor cabs and other assemblies in its Waterloo, Iowa, plant. Large combine harvesters and hydraulic cylinders and planting equipment were manufactured in East Moline, Illinois. The plant in Valley City, North Dakota, manufactured tilling and seeding equipment. The Davenport, Iowa, plant manufactured wheel loaders, motor graders, dump trucks, and forestry equipment. In neighboring Dubuque, Iowa, production consisted of backhoes, crawlers, tracked forestry equipment, and skid-steer loaders. The Springfield, Missouri, plant manufactured engines.

The Ankeny, Iowa, plant manufactured sprayers, while hay and pull-type mowers were made in Ottumwa, Iowa. Cane harvesting equipment and scrapers were made in Thibodaux, Louisiana. The plant in Horicon, Wisconsin, produced lawn and garden and turf care products, while the plant in Augusta, Georgia, manufactured the 5E, 5EN, and 5M Series tractors. The Fuquay Varina, North Carolina, plant made golf equipment and turf mowers.

International Manufacturing Operations
Expansion plans called for new manufacturing locations in key markets that were to be completed in 2013 and ready in 2014 to support increased production. Deere opened three locations in China to support construction equipment, engines, and large farm equipment; two locations in Brazil, one of which

was in conjunction with Hitachi, for construction equipment; one location in India for manufacturing farm equipment; and one in Russia for manufacturing seeding and tillage machines. Additional plans included expansion into Germany to manufacture cab production and into Brazil to manufacture large tractors. In the United States, the company's expansion included new factories in Moline, Illinois, and Valley City, North Dakota, and extensive modernization at existing plants. Deere sold its landscape operation and purchased a manufacturer of ultrawide planters.

Deere's international manufacturing operations spanned Mexico, India, Argentina, China, Canada, and Europe. Two plants in Mexico (Saltillo and Torreon) manufactured a variety of agricultural tractors. Power systems were manufactured in Fleury-les-Aubrais, France. Tractors, diesel engines, and header models for grain harvesting were built in Granadero Baigorria, Santa Fe, Argentina. The Pune, India, plant manufactured small agricultural tractors, while additional tractors were manufactured in the Mannheim, Germany, plant. The Zweibrücken, Germany, plant manufactured harvesting equipment, and the Horst, Netherlands, plant manufactured spraying equipment. Forwarders and wheeled harvesters were built in the Joensuu, Finland, plant. The Edmonton, Alberta, Canada, plant produced remanufactured equipment. Consumer and commercial lawn equipment was manufactured in Gummersbach, Germany.

Deere's Rivals in the Tractor and Agricultural Equipment Industry

Deere & Company was the world's leading manufacturer of agricultural and forestry equipment, with a market share of 35.4 percent in 2013. Its primary competitors in the tractors and agricultural equipment industry were CNH Industrial N.V., the maker of Case and New Holland tractors and construction equipment; AGCO Corporation, the maker of Massey Ferguson and other brands; and Caterpillar, Inc.

CNH Industrial N.V.

CNH Industrial N.V., based in Basildon, United Kingdom, held an 11.7 percent market share and was

Deere & Company's primary rival in agricultural equipment. CNH Industrial was formed in 2013 as a result of a merger between CNH Global and Fiat Industrial. The company marketed agricultural equipment under 12 global and regional brands, and it had 62 manufacturing plants, 48 research and development centers, and 6,000 dealers in 190 countries. The company's farming/agricultural and construction equipment was marketed under such brands as Case IH Agriculture, New Holland Agriculture, and Steyr. CNH Industrial also manufactured and marketed trucks, busses, and other commercial vehicles under the Iveco and HeuliezBus brands. The company's total revenues in 2014 were 32.56 billion. Approximately 62 percent of the company's revenues and 94 percent of its operating profits were generated from the sale of agricultural and construction equipment in 2013. Exhibit 5 provides a summary of the company's financial performance for 2011 through 2014.

AGCO Corporation

AGCO Corporation, based in Duluth, Georgia, held an approximate 4 percent share of the global farm equipment market in 2013. The company's tractors, combines, planters, grain storage silos, and other agricultural equipment were sold in 140 countries. Sales from North America accounted for approximately 25 percent of the company's revenues in

2014. The company held a strong market presence in emerging markets, such as Brazil and other Latin American markets. Approximately 57 percent of its revenues were generated from tractor sales under brands such as Massey Ferguson, Fendt, and Challenger. The company had approximately 1,300 dealers in North America, 340 dealers in South America, 1,160 dealers in Europe and the Middle East, and 300 dealers in the Asia-Pacific region. A summary of AGCO's financial performance between 2010 and 2014 is presented in Exhibit 6.

Caterpillar, Inc.

Caterpillar, Inc., manufactured construction and mining equipment, diesel and natural gas engines, gas turbines, and diesel-powered locomotives. The company also built and marketed small to medium-sized track-type tractors for use in the construction and mining industries. In 2014, the company's consolidated construction industry recorded sales and operating profit of $19.4 billion and $2.2 billion, respectively. The company's construction equipment sales in North America for 2014 were approximately $8.4 billion, with sales in the Asia-Pacific region approximating $4.2 billion; sales in Europe, Africa, and the Middle East slightly exceeding $4.2 billion; and sales in Latin America approximating $2.4 billion. In 2014, the company's revenues for

---

EXHIBIT 5

Financial Summary for CNH Industrial N.V., 2011–2014 (in millions of euros), except per share amounts)

	2014	2013	2012	2011
Revenues:				
Net sales	€31,196	€32,632	€31,529	€32,224
Finance and interest income	1,359	1,204	1,272	1,256
Total revenues	32,555	33,836	32,801	33,480
Net income	708	828	876	639
Earnings per share	€0.52	€0.54	€0.62	€0.42
Total assets	€51,913	€53,843	€48,965	€48,003
Equity	4,961	4,955	4,825	4,857

Source: CNH Industrial 2014 Annual Report.

EXHIBIT 6

EXHIBIT 6

Financial Summary for AGCO Corporation, 2010–2014 (in millions)

	2014	2013	2012	2011	2010
Net revenues	$9,723.7	$10,786.9	$9,962.2	$8,773.2	$6,896.6
Gross profit	2,066.3	2,390.6	2,123.2	1,776.1	1,258.0
Income from operations	646.5	900.7	693.2	610.3	324.2
Net income	404.2	592.3	516.4	585.3	220.0
Total assets	7,395.9	8,438.8	7,721.8	7,257.2	5,436.9
Total equity	3,496.9	4,044.8	3,481.5	3,031.2	2,259.2

Source: AGCO Corporation 2014 annual report.

its energy and power systems were approximately $201.1 billion, its mining machinery revenues were approximately $8.9 billion, and its financial services revenues were over $3.3 billion. A summary of Caterpillar's financial performance for 2010 through 2014 is presented in Exhibit 7.

Caterpillar's strategy was focused on best-in-industry quality and after-the-sale service. The company maintained 177 global dealers, with an average dealer relationship of more than 88 years. The company's relationship with its dealers and its commitment to unmatched parts availability ensured that the 3 million Caterpillar products around the world were in top-notch operating condition and were able to keep construction projects on schedule. Caterpillar's strategy was also focused on developing new products and improving the company's cost structure to boost profitability. Even though Caterpillar was the industry leader in construction equipment sales, it experienced a dramatic decline in sales and profit in 2013 and another, smaller decline in 2014, due to a slowdown in global construction.

The Future for Deere & Company

Deere's forecast for a challenging 2015 had proven correct at the end of the first six months of the fiscal year. Net sales had fallen 17 percent during the first six months of fiscal 2015 to $14.6 billion, compared to $17.6 billion in the same period in the prior year. Net income of $1.1 billion reflected a year-over-year decline of 35.2 percent from $1.7 billion in 2014. Deere's revised outlook for fiscal 2015 announced in May 2015 was for equipment sales to decrease by about 19 percent for the entire fiscal 2015.

The revised projections by Deere management were based upon a further strengthening U.S. dollar, a severe slump in farm machinery demand that started in 2014, falling crop prices, weakening overseas sales, and reduced U.S. agricultural tax incentives. Industry forces had dampened demand for farm equipment, particularly for large models in the United States and Canada, where Deere dominated the market. In May 2015, Deere aggressively

EXHIBIT 7

Financial Summary for Caterpillar, Inc., 2010–2014 (in millions)

	2014	2013	2012	2011	2010
Net revenues	$55,184	$55,656	$65,875	$60,138	$42,588
Operating profit	5,328	5,628	8,573	7,153	3,963
Net income	3,695	3,789	5,681	4,928	2,700
Total assets	84,681	84,896	88,970	91,218	63,728

Source: Caterpillar, Inc., 2014 annual report.

scaled back equipment production and slashed costs to align the company with lower demand. *Market Watch* reported in May 2015 that Deere had announced plans to lay off 910 workers at plants in Iowa and Illinois.

With the revised forecast, Deere & Company CEO Samuel Allen noted, "John Deere expects to be solidly profitable in 2015, with the year ranking among our stronger ones in sales and earnings despite the pullback in the farm sector. Such an achievement illustrates our success establishing a wider range of revenue sources and a more durable business model. All in all, we remain confident in the company's present direction and in its ability to meet customer needs for advanced machinery and innovative services in the years ahead."[1]

ENDNOTES

[1] As quoted in "Deere Announces Second-Quarter Earnings of $690 million," *PR Newswire*, May 22, 2015.

PepsiCo's Diversification Strategy in 2015

JOHN E. GAMBLE Texas A&M University–Corpus Christi

DAVID L. TURNIPSEED University of South Alabama

PepsiCo was the world's largest snack and beverage company, with 2014 net revenues of approximately $66.7 billion. The company's portfolio of businesses in 2015 included Frito-Lay salty snacks, Quaker Chewy granola bars, Pepsi soft-drink products, Tropicana orange juice, Lipton Brisk tea, Gatorade, Propel, SoBe, Quaker Oatmeal, Cap'n Crunch, Aquafina, Rice-A-Roni, Aunt Jemima pancake mix, and many other regularly consumed products. The company viewed the lineup as highly complementary since most of its products could be consumed together. For example, Tropicana orange juice might be consumed during breakfast with Quaker Oatmeal, and Doritos and a Mountain Dew might be part of someone's lunch. In 2015, PepsiCo's business lineup included 22 $1 billion global brands.

The company's top managers were focused on sustaining the impressive performance through strategies keyed to product innovation, close relationships with distribution allies, international expansion, and strategic acquisitions. Newly introduced products such as Mountain Dew KickStart, Tostitos Cantina tortilla chips, Quaker Real Medleys, Starbucks Refreshers, and Gatorade Energy Chews accounted for 15 to 20 percent of all new growth in recent years. New product innovations that addressed consumer health and wellness concerns were important contributors to the company's growth, with PepsiCo's better-for-you and good-for-you products becoming focal points in the company's new product development initiatives. In 2014, PepsiCo's nutrition business accounted for about 20 percent of the company's net revenue.

In addition to focusing on strategies designed to deliver revenue and earnings growth, the company maintained an aggressive dividend policy, with more than $53 billion returned to shareholders between 2003 and 2012. PepsiCo increased its dividend for the 42nd consecutive year in 2014 and paid $8.7 billion to its shareholders through dividends and stock repurchases, which was a 36 percent increase over 2013. The company bolstered its cash returns through carefully considered capital expenditures and acquisitions and a focus on operational excellence. Its Performance with Purpose plan utilized investments in manufacturing automation, a rationalized global manufacturing plan, reengineered distribution systems, and simplified organization structures to drive efficiency. In addition, the company's Performance with Purpose plan was focused on minimizing the company's impact on the environment by lowering energy and water consumption, and reducing its use of packaging material, providing a safe and inclusive workplace for employees, and supporting and investing in the local communities in which it operated. PepsiCo had been listed on the Dow Jones Sustainability World Index for eight consecutive years and listed on the North America Index for nine consecutive years as of 2014.

Even though the company had recorded a number of impressive achievements over the past decade, its growth had slowed since 2011. In fact, the spikes in the company's revenue growth since 2000 had resulted from major acquisitions, such as the $13.6 billion acquisition of Quaker Oats in 2001, the 2010 acquisition of the previously independent Pepsi Bottling Group and PepsiCo Americas for $8.26 billion, and the acquisition of Russia's leading food-and-beverage company, Wimm-Bill-Dann (WBD) Foods, for $3.8 billion in 2011. A summary of PepsiCo's financial performance for 2005 through 2014 is shown in Exhibit 1. Exhibit 2 tracks PepsiCo's market performance between 2004 and July 2014.

Company History

PepsiCo, Inc., was established in 1965 when Pepsi-Cola and Frito-Lay shareholders agreed to a merger between the salty-snack icon and the soft-drink giant. The new company was founded with annual revenues of $510 million and such well-known brands as Pepsi-Cola, Mountain Dew, Fritos, Lay's, Cheetos, Ruffles, and Rold Gold. PepsiCo's roots can be traced to 1898, when New Bern, North Carolina, pharmacist Caleb Bradham created the formula for a carbonated beverage he named Pepsi-Cola. The company's salty-snack business began in 1932, when Elmer Doolin, of San Antonio, Texas, began manufacturing and marketing Fritos corn chips and Herman Lay started a potato chip distribution business in Nashville, Tennessee. In 1961, Doolin and Lay agreed to a merger between their businesses to establish the Frito-Lay Company.

During PepsiCo's first five years as a snack and beverage company, it introduced new products such as Doritos and Funyuns, entered markets in Japan and eastern Europe, and opened, on average, one new snack-food plant per year. By 1971, PepsiCo had more than doubled its revenues to reach $1 billion. The company began to pursue growth through acquisitions outside snacks and beverages as early as 1968, but its 1977 acquisition of Pizza Hut significantly shaped the strategic direction of PepsiCo for the next 20 years. The acquisitions of Taco Bell in 1978 and Kentucky Fried Chicken in 1986 created a business portfolio described by Wayne Calloway (PepsiCo's CEO between 1986 and 1996) as a balanced three-legged stool. Calloway believed the combination of snack foods, soft drinks, and fast food offered considerable cost-sharing and skill-transfer opportunities, and he routinely shifted managers among the company's three divisions as part of the company's management development efforts.

PepsiCo strengthened its portfolio of snack foods and beverages during the 1980s and 1990s with the acquisitions of Mug Root Beer, 7-Up International, Smartfood ready-to-eat popcorn, Walker's Crisps (United Kingdom), Smith's Crisps (United Kingdom), Mexican cookie company Gamesa, and Sunchips. Calloway added quick-service restaurants Hot-n-Now in 1990; California Pizza Kitchens in 1992; and East Side Mario's, D'Angelo Sandwich Shops, and Chevy's Mexican Restaurants in 1993. The company expanded beyond carbonated beverages through a 1992 agreement with Ocean Spray to

---

EXHIBIT 1

Financial Summary for PepsiCo, Inc., 2005–2014 (in millions, except per share amounts)

	2014	2013	2012	2011	2010	2009	2008	2007	2006	2005
Net revenue	$66,683	$66,415	$65,492	$66,504	$57,838	$43,232	$43,251	$39,474	$35,137	$32,562
Net income	6,558	6,787	6,214	6,443	6,320	5,946	5,142	5,599	5,065	4,078
Income per common share—basic, continuing operations	$4.31	$4.37	$3.96	$4.08	$3.97	$3.81	$3.26	$3.38	$3.00	$2.43
Cash dividends declared per common share	$2.53	$2.24	$2.13	$2.03	$1.89	$1.78	$1.65	$1.42	$1.16	$1.01
Total assets	$70,509	77,478	74,638	72,882	68,153	39,848	35,994	34,628	29,930	37,727
Long-term debt	23,821	24,333	23,544	20,568	19,999	7,400	7,858	4,203	2,550	2,313

Source: PepsiCo 10-K reports, various years.

EXHIBIT 2

Monthly Performance of PepsiCo, Inc.'s Stock Price, 2005–July 2015

(a) Trend in PepsiCo, Inc.'s Common Stock Price

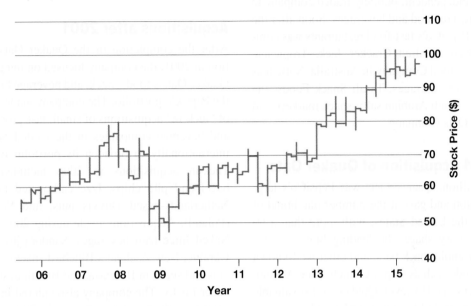

(b) Performance of PepsiCo, Inc.'s Stock Price Versus the S&P 500 Index

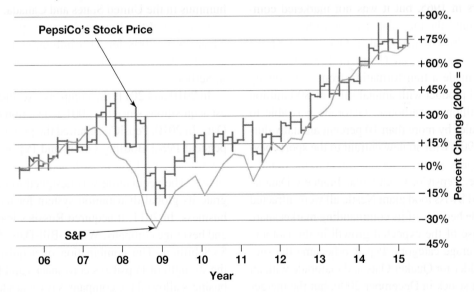

distribute single-serving juices, the introduction of Lipton ready-to-drink (RTD) teas in 1993, and the introduction of Aquafina bottled water and Frappuccino ready-to-drink coffees in 1994.

By 1996, it had become clear to PepsiCo management that the potential strategic-fit benefits existing between restaurants and PepsiCo's core beverage and snack businesses were difficult to capture. In

LIABILITIES AND EQUITY		
Short-term obligations	$5,076	$5,306
Accounts payable and other current liabilities	13,016	12,533
Liabilities, current	18,092	17,839
Long-term debt obligations	23,821	24,333
Other liabilities, noncurrent	5,744	4,931
Deferred income taxes	5,304	5,986
Liabilities	52,961	53,089
Commitments and contingencies		
Preferred stock, no par value	41	41
PepsiCo common shareholders' equity		
Common stock, value, issued	25	25
Additional paid in capital, common stock	4,115	4,095
Retained earnings (accumulated deficit)	49,092	46,420
Accumulated other comprehensive loss	(10,669)	(5,127)
Stockholders' equity attributable to parent	17,578	24,409
Stockholders' equity attributable to noncontrolling interest	110	110
Total equity	17,548	24,389
Liabilities and equity	$70,509	$77,478

Source: PepsiCo, Inc., 10-K report, 2013.

EXHIBIT 5

Net Cash Provided By PepsiCo's Operating Activities, 2011–2014

	2014	2013	2012	2011
Net cash provided by operating activities	$10,506	$9,688	$8,479	$8,944
Capital spending	(2,859)	(2,795)	(2,714)	(3,339)
Sales of property, plant, and equipment	115	109	95	84
Free cash flow	$7,762	$7,002	$5,860	$5,689

Source: PepsiCo, Inc., 2014 10-K report.

Building Shareholder Value in 2015

Three people had held the position of CEO since the company began its portfolio restructuring in 1997. Even though Roger Enrico was the chief architect of the business lineup as it stood in 2007, his successor, Steve Reinemund, and Indra Nooyi, the company's CEO in 2007, were both critically involved in the restructuring. Nooyi joined PepsiCo in 1994 and developed a reputation as a tough negotiator who engineered the 1997 spin-off of Pepsi's restaurants, spearheaded the 1998 acquisition of Tropicana, and played a critical role in the 1999 IPO of Pepsi's

bottling operations. After being promoted to chief financial officer, Nooyi was also highly involved in the 2001 acquisition of Quaker Oats. Nooyi was selected as the company's CEO upon Reinemund's retirement in October 2006. Nooyi had emigrated to the United States in 1978 to attend Yale's Graduate School of Business, and she worked with the Boston Consulting Group, Motorola, and Asea Brown Boveri before arriving at PepsiCo in 1994. In the eight years under Nooyi's leadership, PepsiCo's revenues had increased by nearly 90 percent, and its share price had grown by 50 percent.

In 2014, PepsiCo's corporate strategy had diversified the company into salty and sweet snacks, soft drinks, orange juice, bottled water, ready-to-drink teas and coffees, purified and functional waters, isotonic beverages, hot and ready-to-eat breakfast cereals, grain-based products, and breakfast condiments. Most PepsiCo brands had achieved number-one or number-two positions in their respective food and beverage categories through strategies keyed to product innovation, close relationships with distribution allies, international expansion, and strategic acquisitions. The company was committed to producing the highest-quality products in each category and was working diligently on product reformulations to make snack foods and beverages less unhealthy. The company believed that its efforts to develop good-for-you and better-for-you products would create growth opportunities from the intersection of business and public interests.

PepsiCo was organized into six business divisions, which all followed the corporation's general strategic approach. Frito-Lay North America manufactured, marketed, and distributed such snack foods as Lay's potato chips, Doritos tortilla chips, Cheetos cheese snacks, Fritos corn chips, Grandma's cookies, and Smartfood popcorn. Quaker Foods North America manufactured and marketed cereals, rice and pasta dishes, granola bars, and other food items that were sold in supermarkets. Latin American Foods manufactured, marketed, and distributed snack foods and many Quaker-branded cereals and snacks in Latin America. PepsiCo Americas Beverages manufactured, marketed, and sold beverage concentrates, fountain syrups, and finished goods under such brands as Pepsi, Gatorade, Aquafina, Tropicana, Lipton, Dole, and SoBe throughout North and South America. PepsiCo Europe manufactured, marketed, and sold snacks and beverages throughout Europe, while the company's Asia, Middle East, and Africa division produced, marketed, and distributed snack brands and beverages in more than 150 countries in those regions. A full listing of Frito-Lay snacks, PepsiCo beverages, and Quaker Oats products is presented in Exhibit 6. Select financial information for PepsiCo's six reporting units is presented in Exhibit 7.

Frito-Lay North America

As of 2015, three key trends that were shaping the industry were convenience, a growing awareness of the nutritional content of snack foods, and indulgent snacking. A product manager for a regional snack producer explained, "Many consumers want to reward themselves with great-tasting, gourmet flavors and styles. . . . The indulgent theme carries into seasonings as well. Overall, upscale, restaurant-influenced flavor trends are emerging to fill

---

EXHIBIT 6

PepsiCo, Inc.'s Snack, Beverage, and Quaker Oats Brands, 2014

Snack Brands	Beverage Brands	Quaker Oats Brands
• Lay's potato chips	• Pepsi-Cola	• Quaker Oatmeal
• Maui Style potato chips	• Mountain Dew	• Cap'n Crunch cereal
• Ruffles potato chips	• Mountain Dew AMP energy drink	• Life cereal
• Doritos tortilla chips	• Mug	• Quaker 100% Natural cereal
• Tostitos tortilla chips	• Sierra Mist	• Quaker Squares cereal
• Santitas tortilla chips	• Slice	• Quisp cereal
• Fritos corn chips	• Lipton Brisk (partnership)	• King Vitaman cereal
• Cheetos cheese-flavored snacks	• Lipton Iced Tea (partnership)	• Quaker Oh's! cereal
• Rold Gold pretzels and snack mix	• Dole juices and juice drinks (license)	• Mother's cereal
• Funyuns onion-flavored rings	• FruitWorks juice drinks	• Quaker grits
• Go Snacks	• Aquafina purified drinking water	• Quaker Oatmeal-to-Go
• Sunchips multigrain snacks	• Frappuccino ready-to-drink coffee (partnership)	• Aunt Jemima mixes and syrups
• Sabritones puffed-wheat snacks	• Starbucks DoubleShot (partnership)	• Quaker rice cakes
• Cracker Jack candy-coated popcorn	• SoBe juice drinks, dairy, and teas	• Quaker rice snacks (Quakes)

- Chester's popcorn

- Grandma's cookies
- Munchos potato crisps
- Smartfood popcorn
- Baken-ets fried pork skins
- Oberto meat snacks
- Rustler's meat snacks
- Churrumais fried corn strips
- Frito-Lay nuts
- Frito-Lay, Ruffles, Fritos, and Tostitos dips and salsas
- Frito-Lay, Doritos, and Cheetos snack crackers
- Fritos, Tostitos, Ruffles, and Doritos snack kits
- Grain Waves
- Lay's Stax potato crisps
- Miss Vickie's potato chips
- Munchies snack mix
- Stacy's Pita Chips
- Flat Earth fruit and vegetable chips
- Red Rock Deli Chips
- Sabra hummus

Outside North America
- Bocabits wheat snacks
- Crujitos corn snacks
- Fandangos corn snacks
- Hamka's snacks
- Niknaks cheese snacks
- Quavers potato snacks

- Sabritas potato chips

- Smiths potato chips
- Walkers potato crisps
- Gamesa cookies
- Doritos Dippas
- Sonric's sweet snacks
- Wotsits corn snacks
- Red Rock Deli
- Kurkure
- Smiths Sensations
- Cheetos Shots
- Quavers Snacks
- Bluebird Snacks
- Duyvis Nuts
- Müller yogurts
- Lucky snacks
- Penelopa nuts and seeds
- Marbo
- Wimm-Bill-Dann

- SoBe energy drinks (No Fear and Adrenaline Rush)
- H2OH!
- Gatorade
- Propel
- Tropicana
- Tropicana Twister
- Tropicana Smoothie
- Izze
- Naked Juice

Outside North America

- Mirinda

- 7UP

- Pepsi
- Kas
- Teem
- Manzanita Sol
- Paso de los Toros
- Fruko
- Evervess
- Yedigun
- Shani
- Fiesta
- D&G (license)
- Mandarin (license)
- Radical Fruit
- Tropicana Touche de Lait
- Alvalle gazpacho fruit juices and vegetable juices
- Tropicana Season's Best juices and juice drinks
- Loóza juices and nectars
- Copella juices
- Frui'Vita juices
- Sandora juices

- Quaker Chewy granola bars

- Quaker Dipps granola bars
- Rice-A-Roni side dishes
- Pasta Roni side dishes
- Near East side dishes
- Puffed Wheat
- Harvest Crunch cereal
- Quaker baking mixes
- Spudz snacks
- Crisp'ums baked crisps

- Quaker Fruit & Oatmeal bars

- Quaker Fruit & Oatmeal Bites

- Quaker Fruit and Oatmeal Toastables
- Quaker Soy Crisps
- Quaker Bakeries

Outside North America
- FrescAvena beverage powder
- Toddy chocolate powder
- Toddynho chocolate drink
- Coqueiro canned fish
- Sugar Puffs cereal
- Puffed Wheat
- Cruesli cereal
- Hot Oat Crunch cereal
- Quaker Oatso Simple hot cereal
- Scott's Porage Oats
- Scott's So Easy Oats

- Quaker bagged cereals

- Quaker Mais Sabor
- Quaker Oats
- Quaker oat flour
- Quaker Meu Mingau
- Quaker cereal bars
- Quaker Oatbran
- Corn goods
- Magico chocolate powder
- Quaker Vitaly Cookies
- 3 Minutos Mixed Cereal
- Quaker Mágica
- Quaker Mágica con Soja
- Quaker pastas
- Quaker Frut

Source: Pepsico.com.

EXHIBIT 7

Select Financial Data for PepsiCo, Inc.'s Business Segments, 2011–2014 (in millions)

	2014	2013	2012	2011
Net revenue				
Frito-Lay North America	$14,502	$14,126	$13,574	$13,322
Quaker Foods North America	2,568	2,612	2,636	2,656
Latin American Foods	8,442	8,350	7,780	7,156
PepsiCo Americas Beverages	21,154	21,068	21,408	22,418
Europe	13,290	13,752	13,441	13,560
Asia, Middle East, Africa	6,727	6,507	6,653	7,392
Total division	66,683	66,415	65,492	66,504
Operating profit				
Frito-Lay North America	$ 4,054	$ 3,877	$ 3,646	$ 3,621
Quaker Foods North America	621	617	695	797
Latin American Foods	1,211	1,242	1,059	1,078
PepsiCo Americas Beverages	2,846	2,955	2,937	3,273
Europe	1,331	1,293	1,330	1,210
Asia, Middle East, Africa	1,043	1,174	1,330	1,210
Total division	11,106	11,158	10,414	10,866
Capital expenditures				
Frito-Lay North America	$ 519	$ 423	$ 365	$ 439
Quaker Foods North America	58	38	37	43
Latin American Foods	368	384	436	413
PepsiCo Americas Beverages	719	716	702	1,006
Europe	502	550	575	588
Asia, Middle East, Africa	517	531	510	693
Total division	2,683	2,642	2,625	3,182
Total assets				
Frito-Lay North America	$ 5,307	$ 5,308	$ 5,332	$ 5,384
Quaker Foods North America	982	983	966	1,024
Latin American Foods	4,760	4,829	4,993	4,721
PepsiCo Americas Beverages	30,188	30,350	30,889	31,142
Europe	13,902	18,702	19,218	18,461
Asia, Middle East, Africa	5,887	5,754	5,738	6,038
Total division	61,102	65,926	67,146	66,770
Depreciation and other amortization				
Frito-Lay North America	$ 424	$ 430	$ 445	$ 458
Quaker Foods North America	51	51	53	54
Latin American Foods	254	253	248	238
PepsiCo Americas Beverages	856	863	855	865
Europe	471	525	522	522
Asia, Middle East, Africa	313	283	305	350
Total division	2,553	2,553	2,570	2,604
Amortization of other intangible assets				
Frito-Lay North America	$7	$7	$7	$7
Quaker Foods North America	—	—	—	—
Latin American Foods	8	8	10	10
PepsiCo Americas Beverages	45	58	59	65
Europe	28	32	36	39
Asia, Middle East, Africa	4	5	7	12
Total division	92	110	119	133

Source: PepsiCo, Inc., 2014 10-K report.

consumers' desires to escape from the norm and taste snacks from a wider, often global, palate."[1] Most manufacturers had developed new flavors of salty snacks such as jalapeno and cheddar tortilla chips and pepper jack potato chips to attract the interest of indulgent snackers. Manufacturers had also begun using healthier oils when processing chips and had expanded lines of baked and natural salty snacks to satisfy the demands of health-conscious consumers. Snacks packaged in smaller bags not only addressed overeating concerns but also were convenient to take along on an outing. In 2013, Frito-Lay owned the top-selling chip brand in each U.S. salty-snack category and held more than a 2-to-1 lead over the next-largest snack-food maker in the United States. Frito-Lay's 36.6 percent market share of convenience foods sold in the United States was more than five times greater than runner-up Kellogg's market share of 6.9 percent. Convenience foods included both salty and sweet snacks, such as chips, pretzels, ready-to-eat popcorn, crackers, dips, snack nuts and seeds, candy bars, and cookies.

PepsiCo's Performance with Purpose goals applied to all of its business units. Frito-Lay North America's (FLNA's) net revenues increased by 3 percent during 2014, its volume increased by 2 percent, and its operating profit increased by 5 percent. The division's management believed that growth in snack foods remained possible since typical individuals, on average, consumed snacks 67 times per month. On average, consumers chose Frito-Lay snacks only eight times per month. To increase its share of snack consumption, FLNA was focused on developing additional better-for-you (BFY) snacks such as Baked Cheetos and Doritos packaged in smaller portion sizes. Between 2008 and 2014, improving the performance of the division's core salty brands and further developing health and wellness products were key strategic initiatives. The company had eliminated trans fats from all Lay's, Fritos, Ruffles, Cheetos, Tostitos, and Doritos varieties, marketed a wide variety of gluten-free products, and was looking for further innovations to make its salty snacks more healthy. The company had introduced Lay's Classic Potato Chips cooked in sunflower oil that retained Lay's traditional flavor but contained 50% less saturated fat.

Good-for-you (GFY) snacks, such as Flat Earth fruit and vegetable snacks, offered an opportunity for the company to exploit consumers' desires for healthier snacks and address a deficiency in most diets. Americans, on average, consumed only about 50 percent of the U.S. Department of Agriculture's recommended daily diet of fruits and vegetables. Other GFY snacks included Stacy's Pita Chips, Sabra hummus, salsas and dips, and Quaker Chewy granola bars. In 2013, FLNA manufactured and marketed baked versions of its most popular products, such as Cheetos, Lay's potato chips, Ruffles potato chips, and Tostitos Scoops! tortilla chips.

Quaker Foods North America

Quaker Foods produced, marketed, and distributed hot and ready-to-eat cereals, pancake mixes and syrups, and rice and pasta side dishes in the United States and Canada. In 2014, the division recorded sales of approximately $2.56 billion, down 2 percent, and sales volume was even with the prior year. The sales volume of Quaker Foods products decreased by nearly 1 percent annually between 2011 and 2013 with Quaker Oatmeal, Life cereal, and Cap'n Crunch cereal volumes competing in mature industries with weak competitive positions relative to Kellogg's and General Mills. Sales of Aunt Jemima syrup and pancake mix, and Rice-A-Roni rice and pasta kits also declined between 2011 and 2013. Quaker Oats was the star product of the division, with a commanding share of the North American market for oatmeal in 2013. Rice-A-Roni also held a number-one market share in the rice and pasta side-dish segment of the consumer food industry. More than one-half of Quaker Foods' 2013 revenues was generated by BFY and GFY products.

Latin American Foods

PepsiCo management believed international markets offered the company's greatest opportunity for growth since per capita consumption of snacks in the United States averaged 6.6 servings per month, while per capita consumption in other developed countries averaged 4 servings per month and in developing countries averaged 0.4 serving per month. PepsiCo executives expected China and Brazil to become the two largest international markets for snacks. The United Kingdom was estimated to be the third-largest international market for snacks, while developing markets Mexico and Russia were expected to be the fourth- and fifth-largest international markets, respectively.

Developing an understanding of consumer taste preferences was a key to expanding into international markets. Taste preferences for salty snacks were more similar from country to country than were preferences for many other food items, and this allowed PepsiCo to make only modest modifications to its snacks in most countries. For example, classic varieties of Lay's, Doritos, and Cheetos snacks were sold in Latin America. In addition, consumer characteristics in the United States that had forced snack-food makers to adopt better-for-you or good-for-you snacks applied in most other developed countries as well.

PepsiCo operated 50 snack-food manufacturing and processing plants and 640 warehouses in Latin America, with its largest facilities located in Guarulhos, Brazil; Monterrey, Mexico; Mexico City, Mexico; and Celaya, Mexico. PepsiCo was the second-largest seller of snacks and beverages in Mexico, and its Doritos, Marias Gamesa, Cheetos, Ruffles, Emperador, Saladitas, Sabritas, and Tostitos brands were popular throughout most of Latin America. The division's revenues had grown from $7.2 billion in 2011 to $8.4 billion in 2014 and accounted for 11 percent of 2014 total net revenues.

PepsiCo Americas Beverages

PepsiCo was the largest seller of liquid refreshments in the United States, with a 24 percent share of the market in 2013. Coca-Cola was the second-largest nonalcoholic beverage producer, with a 21 percent market share. Dr. Pepper Snapple Group was the third-largest beverage seller in 2013, with a market share of 8.9 percent. Private-label sellers of beverages collectively held an 8 percent market share in 2013. As with Frito-Lay, PepsiCo's beverage business contributed greatly to the corporation's overall profitability and free cash flows.

In 2014, PepsiCo Americas Beverages (PAB) accounted for 32 percent of the corporation's total revenues and 26 percent of its operating profits. The PAB division's $1 billion brands included Gatorade, Tropicana fruit juices, Lipton ready-to-drink tea, Pepsi, Diet Pepsi, Mountain Dew, Diet Mountain Dew, Aquafina, Miranda, Sierra Mist, Dole fruit drinks, Starbucks cold-coffee drinks, and SoBe.

Gatorade was the number-one brand of sports drink sold worldwide; Tropicana was the number-two seller of juice and juice drinks globally; and PAB was the second-largest seller of carbonated soft drinks worldwide, with a 29 percent market share in 2014. Market leader Coca-Cola held a 42 percent share of the carbonated soft-drink (CSD) industry in 2014. Carbonated soft drinks were the most consumed type of beverage in the United States, with industry sales of $20.4 billion, but the industry had declined by 1 to 2 percent annually for nearly a decade. The overall decline in CSD consumption was a result of consumers' interest in healthier food and beverage choices. In contrast, flavored and enhanced water, energy drinks, ready-to-drink teas, and bottled water were growing beverage categories that were capturing a larger share of the stomachs in the United States and internationally.

PepsiCo's Carbonated Soft-Drink Business

Among Pepsi's most successful strategies to sustain volume and share in soft drinks was its Power of One strategy, which attempted to achieve the synergistic benefits of a combined Pepsi-Cola and Frito-Lay envisioned by shareholders of the two companies in 1965. The Power of One strategy called for supermarkets to place Pepsi and Frito-Lay products side by side on shelves. The company was also focused on soft-drink innovation to sustain sales and market share, including new formulations to lower the calorie content of nondiet drinks.

PepsiCo's Noncarbonated Beverage Brands

Although carbonated beverages made up the largest percentage of PAB's total beverage volume, much of the division's growth was attributable to the success of its noncarbonated beverages. Aquafina was the number-one brand of bottled water in the United States. Gatorade, Tropicana, Aquafina, SoBe, Starbucks Frappuccino, Lipton RTD teas, and Propel were all leading BFY and GFY beverages in the markets where they were sold.

PepsiCo Europe

All of PepsiCo's global brands were sold in Europe, as well as its country- or region-specific brands, such as Domik v Derevne, Chjudo, and Agusha. PepsiCo Europe operated 125 plants and approximately 525 warehouses, distribution centers, and offices in eastern and western Europe. The company's acquisition of Wimm-Bill-Dann Foods, along with sales of its long-time brands, made it the number-one food and beverage company in Russia, with a 2-to-1 advantage over its nearest competitor. It was also the leading seller of snacks and beverages in the United Kingdom. PepsiCo Europe management believed further opportunities in other international markets existed, with opportunities to distribute many of its newest brands and product formulations throughout Europe. PepsiCo Europe provided 20% of the corporation's net revenues and 12% of its operating profit in 2014. PepsiCo Europe's net sales fell 3 percent in 2014 over the prior year but contributed 20 percent to the corporation's total revenue.

Asia, Middle East, and Africa

PepsiCo's business unit operating in Asia, the Middle East, and Africa manufactured and marketed all of the company's global brands and many regional brands such as Kurkure and Chipsy. PepsiCo operated 45 plants, 490 distribution centers, warehouses, and offices located in Egypt, Jordan, and China, and was the number-one brand of beverages and snacks in India, Egypt, Saudi Arabia, United Arab Emirates, and China. The division's revenues had declined from $7.4 billion in 2011 to $6.5 billion in 2013 but rebounded to $6.7 billion in 2014, while its operating profit declined from $1,210 to $1,080 over the period 2011 to 2014. In 2014, Asia, Middle East, and Africa provided 10% of the corporation's net revenues and 9% of its operating profit.

Value Chain Alignment Between PepsiCo Brands and Products

PepsiCo's management team was dedicated to capturing strategic-fit benefits within the business lineup throughout the value chain. The company's procurement activities were coordinated globally to achieve the greatest possible economies of scale, and best practices were routinely transferred among its more than 200 plants, over 3,500 distribution systems, and 120,000 service routes around the world.

PepsiCo also shared market research information with its divisions to better enable each division to develop new products likely to be hits with consumers, and the company coordinated its Power of One activities across product lines.

PepsiCo management had a proven ability to capture strategic fits between the operations of new acquisitions and its other businesses. The Quaker Oats integration produced a number of noteworthy successes, including $160 million in cost savings resulting from corporatewide procurement of product ingredients and packaging materials and an estimated $40 million in cost savings attributed to the joint distribution of Quaker snacks and Frito-Lay products. In total, the company estimated that the synergies among its business units generated approximately $1 billion annually in productivity savings.

Pepsico's Strategic Situation in 2015

For the most part, PepsiCo's strategies seemed to be firing on all cylinders in 2015. PepsiCo's chief managers expected the company's lineup of snack, beverage, and grocery items to generate operating cash flows sufficient to reinvest in its core businesses, provide a 7.3 percent increase in cash dividends to shareholders, fund a $4.5 billion to $5 billion share-buyback plan, and pursue acquisitions that would provide attractive returns. Nevertheless, the low relative profit margins of PepsiCo's international businesses created the need for a continued examination of its strategy and operations to better exploit strategic fits between the company's international business units.

The company had developed a new divisional structure in 2008 to combine its food and beverage businesses in Latin America into a common division. Also, the company's international businesses were reorganized to boost profit margins in Europe and Asia, the Middle East, and Africa. However, more than six years after the reorganization, the performance of the company's international businesses continued to lag that of its North American businesses by a meaningful margin. Some food and beverage industry analysts had speculated that additional corporate strategy changes might also be required to improve the profitability of PepsiCo's international operations and to help restore previous revenue and earnings growth rates. Possible actions might include a reprioritization of internal uses of cash, new acquisitions, further efforts to capture strategic fits existing between the company's various businesses, or the divestiture of businesses with poor prospects of future growth and minimal strategic fit with PepsiCo's other businesses.

ENDNOTES

[1] As quoted in "Snack Attack," *Private Label Buyer,* August 2006, p. 26.

Mc Graw Hill Education **connect**   JOSEPH LAMPEL Alliance Manchester Business School

It was in the spring of the second year of his insurrection against the High Sheriff of Nottingham that Robin Hood took a walk in Sherwood Forest. As he walked, he pondered the progress of the campaign, the disposition of his forces, the sheriff's recent moves, and the options that confronted him.

The revolt against the sheriff had begun as a personal crusade. It erupted out of Robin's conflict with the sheriff and his administration. However, alone Robin Hood could do little. He therefore sought allies, men with grievances and a deep sense of justice. Later he welcomed all who came, asking few questions and demanding only a willingness to serve. Strength, he believed, lay in numbers.

He spent the first year forging the group into a disciplined band, united in enmity against the sheriff and willing to live outside the law. The band's organization was simple. Robin ruled supreme, making all important decisions. He delegated specific tasks to his lieutenants. Will Scarlett was in charge of intelligence and scouting. His main job was to shadow the sheriff and his men, always alert to their next move. He also collected information on the travel plans of rich merchants and tax collectors. Little John kept discipline among the men and saw to it that their archery was at the high peak that their profession demanded. Scarlock took care of the finances, converting loot to cash, paying shares of the take, and finding suitable hiding places for the surplus. Finally, Much the Miller's son had the difficult task of provisioning the ever-increasing band of Merry Men.

The increasing size of the band was a source of satisfaction for Robin but also a source of concern. The fame of his Merry Men was spreading, and new recruits were pouring in from every corner of England. As the band grew larger, their small bivouac became a major encampment. Between raids, the men milled about, talking and playing games. Vigilance was in decline, and discipline was becoming harder to enforce. "Why," Robin reflected, "I don't know half the men I run into these days."

The growing band was also beginning to exceed the food capacity of the forest. Game was becoming scarce, and supplies had to be obtained from outlying villages. The cost of buying food was beginning to drain the band's financial reserves at the very moment when revenues were in decline. Travelers, especially those with the most to lose, were now giving the forest a wide berth. This was costly and inconvenient to them, but it was preferable to having all their goods confiscated.

Robin believed that the time had come for the Merry Men to change their policy of outright confiscation of goods to one of a fixed transit tax. His lieutenants strongly resisted this idea. They were proud of the Merry Men's famous motto: "Rob the rich and give to the poor." "The farmers and the townspeople," they argued, "are our most important allies. How can we tax them and still hope for their help in our fight against the sheriff?"

Robin wondered how long the Merry Men could keep to the ways and methods of their early days. The sheriff was growing stronger and becoming better organized. He now had the money and the men. and was beginning to harass the band, probing for its weaknesses. The tide of events was beginning to turn against the Merry Men. Robin felt that the campaign must be decisively concluded before the sheriff had a chance to deliver a mortal blow. "But how," he wondered, "could this be done?"

Robin had often entertained the possibility of killing the sheriff, but the chances for this seemed increasingly remote. Besides, killing the sheriff might satisfy his personal thirst for revenge, but it would not improve the situation. Robin had hoped that the perpetual state of unrest and the sheriff's failure to collect taxes would lead to his removal from office. Instead, the sheriff used his political connections to obtain reinforcement. He had powerful friends at court and was well regarded by the regent, Prince John.

Prince John was vicious and volatile. He was consumed by his unpopularity among the people, who wanted the imprisoned King Richard back. He also lived in constant fear of the barons, who had first given him the regency but were now beginning to dispute his claim to the throne. Several of these barons had set out to collect the ransom that would release King Richard the Lionheart from his jail in Austria. Robin was invited to join the conspiracy in return for future amnesty. It was a dangerous proposition. Provincial banditry was one thing, court intrigue another. Prince John had spies everywhere, and he was known for his vindictiveness. If the conspirators' plan failed, the pursuit would be relentless and retributions swift.

The sound of the supper horn startled Robin from his thoughts. There was the smell of roasting venison in the air. Nothing was resolved or settled. Robin headed for camp promising himself that he would give these problems his utmost attention after tomorrow's raid.

ARTHUR A. THOMPSON The University of Alabama

JOHN E. GAMBLE Texas A&M University—Corpus Christi

In 2014, Southwest Airlines was the market share leader in domestic air travel in the United States; it transported more passengers from U.S. airports to U.S. destinations than any other airline, and it offered more regularly scheduled domestic flights than any other airline. Southwest also had the enviable distinction of being the only major air carrier in the United States that was consistently profitable, having reported a profit every year since 1973.

From humble beginnings as a scrappy underdog with quirky practices that flew mainly to "secondary" airports (rather than high-traffic airports such as Chicago O'Hare, Dallas–Fort Worth, and New York's Kennedy airport), Southwest had climbed up through the industry ranks to become a major competitive force in the domestic segment of the U.S. airline industry. It had weathered industry downturns, dramatic increases in the price of jet fuel, cataclysmic falloffs in airline traffic due to terrorist attacks and economywide recessions, and fare wars and other attempts by rivals to undercut its business, all the while adding more and more flights to more and more airports. Since 2000, the number of passengers flying Southwest had increased from 72.6 million to 115.4 million, whereas domestic passenger traffic had remained flat or declined at American Airlines, Delta Air Lines, United Airlines, and US Airways (see Exhibit 1).

Company Background

In late 1966, Rollin King, a San Antonio entrepreneur who owned a small commuter air service, marched into Herb Kelleher's law office with a plan to start a low-cost, low-fare airline that would shuttle passengers between San Antonio, Dallas, and Houston.[1] Over the years, King had heard many Texas businessmen complain about the length of time that it took to drive between the three cities and the expense of flying the airlines currently serving these cities. His business concept for the airline was simple: Attract passengers by flying convenient schedules, get passengers to their destination on time, make sure they have a good experience, and charge fares competitive with travel by automobile. Kelleher, skeptical that King's business idea was viable, dug into the possibilities during the next few weeks and concluded a new airline was feasible; he agreed to handle the necessary legal work and to invest $10,000 of his own funds in the venture.

In 1967, Kelleher filed papers to incorporate the new airline and submitted an application to the Texas Aeronautics Commission for the new company to begin serving Dallas, Houston, and San Antonio.[2] But rival airlines in Texas pulled every string they could to block the new airline from commencing operations, precipitating a contentious four-year parade of legal and regulatory proceedings. Herb Kelleher led the fight on the company's behalf, eventually prevailing in June 1971 after winning two appeals to the Texas Supreme Court and a favorable ruling from the U.S. Supreme Court. Kelleher recalled, "The constant proceedings had gradually come to enrage me. There was no merit to our competitors' legal assertions. They were simply trying to use their superior economic power to

EXHIBIT 1

Total Number of Domestic and International Passengers Traveling on Select U.S. Airlines, 2000, 2005, 2010–2013 (in thousands)

Carrier	Total Number of Enplaned Passengers[1]					
	2000	**2005**	**2010**	**2011**	**2012**	**2013**
American Airlines						
Domestic	68,319	77,297	65,774	65,253	65,027	65,070
International	17,951	20,710	20,424	20,887	21,430	19,962
Total	86,270	98,007	86,198	86,140	86,457	85,032
Delta Air Lines[2]						
Domestic	97,965	77,581	90,141	92,864	95,641	98,590
International	7,596	8,359	19,390	19,344	19,568	18,925
Total	105,561	85,940	109,531	112,208	115,209	117,515
Southwest Airlines (domestic only, has no international flights)[3]	**72,568**	**88,436**	**106,270**	**110,624**	**112,277**	**115,377**
AirTran (Domestic)[3]	—	—	—	**23,781**	**20,453**	**16,146**
AirTran (International)	—	—	—	**937**	**1,301**	**1,534**
Southwest Airlines total				**135,342**	**134,031**	**133,057**
United Airlines[4]						
Domestic	72,450	55,173	43,323	39,551	67,629	65,221
International	10,625	10,356	9,727	10,091	23,998	22,209
Total	83,075	65,529	53,050	49,642	91,627	87,430
US Airways[5]						
Domestic	56,667	37,040	45,180	46,208	47,481	50,037
International	3,105	4,829	6,670	6,749	6,794	6,480
Total	59,772	41,869	51,850	52,957	54,275	56,517

[1]Includes both passengers who paid for tickets and passengers who were traveling on frequent-flyer awards.

[2]Delta Air Lines and Northwest Airlines merged in October 2008; however, combined reporting did not begin until 2010.

[3]Southwest Airlines acquired AirTran in late 2010; by year-end 2014, all AirTran flights were scheduled to be rebranded as Southwest Airlines flights.

[4]United Airlines acquired Continental Airlines in 2010, and the two companies began joint reporting of passenger traffic in 2012. Prior to 2012, traffic count data are for only United flights.

[5]US Airways and America West merged in September 2005, but joint reporting of traffic counts did not begin until 2007; hence, data for 2000 and 2005 do not include America West, whereas the data for 2010–2013 do include the traffic counts of the combined companies. US Airways and American Airlines merged in December 2013 but continued to operate under their separate names through 2014.

Source: U.S. Department of Transportation, Bureau of Transportation Statistics, "Air Carrier Statistics," Form T-100.

squeeze us dry so we would collapse before we ever got into business. I was bound and determined to show that Southwest Airlines was going to survive and was going into operation."[3]

In January 1971, Lamar Muse was brought in as the CEO to get operations under way. Muse was an aggressive and self-confident airline veteran who knew the business well and who had the entrepreneurial skills to tackle the challenges of building the airline from scratch and then competing head-on with the major carriers. Through private investors

and an initial public offering of stock in June 1971, Muse raised $7 million in new capital to purchase planes and equipment and provide cash for startup. Boeing agreed to supply three new 737s from its inventory, discounting its price from $5 million to $4 million and financing 90 percent of the $12 million deal. Muse was able to recruit a talented senior staff that included a number of veteran executives from other carriers. He particularly sought out people who were innovative, wouldn't shirk from doing things differently or unconventionally, and were motivated by the challenge of building an airline from scratch. Muse wanted his executive team to be willing to think like mavericks and not be lulled into instituting practices at Southwest that imitated what was done at other airlines.

Southwest's Struggle to Gain a Market Foothold

In June 1971, Southwest initiated its first flights with a schedule that soon included 6 round-trips between Dallas and San Antonio and 12 round-trips between Houston and Dallas. But the introductory $20 one-way fares to fly the Golden Triangle, well below the $27 and $28 fares charged by rivals, attracted disappointingly small numbers of passengers. To try to gain market visibility and drum up more passengers, Southwest undertook some creative actions to supplement its ad campaigns publicizing its low fares:

- Southwest decided to have its flight hostesses dress in colorful hot pants and white knee-high boots with high heels. Recruiting ads for Southwest's first group of hostesses headlined "Attention, Raquel Welch: You can have a job if you measure up." Two thousand applicants responded, and those selected for interviews were asked to come dressed in hot pants to show off their legs—the company wanted to hire long-legged beauties with sparkling personalities. Over 30 of Southwest's first graduating class of 40 flight attendants consisted of young ladies who were cheerleaders and majorettes in high school and thus had experience performing skimpily dressed in front of people.

- A second attention-getting action was to give passengers free alcoholic beverages during daytime flights. Most passengers on these flights were business travelers. Management's thinking was that many passengers did not drink during the daytime and, with most flights being less than an hour's duration, it would be cheaper to simply give the drinks away than collect the money.

- Taking a cue from being based at Dallas Love Field, Southwest began using the tagline "Now There's Somebody Else Up There Who Loves You." The routes between Houston, Dallas,

and San Antonio became known as the "Love Triangle." Southwest's planes were referred to as "Love Birds," drinks became "Love Potions," peanuts were called "Love Bites," drink coupons were "Love Stamps," and tickets were printed on "Love Machines." The "love" campaign set the tone for Southwest's approach to its customers and its efforts to make flying Southwest Airlines an enjoyable, fun, and differentiating experience. (Later, when the company went public, it chose "LUV" as its stock-trading symbol.)

- To add more flights without buying more planes, the head of Southwest's ground operations came up with a plan for ground crews to off-load passengers and baggage, refuel the plane, clean the cabin and restock the galley, on-load passengers and baggage, do the necessary preflight checks and paperwork, and push away from the gate in 10 minutes. The 10-minute turnaround became one of Southwest's signatures during the 1970s and 1980s. (In later years, as passenger volume grew and many flights were filled to capacity, the turnaround time gradually expanded to 30 minutes because it took more time to unload and load 135 passengers compared to a half-full plane with just 60 to 65 passengers. Even so, the average turnaround times at Southwest during the 2000–2013 period were shorter than the 35- to 50-minute turnarounds typical at other major airlines.)

- In late November 1971, Lamar Muse came up with the idea of offering a $10 fare to passengers on the Friday night Houston-Dallas flight. With no advertising, the 112-seat flight sold out. This led Muse to realize that Southwest was serving two quite distinct types of travelers in the Golden Triangle market: (1) business travelers who were more time-sensitive than price-sensitive and wanted weekday flights at times suitable for conducting business, and (2) price-sensitive leisure travelers who wanted lower fares and had more flexibility about when to fly.[4] He came up with a two-tier on-peak and off-peak pricing structure in which all seats on weekday flights departing before 7 p.m. were priced at $26 and all seats on other flights were priced at $13. Passenger traffic increased significantly—and systemwide on-peak and off-peak pricing soon became standard across the whole airline industry.

• In 1972, the company decided to move its flights in Houston from the newly opened Houston Intercontinental Airport (where Southwest was losing money and where passengers faced a 45-minute trip to the city's downtown area) to the abandoned Houston Hobby Airport, located much closer to downtown Houston. Despite being the only carrier to fly into Houston Hobby, the results were spectacular: business travelers who flew to Houston frequently from Dallas and San Antonio found the Houston Hobby location far more convenient, and passenger traffic doubled almost immediately.

• In early 1973, in an attempt to fill empty seats on its San Antonio–Dallas flights, Southwest cut its regular $26 fare to $13 for all seats, all days, and all times. When Braniff International, at that time one of Southwest's major rivals, announced $13 fares of its own, Southwest retaliated with a two-page ad, run in the Dallas newspapers, headlining "Nobody is going to shoot Southwest Airlines out of the sky for a lousy $13" and containing copy stating that Braniff was trying to run Southwest out of business. The ad announced that Southwest would not only match Braniff's $13 fare but would also give passengers the choice of buying a regular-priced ticket for $26 and receiving a complimentary fifth of Chivas Regal scotch, Crown Royal Canadian whiskey, or Smirnoff vodka (or, for nondrinkers, a leather ice bucket). Over 75 percent of Southwest's Dallas-Houston passengers opted for the $26 fare, although the percentage dropped as the two-month promotion wore on and corporate controllers began insisting that company employees use the $13 fare. The local and national media picked up the story of Southwest's offer, proclaiming the battle as a David versus Goliath struggle in which the upstart Southwest did not stand much of a chance against the much larger and well-established Braniff; grassroots sentiment in Texas swung to Southwest's side.

All these moves paid off. The resulting gains in passenger traffic enabled Southwest to report its first-ever annual profit in 1973.

More Legal and Regulatory Hurdles

During the rest of the 1970s, Southwest found itself embroiled in another round of legal and regulatory battles. One battle involved Southwest's refusal to move its flights from Dallas Love Field, located 10 minutes from downtown, out to the newly opened Dallas–Fort Worth (DFW) Regional Airport, which was 30 minutes from downtown Dallas. Local officials were furious because they were counting on fees from Southwest's flights in and out of DFW to help service the debt on the bonds issued to finance the construction of the airport. Southwest's position was that it was not required to move because it had not agreed to do so or been ordered to do so by the Texas Aeronautics Commission; moreover, the company's headquarters were located at Love Field. The courts eventually ruled that Southwest's operations could remain at Love Field.

A second battle ensued when rival airlines protested Southwest's application to begin serving several smaller cities in Texas; their protest was based on arguments that these markets were already well served and that Southwest's entry would result in costly overcapacity. Southwest countered that its low fares would allow more people to fly and thus would grow the market. Again, Southwest prevailed, and its views about low fares expanding the market proved accurate. In the year before Southwest initiated service, 123,000 passengers flew from Harlingen Airport in the Rio Grande Valley to Houston, Dallas, or San Antonio; in the 11 months following Southwest's initial flights, 325,000 passengers flew to the same three cities.

Believing that Braniff and Texas International were deliberately engaging in tactics to harass Southwest's operations, Southwest convinced the U.S. government to investigate what it considered predatory tactics by its chief rivals. In February 1975, Braniff and Texas International were indicted by a federal grand jury for conspiring to put Southwest out of business—a violation of the Sherman Antitrust Act. The two airlines pleaded "no contest" to the charges, signed cease-and-desist agreements, and were fined a modest $100,000 each.

When Congress passed the Airline Deregulation Act in 1978, Southwest applied to the Civil Aeronautics Board (now the Federal Aviation Administration) to fly between Houston and New Orleans. The application was vehemently opposed by local government officials and airlines operating out of DFW because of the potential for passenger traffic to be siphoned away from DFW. The opponents solicited the aid of Fort Worth congressman Jim Wright, then the majority leader of the U.S. House of Representatives, who took the matter to the floor of the House; a rash of lobbying and maneuvering ensued. What emerged came to be known as the Wright Amendment of 1979: No airline may provide nonstop or through-plane service from Dallas Love Field to any city in any state except for locations in Texas, Louisiana, Arkansas, Oklahoma, and New Mexico. Southwest was prohibited from advertising, publishing schedules or fares, or checking baggage for travel from Dallas Love Field to any city it served outside the five-state "Wright Zone." The Wright amendment was expanded in 1997, when Alabama, Mississippi, and Kansas were added to the five-state zone; in 2005, Missouri was added to the Wright Zone. In 2006, after a heated battle in Congress, legislation was passed and signed into law that repealed the Wright amendment beginning in 2014.

The Emergence of a Combative, Can-Do Culture at Southwest

The legal, regulatory, and competitive battles that Southwest fought in its early years produced a strong esprit de corps among Southwest personnel and a drive to survive and prosper despite the odds. With newspaper and TV stories reporting Southwest's difficulties regularly, employees were fully aware that the airline's existence was constantly on the line. Had the company been forced to move from Love Field, it would most likely have gone under, an outcome that employees, Southwest's rivals, and local government officials understood well. According to Southwest's former president, Colleen Barrett, the obstacles thrown in the company's path by competitors and local officials were instrumental in building Herb Kelleher's passion

for Southwest Airlines and ingraining a combative, can-do spirit into the corporate culture:[5]

> They would put twelve to fifteen lawyers on a case and on our side there was Herb. They almost wore him to the ground. But the more arrogant they were, the more determined Herb got that this airline was going to go into the air—and stay there.
>
> The warrior mentality, the very fight to survive, is truly what created our culture.

When Lamar Muse resigned in 1978, Southwest's board wanted Herb Kelleher to take over as chairman and CEO. But Kelleher enjoyed practicing law, so while he agreed to become chairman of the board, he insisted that someone else be CEO. Southwest's board appointed Howard Putnam, a group vice president of marketing services at United Airlines, as Southwest's president and CEO in July 1978. Putnam asked Kelleher to become more involved in Southwest's day-to-day operations, and over the next three years, Kelleher got to know many of the company's personnel and observe them in action. Putnam announced his resignation in fall 1981 to become president and COO at Braniff International. This time, Southwest's board succeeded in persuading Kelleher to take on the additional duties of CEO and president.

Sustained Growth Transforms Southwest into the Domestic Market Share Leader, 1981–2013

When Herb Kelleher took over in 1981, Southwest was flying 27 planes to 14 destination cities and had $270 million in revenues and 2,100 employees. Over the next 20 years, Southwest Airlines prospered under Kelleher's leadership. When Kelleher stepped down as CEO in mid-2001, the company had 350 planes flying to 58 U.S. airports, annual revenues of $5.6 billion, over 30,000 employees, and 64 million fare-paying passengers annually.

Under the two CEOs who succeeded Kelleher, Southwest continued its march to becoming the market share leader in domestic air travel, growing to 2013 revenues of $17.7 billion and 44,800 employees, flying 680 planes to 96 airports in 41 states and 7 destinations outside the United States, and transporting more than 108 million fare-paying passengers and over 133 million total passengers (including those traveling on frequent-flyer awards) in 2013. In the process, the company won more industry Triple Crown awards—for best on-time record, best baggage handling, and fewest customer complaints—than any other U.S. airline. While Southwest fell short of its on-time performance and baggage-handling goals in 2013, it still led the domestic airline industry in customer satisfaction and received other awards and recognitions, including Best Domestic Airline for Customer Service, one of *Executive Travel Magazine*'s Leading Edge awards; Brand of the Year in the Value Airline Category, from the Harris Poll; and Best Customer Service and Best Loyalty Credit Card, from *InsideFlyer Magazine.*

Exhibit 2 provides a five-year summary of Southwest's financial and operating performance. Exhibit 3 provides select operating and financial data for major U.S. air carriers during the 1995–2013 period.

Herb Kelleher: The Ceo Who Transformed Southwest into a Major Airline

Herb Kelleher majored in philosophy at Wesleyan University in Middletown, Connecticut, graduating with honors. He earned his law degree at New York University, again graduating with honors and serving as a member of the law review. After graduation, he clerked for a New Jersey Supreme Court justice for two years and then joined a law firm in Newark. Upon marrying a woman from Texas and becoming enamored with Texas, he moved to San Antonio, where he became a successful lawyer and came to represent Rollin King's small aviation company.

When Herb Kelleher took on the role of Southwest's CEO in 1981, he made a point of visiting with maintenance personnel, to check on how well the planes were running, and talking with the flight attendants. Kelleher did not do much managing from his office, preferring instead to be out among the troops as much as he could. His style was to listen and observe and to offer encouragement. Kelleher attended most graduation ceremonies of flight attendant classes, and he often helped load bags on "Black Wednesday," the busy travel day before Thanksgiving. He knew the names of thousands of Southwest employees and was held in the highest regard by the employees. When he attended a Southwest employee function, he was swarmed like a celebrity.

Kelleher had an affinity for bold-print Hawaiian shirts, owned a tricked-out motorcycle, and made no secret of his love for smoking and Wild Turkey whiskey. He loved to make jokes and engage in pranks and corporate antics, prompting some people to refer to him as the "clown prince" of the airline industry. He once appeared at a company gathering dressed in an Elvis costume, and he had arm-wrestled a South Carolina company executive at a public event in Dallas for the right to use "Just Plane Smart" as an advertising slogan.[6] Kelleher was well known inside and outside the company for his combativeness, particularly when it came to beating back competitors. On one occasion, he reportedly told a group of veteran employees, "If someone says they're going to smack us in the face, knock them out, stomp them out, boot them in the ditch, cover them over, and move on to the next thing. That's the Southwest spirit at work."[7] On another occasion, he said, "I love battles. I think it's part of the Irish in me. It's like what Patton said, 'War is hell and I love it so.' That's how I feel. I've never gotten tired of fighting."[8]

While Southwest was deliberately combative and flamboyant in some aspects of its operations, when it came to the financial side of the business, Kelleher insisted on fiscal conservatism, a strong balance sheet, comparatively low levels of debt, and zealous attention to bottom-line profitability. While believing strongly in being prepared for adversity, Kelleher had an aversion to Southwest personnel spending time drawing up all kinds of formal strategic plans, saying, "Reality is chaotic; planning is ordered and logical. The meticulous nit-picking that goes on in most strategic planning processes creates a mental straightjacket that becomes disabling in an industry where things change radically from one day to the next." Kelleher wanted Southwest managers to think ahead, have contingency plans, and be ready to act when it seemed that the future held significant risks or when new conditions suddenly appeared and demanded prompt responses.

EXHIBIT 2

Summary of Southwest Airlines' Financial and Operating Performance, 2009–2013 (in millions, except per share and operating data)

	Year Ended December 31				
	2013	**2012**	**2011**	**2010**	**2009**
Financial data					
Operating revenues	$ 17,699	$ 17,088	$ 15,658	$ 12,104	$ 10,350
Operating expenses	16,421	16,465	14,965	11,116	10,088
Operating income	1,278	623	693	988	262
Other expenses (income), net	69	(62)	370	243	98
Income before taxes	1,209	685	323	745	164
Provision for income taxes	455	264	145	286	65
Net income	$ 754	$ 421	$ 178	$ 459	$ 99
Net income per share, basic	$ 1.06	$ 0.56	$ 0.23	$ 0.62	$ 0.13
Net income per share, diluted	$ 1.05	$ 0.56	$ 0.23	$ 0.61	$ 0.13
Cash dividends per common share	$ 0.1300	$ 0.0345	$ 0.0180	$ 0.0180	$ 0.0180
Total assets at period-end	$ 19,345	$ 18,596	$ 18,068	$ 15,463	$ 14,269
Long-term obligations at period-end	2,191	2,883	3,107	2,875	3,325
Stockholders' equity at period-end	7,336	6,992	6,877	6,237	5,454
Operating data					
Revenue passengers carried	108,075,976	109,346,509	103,973,759	88,191,322	86,310,229
Enplaned passengers	133,155,030	133,978,100	127,551,012	106,227,521	101,338,228
Revenue passenger-miles (RPMs) (000s)[1]	104,348,216	102,874,979	97,582,530	78,046,967	74,456,710
Available seat-miles (ASMs) (000s)[2]	130,344,072	128,137,110	120,578,736	98,437,092	98,001,550
Load factor[3]	80.1%	80.3%	80.9%	79.3%	76.0%
Average length of passenger haul (miles)	966	941	939	885	863
Average length of each flight (miles)	703	693	679	648	639
Trips flown	1,312,785	1,361,558	1,317,977	1,114,451	1,125,111

Average passenger fare	$ 154.72	$ 147.17	$ 141.90	$ 130.27	$ 114.61
Passenger revenue yield per RPM (cents)[4]	16.02	15.64	15.12	14.72	13.29
Operating revenue per ASM (cents)[5]	13.58	13.34	12.99	12.30	10.56
Passenger revenue per ASM (cents)[6]	12.83¢	12.56¢	12.24¢	11.67¢	10.09¢
Operating expenses per ASM (cents)[7]	12.60¢	12.85¢	12.41¢	11.29¢	10.29¢
Operating expenses per ASM, excluding fuel (cents)	8.18¢	8.07¢	7.73¢	7.61¢	7.18¢
Operating expenses per ASM, excluding fuel and profit sharing (cents)	8.01¢	7.98	7.65¢	7.45¢	7.15¢
Fuel costs per gallon, including fuel tax	$ 3.16	$ 3.30	$ 3.19	$ 2.51	$ 2.12
Fuel costs per gallon, including fuel tax, economic	$ 3.12	$ 3.28	$ 3.19	$ 2.39	$ 1.97
Fuel consumed, in gallons (millions)	1,818	1,847	1,764	1,437	1,428
Active full-time equivalent employees	44,831	45,861	45,392	34,901	34,726
Aircraft in service at period end[8]	680	694	698	548	537

[1] A revenue passenger-mile is one paying passenger flown 1 mile.

[2] An available seat-mile (ASM) is one seat (empty or full) flown 1 mile; also referred to as "capacity," which is a measure of the space available to carry passengers in a given period.

[3] Revenue passenger-miles divided by available seat-miles.

[4] Calculated as passenger revenue divided by revenue passenger-miles. It represents the average cost paid by a paying passenger to fly 1 mile.

[5] Calculated as operating revenue divided by available seat-miles. It is a measure of operating revenue production based on the total available seat-miles flown during a particular period.

[6] Calculated as passenger revenue divided by available seat-miles. It is a measure of passenger revenue production based on the total available seat-miles flown during a particular period.

[7] Calculated as operating expenses divided by available seat-miles. Also referred to as *unit costs* or *cost per available seat-mile*, this is the average cost of flying an aircraft seat (empty or full) 1 mile.

[8] Includes leased aircraft and excludes aircraft that were not available for service, in storage, held for sale, or held for return to the lessor.

Source: Company 10-K report, 2013.

EXHIBIT 3

Select Operating and Financial Data for Major U.S. Airline Carriers, 1995, 2000, 2005, 2010–2013

	1995	2000	2005	2010	2011	2012	2013
Passengers (millions)	559.0	666.2	738.3	720.5	730.8	736.6	758.9
Flights (thousands)	8,062.0	9,035.0	11,564.0	9,521.0	9,478.0	9,284	9,161
Revenue passenger-miles (billions)	603.4	692.8	778.6	798.0	814.4	823.2	840.4
Available seat-miles (billions)	807.1	987.9	1,002.7	972.6	992.7	994.5	1,011.2
Load factor (%)	67.0	72.4	77.7	82.0	82.0	82.8	83.1
Passenger revenues (millions)	$69,470	$93,622	$93,500	$103,978	$114,299	$115,975	$120,640
Operating profit (loss) (millions)	$ 5,852	$ 6,999	$ 427	$ 9,344	$ 7,035	$ 7,516	$ 12,548
Net profit (loss) excluding one-time charges and gains (millions)	$ 2,283	$ 2,486	($5,782)	$ 3,665	$ 1,392	$ 360	$ 12,771
Total employees	546,987	679,967	562,467	531,224	538,300	547,558	n.a.

n.a. Not available

Source: Air Transport Association, *2005 Economic Report*, p. 7; and U.S. Department of Transportation, Bureau of Transportation Statistics, "Airline Traffic Data" press releases, various years.

Kelleher was a strong believer in the principle that employees—not customers—came first:[9]

> You have to treat your employees like your customers. When you treat them right, then they will treat your outside customers right. That has been a very powerful competitive weapon for us. You've got to take the time to listen to people's ideas. If you just tell somebody no, that's an act of power and, in my opinion, an abuse of power. You don't want to constrain people in their thinking.

Another indication of the importance that Kelleher placed on employees was the message he had penned in 1990 that was prominently displayed in the lobby of Southwest's headquarters in Dallas:

> The people of Southwest Airlines are "the creators" of what we have become—and of what we will be.
> Our people transformed an idea into a legend. That legend will continue to grow only so long as it is nourished—by our people's indomitable spirit, boundless energy, immense goodwill, and burning desire to excel.
> Our thanks—and our love—to the people of Southwest Airlines for creating a marvelous family and a wondrous airline.

In June 2001, Herb Kelleher stepped down as CEO but continued on in his role as the chairman of

Southwest's board of directors and the head of the board's executive committee; as chairman, he played a lead role in Southwest's strategy, expansion to new cities and aircraft scheduling, and government and industry affairs. In May 2008, after more than 40 years of leadership at Southwest, Kelleher retired as chairman (but he remained a full-time Southwest employee until July 2013 and carried the title of chairman emeritus in 2014).

Executive Leadership at Southwest: 2001–2014

In June 2001, Southwest Airlines, responding to anxious investor concerns about the company's leadership succession plans, began an orderly transfer of power and responsibilities from Herb Kelleher, age 70, to two of his most trusted protégés: James F. Parker, 54, Southwest's general counsel, succeeded Kelleher as CEO; Colleen Barrett, 56, Southwest's executive vice president—customers and self-described keeper of Southwest's pep-rally corporate culture, became president and chief operating officer.

James Parker, Southwest's CEO, 2001–2004

James Parker's association with Herb Kelleher went back 23 years to the time when they were colleagues at Kelleher's old law firm. Parker moved over to Southwest from the law firm in February 1986. Parker's profile inside the company as Southwest's vice president and general counsel had been relatively low, but he was Southwest's chief labor negotiator, and much of the credit for Southwest's good relations with employee unions belonged to Parker. Parker and Kelleher were said to think much alike, and Parker was regarded as having a good sense of humor, although he did not have as colorful and flamboyant a personality as Kelleher. Parker was seen as an honest, straight-arrow kind of person who had a strong grasp of Southwest's culture and market niche and who could be nice or tough, depending on the situation. When his appointment as CEO was announced, Parker said:[10]

> There is going to be no change of course insofar as Southwest is concerned. We have a very experienced leadership team. We've all worked together for a long time. There will be evolutionary changes in Southwest, just as there have always been in our history. We're going to stay true to our business model of being a low-cost, low-fare airline.

Parker retired unexpectedly, for personal reasons, in July 2004, stepping down as CEO and vice chairman of the board and resigning from the company's board of directors. He was succeeded by Gary C. Kelly.

Colleen Barrett, Southwest's President, 2001–2008

Barrett began working with Kelleher as his legal secretary in 1967 and had been with Southwest since 1978. As executive vice president–customers, Barrett had a high profile among Southwest employees and spent most of her time on culture building, morale building, and customer service; her goal was to ensure that employees felt good about what they were doing and empowered to serve the cause of Southwest Airlines.[11] She and Kelleher were regarded as Southwest's guiding lights, and some analysts said she was essentially functioning as the company's chief operating officer prior to her formal appointment as president. Much of the credit for the company's strong record of customer service and its strong-culture work climate belonged to Barrett.

Barrett had been the driving force behind lining the hallways at Southwest's headquarters with photos of company events and trying to create a family atmosphere at the company. Believing it was important to make employees feel cared about and important, Barrett had put together a network of contacts across the company to help her stay in touch with what was happening with employees and their families. When network members learned about events that were worthy of acknowledgment, the word quickly got to Barrett; the information went into a database, and an appropriate greeting card or gift was sent. Barrett had a remarkable ability to give gifts that were individualized and connected her to the recipient.[12]

Barrett was the first woman appointed as president and COO of a major U.S. airline. In October 2001, *Fortune* included Colleen Barrett on its list of the 50 most powerful women in American business (she was ranked number 20). Barrett retired as president in July 2008.

Gary C. Kelly, Southwest's CEO, 2004–Present

Gary Kelly was appointed vice chairman of the board of directors and chief executive officer of Southwest effective July 15, 2004. Prior to that time, Kelly was executive vice president and chief financial officer from 2001 to 2004 and vice president–finance and chief financial officer from 1989 to 2001. He joined Southwest in 1986 as its controller. In 2008, effective with the retirement of Kelleher and Barrett, Kelly assumed the titles of chairman of the board and president, in addition to serving as CEO.

When Kelly was named CEO in 2004, Herb Kelleher said:[13]

> Gary Kelly is one of our brightest stars, well respected throughout the industry and well known, over more than a decade, to the media, analyst, and investor communities for his excellence. As part of our Board's succession planning, we had already focused on Gary as Jim Parker's successor, and that process has simply been accelerated by Jim's personal decision to retire. Under Gary's leadership, Southwest

has achieved the strongest balance sheet in the American airline industry; the best fuel hedging position in our industry; and tremendous progress in technology.

In his first two years as CEO, Kelly and other top-level Southwest executives sharpened and fine-tuned Southwest's strategy in a number of areas, continued to expand operations (both adding more flights and initiating service to new airports), and worked to maintain the company's low-cost advantage over its domestic rivals.

Kelly saw four factors as keys to Southwest's recipe for success:[14]

- Hire great people, treat 'em like family.
- Care for our Customers warmly and personally, like they're guests in our home.
- Keep fares and operating costs lower than anybody else by being safe, efficient, and operationally excellent.
- Stay prepared for bad times with a strong balance sheet, lots of cash, and a stout fuel hedge.

To guide Southwest's efforts to be a standout performer on these four key success factors, Kelly had established five strategic objectives for the company:[15]

- Be the best place to work.
- Be the safest, most efficient, and most reliable airline in the world.
- Offer customers a convenient flight schedule with lots of flights to lots of places they want to go.
- Offer customers the best overall travel experience.
- Do all of these things in a way that maintains a low-cost structure and the ability to offer low fares.

In 2008–2009, Kelly initiated a slight revision of Southwest's mission statement and spearheaded a vision statement that called for a steadfast focus on a triple bottom line of "Performance, People, and Planet" (see Exhibit 4).

In 2010, Kelly initiated one of the biggest strategic moves in the company's history: the acquisition of AirTran Airways, a low-fare, low-cost airline that served 70 airports in the United States, Mexico, and the Caribbean (19 of the airports AirTran served coincided with airports served by Southwest). In 2011, Kelly initiated a five-year strategic plan that featured five strategic initiatives:

- Integrating AirTran into Southwest.
- Modernizing Southwest Airlines' existing aircraft fleet.
- Adding over 100 new Boeing 737-800 aircraft to the Southwest fleet.
- Launching international service and a new reservation system.
- Growing membership in the company's Rapid Rewards frequent-flyer program.

In his Letter to the Shareholders in Southwest's 2013 annual report, Kelly said:

We are now in the fourth year of a bold five-year strategic plan that began in 2011. We believe our five Strategic Initiatives are transformative with the potential to drive more revenue, reduce unit costs, and make Southwest more competitive. The world has changed dramatically since 2000. Our competitors took draconian measures, including massive layoffs and pay cuts, to adjust to today's economic realities and have been given new life through the use of federal bankruptcy laws. Thanks to the hard work and extraordinary efforts of our Southwest Warriors, Southwest has adjusted through incredible Teamwork and unwavering resolve to execute our strategic plan. We have survived the onslaught of challenges to remain profitable for 41 consecutive years, remain the nation's largest airline in terms of domestic originating passengers boarded, and operate the largest Boeing fleet in the world. The transformation hasn't been easy, but it was necessary, and we made significant and successful progress in 2013.

Southwest Airlines' Strategy in 2014

From day one, Southwest had pursued a low-cost, low-price, no-frills strategy to make air travel affordable to a wide segment of the population. While specific aspects of the strategy had evolved over the years, three strategic themes had characterized the company's strategy throughout its existence and still had high profiles in 2014:

EXHIBIT 4

Southwest Airlines' Mission, Vision, and Triple-Bottom-Line Commitment to Performance, People, and Planet

THE MISSION OF SOUTHWEST AIRLINES The mission of Southwest Airlines is dedication to the highest quality of Customer Service delivered with a sense of warmth, friendliness, individual pride, and Company Spirit.
OUR VISION Become the world's most loved, most fl own, and most profitable airline.

TO OUR EMPLOYEES We are committed to provide our Employees a stable work environment with equal opportunity for learning and personal growth. Creativity and innovation are encouraged for improving the effectiveness of Southwest Airlines. Above all, Employees will be provided the same concern, respect, and caring attitude within the organization that they are expected to share externally with every Southwest Customer.

TO OUR COMMUNITIES Our goal is to be the hometown airline of every community we serve, and because those communities sustain and nurture us with their support and loyalty, it is vital that we, as individuals and in groups, embrace each community with the SOUTHWEST SPIRIT of involvement, service, and caring to make those communities better places to live and work.

TO OUR PLANET We strive to be a good environmental steward across our system in all of our hometowns, and one component of our stewardship is efficiency, which, by its very nature, translates to eliminating waste and conserving resources. Using cost-effective and environmentally benefi cial operating procedures (including facilities and equipment) allows us to reduce the amount of materials we use and, when combined with our ability to reuse and recycle material, preserves these environmental resources.

TO OUR STAKEHOLDERS Southwest's vision for a sustainable future is one where there will be a balance in our business model between Employees and Community, the Environment, and our Financial Viability. In order to protect our world for future generations, while meeting our commitments to our Employees, Customers, and Stakeholders, we will strive to lead our industry in innovative efficiency that conserves natural resources, maintains a creative and innovative workforce, and gives back to the Communities in which we live and work.

Source: Southwest Airlines, "One Report, 2009," www.southwest.com (accessed August 20, 2010).

- Charge fares that were very price-competitive and, in some cases, appealingly lower than what rival airlines were charging.
- Create and sustain a low-cost operating structure.
- Make it fun to fly on Southwest, and provide customers with a top-notch travel experience.

Fare Structure Strategy

Southwest employed a relatively simple fare structure displayed in ways that made it easy for customers to choose the fare they preferred. In 2014, Southwest's fares were bundled into four major categories: "Wanna Get Away," "Anytime," "Business Select," and fares for seniors (people 65 and older):

1. Wanna Get Away fares were always the lowest fares and were subject to advance purchase requirements. No fee was charged for changing a previously purchased ticket to a different time or day of travel (rival airlines charged a change fee of $100 to $175), but applicable

fare differences were applied. The purchase price was nonrefundable, but the funds could be applied to future travel on Southwest, provided the tickets were not canceled or changed within 10 minutes of a flight's scheduled departure.

2. *Anytime* fares were refundable and changeable, and funds could be applied toward future travel on Southwest. Anytime fares included a higher frequent-flyer point multiplier under Southwest's Rapid Rewards frequent-flyer program than did Wanna Get Away fares.

3. *Business Select* fares were refundable and changeable, and funds could be applied toward future travel on Southwest. Business Select fares included additional perks such as priority boarding, a higher frequent-flyer point multiplier than other Southwest fares (including twice as many points per dollar spent as compared to Wanna Get Away fares), priority security and ticket counter access in select airports, and one complimentary adult beverage

coupon for the day of travel (for customers of legal drinking age). The Business Select fare had been introduced in 2007 to help attract economy-minded business travelers.

4. *Senior* fares were typically priced between the Wanna Get Away and Anytime fares. No fee was charged for changing a previously purchased ticket to a different time or day of travel, but applicable fare differences were applied. The purchase price was nonrefundable, but funds could be applied to future travel on Southwest, provided the tickets were not canceled or changed within 10 minutes of a flight's scheduled departure. Fares for seniors were not displayed on the list of fare options at the company's website unless customers checked a box indicating that one or more passengers were 65 years of age or older.

In 2008, rival airlines instituted a series of add-on fees—including a fuel surcharge for each flight, fees for checking bags, fees for processing frequent flyer travel awards, fees for buying a ticket in person at the airport or calling a toll-free number to speak with a ticket agent to make a reservation, fees for changing a previously purchased ticket to a different flight, and fees for certain in-flight snacks and beverages—to help defray skyrocketing costs for jet fuel (which had climbed from about 15 percent of operating expenses in 2000 to 40 percent of operating expenses in mid-2008) and try to bolster their operating performance. In 2014, Frontier Airlines announced that it would begin charging passengers fees of $20 to $50 for using the overhead bins to store carry-on luggage and other items and fees of $3 to $15 to preselect a seat; Frontier also charged $1.99 for bottled water and soft drinks on its flights. Southwest, however, chose to forgo "à la carte" pricing and stuck with an all-inclusive fare price. During 2009 and periodically thereafter, Southwest ran "Bags Fly Free" ad campaigns to publicize the cost savings of flying Southwest rather than paying the $20 to $50 fees that rival airlines charged for a first or second checked bag. Southwest also ran ads promoting its policy of not charging a fee for changing a previously purchased ticket to a different flight.

When advance reservations were weak for particular weeks or times of the day or on certain routes, Southwest made a regular practice of initiating special fare promotions to stimulate ticket sales on flights that otherwise would have had numerous empty seats. The company's use of special fare sales and Bags Fly Free ads to combat slack air travel during much of the Great Recession in 2008–2009 resulted in company-record load factors (the percentage of all available seats on all flights that were occupied by fare-paying passengers) for every month from July through December 2009.

Southwest was a shrewd practitioner of the concept of price elasticity, proving in one market after another that the revenue gains from increased ticket sales and the volume of passenger traffic would more than compensate for the revenue erosion associated with low fares. When Southwest entered the Florida market with an introductory $17 fare from Tampa to Fort Lauderdale, the number of annual passengers flying the Tampa–Fort Lauderdale route jumped 50 percent, to more than 330,000. In Manchester, New Hampshire, passenger counts went from 1.1 million in 1997, the year prior to Southwest's entry, to 3.5 million in 2000, and average one-way fares dropped from just over $300 to $129. Southwest's success in stimulating higher passenger traffic at airports across the United States via low fares and frequent flights was coined the "Southwest Effect" by personnel at the U.S. Department of Transportation. (See Exhibit 6 for a list of the cities and airports Southwest Airlines served in July 2014.)

AirTran's Fare Structure AirTran had a fare structure that included business class fares and competitively priced economy class fares. AirTran business class fares were refundable and changeable, and included such perks as priority boarding, oversized seats with additional leg room, bonus frequent-flyer credit, no first- or second-bag fees, and complimentary cocktails on board. Business class upgrades could be purchased within 24 hours of travel for a fee ranging from $69 to $139 (depending on the length of the flight). All other AirTran fares were nonrefundable but could be changed prior to departure for a service fee of $150 per person. AirTran also imposed fees for checked baggage ($25 for the first checked bag and $35 for the second checked bag), advance seat assignments, priority boarding, ticket booking through the customer call center, ticket cancellation ($150 per ticket), and assorted other services.

Southwest's Strategy to Create and Sustain Low-Cost Operations

Southwest management fully understood that earning attractive profits by charging low fares necessitated the use of strategy elements that would enable the company to become a low-cost provider of commercial air service. There were three main components of Southwest's strategic actions to achieve a low-cost operating structure: using a single aircraft type for all flights, creating an operationally efficient point-to-point route structure, and striving to perform all value chain activities in a cost-efficient manner.

Use of a Single Aircraft Type

For many years, Southwest's aircraft fleets had consisted only of Boeing 737 aircraft. Operating only one type of aircraft produced many cost-saving benefits: minimizing the size of spare-parts inventories, simplifying the training of maintenance and repair personnel, improving the proficiency and speed with which maintenance routines could be done, and simplifying the task of scheduling planes for particular flights. In 2013, Southwest operated the biggest fleet of Boeing 737 aircraft in the world. Exhibit 5 provides information about Southwest's aircraft fleet.

Southwest's Point-to-Point Route Structure Strategy

Southwest's point-to-point scheduling of flights was more cost-efficient than the hub-and-spoke systems used by almost all rival airlines. Hub-and-spoke systems involved passengers on many different flights coming in from spoke locations (and sometimes another hub) to a central airport or hub within a short span of time and then connecting to an outgoing flight to their destination—a spoke location or another hub. Most flights arrived at and departed from a hub during a two-hour window, creating big peak-valley swings in airport personnel workloads and gate utilization; airport personnel and gate areas were very busy when hub operations were in full swing and then were underutilized in the interval awaiting the next round of inbound and outbound flights. In contrast, Southwest's point-to-point routes permitted scheduling aircraft so as to minimize the time aircraft were at the gate, currently approximately

25 minutes, thereby reducing the number of aircraft and gate facilities that would otherwise be required. Furthermore, with a relatively even flow of incoming and outgoing flights and gate traffic, Southwest could staff its terminal operations to handle a fairly steady workload across a day, whereas hub-and-spoke operators had to staff their operations to serve three to four daily peak periods.

Exhibit 6 shows the cities and airports served by Southwest in mid-2014. Going into 2014, Southwest had nonstop service between 524 airports. In 2013, Southwest's average passenger airfare was $154.72 one way, and the average passenger trip length was approximately 966 miles.

Striving to Perform All Value Chain Activities Cost-Effectively

Southwest made a point of scrutinizing every aspect of its operations to find ways to trim costs. The company's strategic actions to reduce or at least contain costs were extensive and ongoing:

- Sharply rising prices for jet fuel over the past 12 years that caused fuel expenses to rise from 16.5 percent of total operating expenses in 2003 to between 28 and 38 percent of total operating expenses since 2006 had prompted a number of projects to increase fuel efficiency, including:

  - Installing "blended winglets" on all of Southwest's planes beginning in 2007 and then, in 2014, starting to upgrade its aircraft fleet with newly designed split-scimitar winglets (see Exhibit 7). These winglets reduced lift drag, allowed aircraft to climb more steeply and reach higher flight levels quicker, improved cruising performance, helped extend engine life and reduce maintenance costs, and reduced fuel burn.

  - Using auto-throttle and vertical navigation procedures to maintain optimum cruising speeds.

  - Introducing new engine start procedures to support using a single engine for runway taxiing.

  - Reducing engine aircraft idle speed while on the ground.

- Southwest was the first major airline to introduce ticketless travel (eliminating the need to

EXHIBIT 5

Southwest's Aircraft Fleet as of December 31, 2013

Type of Aircraft	Number	Seats	Average Age (years)	Comments
Boeing 717-200	66	117	12	All of these were AirTran aircraft that were in the process of being removed from the Southwest fleet and leased or subleased to Delta Air Lines.
Boeing 737-300	122	137/143	20	Southwest was Boeing's launch customer for this model.
Boeing 737-500	15	122	22	Southwest was Boeing's launch customer for this model.
Boeing 737-700	425	137/143	9	Southwest was Boeing's launch customer for this model in 1997. As of April 2013, all were equipped with satellite-delivered broadband Internet-reception capability.
Boeing 737-800	52	175	1	As of April 2013, all were equipped with satellite-delivered broadband Internet-reception capability.
Total	541			

Other Fleet-Related Facts

Average age of aircraft fleet	Approximately 11 years
Average aircraft trip length	708 miles, with an average duration of 1 hour and 59 minutes
Average aircraft utilization per day	Nearly 6 flights and 10 hours and 43 minutes of flight time
Fleet size:	106
1990	224
1995	344
2000	537
2009	
Firm orders for new aircraft:	33
2014	19
2015	31
2016	225
2017–2024:	

Source: Information at www.southwest.com (accessed May 7, 2014).

EXHIBIT 6

Airports and Cities Served by Southwest Airlines, July 2014

Southwest's Top-10 Airports, by Departures

Airport/City	Daily Departures	Gates	Nonstop Cities Served
Chicago Midway	233	32	64
Las Vegas	210	19	54
Baltimore/Washington	206	28	57

Denver	167	19	56
Houston (Hobby)	161	19	45
Atlanta	165	31	44
Phoenix	162	24	46
Dallas (Love Field)	124	15	18
Orlando	120	20	43
Los Angeles	104	12	23

Other Airports Served by Southwest Airlines

Akron, OH	Fort Myers/Naples	Norfolk	San Francisco
Albany	Greenville/Spartanburg, SC	Oakland	San Jose
Albuquerque	Harlingen/South Padre Island, TX	Oklahoma City	Seattle/Tacoma
Amarillo	Grand Rapids, MI	Omaha	Spokane
Austin	Hartford/Springfield	Ontario, CA	Tampa
Birmingham	Indianapolis	Orange County, CA	Tucson
Boise	Jacksonville	Panama City, FL	Tulsa
Boston Logan	Kansas City	Pensacola, FL	Washington, DC (Dulles)
Buffalo	Little Rock	Philadelphia	Washington, DC (Reagan
Burbank, CA	Long Island	Pittsburgh	National)
Charleston	Louisville	Portland, OR	West Palm Beach
Charlotte	Lubbock	Portland, ME	Wichita, KS
Cleveland	Manchester, NH	Providence	International
Columbus, OH	Memphis	Raleigh-Durham	Aruba
Corpus Christi, TX	Midland/Odessa, TX	Reno/Tahoe	Cabo San Lucas, Mexico
Dayton, OH	Milwaukee	Richmond	Cancun, Mexico
Detroit Metro	Minneapolis/St. Paul	Rochester	Mexico City
Des Moines	Nashville	Sacramento	Montego Bay, Jamaica
El Paso	Newark	St. Louis	Nassau, Bahamas
Flint, MI	New Orleans	Salt Lake City	Punta Cana, Dominican Republic
Fort Lauderdale	New York (LaGuardia)	San Antonio	San Juan, Puerto Rico

Source: Company 10-K report, 2013; and information at www.southwest.com (accessed April 29, 2014).

EXHIBIT 7

Southwest's Fuel-Saving Blended Winglets and Split-Scimitar Winglets

Southwest Airlines plane on runway

Southwest Airlines, tail of plane

print and process paper tickets); by 2007, ticket-less travel accounted for more than 95 percent of all ticket sales.

- Southwest was also the first airline to allow customers to make reservations and purchase tickets at the company's website (thus bypassing the need to pay commissions to travel agents for handling the ticketing process and reducing staffing requirements at Southwest's reservation centers). Selling a ticket on its website cost Southwest roughly $1 versus $3 to $4 for a ticket booked through its own internal reservation system and as much as $15 each for tickets purchased through travel agents and professional business travel partners. Online ticket sales at Southwest's website grew swiftly, accounting for 74 percent of Southwest's revenues in 2009 and 80 percent of all company bookings in 2013.

- For most of its history, Southwest stressed flights into and out of airports in medium-sized cities and less congested airports in major metropolitan areas (Chicago Midway, Detroit Metro, Houston Hobby, Dallas Love Field, Baltimore-Washington International, Burbank, Manchester, Oakland, San Jose, Providence, and Ft. Lauderdale–Hollywood). This strategy helped produce better-than-average on-time performance and reduce the fuel costs associated with planes sitting in line on crowded taxiways or circling airports waiting for clearance to land. It further allowed the company to avoid paying the higher landing fees and terminal gate costs at such high-traffic airports as Atlanta's Hartsfield International, Chicago's O'Hare, and Dallas–Fort Worth, where landing slots were controlled and rationed to those airlines willing to pay the high fees. More recently, however, having already initiated service to almost all of the medium-sized cities and less congested airports where there were good opportunities for sustained growth in passenger traffic and revenues, Southwest had begun initiating service to airports in large metropolitan cities where air traffic congestion was a frequent problem, such as Los Angeles (LAX), Boston's Logan International, New York LaGuardia, Denver, San

Francisco, Philadelphia, and Atlanta (when it acquired AirTran).

- To economize on the amount of time it took terminal personnel to check passengers in and to simplify the whole task of making reservations, Southwest dispensed with the practice of assigning each passenger a reserved seat. Initially, passengers were given color-coded plastic cards marked with the letter *A, B,* or *C* when they checked in at the boarding gate. Passengers then boarded in groups, according to their card color and letter, and sat in any seat that was vacant when they got on the plane. In 2002, Southwest abandoned the use of plastic cards and began printing a big, bold *A, B,* or *C* on the boarding pass when the passenger checked in at the ticket counter; passengers then boarded in groups according to the letter on their boarding pass. In 2007–2008, Southwest introduced an enhanced boarding method that automatically assigned each passenger a specific number within the passenger's boarding group at the time of check-in; passengers then boarded the aircraft in that numerical order. All passengers could check in online up to 24 hours before departure time and print out a boarding pass, thus bypassing counter check-in (unless they wished to check baggage).

- Southwest flight attendants were responsible for cleaning up trash left by deplaning passengers and otherwise getting the plane presentable for passengers to board for the next flight. Rival carriers had cleaning crews come on board to perform this function until they incurred heavy losses in 2001–2005 and were forced to institute stringent cost-cutting measures that included abandoning use of cleaning crews and copying Southwest's practice.

- Southwest did not have a first-class section in any of its planes and had no fancy clubs for its frequent flyers to relax in at terminals.

- Southwest did not provide passengers with baggage transfer services to other carriers: passengers with checked baggage who were connecting to other carriers to reach their destination were responsible for picking up their luggage at Southwest's baggage claim and then getting it to the check-in facilities of the connecting carrier. (Southwest booked tickets involving only its own flights; customers connecting to flights on other carriers had to book such tickets through either travel agents or the connecting airline).

- Starting in 2001, Southwest began converting from cloth to leather seats; the team of Southwest employees that investigated the economics of the conversion concluded that an all-leather interior would be more durable and easier to maintain, more than justifying the higher initial costs.

- Southwest was a first mover among major U.S. airlines in employing fuel hedging and derivative contracts to counteract rising prices for crude oil and jet fuel. From 1998 through 2008, the company's fuel-hedging activities produced fuel cost savings of about $4 billion over what the company would have spent had it paid the industry's average price for jet fuel. But unexpectedly large declines in jet fuel prices in late 2008 and 2009 resulted in reported losses of $408 million on the fuel-hedging contracts that the company had in place during 2009. Since then, the company's fuel-hedging activities had continued to be ineffective in reducing fuel expenses; the company recognized losses on its fuel-hedging activities of $324 million in 2010, $259 million in 2011, $157 million in 2012, and $118 million in 2013. Southwest's fuel-hedging strategy involved modifying the amount of its future fuel requirements that were hedged based on management's judgments about the forward market prices of crude oil and jet fuel. As of January 2014, the company had fuel derivative contracts in place for about 20 percent of its expected fuel consumption in 2014, about 40 percent of its expected fuel consumption in 2015, and about 35 percent of its expected fuel consumption in 2016.

- Southwest regularly upgraded and enhanced its management information systems to speed data flows, improve operating efficiency, lower costs, and upgrade its customer service capabilities. In 2001, Southwest implemented the use of new software that significantly decreased the time required to generate optimal crew schedules and helped improve on-time performance. In 2007–2008, Southwest invested in next-generation technology and software to improve its ticketless system and its back-office accounting, payroll, and human resource information systems. During 2009, the company replaced or enhanced its point-of-sale, electronic ticketing and boarding, and revenue accounting systems. During 2010, it completed an initiative to convert to a new SAP enterprise resource planning application that would replace its general ledger, accounts payable, accounts receivable, payroll, benefits, cash management, and fixed-asset systems; the conversion was designed to increase data accuracy and consistency and lower administrative support costs.

For many decades, Southwest's operating costs had been lower than those of rival U.S. airline carriers; see Exhibit 8 for comparative *costs per revenue passenger-mile* among the five major U.S. airlines during the 1995–2013 period. Exhibit 9 shows trends in Southwest's operating *costs per available seat-mile* rather than per passenger-occupied seat.

Making It Fun to Fly Southwest: The Strategy to Provide a Top-Notch Travel Experience

Southwest's approach to delivering good customer service and building a loyal customer clientele was predicated on presenting a happy face to passengers, displaying a fun-loving attitude, and doing things in a manner calculated to provide passengers with a positive flying experience. The company made a special effort to employ gate personnel who enjoyed interacting with customers, had good interpersonal skills, and displayed cheery, outgoing personalities. A number of Southwest's gate personnel let their wit and sense of humor show by sometimes entertaining those in the gate area with trivia questions or contests such as "Who has the biggest hole in their sock?" Apart from greeting passengers coming onto planes and assisting them in finding vacant seats and stowing baggage, flight attendants were encouraged to be engaging, converse and joke with passengers, and go about their tasks in ways that made passengers smile. On some flights, attendants sang announcements to

EXHIBIT 8

Comparative Operating Cost Statistics per Revenue Passenger-Mile, Major U.S. Airlines, 1995, 2000, 2005, 2010–2013

	Total Salaries and Fringe Benefits		Costs Incurred per Revenue Passenger-Mile (in cents)								
	Pilots and Copilots	All Employees	Fuel and Oil	Maintenance	Rentals	Landing Fees	Advertising	General and Administrative	Other Operating Expenses	Total Operating Expenses
American Airlines										
1995	0.94¢	5.59¢	1.53¢	1.34¢	0.59¢	0.22¢	0.19¢	1.14¢	3.65¢	14.25¢
2000	1.16	5.77	2.04	1.90	0.48	0.23	0.18	0.58	3.30	14.48
2005	0.90	4.65	3.67	1.42	0.41	0.32	0.10	0.95	3.66	15.18
2010	0.88	5.18	4.57	1.92	0.47	0.35	0.13	1.23	3.68	17.53
2011	0.89	5.27	5.82	1.91	0.51	0.31	0.15	1.82	4.07	19.87
2012	0.86	5.17	6.10	1.87	0.43	0.30	0.12	1.91	3.70	19.61
2013	0.91	4.39	5.94	1.82	0.57	0.31	0.14	1.35	4.38	18.90
Delta Air Lines										
1995	1.27¢	4.97¢	1.70¢	1.16¢	0.71¢	0.30¢	0.18¢	0.43¢	4.07¢	13.53¢
2000	1.27	5.08	1.73	1.41	0.54	0.22	0.12	0.74	3.03	12.85
2005	0.93	4.31	3.68	1.10	0.38	0.22	0.16	0.84	6.01	16.69
2010	0.91	4.15	4.51	1.33	0.14	0.28	0.10	0.64	6.26	17.41
2011	0.95	4.27	5.77	1.41	0.15	0.28	0.13	0.54	7.09	19.65
2012	0.99	4.57	5.97	1.53	0.15	0.28	0.14	0.71	6.85	20.21
2013	1.11	4.82	5.42	1.58	0.13	0.28	0.13	0.68	6.61	19.65
Southwest Airlines										
1995	0.92¢	3.94¢	1.56¢	1.21¢	0.79¢	0.35¢	0.41¢	1.09¢	1.56¢	10.91¢
2000	0.86	4.22	1.95	1.22	0.48	0.31	0.35	1.42	0.96	10.91
2005	1.18	4.70	2.44	1.17	0.31	0.34	0.29	0.73	1.23	11.21
2010	1.37	4.97	4.63	1.47	0.28	0.46	0.26	0.83	1.32	14.23
2011	1.37	4.99	5.76	1.47	0.23	0.45	0.26	0.98	1.35	15.50
2012	1.57	5.66	6.70	1.86	0.42	0.51	0.26	1.29	1.72	18.43
2013	1.59	5.87	6.38	1.85	0.46	0.52	0.23	1.21	1.68	18.19

United Airlines									
1995	0.86¢	4.73¢	1.51¢	0.90¢	0.17¢	0.29¢	0.53¢	2.92¢	12.58¢
2000	1.15	5.75	1.84	0.73	0.21	0.28	0.76	3.09	14.65
2005	0.62	3.72	1.60	0.35	0.16	0.30	0.60	5.09	15.35
2010	0.67	4.34	1.86	0.32	0.06	0.38	1.31	5.24	17.96
2011	0.69	4.38	2.14	0.32	0.08	0.36	1.38	6.07	20.34
2012	0.74	4.71	1.72	0.44	0.09	0.35	1.57	5.84	20.69
2013	0.95	5.01	1.70	0.41	0.10	0.35	1.38	6.19	20.74
US Airways									
1995	1.55¢	7.53¢	2.09¢	1.05¢	0.13¢	0.29¢	0.73¢	4.32¢	17.73¢
2000	1.36	7.59	2.30	0.97	0.19	0.28	1.10	4.81	19.68
2005	0.78	3.74	1.50	1.06	0.06	0.31	0.66	7.26	18.49
2010	0.74	4.03	1.82	1.17	0.02	0.27	1.07	6.93	19.36
2011	0.72	3.96	1.82	1.09	0.03	0.27	1.02	7.47	21.24
2012	0.76	4.20	1.78	1.06	0.02	0.28	1.30	7.10	21.30
2013	0.75	4.29	1.69	0.93	0.02	0.29	1.93	6.68	21.06

Note 1: Cost per revenue passenger-mile for each of the cost categories in this table is calculated by dividing the total costs for each cost category by the total number of revenue passenger-miles flown, where a revenue passenger-mile is equal to one paying passenger flown 1 mile. Costs incurred per revenue passenger-mile thus represent the costs incurred per ticketed passenger per mile flown.

Note 2: US Airways and America West started merging operations in September 2005, and joint reporting of their operating costs began in late 2007. Effective January 2010, data for Delta Air Lines include the combined operating costs of Delta and Northwest Airlines; the merger of these two companies became official in October 2008. United Airlines acquired Continental Airlines in 2010, and the two companies began joint reporting of operating expenses in 2012.

Source: U.S. Department of Transportation, Bureau of Transportation Statistics, "Air Carrier Statistics," Form 298C, "Summary Data," and Form 41, Schedules P-6, P-12, P-51, and P-52, all for various years.

passengers on takeoff and landing. On one flight, while passengers were boarding, an attendant with bunny ears popped out of an overhead bin exclaiming "Surprise!" The repertoires to amuse passengers varied from flight crew to flight crew.

During their tenure, both Herb Kelleher and Colleen Barrett had made a point of sending congratulatory notes to employees when the company received letters from customers complimenting particular Southwest employees; complaint letters were seen as learning opportunities for employees and reasons to consider making adjustments. Employees were provided the following policy guidance regarding how far to go in trying to please customers:

> No Employee will ever be punished for using good judgment and good old common sense when trying to accommodate a Customer—no matter what our rules are.[16]
>
> When you empower People to make a positive difference everyday, you allow them to decide. Most guidelines are written to be broken as long as the Employee is leaning toward the Customer. We follow the Golden Rule and try to do the right thing and think about our Customer.[17]

Southwest executives believed that conveying a friendly, fun-loving spirit to customers was the key to competitive advantage. As one Southwest manager put it, "Our fares can be matched; our airplanes and routes can be copied. But we pride ourselves on our customer service."[18]

Southwest's emphasis on point-to-point flights enabled many passengers to fly nonstop to their destinations, thereby cutting total trip time and avoiding not only the added built-in travel time needed to make connections but also the oft-encountered delays associated with connecting flights (late incoming flights, potential equipment failures requiring repairs at the gate, and late departures). In recent years, about 72 percent of Southwest's passengers flew nonstop to their destination. Nonstop travel was a major contributor to providing customers with a top-notch travel experience.

In 2007, Southwest invested in an "extreme gate makeover" to improve the airport experience of customers. The makeover included adding (1) a business-focused area with padded seats, tables with power outlets, power stations with stools, and a large-screen TV with news programming and (2) a family-focused area with smaller tables and chairs, power stations for charging electrical devices, and kid-friendly TV programming. Later, Southwest added free wireless Internet service for passengers waiting in its gate areas.

In 2013–2014, Southwest began offering in-flight satellite-based Internet service on all of its 737-700 and 737-800 aircraft, representing over 75 percent of Southwest's fleet. Southwest's arrangement with its Internet service provider enabled the company to control the pricing of in-flight Internet service (which in 2014 was $8 a day per device, including stops and connections). The addition of in-flight Internet service, coupled with the free wireless service available in all of Southwest's gate areas, meant that passengers traveling on a Southwest airplane equipped with satellite Internet service had gate-to-gate connectivity for small portable electronic devices. In early 2014, Southwest was the only carrier currently offering gate-to-gate connectivity on 75 percent of its total aircraft fleet.

In 2013, Southwest joined with DISH Network to give customers free access to 17 live channels and 75 on-demand recorded episodes from various TV series at no additional charge. This promotion was later extended through the end of 2014. Shortly thereafter, Southwest added a selection of movies on demand (currently priced at $5 per movie) to its entertainment offerings and, in December 2013, became the first airline to offer a messaging-only option for $2 a day per device, including all stops and connections. Passengers did not have to purchase in-flight Internet service to access television offerings, movies on demand, or the messaging-only service.

In 2013, Southwest introduced a completely redesigned Southwest mobile website and app for iPhone and Android that had more features and functionality. The app enabled passengers to begin using mobile boarding passes.

Strategic Plan Initiatives, 2011–2015

Integrating Southwest's and AirTran's Operations
The process of integrating AirTran into Southwest's operation began in 2013 and was expected to be completed by year-end 2014. Headed

into 2014, Southwest had completed a number of integration milestones:

- Connecting capabilities between AirTran and Southwest flights had been fully deployed, thereby enabling customers of both Southwest and AirTran to book connecting itineraries between the two carriers and fly between any of the combined 96 Southwest and AirTran destinations on a single itinerary.
- Because AirTran utilized mainly a hub-and-spoke network system, with approximately half of its flights historically originating or terminating at its hub at Hartsfield-Jackson Atlanta International Airport, Southwest had begun gradually transitioning AirTran's Atlanta hub into a point-to-point operation to capture the efficiencies related to the scheduling of aircraft, flight crews, and ground staff. Converting AirTran's flight network into a point-to-point operation was in the final stages.
- In addition to converting AirTran's flight schedules into a point-to-point operation, Southwest had made excellent progress in merging and optimizing the combined Southwest-AirTran flight schedules. The optimization effort involved using a set of Southwest-developed tools for managing revenues and profitability to (1) discontinue service to unprofitable destinations (service to 15 AirTran destinations and four Southwest destinations was discontinued in 2011–2013) and redeploy the aircraft to other routes and markets, (2) adjust the frequencies and arrival-departure times of Southwest and AirTran flights to airports served by both Southwest and AirTran (to avoid having too many unsold seats and better optimize profitability), (3) establish point-to-point flights from airports currently served only by AirTran to select destinations currently served only by Southwest, and (4) establish point-to-point flights from airports currently served only by Southwest to destinations currently served only by AirTran. Southwest had established a Southwest presence in all AirTran cities not currently served by Southwest in preparation for rebranding all AirTran operations and activities as Southwest; already, AirTran operations in

several airports had been rebranded as Southwest. Southwest management expected that optimization and alignment of the Southwest and AirTran flight schedules would produce significant cost savings, enable more efficient scheduling of airport employees, and free up aircraft for redeployment either to new destinations that looked appealing or to existing destinations where more flights were needed to serve the growing numbers of people choosing to fly Southwest Airlines.

- A total of 52 of AirTran's Boeing 737-700 aircraft had completed the process of being converted to the Southwest fleet. Conversion of AirTran's remaining 35 Boeing 737-700 aircraft was scheduled to occur when AirTran's flights to seven international destinations were redesignated as Southwest flights.
- Approximately 65 percent of AirTran employees had been converted to Southwest employees. The transfer of all remaining AirTran employees, including flight crews and dispatchers whose transitions were aligned with aircraft conversion, was scheduled for 2014.
- Southwest had made considerable headway in integrating Southwest's and AirTran's unionized workforces. AirTran's flight attendants, represented by the Association of Flight Attendants—CWA (AFA), had voted to ratify a new collective bargaining agreement with Southwest. The agreement with AFA applied to AirTran flight attendants until they transitioned to Southwest by the end of 2014 and automatically became members of the Transportation Workers of America union representing Southwest's flight attendants.

Southwest's Fleet Modernization Initiative

Southwest had multiple efforts underway to modernize its aircraft fleet. One effort, referred to by Southwest as *Evolve—The New Southwest Experience,* entailed retrofitting and refreshing the cabin interior of its fleet of 425 Boeing 737-700 planes. The goal of the Evolve program was to enhance customer comfort, personal space, and the overall travel experience while improving fleet efficiency and being environmentally responsible. The cabin refresh featured recyclable carpet, a brighter color scheme, and more durable, eco-friendly, and comfortable seats that weighed less than the prior seats. By maximizing the space inside the plane, Evolve allowed for six additional seats on each retrofitted aircraft, along with more climate-friendly and cost-effective materials. Southwest retrofitted 78 of its 737-300 aircraft through Evolve in 2013. In addition, the new 737-800 aircraft entering the company's fleet had the Evolve interior. The 17 AirTran 737-700 aircraft that were transferred to Southwest's fleet at year-end 2013 were refreshed with the new Evolve interior, and the remaining 35 AirTran 737-700 aircraft were scheduled to be refreshed with the Evolve interior when they became a part of the Southwest fleet in the second half of 2014.

Furthermore, Southwest was divesting AirTran's fleet of Boeing 717-200 aircraft. It had negotiated an agreement with Delta Air Lines, Inc., and Boeing Capital Corp. to lease or sublease AirTran's 88 Boeing 717-200 aircraft to Delta. Deliveries to Delta began in September 2013 and were scheduled to continue at the rate of about three aircraft per month. The seating capacity of the AirTran Boeing 717-200 planes was being replaced by (1) extending the retirement dates for a portion of Southwest's 737-300 and 737-500 aircraft, (2) acquiring used Boeing 737 aircraft from other sources, and (3) the forthcoming deliveries of new Boeing 737 aircraft. The company did not want to keep Boeing 717-200 planes in its aircraft fleet because of the added maintenance and repair costs associated with having a second type of plane in the fleet. Moreover, replacing the Boeing 717 aircraft capacity with Boeing 737 capacity provided incremental revenue opportunities because the latter had more seats per aircraft yet cost approximately the same amount to fly on a per-trip basis as the smaller Boeing 717 aircraft.

Incorporating Larger Boeing Aircraft into Southwest's Fleet Starting in 2012, Southwest began a long-term initiative to replace older Southwest aircraft with a new generation of Boeing aircraft that had greater seating capacity, a quieter interior, LED reading and ceiling lighting, improved security features, reduced maintenance requirements, increased fuel efficiency, and the capability to fly longer distances without refueling. Of the

680 active aircraft in Southwest's fleet at year-end 2013, the company had plans to remove 122 Boeing 737-300 aircraft (with 143 seats and an average age of 20 years), 15 Boeing 737-500 aircraft (with 122 seats and an average age of 22 years), and 12 Boeing 717-200 aircraft (with 117 seats and an average age of 12 years) from its fleet over the next five years and replace them with new Boeing 737-700s (143 seats), 737-800s (175 seats), and 737-MAX aircraft (up to 189 seats). While Southwest had added 54 new Boeing 737-700 and 737-800 planes to its fleet in 2012–2013, even bigger additions of new planes were scheduled for future delivery. As of early 2014, Southwest had placed firm orders for 52 Boeing 737-800 aircraft to be delivered in 2014–2015, 56 Boeing 737-700 aircraft to be delivered in 2016–2018 (with options to take delivery on an additional 36 planes), and 200 737-MAX aircraft to be delivered during 2017–2024 (with options to take delivery on an additional 83 planes—Southwest was Boeing's launch customer for the 737-MAX). Plans called for some of the new aircraft to be leased from third parties rather than be purchased; of the company's current fleet of 680 aircraft, 516 were owned and 164 were leased.

Southwest expected that the new Boeing 737-800 and 737-MAX aircraft would significantly enhance the company's capabilities to (1) more economically fly long-haul routes (the number of short-haul flights throughout the domestic airline industry had been declining since 2000), (2) improve scheduling flexibility and more economically serve high-demand, gate-restricted, slot-controlled airports by adding seats to such destinations without increasing the number of flights, and (3) boost overall fuel efficiency to reduce overall costs. Additionally, the aircraft would enable Southwest to profitably expand its operations to new, more distant destinations (including extended routes over water), such as Hawaii, Alaska, Canada, Mexico, and the Caribbean. Southwest management expected that the new Boeing 737-MAX planes would have the lowest operating costs of any single-aisle commercial airplane on the market.

Launching International Service and a New Reservation System In January 2014, Southwest launched an international reservation system separate from its domestic reservation system (but linked to and accessible from www.southwest.com) and began selling tickets for its inaugural international daily nonstop service on Southwest aircraft beginning July 1, 2014, to Jamaica (Montego Bay), the Bahamas (Nassau), and Aruba (Oranjestad). During this first phase of Southwest's international conversion plan, AirTran continued service between Atlanta and Nassau and between Chicago Midway and Montego Bay, as well as flights to and from Cancun, Mexico City, and Cabo San Lucas, Mexico, and Punta Cana, Dominican Republic. AirTran service to all these destinations was scheduled to be converted to Southwest in the second half of 2014. Southwest worked with an outside vendor, Amadeus IT Group, to create and support its international reservation service. In 2014, Southwest was in the planning stages of replacing its existing domestic reservation system with a comprehensive domestic and international system; in May 2014, Southwest chose Amadeus IT Group to be the vendor for this multiyear project.

Growing Southwest's Rapid Rewards Frequent-Flyer Program

Southwest's current Rapid Rewards frequent-flyer program, launched in March 2011, linked free-travel awards to the number of points members earned purchasing tickets to fly Southwest (the previous version of the Rapid Rewards program had tied free-travel awards to the number of flight segments flown during a 24-month period). The amount of points earned was based on the fare and fare class purchased, with higher-fare products (such as Business Select) earning more points than lower-fare products (such as Wanna Get Away). Likewise, the amount of points required to be redeemed for a flight was based on the fare and fare class purchased. Rapid Rewards members could also earn points through qualifying purchases with Southwest's Rapid Rewards Partners (which included car rental agencies, hotels, restaurants, and retail locations), and they could purchase points. Members who opted to obtain a Southwest co-branded Chase Visa credit card, which had an annual fee of $99, earned two points for every dollar spent on purchases of Southwest tickets and on purchases with Southwest's car rental and hotel partners, and they earned one point on every dollar spent everywhere else. Holders of Southwest's co-branded Chase Visa credit card could redeem credit card points for items other than travel on Southwest, including international flights on other airlines, cruises, hotel stays, rental cars, gift cards, event tickets, and other items. The most active members of Southwest's Rapid Rewards program qualified for priority check-in and security lane access (where available), standby priority, and free in-flight WiFi. In addition, members who flew 100 qualifying flights or earned 110,000 qualifying points in a calendar year automatically received a Companion Pass, which provided unlimited free round-trip travel for one year to any destination available via Southwest for a designated companion of the qualifying Rapid Rewards member.

Rapid Rewards members could redeem their points for any available seat, on any day, on any flight, with no blackout dates. Points did not expire as long as the Rapid Rewards member had points-earning activity during the most recent 24 months.

Headed into 2014, the current Rapid Rewards program had exceeded management's expectations with respect to the number of frequent-flyer members added, the amount spent per member on airfare, the number of flights taken by members, the number of Southwest's co-branded Chase Visa credit card holders added, the number of points sold to business partners, and the number of frequent-flyer points purchased by program members.

Southwest allowed both its Rapid Rewards members and the members of AirTran's A1 Rewards frequent-flyer program to transfer their loyalty rewards between the Southwest and AirTran frequent-flyer programs, thus giving them access to the benefits of the combined programs.

In 2013, members of the Southwest and AirTran frequent-flyer programs redeemed approximately 5.4 million flight awards, accounting for approximately 9.5 percent of the revenue passenger-miles flown. This was significantly higher than the 2012 redemptions of approximately 4.5 million flight awards (accounting for approximately 9.0 percent of the revenue passenger-miles flown) and the 2011 redemptions of approximately 3.7 million flight awards (accounting for approximately 8.6 percent of the revenue passenger-miles flown). Southwest's Rapid Rewards members redeemed 2.4 million free-ticket awards during 2009 and 2.8 million free-ticket awards in both 2007 and 2008.

Southwest's Growth Strategy

Southwest's strategy to grow its business consisted of (1) adding more daily flights to the cities and airports it currently served and (2) adding new cities and airports to its route schedule.

It was normal for customer traffic to grow at the airports Southwest served. Hence, opportunities were always emerging for Southwest to capture additional revenues by adding more flights at the airports already being served. Sometimes these opportunities entailed adding more flights to one or more of the same destinations, and sometimes the opportunities entailed adding flights to a broader selection of Southwest destinations, depending on the mix of final destinations the customers departing from a particular airport were flying to.

To spur growth beyond that afforded by adding more daily flights to cities and airports currently being served, it had long been Southwest's practice to add one or more new cities and airports to its route schedule annually. In selecting new cities, Southwest looked for city pairs that could generate substantial amounts of both business and leisure traffic. Management believed that having numerous flights flying the same routes appealed to business travelers looking for convenient flight times and the ability to catch a later flight if they unexpectedly ran late.

As a general rule, Southwest did not initiate service to a city and/or airport unless it envisioned the potential for originating at least eight flights a day there and saw opportunities to add more flights over time; in Denver, for example, Southwest had boosted the number of daily departures from 13 in January 2006 (the month in which service to and from Denver was initiated) to 79 daily departures in 2008, 129 daily departures in May 2010, and 167 daily departures in 2014.

On a number of occasions when rival airlines had cut back flights to cities that Southwest served, Southwest had quickly moved in with more flights of its own, believing its lower fares would attract more passengers. When Midway Airlines ceased operations in November 1990, Southwest moved in overnight and quickly instituted flights to Chicago's Midway Airport. Southwest was a first mover in adding flights on routes where rivals cut their offerings following 9/11. When American Airlines closed its hubs in Nashville and San Jose, Southwest immediately increased the number of its flights into and out of both locations. When US Airways trimmed its flight schedule for Philadelphia and Pittsburgh, Southwest promptly boosted its flights into and out of those airports. Southwest initiated service to Denver when United, beset with financial difficulties, cut back operations at its big Denver hub. In 2014, it was clear that Southwest intended to pick up the pace in adding service to more locations, particularly larger metropolitan airports, places such as Hawaii and Alaska, and international destinations.

Marketing, Advertising, and Promotion Strategies

Southwest was continually on the lookout for novel ways to tell its story, make its distinctive persona come alive, and strike a chord in the minds of air travelers. Many of its print ads and billboards were deliberately unconventional and attention-getting to create and reinforce the company's maverick, fun-loving, and combative image. Previous campaigns had promoted the company's performance as "The Low-Fare Airline" and "The All-Time On-Time Airline" and its Triple Crown awards. One of the company's billboard campaigns touted the frequency of the company's flights with such phrases as "Austin Auften," "Phoenix Phrequently," and "L.A. A.S.A.P." Each holiday season since 1985 Southwest had run a "Christmas card" ad on TV featuring children and their families from the Ronald McDonald Houses and Southwest employees. Fresh advertising campaigns were launched periodically. Exhibit 9 shows four representative ads.

Southwest tended to advertise far more heavily than any other U.S. carrier. According to The Nielsen Company, during the first six months of 2009, Southwest boosted its ad spending by 20 percent to hammer home its "bags fly free" message. Passenger traffic at Southwest subsequently rose, while passenger volumes went in the opposite direction at Southwest's largest competitors—all of which had recently introduced or increased fees for checked baggage.

During 2010–2013, the company periodically launched national and local advertising and promotional campaigns to highlight what management

EXHIBIT 9

Four Samples of Southwest's Ads

Southwest Airlines Ad, "We Came. We Saw. . ."

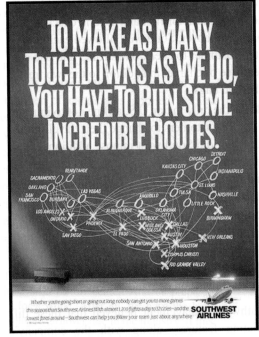

Southwest Airlines Ad, "To Make as Many. . ."

Southwest Airlines Ad, "Bags Fly Free. . ."

Southwest Airlines Ad, "We'd Like to Match Their New. . ."

Source: Southwest Airlines.

company's Annual Awards Banquet, and supporting the Corporate Culture Committee. Each major department and geographic operating unit had a Local Culture Committee charged with organizing culture-building activities and nurturing the Southwest Spirit within its unit. More recently, the company created a new position in each of its major operating departments and largest geographic locations called *culture ambassador;* the primary function of culture ambassadors was to nurture the Southwest Spirit by helping ensure that the Local Culture Committee had the resources needed to foster the culture at its location, planning and coordinating departmental celebrations and employee appreciation events, and acting as a liaison between the local office and the corporate office on culture-related matters.

Efforts to Nurture and Sustain the Southwest Culture

Apart from the efforts of the Corporate Culture Committee, the Local Culture Committees, and the cultural ambassadors, Southwest management sought to reinforce the company's core values and culture via a series of employee recognition programs to single out and praise employees for their outstanding contributions to customer service, operational excellence, cost efficiency, and display of the Southwest Spirit. In addition to Kick Tail awards, there were "Heroes of the Heart" awards, *Spirit* magazine Star of the Month awards, President's awards, and LUV Reports whereby one or more employees could recognize other employees for an outstanding performance or contribution.

Other culture-supportive activities included the CoHearts mentoring program; the Day in the Field program, in which employees spent time working in another area of the company's operations; the Helping Hands program, in which volunteers from around the system traveled to work two weekend shifts at other Southwest facilities that were temporarily shorthanded or experiencing heavy workloads; and periodic Culture Exchange meetings to celebrate the Southwest Spirit and company milestones. Almost every event at Southwest was videotaped, which provided footage for creating multipurpose videos, such as *Keepin' the Spirit Alive,* that could be shown at company events all over the system and used in

training courses. The concepts of LUV and fun were spotlighted in all of the company's training manuals and videos.

Southwest's monthly employee newsletter often spotlighted the experiences and deeds of particular employees, reprinted letters of praise from customers, and reported company celebrations of milestones. A quarterly news video, *As the Plane Turns,* was sent to all facilities to keep employees up to date on company happenings, provide clips of special events, and share messages from customers, employees, and executives. The company had published a book for employees that described "outrageous" acts of service.

In 2012, Southwest launched the Southwest Airlines Gratitude (SWAG) initiative, which included a software tool that enabled each employee to set up a profile that listed all the recognitions and awards she or he received. This tool also allowed the employee to send commendations to other employees, recognizing their hardworking efforts and/or exemplary performance. Employees who won Kick Tail, Heroes of the Heart, Star of the Month, or President's awards were credited with SWAG points that could be redeemed in the company's SWAG Shop, which contained thousands of items and enabled employees to reward themselves in ways they found most meaningful.

Employee Productivity

Management was convinced the company's strategy, culture, esprit de corps, and people management practices fostered high labor productivity and contributed to Southwest having low labor costs in comparison to the labor costs at its principal domestic rivals (Exhibit 8). When a Southwest flight pulled up to the gate, ground crews, gate personnel, and flight attendants hustled to perform all the tasks required to turn the plane around quickly; employees took pride in doing their part to achieve good on-time performance. Southwest's turnaround times were in the 25-to-35-minute range, versus an industry average of around 45 minutes. In 2013, just as had been the case for many years, Southwest's labor productivity compared quite favorably with its chief domestic competitors:

	Productivity Measure	
	Passengers Enplaned per Employee, 2013	Employees per Plane, 2013
Southwest Airlines	2,412	66
American Airlines	1,461	96
Delta Air Lines	1,553	107
United Airlines	1,038	127
US Airways	1,775	98

Source: Information at www.airlinesfinancials.com (accessed May 22, 2014).

System Operations

Under Herb Kelleher, instituting practices, procedures, and support systems that promoted operating excellence had become a tradition and a source of company pride. Much time and effort over the years had gone into finding the most effective ways to do aircraft maintenance, to operate safely, to make baggage handling more efficient and baggage transfers more accurate, and to improve the percentage of on-time arrivals and departures. Believing that air travelers were more likely to fly Southwest if its flights were reliable and on time, Southwest's managers constantly monitored arrivals and departures, making inquiries when many flights ran behind and searching for ways to improve on-time performance. One initiative to help minimize weather and operational delays involved the development of a state-of-the-art flight dispatch system.

Southwest's current CEO, Gary Kelly, had followed Kelleher's lead in pushing for operating excellence. One of Kelly's strategic objectives for Southwest was "to be the safest, most efficient, and most reliable airline in the world." Southwest managers and employees in all positions and ranks were proactive in offering suggestions for improving Southwest's practices and procedures; suggestions with merit were quickly implemented. Southwest was considered to have one of the most competent and thorough aircraft maintenance programs in the commercial airline industry and, going into 2008, was widely regarded as the best operator among U.S. airlines. Exhibit 13 presents data comparing Southwest against its four domestic rivals on four measures of operating performance.

The First Significant Blemish on Southwest's Safety Record While no Southwest plane had ever crashed and there had never been a passenger fatality, there was an incident in 2005 in which a Southwest plane landing in a snowstorm with a strong tailwind at Chicago's Midway airport was unable to stop before overrunning a shorter-than-usual runway and rolled onto a highway, crashing into a car, killing one of the occupants, and injuring 22 of the passengers on the plane. A National Transportation Safety Board investigation concluded that "the pilot's failure to use available reverse thrust in a timely manner to safely slow or stop the airplane after landing" was the probable cause.

Belated Aircraft Inspections Further Tarnish Southwest's Reputation In early 2008, various media reported that Southest Airlines had, over a period of several months in 2006 and 2007, knowingly failed to conduct required inspections for early detection of fuselage-fatigue cracking on 46 of its older Boeing 737-300 jets. The company had voluntarily notified the FAA about the lapse in checks for fuselage cracks, but it continued to fly the planes until the work was done—about eight days. The belated inspections revealed tiny cracks in the bodies of six planes, with the largest measuring 4 inches; none impaired flight safety. According to CEO Gary Kelly, "Southwest Airlines discovered the missed inspection area, disclosed it to the FAA, and promptly reinspected all potentially affected aircraft in March 2007. The FAA approved our actions and considered the matter closed as of April 2007." Nonetheless, on March 12, 2008, shortly after the reports in the media surfaced about Southwest not meeting inspection deadlines, Southwest canceled 4 percent of its flights and grounded 44 of its Boeing 737-300s until it verified that the aircraft had undergone required inspections. Kelly then initiated an internal review of the company's maintenance practices; the investigation raised "concerns" about the company's aircraft maintenance procedures, prompting Southwest to put three employees on leave. The FAA subsequently fined Southwest $10.2 million for its transgressions. In an effort to help restore customer confidence, Kelly publicly apologized for the company's wrongdoing, promised that

EXHIBIT 13

Comparative Statistics on On-Time Flights, Mishandled Baggage, Boarding Denials Due to Oversold Flights, and Passenger Complaints for Major U.S. Airlines, 2000, 2005, 2010–2013

Percentage of Scheduled Flights Arriving Within 15 Minutes of the Scheduled Time
(during the previous 12 months ending in May of each year)

Airline	2000	2005	2010	2011	2012	2013
American Airlines	75.8%	78.0%	79.6%	77.8%	76.9%	77.6%
Delta Air Lines	78.3	76.4	77.4	82.3	86.5	84.5
Southwest Airlines	**78.7**	**79.9**	**79.5**	**81.3**	**83.1**	**76.7**
United Airlines	71.6	79.8	85.2	80.2	77.4	79.3
US Airways	72.7	76.0	83.0	79.8	85.9	81.5

Mishandled Baggage Reports per 1,000 Passengers
(in May of each year)

Airline	2000	2005	2010	2011	2012	2013
American Airlines	5.44	4.58	4.36	3.23	2.92	3.02
Delta Air Lines	3.64	6.21	4.9	2.28	2.22	2.15
Southwest Airlines	**4.14**	**3.46**	**4.97**	**3.59**	**3.08**	**3.72**
United Airlines	6.71	4.00	4.13	4.25	3.87	3.47
US Airways	4.57	9.73	3.49	2.42	2.14	2.52

Involuntary Denied Boardings per 10,000 Passengers Due to Oversold Flights
(January–March of each year)

Airline	2000	2005	2010	2011	2012	2013
American Airlines	0.59	0.72	0.75	0.78	0.75	0.36
Delta Air Lines	0.44	1.06	0.29	0.3	0.79	0.52
Southwest Airlines	**1.70**	**0.74**	**0.76**	**0.49**	**0.75**	**0.66**
United Airlines	1.61	0.42	1.00	0.94	1.52	1.37
US Airways	0.8	1.01	0.91	0.87	0.79	0.55

Complaints per 100,000 Passengers Boarded
(in May of each year)

Airline	2000	2005	2010	2011	2012	2013
American Airlines	2.77	1.01	1.08	0.87	1.86	1.99
Delta Air Lines	1.6	0.91	1.21	0.9	0.43	0.53
Southwest Airlines	**0.41**	**0.17**	**0.29**	**0.14**	**0.20**	**0.36**
United Airlines	5.07	0.87	1.47	2.14	1.93	1.89
US Airways	1.63	0.99	1.15	1.56	0.91	1.27

Source: Office of Aviation Enforcement and Proceedings, "Air Travel Consumer Report," various years.

it would not occur again, and reasserted the company's commitment to safety; he said:

> From our inception, Southwest Airlines has maintained a rigorous Culture of Safety—and has maintained that same dedication for more than 37 years. It is and always has been our number one priority to ensure safety.
>
> We've got a 37-year history of very safe operations, one of the safest operations in the world, and we're safer today than we've ever been.

In the days following the public revelation of Southwest's maintenance lapse and the tarnishing of its reputation, an industrywide audit by the FAA revealed similar failures to conduct timely inspections for early signs of fuselage fatigue at five other airlines. An air travel snafu ensued, with over a thousand flights subsequently being canceled due to FAA-mandated grounding of the affected aircraft while the overdue safety inspections were performed.

Further public scrutiny, including a congressional investigation, turned up documents indicating that, in some cases, planes flew for 30 months after the inspection deadlines had passed. Moreover, high-level FAA officials were apparently aware of the failure of Southwest and other airlines to perform the inspections for fuselage skin cracking at the scheduled times and chose not to strictly enforce the inspection deadlines—according to some commentators, because of allegedly cozy relationships with personnel at Southwest and the other affected airlines. Disgruntled FAA safety supervisors in charge of monitoring the inspections conducted by airline carriers testified before Congress that senior FAA officials frequently ignored their reports that certain routine safety inspections were not being conducted in accordance with prescribed FAA procedures. Shortly thereafter, the FAA issued more stringent procedures to ensure that aircraft safety inspections were properly conducted.

ENDNOTES

[1] Kevin Freiberg and Jackie Freiberg, *NUTS! Southwest Airlines' Crazy Recipe for Business and Personal Success* (New York: Broadway Books, 1998), p. 15.

[2] Ibid., pp. 16–18.

[3] Katrina Brooker, "The Chairman of the Board Looks Back," *Fortune,* May 28, 2001, p. 66.

[4] Freiberg and Freiberg, *NUTS!* p. 31.

[5] Ibid., pp. 26–27.

[6] Ibid., pp. 246–247.

[7] As quoted in *Dallas Morning News,* March 20, 2001.

[8] Quoted in Brooker, "The Chairman of the Board Looks Back," p. 64.

[9] Ibid., p. 72.

[10] As quoted in the *Seattle Times,* March 20, 2001, p. C3.

[11] Speech at Texas Christian University, September 13, 2007, www.southwest.com (accessed September 8, 2008).

[12] Freiberg and Freiberg, *NUTS!* p. 163.

[13] Company press release, July 15, 2004.

[14] Speech to Greater Boston Chamber of Commerce, April 23, 2008, (accessed September 5, 2008).

[15] Speech to Business Today International Conference, November 20, 2007, www.southwest.com (accessed September 8, 2008).

[16] As cited in Freiberg and Freiberg, *NUTS!* p. 288.

[17] Speech by Colleen Barrett on January 22, 2007, www.southwest.com (accessed September 5, 2008).

[18] Brenda Paik Sunoo, "How Fun Flies at Southwest Airlines," *Personnel Journal* 74, no. 6 (June 1995), p. 70.

[19] Statement in the Careers section at www.southwest.com (accessed May 16, 2014). Kelly's statement has been continuously posted on www.southwest.com since 2009.

[20] As quoted in James Campbell Quick, "Crafting an Organizational Structure: Herb's Hand at Southwest Airlines," *Organizational Dynamics* 21, no. 2 (Autumn 1992), p. 51.

[21] Southwest's ad entitled "Work in a Place Where Elvis Has Been Spotted"; Sunoo, "How Fun Flies at Southwest Airlines," pp. 64–65.

[22] Speech to the Paso Del Norte Group in El Paso, Texas, January 22, 2007, www.southwest.com (accessed September 5, 2008).

[23] Quick, "Crafting an Organizational Structure," p. 52.

[24] Southwest Airlines, 2013 One Report, p. 42, www.southwest.com (accessed May 16, 2014).

[25] Sunoo, "How Fun Flies at Southwest Airlines," p. 72.

[26] Brooker, "The Chairman of the Board Looks Back," p. 72.

[27] Freiberg and Freiberg, *NUTS!* p. 273.

[28] Ibid., p. 76.

[29] Roger Hallowell, "Southwest Airlines: A Case Study Linking Employee Needs Satisfaction and Organizational Capabilities to Competitive Advantage," *Human Resource Management* 35, no. 4 (Winter 1996), p. 524.

[30] Speech to Business Today International Conference, November 20, 2007, www.southwest.com (accessed September 8, 2008).

[31] Freiberg and Freiberg, *NUTS!* p. 165.

TOMS Shoes: A Dedication to Social Responsibility

MARGARET A. PETERAF Tuck School of Business, Dartmouth College

SEAN ZHANG Dartmouth College, Research Assistant

MEGHAN L. COONEY Dartmouth College, Research Assistant

While traveling in Argentina in 2006, Blake Mycoskie witnessed the hardships that children without shoes experienced, and he became committed to making a difference. Rather than focusing on charity work, Mycoskie sought to build an organization capable of sustainable, repeated giving, through which children would be guaranteed shoes throughout their childhood. He established Shoes for a Better Tomorrow, better known as TOMS, as a for-profit company based on the premise of the "One for One" pledge. For every pair of shoes TOMS sold, TOMS would donate a pair to a child in need. By year-end 2013, TOMS had given away over 10 million pairs of shoes in more than 40 different countries.[1]

As a relatively new and privately held company, TOMS experienced consistent and rapid growth despite the global recession that began in 2007. In 2013, TOMS had matured into an organization with nearly 400 employees and $210 million in revenues. TOMS shoes could be found in several major retail stores, such as Nordstrom, Bloomingdale's, and Urban Outfitters. In addition to providing shoes for underprivileged children, TOMS also expanded its mission to include restoring vision to those with curable sight-related illnesses by developing a new line of eyewear products. Exhibit 1 illustrates how quickly TOMS expanded in its first eight years of business.

Company Background

While attending Southern Methodist University, Blake Mycoskie founded the first of his six startups, a laundry service company that encompassed seven colleges and staffed over 40 employees.[2] Four startups and a short stint on *The Amazing Race* later, Mycoskie found himself vacationing in Argentina, where he not only learned about the Alpargata shoe originally used by local peasants in the 14th century but also witnessed the extreme poverty in rural Argentina.

Determined to make a difference, Mycoskie believed that providing shoes could more directly impact the children in these rural communities than delivering medicine or food. Aside from protecting children's feet from infections, parasites, and diseases, shoes were often required for a complete school uniform. In addition, research had shown that shoes were found to significantly increase children's self-confidence, help them develop into more active community members, and lead them to stay in school. Thus, by ensuring access to shoes, Mycoskie could effectively increase children's access to education and foster community activism, raising the overall standard of living for people living in poor Argentinian rural areas.

Dedicated to his mission, Mycoskie purchased 250 pairs of Alpargatas and returned home to Los Angeles, where he subsequently founded TOMS Shoes. He built the company on the promise of "One for One," donating a pair of shoes for every pair sold. With an initial investment of $300,000, Mycoskie's business concept of social entrepreneurship was simple: Sell both the shoe and the story behind it. Building on a simple slogan that effectively communicated his goal, Mycoskie championed his personal

EXHIBIT 1

TOMS' Growth in Sales and Employees, 2006–2013

Year	Total Employees	Pairs of Shoes Sold
2006	4	10,000
2007	19	50,000
2008	33	110,000
2009	46	230,000
2010	72	700,000
2011	250	1,200,000
2012	320	2,500,000
2013	400	6,000,000

Source: PrivCo, "Private Company Financial Report: TOMS Shoes, Inc.," May 30, 2014.

experiences passionately and established deep and lasting relationships with customers.

Operating from his apartment with three interns he found through Craigslist, Mycoskie quickly sold out his initial inventory and expanded considerably, selling 10,000 pairs of shoes by the end of his first year. With family and friends, Mycoskie ventured back to Argentina, where they hand-delivered 10,000 pairs of shoes to children in need. Because he followed through on his mission statement, Mycoskie was able to subsequently attract investors to support his unique business model and expand his venture significantly.

When TOMS was initially founded, it operated as the for-profit financial arm while a separate entity entitled "Friends of TOMS" focused on charity work and giving. After 2011, operations at Friends of TOMS were absorbed into TOMS' own operations as TOMS itself matured. In Friends of TOMS' latest accessible 2011 501(c)(3) filing, assets were reported at less than $130,000.[3] Moreover, as of May 2013, the Friends of TOMS website was discontinued, while TOMS also ceased advertising its partnership with Friends of TOMS in marketing campaigns and on its corporate website. The developments suggested that Friends of TOMS became a defunct entity as TOMS incorporated all of its operations under the overarching TOMS brand.

Industry Background

Even though Mycoskie's vision for his company was a unique one, vying for a position in global footwear manufacturing was a risky and difficult venture. The industry was both stable and mature—one in which large and small companies competed on the basis of price, quality, and service. Competitive pressures came from foreign as well as domestic companies, and new entrants needed to fight for access to downstream retailers.

Further, the cost of supplies was forecast to increase between 2013 and 2020. Materials and wages constituted over 70 percent of industry costs—clearly a sizable concern for competitors. Supply purchases included leather, rubber, plastic compounds, foam, nylon, canvas, laces, and so on. While the price of leather rose steadily each year, the price of rubber also began to climb, at an average annual rate of 7.6 percent. Wages were expected to increase at a rate of 5.8 percent over a five-year period due to growing awareness of how manufacturers took advantage of cheap, outsourced labor.[4]

To thrive in the footwear manufacturing industry, firms needed to differentiate their products in a meaningful way. Selling good-quality products at a reasonable price was rarely enough; they needed to target a niche market that desired a certain image. Product innovation and advertising campaigns therefore became the most successful competitive weapons. For example, Clarks adopted a sophisticated design, appealing to a wealthier, more mature customer base. Nike, adidas, and Skechers developed athletic footwear and aggressively marketed their brands to reflect that image. Achieving economies of scale, increasing technical efficiency, and developing a cost-effective distribution system were also essential elements for success.

Despite the presence of established incumbents, global footwear manufacturing was an attractive industry to potential entrants based on the prediction of increased demand and therefore sales revenue. Moreover, the industry offered incumbents one of the highest profit margins in the fashion industry. But because competitors were likely to open new locations and expand their brands in order to discourage competition, new companies' only option was to attempt to undercut them on cost. Acquiring capital equipment and machinery to manufacture footwear on a large scale was expensive. Moreover, potential entrants also needed to launch costly large-scale marketing campaigns to promote brand awareness. Thus, successful incumbents were traditionally able to maintain an overwhelming portion of the market.

Building the TOMS Brand

Due to its humble beginnings, TOMS struggled to gain a foothold in the footwear industry. While companies such as Nike had utilized high-profile athletes such as Michael Jordan and Tiger Woods to establish brand recognition, TOMS had relatively limited financial resources and tried to appeal to a more socially conscious consumer. Luckily, potential buyers enjoyed a rise in disposable income over time as the economy recovered from the recession. As a result, demand for high-quality footwear increased for affluent shoppers, accompanied by a desire to act (and be *seen* acting) charitably and responsibly.

While walking through the airport one day, Mycoskie encountered a girl wearing TOMS shoes. Mycoskie recounts:

> I asked her about her shoes, and she went on to tell me this amazing story about TOMS and the model that it uses and my personal story. I realized the importance of having a story today is what really separates companies. People don't just wear our shoes, they tell our story. That's one of my favorite lessons that I learned early on.

Moving forward, TOMS focused more on selling the story behind the shoe rather than depending on product features or celebrity endorsements. Moreover, rather than relying on mainstream advertising, TOMS emphasized a grassroots approach using social media and word of mouth. With nearly 2 million Facebook "Likes" and over 2 million Twitter "Followers" in 2013, TOMS' social media presence eclipsed that of its much larger rivals, Skechers and Clarks. Based on 2013 data, TOMS had fewer Followers than Nike and fewer Likes than both Nike and adidas. However, TOMS had more Followers and Likes per dollar of revenue. Therefore, taking company size into account, TOMS also had a greater social media presence than the industry's leading competitors (see Exhibit 2).

TOMS' success with social media advertising can be attributed to the story crafted and championed by Mycoskie. Industry incumbents generally dedicated a substantial portion of revenue and effort to advertising since they were simply selling a product. TOMS, on the other hand, used its mission to ask customers to buy into a *cause,* limiting its need to devote resources to brand building. TOMS lets its charitable work and social media presence generate interest for the company organically. This strategy also increased the likelihood that consumers would make repeat purchases and share the story behind their purchases with family and friends. TOMS' customers took pride in supporting a grassroots cause instead of a luxury-footwear supplier and encouraged others to share in the rewarding act.

EXHIBIT 2

TOMS' Use of Social Media Compared to Select Footwear Competitors, 2013

	2013 Revenue (millions)	Facebook		Twitter	
		Number of Likes	Likes per Million $ in Revenue	Number of Followers	Followers per Million $ in Revenue
TOMS	$210 (est.)	2,215,283	7,384	2,173,377	7,245
Clarks	1,400	241,355	172	22,184	16
Skechers	1,854	1,200,911	648	18,005	10
adidas	19,640	16,340,675	832	961,065	49
Nike	25,280	18,020,656	713	3,138,584	124

Source: Author data.

A Business Model Dedicated to Socially Responsible Behavior

Traditionally, the content of advertisements for many large apparel companies focused on the attractive aspects of the featured products. TOMS' advertising, on the other hand, showcased its charitable contributions and the story of its founder, Blake Mycoskie. While the CEOs of Nike, adidas, and Clarks rarely appeared in their companies' advertisements, TOMS ran as many ads with its founder as it did without him, emphasizing the inseparability of the TOMS product from Mycoskie's story.

In all of his appearances, Mycoskie was dressed in casual and friendly attire so that customers could easily relate to him and his mission. This advertising method conveyed a small-company feel and encouraged consumers to connect personally with the TOMS brand. It also worked to increase buyer patronage through differentiating the TOMS product from others. Consumers were convinced that every time they purchased a pair of TOMS, they became instruments of the company's charitable work. Exhibit 3 provides examples of TOMS' advertisements used in 2013.

The company's social message fueled buyer enthusiasm and led to repeat purchases by many customers. One reviewer commented, "This is my

EXHIBIT 3

Examples of TOMS' Advertisements

TOMS ad, Worn blue shoe

TOMS ad, This holiday season . . .

TOMS ad, GIVE

TOMS ad, With every pair you purchase . . .

third pair of TOMS and I absolutely love them! . . . I can't wait to buy more!"[5] Another wrote, "Just got my 25th pair! Love the color! They . . . are my all-time favorite shoe for comfort, looks & durability. AND they are for a great cause!! Gotta go pick out my next pair."[6]

Virtually all consumer reports on TOMS shoes shared similar themes. Though not cheap, TOMS footwear was priced lower than rivals' products, and customers overwhelmingly agreed that the value was worth the cost. Reviewers described TOMS as comfortable, true to size, lightweight, and versatile ("go with everything"). The shoes had "cute shapes and patterns" and were made of canvas and rubber that molded to customers' feet with wear. Because TOMS products were appealing and trendy yet also basic and comfortable, they were immune to changing fashion trends and consistently attracted a variety of consumers.

In addition to offering a high-quality product that people valued, TOMS was able to establish a positive repertoire with its customers through efficient distribution. Maintaining an online shop helped TOMS save money on retail locations and allowed it to serve a wide geographic range. Further, the company negotiated with well-known retailers such as Nordstrom and Neiman Marcus to assist in distribution. Through thoughtful planning and structured coordination, TOMS limited its operation costs and provided prompt service for its customers.

Giving Partners

As it continued to grow, TOMS sought to improve its operational efficiency by teaming up with "Giving Partners," nonprofit organizations that helped to distribute the shoes that TOMS donated. By teaming up with Giving Partners, TOMS streamlined its charity operations by shifting many of its distributional responsibilities to organizations that were often larger and more resourceful and were able to distribute TOMS shoes more efficiently. Moreover, these organizations possessed more familiarity and experience in dealing with the communities that TOMS was interested in helping and could therefore better allocate shoes that suited the needs of children in the area. Giving Partners also provided feedback

to help TOMS improve upon its giving and distributional efforts.

Each Giving Partner also magnified the impact of TOMS shoes by bundling their distribution with other charity work that the organization specialized in. For example, Partners in Health, a nonprofit organization that spent almost $100 million in 2012 on providing health care for the poor (more than TOMS' total revenue that year), dispersed thousands of shoes to schoolchildren in Rwanda and Malawi while also screening them for malnutrition. Cooperative giving further strengthened the TOMS brand by association with well-known and highly regarded Giving Partners. Complementary services expanded the scope of TOMS' mission, enhanced the impact that each pair of TOMS had on a child's life, and increased the number of goodwill and business opportunities available to TOMS.

To ensure quality of service and adherence to its fundamental mission, TOMS maintained five criteria for Giving Partners:[7]

- *Repeat giving.* Giving Partners must be able to work with the same communities in multiyear commitments, regularly providing shoes to the same children as they grow.
- *High impact.* Shoes must aid Giving Partners with their existing goals in the areas of health and education, providing children with opportunities they would not have otherwise.
- *Consideration of local economy.* Providing shoes cannot have negative socioeconomic effects on the communities where shoes are given.
- *Large-volume shipments.* Giving Partners must be able to accept large shipments of shoes.
- *Focus on health and education.* Giving Partners must give shoes only in conjunction with health and education efforts.

As of 2013, TOMS had built relationships with over 75 Giving Partners, including Save the Children, U.S. Fund for UNICEF, and IMA World Health. To remain accountable to its mission in these joint ventures, TOMS also performed unannounced audit reports that ensured shoes were distributed according to the One for One model.

Building a Relationship with Giving Partners

Having Giving Partners offered TOMS the valuable opportunity to shift some of its philanthropic costs onto other parties. However, TOMS also proactively maintained strong relationships with its Giving Partners. Kelly Gibson, the program director of National Relief Charities, a Giving Partner and nonprofit organization dedicated to improving the lives of Native Americans, highlighted the respect with which TOMS treated its Giving Partners:

> TOMS treats their Giving Partners (like us) and the recipients of their giveaway shoes (the Native kids in this case) like customers. We had a terrific service experience with TOMS. They were meticulous about getting our shoe order just right. They also insist that the children who receive shoes have a customer-type experience at distributions.

From customizing Giving Partners' orders to helping pick up the tab for transportation and distribution, TOMS treated its Giving Partners as valuable customers and generated a sense of goodwill that extended beyond its immediate One for One mission. By ensuring that its Giving Partners and recipients of shoes were treated respectfully, TOMS developed a unique ability to sustain business relationships that other for-profit organizations more concerned with the financial bottom line did not.

Maintaining a Dedication to Corporate Social Responsibility

Although TOMS manufactured its products in Argentina, China, and Ethiopia (countries that have all been cited as areas with a high degree of child and forced labor by the Bureau of International Labor Affairs), regular third-party factory audits and a Supplier Code of Conduct helped to ensure compliance with fair labor standards.[8] Announced and unannounced audits were conducted, and the Supplier Code of Conduct was publicly posted in the local language of every work site. The Supplier Code of Conduct enforced standards such as minimum work age, requirement of voluntary employment, nondiscrimination, maximum work-week hours, and right to unionize. It also protected workers from physical, sexual, verbal, or psychological harassment in accordance with a country's legally mandated standards. Workers were encouraged to report violations directly to TOMS, and suppliers found in violation of TOMS' Supplier Code of Conduct faced termination.

In addition to ensuring that suppliers met TOMS' ethical standards, TOMS also emphasized its own dedication to ethical behavior in a number of ways. TOMS was a member of the American Apparel and Footwear Association (AAFA) and was registered with the Fair Labor Association (FLA). Internally, TOMS educated its own employees on human trafficking and slavery prevention, and partnered with several organizations dedicated to raising awareness about such issues, including Hand of Hope.[9]

Giving Trips

Aside from material shoe contributions, TOMS also held a series of "Giving Trips" that supported the broader notion of community service. Giving Trips were firsthand opportunities for employees of TOMS and selected TOMS' customers to participate in the delivery of TOMS shoes. These trips increased the transparency of TOMS' philanthropic efforts, further engaging customers and employees. They generated greater social awareness as well, since participants on these trips often became more engaged in local community service efforts at home.

From a business standpoint, the Giving Trips also represented a marketing success. First, a large number of participants were customers and journalists unassociated with TOMS who circulated their stories online through social media upon their return. Second, TOMS was able to motivate participants and candidates to become more involved in its mission by increasing public awareness. In 2013, instead of internally selecting customers to participate on the Giving Trips, TOMS opted to hold an open voting process that encouraged candidates to reach out to their known contacts and ask them to vote for their inclusion. This contest drew thousands of contestants and likely hundreds of thousands of voters, although the final vote tallies were not publicly released.

Environmental Sustainability

Dedicated to minimizing its environmental impact, TOMS pursued a number of sustainable practices that included offering vegan shoes, incorporating recycled bottles into its products, and printing with soy ink. TOMS also used a blend of organic canvas and post-consumer recycled plastics to create shoes that were both comfortable and durable. By utilizing natural hemp and organic cotton, TOMS eliminated pesticide and insecticide use that adversely affected the environment.

In addition, TOMS supported several environmental organizations such as Surfers Against Sewage, a movement that raised awareness about excess sewage discharge in the United Kingdom. TOMS was a member of the Textile Exchange, an organization dedicated to textile sustainability and protecting the environment. The company also participated actively in the AAFA's Environmental Responsibility Committee.

Creating the TOMS Workforce

When asked what makes a great employee, Mycoskie blogged:

> As TOMS has grown, we've continued to look for these same traits in the interns and employees that we hire. Are you passionate? Can you creatively solve problems? Can you be resourceful without resources? Do you have the compassion to serve others? You can teach a new hire just about any skill . . . but you absolutely cannot inspire creativity and passion in someone that doesn't have it.[10]

The company's emphasis on creativity and passion was part of the reason that TOMS relied so heavily on interns and new hires rather than experienced workers. By hiring younger, more inexperienced employees, TOMS was able to be more cost-effective in terms of personnel. The company could also recruit young and energetic individuals who were more likely to think innovatively and out of the box. These employees were placed in specialized teams under the leadership of strong, experienced managerial talent. This human intellectual capital generated a competitive advantage for the TOMS brand.

Together with these passionate individuals, Mycoskie strove to create a family-like work atmosphere where openness and collaboration were celebrated. With his cubicle located in one of the most highly trafficked areas of the office (right next to customer service), Mycoskie made a point to interact with his employees on a daily basis, in all-staff meetings, and through weekly personal e-mails while traveling. Regarding his e-mails, Mycoskie reflected:

> I'm a very open person, so I really tell the staff what I'm struggling with and what I'm happy about. I tell them what I think the future of TOMS is. I want them to understand what I'm thinking. It's like I'm writing to a best friend.[11]

The notion of "family" was further solidified through company dinners, ski trips, and book clubs through which TOMS employees were encouraged to socialize in informal settings. These casual opportunities to interact with colleagues created a "balanced" work atmosphere where employees celebrated not only their own successes but also the successes of their co-workers

Diversity and inclusion were also emphasized at TOMS. For example, cultural traditions such as the Chinese Lunar New Year were celebrated publicly on the TOMS company blog. Moreover, as TOMS began expanding and distributing globally, the company increasingly sought to recruit a more diverse workforce by hiring multilingual individuals who were familiar with TOMS' diverse customer base and could communicate with its giving communities.[12]

The emphasis that Mycoskie placed on each individual employee was one of the key reasons why employees at TOMS often felt "lucky" to be part of the movement.[13] Coupled with the fact that TOMS employees knew their efforts fostered social justice, these "Agents of Change," as they referred to themselves, were generally quite satisfied with their work, making TOMS *Forbes*'s 18th "Most Inspiring Company" in 2011. Overall, the culture allowed TOMS to recruit and retain high-quality employees invested in achieving its social mission.

Financial Success at Toms

While TOMS remained a privately held company with limited financial data, the estimated growth rate of TOMS' revenue was astounding. In the eight years after his company's inception, Mycoskie was able to turn his initial $300,000 investment into a company with estimated 2013 revenues of $210 million. Exhibit 4 presents the company's estimated revenues for 2006 through 2013. The exhibit also provides total footwear industry revenues for 2006 through 2013.

The fact that TOMS was able to experience consistent growth despite financial turmoil post-2008 illustrates the strength of the One for One movement to survive times of recession. Mycoskie attributed his success during the recession to two factors: (1) As consumers became more conscious of their spending during recessions, products such as TOMS that gave to others actually became *more* appealing (according to Mycoskie); and (2) the giving model that TOMS employed is not "priced in." Rather than commit a percentage of profits or revenues to charity, Mycoskie noted that TOMS simply gave away a pair for every pair it sold. This way, socially conscious consumers knew exactly where their money was going without having to worry that TOMS would cut back on its charity efforts in order to turn a profit.[14]

Production at TOMS

Although TOMS manufactured shoes in Argentina, Ethiopia, and China, only shoes made in China were brought to the retail market. Shoes made in

Argentina and Ethiopia were strictly used for donation purposes. TOMS retailed its basic Alpargata shoes in the $50 price range, even though the cost of producing each pair was estimated at around $9.[15] Estimates for the costs of producing TOMS' more expensive lines of shoes were unknown, but the shoes retailed for more than $150.

In comparison, manufacturing the average pair of Nike shoes in Indonesia cost around $20, and they were priced around $70.[16] Factoring in the giving aspect, TOMS seemed to have a slightly smaller markup than companies such as Nike, yet it still maintained considerable profit margins. More detailed information on trends in TOMS' production costs and practices is limited due to the private nature of the company.

The Future

Because demand and revenues were predicted to increase in the global footwear manufacturing industry, incumbents like TOMS needed to find ways to defend their position in the market. One method was to continue to differentiate products based on quality, image, or price. Another strategy was to focus on R&D and craft new brands and product lines that appealed to different audiences. It was also recommended that companies investigate how to mitigate the threat posed by an increase in supply costs.

In an effort to broaden its mission and product offerings, TOMS began to expand both its consumer base and charitable-giving product lines. For its customers, TOMS started offering stylish wedges, ballet flats, and even wedding apparel in an effort to reach more customers and satisfy the special needs of current ones. For the children it sought to help, TOMS expanded past its basic, black canvas shoe offerings to winter boots in order to help keep children's feet dry and warm during the winter months in cold-climate countries.

On another front, TOMS entered the eyewear market in hopes of restoring vision to the 285 million blind or visually impaired individuals around the world. For every pair of TOMS glasses sold, TOMS restored vision to one individual either through donating prescription glasses or offering medical treatment for those suffering from cataracts and eye infections. TOMS recently focused

EXHIBIT 4

Estimated Annual Revenues for TOMS and the Footwear Industry, 2006–2013

	TOMS		Footwear Industry	
Year	Revenue (millions)	Annual Growth Rate	Revenue (millions)	Annual Growth Rate
2006	$ 0.2	—	$ 74	12.4%
2007	1.2	457%	87	16.8
2008	3.1	156	94	8.5
2009	8.4	168	98	4.0
2010	26.2	212	100	1.6
2011	43.5	66	106	6.2
2012	97.5	124	108	2.6
2013	210.0	115	117	7.5

Source: PrivCo; and "Global Footwear Manufacturing," *IBISWorld*, June 2, 2013, clients1.ibisworld.com/reports/gl/industry/currentperformance .aspx?entid500.

its vision-related efforts in Nepal and planned to expand globally as the TOMS eyewear brand grew. As of 2013, TOMS had teamed up with 15 Giving Partners to help restore sight to 150,000 individuals in 13 countries. A challenge for Blake Mycoskie would be to remain focused on the company's social mission while meeting the managerial demands of a high-growth international company.

ENDNOTES

[1] Claire Groden, "TOMS Hits 10 Million Mark on Donated Shoes," *Time*, June 26, 2013, accessed at http://www.huffingtonpost.com/blake-mycoskie/.

[2] Blake Mycoskie, blog post, *The Huffington Post,* May 26, 2013, accessed at http://style.time.com/2013/06/26/toms-hits-10-million-mark-on-donated-shoes/.

[3] 501c3Lookup, June 2, 2013, accessed at http://501c3lookup.org/FRIENDS_OF_TOMS/.

[4] "Global Footwear Manufacturing." *IBISWorld,* March 2014, accessed at http://clients1.ibisworld.com/reports/gl/industry/keystatistics.aspx?entid=500.

[5] Post by "Alexandria," TOMS website, June 2, 2013, accessed at http://www.toms.com/red-canvas-classics-shoes-1.

[6] Post by "Donna Brock," TOMS website. January 13, 2014, accessed at http://www.toms.com/women/bright-blue-womens-canvas-classics.

[7] TOMS website, June 2, 2013, accessed http://www.toms.com/our-movement-giving-partners.

[8] "Trafficking Victims Protection Reauthorization Act." U.S. Department of Labor, June 2, 2013, accessed at http://www.dol.gov/ilab/programs/ocft/tvpra.htm; TOMS website, June 2, 2013, accessed at http://www.toms.com/corporate-responsibility.

[9] Hand of Hope, "Teaming Up with TOMS Shoes," *Joyce Meyer Ministries,* June 2, 2013, accessed at http://www.studygs.net/citation/mla.htm.

[10] Blake Mycoskie, "Blake Mycoskie's Blog," *Blogspot,* June 2, 2013, accessed at http://blakemycoskie.blogspot.com/.

[11] Tamara Schweitzer, "The Way I Work: Blake Mycoskie of TOMS Shoes," *Inc.,* June 2, 2013, accessed at http://www.inc.com/magazine/20100601/the-way-i-work-blake-mycoskie-of-toms-shoes.html.

[12] TOMS Jobs website, June 2, 2013, accessed at. http://www.toms.com/jobs/l

[13] Daniela, "Together We Travel," *TOMS Company Blog,* June 3, 2013, accessed at http://blog.toms.com/post/36075725601/together-we-travel.

[14] Mike Zimmerman, "The Business of Giving: TOMS Shoes," *Success,* June 2, 2013, accessed at http://www.success.com/articles/852-the-business-of-giving-toms-shoes.

[15] Brittney Fortune, "TOMS Shoes: Popular Model with Drawbacks," *The Falcon,* June 2, 2013, accessed at http://www.thefalcononline.com/article.php?=id159.

[16] Jim Keady, director, *Behind the Swoosh,* 1995. Film.

GLOSSARY

B

backward integration   Backward integration involves performing industry value chain activities previously performed by suppliers or other enterprises engaged in earlier stages of the industry value chain

balanced scorecard   The balanced scorecard is a widely used method for combining the use of both strategic and financial objectives, tracking their achievement, and giving management a more complete and balanced view of how well an organization is performing.

benchmarking   Benchmarking is a potent tool for learning which companies are best at performing particular activities and then using their techniques (or "best practices") to improve the cost and effectiveness of a company's own internal activities.

best-cost provider strategies   Best-cost provider strategies are a *hybrid* of low-cost provider and differentiation strategies that aim at satisfying buyer expectations on key quality/features/performance/service attributes and beating customer expectations on price.

blue ocean strategies   Blue ocean strategies offer growth in revenues and profits by discovering or inventing new industry segments that create altogether new demand.

broad differentiation strategy   The essence of a broad differentiation strategy is to offer unique product or service attributes that a wide range of buyers find appealing and worth paying for.

business ethics   Business ethics involves the application of general ethical principles to the actions and decisions of businesses and the conduct of their personnel.

business model   A company's business model sets forth how its strategy and operating approaches will create value for customers, while at the same time generating ample revenues to cover costs and realizing a profit. The two elements of a company's business model are its (1) customer value proposition and (2) its profit formula.

business strategy   Business strategy is primarily concerned with strengthening the company's market position and building competitive advantage in a single business company or a single business unit of a diversified multibusiness corporation.

C

capability   Capability is the capacity of a company to competently perform some internal activity. Capabilities are developed and enabled through the deployment of a company's resources.

cash cow   A cash cow generates operating cash flows over and above its internal requirements, thereby providing financial resources that may be used to invest in cash hogs, finance new acquisitions, fund share buyback programs, or pay dividends.

cash hog   A cash hog generates operating cash flows that are too small to fully fund its operations and growth; a cash hog must receive cash infusions from outside sources to cover its working capital and investment requirements.

competitive strategy   A competitive strategy concerns the specifics of management's game plan for competing successfully and securing a competitive advantage over rivals in the marketplace.

corporate culture   Corporate culture is a company's internal work climate and is shaped by its core values, beliefs, and business principles. A company's culture is important because it influences its traditions, work practices, and style of operating

corporate restructuring   Corporate restructuring involves radically altering the business lineup by divesting businesses that lack strategic fit or are poor performers and acquiring new businesses that offer better promise for enhancing shareholder value.

corporate social responsibility (CSR)   Corporate social responsibility (CSR) refers to a company's *duty* to operate in an honorable manner, provide good working conditions for employees, encourage workforce diversity, be a good steward of the environment, and actively work to better the quality of life in the local communities in which it operates and in society at large.

corporate social responsibility strategy   A company's corporate social responsibility strategy is defined by the specific combination of socially beneficial activities it opts to support with its contributions of time, money, and other resources.

corporate strategy   Corporate strategy establishes an overall game plan for managing a *set of businesses* in a diversified, multibusiness company.

cost driver   A cost driver is a factor having a strong effect on the cost of a company's value chain activities and cost structure.

D

driving forces   Driving forces are the major underlying causes of change in industry and competitive conditions.

dynamic capability   A dynamic capability is the ability to modify, deepen, or reconfigure the company's existing resources and capabilities in response to its changing environment or market opportunities.

E

economic risks   Economic risks stem from the stability of a country's monetary system, economic and regulatory policies, and the lack of property rights protections.

economies of scope   Economies of scope are cost reductions stemming from strategic fit along the value chains of related businesses (thereby, a larger scope of operations), whereas *economies of scale* accrue from a larger operation.

environmental sustainability   Environmental sustainability involves deliberate actions to protect the environment, provide for the longevity of natural resources, maintain ecological support systems for future generations, and guard against the ultimate endangerment of the planet.

ethical relativism   According to the school of ethical relativism, different societal cultures and customs create divergent standards of right and wrong; thus, what is ethical or unethical must be judged in the light of local customs and social mores, and can vary from one culture or nation to another.

ethical universalism   According to the school of ethical universalism, the same standards of what's ethical and what's unethical resonate with peoples of most societies, regardless of local traditions and cultural norms; hence, common ethical standards can be used to judge employee conduct in a variety of country markets and cultural circumstances.

F

financial objectives   Financial objectives relate to the financial performance targets management has established for the organization to achieve.

first-mover advantages   Because of first-mover advantages and disadvantages, competitive advantage can spring from *when* a move is made as well as from *what* move is made.

forward integration   Forward integration involves performing industry value chain activities closer to the end user.

G

global strategies   Global strategies employ the same basic competitive approach in all countries where a company operates and are best suited to industries that are globally standardized in terms of customer preferences, buyer purchasing habits, distribution channels, or marketing methods. This is the think global, act global strategic theme.

H

horizontal scope   Horizontal scope is the range of product and service segments that a firm serves within its focal market.

I

integrative social contracts theory   According to integrative social contracts theory, universal ethical principles based on collective views of multiple cultures combine to form a "social contract" that all employees in all country markets have a duty to observe. Within the boundaries of this social contract, there is room for host-country cultures to exert *some* influence in setting their own moral and ethical standards. However, *"first-order"* universal ethical norms always take precedence over *"second-order"* local ethical norms in circumstances in which local ethical norms are more permissive

internal capital market   A strong internal capital market allows a diversified company to add value by shifting capital from business units generating *free cash flow* to those needing additional capital to expand and realize their growth potential.

international strategy   A company's international strategy is its strategy for competing in two or more countries simultaneously.

J

joint venture   A joint venture is a type of strategic alliance that involves the establishment of an independent corporate entity that is jointly owned and controlled by the two partners.

K

key success factors   Key success factors are the strategy elements, product attributes, competitive capabilities, or intangible assets with the greatest impact on future success in the marketplace.

L

low-cost leader   A low-cost leader's basis for competitive advantage is lower overall costs than competitors'. Success in achieving a low-cost edge over rivals comes from eliminating and/or curbing "nonessential" activities and/or outmanaging rivals in performing essential activities.

M

macro-environment   The macro-environment encompasses the broad environmental context in which a company is situated and is comprised of six principal components: political factors, economic conditions, sociocultural forces, technological factors, environmental factors, and legal/regulatory conditions.

mission statement   A well-conceived mission statement conveys a company's purpose in language specific enough to give the company its own identity.

multidomestic strategy   A multidomestic strategy calls for varying a company's product offering and competitive approach from country to country in an effort to be responsive to significant cross-country differences in customer preferences, buyer purchasing habits, distribution channels, or marketing methods.

N

network structure   A network structure is the arrangement linking a number of independent organizations involved in some common undertaking.

O

objectives   Objectives are an organization's performance targets—the results management wants to achieve.

outsourcing   Outsourcing involves contracting out certain value chain activities to outside specialists and strategic allies.

P

PESTEL analysis   PESTEL analysis can be used to assess the strategic relevance of the six principal components of the macro-environment: political, economic, sociocultural, technological, environmental, and legal forces.

political risks   Political risks stem from instability or weakness in national governments and hostility to foreign business

R

realized strategy   A company's realized strategy is a combination *deliberate planned elements* and *unplanned emergent elements*. Some components of a company's deliberate strategy will fail in the marketplace and become *abandoned strategy elements*.

related businesses   Related businesses possess competitively valuable cross-business value chain and resource matchups

resource   A resource is a competitive asset that is owned or controlled by a company

resource and capability analysis   Resource and capability analysis is a powerful tool for sizing up a company's competitive assets and determining if the assets can support a sustainable competitive advantage over market rivals.

resource bundles   Companies that lack a stand-alone resource that is competitively powerful may nonetheless develop a competitive advantage through resource bundles that enable the superior performance of important cross-functional capabilities.

resource fit   A diversified company exhibits resource fit when its businesses add to a company's overall mix of resources and capabilities and when the parent company has sufficient resources to support its entire group of businesses without spreading itself too thin.

S

scope of the firm   The scope of the firm refers to the range of activities the firm performs internally, the breadth of its product and service offerings, the extent of its geographic market presence, and its mix of businesses.

strategic alliance   A strategic alliance is a formal agreement between two or more companies to work cooperatively toward some common objective.

strategic fit   Strategic fit exists when value chains of different businesses present opportunities for cross-business skills transfer, cost sharing, or brand sharing.

strategic group   A strategic group is a cluster of industry rivals that have similar competitive approaches and market positions.

strategic group mapping   Strategic group mapping is a technique for displaying the different market or competitive positions that rival firms occupy in the industry.

strategic objectives   Strategic objectives relate to target outcomes that indicate a company is strengthening its market standing, competitive vitality, and future business prospects.

strategic vision   A strategic vision describes "where we are going"—the course and direction management has charted and the company's future product-customer-market-technology focus.

strategy   A company's strategy explains why the company matters in the marketplace by specifying an approach to creating superior value for customers and determining how capabilities and resources will be utilized to deliver the desired value to customers.

sustainable business practices   Sustainable business practices are those that meet the needs of the present without compromising the ability to meet the needs of the future.

sustainable competitive advantage   A company achieves sustainable competitive advantage when an attractively large number of buyers develop a durable preference for its products or services over the offerings of competitors, despite the efforts of competitors to overcome or erode its advantage.

SWOT analysis   SWOT analysis is a simple but powerful tool for sizing up a company's internal strengths and competitive deficiencies, its market opportunities, and the external threats to its future well-being.

T

think local, act local   Think local, act local strategy-making approaches are also essential when host-government regulations or trade policies preclude a uniform, coordinated worldwide market approach.

transnational strategy   A transnational strategy is a think global, act local approach to strategy making that involves employing essentially the same strategic theme (low-cost, differentiation, focused, best-cost) in all country markets, while allowing some country-to-country customization to fit local market conditions.

U

uniqueness driver   A uniqueness driver is a value chain activity or factor that can have a strong effect on customer value and creating differentiation.

unrelated businesses   Unrelated businesses have dissimilar value chains and resources requirements, with no competitively important cross-business value chain relationships.

V

value chain   A company's value chain identifies the primary activities that create customer value and related support activities.

values   A company's values are the beliefs, traits, and behavioral norms that company personnel are expected to display in conducting the company's business and pursuing its strategic vision and mission.

vertical scope   Vertical scope is the extent to which a firm's internal activities encompass one, some, many, or all of the activities that make up an industry's entire value chain system, ranging from raw-material production to final sales and service activities.

vertically integrated   A vertically integrated firm is one that performs value chain activities along more than one stage of an industry's overall value chain.

VRIN tests for sustainable competitive advantage   The VRIN tests for sustainable competitive advantage ask if a resource or capability is valuable, rare, inimitable, and nonsubstitutable.

INDEXES

Organization

a

A. T. Kearney, 77
Aabar Investments, 336
ABC News, 232
ABC World News Tonight, 231, 233
Accenture, 77
Acer, 273
AC Hotels by Marriott, 105
Adidas, 69, 431, 433
AGCO Corporation, 370, 373
    description, 374
    financial data, 375
Agusha, 387
AirTran Airways, 414, 415, 422
    acquired by Southwest, 402
    fare structure, 404–405
    integrated into Southwest, 412–413
Albertsons, 41
Alcoa, 24
Algenist, 141
Allstate Insurance, 123
Amadeus ITGroup, 415
Amazon, 70, 75, 112, 121, 222
Amazon Kindle, 113, 114
American Airlines, 33, 119, 393, 416, 422, 428
American Apparel, 107
American Apparel and Footwear Association, 435, 436
American Express, 116
American Giant Clothing Company, 75, 76, 106, 107
AMR Corporation, 119
Android, 117, 158, 412
Anheuser-Busch InBev, 42, 56, 92
Animal Compassion Foundation, 192
Ann Taylor, 23
AOL Time Warner, 29
APC, 77
Apple Inc., 5, 96, 126, 159, 218
Apple Inc., case
    competitive position
        in computer industry, 271–273
        in personal media player industry, 276–277
        in smartphone market, 274–276
    financial performance 2010-2014, 270
    launch of Apple Watch, 277–278

    leadership change, 268
    management changes, 269
    performance in 2015, 277–278
    revenue growth, 268
    rivals in computer industry
        Acer, 273
        Dell Inc., 274
        Hewlett-Packard, 273–274
    sales by segment 2012-2014, 271
    Steve Jobs' leadership, 268–270
Aquafina, 377, 383, 387
Aral, 143
Aravind Eye Care System, 103, 104
Arby's, 49, 121
Arco, 143
Asea Brown Boveri, 382
AT&T, 155, 236
Audi, 334, 357, 364
Audi A8, 364
Aunt Jemima, 377, 380, 386
Autograph Collection hotels, 105
Autonation, 112

b

Baked Cheetos, 386
Banana Republic, 107
Barnes & Noble, 70
BASF, 94
Bell helicopters, 160
Benchmarking Exchange, 77
Benchnet, 77
Bentley, 100
Best Buy, 41, 109
Best Practices. LLC, 77
BillCutterz.com, case
    balance sheet, 234
    in bill negotiation industry, 233–234
    business model, 231, 232–233
    business model modification, 236
    capabilities, 235
    company history, 231–232
    competitive resources, 235
    employee training, 235
    income statement, 233–234
    profit formula, 232–233
    strategy, 232–233
BlackBerry, 117
Bloomingdale's, 420

Bluebird snacks, 380
BMW, 20, 57, 71, 97, 100, 101, 133, 334, 343, 357, 364
BMW i3, 351
BMW i3 Hatchback, 364
BMW 7 series, 360–361, 364
Boeing 717, 406, 414
Boeing 737, 405, 406, 414, 427
Boeing Capital Group, 414
Boeing Company, 393
Bosch, 97
Boston Beer, 56
Boston Consulting Group, 202, 382
BP, 143
Braniff International, 395, 396
Bridgestone/Firestone, 41
British Telecommunications, 155, 189
BTR, 171
Bud Light, 92
Budweiser, 92
Burger King, 49
Burt's Bees, 189, 190, 195

c

Cadillac, 364
Caesars Entertainment, 212
Caesars Palace, 212
California Pizza Kitchen, 378
Campbell Soup Company, 97
Cap'n Crunch, 377, 380, 386
Carolina Cotton Works, 107
Cartier, 100
Case IH Agriculture, 374
Case tractors, 373
Caterpillar, Inc., 19, 96, 373
    description, 374–375
    financial data, 375
Cessna aircraft, 160
CGA, Inc., 103
Challenger, 374
Chanel, 58, 97
Chaps, 119
Charles Schwab, 97
Chase Visa card, 415
Cheetos, 383, 387
Chevrolet Spark, 364
Chevrolet Volt, 362, 363, 364
Chevy's Mexican Restaurants, 378

Subject